LEO BAECK INSTITUTE
YEAR BOOK

1979

MOSES MENDELSSOHN
was born 250 years ago in 1729

From a miniature painting, artist unknown

*By courtesy of the owner, Professor Felix Gilbert, Princeton,
reproduced from a photo in the Archives of the
Leo Baeck Institute, New York*

PUBLICATIONS OF THE
LEO BAECK INSTITUTE

YEAR BOOK XXIV

1979

SECKER & WARBURG · LONDON
PUBLISHED FOR THE INSTITUTE
LONDON · JERUSALEM · NEW YORK

FOUNDER EDITOR: ROBERT WELTSCH
CO-EDITOR: ARNOLD PAUCKER

OFFICES OF THE
LEO BAECK INSTITUTE

JERUSALEM (ISRAEL): 33 Bustanai Street
LONDON: 4 Devonshire Street, W.1
NEW YORK: 129 East 73rd Street

THE LEO BAECK INSTITUTE
was founded in 1955 by the
COUNCIL OF JEWS FROM GERMANY
for the purpose of collecting material on and sponsoring research into the history of the Jewish Community in Germany and in other German-speaking countries from the Emancipation to its decline and new dispersion. The Institute is named in honour of the man who was the last representative figure of German Jewry in Germany during the Nazi period.

The Council of Jews from Germany was established after the war by the principal organisations of Jews from Germany in Israel, USA and UK for the protection of their rights and interests.

THIS PUBLICATION WAS SUPPORTED
BY A GRANT FROM THE
MEMORIAL FOUNDATION FOR JEWISH CULTURE

© Leo Baeck Institute 1979
Published by Martin Secker & Warburg Limited
54 Poland Street, London W1V 3DF
SBN 436 24432 2
Printed in Great Britain by
Fletcher & Son Ltd, Norwich

Contents

Preface ... VII

I. HISTORIOGRAPHY

WERNER E. MOSSE: Judaism, Jews and Capitalism – Weber, Sombart and Beyond .. 3
LAWRENCE SCHOFER: The History of European Jewry – Search for a Method .. 17
KONRAD KWIET: Problems of Jewish Resistance Historiography .. 37

II. CULTURAL RAPPROCHEMENT

EVA ENGEL: The Emergence of Moses Mendelssohn as Literary Critic .. 61
MOSHE PELLI: The Beginning of the Epistolary Genre in Hebrew Enlightenment Literature in Germany – The Alleged Affinity between Lettres Persanes and 'Igrot Meshulam .. 83

III. EMANCIPATION AND ASSIMILATION

JULIUS CARLEBACH: The Forgotten Connection – Women and Jews in the Conflict between Enlightenment and Romanticism .. 107
MICHAEL A. MEYER: The Religious Reform Controversy in the Berlin Jewish Community, 1814–1823 .. 139
PETER FREIMARK: Language Behaviour and Assimilation – The Situation of the Jews in Northern Germany in the First Half of the Nineteenth Century .. 157
STEVEN M. LOWENSTEIN: The Yiddish Written Word in Nineteenth-Century Germany .. 179

IV. AUTOBIOGRAPHY AND GENEALOGY

PETER FRAENKEL: The Memoirs of B. L. Monasch of Krotoschin .. 195
DOLF MICHAELIS: The Ephraim Family and their Descendants (II) .. 225
HELMUT GERNSHEIM: The Gernsheims of Worms .. 247

V. GERMANY AND PALESTINE

JEHUDA REINHARZ: The Esra Verein and Jewish Colonisation in Palestine .. 261
ISAIAH FRIEDMAN: The Hilfsverein der deutschen Juden, the German Foreign Ministry and the Controversy with the Zionists, 1901–1918 .. 291
FRANCIS R. J. NICOSIA: Weimar Germany and the Palestine Question .. 321

VI. JEWISH NATIONALISM

PHILIP L. UTLEY: Siegfried Bernfeld's Jewish Order of Youth, 1914–1922 .. 349
JOSEPH WALK: Profile of a Local Zionist Association 1903–1904 – On the Social History of German Zionism .. 369

VI	Contents							
VII.	BIBLIOGRAPHY	..	..	..	..	..	..	.. 375
VIII.	LIST OF CONTRIBUTORS		..	..	..	..	..	.. 459
IX.	INDEX	..	..	..	..	..	..	.. 463

Illustrations

Moses Mendelssohn .. .. Frontispiece

Hans Liebeschütz
Max Kreutzberger
Hans Tramer
Jochanan Ginat
} following preface

Geschichte der Jehudim
Antisemitic comic book
Yiddish dialect joke books
1848 Yiddish dialect poster
} between pp. 184–185

Hagadah
Baer Loew Monasch
Mathilde Monasch
} between pp. 216–217

Ephraim Marcus Ephraim
Jacob Ephraim/Dufresne, Isaac Jacob Gans
Ida Stern and children
} between pp. 232–233

Judenbischof, Friedrich Gernsheim,
Wilhelm Gernsheim
Courtyard, the Gernsheim House, Worms
} between pp. 248–249

Willy Bambus, Hirsch Hildesheimer, Otto Warburg   opp. p. 280

Pro-Palästina-Komitee .. ..   opp. p. 328

Preface

Our twenty-fourth Year Book is without the Introduction to which our readers have for so long been accustomed and which Robert Weltsch has written for almost every volume since 1956. At the age of eighty-eight he has, for personal reasons, moved to Jerusalem. This does not mean however that the Editor will from now on dispense with the Introductions altogether. It is intended that some future volumes will carry on the tradition. Different scholars will be asked to write them on special occasions, or to introduce a particular theme. Moreover a likely feature of such Introductions would be an analysis of recent trends in, or an assessment and summing up of the present state of research in German-Jewish history.

Here it should be noted that of late a number of our contributors have paid increasing attention to methods of research and problems of historiography. This volume begins with a section dedicated to questions of methodology appertaining to the economic, social and political history of the German Jews. A further broadening of the scope of the Year Book may also be discerned in the essays on the factor of linguistic conflict and language problems in the process of Jewish emancipation in Germany, such as the persistence of Yiddish in certain regions throughout the nineteenth century; or in the contribution which attempts a comparative treatment between the "Jewish Question" and the *Frauenfrage*. Furthermore German and Israeli archives yield rich material on the position of Palestine in German and German-Jewish politics both in the Wilhelminian and in the Weimar era and considerable space has been allotted to this in our current volume.

Social and economic history will, we hope, be given a prominent place in the Year Books now being planned. We shall also continue to print important papers on aspects of German-Jewish history delivered at the historians' conventions, or the records of sessions sponsored by the Leo Baeck Institute itself. We will try to make more original documentation accessible, both from our large holdings in New York and other archives. On those subjects which could be regarded as rather outside the Institute's immediate concern, such as that of the more general research on the development of antisemitism in Central Europe and the mounting preoccupation with local and communal history we shall resume the earlier reviews and surveys.

This year the Leo Baeck Institute mourns the death of some of the distinguished men who founded it almost a quarter of a century ago. Those commemorated in the following pages were truly shaping spirits who inspired our activities and were instrumental in giving a decisive impetus to what is by now a flourishing academic subject: German-Jewish studies.

Arnold Paucker

HANS LIEBESCHÜTZ
(1893–1976)

Hans Liebeschütz, Member of the Executive of the London Board of the Leo Baeck Institute, died on 28th October 1978 in Liverpool in his 85th year. A distinguished mediaevalist and historian, he was amongst the founders of the Institute in 1955. A lecturer at the *Hochschule für die Wissenschaft des Judentums*, after his dismissal from school and university posts by the Nazis, Hans Liebeschütz emigrated to England in 1939 where he eventually became Reader in Mediaeval History at Liverpool University and later a Professor at the University of Hamburg. He wrote extensively on the Intellectual History of the Middle Ages; and to the Institute's work he contributed numerous essays published in the Year Book and elsewhere and two outstanding monographs, *Das Judentum im deutschen Geschichtsbild von Hegel bis Max Weber* (1967) and *Von Georg Simmel zu Franz Rosenzweig. Studien zum jüdischen Denken im deutschen Kulturbereich* (1970). One of the guiding spirits of the London Leo Baeck Institute, his loss is immeasurable.

JOCHANAN GINAT
(1908–1979)

Jochanan Ginat (Hans Gaertner), Director of the Leo Baeck Institute in Jerusalem from 1970 to 1978, died on 22nd February 1979 in Jerusalem in his 72nd year. A teacher and Co-Director of the Theodor Herzl Schule in Berlin during the Nazi era until 1939, he became after his emigration Director of the Ludwig Tietz School in Israel (1939–1950). Associated with the Youth Aliyah movement since its inception in the 1930s, he served it in various capacities after 1950, eventually as its Director-General from 1967 to 1970. Jochanan Ginat was an authoritative voice on Jewish education in the Weimar and Nazi periods, on which he contributed studies to the Year Book, in particular *The Jewish Teacher in Germany* (1974). In the years before his death he edited (with Miriam Sambursky) the correspondence of Kurt Blumenfeld, *Im Kampf um den Zionismus. Briefe aus fünf Jahrzehnten* (1976), on behalf of the Leo Baeck Institute (the directorship of which he had assumed on the retirement of Shalom Adler-Rudel). A stimulating colleague, his forceful presence will be greatly missed.

Historiography

Judaism, Jews and Capitalism
Weber, Sombart and Beyond

BY WERNER E. MOSSE

When Weber and Troeltsch, in the age of *Hochkapitalismus*, in their epoch-making attempt to link religion and the rise of capitalism, created the concept of the "Protestant ethic", Sombart, as is well known, felt impelled to explore possible links between Judaism and capitalism.* Indeed he presently concluded that the "Protestant ethic" was, in fact, of Old-Testamentary derivation. However, as indicated already by the title of his study, *Die Juden und das Wirtschaftsleben*,[1] he readily slipped into an examination not of the Jewish religious tradition but rather of the share of Jews in the development of capitalism.[2] The two aspects, of course, are to some extent complementary. Thus while Sombart laid stress on the allegedly hereditary (that is racial) economic characteristics of Jews, one chapter in his book – not as it happens the most persuasive – deals with "the significance of the Jewish religion in economic life". Weber in his turn,[3] transcending his reflections on the economic implications of the ethic of ancient Israel, supplements this with applying to the Jews his concepts of a "pariah people" and "pariah capitalism". Religious and ethnic aspects in fact are closely intertwined. What both Weber and Sombart play down – though not unaware of its existence – is the impact on economic behaviour of the status of Jews as members of a tolerated religious minority group. But though the theories of Weber and Sombart were one-sided and, at times, questionable in their methodology, there can be no doubt about the interest and importance of the debate they provoked. This was the first and, to-date, most systematic attempt to elucidate some of the reasons for the palpably disproportionate prominence (by whatever yardstick it is measured) of Jews and people of Jewish extraction[4] at the highest level of economic activity, more particularly in Germany. This was a phenomenon which did indeed call for some explanation. While the answers provided may have been less than satisfactory, the question posed was real and remains an open one. The problems of "Judaism and capitalism" and "the Jewish role in economic life" invite reconsideration.

---

*This essay is based on a paper read to an international conference of economic and social historians held in the summer of 1978 at the *Zentrum für Interdisziplinäre Forschung* of the University of Bielefeld. The author is indebted to Rabbi C. E. Cassel, London, and Rabbi Dr. Albert Friedlander, London, for a number of valuable suggestions.

[1] Leipzig 1911.
[2] For a recent discussion of aspects of Sombart's study see Paul R. Mendes-Flohr, 'Werner Sombart's: The Jews and Modern Capitalism. An Analysis of its Ideological Premises', in *LBI Year Book XXI* (1976), pp. 87–107.
[3] Weber's views are discussed by Freddy Raphael in his essay 'Max Weber and Ancient Judaism', in *LBI Year Book XVIII* (1973), pp. 41–62.
[4] In the following, both categories will be designated by the term Jews.

I

The problem of the economic articulation of the Old Testament raised in the eleventh chapter of Sombart's study can be dealt with briefly. Sombart imagines "old Amschel Rothschild" on a Friday evening after having "earned" that day a million on the Stock Exchange, turning to his Bible for edification and legitimation of his activity. He reads with satisfaction a number of passages (mainly in Deuteronomy and Proverbs), in which wealth is described as God's reward for piety. Amschel might indeed feel some disquiet at certain texts deprecating the pursuit of wealth (furnished to Sombart by an unnamed rabbi), but these pale into insignificance before "the numerous passages in this very book (Proverbs) which commend riches. So numerous indeed that they may be said to set the tone of the whole of Proverbs".[5] The actual facts, however, hardly bear out this claim. Examination of the relevant passages in Deuteronomy and Proverbs reveals, instead, an ambivalent attitude to both riches and their acquisition. There are indeed passages which represent wealth as the gift of God, such as *Prov. XX: 4*, "By humility and the fear of the Lord are riches, honour and life," or *Deut. XXVI: 11*, "And thou shalt rejoice in every good thing which the Lord hath given unto thee, and unto thine house . . ." But equally, there are warnings against the pursuit of gain like *Prov. XXIII: 4*, "Labour not to be rich: cease from thine own wisdom," *Prov. XV: 16*, "Better is little with the fear of the Lord than great treasure and trouble therewith," *Prov. I: 19*, "So are the ways of everyone that is greedy of gain; which taketh away the life of the owners thereof," or *Prov. XVI: 8*, "Better is little with righteousness than great revenues without right." In fact, the characteristic attitude of the Bible would appear to be a combination of both views. Wealth is indeed the gift of God, but its pursuit is an activity of an inferior order. Thus *Prov. VIII: 10* declares "Receive my instruction, and not silver; and knowledge rather than choice gold." There is, indeed, a relationship between fear of the Lord and the wealth he bestows, but it is not, as Sombart claims, a direct causal – let alone a contractual one. The relevant texts at any rate imply – what, as is well known, is proclaimed explicitly by the major prophets – that one can, at the same time, be rich and anything but pleasing to God. To take up Sombart's picture once more, Rothschild can find in the Bible legitimation for his wealth (though not, specifically its pursuit) only to the extent that he is conscious of leading a life pleasing to God for which he may consider his wealth a reward. Biblical approval of wealth, in effect, is subordinated strictly to righteous conduct. As for the actual pursuit of gain, the attitude of the Bible may best be described as one of neutrality.

Uncharacteristic of the conceptual framework of Proverbs is the somewhat isolated text *Prov. XIII: 11* chosen by the Frankfurt banker Moritz B. Goldschmidt in 1870 as the motto for a paternal letter of advice to his sons: "Wealth gotten by vanity shall be diminished; but he that gathereth by labour shall increase."[6] What stands out is the distinction between two kinds of wealth (if

---
[5]*Die Juden und das Wirtschaftsleben*, p. 255
[6]Moritz B. Goldschmidt to his sons, Homburg, 10th August 1870. Salomon Benedict Goldschmidt Collection, AR 100, Archives of the Leo Baeck Institute in New York.

indeed the second type of effort is held to lead to wealth) defined by method of acquisition (deceit or fraud, with also the connotation of "a quick penny", against laborious "honest effort"). No less significant is the moralistic assertion that, whereas wealth acquired by the first method diminishes, that gained by the second is increased – curiously without any explicit reference to the Lord. The underlying concept would appear to be that of wealth (or is it merely sufficiency or "a modest prosperity"?) as the reward of honest effort. Untypical though this passage may be of the general tenor of Proverbs, it is not without interest that it should have been chosen at the end of his career (he was then seventy-one) by a religious Jewish banker of the nineteenth century as the moral legitimation of his life's work.

II

No less important than the attitude of the Bible – also in Sombart's view – is that of the Talmud. Its background is described in Lujo Brentano's lucid critique of Sombart's book. The pre-exilic Israelites, he argues, were a pastoral and agricultural people little given to commercial pursuits. Their situation, however, changed dramatically when, in Babylonian exile, they were brought into sudden and traumatic contact with an advanced commercial civilisation. Under the impact of their new environment some Jews – rather than sit weeping by the waters of Babylon – joined in the economic pursuits of the surrounding peoples, sometimes to good effect.[7] If Brentano's view is correct, the substantial involvement of Jews in commercial activities and the transformation of some into traders was the fruit in the first place less of religious belief than of a changed environment. It would have occurred moreover – significantly – while Jews were a tolerated religious minority in a foreign environment. Commercial activity then continued among Babylonian Jews even after Esra and Nehemia had led back some of the exiles (possibly the economically less successful) to Jerusalem.

It was in Babylonian exile that Jewish scholars, besides undertaking the codification of the Jewish religious canon, embarked upon the compilation of Jewish laws and customs later known as the Babylonian Talmud. Here it is significant that, since Jewish tradition forbade making profit out of religious pursuits (though rabbis occasionally did engage in trade in order to enable them to work for the community without remuneration), the men who compiled, taught and interpreted talmudic law tended to be traders, artisans or professional men. They were thus engaged in economic activity and were familiar with economic practice. As Sombart notes with ill-concealed distaste, the most learned Talmudists were also often the most skilled financiers, doctors, jewellers and merchants.[8] The Talmudic law, therefore, was compiled, interpreted and applied by men with a positive economic motivation – in this respect very unlike the early Fathers of the Christian Church, who tended to reject on grounds of

[7] Lujo Brentano, 'Judentum und Kapitalismus', in *Der wirtschaftende Mensch in der Geschichte. Gesammelte Reden und Aufsätze*, Leipzig 1923, pp. 426–490, esp. p. 476.
[8] *Die Juden und das Wirtschaftsleben*, p. 230.

religious principle preoccupation with the acquisition of worldly goods, "vile mammon", thus incorporating a strong anti-economic strain in the Christian religious tradition.

However, while the pursuit of gain was thus clearly sanctioned by the Jewish religious tradition it was, in the Biblical spirit, never accepted as the primary purpose of life. As is well known, the overriding duty of the pious Jew was the acquisition of "learning" – the study of the Bible and Talmud. The Jewish cultural tradition, until the dawn of the modern era, was orientated towards scholarship. While this might, on the one hand, place some limits on acquisitive motivation. it at the same time would contribute also to economic success. Jewish study in the first place made for almost complete Jewish literacy in a world where literacy in general remained a rare attainment especially among the laity. Moreover, as has often been pointed out, the training offered in Jewish religious schools tended to sharpen the minds of the pupils. Although not specifically directed towards economic objects, his schooling would provide the young Jew with attainments which enhanced his competitiveness in the economic sphere.

Indeed, notwithstanding the theoretical primacy of "learning", the Jew also had to earn his (often precarious) living. As is well known, social institutions like the guild system and the interest of princes secular and ecclesiastical, forced the majority of Jews into marginal petty trade, a smaller number into money-lending, stigmatised as "usury". Money-lending, moreover, due to the Christian prohibition[9] was left largely – if by no means wholly[10] – to Jews. What is worth noting in the present context is the fact that the growing Jewish involvement in money-lending and usury (later, under changed economic and social conditions legitimised as banking) was the result neither of Jewish religious attitudes nor of a special Jewish preference for this particular pursuit, nor yet of specific racial aptitudes, but predominantly of outside forces,[11] among them the economically retarding effect of distinctive Christian attitudes.

It was in fact above all as a consequence of Christian economic policy that at least the Ashkenazic Jews of Central Europe entered the age of industrial capitalism in their great majority as marginal petty traders with a thin layer of (often wealthy) Court Jews. The latter, moreover, controlled a not insignificant part of scarce urban mobile capital – the potential "investment capital"

[9]Characteristic is the statement incorporated by the Hohenstaufen Emperor Frederick II in the Constitutions of Melfi (1231): "Von der Verbindlichkeit dieses unseres Wuchergesetzes nehmen wir allein die Juden aus, die des unerlaubten Zinsnehmens, durch Gottesgesetz verboten, nicht zu zeihen sind, da sie – wie bekannt – nicht unter dem Gesetz der seligen Kirchenväter stehen" (Kant. 245).

[10]While it is well known that by means of the doctrines of *lucrum cessans* and *damnum emergens* money-lending was legitimised also among Christians, it is perhaps less widely realised that by means of analogous doctrines Jews overcame the inner-Jewish prohibition of the taking of interest contained in *Deut. XXIII:21*.

[11]Moses Mendelssohn, for example, characteristically complained that his son Joseph, whom he considered exceptionally gifted as a scientist, was permitted only to study medicine. As this did not interest him, he had no choice but to go into business. Cf. Felix Gilbert (Hrsg.), *Bankiers, Künstler und Gelehrte. Unveröffentlichte Briefe der Familie Mendelssohn aus dem 19. Jahrhundert*, Tübingen 1975 (Schriftenreihe wissenschaftlicher Abhandlungen des Leo Baeck Instituts 31), p. XVII.

– available in society. Jews, moreover, as a result of their religious-cultural ethnicity, reinforced by the mutual exclusiveness of Jew and Christian, entered industrialising society from the decaying ghetto as a largely closed ethnic and social community. They left the pre-industrial age as a "magic nation" in the Spenglerian sense. How, it may be asked, were members of this group prepared for participation in the activities of the approaching age of industrial capitalism?

III

A number of elements in the Jewish cultural tradition may well have influenced the economic role of Jews in the age of early industrialisation. Thus Sigmund Freud stresses the element of *Weltbejahung* which, indeed, constitutes for him the central collective characteristic of Judaism and Jewry.[12] What he says about the Jewish rejection of magic and mysticism, moreover, finds a striking parallel in what Sombart had written in 1911 about the Jewish rejection of mysticism, mysteries and artistic inspiration based on the world of sensual passion.[13]

The attempt has been made – its success is debatable – to give to this *Weltbejahung* which almost certainly distinguishes Judaism from Christianity – in the Jewish tradition the "next world" and life after death also are reduced to a minimal role – an economic significance. Thus Sombart after drawing a somewhat crude parallel between rationalism and capitalism, goes on to conclude that since the Jewish religion had rationalistic features, there existed among Jews a natural affinity for equally rationalistic capitalism. Weber on the other hand links the alleged Jewish rationalism directly to the Jewish way of life, and the Jewish attitude to work and economic activity. In particular it is claimed, the rationality of their way of life led Jews – as the only people in antiquity – to consider occupation and work as a divine calling or service (Melocho).[14] The

[12]Already in 1882, Freud had written to his bride Martha Bernays concerning his conception of the essence of Judaism: "... Wenn die Form in der die alten Juden sich wohl fühlten, auch für uns kein Obdach mehr bietet, etwas vom Kern, das Wesen des sinnvollen und lebensfrohen Judentums, wird unser Haus nicht verlassen." (Freud to Martha Bernays, 23rd July 1882, in Ernst und Lucie Freud [Hrsg.], *Sigmund Freud Briefe 1873–1939*, Frankfurt a. Main 1968, p. 32.)

And, towards the end of his life, more than half a century later, he would elaborate the same view: "Ich war überrascht zu finden, dass schon das erste, sozusagen embryonale Erlebnis des Volkes, der Einfluss des Mannes Moses und der Auszug aus Ägypten, die ganze weitere Entwicklung bis auf den heutigen Tag festgelegt hat – wie ein richtiges frühkindliches Trauma in der Geschichte des neurotischen Individuums. Voran steht hier die Diesseitigkeit der Lebensauffassung und die Überwindung des magischen Denkens, die Absage an die Mystik, beides auf Moses selbst zurückzuführen, und vielleicht nicht mit aller wünschenswerten historischen Sicherheit ein Stück weiter ..." (Freud to N. N., 14th December 1937, *ibid.*, pp. 454 f.) It should be noted that *Weltbejahung* is a basic aspect of a persecuted community which asserted the present over the future. In religious terms, the Jews always stressed *this* world over "the world to come". The man of "this world" was a familiar type in Jewish life and literature.

[13]*Die Juden und das Wirtschaftsleben*, pp. 261–269.

[14]In the words of Kurt Zielenziger: "Die strenge Rationalisierung ihrer Lebensführung, ihnen eingeimpft durch ihre Lehren, lässt ihnen als einziges Volk der Antike – darin stimmen wir Max Weber zu – den Beruf zur göttlichen Berufung, zum 'Melocho' (Dienst) werden. Diese religiöse Bewertung der Arbeit führt die Juden zu rastlosem Vorwärtsstreben, das ihnen sittliche Aufgabe wird." K. Zielenziger, *Juden in der deutschen Wirtschaft*, Berlin 1930, p. 16.

validity of the observation, derived of course from the concept of the "Protestant ethic", for a later age, is doubtful. It is not clear which elements in their religious doctrine are supposed to have implanted in Jews the idea of labour as a divine calling. *Ora et labora* is not a peculiarly Jewish juxtaposition. Indeed had not God decreed, as a punishment for sin, on expulsion from Paradise: "In the sweat of thy brow shalt thou eat thy bread"? Work, originally, was more punishment, than vocation. Nor do the autobiographical writings of poor Jewish pedlars and traders presented by Monika Richarz,[15] suggest that they regarded their labours as anything but a necessary evil. In the only instance, that of Isaac Thannhäuser from Fellheim in Ostschwaben, where there is a direct juxtaposition of religion and labour, the connection between the two is – and perhaps not accidentally – obscure.[16] However one interprets the link in the writer's mind between God and his "peddling business", there is no evidence that Thannhäuser understood his labours as a divine calling or service. Nor is there reason to believe that Rothschilds or Bleichröders – though religious Jews – regarded their money-making as a religious act. Charity, on the other hand, was a religious-moral command which the great majority of wealthy Jews accepted. When, later on, Carl Fürstenberg sought to legitimise his activities as a banker he did so in terms of the development of productive forces and of the national economy.[17] It is in a similar vein that Sombart too provides a legitimation of Jewish economic activity.[18] By this time, in any case, such legitimation would, of course, be expressed in secular terms. The emphasis on labour and profession as divine callings is thus, almost certainly, misconceived.

What Jews, far more concretely, brought with them from their past into the industrial age was, as has often been noted, their particular appreciation of the value of money. The reasons for this phenomenon are hardly to be sought in the Jewish religious tradition. Nor are they convincingly explained in terms of Sombart's alleged racial characteristics. Weber's concepts of a "pariah people" and "pariah capitalism" in turn are only marginally relevant. The most probable reasons – they are, naturally, incapable of proof – were quite well understood also by Sombart himself. In his study of the German economy in the nineteenth century, after referring to the centuries-old legal discrimination against Jews (he might have said rather economic discrimination – the need to pay extra taxes, dues, tolls, ransoms and protection money) and their exclusion from offices and

---

[15]Monika Richarz (Hrsg.), *Jüdisches Leben in Deutschland. Selbstzeugnisse zur Sozialgeschichte 1780–1871*, Stuttgart 1976, Veröffentlichung des Leo Baeck Instituts, pp. 70 ff.

[16]He writes: "Indessen war doch die Religion immer wieder meine Trösterin. Ich nahm meine Zuflucht zu Gott; bat ihn, er möchte mir doch einen Weg zeigen, der mir eine sichere Existenz verschaffe. Dabei war ich immer fleissig in meinem Hausiergeschäft, schlug mich so ziemlich gut hindurch . . ." (*ibid.*, pp. 106–107).

[17]Hans Fürstenberg, *Carl Fürstenberg. Die Lebensgeschichte eines deutschen Bankiers 1870–1914*, Berlin 1931. Neuaufl. Unveränd. Nachdruck der Erstauflage, Wiesbaden 1961, p. 180.

[18]He writes: "Stellt man sich auf den Standpunkt der neuzeitlichen Entwicklung des Wirtschaftslebens, betrachtet man die Entfaltung kapitalistischen Lebens und damit die Freisetzung starker produktiver Kräfte als einen Fortschritt, legt man Wert auf den Rang, den ein Land heute auf dem Weltmarkt einnimmt, so kann man garnicht umhin, die Existenz jüdischer Wirtschaftssubjekte als einen der grössten Vorzüge anzuerkennen, über die dieses Land in ethnischer Hinsicht verfügt: Si le juif n'existait pas, il faudrait l'inventer." W. Sombart, *Die deutsche Volkswirtschaft im neunzehnten Jahrhundert*, 4 Aufl., Berlin 1919 p. 112.

dignities of Christian society, he describes money as a means for providing themselves with that of which the fiat of the law deprived them: importance, status and prestige.[19] In very similar terms, Lion Feuchtwanger sees the possession of money as the only Jewish key to a degree of security, freedom and respect.[20] Toury, finally, stresses – certainly rightly – that for the Jew, in uncertain times, money was the major source of a feeling of security.[21]

It is thus the symbolic and also highly practical value of money in the Jewish situation – and neither Jewish religion nor race – which is the true cause of the oft-described Jewish pursuit of gain, of Jewish frugality, sobriety, hard work, determination to succeed, the "rationality" of the Jewish life-style, in short of the Jewish "Protestant ethic" or of Jewish "pariah capitalism". If the ethic of Protestantism (or Puritanism or Calvinism) was indeed a factor in the emergence of a capitalist mentality, it should almost certainly be distinguished from a Jewish capitalism determined more by the legal and economic situation of the Jewish people than by its religious traditions and attitudes. The Jewish religion was indeed involved, but mainly negatively as the cause of persecution and discrimination. The Jews (like the Protestants in France but unlike the Calvinists in Geneva or the Netherlands) were adherents of a "tolerated religion". As such, they formed just one instance of a wider "religio-socio-economic" phenomenon. This had been noted already by that wise old proto-sociologist Montesquieu, when he wrote in his *Lettres Persanes*:

> "On remarque que ceux qui vivent dans des religions tolérées se rendent ordinairement plus utiles à leur patrie que ceux qui vivent dans la religion dominante, parce que, éloignés des honneurs, ne pouvant se distinguer que par leur opulence et leurs richesses, ils sont portés à acquérir par leur travail et à embrasser des emplois de la Société les plus pénibles."[22]

In short, it is membership of a "tolerated" religious minority group rather than a specific religious dogma which in many cases, including that of the Jews, creates the so-called "puritan" life-style and the psycho-economic attitudes in which it expresses itself. (Much of Synagogue architecture – plain outside and lavish inside – is a graphic illustration of this.)

---

[19] "Da lernten sie denn im Geld ein Mittel kennen, dass ihnen zum grossen Teil ersetzte, was sie durch den Machtspruch der Gesetzgebung entbehren mussten: Geltung und Ansehen. Und daraus ergab sich natürlich abermals eine gesteigerte Wertung dieses Stillers aller Schmerzen, dieses Heilers aller Wunden, dieses wunderbaren Trösters in allen Leiden: des Geldes." Sombart, *Die deutsche Volkswirtschaft*, p. 115.

[20] "Sie hatten es erfahren; in Unsicherheit, Rechtlosigkeit, Fährnis, gab es einen einzigen Schild zwischen lauter wankendem, versagendem Grund, ein einziges Festes: Geld. Den Juden mit Geld hielten die Wächter nicht an den Toren des Ghetto, der Jude mit Geld stank nicht mehr, keine Behörde setzte ihm einen lächerlichen spitzen Hut auf. Die Fürsten und die grossen Herren brauchten ihn, sie konnten nicht Krieg und Regiment führen ohne ihn." Lion Feuchtwanger, *Jud Süss*, quoted in Zielenziger, *op. cit.*, p. 14.

[21] "Darum löste sich die Mehrzahl auch nicht von dem Notanker der ihr in vorbürgerlicher Zeit als einziger Hort der stets gefährdeten Sicherheit und der persönlichen Freiheit gegolten hatte: vom Geld im konkreten Sinn." Jacob Toury, 'Der Eintritt der Juden ins deutsche Bürgertum', in *Das Judentum in der Deutschen Umwelt 1800–1850. Studien zur Frühgeschichte der Emanzipation*, herausgegeben von Hans Liebeschütz und Arnold Paucker, Tübingen 1977 (Schriftenreihe wissenschaftlicher Abhandlungen des Leo Baeck Instituts 35), p. 151.

[22] Charles Louis de Secondat, Baron de la Brède et de Montesquieu, *Lettres Persanes*, Lettre LXXXV, Paris 1960, p. 179.

Where religious attitudes are of real importance in influencing economic conduct – Montesquieu implies it, R. H. Tawney develops the argument – is in the case of the majority religions, in the present instance the Roman Catholic and also the Lutheran. These did, in fact, have a strong anti-economic and anti-capitalist bias based on a rejection of the acquisitive motive.[23] This, moreover, was reinforced by close links with the feudal-aristocratic attitudes of the old ruling classes. The result was a disapproval of commercial activity which was, almost certainly, a retarding influence on economic life.[24] It may be, therefore, that religion provided a negative rather than a positive incentive to Jewish economic activity.

IV

Specifically Jewish institutions and attitudes which affected economic potentialities, are well known and need be considered only briefly. In the first place it is significant that Jews entered the age of industrialisation as a virtually closed community – with a close social network based on solidarity in the face of adversity, a common religion, common social institutions, a closely knit extensive family- and kinship structure. Membership, at most levels, constituted a substantial economic asset, whether actual or potential. David Landes has described some aspects of communities of this kind:[25]

> "I have had occasion [he writes] to discuss elsewhere the success in trade and banking of such dispersed but cohesive religious or ethnic groups as the Jews, Calvinists, Greeks or Parsees. Their effectiveness rested on mutual confidence, especially precious before the days of institutionalized credit ratings and easy communication; on mutual support; and on superior intelligence (in the military sense). Everywhere, they prospered out of proportion to their numbers; but their role was most important in those societies that were either incapable or scornful of trade – areas of backwardness or illiteracy, for example, or countries in which business was looked upon as a degrading activity."

The greater part of Germany, when Jews became involved in economic activities on a substantial scale and at a level above that of subsistence "peddling", was economically underdeveloped and the prejudice against commercial pur-

---

[23]Thus Luther informs the rebellious peasants that "das Evangelium sich weltlicher Sachen gar nicht annimmt und das äusserliche Leben allein in Leiden, Unrecht, Kreuz, Geduld und Verachtung zeitlicher Güter und Lebens setzt . . ." (*Ermahnungen zum Frieden auf die Zwölf Artikel der Bauernschaft in Schwaben*, 1525, as quoted in Wolfgang Venohr/Friedrich Kabermann, Brennpunkte deutscher Geschichte 1450–1850, Kronberg 1978, p. 39.)

[24]Jacob Toury, on the basis of a report from Berlin by a correspondent of *The Times* in the eighteen-sixties writes: "Es muss angenommen werden, dass es einerseits die wirtschaftlichen Möglichkeiten der fünfziger und sechziger Jahre waren, die von den Juden schnell und unternehmungslustig wahrgenommen wurden, während das nichtjüdische Bürgertum, 'der christliche Teil der Kaufmannschaft', aus 'Mangel an herzlicher Sympathie mit den neuen Institutionen' und Tendenzen der Entwicklung nur langsam folgte." Jacob Toury, *Soziale und politische Geschichte der Juden in Deutschland 1847–1871*, Düsseldorf 1977, p. 114. And again: "In weiten Kreisen des deutschen Publikums bestanden wohl langgehegte Voruteile gegen den Beruf des 'Koofmich'. Das konnte den *wirtschaftlichen* Aufstieg der Juden erleichtern, erschwerte dagegen um so mehr ihre *gesellschaftliche* Anerkennung" (*ibid.*, pp. 117–118).

[25]David S. Landes, 'The Bleichröder Bank: An Interim Report', in *LBI Year Book V* (1960), p. 203.

suits among the ruling-classes was widespread. Once economic life accelerated, accompanied by the removal of restrictions on both enterprise and Jews, Germany seemed predestined to become an area of significant Jewish economic activity (the only comparable minority group of the kind described by Landes being the less numerous and possibly less compact Huguenots and, possibly, Protestants in parts of the country that were predominantly Catholic).

Significant also is the sense of Jewish solidarity[26] overriding even intense economic competition. What gives this solidarity a special economic significance is the dispersal of Jews across national boundaries. Their advantage over non-Jewish competitors in international commerce, banking and finance is evident. So are the economic advantages of the well-known family solidarity (which, however, must not be exaggerated – there were frictions among Mendelssohns and Bleichröders – though the exemplary solidarity of the House of Rothschild is perhaps the more typical), exemplified in the remarkable cooperation among members of the Tietz family or, in a different form in the cousin marriages of the Rothschilds, the Mendelssohns or the Hirschs. In general, notwithstanding conversions and mixed marriages, the degree of endogamy within the business community until the end of the nineteenth century is striking (even converts, not infrequently, intermarry). Again, where outsiders are taken into partnership by established Jewish firms, they are frequently (one is almost tempted to say usually) Jews (sometimes also sons-in-law). There are firms with largely Jewish management – the AEG – sometimes referred to by antisemites as "Allgemeine Judengesellschaft"[27] – is an outstanding example – where Jews are prominent also on the Board (*Aufsichtsrat*), betokening close links with other Jewish economic interests. Even in large non-Jewish joint stock enterprises like the *Deutsche Bank*, it is possible to trace from beginning to end (so far as Jews are concerned) a "Jewish" directorial "dynasty"[28], based on a kind of "apostolic succession" and adoption.[29]

There is little doubt that Jewish cohesion and solidarity were a factor – its importance awaits assessment – in German-Jewish economic life and in the evolution of German capitalism and industrialisation. This poses the further question as to the possible existence of a distinctive "Jewish" variant of capitalism, distinguishable from, though of course in close symbiotic relationship with,

---

[26] Freud speaks of tribal and family solidarity, particularly developed among Jews, the product not only of a close community of fate but also of "viele dunkle Gefühlsmächte, umso gewaltiger, je weniger sie sich in Worten erfassen liessen, ebenso wie die klare Bewusstheit der inneren Identität, die Heimlichkeit der gleichen seelischen Konstruktion". Freud an die Mitglieder des Vereins B'nai B'rith (6th May 1926) Freud, *op. cit.*, p. 381. As one of the English Rothschilds, rather more prosaically, put it to a British journalist: "I enjoy Jewish characteristics and like doing business with Jewish people". Stephen Aris, *The Jews in Business,* London 1970, p. 73.

[27] Ernst Schulin, 'Die Rathenaus. Zwei Generationen jüdischen Anteils an der industriellen Entwicklung Deutschlands', in *Juden im Wilhelminischen Deutschland 1890–1914*. Ein Sammelband herausgegeben von Werner E. Mosse unter Mitwirkung von Arnold Paucker, Tübingen 1976 (Schriftenreihe wissenschaftlicher Abhandlungen des Leo Baeck Instituts, 33), p. 123.

[28] At first subsidiary, later primary.

[29] It runs from Ludwig Bamberger through Hermann Wallich and Max Steinthal to Paul Mankiewitz and Oskar Wassermann to end with the (baptised) Georg Solmssen. Moreover, even under the Third *Reich*, after Solmssen was forced to resign, he was succeeded by a man with Jewish blood.

that of the non-Jewish world. The *prima facie* evidence suggests – whether by the distribution of Jews in different fields of commercial activity, or different branches of industry, or by geographical spread and by the network of relations between various commercial enterprises – a certain Jewish specificity. In this connection, the prominent role of Jews or men of Jewish extraction in German banking from the days of Napoleon to those of Hitler has a special significance. Again the Jewish role in the wholesale commodities trade ranging from coal and non-ferrous metals to cotton and cotton goods, colonial produce, grain and hops, as well as the Jewish near-monopoly in retail distribution through department stores, suggests an element of specificity. But investigation of the contours and structure of German-Jewish capitalist enterprise is still in its early stages.

V

Compared to these broader aspects, distinctive Jewish institutions and attitudes derived from the Jewish cultural tradition may be of lesser significance. Their impact is, moreover, not easy to assess, even with the aid of the invaluable *Selbstzeugnisse* edited by Monika Richarz. For instance, observance of the Jewish sabbath might be expected, at least in theory to handicap the Jewish trader as against his non-Jewish competitor. The evidence hardly supports this view. In fields where Jewish participation was a heavy one and where a majority of Jews observed the sabbath, competitiveness of the Jewish individual or family would hardly be impaired. Then, at least from the middle of the nineteenth century onwards, sabbath observance rapidly declined – a fact of life not infrequently accepted by rabbis. Attention, moreover has been drawn to the psychic and recuperative value of the strict observance of the sabbath and its attendant ceremonial, as well as its contribution to family stability. The evidence of the *Selbstzeugnisse* lends some support to this view. In fact the sabbath, when it was observed, may well, overall, have been an economic asset.

As for observance of the Jewish dietary laws, its effects were probably economically ambivalent. It would, while tending to separate Jews from non-Jews, at the same time, draw the former closer together at least to the extent to which sociability impinged on economic dealings. Of course, business contacts were entirely possible without the element of sociability. In any case, with growing assimilation, rigorous observance of the dietary laws, like that of the sabbath, rapidly declined from the middle of the nineteenth century. Some Jewish businessmen reached the compromise of combining the observance of ritual laws at home with disregard outside.

The reasons for the well-known Jewish sobriety, an economic factor of some importance, are not clear. It has been suggested that the semi-sacral character of wine in Jewish ritual helped the emergence of a social tradition hostile to the abuse of alcohol. (It is suggestive that Jewish social restraint recalls the religious prohibition of Islam.) On the other hand, the reasons for moderation in the consumption of alcohol may equally have been economic. In fact, avoidance of drunkenness helped to avoid expense and thus assisted the primary accumulation of capital. It had a beneficial effect on both health and family relations. In mixed business dealings conducted in a convivial atmosphere, the more abstemious Jew was more likely to remain sober and alert than his non-Jewish counterpart. He would also wake up with a clear head the next morning. Overall, whatever its causes, moderation in the consumption of alcohol was an undoubted asset.[30]

So, especially in the early part of the nineteenth century were the distinctive Jewish communication media, the Yiddish language and the Hebrew alphabet. These were significant elements – though of diminishing importance – in a Jewish communications network, from which "outsiders" were largely excluded. Hebrew lettering is to be met with from time to time in intra-Jewish correspondence, both business and private, and an instance is recorded in the *Selbstzeugnisse* of Jews speaking the jargon to prevent the servant from following their conversation.

Structure and role of the Jewish family, and particularly the place of the woman, also in business affairs, remains largely unexplored. There is some evidence that, especially at the level both of peddling and of retail trade in open shops, i.e., in the early stages of the economic (and social) ascent of a family, women would, on occasion, play a crucial role. There is, moreover, a suggestion that, not infrequently, they were a good deal more "down to earth" than their sometimes dreamy, studious and "other-worldly" husbands. The role of the woman in Jewish economic life deserves further investigation, as does the impact of family cohesion and kinship on Jewish business achievement.

VI

To return to the point of departure. The discussion on the subject of Judaism and capitalism opened up by Sombart and Weber on the eve of the First World War was the first and perhaps to-date the only serious attempt to investigate in some detail a curious and important phenomenon. The discussion, however, faltered and faded – as indeed did the wider debate on religion and capitalism of which it formed a part, without leaving behind much more than the concept of the "Puritan ethic" (which Sombart saw as a Jewish one). Nor did Marxism – whether classical or post-classical – provide an explanatory model. Indeed, its preferred categories fail even to reach phenomena like "Judaism" or "Jews". Hence perhaps Karl Marx's early and forced attempt to equate the terms "Jew" and "capitalist" – now shamefacedly shrugged off by his disciples as a youthful "peccadillo".

Thus one is led to ask how far any of the concepts inherited from the earlier debate can today assist the scholarly investigation. Here it is hard to escape the conclusion that past explanations, whether in terms of religion, race, class or

---

[30]Jews at the same time were prominent in the brewery industry. Schultheiss–Patzenhofer, for instance, the largest German (and probably European) brewery concern, could without exaggeration be described as a "Jewish firm" (in terms of management, Board membership and financial links).

ideology have lost such usefulness as they may once have possessed. Instead, if research today tries to come to grips with the problem, it must do so from new points of view and with a new methodology. Thus it may prove fruitful to study comparatively the economic behaviour of certain types of religious and ethnic minority. Equally, it may help to study selected economic élites drawn from such minorities – and Jewish élites in particular.

So far as methodology is concerned, a measure of quantification appears essential, at least as a first stage. This, necessarily, must precede any attempt at explanation or model-building (though of course broad working hypotheses are not ruled out even at the earlier stage). What with respect to the German-Jewish economic élite (and perhaps to other similar élite groups as well) could be established as a start would be not only its proportional strength but also its distribution through different branches of the economy and thus, with the help of a non-Jewish control group, its distinctive character. To give an illustration. The data presented by Rudolf Martin[31] (to be treated, however, with due caution) reveal the presence in 1908, among 747 people in Prussia with fortunes in excess of 5 million marks of 162 Jews – that is, roughly one in five (of only the 100 wealthiest people, twenty-nine were Jewish).[32] If one then analyses the Jewish millionaires according to the type of economic activity through which they acquired their fortunes and compares this with a non-Jewish control sample, light is thrown on the specificity of Jewish capitalism within the general economy.

A somewhat different approach containing a quantitative element is through an examination of the representation of Jews – at different dates – among the directors and on the boards of the major commercial enterprises. Again, a distinctively "Jewish" distribution emerges. Moreover, while distribution on different dates makes it possible to establish trends, the interlocking nature of board memberships reveals specific patterns of Jewish capitalist enterprise at the highest level of economic activity.

Again, once a group like the German-Jewish economic élite has been defined (several different criteria of membership are possible) and the actual members identified, it becomes amenable to quantitative analysis in terms of standard categories of élite studies like social origin, education, career structures, turnover, recruitment etc.

Such quantitative approaches of course, cannot answer the question why. Why were Jews prominent in business activities in general? Why were they more strongly represented in certain fields of activity than in others? In answer to the first question, it is still tempting to accept Montesquieu's hypothesis – though it may need refining – about the distinctive economic motivation and behaviour of members of tolerated religious groups. His is a model which has since been developed and "secularised" by Gottfried Schramm who in a specific instance, that of *Ostjuden*, sees Jewish economic achievement as the outcome of a fruitful

---

[31]Rudolf Martin, *Jahrbuch des Vermögens und Einkommens der Millionäre in Preussen*, Berlin 1912. Similar data are available for other parts of Germany.

[32]For some further detail see Werner E. Mosse, 'Die Juden in Wirtschaft und Gesellschaft', in *Juden im Wilhelminischen Deutschland, op. cit.*, pp. 77 f.

balance between disabilities and opportunities.[33] Both were, indeed, conspicuously present in Germany in the age of industrialisation.

The reasons for the uneven (and perhaps significant) distribution of Jews between different sectors of the economy are almost certainly the result both of a traditional Jewish occupational pattern (largely determined by influences outside the Jewish sphere) and of the economic structure and motivations of non-Jewish society. One interesting approach with regard to the latter would be a comparative examination of the legal, economic, political and social framework within which Jewish economic élites rose and operated in different countries at roughly comparable stages of economic development. This might throw some light on the reasons why the Jewish role would almost certainly be found to be greater in Germany than in the U.S.A. and greater in the latter country than in England or France. A comparison of distribution over different branches of the economy here would also be revealing: both similarities and differences would be of equal significance. Such an approach might, in the end, provide the basis for a general statement about the specific functions (if any) of Jewish economic élites in the different economies.

In conclusion, it would appear that progress in the study of the Jewish role in capitalist society can best be achieved not through the attempt to adapt the cosmic categories inherited from the pre-war debate but through the detailed examination and comparative analysis of Jewish economic élites. New syntheses can be achieved only on the basis of work – as yet only beginning – on their structure, their functions and their motivations.

---

[33]"Die Paarung von Schwierigkeiten die man ihnen machte, [writes Schramm] und bedeutenden Möglichkeiten, die man ihnen nach und nach einräumte, spornte ihre Tüchtigkeit an und führte dazu, dass Juden in dem begrenzten Bereich der ihnen offen stand, im Durchschnitt mehr leisteten als Nichtjuden ... Die Gesellschaft vermochte nicht einzusehen, dass diese Leistung im Grunde das Produkt des Antisemitismus in Rahmen von wirtschaftlich regen Rechtsstaaten war ..." Gottfried Schramm, 'Die Ostjuden als soziales Problem des 19. Jahrhunderts' in Heinz Maus (Hrsg.), *Gesellschaft, Recht und Politik*, Neuwied-Berlin 1968, p. 367.

The History of European Jewry
Search for a Method

BY LAWRENCE SCHOFER

I

Jews, both as individuals and as groups, have played so noticeable a role in the histories of various European countries that they constitute leading candidates for students interested in the interaction of cultural life, economic development and social conflict, in short, in meaningful comparative history.* Everywhere in Central European societies Jews played special and important roles. To know Prussian men of business, the historian must be acquainted with Jewish activity. To comprehend Polish society, the historian must assimilate the notion that next to the peasant "problem" the Jewish "question" overshadowed most other social issues. Yet the history of Jewish "society" remains a stunted enterprise, for the powerful and often admirable tradition of Jewish history has primarily emphasised intellectual developments. The intriguing web of social interrelationships within various national Jewries and between those Jewries and their surrounding societies can be examined with the help of approaches suggested by social-science orientated history.

To this day the economic history of European Jewry figures as something episodic, anecdotal and ill-organised. It is not hard to delineate the main contributions. Salo Baron's great synthesis has stimulated some others, but he has not yet delved into the industrial period. The multi-volume *Social and Religious History of the Jews* is replete with suggestions for further work in demography, economics and social stratification, but much of that new work can come only when others realise the frameworks implicit in the theoretical and methodological statements of non-historians and non-specialists in Jewish studies. From another angle, Raphael Mahler's Marxism has allowed him to conceptualise the place of Jews in modern society. Simply put, class struggle was the prime mover in East European Jewish society in the eighteenth and nineteenth centuries. The artisans receive most attention, functioning here as a proletariat oppressed by the wealthier merchants and small-scale manufacturers. This framework puts blinkers on the author by forcing him to focus on the urban, proto-industrial sectors of Jewry while ignoring trade and other occupations. Moreover, Mahler's Jewish nationalism does not always fit in with his notions of class struggle within the Jewish community, and sometimes his sympathy for

*Much of this material was surveyed while I was a fellow of the Alexander von Humboldt-Stiftung (Bonn). The American Philosophical Society provided some funds for travel and reproduction costs. Some of the writing was done while I was a fellow of the National Endowment for the Humanities. I should like to thank the following for their helpful comments: Mike Zuckerman, Fred Marquardt, Peter Stearns, and the members of the Leo Baeck Institute faculty seminar and the University of Pennsylvania history department workshop.

the oppressed of the world takes second place to his visions of the rightful place of the Jewish nation. Internal contradictions and ideological pleading abound, and as a result Mahler does not provide a systematic guide to ways of studying history. On the whole, the field stands virtually as virgin soil, in part because of ". . . the relative scarcity of mature scholars versed in history *and* economics *and* Jewish studies."[1]

It is sometimes observed that for European historians, "social class" stands out as the major explanatory variable of social action in the last two centuries, while for Americanists "ethnicity" dominates accounts of change. Historians of the European Jews tend to fall into the Americanist camp. Even when writings about Jews do not fall into the realm of apologetic praise of one's own group, these studies usually do not address themselves to the issue of class, which so obsesses other Europeanists. Mahler writes openly as a Marxist, but his conflicting loyalties to class struggle and to Jewish nationalism often lead him into tortuous explanations. Nonetheless, he perceives that in one sense ethnicity is not the answer; it is the question. It does not explain all; it needs to be explained.[2]

Being Jewish meant being part of a corporate state, even in emancipated Prussia and other German states, to say nothing of Eastern Europe in the nineteenth century and in the period between the two world wars. Ethnicity clearly cut across class lines, as it did with every European group experiencing a nationalist revival in the nineteenth or twentieth century. A society of equal citizens could hardly be achieved in this milieu, and in this sense emancipation was incomplete. It could be complete only when the economic strength of Jews (and other groups) could be freely translated into social prestige and when Jews would no longer participate solely in their own separate system of social stratification.[3]

[1] Salo W. Baron, *A Social and Religious History of the Jews*, 2nd edn., 16 vols., New York and Philadelphia 1952–1976; Raphael Mahler, *A History of Modern Jewry*, New York 1971, translation and abridgement of the four-volume Hebrew original, Tel-Aviv 1960. "Scarcity of mature scholars"; Salo W. Baron, Arcadius Kahan, and others, *Economic History of the Jews*, ed. Nachum Gross, New York 1975, p. ix. See the harsh but well-taken critique by Benjamin Braude, 'Jewish Economic History – Review Essay', in *Association for Jewish Studies Newsletter*, 19 (1977), pp. 25–28. Other important works: Bernard Weinryb *Neueste Wirtschaftsgeschichte der Juden in Russland und Polen*, Breslau 1934, 2nd edn., 1972. This study is over 40 years old; the second edition differs but little from the first. Weinryb, *The Jews of Poland*, Philadelphia 1973. Simon Kuznets, 'Economic Structure and Life of the Jews', in Louis Finkelstein, ed., *The Jews. Their History, Culture and Religion*, 3rd edn., Philadelphia 1966, vol. II, pp. 1597–1666 – emphasis on aggregate trends, large-scale population movements, and general occupational preferences of Jews over a large number of countries; an excellent overview. On German Jewry in particular: Esra Bennathan, 'Die demographische und wirtschaftliche Struktur der Juden', in *Entscheidungsjahr 1932. Zur Judenfrage in der Endphase der Weimarer Republik*. Ein Sammelband herausgegeben von Werner E. Mosse unter Mitwirkung von Arnold Paucker, Tübingen 1966 (Schriftenreihe wissenschaftlicher Abhandlungen des Leo Baeck Instituts 13), pp. 87–131. Very generally: Peter D. McClelland, *Causal Explanation and Model Building in History, Economics, and the New Economic History*, Ithaca – New York 1975.

[2] A useful start in a new direction: Thomas Kessner, *The Golden Door. Italian and Jewish Immigrant Mobility in New York City 1880–1915*, New York 1977. An imaginative introduction to the Western context: Monika Richarz, 'Social Mobility in Germany during the Time of Emancipation', in *LBI Year Book XX* (1975), pp. 69–77.

[3] On equal citizenship: T. H. Marshall, 'Citizenship and Social Class', in Marshall, *Class Citizen-*

On the other hand, social classes were not alien to Jewish reality. It is obvious that internally the Jewish community in any given era was stratified by wealth and power, if not by ownership of or control over the means of production. Evidence abounds – the functioning of the *kehillah* (self-government institution) in Central and Eastern Europe; the position of the *Ostjuden* in Germany; the Jewish industrialists and wealthy merchants in Berlin and Leipzig, Warsaw and Lodz, Vienna and Budapest, Vilna and Odessa.[4] What marked those communities was a two-fold stratification system that has received little attention from social theorists or historians. The Jews and other ethnic groups, particularly minority groups, formed corporate estates within particular societies, but they also exhibited internal stratification best perceived through class analysis. The transition to equal citizen status was difficult; it was achieved in Germany only in the short-lived Weimar Republic, but for a long time before that clashes based on socio-economic position were endemic to the Jewish community.[5]

Theorists, influenced by Marx and by non-Marxist spokesmen for "modernisation", have assumed that estate society inevitably will wither away. Perhaps, perhaps not. The central European nationalisms of the late nineteenth century clearly resurrected social divisions based on birth, and the minority treaties developed at the end of the First World War attempted to guarantee the safety of corporate entities in the bodies politic of the newly formed states of Eastern Europe. Post-1945 multi-national societies show no signs of erasing these ascribed distinctions. Even if estates are doomed, it is incumbent on scholars to deal with the complex realities of a particular age instead of sticking with the presumed inexorable prototypes of the future. Because of the hoary tradition of Jewish historiography and because of the peculiar position of the Jews as a minority group everywhere in Europe, Jewish historians are in a good position to work out models for study of this particular problem: estate and class interacting and producing new types of social action.

Perhaps the gravest weakness of Jewish history – and that of other ethnic groups as well – has lain in the assumption that when Jews as a group are different from other groups, the explanation must be found in the manifold qualities of "Jewishness". Such oft-described European Jewish patterns as concentration in urban areas, predilections towards trade and commerce and concentration in the needle trades are seen solely as the result of some longstanding Jewish preferences instead of being regarded as the result of the complex interaction of Jewish preferences and the forces of supply and demand in the

---

ship, and Social Development, Garden City, N.Y. 1964, pp. 65–122. On prestige: Jacob Katz, *Tradition and Crisis*, New York 1971, chapter 19.

[4] On the *kehillah*, see Katz, *Tradition*, and Isaac Levitats, *The Jewish Community in Russia, 1772–1844*, New York 1943. On Germany: Jacob Toury, *Soziale und politische Geschichte der Juden in Deutschland 1847–1871*, Düsseldorf 1977; Werner E. Mosse, 'Die Juden in Wirtschaft und Gesellschaft', in *Juden im Wilhelminischen Deutschland 1890–1914. Ein Sammelband* herausgegeben von Werner E. Mosse unter Mitwirkung von Arnold Paucker, Tübingen 1976 (Schriftenreihe wissenschaftlicher Abhandlungen des Leo Baeck Instituts 33), pp. 57–113; Bennathan, *loc. cit.* (note 1). On the twentieth century in Eastern Europe: Celia S. Heller, *On the Edge of Destruction. Jews of Poland Between the Two World Wars*, New York 1977.

[5] On the mixture of class and ethnic status, cf. Milton Gordon's notion of the "ethclass" in *Assimilation in American Life*, New York 1964, pp. 51–54.

markets for labour and commodities. Similar comments abound when one writes of Poles or Hungarians or Italians or Chinese or whomever. Somehow the analytic tools available to historians become useless in the face of linguistic difficulties, close-knit societies, and the demands of group honour.

One fruitful way of conceptualising this problem is to attempt to explain economic activity by economic and social variables – labour supply and demand, changing technology, shifting markets for goods produced, developing demographic trends, patterns common to minority ethnic groups, etc. One may then turn to what is left unexplained and use cultural and even social variables tied up with the quality of being Jewish. Ultimately, the socio-economic and cultural factors interact. This approach has not been spelled out in great detail, but the more sophisticated of the new social historians clearly pursue this task in their work. I have no doubts that this individualised area will be extensive and probably crucial in understanding the items at hand. However, the more general approach has the advantage of restricting "overdetermined" situations, where there are several sufficient causes available for any one effect. It is not intellectually satisfying to know that Jews in Berlin at the end of the nineteenth century showed a heavy concentration in commerce – 58 per cent of heads of household in 1907[6] – because Jews traditionally had been in commerce and because some occupations were closed to Jews and because the service sector of the economy was underdeveloped and because industry imposed heavy capital requirements and because antisemitism kept Jews out of public service and because . . . These statements are probably all true, but we need a way to establish a hierarchy of causation that will replace this overly impressionistic view of social action.

New economic history, as well as other forms of social science history, for all the pretensions and naïve optimism about making history a true social science, suggest ways of looking at situations in Jewish history that allow the historian to regard Jews as something more than a unique element in human experience. Without abandoning the empirical orientation of the historian, one may follow up the suggestions of theoreticians and econometricians. In this essay I will draw my examples primarily from the German context and secondarily from the East European one, but the method and approach have wider applicability.

II

Is there – or was there – a "Jewish economy"? A basic but essentially unexplored question, this is one that strikes to the heart of that "individualised" sphere of activity. Did a variety of "economic men" populate Central Europe, or was there just one economic man in a variety of cultures? Too often the question of group activity becomes confused with that of the activity of individuals belonging to that group. The problem may lie in a misconception as to what Jewish history should be about. In Eastern Europe, Jews may have

[6]Membership list of the Jewish Community of Berlin, 1907, in the Central Archives for the History of the Jewish People, Jerusalem.

formed a separate entity in the economy. But in Germany? Or France, or England, or anywhere else in Western Europe? The case is not so easy to make.

The activities of Jews on the supply side of particular economies have received much more attention than those on the demand side. This, after all, is the customary realm of economic history, old and new, but here much of the work done has involved Jews as individuals without due consideration of whether or not "Jewish" history is involved. By "supply" I refer to all the goods and services offered by Jews, both to the society at large and to Jews in particular.

Arcadius Kahan has proposed that we treat Jews and Poles in inter-war Poland as subjects of two separate economies to be understood with the help of international trade theory.[7] The Jewish sector and the Polish sector of the economy are to be regarded as separate trading areas, each distinct enough to supply specific goods and to demand others from the outside. Leaving aside for the moment the question of whether Kahan supplies adequate data for evaluating his assertions in the Polish context, let us pose similar questions about German Jewry. In contrast to the situation in Poland, Jews formed a much smaller percentage of the total population. Moreover, nowhere except in Poznań before the 1870s and in Berlin after about 1890 did they form a compact mass large enough to demand particular kinds of goods and to supply other goods to the economy as a whole. Margarine manufacturers, for example, turned to them as a specific market, while the fur trade produced a picture of Jewish employers and employees producing for a general German public. There were other "Jewish" trades as well – scrap metal, clothing, private banking, grain trading, cattle dealing, department stores, for example, but these groups provided goods and services to all comers. They were not part of a *total* Jewish economy.[8]

Of course we all knew much of this before – why get bogged down in the theory of comparative advantage (each economy produces what it produces best and trades for other goods)? How does it help us understand Jewish economic life in Germany?

First of all, Jews were integrated into the national economy only gradually during the nineteenth century. South German Jews may have been living in widely separated settlements before the eighteenth century, but the masses of small-town Jews in the Great Poland annexed by Prussia lived in a different sort of existence. Exempted from most of the emancipatory legislation before 1847, these Poznań Jews lived in relatively compact communities and presented an apparently solid front to the outside world. That Jewish world "manufactured" a few items – kosher meat – and provided some services locally – tailoring, baking. It also provided a service for the entire community, retail sales of clothing and other small goods, primarily through peddling. To mention only a few localities, close to 50 per cent of the local Jewish heads of household lived as tradesmen and pedlars in Schönlanke in 1833 and all through the nineteenth

---

[7]Arcadius Kahan, 'A Note on Methods of Research on the Economic History of the Jews', in *For Max Weinrich on His Seventieth Birthday*, The Hague 1964, pp. 173–181.
[8]On fur: Wilhelm Harmelin, 'Jews in the Leipzig Fur Industry', in *LBI Year Book IX* (1964), pp. 239–266. On other trades: the books and articles of Alfred Marcus are an important source of data – e.g., *Die wirtschaftliche Krise der deutschen Juden*, Berlin 1931.

century (approximately 125 Jewish families resident in the town); the numbers ran to over 70 per cent in tiny Schlichtingsheim and in Meseritz.[9] In fact, these itinerant salesmen constituted a distinct and necessary part of the German economy of the day. Like their counterparts in South and Southwest Germany, they performed their work at a relative cost less than the cost to the rural population of buying goods in some other way. In the last quarter of the nineteenth century, improved transport and the rise of Polish and German cooperative associations undercut the relative advantage of the Jews and drove them out of the trade.[10] The Jews in turn had two choices: to take up other occupations or to leave the area. They left.

Why didn't they involve themselves in other occupations? Here the economic analysis must be interwoven with the specifically cultural elements. Jews in the main had avoided farming for many centuries; that point demands no documentation. Poznań in the late nineteenth century provided no such opportunity anyway because the Polish–German nationality struggle had taken on the cast of a struggle over land ownership. The two communities had mobilised enough capital to keep out any interested outsiders.

Artisan occupations also provided little relief. Despite attempts to rehabilitate the Jews from the charge of avoiding manual labour, it seems obvious that most Jewish artisans in this area serviced primarily Jewish customers. Craft guilds, still of some importance in the Prussian East, successfully kept Jews out. The Jewish butchers, bakers and cobblers formed no affluent group; their low tax assessments in several small towns attest to this situation.[11] Any influx of newcomers would have so diluted the available customers as to ruin everyone.

Models of a whole economy often pose intractable problems for historians (and for economists). It is simpler and initially more workable to deal with questions of supply and demand for goods and services from the Jewish population. In this instance, I want to ask what Jews provided for the economies in which they lived. In so doing, we may perceive how better to use the notion of the "Jewish economy" and "Jewish society".

Jewish activity as businessmen, as wholesalers and retailers both small and large, marked Central and East European societies for centuries. Sometimes innovative empire-builders, more often small shopkeepers or petty traders and pedlars, Jews played a role in the economic life of Germany, Poland–Lithuania- and other Eastern European areas that economic historians usually overlook in their frantic search for the components of economic growth. Not only are the language skills in short supply, but also the problem areas popular now are not helpful in discussing those areas of the economy where Jews have been most active. The service industries cannot be measured like the manufacturing ones; they have hardly figured in accounts of industrialising societies.

---

[9]Preussisches Geheimes Staatsarchiv (Berlin–Dahlem): Schönlanke – B Rep. 30, 1130 and 1131; Schlichtingsheim – B Rep. 32, 245 and 248; Meseritz, B Rep. 32, 124.

[10]Ludwig Bernhard, *Die Polenfrage*, Leipzig 1910. More generally, Aleksander Gieysztor *et al.*, *History of Poland*, Warsaw 1968, pp. 536–540, 563–577, 600–602. Jews are generally ignored in these works.

[11]YIVO Institute for Jewish Research archive, files on the towns of Briesen and Ostrowo; Preussisches Geheimes Staatsarchiv, as in note 9.

Recently economic historians have returned to the study of entrepreneurship, so modish in the 1940s and 1950s, but with a new slant. Whereas formerly businessmen in history were seen to act oddly and against their own economic interests, now historians turn to complicated measuring techniques to see whether these anti-heroes might have known what they were doing after all. And in fact the thrust of many of the latest studies lies in the re-affirmation of an old economist's assumption, that men act rationally and in their own economic self-interest (until proven otherwise). Much of the controversy over assumptions and methods of historical analysis passed over the framework of historians of Germany and Eastern Europe, including historians of the Jews. Times are changing, but we are still being treated to pictures of heroic or nasty businessmen with little insight into group behaviour and the influence of such groups on economic development and social action.

Tales of Jewish entrepreneurs are numerous, sometimes bordering on hagiography. They often neglect to ask the question of the significance of the subject. It seems irrelevant to relate the electricity magnates Emil and Walther Rathenau, or even their adviser Felix Deutsch, to Jewish economic history. By no stretch of the imagination was their AEG (German Edison) a Jewish firm, either in terms of management or in terms of the customer base. Likewise Albert de Rothschild, perhaps the most important single banker in Austria at the turn of the twentieth century, hardly headed a "Jewish" bank. Gerson Bleichröder, Bismarck's banker, definitely did not head a "Jewish" banking house in the sense of a discrete Jewish supply sector of the economy. The on-going fascination with Jewish bankers has not managed to take historical knowledge very far beyond the individual.[12]

A systematic approach to economic and social history leads to other research areas. What methods did the Jewish pioneers use to build their businesses? How did they find their suppliers? Hermann Tietz of Hertie department stores and Michael Marks of England's Marks & Spencer had to break down inefficient supply patterns and invent new ones. Why were existing institutions so inflexible, especially in the light of the claim that economic men act rationally? Tietz designed his own goods and went out into the Poznań countryside looking for workmen willing to execute his designs, while Marks, a Russian Jew, had to invent ways to deceive English suppliers unwilling to sell to an enterprise so

---

[12]For a useful survey of the literature on entrepreneurs, see Peter Kilby, 'Hunting the Heffalump', in Peter Kilby, ed., *Entrepreneurship and Economic Development*, New York 1971, pp. 1–40. A notable exception to the heroic entrepreneur thesis: Hartmut Kaelble, *Berliner Unternehmer während der frühen Industrialisierung*, Berlin 1972, including many data on Jews. My own work includes discussion of the behaviour patterns of businessmen and managers in Germany: Lawrence Schofer, *The Formation of a Modern Labor Force. Upper Silesia, 1865–1914*, Berkeley 1975, esp. chapters 9 and 10. On the much discussed Rathenaus, see Ernst Schulin, 'Die Rathenaus. Zwei Generationen jüdischen Anteils an der industriellen Entwicklung Deutschlands', in '*Juden im Wilhelminischen Deutschland, op. cit.*, pp. 116–142. On bankers, Bernard Michel, *Banques et banqiers en Autriche au début du 20ᵉ siècle*, Paris 1976, pp. 309–318. Stress on the individual banker: Fritz Stern, *Gold and Iron. Bismarck, Bleichröder, and the Building of the German Empire*, New York 1977. Sketchy, but suggestive of an approach towards Jewish bankers as a group: Kurt Grunwald, 'Three Chapters of German-Jewish Banking History', in *LBI Year Book XXII* (1977), pp. 191–208.

"morally repugnant" as a department store.[13] What about the other owners – Leonhard Tietz, the Wertheimers, and the rest? Did they introduce a "Jewish" mode of business? As they flourished, did they establish well-functioning bureaucratic institutions? Business historians today find the organisation of enterprise to be the key to successful economic growth. How did these Jewish retailers treat their employees? Did the owners establish new patterns of paternalism, or were their practices indistinguishable from those of other large firms? Can one see similarities between these retailers and big manufacturers, or did the character of the enterprise demand different kinds of bureaucratic patterns?

These retailing giants were not the only Jews involved in sales to the public, and in fact the search for the medium and small Jewish storekeeper is potentially more important for studying Jewish social and economic history. On this point one may refer to other areas of Central and Eastern Europe as well. There were no big Jewish department stores in Poland or Hungary or Romania or the Ukraine, but there were many Jewish stores and Jewish shopkeepers in these areas.

The search for shopkeepers might well begin with the ubiquitous Jewish pedlar, who in the early nineteenth century (and even later) travelled constantly. He moved on foot or by hitching a ride on a wagon, eating his black, often frozen bread, rancid butter, tasteless cheese, ground coffee, sometimes a bit of beef seasoned in garlic. Those eating only kosher food could eat in no one's house, not even that of a relative. Sleeping meant collapsing on straw in wet clothes in some out-of-the-way inn. Jacob Adam stands as a representative Jewish tradesman. Jacob was born in Poznań province while his father was on the road peddling, "like other Jews". His older brother at the age of thirteen joined his father in door-to-door peddling, and he too eventually became a travelling trader in East Prussia. In the home villages, most Jewish wives were grass widows, sitting in sewing circles waiting for their husbands to return from the road. The wait could be long. When one of Jacob's brothers died, it was some time before the father heard of the misfortune. This story typifies Germany, the Pale, and even the United States before the great immigration starting in the 1870s.[14]

As illuminating as such vignettes may be, the image of that society is incomplete unless we address novel questions to some of the same material, questions based on family connections, on capital and credit, and on the quality of their products. How did family connections help a trader on the rise? How much capital did these salesmen have, and how did they use it? Was there any network of credit available specifically to Jews in this age before country banking and

---

[13]Georg Tietz, *Hermann Tietz. Geschichte einer Familie und ihrer Warenhäuser*, Stuttgart 1965, Veröffentlichung des Leo Baeck Instituts; Goronwy Rees, *St. Michael. A History of Marks and Spencer*, London 1969.

[14]The pedlar: Aron Hirsch Heymann, *Lebenserinnerungen*, Berlin 1909, pp. 134–141 (private printing available at the LBI New York). Memoirs: Monika Richarz, ed., *Jüdisches Leben in Deutschland, 1780–1871. Selbstzeugnisse zur Sozialgeschichte*, Stuttgart 1976, Veröffentlichung des Leo Baeck Instituts. Richarz's introduction to this volume is probably the best introductory survey of the German-Jewish history of the period. Jacob Adam, *Tagebuch*, unpublished memoir, LBI New York, pp. 2–4, 39, 43.

mutual aid societies? Did the prominence of Jews in urban private banking aid the small traders? On a different level, what kinds of goods did the pedlars peddle? Were the Jews specialists in the cheap and shoddy, as was their reputation in Eastern Europe? Can one trace any change in type of goods over time, research which would in turn highlight the evolution of the standard of living in the countryside? When did Christians start becoming interested in these occupations? Were the newcomers Germans or Poles, and how was this economic shift related to the emergence of politically potent antisemitism?

These questions ranging over large areas of social and economic activity cannot be answered by any one study. Nevertheless, they all relate to the core problem of the parameters of a Jewish economy. The individualised areas of economic activity can be understood in terms of patterns of supply to consumers and industries. The organisation of this activity played a major role in determining the interaction between Jews and other groups, who had their own individualised traits. In Central Europe such analyses are vital in understanding how class conflict was joined by ethnic conflict to become the major social issues from the turn of the century to the age of the depradations of the Nazis and their imitators.

The pedlar belonged to the world of the small and medium businessman in Germany, the world of the *Mittelstand*, which has once again come to the fore in historical research. Long pilloried as the major electoral support of the Nazis, this amorphous conglomeration of artisans, small-scale merchants and white-collar workers now figures in the work of more analytical and simultaneously more sympathetic historians.[15] The whole topic demands more extensive justification of the lumping together of such disparate groups, despite the many cases of artisans (e.g., bakers) acting as merchants of their own goods. In the main, it might be better to separate artisans and shopkeepers, particularly as one looks at the unfolding of industrial society. Early in the nineteenth century, many may have functioned as their own retailers, but most historians have dwelled on the artisans alone. Before the 1840s Jewish artisans lived in the small towns of the East, and one is probably justified in seeing this band of Jewish suppliers serving mainly Jewish customers. Thus the glaziers, tailors, bakers and others of Poznań may well have formed an identifiable sub-sector of the economy before the middle of the century.

Once having migrated to the cities, these craftsmen abandoned any participation in a strictly Jewish economy. Even where they held on to their old trades, they can hardly have subsisted on the basis of their Jewish customers alone. This generalisation may not hold for the *Ostjuden*, the newcomers from Eastern Europe after 1890 and especially after 1900. A comparative investigation of the possibilities for a separate Jewish supply and demand sector of the local economy might reveal a great deal about the dynamics of urbanisation among Jews and Germans.

---

[15]Shulamit Angel-Volkov, 'The Social and Political Function of Late 19th Anti-Semitism: The Case of the Small Handicraft Masters', in Hans-Ulrich Wehler, ed., *Sozialgeschichte Heute. Festschrift für Hans Rosenberg*, Göttingen 1974, pp. 416–432. Heinrich August Winkler, *Mittelstand, Demokratie und Nationalsozialismus*, Cologne 1972.

Merchants, traders, travelling salesmen, salespeople, commercial apprentices formed a second and less well understood segment of the *Mittelstand*. From the standpoint of class analysis, they did not form a coherent group, for they were a mixture of employers and employees, independent and quasi-independent businessmen, budding entrepreneurs and frustrated shopowners, and white-collar workers. Upwardly mobile artisans and downwardly mobile bourgeois fleshed out this protean and growing mass known as the "lower middle class". The divide between the *Mittelstand* and the proletariat remained wide, a gap widened in German politics by the open antisemitism of some of these white-collar groups.

The topic here is not antisemitism, which is hardly a neglected subject among historians of the Jews. But one does need to ask about the social and economic status of this lower middle class among German Jews, who differed significantly from the Jews of the Pale. If one eventually succeeds in demarking a specific Jewish area of labour supply to the market, it will obviously be in this sector of the economy. While Eastern European Jews engaged extensively in handicrafts as well as in trade, the German Jews (including those in Poznań) moved more and more exclusively into the realm of trade. The Jewish middleman – the cattle dealer, the grain trader, the pedlar – was a familiar sight all over Central and Eastern Europe; alternative occupations were few. Social mobility can be discussed in terms of small-time pedlars (*Handelsmann*) and merchants (*Kaufmann*). The invidious distinction between the two levels of merchant emerges clearly when one traces the self-definition of occupations over a period of time. For example, the designation *Handelsmann* became less and less common in the Prussian towns of Briesen and Ostrowo, and *Kaufmann* came to dominate, even though gradations of taxes based on income suggest a continuing split among poorer and wealthier merchants. By the time people moved to Berlin, practically no one admitted to being a *Handelsmann* any more.[16]

The reality behind this notation presents intriguing questions for historical research. It might be possible to grade this Jewish lower middle class by wealth alone, and in that sense social mobility is easy to grasp. Prestige and social ranking, however, must be introduced into the equation, and they are hard to define. Nonetheless, studies of mobility here would carry over into general German society. Was the malaise said to be afflicting the lower middle class at the end of the nineteenth century applicable to Jews as well? Were Jews more likely to be upwardly mobile than non-Jews, or were they less pessimistic because they were not bound emotionally and economically to a pre-industrial order? If the economic argument proves to be valid, then historians of Germany must be more careful than hitherto to differentiate between the artisan and shopkeeper segments of the *Mittelstand*. Most artisans suffered from or felt threatened by industrialisation; shopkeepers and traders profited from the increasing prosperity of their customers. All the old *Mittelstand* shopkeepers and artisans alike supported the punitive taxes on department stores that state after state enacted after the turn of the century, but those engaged in commerce could not but

---

[16]Briesen and Ostrowo from the YIVO archives; Berlin – see any available list of community members. The earliest one I have been able to locate dates from 1886.

profit from the new factory-made consumer products entering the market. Shopkeepers and artisans did not share the same fate. As the "anti-capitalist" programmes became tinged with antisemitic ideology, the Jewish merchantry tended to identify itself with the new and against the anti-modernist groups. Jews *qua* Jews acted distinctly in this area; this Jewish sector of the economy is ripe for investigation. It would also be important to know how parallel groups of Germans and Jews behaved during these years. As elsewhere, the questions should not be confined to "mere" ethnic history.[17]

I have only a few words to say about the analysis of demand. One may ask whether there existed any definable Jewish subsectors of an economy. From the consumer (demand) side, did Jews demand specific products wanted by no other people? The example of kosher food is obvious, but we know little about that market. Of course Jewish ritual slaughterers and butchers abounded in Poznań and in other areas of Jewish settlement in Germany, to say nothing of Europe farther east. But quantitatively, who ate what where? Changing consumption patterns, presumably identifiable from German data on cattle production, wholesale prices, and retail sales, might be developed for the Jewish population. Such information would be quite helpful in understanding the changing material position of German Jews. Data on Poland and Russia are scarcer, but information most likely can be found in scattered regional records. How good was the Jewish diet? Does the diet help explain why Jewish population growth differed from that of other ethnic groups, assuming that one can verify the oft-held notion about the relatively rapid Jewish population growth in the nineteenth century.[18]

Tantalising clues of other sorts emerge from unexpected sources. For example, the chance introduction in 1899 of *Sana* brand margarine, an all-vegetable oil product, provoked an enormous response from German Jews, opening up retailing possibilities undreamed of earlier.[19] Can other goods be classified as "Jewish" – ritual garments, certain types of cloth, ritual paraphernalia, specific types of books, etc.? Taken together, these kinds of items would help one construct a picture of the Jewish consumer demand in specific countries. This is a question for research prompted by the most basic sort of economic theory, but proposed answers can be supplied only by persistent research in records of all sorts, research supplemented by statistical techniques of averaging, interpolation, index prices, and the like. Even more difficult is the task of identifying Jewish con-

---

[17]Good general statements, but lacking the distinction between artisans and shopkeepers: Herman Lebovics, ' "Agrarians" versus "Industrializers". Social Conservative Resistance to Industrialism and Capitalism in Late Nineteenth Century Germany', in *International Review of Social History*, XII (1967), pp. 31–65; Thomas Childers, 'The Social Bases of the National Socialist Vote', in *Journal of Contemporary History*, XI (1976), pp. 17–42. Even Hans Rosenberg, who recognises the separateness of the two groups, generally treats them as a whole – *Grosse Depression und Bismarckzeit*, Berlin 1967, pp. 102, 150, 178. The distinction is made by Robert Gellately, *The Politics of Economic Despair. Shopkeepers and German Politics 1890–1914*, London 1974.

[18]Assertions on the general health of the Jews, Gottfried Schramm, 'Die Ostjuden als soziales Problem des 19. Jahrhunderts', in Heinz Maus *et al.*, eds., *Gesellschaft, Recht und Politik*, Neuwied 1968, pp. 362–364.

[19]Charles Wilson, *The History of Unilever*, London 1954, vol. 2, p. 73.

sumer taste for items not ritually linked – herring, for example. The mere compilation of a list of such items would be an interesting and rewarding but arduous task.

III

When a local labour market is saturated, when labour supply far outstrips demand, labour usually migrates. The rapid move out of the villages and small towns of Eastern Prussia after the middle of the nineteenth century suggests that economic conditions were quite strained even before Prussia began to industrialise in the 1830s. Support for this perception comes from the records of Jewish communities, debt-ridden and unable to improve their situation. Such was the case of the township of Samter, to cite but one example. Large debts to monasteries and nunneries remained unpaid, while local Jews hoped for repayment of smaller loans they had made to the community.[20] Once the institutional constraints on the labour market fell (free migration after 1847), the personnel of the specifically Jewish labour market marched off in search of a better life. This "push" from the local economy sufficed to account for what was happening. Antisemitism in the Polish national movement did not trigger the move. Indeed, Polish nationalism in Poznań emerged as a significant social force only somewhat later, in the 1860s; it was fuelled by a struggle between the Polish and German subsectors of the national economy.

European migration in the nineteenth century was primarily a rural to urban phenomenon, a result of the unprecedented population increase following a rapid decline in the death rate. Everywhere people were on the move. First the English, Scots and Irish moved, then the Germans and Scandinavians, and then in the second half of the century the Jews, Poles, Ukrainians, Italians and the many others living in Eastern and Southern Europe. When the Southwest Germans moved, so did the Jews of Southwest Germany; when the Eastern Europeans moved, so did the Eastern European Jews. This is a clear case of a general European phenomenon, not of some specific ethnic peculiarity stemming from pogroms or general antisemitism. A familiar story, but one that bears repeating; it is a clear example of the utility of a truly comparative history.

Truly comparative? I refer to the process of delineating lines of development apparent in similar processes and of formulating hypotheses based on these similarities. So the European migrations of the nineteenth century seem to stem from economic motivations in all countries. This is in short an explanation stripped of arguments based on infinite peculiarities of individuals and groups. The universality of this approach obviously leaves a lot to be considered; this is that individualised area of values and tastes that form so important an element in human activity. On the whole the Jews, Irish and Scandinavians migrated to the United States in family groups; the Poles, Ukrainians, Italians and most others supplied young working males who intended eventually to return to the

[20]Preussisches Geheimes Staatsarchiv B Rep. 32, 215. See also Michael Zarchin, *Jews in the Province of Posen*, Philadelphia 1939, p. 46 ff.

homeland. Other family members followed only after a long lag. That is one step in inserting group values into an understanding of the migratory process. We can become even more specific by talking about land hunger in Sweden, the loss of Jewish tavern-keeping privileges in Galicia and the Russian Pale of Settlement, and the expulsion of Jews from rural areas of the Pale. Instead of seeing the world of the past atomised into fragments labelled solely by ethnicity, we can say with more accuracy and with greater confidence how Jews (and other groups) expressed their own peculiar values by first sorting out universal processes and then moving to the particulars.[21]

The emigrants flocked to find economic opportunities; for Jews in Germany that meant the cities, particularly Berlin (see Table I), but also Breslau, Frankfurt, Cologne, Hamburg, Leipzig and Munich.

TABLE I
The Jewish Population of Berlin, 1811–1910

Year	Total population	Jews	Jews as % of total
1811	169,763	3,292	1·94
1840	328,692	6,456	1·96
1871	825,937	36,015	4.36
1890	1,578,794	79,286	5·02
1910	2,071,257	90,013	4·34

SOURCE: Jacob Segall, 'Die Entwicklung der jüdischen Bevölkerung in Berlin von 1811–1910', Zeitschrift für Demographie und Statistik der Juden, IX (1913), p. 9.

Who left and who stayed? Small town Jewry in Poznań declined precipitously in the second half of the nineteenth century; town after town lost large numbers of Jews, often culminating in the extinction of Jewish community life. A few examples are given in Table II.

However, there may well have been a pattern of exit. Did the affluent or the poor or the artisans or whoever leave first? Manuscript censuses or other un-

[21] On immigrant peculiarities, Josef J. Barton, *Peasants and Strangers. Italians, Rumanians, and Slovaks in an American City, 1890–1950*, Cambridge, U.S.A. 1975. General model of migration, with broad implications for social and economic change: Richard A. Easterlin, *Population, Labor Force, and Long Swings in Economic Growth*, New York 1968. Broad overview of the population problems of Eastern European Jews: Schramm, 'Die Ostjuden', (note 18), pp. 353–380. A broad look at Jewish migration: Kuznets, 'Economic Structure', (note 1). More particularly on Germany: Heinrich Silbergleit, *Die Bevölkerungs- und Berufsverhältnisse der Juden im Deutschen Reich*, vol. 1, Berlin 1930; Klara Eschelbacher, 'Die ostjüdische Einwanderungsbevölkerung der Stadt Berlin', in *Zeitschrift für Demographie und Statistik der Juden*, XVI (1930), pp. 2–20. On Poland, see the extraordinarily interesting collection of letters from the New World to the Old, including a number by Jewish settlers: *Listy emigrantów z Brazylii i Stanów Zjednoczonych 1890–1891* (Letters from emigrants from Brazil and the United States 1890–1891), Warsaw 1973. Also Bohdan Wasiutynski, *Ludność żydowska w Polsce w wiekach XIX i XX* (The Jewish population in Poland in the 19th and 20th centuries), Warsaw 1930; Szyja Bronsztejn, *Ludność żydowska w Polsce w okresie międzywojennym* (The Jewish population in Poland in the inter-war period), Wroclaw 1963. On migration in particular: Artur Eisenbach, 'La mobilité territoriale de la population juive du Royame de Pologne', in *Revue des études juives*, CXXVI (1967), pp. 55–111, 435–471; CXXVII (1968), pp. 39–95. Most recently: Simon Kuznets, 'Immigration of Russian Jews to the United States. Background and Structure', in *Perspectives in American History*, IX (1975) pp. 33–124.

published census materials would provide some answers. For students of German-Jewish history, that means being subjected to the vagaries of the East German archives; elsewhere in Eastern Europe, conditions vary by country. The Poles, for example, are usually cooperative, but they lost huge amounts of material during the Second World War; the Russians are recalcitrant in general, let alone on Jewish topics. Even for Poland one may entertain hopes of finding novel material, a hope nourished by a recent study of Christian marriage certificates in the Warsaw of the 1850s.[22]

Nevertheless, scattered materials do exist which may supply the data demanded by the new techniques. Jews in Germany belonged to formally recognised communities, and many such lists of people can be found for communities

TABLE II

Jews in Cities in Poznań Province, 1849–1905

Settlement	Number of Jews		% of local population	
	1849	1905	1849	1905
Posen City	7,651	5,761	20	5
Samter	990	537	38	10
Grätz	1,360	250	29	7
Brätz	180	1	12	—

SOURCE: Bernhard Breslauer, *Die Abwanderung der Juden aus der Provinz Posen*, Berlin 1909, Tables A and B.

large and small. Hints of mortality and fertility emerge in these documents, as well as suggestions of marriage patterns. Most clearly one sees evidence of income and of social and occupational stratification.

In the archives of the YIVO Institute for Jewish Research (New York) I found lists of members of the community of Briesen (West Prussia) and their tax assessments from the early 1880s to the First World War. (The German church tax was compulsory.) I now propose to undertake an inventory of the names found in the early list and compare individual names with subsequent lists to find out who left when. With occupations and tax assessments given, I will be able to make some judgment about the pattern of emigration and about the changing relative wealth of the Jewish community. Who left first, rich or poor? Was emigration balanced by an immigration? How did the occupational preferences of Jews compare with those of the Christian population? Can one identify those separate economies postulated by the theory of international trade? A small beginning, but a beginning nevertheless.

The Jewish Community of Berlin published membership lists too, although only archival sources will reveal the tax assessments. In the future I hope to trace some of the people from Eastern Germany to Berlin itself, and there is reason to hope that regional archives in Poznań will yield more information.

---

[22]Stefania Kowalska-Glikman, *Ruchliwość społeczna i zawodowa mieszkańców Warszawy w latach 1845–1861* (The Social and Occupational Mobility of the Inhabitants of Warsaw 1845–1861), Wroclaw 1971.

Mortality has not received great attention from theorists, but one cannot explain the great population explosion of the nineteenth century – the demographic transition – without tracing the sources of mortality decline. Historians have noted a lower death rate of Jews than that of other Eastern Europeans. Given our knowledge of high urban mortality in the nineteenth century, one is hard put to fathom the reputation of Jews for surviving better than other groups. We need a more detailed study of health and illness among Jews and among other groups to understand this component of population change and its relationship to group mores.

Similarly, Jewish birth rates seemed to diverge from the average in both Germany and Central Europe. Why so? Urban life, lower infant mortality rates, low rates of illegitimacy can all be proposed as explanations. They all seem warranted, but doors lie open before ingenious researchers to spell out the peculiarities of group life which account for perceptible separatism in demographic behaviour. Jews might also be drawn into the realm of the historical demographers' favourites: (1) What caused the sharp decline in European fertility that started around 1880? (2) Are there any discernible trends in pre-1880s fertility?

By studying fertility and mortality, one will be able to say with some confidence if and how Jews differed from other ethnic groups. If indeed they were healthier, why? Was it the tradition of community welfare, of care for the poor? Did German Jews show patterns of mortality similar to Germans or to East European Jews? Did German-Jewish fertility decline earlier than German fertility, or do ethnic differences become irrelevant when one accounts for socio-economic variables? A whole host of hypotheses can be supported or refuted by answering carefully phrased comparative questions. All of this needs to be done with control groups, that is, with other parts of the population subject to the same trends being used for comparison. In this way we can learn what was distinctively Jewish about Central European Jews, and we will also be learning what was distinctively German or Polish or whatever about other ethnic groups.[23]

For a number of writers, the family economy represents a vehicle for testing the impact of urban life on new immigrants, often differentiated by ethnic group. In particular the city locale and/or factory employment seem to have led to the break-up of the traditional arrangement of husband, wife, and children all sharing common work tasks and participating in a family division of labour. This was true in farming and was true of the textile industry and other artisan trades. When the peasant family entered the city or when factory division of labour prevented the handicraftsman from using his children as helpers, the

[23] For a very sophisticated general treatment of all these demographic questions, cf. Calvin Goldscheider, *Population, Modernization and Social Structure*, Boston 1971, and his articles noted there on the fertility of the Jews. On Germany: John E. Knodel, *The Decline of Fertility in Germany, 1871–1939*, Princeton 1974, and his articles noted there. Also see many of the articles in the pre-First World War *Zeitschrift für Demographie und Statistik der Juden* and several still unpublished articles by Steven Lowenstein, including 'Voluntary and Involuntary Fertility in Nineteenth Century Bavarian Jewry'. Another source is mined in Alice Goldstein, 'Some Demographic Characteristics of Village Jews in Germany. Nonnenweier, 1800–1931', unpublished paper, Brown University (using *Ortssippenbücher*).

whole framework for intra-familiar economic relations changed. Married women stayed at home or worked sporadically; children went out on their own.[24]

Jews, however, did not participate in the same way in the urbanising process. For those with previous experience in commerce, the change of setting did not prove so unsettling. Women, men and children had not lived and worked in the same kind of farm or workshop milieu as had their Central European neighbours. The Jews' urban-style occupations made it much easier for them to shift to a new setting of service industries; this may account for their success in rapidly building viable and prosperous communities in German big cities. For those in artisan occupations or in inn-keeping, the shock was more severe. The innkeepers in Poland, Russia and Galicia were driven into poverty starting early in the nineteenth century. Artisans held on longer, especially where they could supply a specifically Jewish market, but by the 1890s, and certainly by the 1920s, they were being rapidly squeezed out of the market-place. Industrial opportunities did not open up on any great scale for Eastern European Jews, and only the possibility of overseas migration delayed the onset of a great economic catastrophe. That catastrophe had come over the horizon in Poland well before the entry of the Nazis.[25]

It seems obvious then that in the case of the family economy one must differentiate clearly among ethnic groups. Life experiences peculiar to Jews in pre-industrial times paved the way for many of them to rapidly shift into urban life; other national groups did not enjoy the same advantages and often underwent more painful adjustments in the new environment.

IV

From the world of work many have moved to more "exotic" areas, areas stemming from the conviction that people are best understood by popular phenomena like leisure-time activities, sex-life, interpersonal communication. The working poor, the beggars and the underworld, groups apart from high culture, emerge as favoured subjects. When Alfred Döblin chronicled the life of Franz Bieberkopf in *Berlin Alexanderplatz*, he turned to the slum and underworld quarter known as the *Scheunenviertel*, the same streets around which centred the life of the Berlin *Ostjuden*. One must assume that Jews in Germany were not all

---

[24]On farming in an ethnically distinct context: Lyn Lees, 'Mid-Victorian Migration and the Irish Family Economy', in *Victorian Studies*, XX (1976), pp. 26–29. General statement on women's work: Joan W. Scott and Louise A. Tilly, 'Women's Work and the Family in Nineteenth-Century Europe', in *Comparative Studies in Society and History*, XVII (1975), pp. 36–64.

[25]On the pace of change in Germany, see Toury, *Soziale und politische Geschichte* (note 4) and his 'Der Eintritt der Juden ins deutsche Bürgertum', in *Das Judentum in der deutschen Umwelt 1800–1850. Studien zur Frühgeschichte der Emanzipation*, herausgegeben von Hans Liebeschütz und Arnold Paucker, Tübingen 1977 (Schriftenreihe wissenschaftlicher Abhandlungen des Leo Baeck Instituts 35). Cf. the study of Warsaw by Jacob Lestschinsky, 'Hayishuv hayehudi behithpathchutho hakalkalith', (The economic development of the Jewish community) in *Entsyklopedia shel Galuyot*, vol. 1: *Varshah*, Jerusalem 1959, pp. 125–218. Extremely useful: Steven M. Lowenstein, 'The Pace of Modernisation of German Jewry in the Nineteenth century', in *LBI Year Book XXI* (1976), pp. 41–56.

part of the respectable bourgeoisie; as in other countries, they certainly formed part of the poor, the lumpenproletariat, and the underworld. That image has been obscured by romantic filiopietism, but it is only too clear from autobiography and fiction, such as Isaac Bashevis Singer on Warsaw and elsewhere and Isaac Babel on Odessa.[26]

Possibilities for studies of social life are legion, but precisely in this area new social historians can lapse into antiquarianism or filiopietism or triviality. To avoid such pitfalls, the historian of ethnic groups must constantly keep in mind the general trends of the larger society. Once again, individualised areas provide the flavour of historical study, but certain developments in the national economy and society are inescapable. One way of drawing together many of the diverse strands mentioned here is to turn to the city as the crucible of a new society.

Three general approaches dominate the way historians, sociologists, geographers, planners and others deal with the city.[27] The first, the most traditional and the most common among historians, is to treat people who live in a city and events that occur there as urban history: urban context=urban history. This assumption certainly characterises studies of the Jews, who in the context of nineteenth- and twentieth-century Europe were associated primarily with things urban. Not that all Jews lived in cities – South German Jews lived in villages until the First World War, and perhaps 25 per cent of the Polish Jews were living in rural communes in 1931. However, the Jews pursued non-agricultural callings, and that trait prepared them for the move to cities when the opportunities arose. This is not urban history as such; there is nothing "new" about it. This type of history may be sensitively done, or it may be purely antiquarian. Among students of Jewish studies, the latter have predominated. In either case, writers have omitted the specifically urban character of their subject.[28]

The other two approaches comprise really new ways of dealing with the subject. One method takes its cue from geography and demography; it emphasises the use of space within the city with special emphasis on population movements in the aggregate.[29] Although some urbanists are particularly fond of this approach, the generalising nature of the theory tends to blot out the individuality and idiosyncracies of individual groups in favour of broader social processes. In fact, it is "urbanisation" as a broad process that draws interest here, and specific cities or specific social groups emerge only as examples of something more general. If Jews were the subject at hand, the practitioner of this approach would seek to use them as examples of migration or urban occupational distribution or the like. On the whole, this kind of analysis seems in-

---

[26]Todd M. Endelman, *The Jews of Georgian England*, Philadelphia 1978, based on trial records of Old Bailey. Cf. Rudolf Glanz, *Geschichte des niederen deutschen Volkes in Deutschland*, New York 1968. Pre-First World War – cf. the setting of I. B. Singer, *In My Father's Court*, New York 1962. Integration in the 1920s: the memoir account of Bernard Goldstein, *Tsvantsig yor in varshever "Bund", 1919–1939*, New York 1960.

[27]Roy Lubove, 'The Urbanization Process. An Approach to Historical Research', in *Journal of the American Institute of Planners*, XXXIII (1967), pp. 33–39.

[28]A mixture of the sensitive and antiquarian: Jacob Shatzki, *Geshikhte fun Yidn in Varshe*, 3 vols., New York 1947–53. Cf. Lestschinsky, 'Hayishuv' (note 25).

[29]See especially Eric Lampard, 'History of Cities in the Economically Advanced Areas', in *Economic Development and Cultural Change*, III (1955), pp. 86–102.

hospitable to the kinds of case studies that interest students of Jewish history, but there is no theoretical reason why the two foci cannot be combined. Students of German history have provided some raw material for such work, but even the long series of publications by the Historical Commission of Berlin has not presented any really forceful conceptual analyses.

One might find more accommodating the other half of the new urban history, the notion of the city as "artifact", the city as a peculiar and differentiated form for living in which social groups and institutions both social and physical interact to create new forms of civilisation. For example, how do specific ethnic groups fit into the evolving nature of the city? What institutions do they create to help them make the new surroundings livable? An historian of the Jews then can ask how "Jewishness" changed the character of specific cities – the bourgeois Jews of Berlin/Charlottenburg; the proletarians and immigrants of Warsaw; the manufacturers and workers of Lodz; and so on down the line of cities of Jewish concentration large and small, from Vienna, Budapest and Odessa to Gnesen (Germany), Chrzanów (Russian Poland) and Minsk (Russia). One must be careful to continue phrasing problems in terms of a peculiarly urban environment. Studies emphasising land use give evidence on the process of city-building over time; the result will be less the case of Jews who happened to live in Berlin or Munich and more that of Jewish colouration of the city. If Jews were not concentrated enough and not important enough to influence the character of the city, as in Munich, it might still be worthwhile using this physically orientated framework to understand Jewish communal life.

Anti-capitalist and anti-urban propagandists of course use the Jewish quarters of these cities as evidence for their tirades against the new industrial, emancipated world, but how real were their charges? What reality underlay the perception of the "Jewish city"? This is the obverse side of the question of how the city affected the Jews, and some of the issues involved are not difficult to pose. They would, for example, take the form of an investigation of Jewish support for the arts, or Jewish urban philanthropy as it affected the society as a whole. It should be noted that this is not the same as investigating Jewish capitalists or Jewish importance in German textiles, metal trading, private banking, and grain trading. These are older topics still worth investigating, but they do not make use of the formation of the urban environment as a way to understand Jewish life.[30]

How did the Jews affect the city? Not an easy question to answer. Students of the Jews and other ethnic groups too readily assume that their particular group made an obvious, indelible, and lasting impact, but the comparative work necessary to substantiate such hypotheses usually is not done. To know whether the Jews shaped or re-shaped urban life in Berlin or Vienna or Budapest, one must articulate the underlying general processes and study them in other contexts as well. One might well hypothesise that the key variables in modern

---

[30]Jewish capitalists: Hugo Rachel and Paul Wallich, *Berliner Grosskaufleute und Kapitalisten*, vol. 3, revised edn., Berlin 1967; Kaelbe, *Berliner Unternehmer* (note 12). More specifically Jewish: Alfred Marcus, 'Jews as Entrepreneurs in Weimar Germany', in *YIVO Annual of Jewish Social Science*, VII (1952), pp. 175–203.

city-building lie in technology, the type of economic activity supported by the physical environment, the shape of the labour market and in migratory patterns. One is then hard put to talk of the Jewish influence on Berlin, or even on Warsaw or Lodz, when developments in St. Petersburg and London and Lille seem so similar. This is not to deride the study of Jewish economic and social history, but to caution against inflated claims on the basis of intense self-interest.

The new urban history and the new social history are promising approaches, but their methods and concepts stand as empty boxes unless filled with empirical reality. There is a certain amount of work going on, much of it by younger historians, that may fit into these categories. To give a sense of the possibilities, I will turn here to my own current project on European Jewish history: 'The Jews of Berlin and Warsaw, 1850–1939. Migration, Urbanisation, and Occupational Stratification'.

I pose a series of interrelated questions about the Central European experience of Jews from the middle of the nineteenth century (beginning of mass migration to these capital cities) to the take-over by the Nazis. What prompted large numbers of people, Jews and Germans and Poles, to move from farm, village and small town to the big city? In particular, how did the metropolises of Berlin and Warsaw act as magnets for huge numbers of people, especially after the onset of industrialisation in these countries? The answers are not to be found simply in an account of population growth, changing health standards, shifts in the labour market and differential growth of industry. Jews in Germany acted differently from other Germans; Jews in Poland acted differently from other Poles. Was there a wholly different system of values and tastes which led to these variations in behaviour? In other words, did German Jews act from the same motives as Polish Jews? Were the observed differences merely a reflection of different opportunities, or were they simply like other Germans and Poles in similar socio-economic situations? Answering these queries means establishing more precisely than we have till now the economic structure of the Jewish community and comparing it to the general trends of the societies in which they lived.

Secondly, under what auspices did people move? Was it the need for work that prompted them to go, or did kinship and neighbourly ties attract them to new homes? Or was it a combination of these, whereby small town and rural people looking for work moved to those places where they could expect a welcome. Did the three ethnic groups differ? I suspect they did; I suspect that the Jews were much more dependent on an informal network of family and countrymen than were the other groups. It was only with the newcomers after 1900 in Berlin (earlier in Warsaw) that hospitality flagged, and one catches glimpses of a whole new set of institutions for "Eastern Jews" (*Ostjuden*). Indeed, two Jewish sub-cultures seemed to emerge in Berlin, and I should like to learn about parallel processes in Poland.[31]

Other issues, particularly those revolving around the choice of occupation and

---

[31]See the highly instructive Charles Tilly and C. Harold Brown, 'On Uprooting, Kinship, and the Auspices of Migration', *International Journal of Comparative Sociology*, VII (1967), pp. 139–164.

around the urban life experience, emerge as significant ones for expanding our understanding of Jewish activity in big-city industrial life. There is no need to list them all here. Work similar to this project has been done for England and France, but there is hardly anything available for Germany or Slavic Central Europe. Certainly little has appeared from the pens of historians of the Jews. In the end, I hope to have said a good deal about the general processes of migration, urbanisation, and the interaction of cultural values and economic activity. In this case I have the opportunity of generating hypotheses about comparative history, a comparative history that will be more than a mere juxtaposition of national experiences.

V

The "newness" of the new economic, social and urban histories may in many cases be more semantic than actual. However, some imaginative scholars and their disciples have been able to shift the focus of work in their fields in ways that should be beneficial to the future of Jewish historiography. Examples here derive primarily from Germany, but the concepts and approaches are similar for most European countries and for the United States.

Many useful and exciting approaches emerge from these recent developments, but historians of the Jews must clarify the status of the Jews in the whole enterprise. Is the condition of "Jewishness" to be the independent variable, that item which explains the eccentricities, idiosyncrasies and oddities of the group under discussion? Or is Jewishness to be the dependent variable, something to be explained in terms of more basic and universal developments, such as overpopulation, fertility decline and the like? Historical change is probably the result of "Jewishness" working in both capacities in various contexts, and it is the interplay of the two roles that gives a specific culture or ethnic group its particular place in history.

Problems of Jewish Resistance Historiography

BY KONRAD KWIET

I

When one considers all the research on fascism and anti-fascism within the Federal Republic of Germany, it is evident that the problem area of a German-Jewish resistance has so far largely been passed over in silence. For many years, the German historians had in any case felt bound by a long tradition and had left the historical investigation and interpretation of the history of the German Jews, of antisemitism and of the persecution of the Jews to those directly affected: to the Jews themselves.[1] Behind a protective shield of their own making German historians, feeling themselves affected only indirectly, shunned the obligation and responsibility of providing information on and giving an account of a society which had posed the "Jewish question" – and answered it with Auschwitz. Not until the 1960s did this picture change. Against the background of the West German trials of the murderers of Jews, antisemitic excesses and the Eichmann trial in Jerusalem, antisemitism and the persecution of the Jews moved to the centre of attention for the general public and for research and teaching in the universities. Initially that attention was centred on the structure and development of the Nazi ruling system and the course of the processes of persecution both at the central and the regional level. It is only very recently that there has been a tendency to include the German-Jewish organisations and the conduct of the Jewish population within the canon of subjects worthy of research.[2] Nonetheless, the mass of monographs and essays, documentary and memorial books cannot conceal the fact that both the empirical–historical sorting out of details and the formulation of a theory are still very much in a fragmentary state.[3] The same is essentially true of the Marxist–Leninist historiography in the German Democratic Republic, the state of which was examined critically in this Year Book in 1976.[4] It was only later that historians in other

---

[1]Werner Schochow, *Deutsch-Jüdische Geschichtswissenschaft. Eine Geschichte ihrer Organisationsformen unter besonderer Berücksichtigung der Fachbibliographie*, Berlin 1969; Hans Joachim Bieber, 'Zur bürgerlichen Geschichtsschreibung und Publizistik über Antisemitismus, Zionismus und den Staat Israel', in *Das Argument*, 75 (1972); Reinhard Rürup, *Emanzipation und Antisemitismus. Studien zur "Judenfrage" der bürgerlichen Gesellschaft*, Göttingen 1975.

[2]Herbert S. Levine, 'Die wissenschaftliche Untersuchung des Verhaltens der Juden zur Zeit der nationalsozialistischen Verfolgungen und die Hemmungen einer unbewältigten Vergangenheit', in *Tradition and Neubeginn*. Internationale Forschungen zur deutschen Geschichte im 20. Jahrhundert, Referate und Diskussionen eines Symposiums der Alexander von Humboldt-Stiftung, 10.-15. September 1974 in Bad Brückenau, ed. by J. Hütter (a.o.), Köln 1975, pp. 409–429.

[3]See Ino Arndt/Wolfgang Scheffler, 'Organisierter Massenmord an Juden in nationalsozialistischen Vernichtungslager', in *Vierteljahrshefte für Zeitgeschichte*, 24 (1974), p. 105.

[4]Konrad Kwiet, 'Historians of the German Democratic Republic on Antisemitism and Persecution', in *LBI Year Book XXI* (1976), pp. 173–198.

countries addressed themselves to research into the behaviour patterns of the Jews under persecution and in particular to the vexed question of Jewish resistance. But it remained characteristic that research work continued to be concentrated on the events within the areas occupied by the German Forces during the Second World War, in Eastern Europe especially, because, it was here, in the main centres of European Jewry that the special pre-conditions and forms of a specifically Jewish resistance could be shown and evaluated by examples of attempted escapes, revolts in the ghettos and extermination camps as well as active participation in partisan warfare.[5]

Apart from this general trend which was doubtless influenced by a number of personal factors (e.g. origins, language), much more attention began now to be devoted anyway to the history of the German Jews for which the decisive foundations were laid by the publications of the Leo Baeck Institute which, however, occupied itself largely (though not entirely) with the period up to 1933.[6] In our context Arnold Paucker has shown how the Jews resisted the growing danger of Nazism and outlined the history and problems of Jewish self-defence in the years leading to Hitler's rise to power.[7] H. G. Adler has discussed the question of resistance in sections of his monumental work on the deportation of German Jews.[8]

Israeli historians have of late concerned themselves more and more with areas of German-Jewish history after 1933. In the wake of Ball-Kaduri and Esh, Freeden, Ginat and Adler-Rudel, further gaps in research have been closed by the most recent studies and documentations by Margaliot on the role and activities of German-Jewish organisations, those by Ophir on the Jewish com-

---

[5]Apart from the early contributions in the *Yad Vashem Studies*, *Yad Vashem Bulletin* and *Bulletin of the Wiener Library* see: *Jewish Resistance during the Holocaust. Proceedings of the Conference on Manifestations of Jewish Resistance*, Jerusalem, April 7–11, 1968, Yad Vashem Jerusalem 1971; Lucien Steinberg, *La Révolte des Justes*, Paris 1970 (English edition: *Not as a Lamb*, Farnborough 1974); A. Latour, *La Résistance juive en France*, Paris 1970; Leni Yahil, *The Rescue of Danish Jewry*, Philadelphia 1969; Jacob Presser, *Ondergang. De vervolging en verdelging van het Nederlandse Jodendom 1940–1945*, 's-Gravenhage 1965 (English edition: *The Destruction of Dutch Jews*, New York 1969); I. Trunk, *Judenrat*, New York–London 1972; Yuri Suhl, *They fought back*, New York 1967 (1975); E. Ringelblum, *Polish-Jewish relations during the Second World War*, ed. by J. Kermish and Sh. Krakowski, Jerusalem 1974; Reuben Ainsztein, *Jewish Resistance in Nazi-occupied Eastern Europe*, London 1974; N. Benchley, *Bright Candles*, New York 1974; B. Stadler, *The Holocaust. A History of Courage and Resistance*, New York 1974; Gilles Lambert, *Operation Hazalah*, New York 1974; P. Mann/R. Kluger, *The Last Escape*, New York 1973; B. Mark, *Uprising in the Warsaw Ghetto*, New York 1975; Yehuda Bauer, *Flight and Rescue*, *Brichah*, New York 1970; *They chose Life*, New York 1973; *My Brother's Keeper*, Philadelphia 1974; 'Onkel Saly' – Die Verhandlungen des Saly Meyer zur Rettung der Juden 1944/1945', in *Vierteljahrshefte für Zeitgeschichte*, 25 (1977), pp. 188–219.

[6]Cf. *Publikationen des Leo Baeck Instituts aus zwei Jahrzehnten*, ed. by Max Kreutzberger, Jerusalem–New York–London 1977.

[7]Arnold Paucker, *Der jüdische Abwehrkampf gegen Antisemitismus und Nationalsozialismus in den letzten Jahren der Weimarer Republik*, Hamburg 1968, 1969', 'Jewish Defence against Nazism in the Weimar Republic', in *The Wiener Library Bulletin*, vol. XXVI, Nos. 1 and 2, New Series, Nos. 26 and 27 (1972), pp. 21–31; 'Documents on the Fight of Jewish Organisations against Right-Wing Extremism', in *Michael. The Diaspora Research Institute*, Tel-Aviv University, vol. II (1973), pp. 216–246.

[8]H. G. Adler, *Der verwaltete Mensch. Studien zur Deportation der Juden aus Deutschland*, Tübingen 1974.

munities in Bavaria and by Walk on the Jewish education system.[9] Other research projects are planned or are about to be concluded.

But even today there is no comprehensive and systematic investigation or documentation of the actual resistance of German Jews in the Nazi period. A search for contributions concerned with this problematical aspect of Jewish existence under Nazi rule in the vast literature on the persecution of the Jews and on resistance, reveals only a minimal number, apart from the odd reference here and there.

It was Ball-Kaduri who, in 1959, first posed the question as to whether there had in fact been such a resistance among the German Jews.[10] His brief answer was in the affirmative. This Israeli Historian (of German-Jewish origin) based his work on "certain resistance operations" of the *Reichsvertretung* and on the activities of the Herbert Baum Group. Special characteristics and examples of a German-Jewish resistance in the Rhineland were described by Kurt Düwell.[11] Authors like Ernst Simon and Herbert Freeden had denied the existence of an "active" resistance. They coined the concept of a "spiritual resistance" and spoke of a Jewish desire for self-assertion which manifested itself in activity in publishing, culture and education.[12] Personal experience determined the historical perspective, something which could also be observed in the reports written about the underground activities of Zionist youth groups.[13] The Polish historian Bernhard Mark was the first, in 1961, to write a history of the Herbert Baum Group and showed the specifically Jewish nature of its problems.[14] A few years later Lucien Steinberg, working with the Paris-based *Centre de Documentation Juive Contemporaine* drew attention to 'The Part played by the Jews in the Resistance in Germany'.[15] Basing his work on Gestapo and Nazi legal files accessible to him, as a member of the French Communist Party, in the archives of the G.D.R., he was the first to describe a typology of 'Jewish Resistance

[9] Baruch Zvi Ophir, *Pinkas Hakehillot*. Encyclopedia of Jewish Communities from their foundation till after the Holocaust (Germany–Bavaria), Jerusalem 1971 (in Hebrew); Joseph Walk, *The Education of the Jewish Child in Nazi Germany*. The Law and its Execution, Jerusalem 1975 (in Hebrew; a German edition is being prepared); Abraham Margaliot, 'The Dispute over the Leadership of German Jewry (1933–1938)', in *Yad Vashem Studies*, X (1974), pp. 129–148; Introduction (English abstracts of Margaliot's study in Hebrew on the policies and activities of German-Jewish organisations).

[10] Kurt Jakob Ball-Kaduri, 'Did the Jews of Germany resist?', in *Yad Vashem Bulletin*, 4/5 (1959), pp. 31–32.

[11] Kurt Düwell, 'Das Schicksal der Juden am Rhein im nationalsozialistischen Einheitsstaat', in *Monumenta Judaica*. Handbuch, ed. by Konrad Schilling, Köln 1963; pp. 625 ff.; *Die Rheingebiete in der Judenpolitik des Nationalsozialismus vor 1942*, Köln 1968.

[12] Ernst Simon, *Aufbau im Untergang. Jüdische Erwachsenenbildung im nationalsozialistischen Deutschland als geistiger Widerstand*, Tübingen 1959; Herbert Freeden, *Jüdisches Theater in Nazideutschland*, Tübingen 1964 (Schriftenreihe wissenschaftlicher Abhandlungen des Leo Baeck Instituts 2 & 12); *Vom geistigen Widerstand der Juden. Ein Kapitel jüdischer Selbstbehauptung in den Jahren 1933/1938*, Jerusalem 1963.

[13] Jizchak Schwersenz/Edith Wolff, 'Jüdische Jugend im Untergrund. Eine zionistische Gruppe in Deutschland während des Zweiten Weltkrieges', in *Bulletin des Leo Baeck Instituts*, XII (1969), No. 45, pp. 5–100, Eliyahu Maoz, 'The Werkleute', in *LBI Year Book IV* (1959), pp. 165–182.

[14] Bernhard Mark, 'Die Gruppe von Herbert Baum. Eine jüdische Widerstandsgruppe in den Jahren 1937–1942', in *Blätter für Geschichte*, 14, Warschau 1961 (in Yiddish).

[15] Cf. 'Der Anteil der Juden am Widerstand in Deutschland', in *Studien und Berichte aus dem Forschungsinstitut der Friedrich–Ebert–Stiftung*, Bad Godesberg 1965, pp. 113–140.

Fighters and the Resistance Fight'. This French historian distinguished between anti-fascists of Jewish origin, who fought in the working-class resistance as members of their party and "had obviously appeared as German resistance fighters" and "closed Jewish resistance groups", exemplified by the Baum Group and the resistance organisations within the concentration camps, and a "mixed resistance group" which was led by a Jew. Steinberg's typology needs to be corrected and extended. His distinctions are in reality very much more vague and in addition exclude other forms and areas of resistance. His explanatory model also contains a brief general statement on factors which prevented a "greater and more broadly based resistance activity" of German Jews. These he sees firstly in the degree of assimilation which went so far that the German Jews were "not at all capable of acting in a way different from that of the rest of the population"; secondly in the Nazi terror and the complete isolation of the Jews; thirdly in the lack of help from abroad; and fourthly in a long Jewish tradition which was determined by the consciousness of a "common fate of the Jews" and in which there was no place for a conception of a hopeless "armed and straightforward active resistance".

Finally at the end of the 1960s Helmut Eschwege produced his work on the *Resistance of German Jews against the Nazi Regime*. This outsider among the G.D.R. historians had cast doubt on the hitherto hallowed doctrine of fascism and anti-fascism and had in this way infringed upon one of the basic political and ideological truths of the G.D.R. Evidently just as serious was his transgression in expounding the merits and particular nature of a Jewish anti-fascism at a time when the leaders of state and party in the G.D.R. were in the process of intensifying once again their anti-Zionist campaigns. The G.D.R. censors imposed a veto and the manuscript could not find a publisher in the G.D.R. But the work was not greeted with unmixed applause in the West either. Form, style and the documentary basis were criticised. The phrase "biographical quarry" was used. Scepticism and rejection came from Israel in particular. Noted historians and social scientists denied the very existence of a resistance by German Jews and took exception to the fact that the anti-fascism of Socialists of Jewish origin had been upgraded to a *Jewish* resistance. The fear was expressed that the treatment of the topic was pointless and unproductive from the historical, political and pedagogical point of view, indeed that it would ultimately only serve to foster Jewish apologetics.

A revised extract from the manuscript was published in 1970 in this Year Book. It provoked a discussion which centred around the whole problem of a German-Jewish resistance and with it the question of the premises and conditions, the possibilities and manifestations of a resistance by German Jews.[16]

The answer to this question presupposes the clarification of two basic concepts. What is resistance? Who is a Jew? It also requires the establishment of a concrete historical framework as well as the detailing out of what has been preserved in archives and documents.

---

[16]Helmut Eschwege, 'Resistance of German Jews against the Nazi Regime', in *LBI Year Book XV* (1970), pp. 134–180; Arnold Paucker/Lucien Steinberg, 'Some Notes on Resistance', in *LBI Year Book XVI* (1971), pp. 239–248.

The problem in the definition of these concepts lies in the fact that social research does not possess a catalogue of definitive or objective criteria which can be regarded as generally acceptable. Criteria are chosen according to the political or theoretical position of the writers. There is no lack of formal or evaluative categorisations, nor in very recent times of attempts to operate with an "open" notion of resistance and of examining theoretical models as to their workability. In this context Peter Hüttenberger's 'Vorüberlegungen zum Widerstandsbegriff' (Preliminary Reflections on the Concept of Resistance) have proved to be seminal for all resistance research with an orientation towards the social sciences.[17] I would suggest the following definitions for the empirically accessible activities under Nazi rule:

(a) Any action aimed at countering the ideology and policies of National Socialism is described as being resistance. This includes activities – relating now to concrete groups of people – by Jewish individuals and organisations, which, even without that intention, were none the less directed against National Socialism and are thus objectively seen as a threat and a danger to the Nazi power. These are actions which contradict the general pattern of behaviour or role-playing ordained for the Jewish section of the population by the Nazi authorities. In a wider sense this resistance is defined with reference to Ger van Roon[18] as an open deviation from the prescribed model. It was an offence against the expectations of the Nazis and included the element of personal risk, that is to say, it was carried out taking into account the danger of threats to or annihilation of personal or collective existence. Resistance in this restricted sense is regarded as political anti-fascism. It is associated with a political programme and organisation. It strives to reach certain sectors of the population and mobilise them in order to achieve qualitative changes in accordance with the intentions of the resistance organisations.

(b) If one defines a Jew as a person who professes to belong to the Jewish community, this definition would in the first instance include only the 499,683 German Jews (0·77 per cent of the total population) counted and described by the National Socialists in 1933 as "Adherents to the Jewish faith" or "*Volljuden* of the Mosaic faith". Such a definition does not of course face up to the historical reality. It excludes the relatively large group of those who had themselves severed their ties with Judaism but none the less were seen as and remained classified by the people around them as Jews and were treated accordingly. For this group I prefer to use the description of Germans of Jewish origin. A statistic of the Ministry of the Interior from the year 1935 quotes as 300,000 the number of *Volljuden* or of "non-Aryans not of the Mosaic faith".[19] This official "estimate" must be used with care. It is most probably greatly exaggerated and was used to demonstrate the extent of the "Jewish danger". The census of 1939, which was not published until 1944, showed that at the out-

---

[17]In *Geschichte und Gesellschaft*, Sonderheft 2 (1977), pp. 117–139.
[18]Cf. G. v. Roon, *Neuordnung im Widerstand. Der Kreisauer Kreis innerhalb der deutschen Widerstandsbewegung*, München 1967, p. 1.
[19]Bundesarchiv Koblenz (BA) R 43 II 595. Letter of the *Reichs- und Preuß. Minister des Inneren an die Adjudantur der Wehrmacht beim Führer und Reichskanzler*, 3rd April 1935.

break of the war there remained 233,000 "Race-Jews" in Germany, and of these only 19,700 (18·5 per cent) were "not of the Mosaic faith". The differentiation between German Jews and Germans of Jewish origin allows us to take all those German anti-fascists of Jewish origin into consideration who fought in the ranks of the various political resistance organisations.

II

A further presupposition for the classification of German-Jewish resistance is the concrete historical frame of reference. The initial starting point is the recognition that there neither was nor could there have been anything like the organised and centralised resistance of the German-Jewish community as a whole against National Socialism. This statement implies the question as to which factors determined the situation and reactions of the Jewish sector of the population. In this way, resistance appears only as a segment of a broad, general typology of behaviour which stretches all the way from accommodation and passivity, emigration and escape, to suicide and "submergence" and the marginal phenomena of collaboration and treachery.

One basic factor determining the situation and behaviour of the Jews was made clear immediately in 1933. The destruction of the Weimar Republic also meant the destruction of the Jewish defensive struggle against antisemitism and National Socialism.[20] This struggle, based on democratic and constitutional principles, had been carried on for years. With the political abdication of the liberal bourgeoisie and the helplessness and rapid liquidation of the organised labour movement, the German Jews, the overwhelming majority of whom had become assimilated, i.e. had adapted to their environment almost entirely in their socio-economic situation and their political and ideological attitudes, lost the two social forces which had been first and foremost in propagating and supporting their emancipation. The seizure of power by the Nazis completely destroyed the "image" – or if we like to call it that – the "myth" – of a German-Jewish symbiosis.[21] Antisemitism, which had now become the doctrine of the state, and the officially organised terror brought about a Jewish *Zwangsgemeinschaft* in which various directions and aims initially continued to dominate. The political, social and religious heterogeneity of German Jewry precluded a unified, inner-Jewish defence plan. The attitudes and activities of the German-Jewish organisations and their representatives were characteristic in this regard. Under the impact of the preparations, events and consequences of the "April boycott" of 1933 they endeavoured to establish what their situation was.[22] The

---

[20] Cf. Paucker, *Der jüdische Abwehrkampf, op. cit.*

[21] For the inner-Jewish debate on the German-Jewish "symbiosis" see Gershom Scholem, 'Wider den Mythos vom deutsch-jüdischen Gespräch", in *Bulletin des Leo Baeck Instituts*, VII (1964), No. 27, pp. 278–281 and Eva G. Reichmann, *Größe und Verhängnis deutsch-jüdischer Existenz. Zeugnisse einer tragischen Begegnung*, Heidelberg 1974.

[22] The official statements and memoranda are preserved in the BA Koblenz R 43 II. Klaus J. Hermann's 'Documentation' *Das Dritte Reich und die deutsch-jüdischen Organisationen 1933–1934*, Köln 1964, is one-sided, faulty and useless. It contains selected statements, printed in a con-

common ground between them was exhausted in the general declaration of loyalty to the German people, in the loudly proclaimed assurances that they had opposed the "foreign calls for a boycott" and "attempted interference" (though here, admittedly, one has to differentiate between the official stance and information channelled abroad by devious means) and in the efforts to reach some sort of *modus vivendi* with the Nazi régime which now constituted the "legal" government of Germany.

But from the very beginning, the German-Jewish organisations, especially the *Reichsvertretung* established in 1933 and under the leadership of Leo Baeck and Otto Hirsch, made it quite clear that their activities would remain strictly within the limits of legality. It is important to distinguish two attitudes here: that directed to the outside world and that within the Jewish community. Externally – the attitude towards the official, police channels which controlled and communicated with them was determined by the concern that any open deviation, any behaviour that might be interpreted as "disloyal" or "lawless" must necessarily result in a further endangering of the Jewish community. This was the result of an element of tradition: the recognition of the necessity of renouncing a hopeless militant resistance in the interests of collective survival and solidarity. The possibility of militant resistance was considered and rejected. Jewish representatives spurned a suggestion of Moshe Shapira who had hurried across from Palestine and recommended the establishment of a Jewish self-protection organisation to confront antisemitic hostility.[23] They were just as unwilling to accept the advice of Gandhi and call upon German Jews to carry out a mass suicide as a spectacular act of a passive, non-violent resistance. A different way was adopted. Internally – in the Jewish community – they trusted that they would be able to ward off moral defamation and social discrimination by responding in the traditional way. As in earlier times of crisis and persecution in Jewish history this response lay in an intensification of Jewish life and creativity. Work in Jewish education and culture, loyalty to the faith and steadfastness, vocational retraining and pioneer work for Palestine are all evidence of this will to self-assertion, to describe which Jewish historians have used the expression "construction in destruction" (*Aufbau im Untergang*).

The behaviour patterns and especially the defensive and survival strategies of the Jewish sectors of the population – as also of other persecuted minorities – cannot be described only in terms of themselves. They depend to a decisive degree on the behaviour of society. It is thus necessary to explore the relationship between the Jewish population and German society. The starting point here is the realisation that the German Jews received no adequate assistance, support or solidarity from German society or from abroad. The exceptions only prove the rule. A general thesis is: the attitude of the world facilitated and indeed made it possible for the Nazi leadership gradually to exclude and expel the Jews and to

---

fused order, mainly manifestations of the *Reichsbund jüdischer Frontsoldaten* (RjF) and the marginal Naumann-group (*Verband nationaldeutscher Juden*, VNJ).

[23]Cf. A. Margaliot, Introduction, op. cit., p. VI.

exterminate them systematically from 1941 on.[24] The outlawed, socially degraded and isolated German Jews – as also later the Jews in the occupied territories – were delivered up unprepared and helpless into the hands of a ruling system and a society which gave them no opportunities for a collective strategy of defence.

The Nazi ruling system was itself based on several "pillars of power" which often fought and blocked each other. The bearers of power or central power channels of this Nazi polycracy[25] can be listed as follows: the Nazi leadership and the mass movement (NSDAP), the bureaucracy, the SS, the Army, economic leaders and Churches. If we accept this structural model for the explanation of German fascism, then it becomes clear that the "pact" between National Socialism and the old social élites manifested and proved itself again in the persecution of the Jews. In any case, it is certain that the basic decisions were made by the Nazi leadership.[26] Added to this is the army of helpers' helpers and those who stood to gain. It is possible to provide an outline of the various social and professional groups who could not resist the opportunity of campaigning against the *undeutschen Geist* and of participating in the defamation, separation and destruction of the *artfremden* Jews of which they were the beneficiaries. This also raises the further question of the attitudes of the German population, a complex which is of central importance for the analysis of the situation of the Jews as well. There are significant gaps in the research here too, which in its present state allows no more than a sketch of a general typology of behaviour which distinguishes three basic patterns: solidarity, aggression and indifference.

The first thing to observe is that the defamation, segregation and expulsion of the Jewish sector of the population occurred in full view of everyone until 1941. It aroused no general, massive opposition in the population. What can be demonstrated in all parts of Germany and up to the time of the deportations are only single, spontaneous acts of solidarity and humanitarian aid. They were verbal or written expressions of protest and disgust, regret and pity. As far as is known, the most vehement form of a public revolt displayed was in one single demonstration of protest. In February 1943 a group of German women in Berlin were able to force the release of their Jewish husbands who were under arrest. Other manifestations of sympathy were restricted to small acts of friendliness and other gestures. But in addition to this there were, finally, Germans who continued to have personal contact with their Jewish acquaintances and who, fully aware of the risk to themselves, from 1941 onwards, stood up for the rescue of Jews.[27]

[24]For the comprehensive works see Raul Hilberg, *The Destruction of European Jews*, Chicago 1961; Gerald Reitlinger, *Final Solution*, London 1971; *Holocaust*, Jerusalem 1974 (Israel Pocket Library); N. Levin, *The Holocaust. The Destruction of European Jewry 1933–1945*, New York 1975; Lucy S. Dawidowicz, *The War against the Jews 1933–1945*, London–New York 1975 (Pelican Book 1977).

[25]Cf. Martin Broszat, *Der Staat Hitlers*, München 1969; P. Hüttenberger, 'Nationalsozialistische Polykratie', in *Geschichte und Gesellschaft*, 2 (1976), pp. 417–442.

[26]Cf. Uwe Dietrich Adam, *Judenpolitik im Dritten Reich*, Düsseldorf 1972; Martin Broszat, 'Hitler und die Genesis der "Endlösung" ', in *Vierteljahrshefte für Zeitgeschichte*, 25 (1977), pp. 737–775.

[27]Kurt Jakob Ball-Kaduri, 'Berlin wird judenfrei', in *Jahrbuch für die Geschichte Mittel- und*

The open aggressions were discharged in anti-Jewish demonstrations and abuse (vilification), in maltreatment and plundering. The intensity and scope of these attacks varied. They appeared especially in the initial phase of the persecution and they were obviously less in evidence in the large cities and industrial centres than in those regions where antisemitism was firmly rooted in long tradition. This applies particularly to areas of Hessen, Franconia, Upper and Lower Bavaria and Silesia. Of course intensive research is still required to clarify regional differences and peculiarities and to determine the specific causes manifestations and consequences. We can expect statements on and interpretations of the "daily life" during the time of persecution and perhaps also the empirical establishment of a thesis based on the supposition that proportionally more Jews from rural antisemitic areas were saved. This hypothesis is supported by the fact that Jews in the countryside saw themselves exposed to very much more public and active hostility and thus resorted to rapid, timely emigration. There was a further specific mode of behaviour which was part of daily life under the Nazis: spying and denunciation. At the beginning of 1939 this reached such an extent that the administrative "solution of the Jewish question" was hampered and forced the Nazi authorities to intervene.[28]

Both reactions – solidarity and aggression – only mark the extreme poles and they can probably be estimated as covering no more than a few per cent of the population. The overwhelming majority of Germans remained passive, indifferent, and adopted the role of the silent spectator. The same is true of the population of the occupied areas with, however, significant variations within the limits defined above. Quite general was the indifference with which people took cognisance of the process of segregation and expulsion. Quite general also were the surprise and perplexity after the introduction of the Yellow Star, as to who was suddenly recognisable as a "Jew" and how many of them there were still living among them. This is an indication of how few Germans had any direct contact with Jews by the autumn of 1941.

Passivity and indifference as a dominant behaviour pattern can hardly be said to result from a tradition and firm foundation of antisemitism as a basic attitude. One possible starting point for an explanation can be derived from a

---

Ostdeutschlands, 22 (1973), pp. 208 ff.; M. Wolfson, 'Zum Widerstand gegen Hitler. Umriss eines Gruppenporträts deutscher Juden', in *Tradition und Neubeginn, op. cit.*, pp. 391–407; I. Rewald, *Berliner, die uns halfen*, Berlin 1975.

[28]Thus Göring in his capacity as plenipotentiary for the Four Year Plan complained "of the many denunciations ... in the Jewish question" and had the *Reichsstatthalter* instructed through the Ministry of the Interior on 10th January 1939 to take action against the "unpleasant inconveniences" in the interests of the "absolutely necessary, even and uninterrupted execution" of the Four Year Plan. BA Koblenz R 58 276. Despite this intervention, spying and denunciations continued. Hundreds of Jews and non-Jews were still to fall victim to them. The fragmentary transmission of accounts and experiences and Gestapo files precludes a complete, well-founded quantification, and allows statements only of a relative nature. It is authenticated that the overwhelming majority of the personal files of German Jews examined show entries and other proofs of denunciations. From the Düsseldorf collection (cf. note 45, p. 51) alone, 150 personal files were examined which are connected with "seditious behaviour" and "seditious utterances". An examination showed that in only thirty cases was a real "offence" proven against the Jews. In 120 cases there was insufficient evidence.

description of the function ascribed to Nazi antisemitism. This form of antisemitism is characterised not only by the fact that it, along with anti-communism, functioned as a central ideology for mobilisation and justification but was also raised to be the prototype of despotism and was used as a direct and indirect instrument of power.[29] In other words, the open and direct terrorising of the Jews – as also of other "enemies of the people and of the nation" – rebounded indirectly on the rest of the population. It was intended that the whole society was to see by the treatment of the outlawed and socially degraded Jewish population what would happen to anyone not approved of by the system. The deterrent effect of this terror forced people to accommodation, submission and acceptance of the Nazi power. In addition, there were indoctrination and propaganda. These provided a positive counterpart, as it were – the non-Jews could have the satisfaction of belonging to a privileged "chosen master race". This identification excluded any solidarity, any siding with those persecuted. People saw their situation and from 1941 suspected their "uncertain" fate, which they did not wish to share. They retreated into safe indifference and thus conformed to the behaviour prescribed by the Nazi leadership.

One further aspect needs to be considered in order to understand the situation and behaviour of the Jewish section of the population. This concerns the position of the German resistance and the possibility of any participation in it by the German Jews.

At no time did the organised resistance to the Nazis adopt the forms of a mass movement. There were of course isolated instances of protest against the anti-Jewish measures and of humanitarian help within the resistance movement. Nonetheless it can be argued that the individual centres of resistance, harried and hunted by the Gestapo and isolated from the population as they were, were neither in a position nor willing to place the struggle against the persecution of the Jews at the centre of their anti-fascism. This may be elucidated by a brief description.

The resistance in the Churches began in the first instance with basic questions of theology and these were decided within the framework of a "church struggle". There could clearly be no participation of the Jews here. Nor did they have access to the conservative bourgeois resistance which was in the hands of dignitaries, bureaucrats and military men. These circles hardly stirred when the Jewish emancipation was revoked and the Jews put outside the law after 1933. This state of affairs only began to change immediately before the war, at a time when the Jews had already been cast out of society and demoralised. The problem of the "Jewish question" appeared only on the periphery. Concrete connections can be shown in the internal discussions, protests or individual acts of assistance by the Kreisauer Circle, the Oster Circle, the groups around the Scholls and other smaller groups.[30] The connections which existed between Jewish representatives and the Goerdeler Circle are still largely unexplored. Almost entirely unknown is such a fact as that of the executive director of the

---

[29]M. v. Brentano, 'Die Endlösung – Ihre Funktion in Theorie und Praxis des Faschismus', in *Antisemitismus*, ed. by H. Huss and A. Schroeder, Frankfurt a. Main 1965, pp. 35–76.
[30]Roon, *op. cit.*; P. Hoffmann, *Widerstand Staatsstreich Attentat*, München 1971.

Robert Bosch Works, Hans Walz, making money available and assisting in the rescue of persecuted Jews. Leo Baeck was asked, apparently by Carl Goerdeler, to write a 'Manifesto' which was to be presented to the "German People" after a successful coup.[31] Despite these connections, it remains a fact that there was really no room for a Jew within the conservative bourgeois resistance. A further indication of its "exclusiveness" can be found in its political and ideological programme. Goerdeler's famous memoranda are interwoven with traditional power political demands, nationalistic strains and illiberal sentiments. Here and in other "plans for a new order" of conservative bourgeois origins it becomes only too plain that any discussion of the attempted destruction of European Jewry had only marginal significance.

From the very beginning, members of the smashed and divided German workers' movement had been concerned with the organising and development of resistance. But here too the "Jewish question" played no decisive role. The traditional Marxist model of interpretation prescribed the line along which the attitude and the "solution" had to be orientated.[32] A further barrier which prevented the participation of the German Jews in the workers' resistance was their social and political affinity with the bourgeoisie. In contradistinction to the bourgeois opposition, however, the workers' resistance offered party members or sympathisers of Jewish origin a political and organisational platform for taking up the active struggle against National Socialism. Here it is important to note that this decision was determined not by any "Jewish" motivation but entirely by political conviction. Or, to put it in another way: they joined the various resistance organisations not as Jews but as convinced Communists, undogmatic Marxists, Social Democrats, unionists, Trotskyites or Anarcho-syndicalists. This state of affairs explains why in the initial phases of the Nazi régime no specifically Jewish resistance organisations were established. Their anti-fascism was part of the general German resistance and was decided within the framework of the particular German workers' resistance.

III

These methodological questions must be able to withstand empirical scrutiny. This raises the question as to the state of source material. The main problem here is that the archival and documentary transmission of material is fragmentary and scattered and is in part still not accessible for research on contemporary history. Properly founded quantifying statements can only be made

---

[31]Hans Reichmann, 'The Fate of a Manuscript', in *LBI Year Book III* (1958), pp. 361–363. In his biography of Goerdeler G. Ritter does not mention this "order". Goerdeler's *Nachlaß* does not contain any hints. Despite intensive investigations Baeck's "proclamation" has not yet been found. On Baeck's connection with the Stuttgart Bosch circle see now also Leonard Baker, *Days of Sorrow and Pain. Leo Baeck and the Berlin Jews*, New York 1978, pp. 249–251. There is a letter from Hans Walz, dated 16th June 1967 with information provided for the Leo Baeck Institute in the Institute's Archives in New York.

[32]For the period till 1933 see Hans-Helmuth Knütter, *Die Juden und die deutsche Linke in der Weimarer Republik 1918–1933*, Düsseldorf 1971.

to a minimal extent on this basis. The examination and evaluation of the archival materials in question provide an empirical basis,[33] which is sustained by various source complexes.

The first source complex embraces the so-called *Lage- und Stimmungsberichte*, reports on the position and mood of the population. These are among the most important sources for research into German fascism and anti-fascism. They can be divided into several groups, though behind them are the different authorities of the Nazi system of government. From the beginning, and lasting partly into the Second World War the government bureaucracy, the SS, the Nazi Party as well as the Army and industry all had their own competing sources of information. All these secret reports ran through particular official channels. They were written at regular intervals and according to a prescribed fixed pattern. They provided information – adjusted according to the views and interests of the authority in question and those of its recipients higher up, as well as those of the informants – information about the mood and living conditions of the population, about all "seditious endeavours" and about the situation and behaviour of the Jews.

The reports of the *Regierungspräsidenten/Oberpräsidenten* in Bavaria and Prussia have largely survived.[34] The size and completeness of these files allow a description of various acts of resistance at least for the initial phase of persecution. The reports of the Gestapo and the SD (Security Service) too, have proved to be key documents for the treatment of this topic. Only small remnants are available for research in the Federal Republic,[35] a mere fraction has been printed.[36]

---

[33] The following archives and research centres were visited: Bundesarchiv Koblenz (BA), Bundesarchiv/Militärarchiv Freiburg/Brsg., Staatsarchiv Hamburg, Koblenz, Speyer, München, Berlin (West) and Würzburg; Stadtarchiv Berlin (West), Mainz and Landau; Institut für Zeitgeschichte München, Forschungsstelle für die Geschichte des Nationalsozialismus in Hamburg, Rijksinstituut voor Oorlogsdocumentatie Amsterdam, Wiener Library London, Leo Baeck Institute London and Jerusalem, Yad Vashem Jerusalem, Kibbuz-Archiv Hasorea.

[34] The Bavarian material covering the period from 1933 to 1943 is in the Hauptstaatsarchiv München, Abt. II MA 106 670–704. Cf. H. Witetschek, 'Die Bayerischen Regierungspräsidentenberichte 1933–1943 als Geschichtsquelle', in *Historisches Jahrbuch*, 87 (1967), pp. 355–372. Only parts are published. Within the framework of the project entitled 'Persecution and Resistance in Bavaria 1933–1945' which has been begun by the Institut für Zeitgeschichte München in cooperation with the Bavarian State Archives, the Bavarian materials are being systematically sifted. The first documentary volume has appeared recently. *Bayern in der NS-Zeit. Soziale Lage und politisches Verhalten der Bevölkerung im Spiegel vertraulicher Berichte*, ed. by Martin Broszat, E. Fröhlich, F. Wiesemann, München-Wien 1977. For a survey of the files, cf. *Widerstand und Verfolgung in Bayern 1933–1945. Archivinventare*, München 1975 ff.

The Prussian material may be found in the Geheimes Staatsarchiv Berlin (West), Rep. 90 P. At present it is not open for research as the State Archives are themselves preparing an edition of the files in several volumes, of which two have been published: *Pommern 1934/35 im Spiegel von Gestapo-Lageberichten und Sachakten*, ed. by R. Thevóz, H. Branig, Cécile Lowenthal-Hensel, Köln–Berlin 1974. The volume on Silesia is on the point of completion.

[35] These are in the Federal Archives in Koblenz, in various State archives and in the Institut für Zeitgeschichte, München. Reports of the Gestapo and the SD do exist in considerable numbers in the archives of the G.D.R., but there they are not available for the use of researchers from the West.

[36] B. Vollmer, *Volksopposition im Polizeistaat, Gestapo- und Regierungspräsidentenberichte 1934–1936*, Stuttgart 1957. They refer almost exclusively to resistance in the Church and come from the Stapoleitstelle Aachen; H. Boberich, *Meldungen aus dem Reich. Auswahl aus den geheimen*

On the other hand, only very little is known as to the contents, value as source material and whereabouts of the reports of the *Gauleiter*. It seems that only minimal remnants survived the end of the war. The same is also true of reports stemming from other sources. The military reports on the mood of the populace do not yield very much.

Studies at the military archives in Freiburg/Brsg. concentrated on the reports from the occupied Eastern areas, especially on those of the section *Fremde Heere Ost* (Foreign Armies, East),[37] on the eight volumes of the *Partisanenkampf* (Partisan Struggle) and the information on the *Bandenkrieg* (Gang War), and on the reports of the units in service in the areas in the rear of the army (*Einsatzgruppen, Sicherungs-Divisionen und -Battalione*). These supplied no noteworthy information on acts of resistance by German Jews. But they are of decisive significance for the persecution and behaviour patterns of the Eastern European Jews, particularly the Russian Jews. It is characteristic of the state of research in contemporary history and the interest of historians in this topic that the list of names on the record of those who have made use of the documents on this subject consist almost without exception of investigations from the judicial authorities. To date, I have been unable to ascertain whether the reports of the *Oberlandesgerichte* and *Generalstaatsanwaltschaften* (offices of the Prosecutors-General) contain information on a German-Jewish resistance.[38] In the unpublished *Führer-Informationen* of the Minister of Justice there was but a single reference.[39] Report No. 81, dated 23rd July 1942 informs Hitler of the death sentence passed on the Jewish Communist members of the Herbert Baum Group by the Berlin Special Court a few days previously.

'Reports on the Position and Mood' were also written within the workshops of trade and industry. The reports sent in by those workshops and concerns in which Jews worked as forced labour are probably of special interest. The question as to whether these documents contain any indication of actions of sabotage, refusal to work or other examples of "deviant" behaviour, cannot be answered. The barriers to gaining access to the relevant files in the archives of the companies concerned are simply insurmountable.

The second great complex of source material of central significance is based

---

Lageberichten des Sicherheitsdienstes der SS 1939–1944, Neuwied 1965; J. Schadt, *Verfolgung und Widerstand unter dem Nationalsozialismus in Baden*. Die Lageberichte der Gestapo und des Generalstaatsanwalts Karlsruhe 1933–1940, Stuttgart 1976.

[37]Cf. H. H. Wilhelm, 'Die Prognosen der Abteilung Fremde Heere Ost 1942–1945', in *Zwei Legenden aus dem Dritten Reich*, Stuttgart 1974.

[38]BA Koblenz R 22 3355–3389. The reports cover the years 1940 until the beginning of 1945.

[39]BA Koblenz R 22 4089. The 'Information for the Führer' of the Justice Minister from the years 1942 to 1945 contain 191 references. These are in my opinion among the most interesting and informative documents of National Socialism. In a way that is really "classic" they document the position and "achievements" of German justice as well as the absurdities and atrocities of every-day National Socialism. "Special events, important verdicts and incidents, measures and plans" of the Ministry of Justice were compiled in telegram style and submitted to Hitler. The large print of the 'Information for the Führer' took into account Hitler's weak eyesight, the selected examples, his "taste". A brief survey is provided by G. Gibbom, 'Die Führerinformationen des Reichsjustizministeriums', in *Deutsche Richterzeitung*, 49 (1971), pp. 152–155. Cf. also the references in *Richterbriefe. Dokumente zur Beeinflussung der deutschen Rechtssprechung 1942–1944*, ed. by H. Boberach, Boppard 1975.

on the dossiers of the Gestapo. Part of the routine of the *Stapo–(Leit)–Stellen* was to open a file on every person who had "attracted attention in a political way" and against whom any "measures" had been taken by the Gestapo. As a rule the dossiers contain a questionnaire with a short biography, the record of questioning and results of investigation and, in the case of "persons convicted of a punishable offence" and resistance fighters, the indictment and the sentence (carbon copy), the warrants for arrest and the death notices.

Again, only remnants – about 100,000 dossiers – are available for research in the Federal Republic.[40] Destruction during the war, poor storage and the destruction of files by the Gestapo, as well as confiscation by the Allies are the reasons for this. The small West German remnant comes from the former *Stapoleitstellen* in Neustadt/Weinstraße, Würzburg and Düsseldorf.

The documents from Würzburg were released by the Americans quite early on and passed into the hands of the Bavarian *Verfassungsschutz* (special branch) and were not handed over to the State Archives in Würzburg until 1961.[41] They comprise 18,130 dossiers, about 2,000 of them on Jews. A complete evaluation of the as yet still unsorted documents was not undertaken.[42] The examination of 871 dossiers of German Jews revealed only minimal indications of acts of resistance in the Würzburg area.

The Neustadt documents, which were discovered in the attic of the local administration building in Rheinhessen/Pfalz in 1970 and handed over to the State Archives in Speyer, comprise 12,000 dossiers, 600 of them on Jews.[43] These documents have been catalogued on to a card system, but are as good as closed to research because the administration of the archives in the *Länder* Rheinland-Pfalz and the Saarland is reserving the historical evaluation for itself.[44] The sifting of twelve selected dossiers proved to be unproductive. The archivists in charge gave the assurance that these documents contained no further evidence of a German-Jewish resistance.

The dossiers of the Düsseldorf *Stapoleitstelle* can be consulted with the approval of the Minister for Culture of Nordrheinwestphalen. The Düsseldorf centre, with its regional offices in Duisburg, Essen, Mönchengladbach, Krefeld, Oberhausen and Wuppertal and its border commissariats in Emmerich, Kaldenkirchen and Kleve, covers almost the entire Ruhr area. The approximately 72,000 dossiers which were handed over to the Central State Archive in Düsseldorf by the British Military Government in April 1952, have by now probably been included almost completely in a comprehensive catalogue system

---

[40] It is uncertain whether further dossiers of the Gestapo are kept in the archives of the G.D.R. or of other countries.

[41] For the incomplete transmission of the documents cf. H. G. Adler, who has evaluated them in detail: *Der verwaltete Mensch*, pp. XVII–XIX.

[42] Access to the Jewish files is facilitated by a special (traditional) marking: Jewish names are designated by a red handwritten J. The designation is faulty and incomplete. Of the 478 files it covers only those numbered 1–314. I broke off the investigation after File No. 200, letter L.

[43] Staatsarchiv Speyer H. 91.

[44] Cf. *Dokumentation zur Geschichte der jüdischen Bevölkerung in Rheinland-Pfalz und im Saarland von 1800 bis 1945*, vol. 6, Johannes Simmert (Ed.), *Die nationalsozialistische Judenverfolgung in Rheinland-Pfalz 1933–1945*; Hans-Walter Herrmann, *Das Schicksal der Juden im Saarland 1928 bis 1945*, Koblenz 1974; *Dokumente des Gedenkens*, Koblenz 1974.

which is exemplary and unique of its kind.[45] The catalogue and the files proved to be a veritable goldmine of information on our subject. Several hundred files were inspected. The contents extend to all areas and manifestations of a German-Jewish resistance.

The fourth complex of source material consists of the files of Nazi authorities. These comprise official correspondence, instructions, ordinances, notes of files, minutes of meetings etc. The quantitative yield did not come up to the expectations raised by the volume of the materials examined. In the files concerning the trials and sentences under Nazi justice there were only isolated instances of Jewish resistance fighters, who were sentenced by the *Oberlandesgerichte*, the Nazi *Volksgerichte* and the *Volksgerichtshof*.[46] Investigations at the *Generalstaatsanwaltschaft* (Department of the Attorney-General) in West Berlin proved fruitless. There were no indications of any acts of resistance of German Jews in the card indexes or entries in the registers.[47] It must remain undecided to what extent the very small yield of information is due to the fact that a systematic historical and archival classification of the files of the Justice Department – in any case difficult of access – was never carried out and we can presume that it is unlikely to be undertaken at a future date.

It is obvious that the materials listed here are not of themselves sufficient to reconstruct and interpret the resistance of the German Jews. They merely record what was discovered and registered by the Nazi authorities in charge of control and persecution. There are limits imposed on the extension of the documentary basis. All resistance research faces the basic problem that, since resistance could only exist under conditions of illegality and in a conspiratorial way, any production and preservation of records of resistance activities which had been carried out was contrary to the interests of the safety of the resistance fighters. For this reason, testimonies, the declarations of the anti-fascists themselves are only fragmentary. Among these are illegal pamphlets and other printed works, letters and diary entries, eye-witness reports and descriptions of personal experiences. The search for and viewing of these "historical reports of witnesses"[48] are concentrated on the memoir literature and on the two largest and probably most important collections: the witnesses' literature of the Wiener Library (London) and of the Yad Vashem (Jerusalem). Further information was collected with the aid of correspondence and "oral history". These revealed hardly any concrete certifiable dates or facts. What the few survivors were still able to give in the way of evidence after three decades were memories and experiences of their own battle for survival, descriptions of their state of mind at that time and the motivation of their own anti-fascism.

---

[45]Cf. G. Vollmer, 'Der Bestand der Gestapoleitstelle Düsseldorf im Hauptstaatsarchiv Düsseldorf', in *Der Archivar*, 16 (1963), pp. 288–294.

[46]For trials and sentences against Jews see: Ernst Noam, *Juden vor Gericht 1933–1945. Dokumente aus hessischen Justizakten*, Wiesbaden 1975; H. Robinson, *Justiz als politische Verfolgung. Die Rechtsprechung in "Rasseschandefällen" beim Landgericht Hamburg 1936–1943*, Stuttgart 1977.

[47]Letter of the Prosecutor-General at the Landgericht (Dr. Spickermann) dated 13th June 1975 to the author.

[48]Cf. Kurt Jakob Ball-Kaduri, 'Wert und Grenzen von Erinnerungen und Zeugenberichten als jüdische Quelle der Hitlerzeit', in *Zeitschrift für die Geschichte der Juden*, 2 (1965), pp. 159–168.

IV

Despite all the gaps, this basis of sources allows the construction of a descriptive model which covers the manifestations, levels and peculiarities of the German-Jewish resistance. In so doing it is important to note that German Jews, or Germans of Jewish origin, practised various forms of resistance simultaneously or successively in the course of the historical process. Furthermore, the empirical findings indicate that the two levels of resistance in the narrower and the broader sense have a tendency to merge after 1935.

Within the realm of resistance in the narrower sense are all activities which were carried out within the framework of politically organised anti-fascism. Anti-fascists of Jewish origin are authenticated – at least in the initial years of Nazi rule – in all the underground organisations of the smashed and dispersed workers' movement. The spectrum extends from the SPD, and SAPD, the KPD, KPD/O and other Marxist splinter parties, to the unionists' and anarcho-syndicalist groups to the socialist non-party organisations *Neu-Beginnen* and *Roter Stoß-Trupp*. The state of the source material makes an accurate statement as to the extent of the "Jewish" share in each case impossible. But with all reservations we can say that the total number did not exceed 2,000 (no mean number, however, when one considers the size of the German resistance). The majority fought in the Communist underground. The group *Neu-Beginnen* also shows a relatively high proportion of Jews. Added to this there are the members of the various Jewish youth organisations who were concerned with the development of a resistance immediately after 1933. For the most part they represented the "Left", the Zionist-Socialist side and were recruited from the *Hashomer Hatzair*, the Left *Poale Zion* and the *Borochow*-Youth, the *Habonim* and *Blau-Weiß* as well as the *Schwarzer Haufen* and the *Werkleute*. Their number can be estimated only with difficulty; it probably comprised no more than a few hundred (which again must be seen in relation to the numbers of German Youth in the underground movement). A special place is occupied by those German anti-fascists of Jewish origin, who fought in the contingents of the International Brigades in the Spanish Civil War[49] and the small band of those who sought and found their way into the "resistance" in the occupied territories during the Second World War.

Anti-fascists of Jewish origins were subject to a dual danger – as Socialists and as Jews. In January 1935 the Gestapo saw fit to instigate special investigations about the "Communist and Marxist activities of Jewish elements"[50] and their part in the resistance. After this time, the authorities in charge of the surveillance and persecution were ordered to place the classification "Jew" after the names of suspected or detained anti-fascists of Jewish origin. Now, one might

---

[49] For the participation of Jews from various countries see Josef Toch, 'Juden im spanischen Krieg 1936–1939', in *Zeitgeschichte* (1974), pp. 157–169, in which, however, the proportion of German anti-fascists of Jewish origin is not worked out.
[50] Forschungsstelle Hamburg. Archiv- LA Schleswig-Reg. Eutin A V a 27 a I. Directive of the Gestapo, dated 11th January 1935. Cf. also Lucien Steinberg, *Der Anteil der Juden, op. cit.*, pp. 121 f.

have expected that this category of resistance fighters would have been handed over to systematic extermination without exception. It is, however, a fact that some of the Germans of Jewish origin in custody for political offences were given a small, limited chance of survival in the prisons and even in the concentration camps. In other words, political prisoners were in principle not subjected to the selections for extermination. Though both Jews and Socialists, they were often assigned duties in the camps which made survival and the continuation of resistance possible. A second peculiarity should be emphasised. Under the conditions of the Nazi terror and of their illegal existence a change of awareness as to their Jewishness took place in some of them.[51] This was the experience of being classified and branded as Jews not only by the Nazi régime and their surroundings but also by non-Jewish comrades in the resistance movement. This emerged at a time when the organised workers' resistance had reached its peak in the mid-1930s and the centres of resistance had moved into exile.

Under the impression of the massive waves of arrest and trials which decimated or totally annihilated the illegal groups, the leaders in exile made certain decisions which deprived the anti-fascists of Jewish origin of an organisational platform and in this way restricted their opportunities of being effective quite decisively. The Socialists decided against the reconstruction of illegal groups. The Communists continued the struggle, but with changed organisational and tactical concepts. The orders of the Communist leadership in exile in Paris to remove Communist members of Jewish origins from the depleted ranks "in the interests of our own safety" belong to this area. In Germany, and in some other countries, in 1936/37 they faced the alternative of either emigrating or forming purely Jewish groups. It was only after this decision – which is passed over in silence in the official party historiography of the G.D.R.[52] – that the way was clear for the formation of a resistance organisation which is regarded as the example par excellence of German-Jewish resistance: this was the Herbert Baum Group. And it is equally characteristic that this Jewish Communist group (which also contained some non-Communist members) did not take up the anti-fascist resistance struggle until after the attack on the Soviet Union and that its structure and programme were orientated largely on the Communist model and not on a specifically "Jewish" basis. A further characteristic was its almost total isolation. An invisible ghetto wall separated the Baum Group from the German population. But in addition, it also operated outside the Jewish community (whose leadership disapproved of its activity, if only for reasons of security) and even in the Communist underground its position was that of an outsider group.

Within the realm of resistance in the wider sense may be included all be-

[51]Eliyahu Maoz in his article 'A Jewish Underground in Germany', *Yalkut Moreshet* (Hebrew), 3, 1965, pp. 79–88 (an English version was issued by the Organisation Department of the World Zionist Organization in the same year) touches on this complex question. His is a particularly sensitive study.

[52]Yad Vashem 01/298. Statement by Charlotte Holzer. A written order has not been found to date. Indications for the existence of such orders can also be found in the memoir literature, This total disregard of G.D.R. historians is well demonstrated by Margot Pikarski, in *Jugend im Berliner Widerstand. Herbert Baum und Kampfgefährten*, Berlin/DDR 1978.

haviour patterns which deviated from the prescribed model. Its manifestations include protests, production and distribution of illegal printed matter as well as attempted escapes and organised rescues. Spying and sabotage occur only marginally. Also marginal are acts of resistance in the concentration and extermination camps and the minimal participation in ghetto uprisings and the partisan war. The description and interpretation of marginal phenomena must be excluded here. I shall concentrate on working out the main forms and special qualities of German-Jewish resistance.

On the first level there is the open protest. It proved to be the first, usually spontaneous attempt at an individual or collective self-assertion and self-defence. It took many forms. In telegrams, letters and memoranda addressed to the Nazi authorities, German Jews and German-Jewish organisations protested against moral defamation and social ostracism. Jewish representatives raised their voices. Speeches and sermons, publications and cultural events are evidence here. German Jews refused to obey Nazi directives. The attempts to oppose the "designation directive" of September 1941 by not wearing or by concealing the Yellow Star are an example of this. Rebellion and indignation was quite publicly expressed – a fact which has largely been ignored by research so far. This protest exploded in verbal utterances, insults and acts of violence. These measures of *Abwehr-Affekt* or defiance already sufficed to transgress against the pattern of behaviour which the Nazi régime prescribed for and expected of the Jewish population. The National Socialists quickly found a way of dressing up in legal terminology and prosecuting legally offences of this kind which initially had been labelled as "evil Jewish agitation", "Jewish cheek", "typically Jewish impudence", "presumption", or "provocation". These now became "seditious utterances", "seditious" or "treacherous attitudes", "malicious gossip" or "atrocity propaganda" which had to be punished "for the protection of the people and the state". The punishments varied. They extended – depending on the severity of the case and the phase of persecution – from a warning to protective custody to the death penalty. Hundreds of cases have become known. They cover the whole of Germany and can be demonstrated from 1933 up to the period of the deportations.

To take just one example, chosen from the wide spectrum of protests to indicate the particular difficulties and problems involved in classifying and interpreting these activities. When, in the beginning of 1935 the Nazis increased the pressure on Jews to emigrate, all propaganda of an "assimilationist" nature was prohibited. Some Jewish representatives of a more "German-National" provenance, especially from the leadership of the RjF and the VNJ opposed this prohibition and persisted in speeches and in print, in continuing to plead for the Jews to stay in Germany. They were punished by being prohibited from speaking or publishing. If we are to follow the definition presented above, then even such behaviour on the part of some Jews must perhaps, with some reservations in this particular instance, be regarded as a deviation from the prescribed model. Paradoxically, however, it was precisely this wish to remain a part of German society which led many to their doom in the following years.

The second form of resistance is the production and distribution of illegal publications. It is well known that this form of anti-fascist propaganda, information and mobilisation was practised by nearly all political resistance groups, especially by the Communists. Their extent and political programmes can be deduced from the carefully kept statistics and reports of the Gestapo and the Security Service. The number of publications confiscated varied from year to year. At the peak of the organised workers' resistance between 1934 and 1936 it reached a record number of over 1·5 million. Equally well established is the fact that the carelessness and openness with which this propagandist activity was carried on often led to the discovery and destruction of illegal groups and centres. It is thus not surprising that the Gestapo again and again caught anti-fascists of Jewish origin in the act of producing or distributing camouflaged publications, journals and pamphlets, and punished them for "high treason". But it is quite unknown that from 1933 up to the time of the deportations polemics, pamphlets and protests written by German Jews continued to appear.

The initial phase consisted of the early defensive writings, documentations and eye-witness accounts, which were written and printed outside the areas of Nazi rule and smuggled into Germany. Added to this was the reading and passing on of other prohibited political and literary works. A special position must be accorded the anonymous Jewish pamphlets and broadsheets, letters and protests which were written as spontaneous replies to particular measures or events in the persecution of the Jews. They fell into the hands of the Gestapo and the postal censors especially after the promulgation of the Nuremberg Laws, during the Olympic Games and after the pogroms of the *Reichskristallnacht*. They were addressed to Nazi authorities and personages, but also to German "comrades-in-arms" and "brothers". The technical side of production was by means of printing or duplicating machines, typewriters or even in handwritten form. Distribution centred on letter-boxes, phone-boxes, public transport, streets, house walls and other public places. What these "inflammatory writings" all had in common was the protest against defamation and discrimination, and the accusation levelled against those in political power. This constituted "incitement", "slander" and "high treason" and set the investigation and prosecution apparatus in motion. In the fragmentary material now in archives, proof of only twenty examples could be found, apart from allusions and conjectures. With the exception of three concrete isolated cases, however, the files reveal nothing about the author or the outcome of the investigations of the police.

The third form of resistance covers all attempts to flee from the grasp of the pursuers by escape. There are four distinctions or problem areas to be differentiated here: emigration, escape, assistance in escape and suicide.

The emigration of German Jews does not represent an act of resistance. Until 1941 it was – despite all the barriers and contradictions – a stated aim of Nazi policy on Jews and thus conformed to a prescribed pattern of behaviour. Furthermore, emigration presupposes a fairly lengthy bureaucratic and official process of gaining approval. Escape on the contrary was a spontaneous act and was associated with illegality and threat to life and limb. Until the present time, it has not been possible to make exact statements as to the number of German emigrants or escapees or to establish the relationship between politically and ideologically motivated emigration or escapes on the one hand, and those motivated by reasons of race. All numbers stated are based on rough estimates, which vary widely in any case.[53] There is general agreement in the literature that the total number of German Jews who left Germany up to 1941 is about 300,000. The numbers of successful and unsuccessful attempts at escape, however, remain totally unknown. The source material permits only relative statements about waves of escapes which increased suddenly in certain phases of persecution. The first massive wave of escapes began immediately after the seizure of power by the Nazis. In September 1933, the Foreign Office estimated the number of Germans who had escaped into other European countries, as 47,350 and emphasised that the "Jewish element" predominated.[54] It can be assumed that the majority left Germany for political reasons. An increase in illegal border crossings was registered by the Nazi authorities after the Nuremberg Laws and the *Reichskristallnacht*. Only very few Jews succeeded in escaping over the hermetically sealed-off borders during the war. After the final prohibition of emigration and the beginning of the deportations in the autumn of 1941, the only alternative left to them was to resist the evacuation orders and to escape into the underground. The possibilities of disappearing were limited. About 10,000 German Jews found a hiding place, 5,000 of them in Berlin alone. 30 per cent of them may have survived the war.[55] All activities concerned with the rescue of Jews can be described as assistance in escape.

This form of resistance comprises attempts to liberate prisoners from prisons and concentration camps, making living quarters available and looking after those who had gone into hiding, the provision of money and the production of forged papers as well as finding out about ways of escape and of evading the transports. The rescue operations presupposed the cooperation of both Jews and non-Jews, which took place on two levels. German Jews and Jews of German origin worked in various organisations for the assistance in escape or were in charge of such organisations in Germany and especially also in the occupied territories of Western Europe. Examples for Germany are the underground groups centred around Edith Wolff and J. Schwersenz, the Rast-Organisation or the rescues by Probst Grüber and his associates. In the Netherlands, the Palestine Pioneers under the leadership of Joachim "Schuschu" Simon stand out. He built up a very extensive rescue organisation together with Joop Westerweel. Evidence of similar examples can be cited also for Belgium and for France.

[53]Cf. U. Langkau-Alex, *Volksfront für Deutschland?* vol. 1: *Vorgeschichte und Gründung des "Ausschusses zur Vorbereitung einer deutschen Volksfront"*, *1933–1936*, Frankfurt a. Main 1977, pp. 40 ff.; W. Röder, *Die deutschen sozialistischen Exilgruppen in Großbritannien*, Hannover 1969, pp. 15 ff. For a general outline see: Kurt R. Grossmann, *Emigration. Geschichte der Hitler-Flüchtlinge 1933 bis 1945*, Frankfurt a. Main 1959 and H. E. Tutas, *Nationalsozialismus und Exil. Die Politik des Dritten Reiches gegenüber der deutschen politischen Emigration*, München–Wien 1975.
[54]BA Koblenz R 43 600. Report of the Auswärtiges Amt to the Reichskanzlei dated 27th September 1933.
[55]Stefi Jersch-Wenzel, *300 Jahre jüdische Gemeinde zu Berlin. Leistung und Schicksal*, Katalog Berlin Museum 1971, p. 25.

There is a connecting link to the second level, viz. to the small band of Germans who endeavoured to rescue the Jews. After the end of the war, the Senate of West Berlin bestowed honours on 687 citizens for their part in these activities; Yad Vashem had found 69 further people by 1971 whom it could honour as "Righteous among the Nations".[56]

The last and most radical category of attempts to escape from the Nazi terror is suicide. In Germany, Austria and some of the occupied areas, it attained the proportions of a mass phenomenon, which however has hardly been researched at all so far. There have been isolated calls, especially in contemporary history research in the Netherlands,[57] to include suicide as an act of resistance. There has, however, been opposition to this inclusion and it has not yet been generally accepted (though it could be said that such a solution has many precedents in Jewish tradition in the long history of persecution). There is no question, on the other hand, that suicide "disturbed" or "interfered with" the smooth running of the administration and technical persecution and extermination process. This offence too, this deviation from the prescribed model, was punished. It was one of the duties of the persecutors to prevent the suicide of Jews.

The present state of research allows only a few general statements. The total number of suicides and attempted suicides amounts to several thousand. The significant factors here are old age and a high degree of assimilation. In other words, the fact that it was mostly the younger people who emigrated meant that the Jewish population rapidly came to contain a high proportion of old people; this, together with social and professional degradation, is reflected in the high suicide rate. The course of the suicide curve reveals the connection between persecution and suicide. On the basis of data surviving from Berlin and Württemberg, a rising curve can be drawn which jumped to sudden peaks in the years 1933, 1935, 1938 and 1941/2. More concretely, the "April boycott" and the revocation of the emancipation of the Jews, the Nuremberg Laws and the *Kristallnacht*, the introduction of the Jewish Star and the delivery of the deportation orders mark the "historic" moments in which the burden became too great to bear. Despair and resignation, the feeling of humiliation, deprivation of rights and isolation all culminated in suicide, which must be seen in terms of a defensive measure; (*Abwehr-Affekt*), an ultimate act of defiance.

This outline is the result of an investigation undertaken on behalf of the Leo Baeck Institute into the feasibility, the problematics and the scope of an extensive research project on the resistance of German Jews to Nazism. It is to be hoped that the methodological premises and concepts developed here will assist in the clarification of how such a programme may be carried out, directed as it would be to a question which alas suffers no lack of topicality in a world where, in one part or another, a minority group is only too likely to find itself confronting the danger of persecution.

[56]Yad Vashem. List of Righteous among the Nations from Germany, Recognized by Yad Vashem till 31. 12. 1971. General: A. L. Bauminger, *Roll of Honour*, Jerusalem 1970.
[57]Cf. C. J. E. Stuldreher, 'Samen alleen', in *Bericht van de Tweede Wereldoorlog*, No. 54, deel 4 (1971), *Verzet van Joden*, pp. 1489 ff.

Cultural Rapprochement

The Emergence of Moses Mendelssohn as Literary Critic

BY EVA ENGEL

In another article[1] I have written on Lessing's literary criticism and how decisively it was affected by contact with a mind as different from his as that of his friend Moses of Dessau. The present paper[2] concerns itself with the reverse process: the influence of Lessing, the critic, on Mendelssohn, the metaphysician. The preamble to such an enquiry cannot be brief. It will have to take into account the phenomena of Mendelssohn's self-education, the disproportionate odds against his penetration of an unknown and hostile world, and the acclaim, help and welcome he received from French and German men of learning, wit and taste in the Berlin of the 1750s.

This "revolution" of attitudes, at this period, and in this town, raises many issues, some more puzzling than others. Though none of the issues can be dealt with in detail here, there are three main questions that need to be set down and borne in mind: how could a Jew acquire a secular eighteenth-century education in Berlin? How could he meet non-Jews? Why should this be the time for young German intellectuals to seek out and befriend Mendelssohn, a Jew? Intelligent and informed guesses may shed light on some of the underlying facts and factors, even when no definite answer can be agreed upon.

The first web of queries concerns Mendelssohn's rise to fame as a philosopher/theorist and as a writer of lucid, beautiful German prose. The eighteenth century is rich in remarkable men, some of them rising from poverty and obscurity, and none more so than the Jew from the Dessau ghetto. How could it come about that, having reached Berlin as an adolescent, this man of alien mind and tongue achieved fame as a German metaphysician–aesthetician by the age of twenty-five; and by the age of twenty-eight was accepted as arbiter of taste in matters concerning German and European belletristics?

As we shall show, some of the answers can be found within the historical context: the presence in Berlin of French "esprits", bringing with them tolerance in matters of religion, avid interest in scientific truth, and access to the exchange of learned knowledge, be it in meetings, by prize competitions, or published work. Learned matter was accessible to Mendelssohn also in the special sections of two Berlin journals and through teachers and socratic discussions with friends. Originally books could be had only at the expense of forgoing food; in later years, Mendelssohn could rely on Nicolai's bookshop and on the works owned by his friends Nicolai and Lessing.

As a Jew, Mendelssohn was not alone in his desire to avail himself of non-Jewish learning. By 1750, some of the Jews permitted to settle in Berlin had

[1]'The Transformation of Lessing's Style as a Critic (1749–1755)', in *Lessing Year Book XI*, Ismaning/Munich 1979.
[2]This essay is based on a paper originally read at the Leo Baeck Institute in New York, 19th January 1978.

acquired enough standing in the German community to rebel against the educational isolationism imposed on their young by the rabbis from the East who were averse to any contact with the non-Jewish townsfolk, its speech, its culture. In the 1740s, the use of German speech, of books in modern languages constituted an infringement of rules set by the rabbinic authorities. How could young Moses, about to become Hamann's "sçavant célèbre à Berlin",[3] not only escape the fate of a Baruch Spinoza or Uriel Acosta but indeed use his allegiance to Judaism on behalf of European Jewry – and at the same time, be one of the most fertile minds of European Enlightenment and partner in the iconoclastic literary ventures of Nicolai and Lessing?

What interplay of chance and circumstance was needed to bring about the encounter of Moses with non-Jews? And what, in turn, made two young lively spirits like Nicolai and Lessing be ready to befriend the Jew, to meet for intense discussion "at least twice and thrice weekly",[4] to impart knowledge to him, to benefit from his, and to exchange letters of an intellectual calibre unequalled by any eighteenth-century German writer, except by Schiller with Mendelssohn's erstwhile pupil, Wilhelm von Humboldt.

In several of his writings, Nicolai pointed out[5] that around 1750, he and Lessing were odd men out, that all three of them were young, eager for truth, free from professional ambition, intent only on studies and discussion that led to knowledge for its own sake and eager to sharpen their critical sensibility.

In addition, the death in London of Christlob Mylius in 1754 left Lessing bereft of his collaborator. The feeling of intellectual isolation may have been compounded by Lessing's well-documented desire to be devil's advocate, to defend both sides of any argument, and to protect men left defenceless by circumstances.

By the 1750s, a concatenation of incident, improbability, historic fact and lively thinking brought about the beginning of a new era in Germany. For nearly two centuries German culture was creatively shaped by German Jews to an extent where it became impossible to discount the ferment, fertilisation and endowment they engendered. This process of reciprocated partnership has yet to be fully assessed.

Among the extant Mendelssohn correspondence, two early passages afford insight into the intellect and humanity of the two men who were the key figures in his process of *Bildung*: one Jew, one non-Jew. The first is Aaron Emmerich Gumpertz, the second Gotthold Ephraim Lessing. Gumpertz was six years older than Mendelssohn, Lessing merely eight months his senior. Both men were erudite, both had acquired their learning within a few short years at the university, but largely by their own efforts. To both avid minds Mendelssohn paid tribute all his life. The passages in the letter to Gumpertz and the letter from Lessing are important, not for what they tell us about these two men but for what they tell us about Mendelssohn's ideals and temperament at the age of twenty-four

---

[3] *JubA* (see note 6), XII. 1, p. 277 (letter 256).
[4] Nicolai, *Bildniss* . . . (see note 36), p. 14 ff.
[5] *Ibid.*; L. F. G. von Göckingh, *Friedrich Nicolais Leben und literarischer Nachlass*, Berlin 1820, pp. 17–19.

and twenty-seven years, respectively. It is this time span in Mendelssohn's life that added a new dimension to his achievement, and happens to be one that – so far – has been largely understressed, if not ignored.

In one of his earliest extant letters,[6] Mendelssohn wrote to Gumpertz in June 1754:

> "Whoever knows you, most dear friend, and esteems your talents, surely does not lack proof how freely fortunate minds can ascend without model or teacher. They can expand their valuable gifts, improve mind and heart, and aspire to be ranked with the most outstanding men."[7]

Two and a half years later, and soon after the outbreak of the Seven Years' War, while Lessing was in Leipzig, i.e. in enemy territory, he wrote to Mendelssohn on 2nd February 1957:

> "Like you, I doubt if we have reached even the first confines of our discussion. Are you really as desirous as I am to proceed more deeply inland and to discover this unknown territory – even if we should miss our way a hundred times first? Indeed, why do I ask? If you were not to accompany me from inclination, you would do it to oblige me."[8]

Thus, both friends played thoroughly dissimilar parts in these early years. Gumpertz became Mendelssohn's mentor,[9] introducing him to new learning and new people, while Lessing's friendship and his interests exerted a spell that made Mendelssohn desert metaphysics for a number of years. This spell becomes apparent to us from the correspondence that commenced when Lessing left Berlin in November 1755 and stayed away till May 1758. In order to account for the fascination Lessing held for him, we need to know more about the young Mendelssohn before he made Lessing's acquaintance in 1754 or 1753.

Let us move backwards in time, to the autumn of 1743, when the barely fourteen-year-old Moses of Dessau set out from home, "desert behind – desert ahead", as one of his early biographers, Daniel Jenisch, described it in 1789. There were two Berlin city gates that gave Jews access to the capital of Frederick II's Prussia. Fairly strict regulations governed the admission and settling of Jews in Berlin, but the unprotected, unknown and very poor foreigner Moses had followed his Dessau rabbi David Fränkel on foot, with no other thought in mind but to go on learning from the scholar whom he revered and who, against all precedent, had introduced him to metaphysics. We know that the rabbi found him a place to stay, with a few weekly free meals, that he gave

---

[6]The following abbreviations have been used throughout:

   Jenisch = *Moses Mendelssohn's kleine Philosophische Schriften. Mit einer Skizze seines Lebens und Charakters von D. Jenisch*, Berlin 1789 (quoted from edition of 1830).
   JubA = *Moses Mendelssohn Jubiläumsausgabe*, Stuttgart 1970—.
   LM = *Lessings Werke*, ed. Lachmann-Muncker, 1886–1924.
   LSS = *G. E. Lessings Sämtliche Schriften*, Berlin 1789, specifically *LSS*, XXVII, 1794, pp. 489–520 'Anmerkungen zu Moses Mendelssohns im Jahre 1789 gedrucktem Briefwechsel mit Lessing' (ed. F. Nicolai).

[7]*Jub A*, XI, p. 12 (end of June 1754).
[8]*Ibid.*, p. 105 (Lessing: 2nd February 1757).
[9]*Ibid.*, p. 220 (to Fromet Gugenheim: 16th April 1761).

him manuscripts to copy for pay; in short, that he made a very hard life more tolerable on the physical level. Jenisch records:

> "Mendelssohn used to narrate that he lived on dry bread for days on end, having earned a few groats by copying. The bread he used to mark by lines to make it last in proportion to his income."[10]

In later years, Mendelssohn chose not to remember this period. Except for one brief summary of facts, written in 1774, and giving merely the outline of his by then twenty years in Berlin,[11] all our reports of his contacts, his studying, are secondhand. The main evidence comes from the footnotes with which Friedrich Nicolai annotated the Lessing–Mendelssohn correspondence in 1794. From these notes, it would seem that, intellectually, Mendelssohn came away from the Dessau period and its rabbinic learning soon after he reached Berlin. The aim of such teaching, to produce a new generation of talmudic scholars, had called for pure biblical Hebrew, for study of the Bible, for talmudic disciplines. The Dessau rabbi, by introducing him to Maimonides' controversial *Dalalāt al ḥaïrin* (*Moreh Nebuchim*, i.e. *Guide to the Perplexed*), newly reprinted in 1742, had opened to young Mendelssohn new fields of thought, method and investigation. Maimonides' discussion of metaphysical themes, of comparative philosophies and theologies, of the use of figurative speech highlights the problems the *Guide to the Perplexed* seeks to answer: the conflict of faith with science, of Revelation with reason. For Mendelssohn life in Berlin enhanced the awareness of new intellectual needs, new areas of scholarly exploration. It emphasised the need for new minds as teachers, new texts, new languages. The year in which this new stage of Mendelssohn's development seems to have begun to gather momentum is 1745. Why it should happen just then, and in Berlin of all places, needs investigating. We turn to the happy concatenation of facts and factors that brought it about.

Mendelssohn could hardly have reached Berlin at a more felicitous moment. For the hitherto intellectually bleak capital of the kingdom of Prussia had just then undergone a metamorphosis. In Voltaire's words Sparta had become a new Athens. The accession of Frederick II saw the beginning of an Augustan Age through the revival of the Royal Academy. During the years 1745–1770 the Académie Royale des Sciences et des Belles Lettres de Berlin became a worthy competitor of the Académie in Paris and the Royal Society in London.[12] The promise of a new era of freedom of thought fostered a climate of scientific and scholarly enquiry. Like a magnet it attracted minds of the calibre of men like Maupertuis, the two Eulers, Lambert, LaGrange, Aepinus, Merian,

---

[10] *Jenisch*, p. 18: "Aber wie kümmerlich mußte er hier leben; er pflegte selbst zu erzählen, daß er sich viele Tage hindurch vom trockenem Brod ernährt, wozu er sich einige Groschen mit Abschreiben verdiente: das Brod was er sich kaufte bezeichnete er mit Einschnitten, um nach dem Verhältnis seiner Casse damit auszukommen."

[11] *JubA*, XII, p. 2 (to Joh. Jac. Spiess: 1st March 1774).

[12] By 1744 the Académie Royale . . . de Berlin already had 84 foreign members, including Celsius, Gottsched, Maupertuis, Michaelis, Réaumur, Sloane, Wolff. The number of regular members was kept low – 1750: 35; 1756: 33; during the Seven Years' War: 21; 1763–1775: 27. After 6th January 1774 the King's consent was needed for election. (Adolf von Harnack, *Geschichte der Kgl. Preussischen Akademie in Berlin*, Berlin 1900, vol. I, pt. 1, pp. 394–465 passim.)

Prémontval and Sulzer to the Academy. Voltaire, a Member from 1746, remained the *genius loci*. His ideas on tolerance, on rationalism, his literary skills and style affected the progression of enlightenment that attracted to Potsdam men like d'Alembert, de Catt, the Marquis d'Argens and in Berlin influenced Mylius, Nicolai, Lessing and, in due course, Mendelssohn. The eight or nine years after 1745 shaped the mind of the man whom Lessing encountered and whom, in October 1754, he presented to Johann David Michaelis, of Göttingen University, as a "second Spinoza who without any instruction has gained such great stature in languages, mathematics, philosophy and poetry".[13] Nicolai, too, stressed the autodidactic nature of Mendelssohn's learning: "Moses had become what he was, merely by the exercise of his own thinking and with hardly any books."[14] But it was a paucity of texts, as we shall see, not a complete lack of them that Mendelssohn had to contend with.

However, before he could read books and publications, Mendelssohn had to learn the languages they were written in. He needed German for letters, newspapers, for daily intercourse with educated Germans, he needed Latin for books on philosophy and science topics, and French to have access to the learned papers of the francophile king's Royal Academy. Nicolai described appreciatively how much pain Mendelssohn took over increasing his ability to handle written German and to grasp the nature of this language which was, after all, not his mother tongue.[15] And a book could be written on the excellence of Mendelssohn's style, on the sensitive and flexible quality of his diverse translations, his unremitting care in finding the right nuance, his appreciation of levels of diction, of prose rhythms, and his uncanny gift of adapting his style of writing to that of his recipient, to the point of mimicry.

The adolescent who was so eager to learn, was fortunate in finding able schoolmasters and teachers. There was the Hebrew-speaking Israel Samocz who excelled in mathematics and poetics and who, above all, was an original thinker. Whether this man taught Mendelssohn, or whether the chain reaction in his development began with Samocz's student Gumpertz, is now immaterial. For Mendelssohn would in any case have heard of him through Gumpertz; and Gumpertz Mendelssohn encountered at a time when he had discovered his ability to think, but probably before he realised that there were philosophies other than that of Maimonides. As Nicolai reports: "And still he knew nothing of those philosophers and their theories that came between Maimonides and Locke, and after Locke."[16] But how had he come across Locke?

About the year 1745, Mendelssohn had the chance to listen to lectures by the headmaster of the *Joachimsthaler Gymnasium* where young Louis Beausobre, son of the royal chaplain, had taken Gumpertz and Mendelssohn. Heinius, the rector of the school, taught philosophy, ancient languages and the history of philosophy. He lectured in Latin, but apparently by then Mendelssohn was able

---

[13]*LM*, XVII, p. 40 (Lessing to Michaelis: 16th October 1754).
[14]*LSS*, XXVII. p. 125 f.: "Moses war bloß durch Selbstdenken, fast ohne Bücher geworden, was er war."
[15]*Ibid.*, p. 493.
[16]*Ibid.*, p. 492 f.

to hold his own, thanks to Abraham Kisch. Kisch, one year younger than Mendelssohn, had helped him acquire the rudiments of Latin, not as an end in itself but for the express purpose of reading modern philosophers. Over a period of six months, he had taught Mendelssohn for fifteen minutes a day. Mendelssohn saved up quite a while for a second-hand grammar and dictionary, and then first tried his hand, unsuccessfully, at Cicero, and then laboriously, at Locke's *Essay on Human Understanding*. "This work", said Nicolai:

> "he tried to decipher with incredible effort. He looked up every word that he did not understand (and that meant most words), and then wrote them down till he had a few clauses. Then he thought about their content. By pondering he tried to guess at the meaning of the passage, and when he thought he had found it, he compared that to the meaning of the words – as far as his knowledge of the language would let him."[17]

As he grew more familiar with Latin, a vast arsenal of texts became accessible, including works on all aspects of mathematics, such as Leonhard Euler's theory of music (*Tentamen theoriae musicae*, 1739). This leads to two interesting asides. The first refers to a short but eloquent passage in Jenisch in which he ascribes Mendelssohn's first contact with mathematics to Israel Samocz's Hebrew translation of the first six books of Euclid. Jenisch continued:

> "The spirit of thoroughness and profundity that is so characteristic of all of Mendelssohn's writings, is the result of his study of mathematics."[18]

The second aside provides a tentative answer to those interested in tracing Felix Mendelssohn's musical inheritance. If one looks up 'Temperament' in the *Harvard Dictionary of Music*, one notices that Mendelssohn's piano teacher, Johann Philipp Kirnberger is credited with that century's second important contribution to the theory of constructing a well-tempered clavier. But could he have written it? Moses Mendelssohn had started taking piano lessons with Kirnberger in October 1756. Kirnberger was a self-taught musician, making the most of any source of learning open to him. So he earnestly quizzed Mendelssohn on the philosophy of music.[19] The treatise in question, published anonymously in

---

[17] *Ibid.*, "Moses bekam auch einen alten Band, worin einige Schriften des Cicero enthalten waren, die er der Sprache wegen zu studiren suchte, aber nicht recht verstehen konnte. Der Zufall führte ihm bey einem Verkäufer alter Bücher eine lateinische Uebersetzung von Locke's Werk vom menschlichen Verstande zu . . . welches ihm große Freude machte. Dies Werk suchte er mit unbeschreiblicher Mühe zu entziffern; er schlug jedes Wort, das er nicht verstand (und das waren die meisten) im Lexicon nach, und schrieb es auf, bis ein Paar Perioden da waren. Alsdann dachte er über den Inhalt nach. Durch Nachdenken suchte er den Verstand zu errathen, und wenn er ihn gefunden zu haben glaubte, verglich er ihn wieder, so weit seine Kenntniß der Sprache reichte mit dem Wortverstande."

[18] *Jenisch*, p. 22f.: "Einen neuen Schwung erhielt sein philosophisches Genie durch das Studium der Mathematik, da er durch R. Israel Moses die ersten 6 Bücher des Euklides, welche dieser ins Ebräische übersetzt hatte, kennen lernte. Der Geist der Gründlichkeit und der Tiefe, der allen Schriften Mendelssohns durchgängig eigen ist, war gewiss eine Folge seines Studiums der Mathematik, welche er nach so vielen Beispielen, die wir davon in seinen philosophischen Abhandlungen finden, bis zu einer Tiefe bearbeitet zu haben scheint, auf welche unsere historische Philosophen, . . . nicht einmal Anspruch machen wollen."

[19] *LSS*, XXVII, p. 506: "Moses hatte alle Theile der Mathematik gründlich studirt, und auch die mathematische Musik in L. Eulers großem Werke. Dadurch kam er auf den Gedanken, sich auch einige Kenntniß von der praktischen Musik erwerben zu wollen. Er ließ sich im Jahr 1756 von dem Musiker Kirnberger Unterricht im Klavierspielen geben. Kirnberger dünkte

1761, could not have been written by Kirnberger. We have Jenisch's account of Sulzer's and Mendelssohn's vain attempts to make sense of the musings and theorisings of this self-styled philosopher of music. On the basis of its mathematical argumentation and its concise style, as well as on the evidence offered by the editor of the periodical in which the treatise first appeared,[20] Haim Bar Dayan attributes the treatise, 'Versuch eine vollkommen gleichschwebende Temperatur durch die Construction zu finden' to Mendelssohn.[21]

Nicolai gave an entertaining description of the clash between the mathematician Mendelssohn and the musician Kirnberger:

> "Kirnberger conversed with Moses about the philosophical aspect of music. Mendelssohn imagined that he grasped what Kirnberger said, because his own wisdom made up for the man's muddleheadedness, and Kirnberger for his part swore that Mendelssohn had a superb grasp of all musical matters. At the beginning of the lessons, Kirnberger wanted to explain the difference in rhythms to his pupil. But they could not reach an understanding about the difference between the three-quarter time and six-eight time. Mendelssohn said: 'How is it that 3/4 is not identical with 6/8?' Kirnberger replied: 'Because one is triple metre, and the other simple metre.' 'How so, and how could this be?' Moses went on. Kirnberger sat down at the piano and played both 3/4 and 6/8 and said magisterially: 'Well then, now you do hear that the first is in triple metre?' 'No,' replied Moses. 'I can't hear any difference.' Kirnberger played both kinds of rhythms in some six different ways but the student was as puzzled as before. Finally, Kirnberger said with some impatience: 'I cannot understand how you, a mathematician, cannot measure 3/4 so that it is in triple metre.' Moses smiled and said 'as a mathematician I do not know of any 3/4 that would not be 6/8, but since this is supposed to be different in music, I begin to imagine that I do not have the ear for music and cannot sense the difference.' The lessons ended after a few months, but Mendelssohn came away from them with the ability to play one minuet rather slowly on the piano. 'Strange,' he said and smiled, 'I can play triple metre but I cannot hear it.'"[22]

---

sich ein philosophischer Musiker zu seyn. Er hatte auch wirklich über seine Kunst mehr nachgedacht als andere Musiker. Indessen hatte er doch von vielen Dingen nicht deutliche, noch weniger philosophisch richtige Begriffe. Da er gar keine Schulstudien besaß und wenig gelesen hatte, so fehlten ihm manche nöthige Kenntnisse, die er sich durch Umgang mit Gelehrten erst mit vieler Mühe erwerben mußte; daher konnte er zuweilen ziemlich gemeine Dinge nicht deutlich aus einander setzen. Gelehrte, welche sich mit ihm darüber verständigen wollten, mußten seinen Sinn errathen; daher auch Sulzer, der von der Musik gar nichts verstand, und Kirnbergern nachher bey seinem Wörterbuche brauchte, in ein Paar musikalischen Artikeln (in der ersten Ausgabe) falsch gerathen hat."
[20]F. W. Marpurg, *Historisch-Kritische Beyträge zur Aufnahme der Musik*, vol. V. 2, pp. 95–97.
[21]*JubA*, II, pp. 187–196, 455 f.
[22]*LSS*, XXVII, p. 506: "Kirnberger unterhielt sich mit Moses über den philosophischen Theil der Musik. Moses glaubte ihn zu verstehen, weil sein eigener Scharfsinn Kirnbergers Undeutlichkeit ersetzte, und K. hingegen versicherte, daß Moses alles Musikalische trefflich fasse. Im Anfange der Unterweisung wollte K. seinem Schüler Moses die verschiedenen Taktarten erklären. Ueber den Unterschied von 3/4 und 6/8 Takt, konnten sie sich nicht verständigen. Moses fragte: 'Wie es zugehe, daß 3/4 nicht 6/8 machen sollten?' K. sagte: 'weil der eine im Tripeltakt und der andere ein gerader Takter ist.' Aber warum? und wie geht das zu? fragte Moses weiter. Kirnberger setzte sich ans Klavier, spielte ihm 3/4 and 6/8 gegen einander vor, und sagte belehrend: 'Nicht wahr, nun hören Sie doch, daß das erstere Tripeltakt ist?' 'Nein!' sagte Moses, 'ich kann keinen Unterschied hören. Kirnberger spielte beide Taktarten wohl auf sechserley Art; es blieb aber mit dem Schüler wie vorher. Endlich sagte K. ungeduldig: 'Ich kann nicht begreifen, wie Sie ein Mathematiker seyn und nicht 3/4 abmessen können, daß es ein Tripeltakt ist?' Moses sagte lächelnd: 'Als Mathematiker kenne ich keine 3/4, die nicht = 6/8 wären; aber da dieß in der Musik unterschieden seyn soll, so fange ich an zu glauben, daß ich kein musikalisches Ohr habe, um den Unterschied zu empfinden.' Der Unterricht endigte

We turn back to Mendelssohn's reading. At first, it was restricted to what he could afford to buy, to what he heard discussed at the *Joachimsthaler Gymnasium*, and to what the men of his acquaintance suggested.

From Nicolai we know of the impetus Mendelssohn received through the chance acquisition at a pawnbroker's of Reinbeck's *Betrachtungen über die Augsburger Confession*. Nicolai reported:

> "Here suddenly, he found himself in a totally different world; for till then he had not the slightest notion of Christian theology, or of a philosophy that was more recent than that of Maimonides. Hence, the philosophical part of Reinbeck's book, for instance the proofs of the existence of God, attracted him irresistibly."[23]

At once he sought someone with an open mind, in order to discuss the book. It was a dangerous step to take, for at that time the Jewish community still actively discouraged attempts to read any German texts, let alone a book dealing with Christian doctrine. Abraham Kisch, however, grasped Mendelssohn's desire to find out more about recent philosophers, and it was at this point that he advised and helped him to learn Latin forthwith. This opened the way to John Locke, and subsequently to other modern philosophers. It was Gumpertz who introduced Mendelssohn to Leibniz, and to Leibniz's disciple, Christian Wolff.[24]

By 1754, correspondence and publications help to provide evidence of Mendelssohn's reading. Before that time we are safe only in including the Bible, the Talmud, Maimonides *Guide to the Perplexed*, Reinbeck on Christian doctrine, Cicero, Locke *On Human Understanding*, Leibniz's *Théodicée*, Wolff's books on metaphysics, ethics and ontology, six books of Euclid, Spinoza's *Ethica more geometrica demonstrata*, and the treatise by Spinoza's fierce refuter, Pierre Bayle.

From 1754 onwards, the picture changes, as if overnight, and the volume of Mendelssohn's reading fans out unbelievably. Shaftesbury, Baumgarten, Prémontval, enter into Mendelssohn's letters. In 1755, Mendelssohn's earliest publication reflects *Recherche sur l'origine des sentiments agréables et désagréables* by Sulzer, Pouilly's *Théorie des sentiments agréables*, G. F. Meier's *Anfangsgründe der schönen Wissenschaften*, and the book to which this was transcription and commentary: Baumgarten's first volume of *Aesthetica*. Letters mention Déscartes' *Les passions de l'âme*, Aristotle's *Poetics*, Newton's *Optics*, Voltaire's *Zaïre*, Lessing's *Miss Sara Sampson*, Corneille, Hutcheson, Goldoni. We could go on with Malebranche, Réaumur, Bernouilli, Hogarth, Dubos and others. An incredibly vast number of books filled those few morning hours between 5 a.m. and 8 a.m. that Mendelssohn could set aside for study. Some intimation of it emerges in the appendix to Volume IV, *Jubiläumsausgabe* which lists the authors and books Mendelssohn referred to in just twenty-one review articles written between the

---

sich in ein Paar Monaten; doch trug Moses eine Menuet davon, die er ziemlich langsam auf dem Klaviere spielen lernte. 'Es ist sonderbar', sagte er lächelnd; 'ich kann den Tripeltakt spielen, aber nicht hören!' " See also *JubA*, XII, 1, p. 60: to Abbt, August 1764.
[23]*LSS*, XXVII, p. 491 f.
[24]*Ibid.*; "Immer aber wußte er noch nichts von denjenigen Philosophen und ihren Lehren, die zwischen Maimonides und Locke und nach dem leztern existirt hatten. Durch Gumpertz lernte er zuerst Leibnitz und Wolf kennen, deren Philosophie damals im stärksten Gange war."

summer of 1756 and thirty months later. The names of these authors fill thirteen pages of small print.

Mendelssohn had been fortunate from boyhood on, in finding men to help his mind develop: first his father, then the teachers Hirsch and David Fränkel in Dessau. Mendelssohn joined Fränkel in Berlin in what was probably his fourth year of talmudic studies. Soon afterwards, he met Abraham Kisch[25] and Aaron Gumpertz, the teacher and friend[26] of whom he wrote in 1761 to Fromet Gugenheim, his wife-to-be: "ihm allein habe ich alles zu danken, was ich in den Wissenschaften profitirt habe."

When they first met, probably in 1745, Gumpertz then aged twenty-two and Mendelssohn sixteen, Mendelssohn encountered in Gumpertz a widely educated young man who could help him with mathematics, philosophy, with literary German, with French and English. Through him, Mendelssohn had had access to classes held in Latin and in fields altogether new to him. Gumpertz was well-to-do and so confident of his learning that he moved with ease among the French scientists and Royal Academy scholars whom Frederick II had invited to Berlin. It was through Gumpertz that Mendelssohn was introduced to the mathematician and philosopher Maupertuis, president of the Royal Academy since 1745, to the Marquis d'Argens who employed Gumpertz as secretary after 1752, and to Lessing who reached Berlin in late October 1748. But before the meetings with Maupertuis and d'Argens took place around 1754/1755, Gumpertz, in his constant search for new experience, had planned to study philosophy and theory of literature under Gottsched in Leipzig, the Athens of the East. But the Second Silesian War which began in August 1744 made a move to Saxony unwise. Instead, he stayed in Berlin. The meeting with Lessing is thought to have taken place in 1748, for it is assumed that the good traveller, a Jew, in Lessing's comedy *Die Juden*, was modelled on Gumpertz, and the date of the comedy is 1749. Ultimately, Gumpertz went off to Frankfurt an der Oder, to study medicine. From there he returned with a diploma as doctor of medicine in 1750. In that same year Mendelssohn entered the family of the silk merchant and manufacturer Isaac Bernhard as tutor to his children. He held this post for four years. Gumpertz's stay in Frankfurt coincided with that of Friedrich Nicolai. Nicolai, ten years younger than Gumpertz, had been sent by his father to learn the book-trade, but he used the time mainly to profit from the lectures by men like Alexander Baumgarten. It is conceivable that Gumpertz and Nicolai met in Frankfurt an der Oder, and that Gumpertz thus knew Mendelssohn, Nicolai and Lessing before these met each other in Berlin.

On Nicolai's evidence, Lessing was introduced to Mendelssohn by Gumpertz early in 1754 through their shared interest in chess. If that was the year, Lessing was then twenty-five, Nicolai twenty-two and Mendelssohn, who had just ended his years of tutoring and had become Bernhard's accountant, was in his twenty-fifth year. The meeting between Lessing and Nicolai took place at the

[25]Alexander Altmann, *Moses Mendelssohn. A Biographical Study*, University of Alabama Press 1973, p. 766, note 44.
[26]*JubA*, XI, p. 220.

printing press of the bookseller Voss who chanced to have obtained the proof sheets of young Nicolai's anonymous treatise, *Briefe über den itzigen Zustand der schönen Wissenschaften in Deutschland*. Lessing befriended Nicolai and then introduced his two new friends, Mendelssohn and Nicolai, to each other late in 1754. This is Nicolai's recollection. Actually, Lessing and Mendelssohn may have met earlier, on Lessing's return to Berlin in November 1752, after a year's absence to study and write in Wittenberg. At the latest, I think, they met in the autumn of 1753. This is my reason: the first of Mendelssohn's extant letters, dating from January 1754, is addressed to Naumann, Lessing's close friend since 1746 and with whom he shared a room in the early years in Berlin. This letter responds to Naumann's plea for advice on a treatise of his which appeared in print (with Mendelssohn's advice incorporated) in early February 1754.[27] Lessing must have known Mendelssohn some weeks, if not months before then. There had to be time for Lessing to bring Naumann and Mendelssohn together, and time for the friendship to ripen; for this kind of advice is hardly sought at a first encounter. Naumann seems to have been among the earliest of Lessing's circle of which Mendelssohn suddenly found himself a member. There were also other old friends of Lessing's, the musician and editor of various musicological periodicals, Marpurg, and von Breitenbauch, a cultured, far-travelled man with a gift for caricature. Above all, there were gatherings of educated Germans in clubs and coffee houses. For instance, at this time the chairman of the so-called Monday Club was Sulzer, the Swiss scholar and member of the Berlin Academy. Mendelssohn never formally joined this group because the twenty-four artists, writers and scholars met for dinner, but he certainly knew some of the members, for instance Sulzer and the poet Ramler.

However, Mendelssohn did belong to the Learned Coffee-house which was founded early in 1756. The members of this quite large group of more than forty men included Gumpertz, the mathematician Johann Albrecht Euler, Resewitz (then a theological student), the mathematician and member of the Academy, Lieutenant Jacobi, and a young Scottish nobleman, named Middleton. The society owned two rooms, one of them given over to a billiard table. Apart from a weekly meeting for all members and their guests, there was a meeting every four weeks at which a member's treatise on a topic from mathematics, physics or philosophy was read to the assembled company "to increase their knowledge and scholarship". The standard was high, if we are to judge it by the quality of papers such as Mendelssohn's on Probability. Of this paper Nicolai reported:[28]

> "In Moses's treatise on probability there are some equations. Towards the end where the author is refuting those philosophers who postulate *aequilibrium indifferentiae*, Mendelssohn deduced that their opinion led to assuming that the degree of divine foreknowledge amounts to nought. Moses did not read his own treatise because he was too shy to trust his own voice. The man whom Moses had asked to read it aloud, made a funny mistake. When he got to the equation just referred to, he mistook the zero for an O. When all of a sudden this O rang out, all listeners looked at each other, some laughed. For though there is an a, b, n, x, y in the treatise, there is no O. In those years a Scot called Middleton, reputedly the younger son of a Lord, was living in Berlin . . . He was an eccentric,

[27] *Ibid.*, p. 386.
[28] *LSS*, XXVII, p. 504 f.

humorous young man with many good qualities. He studied German literature with much zeal ... he also wrote in German ... he translated Moses's letters *Über die Empfindungen*. Being an enthusiastic member of the Learned Coffee-house, he was rarely absent from its meetings, especially when it came to the lectures. On the day the treatise on probability was being read, he turned up as the reading began. After he had listened for a while, he moved next to Moses and asked him in a low voice, whose treatise this was. Moses gestured that he should not interrupt proceedings, and pointed to the reader as being the author. Middleton shook his head, because he did not feel he could expect such a treatise from this reader. He went on listening assiduously, and when another few pages had been read, he whispered into Moses' ear that he took *him* to be the author, and he should not go on denying it. Again Moses shook his head and pointed to the reader as being the author. When now eventually the O rang out, Middleton was the first to laugh heartily, and he asked Moses whether he would still deny being the author of the paper?"

This essay on Probability appeared under Mendelssohn's name only in 1761, in part II of *Philosophische Schriften*. It had appeared anonymously in the autumn of 1756[29] but it was by no means Mendelssohn's first venture into having his original ideas published in German. According to Mendelssohn himself, this had come about in the following manner – the narrator is Daniel Jenisch in 1789:

"One fine day, Lessing gave Mendelssohn an essay by a foreign scholar. Mendelssohn returned this soon with the comment 'this is a topic about which I might trust myself to have something to say'. Lessing replied: 'I should love to see it.' Mendelssohn remained silent but a while later, brought him the first of his *Philosophische Gespräche*. Lessing took it, giving the excuse that he had no time to read it now. Several weeks went by without Mendelssohn catching sight of his manuscript. Once, when he was in Lessing's rooms, he asked if Lessing had read the essay yet. In lieu of an answer, Lessing pointed and said: 'Take the small book over there' and Mendelssohn saw his manuscript in print."[30]

When Mendelssohn's eldest son Joseph quoted this story in *Gesammelte Schriften* as his father was supposed to have told it, he stated that the "foreign scholar" was Shaftesbury, that Mendelssohn asserted "he could write essays like that too", that not weeks but months went by before Lessing handed him, not a copy of the first *Philosophic Dialogue*, but of all of them. In essence the two accounts tally.

A look at the Appendix will show that until 1756 Mendelssohn's written work focused on metaphysics. This early work on metaphysics has received detailed, scholarly treatment in Alexander Altmann's *Moses Mendelssohns Frühschriften zur Metaphysik*.[31] So it would be both impertinent and superfluous to

[29] *Vermischte Abhandlungen und Urtheile über das Neueste aus der Gelehrsamkeit*, vol. III, Berlin, 1756, pp. 3–26 (cf. *JubA*, I, p. 340).
[30] Jenisch, p. 28 f.: "Nikolai gab damals die Bibliothek der freien Künste heraus, wozu Mendelssohn ihm Beiträge gegeben. Als Lessing und Nikolai seine Aufsätze sahen, baten sie ihn, etwas wissenschaftliches zu schreiben; aber dies erlaubte ihm seine natürliche Schüchternheit nicht. Lessing gibt ihm einst einen Aufsatz von einem auswärtigen Gelehrten zu lesen, welchen er ihm aber bald zurückstellte, mit der Äußerung: ich getraue mir allenfalls etwas darüber aufzusetzen. Das möchte ich wohl sehen, erwiederte Lessing. Mendelssohn schweigt stille, und bringt ihm einige Zeit nachher die erste seiner bekannten philosophischen Gespräche. Lessing nimmt es zu sich, mit der Entschuldigung, er habe jetzt keine Zeit zu lesen, – und so verstrichen einige Wochen, ohne daß Mendelssohn das Manuscript wieder bekam. Indem er einst auf Lessings Stube ist, und ihn fragt, ob er bereits seinen Aufsatz gelesen? sagt Lessing ihm statt der Antwort: Nehmen sie dort das kleine Büchelchen – und Mendelssohn steht erstaunet da, sein Manuscript gedruckt zu sehen."
[31] Tübingen 1969.

treat these writings here. These early treatises were indicative of a very promising and natural bent: Mendelssohn is clearly in his element. What were the reasons, therefore, that caused Mendelssohn to desert metaphysics in 1754 for a number of years? The key to this perplexing turn-around in intellectual interests is to be sought in Mendelssohn's friendship with Lessing and Nicolai.

The Berlin of 1754 boasted no university, no theatre; it had only limited access to news about the world outside: it offered freedom of speech only in matters of learning and religion. The educated had a surfeit of French and English literature to feast on; even scholarly and scientific matters, in the guise of Academy lectures, were accessible only in French. Was it surprising that the lively minds of the young generation turned to opposition and criticism, and that since they could not voice it in national politics, they turned to national literature? Or that they tried to instil the rudiments of critical thinking into their contemporaries?

Certainly, this had been the case with Lessing and with Nicolai. By the time he made Mendelssohn's acquaintance, Lessing was an acknowledged critic. His anonymous reviews in the two Berlin journals that had the Royal privilege and permission to publish three issues a week, were mostly brief, sharp and descriptive rather than analytical. But by 1745 Lessing's days of anonymity were over. He had begun to edit those of his writings he wished to acknowledge as his. Lessing had not yet turned to the theory of literature, or to the writing of drama of any real profundity.

By 1754, Nicolai was enjoying the only years of his life in which he was totally free, free to study, free from any kind of responsibility for the family's publishing firm and bookshop. It was in 1754 that he wrote the remarkable eighteen *Briefe über den itzigen Zustand der schönen Wissenschaften in Deutschland* which logically and stylistically were so pungent that the anonymous treatise was ascribed to Lessing.

Lessing had been to the University of Leipzig for two years and at Wittenberg for one. Nicolai, though not formally enrolled at a university, had similarly had the chance to profit from university lectures in logic, metaphysics, aesthetics and history for three years. Like Lessing, he knew a number of languages, had tried his hand at translating, had come in contact with the teachings of Wolff and had developed a style that showed the influence of Voltaire.

While Lessing and Nicolai had had their lively intelligence disciplined by systematic study and training in their late teens, Mendelssohn had been left to browse at will, and needed direction. It was particularly in drawing attention to modern languages and their literatures that Lessing took over from Gumpertz. He guided Mendelssohn so totally, that after Lessing's death, Mendelssohn wrote to Karl Lessing in 1781:

> "I thank providence for the benefice of letting me get to know so early in life a man who formed my soul and to whom I looked and shall look as friend and judge at each action I do, at each line of text I write . . ."[32]

This meant in no way, however, that Mendelssohn's integrity was at stake. Here is Nicolai in 1786:

[32] *JubA*, XIII, p. 6.

"We agreed in metaphysical, aesthetic and moral principles, but each individual's point of view was so divergent, that every one of our observations opened up new prospects, and lent itself so richly to further thought and satisfying results, even if we ended up – as we generally did – by sticking to different opinions on secondary points. This sincere agreement in matters of moment, the disagreement on many subsidiary points despite fierce arguing, is still my surest yardstick of our tireless love of truth. Each one of us remained true to his individual character, his individual way of thinking, without any pretension or hypocrisy."[33]

In short, the friends argued not to best each other, but to train their critical faculties and widen their mental horizons. There are several other accounts that ring just as true:

"Almost daily, we spent some time together. Again and again, we went back to those concepts which we were developing by constant discussion. We did this especially by virtue of Moses acting out the part of the Chorus in ancient drama. Generally, he listened to our hot-headed disputes calmly, and suddenly, when we still deemed ourselves far from reaching any conclusion, he provided a summing up by means of a few striking phrases that left all of us content. This went on for more than a year."[34]

Nicolai also gave a vivid description of their method of discussing. In 1799, he outlined Lessing's habit of either taking the devil's advocate point of view, or by deliberately and ingeniously refuting a point of view just presented. And he did this, said Nicolai:

"not as a deliberate exercise in refutation but from conviction – which we shared – that in speculative thought to find the truth is not as important as the exercising of one's mind in ferreting it out."[35]

"And in order to develop their mental vigour, they looked at both sides of any question, maintaining scepticism to the very end. Each participant in the discussion retained his integrity, and each emerged from this amicable discoursing less prejudiced and clearer, and more definite in mind . . . Lessing and Moses equalled each other in frank rejection of all prejudice, both were equally pure in heart, equally magnanimous, equally free of all pretentiousness, equally penetrating in the swift developing, exact differentiating, clear defining of concepts. Lessing was more ardent in his search for truth . . . and quite frequently used his wits to defend or refute what yet seemed to lack defence or refutation. Moses was more circumspect and more attentive to the outcome; and Nicolai at least their equal in vivacious love of truth, good will and candour, and as avid to increase those insights which can be obtained by the lucidity of statements. All three were of lively mind, so that their talk was frequently spiced by wit and joke."[36]

---

[33]Nicolai, *Allgemeine Deutsche Bibliothek*, vol. 65.2, 1786, p. 628.
[34]*LSS*, XXVI, p. 19*f.: "Da wir fast täglich beysammen waren, so kamen wir immer wieder auf eben die Gedanken zurück, welche sich durch beständige Erörterung immer mehr entwickelten, besonders durch unsern lieben *Moses*, der bey uns war, was bey den alten Schauspielen der Chor. Er war gewöhnlich unserer lebhaften Disputen kaltblütiger Zuhörer, und zog unvermuthet, und wenn wir noch weit vom Ziele zu seyn glaubten, in wenig Worten ein treffendes Resultat, das uns alle befriedigte. Dies währte über ein Jahr. Fast bey jedem neuen Buche, über das wir sprachen, erneuerte sich der Verdruß über die schiefe Wendung, die alles nahm. Hierauf entstand endlich das Verlangen, diesem Uebel abzuhelfen."
[35]Nicolai, *Über meine gelehrte Bildung*, 1799, pp. 40–2: "Diese Manier Lessings entstand nicht aus Liebe zum Widersprechen, sondern um Begriffe dadurch noch heller und bestimmter zu entwickeln, daß man sie von mehreren Seiten betrachtete; denn er war, so wie wir alle überzeugt, daß in spekulativen Dingen sehr oft die gefundene Wahrheit nicht so viel werth ist, als die Uebung des Geistes, wodurch man sie zu finden sucht."
[36]Nicolai, *Bildniss und Selbstbiographie* (ed. M. S. Lowe), Berlin–Leipzig 1806, pp. 14–18: "Desto weniger galt bei ihnen allen irgend eine Autorität oder anderweitige Rücksicht, und Vorurtheil galt gar nicht. Von allen aufgeworfenen Fragen ward beständig das *Dafür* and *Dawider* von

When Nicolai said "this went on for more than a year", he referred to the span of time before Lessing left Berlin for Leipzig in November 1755 and was gone for two and a half years. By the time Lessing left Berlin, quite a few people already knew of the author of *Über die Empfindungen* and of *Philosophische Gespräche*. Some even knew who he was. Sulzer in a letter to Bodmer spoke of Mendelssohn as "starkdenkender Kopf", Gellert (to Rabener) as "witziger Kopf". Zimmermann, early in 1756, quoted from the second dialogue of *Philosophische Gespräche* in *Betrachtungen über die Einsamkeit*, and ascribes them to an "exceptionally sagacious and gentle scholar". Prémontval told Michaelis: "Je le trouve homme d'esprit et de mérite, et je vous dois cette connoissance." Gleim even mentions Mendelssohn's name in a letter to Uz: "The author of *Philosophische Gespräche* and the little treatise *Über die Empfindungen* is not an imaginary, but a real Jew, very young as yet, and of excellent talent. He never had a teacher, and yet got exceedingly far in all branches of knowledge. He uses algebra to while away time, as the likes of us use poetry, and yet from his early years he had to earn his living and work for a Jewish merchant. This much I know from Mr. Lessing. His name is Moses."[37]

Before the meeting of Lessing and Mendelssohn came about, Mendelssohn had written one essay. This is 'Von den ongefähren Zufällen'. In 1754 and 1755 eight pieces of work attest to the intensification of reading, the increase in flexibility of style and structure that Lessing's encouragement brought about. Indeed, one piece of work, *Pope, ein Metaphysiker!* is evidence of their successful collaboration. Another, the translation of Rousseau's *Second Discourse* (*Sur l'origine de l'inégalité parmi les hommes*) is rounded off by an intensive critique of its thought content. Mendelssohn accounted for his own motives in an Open Letter, addressed to 'Magister Lessing in Leipzig'. The translation of the essay was done by the time Lessing left in November. The Open Letter was begun soon after

---

Einem oder dem Andern der Unterredenden aufgenommen, niemal aber darauf ausgegangen, Einen zu Meinung des Andern schlechterdings zu bekehren; sonder Jeder blieb selbständig, ging nur aus dem freundschaftlichen Dispute vorurtheilsfreier nach Hause, oft unter eigenem weiterm Nachdenken darüber, welches nicht selten in der nächsten Versammlung zu neuem Gedankenwechsel Anlaß gab. Lessing und Moses waren sich einander ganz gleich an freymüthiger Verwerfung aller Vorurtheile, beide gleich reinen Herzens, gleich edelmüthig, gleich frey von aller Prätension, gleich scharfsinnig im schnellen Entwickeln im genauen Unterscheiden und deutlichen Bestimmen der Begriffe. Lessing war lebhafter beym Suchen nach Wahreit, und bot seinen Scharfsinn nicht selten auf, bloß um zu vertheidigen oder zu widerlegen was etwa noch nicht stark genug vertheidigt oder widerlegt schien; Moses war bedächtiger, mit deutlicherer Rücksicht auf Resultate; Nicolai ihnen wenigstens gleich an lebhafter Wahrheitsliebe, an gutem Willen und Freymüthigkeit, gleich ihnen begierig nach jedem Wachsthume der Erkenntnisse, welcher durch Deutlichkeit der Begriffe erlangt werden kann. Alle drey waren heitern Geistes, so daß ihre Unterhaltung oft mit Scherze und Witze gewürzt war, ohne daß je die wechselseitige Achtung wäre vergessen worden . . ."

[37]Sulzer to Bodmer: early November 1755; Gellert to Rabener: 24th January 1756; Gleim to Uz: 12th February 1756; Prémontval to Michaelis: 6th January 1756; Zimmermann, *Betrachtungen über die Einsamkeit*, Zürich 1756, p. 66 ff. Gleim: "Der Verfaßer der philosophischen Gespräche und des Werckchens, über die Empfindungen, ist kein erdichteter, sondern ein würklicher Jude, noch sehr jung, und von einem treflichen Genie, der es, ohne Lehrer, in allen Wißenschaften sehr weit gebracht hat, die Algebra zum Zeitvertreib gebraucht, wie wir die Poesie, und doch von Jugend auf, in einer jüdischen Handlung sein Brod verdienet hat. So viel hat Herr Leßing von ihm gesagt. Sein Nahme ist Moses."

the good-byes had been said to the first real friend Mendelssohn had ever had, and to the first non-Jewish German who welcomed, accepted, valued and encouraged him. Mendelssohn was aching to hear what the friend had to say about the Rousseau critique. "Grant me a little of your attention", he pleaded, "and enter into one of those speculative studies by means of which we used to shed imaginary cares."[38] Mendelssohn extolled friendship for its "pleasant quickening of minds, in the absence of which nature and art, despite all their splendour, let us languish in the utmost need . . ."[39] Therefore, "if no country can offer what Rousseau desires to find in his, I should be content to be born in one where Socrates can be my model, and Lessing my friend".[40] The strength of this feeling of friendship completely overwhelmed Mendelssohn. We cannot hope to understand his relinquishment of metaphysics, unless we take this force into account:

> "Far too well do you know . . . how wide open my heart is to the feelings of friendship. Far too often, you noticed, and with pleasure, how one friendly glance from you affected my state of mind, how it sufficed to banish melancholy and make my face light up in gladness. How could your recent absence have turned my heart to stone, no, most cherished friend – it is this very omnipotent force of friendship that bewilders me."[41]

We have to turn to Mendelssohn's letters to trace how he coped with this perplexity and how it resulted in growing disenchantment with metaphysics in the absence of the friend who would have been discussant and critic. In January 1756 Mendelssohn wrote:

> "Some people want to persuade me to write a whole system of metaphysics. But I am determined not to undertake such a work until I have the pleasure of being with you. I thought such a time was close at hand, and though it now looks as if it were further afield, I have not given up hope entirely. Till such a time comes about, I shall go on to get more firmly ensconced in mathematics and to let my philosophical notions reach their essential maturity. The world will not miss my system of metaphysics, if I should never come to write it, and as far as I am concerned, I would hardly have a calm moment, if I had published one without having the frank judgment of a Lessing."[42]

But by early May 1756, there was still no word from Lessing in response to the Rousseau criticism, and, on Mendelssohn's part, the same intense devotion to the memory of the past, together with the first indication of a ripening acquaintance with Sulzer and Nicolai. Thus we reach stage two of this turning away from metaphysics. After Lessing's brief absence from Leipzig and his subsequent return there in late September 1756, Mendelssohn was even more disconsolate than when Lessing had first gone away. As a result, Mendelssohn set out to seek and see in Nicolai what Lessing might have found so attractive. On 2nd August, 1756 he reported:

> "I have become unfaithful to the brooding pursuit of metaphysics. I visit Mr. Nicolai very frequently in his garden. I truly like him and believe that our friendship, yours and mine, should be strengthened by it, because in him I like a man who is your true friend. We read poems, Nicolai reads me his compositions, and I sit there as judge and critic, admire, laugh, approve, reprove till evening falls. Indeed, I am beginning to boast quite

[38]*JubA*, II, p. 86.
[39]*Ibid.*, p. 90 f.
[40]*Ibid.*, p. 95 f.
[41]*Ibid.*, p. 90 f.
[42]*JubA*, XI, p. 52 (10th January 1756).

the makings of a *Belesprit*. Who knows but that I may even produce poetry. May Madame Metaphysica be a forgiving lady. According to her, friendship is based on equality of propensities, but inversely, I find that equality of tastes can be based on friendship. Your friendship and Nicolai's has brought it about that I have withdrawn a part of my affections from this venerable matron and have bestowed it on *Belles Lettres*. Our friend has even asked me to be his collaborator."[43]

In short, Mendelssohn's arguments had been: without your presence and your criticism I will not philosophise; I regard Nicolai as your friend and I have tried to see in him what you do. Apparently, he approves of me as a critic of his literary compositions; he has even asked me to become his collaborator. In other words, you and Nicolai have turned me from metaphysics to *belles lettres*.

To this Lessing rejoined: You are my friend, your ability is also part of me, I need your help to examine my thoughts and to correct them (13th November 1756), and I need your rejoinders to keep this exchange of opinions going (13th and 28th November 1756):

> "It pleases me quite a bit that my Friend the metaphysician has spread out into a *belesprit*. If only his friend the *belesprit* could, or would contract, if only a little, into being a metaphysician. What are we to do? Meanwhile the *belesprit* seeks comfort in the conceit – for what else could a *belesprit* seek comfort in, but in conceits – that if friends are to share everything, your knowledge would be mine too, and that you would not be able to be a metaphysician without my being one too ... With this I conclude. You are my friend; I want to have my thoughts examined by you, not praised. I look forward to your future objections with all the pleasure with which one ought to anticipate improvement. As far as letter writing is concerned, I have filled my lungs – you know what you will have to do, to let me go on breathing."[44]

The fact that Mendelssohn had a very considerable effect on Lessing's style, thinking and method, is not the subject of this study, nor does such influence negate Lessing's perceptive judgment, quoted at the outset,[45] which Mendelssohn confirmed in a most exciting way on 19th April 1757 when he wrote to von Breitenbauch:

> "You are right, my life in the realm of pure scholarship was not of long duration – but I am not quite dead yet. Currently, I am undergoing my transformation, and once this is accomplished, who knows but I will not even boast wings then?"[46]

We heard that Nicolai invited his friend to become his collaborator. Collaborator in what? Clearly it was the periodical which Nicolai had planned as the natural follow-up of his own conclusions to *Briefe über den itzigen Zustand der schönen Wissenschaften in Deutschland*, and as the outcome of the growing frustration which all three young men had experienced in their discussion of current German literature.[47] The postulates of Nicolai's eighteenth chapter of his treatise form the programme of the periodical. In 1756 an explicit announce-

---

[43]*Ibid.*, p. 55 (2nd August 1756).
[44]*Ibid.*, p. 69 (Lessing: 13th November 1756); *Ibid.*, p. 79 (Lessing: 28th November 1756); *Ibid.*, p. 162 (Lessing: 22nd May 1757).
[45]See above p. 63.
[46]*JubA*, XI, p. 116.
[47]*LSS*, XXVII, p. 21: "Fast bey jedem neuen Buche, über das wir sprachen, erneuerte sich der Verdruß über die schiefe Wendung, die alles nahm. Hierauf entstand endlich das Verlangen, diesem Uebel abzuhelfen."

ment declared that the new periodical would be aimed at examining contributions to *belles letteres* and *beaux arts*. Reader, writer and critic were to be guided into developing critical faculties among the Germans. The periodical, *Bibliothek der schönen Wissenschaften und der freyen Künste*, was to teach but not to preach. It was to look out for promising young authors, for new definitions in aesthetics and in literary theory, to provide a platform for literary discussion, and be particularly concerned about the handling of language. It was a successful venture, and a mighty one. With the exception of three articles and the translations of treatises by Dubos and Shaftesbury, *all* other articles in the first four volumes were the work of Nicolai and Mendelssohn. Mendelssohn contributed two long and very important essays, and twenty-one review articles of varying length; the shortest was five pages long, the longest covered seventy pages of octavo print. All this material was produced by Mendelssohn in his spare morning hours, in just over two and a half years, between the summer of 1756 and the end of 1758.

Mendelssohn discussed the works of two Swiss, two French, four English, ten German authors and of one medieval Jewish writer of fables. The languages of the books discussed included Hebrew and Latin, French and English. Categories like Didactic Poetry (by Withof, Dusch, Lichtwer, Gleim, Berachya, Akenside, Pope), Biblical Drama (by Klopstock, Gessner), Historical Drama (Wieland's), Aesthetic Theory (by Burke, Baumgarten, G. F. Meier), Literary Theory (by Mallet, Batteux) and Rhetoric (by Basedow) tell little about the novelty and excitement of the articles to be found *in toto* in volume IV of the *Moses Mendelssohn Jubiläumsausgabe*.

All of Mendelssohn's articles were anonymous, the discussion they aroused was wide spread, and the echo both immediate and affecting the rest of the eighteenth century. For a close study of the material stimulus and the effect of a considerable number of novel ideas, it would be essential to interrelate the literary discussion as it finds its echo in the letters of Mendelssohn, Nicolai and Lessing, in Mendelssohn's two essays of the summer of 1757,[48] and in the twenty-one review articles in the first four volumes of *Bibliothek*.

In 1767, Herder, whose attitude towards Mendelssohn was at best ambivalent, had this to say of Mendelssohn:

> "Here we have the philosopher-writer of our nation who is said to have wedded philosophy to beauty. Yes, the author of *Philosophische Schriften* [1761] is the man who can place philosophy in such lucid clarity as if the muse herself had chosen his words. Where others are content merely to sense beauty, he thinks it, and among the Germans, it is he who has propagated the art of criticism."[49]

By deductive analysis in these belletristic essays and studies, Mendelssohn gave new substance and definition to fields as diverse as comparative literature,

---

[48](1) 'Betrachtungen über die Quellen und die Verbindungen von den schönen Künsten und Wissenschaften' (sent to Lessing between 14th May and 1st July 1757), *Bibliothek der schönen Wissenschaften und der freyen Künste*, I, 2, July 1757, pp. 23–68 (=*JubA*, I, pp. 165–190).
(2) 'Betrachtungen über das Erhabene und das Naive in den schönen Wissenschaften' (sent to Lessing 11th August 1757), *Bibliothek der schönen Wissenschaften* ... II, 2, January 1758, pp. 229–267 (=*JubA*, I, pp. 191–218).
[49]Herder, ed. Suphan, I, p. 224 f.

literary history, literary criticism, semantics and aesthetics. He discussed fable, biblical drama, the Bible as poetry, didactic poetry. He defined and communicated his enthusiasm for writers of genius such as Shakespeare and Shaftesbury. Their reception into eighteenth-century Germany is due to him beyond all others. He introduced Edmund Burke, though he did not know him by name. In literary criticism he formulated definitions for "genius", for "poetic", for the limitation of poetry and painting. He described the autonomy of art, explored that strange artist, the "philosophical poet"; he passed on Shaftesbury's concepts of the artist as "Second Prometheus", as "virtuoso" and Shaftesbury's idea of *Bildung*. He concerned himself with dramatic structure, with historic verity in drama. He knew of "sublime silence", of language apposite to different levels of age and situation, he is the most demanding translator of authors ranging from Isaiah to Dante, Shakespeare, Shaftesbury, Akenside, Pope and Rousseau. In aesthetics he has more, and more valid, things to say on the "sublime" than Burke. He analysed the concept "naive", he probed the meaning of "beautiful", "perfect", "terrible", "ridiculous", of "compassion", "fear", of "aesthetic enjoyment" in tragedy. His influence radiated to Winckelmann, Lessing, Herder, Gerstenberg, to the dramatists of the *Sturm und Drang*. It affected thinkers like Kant, Hamann, K. P. Moritz, and aestheticians like Goethe and Schiller.

At the time when all these formulations and innovations enriched literary history and aesthetics, the man from whom they sprang was not even thirty years of age. It was an intellectual achievement beyond belief. It helped to lay the foundations for making Berlin the intellectual centre of the German-speaking world. In human terms, it was just as incredible a story of success. The young foreign Jew who fifteen years earlier had known just one person in the whole of Berlin, by 1758 was befriended, acclaimed and consulted by a throng of Germans then famous and respected. Originally, the anonymity of Mendelssohn's authorship had added spice to the feast but this reaction was eclipsed by substantive recognition of *Philosophische Gespräche* and *Über die Empfindungen* for their ideas, as well as for elegance of style and structure. Similar acclaim attended the publication of *Bibliothek der schönen Wissenschaften und der freyen Künste* during the years that Mendelssohn and Nicolai were its editors. The critical, objective discussion of literary judgments, the formulation of aesthetic concepts, combined with a resolute rejection of literary mediocrity were revolutionary in the Germany of the 1750s. From the sheer volume and the quality of Mendelssohn's contributions, it is clear that the daring venture of the two young men would not have achieved national fame, importance and effect, without Mendelssohn's collaboration and the high standards that his work set. But is it true to say that by his work for this literary periodical Mendelssohn truly "deserted Madame Metaphysica", that he had turned to belletristics for the sake of friendship with Lessing?

Both rhetorical questions belittle a multi-level, complex progression of causal factors, such as contacts with learned men and with current literature transmitted via the thought processes of an analytical mind, trained in the Wolffian and the Talmudic tradition, and consistently applied to whatever issue confronted him. In the years 1755–1757 Mendelssohn's learned, self-taught, probing mind partly found itself well-received and at ease with the mathematician-physicist members of the Royal Academy, and partly puzzled by the literary figures of his day with their interest in philology, in antiquity and always bedevilled by their lacking a sense of vocation as poets. Among contemporary German writers, of whom he had met quite a few in Berlin, men like Ramler, Gessner, Gleim, even E. v. Kleist, A. v. Haller, and the young Wieland were then in thrall to a didactic bent that evoked Mendelssohn's outright pity for such hybrids: philosophising poets who neither were, nor ever could be genuine philosophers, or seemingly, even good poets. Nicolai and Lessing shared Mendelssohn's unease and dismay over the state of literature in the Germany of their day. Nicolai had attempted to provide a therapeutic programme of training and *Bildung*[50]; Lessing – witness his many brief, forthright reviews in Berlin newspapers – had attacked poor writing whenever and wherever he encountered it.

Mendelssohn neither reproached, nor prescribed, he probed for underlying causes, and from these set up premises, definitions and theory. None of this would have been possible without Mendelssohn's ability to look at a specific problem and spot the generic questions it raised. Primarily, it was the latter which attracted his attention (and for this reason Mendelssohn's review articles contributed so much that was new, arresting and fundamental to literary theory and to aesthetics). But even the occasional *argumentum ad hominem* brought Mendelssohn back to criticism and its function, and to the nature and essence of the writer's work under discussion.

In 1755, Nicolai had quoted Shaftesbury's definition of the essence of criticism and its goals,[51] referring to a passage in *Soliloquy, or Advice to an Author*. Mendelssohn, as we know, had had access to Nicolai's reference to Shaftesbury's views on criticism, and to Shaftesbury's work itself.[52] Moreover, the need for objective criticism had so repeatedly been the subject of discussion among Lessing, Nicolai and Mendelssohn that out of it grew *Bibliothek der schönen Wissenschaften und der freyen Künste* in 1756. However, months elapsed before Mendelssohn's involvement in the new periodical became tangible reality (August 1756), and by then Mendelssohn had experimented repeatedly, both with applying philosophical argumentation to 'Bemühungen der Critik'[53] and philosophical as well as aesthetic judgments to Shaftesburian notions of literature.

In *Über die Empfindungen*, Mendelssohn had tested the use of critical faculties, *more geometrico*, against the concept "Vergnügen". In *Pope, ein Metaphysiker!*, Lessing and Mendelssohn wittily, and more elaborately, applied both philosophic argument and aesthetic criteria to the separate issues of appraising the work of a poet and exposing the fallibility of a syllogism. Late in 1755 Mendelssohn finished his translation into German of Rousseau's *Second Discourse*. In the

[50]See p. 76 above.
[51]*Briefe über den itzigen Zustand der schönen Wissenschaften in Deutschland*, ed. Ellinger, letter 18, p. 137.
[52]See Bamberger in *JubA*, I, XXVIII and *Über die Empfindungen*, *JubA*, I, pp. 165–190.
[53]See note 51.

appended 'Sendschreiben an den Herrn Magister Lessing in Leipzig', it was in keeping with Rousseau's topic that Mendelssohn's argument ceased to deal with abstractions, and turned to Man. In the course of Mendelssohn's moralist objections to the "strange judgment of this sage" on man and man's characteristic qualities, emerge the key-words that indicate Mendelssohn's growing preoccupation with the critique of judgment as it affects our diction ("Sprache unsers Herzens") and the "nature of our soul" (will to strive, pleasure, compassion, harmony, perfectibility). Mendelssohn's 'Sendschreiben' to Lessing was published early in 1756. By August of that year, the precipitation of Shaftesburian themes ("wir waren damals voll von Shaftesbury") [54] became even more discernible in the very important discussion that the three friends carried out by letter between August 1756 and May 1757 on the nature of the tragic, its function, its attendant concepts. Equally perceptible is the influence of Shaftesbury's concepts of "moral truth", "poetic truth", "inward form", "Second Prometheus under Jove" (i.e. the nature of the poet) in the review articles which Mendelssohn began to write in volume for *Bibliothek der schönen Wissenschaften und der freyen Künste* from 1756 onwards.

We watched the philosopher turn moralist in 'Sendschreiben'; in the review essays he was to undergo a further transformation, into literary critic. But at no time did the critic abdicate as a philosopher. Ethics and aesthetics were then still like Siamese twins: indissolubly intertwined, both laying claim to concepts such as good, beautiful, sublime, true; both struggling for independent recognition of their attributes.

Mendelssohn was quite evidently fascinated by this interplay. As early as December 1756,[55] we notice Mendelssohn striving to dissect rational from aesthetic judgments. From these tentative beginnings grew the treatise 'Betrachtungen über die Quellen und Verbindungen der schönen Künste und Wissenschaften'. Its magnificent opening paragraph sums up Mendelssohn's insight into the complex functions of "schöne Künste und Wissenschaften" (beaux arts, belles lettres):[56] their significance for "virtuoso", admirer–onlooker–amateur ("Liebhaber"), and philosopher; their appeal to mind and feeling; and above all, the means of access to our innermost feelings ("tiefsten Geheimnisse unsrer Seele").[57]

It is significant that, deeply affected by feeling at this time, Mendelssohn began to reflect on the impact of feeling on the mind. He regarded this process as catalysis, as unification. It results, he believed, in a refining of judgment, it provides firmer footing from which to define beauty, and above all, it leads to important discoveries in "psychology" (i.e. a theory of feelings). What more cogent grounds could there have been, to go beyond metaphysics and into belletristics, for "die menschliche Seele ist so unerschöpflich als die Natur; das bloße Nachdenken kann unmöglich alles ergründen".[58]

[54] Nicolai, *Berlinische Monatsschrift*, XVII, p. 32 f.
[55] See *JubA*, XI, p: 84.
[56] *JubA*, I, p. 167.
[57] *Ibid.*
[58] *Ibid.*; "Man's soul is as inexhaustible as Nature – and mere thinking cannot possibly fathom it all".

APPENDIX

Writings of Moses Mendelssohn by Date of Completion and/or Publication

			In:	
1.	*1753*, 16 Mch	'Von den ongefähren Zufällen' (cf. Prémontval: De l'Hazard, 1752)	JubA,	II, 3–5
2.	*1754*	*Philosophische Gespräche*, Berlin: Voss, 108 pp. Reviewed: 14. 2. 55 Hamburg. Unpart. Corr. 1. 3. Berl. Priv. Ztg (Lessing) 29. 5. Gött. Gel. Anz. (Michaelis)	,,	I, 1–39
3.	?Autumn	*Pope, ein Metaphysiker!* Danzig: Schuster, 1755, 60 pp.	,,	II, 43–80
4.	*1755*	'Von dem Vergnügen'	,,	I, 125–31
5.	Autumn	*Über die Empfindungen*, Berlin: Voss, 210 pp. Rev. BPZ 4. 9. 1755 GGA 2. 10. 9. 10. (Michaelis)	,,	I, 41–123
6.	ready Oct.	*Abhandlung v.d. Ursprunge d. Ungleicheit unter d. Menschen* Berlin: Voss, 1756 256 pp. (trs. by M. Mendelssohn)		
	ready Jan 1756	'Mit einem Sendschreiben an d. Herrn Magister Lessing in Leipzig' Rev. GGA 5. 2. 1757	,,	II, 81–109
7.		'Sendschreiben an einen jungen Gelehrten in B' in *Verm. Abh. & Urtheile über d. Neueste aus d. Gelehrsamkeit*, Bln: Voss, 1756	,,	I, 133–46
8.		Anmerkungen zu Sulzer: *Essai sur le bonheur des êtres intelligens* (used by S. before essay was published in 1756)	,,	II, 278–96
			,,	II, 27–33
9.	Oct.	'Von der Herrschaft über die Neigungen'	,,	II, 147–55
10.	*1756*	*Der Chamäleon, eine moralische Wochenschrift* Berlin: Birnstiel	,,	II, 111–45
		3. Stück, 33–44 Wie junge Leute d. Alten & Neuen Dichter lesen müssen		
		44–48 Gedanken		
		7. St. 98–103 Schreiben eines eifersüchtigen Ehemannes		
		103–06 Die Furcht vor dem May		
		107–08 Gedanken		
		9. St. 129–44 Ungleichheit & Geselligkeit der Menschen		
		10. St. 158–60 Sokrates Gespräche		
17.	31 Aug. 1756 to 14 May 1757	Correspondence on Trauerspiel	,,	XI, 56–135
18.	Summer	Withof: *Moralische Gedichte*	,,	IV, 5
19.		Lowth: *De sacra poesi Hebraeorum*		20
20.		Dusch: *Drei Gedichte*		63
21.		'Gedanken über die Wahrscheinlichkeit' (a) read in the Gelehrte Kaffeehaus (b) in *Verm. Abh. & Urtheile* ... Voss, III, 1756, 3–26	,,	I, 495–515

1757
22. June	'Betrachtungen über die Quellen & Verbindungen d. schönen Künste & Wissenschaften'		JubA,	I, 165–90
19.	Lowth (cont.)		,,	IV, 43
23. (Aug.)	'Seyn, oder Nichtseyn' trs. of *Hamlet* II, 2		,,	I, 202
24. (Aug.)	'Betrachtungen über das Erhabene & das Naive'		,,	I, 191–218
25. (Oct.)	Basedow: *Lehrbuch der Wohlredenheit*		,,	IV, 72
26.	Akenside: *Pleasures of Imagination*		,,	IV, 95
27.	Wolff: *Historische Lobschrift*		,,	IV, 118
28.	Klopstock: *Der Tod Adams*		,,	IV, 124
29. (5. xi.)	Sermon about the victory at Rossbach		—	

1758
30. (Jan.)	Mallet: *Principes pour la lecture des orateurs*		JubA	IV, 133
(June)	Mallet: (cont.)		,,	IV, 152
31.	Lichtwer: *Aesopische Fabeln*		,,	IV, 171
32.	Berachja: *Fabeln der Füchse*		,,	IV, 185
33.	Dusch: *Schilderungen aus d. Reiche d. Natur*		,,	IV, 189
34.	Meier, G. F. *Anfangsgründe aller schönen Künste*		,,	IV, 196
35. (Oct.)	Lichtwer: *Das Recht der Vernunft*		,,	IV, 202
36.	Burke: *Enquiry into the Origin of the Sublime & Beautiful*		,,	III, 235–67
		&	,,	IV, 216
37.	Gleim: *Lieder, Fabeln u. Romanzen*		,,	IV, 237
38.	Ramler/Batteux: *Einleitung in die schönen Wissenschaften*		,,	IV, 249

Pre Winter
39.	Baumgarten: *Aestheticorum Pars Altera*	,,	IV, 263
40.	Warton, J.: *The Writings & Genius of Pope*	,,	IV, 276
41.	Zimmermann: *Von dem Nationalstolze*	,,	IV, 329

Published in May
1759
40.	Warton: (cont.)	,,	IV, 299
42.	Gessner: *Der Tod Abels*	,,	IV, 348
43.	Wieland: *Lady Johanna Gray*	,,	IV, 375–87

The Beginning of the Epistolary Genre in Hebrew Enlightenment Literature in Germany
The Alleged Affinity between Lettres Persanes and 'Igrot Meshulam

BY MOSHE PELLI

The age of *Haskalah* is an age of change; thus any study of this period must in effect be a study in change.

The goals of that change, which was advocated by the Hebrew and Jewish *Maskilim* [enlighteners] in the last quarter of the eighteenth century in Germany, were in essence to enlighten the Jews, modernise Judaism, and to revive the Hebrew language and its culture. It was, then, a concerted effort on the part of young Jewish intellectuals to reshape and re-form Judaism and the Jews in accordance with the needs of modern times and the ideals of European Enlightenment.

There were some individual works which advocated a renewed interest in the sciences already in mid-century (such as works by Israel Zamosc and Judah Hurwitz). However, they represent single efforts, though important, to introduce certain moderate changes into Jewish society. The beginning of a group's concerted efforts to reach these goals may be traced to Moses Mendelssohn's early attempts in the 1750s to publish a journal of *Haskalah* [Hebrew Enlightenment] in Hebrew. *Qohelet Musar*, of which two issues only appeared, may signal the early start of *Haskalah* effort in Germany.

However, it was not until the publication of *Hame'asef* in the 1780s that the early intimations achieved fruition. Aware of the changes that have taken place in European Enlightenment literature and culture, a group of young intellectuals set out to remedy the condition of their people. Having faith in themselves and in the dire necessity to alleviate the status of the Jews and their culture, the *Maskilim* used the medium of the written word to advocate their desire for change.

The *Maskilim* utilised all means at their disposal to achieve their goal: through fictional and non-fictional writings; through preaching and teaching, directly and indirectly. They battled on a number of fronts. There was an internal struggle against the traditionalists within Judaism, who vehemently rejected the very idea of introducing modernisation into Judaism and into Jewish education, as a means to achieve the goals of Enlightenment ideology. There was also an external struggle with the opponents of Judaism on the European scene, a struggle which, for the *Maskilim*, was essentially a defence of Judaism.

However, the most painful struggle took place within some of the more sensitive Hebrew writers, each one within himself. An echo of it could be found in some of Isaac Euchel's writings, especially in the most tantalising questions expressed in his fictional work *The Letters of Meshulam*.

In this work, one can find the epitome of the problem of this transition period, as the old and the new intertwined, and as ideas of European Enlightenment penetrated into the Hebrew spheres.

It is this latter subject, which falls under the heading of cultural and literary transformation within the *Haskalah*, that concerns the present study.

A student of the period may note some readiness to accept a priori the notion of a total and most exclusive impact of European Enlightenment on the Hebrew *Haskalah*. Coupled with another erroneous notion of the radical inclinations of all the *Maskilim*, this contention ignores – or at least does not take into consideration – the enormous forces from within Judaism that had their impact on the *Maskilim*.

Being products of traditional Judaism, some of these Hebrew enlighteners were rather moderate in their demands for change, while others, extreme as they were in their inclination, continued to exhibit strong ties with the past. It is for this reason that although *Haskalah* owes very much to the literature and thought of European Enlightenment, one must acknowledge the indebtedness of *Haskalah* and the *Maskilim* to intrinsic Judaic influence. Its reliance on medieval Jewish philosophy must be taken into consideration (although an in-depth study of this aspect of *Haskalah* is indeed wanting). Similarly, one must be aware of its strong resemblance in form, contents and, at times, also in its themes, to the Hebrew literature of the past.

Thus, the study of the exchange of ideas between Judaism and European culture in the modern age may indeed recognise the great impact of the latter on the former. However, it is of utmost significance to note that the ways in which ideas penetrated into Judaic spheres in eighteenth-century Germany and elsewhere were quite complicated. An attempt to trace a single source of influence may prove to be futile, for one must take into account the variety of sources, external as well as internal, that have had any bearing on a given idea.

It is my belief that a greater emphasis must be placed on that material which draws on the inner Jewish experience of a given author.

A case in point is the impact of such a seminal work as Montesquieu's *Lettres Persanes* which seems unquestionable; nevertheless, many questions do indeed emerge as to its exclusive influence on Hebrew letters once a thorough probe is conducted.

The following study* purports to deal with this subject, and to serve as a test case for the above considerations.

Some seventy years after the publication of Montesquieu's *Lettres Persanes*, *Hame'asef*, a journal intended to promote the Hebrew *Haskalah* movement, carried a series of fictional letters entitled 'The Letters of Meshulam ben 'Uriyah Ha'eshtemo'i'. These letters, which were written by the Hebrew *Maskil* Isaac

---

*Presented at The Fourth International Congress on the Enlightenment, Yale University, 18th July 1975. This study was made possible with the assistance of Cornell Humanities Faculty Research Grant.

Euchel, constituted the first writing in its genre – the literary epistolary genre – in Modern Hebrew *belles lettres*.¹

Hebrew literary scholarship has assumed an affinity between Montesquieu's *Lettres Persanes* and Euchel's 'Letters of Meshulam'; the alleged dependence of the Hebrew work on its French predecessor has not, however, been demonstrated from a thorough analysis of the two texts themselves. Historians of Hebrew literature, noting a few superficial similarities between the two works, have concluded too hastily that Euchel's epistolary work is indebted to *Lettres Persanes*;² they neither discuss the nature of these similarities nor offer detailed proof of Euchel's alleged indebtedness to Montesquieu. It is not surprising then, that Sha'anan, for example, confronting the many striking dissimilarities, contents himself with stating that Euchel has not always comprehended the pungency of the Frenchman's irony. Whereas Montesquieu, he writes, ridiculed Christian Europe intentionally through the naïve, admiring Moslem, the Hebrew *Maskil*

---

¹ *'Igrot Meshulam ben 'Uriyah Ha'eshtemo'i, Hame'asef*, VI (1790), pp. 38–50, 80, 85, 171–176, 245–249, published anonymously. A list of Euchel's publications and some biographical data – apparently supplied by Euchel himself – were published by V. H. Schmidt and D. G. Mehring, *Neuestes Gelehrtes Berlin*, I, Berlin 1795, pp. 116–117. Among his publications Euchel lists the letters of the oriental travellers. A brief summary of the contents of *'Igrot Meshulam* is included in the second part of my study of Euchel, 'Isaac Euchel: Tradition and Change in the First Generation Haskalah Literature in Germany', *Journal of Jewish Studies*, XXVI, No. 1–2 (Spring-Autumn 1975), pp. 151–167; part two, vol. XXVII, No. 1 (Spring 1976), pp. 54–70. A bibliography on Euchel appears in that study, part one, pp. 151–152. This study is incorporated as chapter X in my book *The Age of Haskalah*, Leiden 1979. A general discussion of Euchel and his work appears also in my article 'Jewish Identity in Modern Hebrew Literature', *Judaism*, XXV, No. 4 (Fall 1976), pp. 448–452.

² Avraham Sha'anan, *'Iyunim Besifrut Hahaskalah* (Studies in the Literature of Haskalah), Merḥavyah, Israel 1952, pp. 75–80, and in his *Hasifrut Ha'ivrit Haḥadashah Lizramehah* (Currents in Modern Hebrew Literature), I, Tel-Aviv 1962), pp. 75–77. Joseph Klausner, *Historyah Shel Hasifrut Ha'ivrit Haḥadashah* (History of Modern Hebrew Literature), I, Jersusalem 1960³, p. 161: "It makes an impression as though it is an imitation of *Lettres Persanes*." Gedalyah Elkoshi, in his articles on Euchel in the *Hebrew Encyclopaedia*, II, Jerusalem 1957, p. 815, and the translated version published in the *Encyclopaedia Judaica*, VI, Jerusalem 1971, p. 957, also suggests that Euchel imitated Montesquieu: "[. . .] and which seemed in some respects to imitate Montesquieu's *Persian Letters*." The Hebrew version has it: "[. . .] which contain signs of imitation of the *Persian Letters*." G. Kressel writes that *'Igrot Meshulam* "are patterned after Montesquieu's *Lettres Persanes* (*Cyclopedia of Modern Hebrew Literature*, I, Merḥavyah, Israel 1965, p. 89 [Hebrew]) Werses is more careful in his observation; he relates *'Igrot Meshulam* to "this kind of 'Persian Letters' and their transformation in German literature" (Shmuel Werses, *Sipur Veshorsho* [Story and Source], Giv'atayim, Israel 1971, p. 11).

In a more recent and more elaborate study, Sha'anan virtually reiterates his contention of a direct influence of *Lettres Persanes* on *'Igrot Meshulam*, although, at times, he would refer to "Montesquieu and others". See his study 'The Letters of Meshullam as Symptom and Genre', *Baruch Kurzweil Memorial Volume*, Tel-Aviv – Ramat Gan 1975 [Hebrew], pp. 355, 356, 363, 364, 366, 368, 369.

In another article which appeared recently, Morris Neiman refers to Euchel's work as "A Hebrew Imitation of Montesquieu's *Lettres Persanes*". See his article bearing that title in *Jewish Social Studies*, XXXVII, No. 2 (Spring 1975), pp. 163–169. Neiman reiterates some of the superficial analogies between the two works, cited already in Sha'anan's *'Iyunim*, and adds a few other cursory similarities without even the slightest attempt to analyse the alleged analogies. Following the completion of the article I received Yehuda Friedlander's excellent essay, 'The Beginning of Satire. Isaac Euchel's "'Igrot Meshulam ben 'Uriyah Ha'eshtemo'i",' published in *Moznayim*, XLIV, No. 2 (January 1977), pp. 107–118 [Hebrew]. Friedlander accepts Sha'anan's affinity theory without reservation.

saw in Europe the seat of wisdom, which should be transplanted into Judaism; thus Euchel emphasised the enlightenment of Europe rather than its darker sides.[3]

According to this view, Euchel is portrayed as insensitive to the satire and irony of *Lettres Persanes*, and to its criticism of the social, cultural and religious institutions and customs of Europe. He is considered to have accepted the literal meaning of the French text, and to have made it the model of his own epistolary work.

Plainly, then, Euchel and his work deserve better and more detailed attention than they have thus far received. One of the very first Hebrew writers of the German *Haskalah* and one of its dominant figures, Isaac Euchel (1756–1804) appeared at the outset of the movement in the last quarter of the eighteenth century. In his personality and his literary and public activities, Euchel may signify many of the cultural changes that took place within the Hebrew intelligentsia in Germany.

As one of the major spokesmen of Hebrew *Haskalah* in Germany, Euchel initiated the first regular Hebrew journal, *Hame'asef*, in 1783, and thus established the enlightenment vehicle for introducing changes into German and European Jewry. He served as its editor for a number of years, contributing articles and creative work continuously even after he had ceased to be editor. Concurrently he established a society of Hebraists, *Hevrat Dorshei Leshon 'Ever* (The Society of the Seekers, or Friends, of the Hebrew Language). This kind of public activity was coupled in the following decade with the establishment of the *Gesellschaft der Freunde*, of which society he was the director from 1797 to 1801.

A follower of Moses Mendelssohn and an apparent student of his, Euchel composed the first book-long biography in Hebrew letters on his admired teacher. Reflecting the attitude of the Hebrew *Maskilim* towards "the Socrates of our time", as they referred to Mendelssohn, this glorifying biography was first serialised in *Hame'asef*, in 1788, and subsequently published as a book.

Among his other contributions, Euchel is credited with the introduction of some European literary genres into Hebrew literature. He wrote the first modern satire, thus utilising the prevalent European genre of the fictional epistolary writing for this purpose. It is *The Letters of Meshulam*, discussed below.

Typically, Euchel's *Haskalah* interests fluctuate between the secular and the sacred in this period of transition. Is there any wonder that he undertook upon himself to translate the traditional prayerbook into German? The *Gebete* (1786), being the first translation into German by a Hebrew writer in modern times (Friedländer published his translation in the same year), highlights the dual nature of Hebrew *Haskalah*, looking both internally as well as externally.

Exemplifying another aspect of the dual nature of Hebrew *Haskalah* is Euchel's contribution to Yiddish literature. He is considered to be the writer of the first modern Yiddish play, *Reb Henoch; oder Was thut men damit*. Clearly, then, the impact of European Enlightenment ideology on such a major writer of *Haskalah* should be thoroughly probed.[4] Such study may shed light on the dissemination

---

[3]*Iyunim*, p. 77; 'The Letters of Meshullam as Symptom', p. 356.
[4]A detailed analysis of his contribution to Hebrew *Haskalah* appears in my study 'Isaac Euchel: Tradition and Change' cited in note 1 above.

of Enlightenment ideas in German Hebrew spheres in general, and may indeed give us a better understanding of Hebrew *Haskalah*.

In this paper I shall first examine the hypothesis of the alleged dependence of *'Igrot Meshulam* solely upon Montesquieu's *Lettres Persanes*. In so doing, I shall not only resort to similarities promulgated by the exponents of this hypothesis, but will attempt to scrutinise the subject by referring to additional similarities not mentioned previously.

My working assumption is that in spite of the apparent impact of Montesquieu's satiric work on Euchel, it is incumbent upon the student of *Haskalah* literature and intellectual history of the Enlightenment to investigate the whole gamut of the epistolary literature in Europe at the time. Only through a thorough probe into the genre would we be able to ascertain the affinity between *'Igrot Meshulam* and *Lettres Persanes*.

Due to the enormous scope of such an undertaking which far exceeds the limitations of a single paper, I have selected a number of representative works in the epistolary, pseudo-oriental genre, and attempted to check whether the alleged similarities could be found in these works as well.

As I have selected works published prior to 1721 – the publication date of *Lettres Persanes* – as well as works published subsequently, the exclusive dependence of *'Igrot Meshulam* on Montesquieu has thus been questioned.

Following this examination, I purport to show that a study of the impact of European cultural milieu and Enlightenment literature on Hebrew *Haskalah* must take into account intrinsic factors as well. In this particular case of alleged literary affinity between a work in Hebrew and its counterpart in European literature, I shall show that a more significant impact will be found internally. Of importance is that *'Igrot Meshulam* is better understood when studied against Euchel's previous writings, *vis-à-vis* Euchel's own experience within the Jewish spheres.

We may study the alleged dependence of Euchel upon Montesquieu in terms of four categories of apparent similarities and one category of dissimilarities between their respective works.

A. The first category comprises those similarities which result from the epistolary genre itself. The very form of epistolary writing necessitates certain literary devices; however, since most are generally found in other such works, they may not be taken as conclusive evidence of the influence of the French on the Hebrew work. One such device is the introduction of the fictional publisher, or editor, of the letters; this is found in both works. However, it is commonly used in other epistolary writings such as the *Turkish Spy*, *Letters from the Dead to the Living* and *Memoirs of the Twentieth Century*,[5] and hence may not be cited as evidence of Euchel's dependence upon Montesquieu.

---

[5]'Introduction', *Lettres Persanes*, *Oeuvres Complètes de Montesquieu*, I, Paris 1875, pp. 51–53; *'Igrot Meshulam*, pp. 38–39. Sha'anan, *'Iyunim*, p. 77, cites the epistolary form as "reminiscent of Montesquieu's invention" (cf. G. L. Van Roosbroeck, *Persian Letters Before Montesquieu*, New York 1972).

In order to substantiate our contention, a number of representative works in the epistolary,

Similarly, the treatment of the letters as translations from an oriental into a European language: this literary convention of pseudo-translation, too, is to be found in both works, as, indeed, in others of the genre.[6] Another technique frequently employed in such writings is the inclusion of stories within the letters.[7] The "foreign observer", too, is conventional in these writings, so that use of this feature does not constitute proof of direct borrowing from *Lettres Persanes*.[8] The genre naturally also has features in common with the travelogue and hence some inherent similarities.

B. The second category includes certain ideas and topics apparently common both to *Lettres Persanes* and *'Igrot Meshulam*. Spaniards, for example, are similarly characterised in both works: they are described as phlegmatic, lazy, having an aversion to work and extremely proud. In addition, the Spanish Inquisition is

---

pseudo-oriental genre, published before 1721 – the publication year of *Lettres Persanes* – and following that year, were examined. See Thomas Brown, *Letters from the Dead to the Living*, 3rd edn., London 1703, preface, p. 3 (my pagination); Giovanni P. Marana, *The Eight Volumes of Letters Writ by a Turkish Spy*, 18th edn., London 1707, vol. I, 'To the Reader', pp. 1–2; *Cf.* Arthur J. Weitzman, ed., 'Introduction', *Letters Writ by a Turkish Spy*, New York 1970, pp. viii, x; Daniel Defoe, *A Continuation of Letters Written by a Turkish Spy at Paris*, London 1718, preface, pp. iii–viii; Samuel Madden, *Memoirs of the Twentieth Century*, London 1733, preface, pp. 18–22; George L. Lyttelton, *Letters from a Persian in England to His Friend at Ispahan*, 4th edn., London 1735, vol. I, p. v, 'To the Bookseller'; Lyttelton, *The Persian Letters* (vol. II of *Letters from a Persian*), London 1735, p. iii.

It should be pointed out that some of the topics compared in these categories were suggested by the Hebrew critics while others are offered in this paper for the purpose of checking any possible connection between the French and Hebrew works.

[6] 'Introduction', *Lettres Persanes*, p. 52; *'Igrot Meshulam*, pp. 38–39. See also Brown, *Letters from the Dead*, preface, p. 4 (my pagination); Marana, *Turkish Spy*, vol. I, 'To the Reader', p. 3 (my pagination); cf. Weitzman, 'Introduction', *Turkish Spy* (1970), p. viii; Defoe, *A Continuation of Letters*, preface, pp. iii–viii; Madden, *Memoirs*, p. 22 ("translating" the twentieth-century English into eighteenth-century English); Lyttelton, *Letters from a Persian*, p. v; Lyttelton, *The Persian Letters*, 'The Translator's Preface', p. iii.

[7] *Lettres Persanes*: Letters 11–14: The story of the Troglodytes; Letter 141: The story of Zuleima; Letter 142: A mythological story; *'Igrot Meshulam* has the story of the expulsion of the Jews from Spain (pp. 81–83), and the story of Don Joseph Pichon (pp. 101–102).

See also: Defoe, *A Continuation*, pp. 34–35: The story of the merchant of Rochel and the skull; pp. 40–41: The story of the woman pope; p. 249: The story of Atlantis; Madden, *Memoirs*, pp. 101–128: A catalogue of relics; Lyttelton, *Letters from a Persian*, pp. 18–25: The love of Ludovico and Honoria; pp. 81–117: The story of Polydore and Emilia; Marquis d'Argens, *The Jewish Spy*, 3rd edn., London, 1766, vol. I, pp. 22–23: The story of the Carmelite father Ange; pp. 52–54: The story of the priest who was canonised through a miracle performed at his grave; pp. 134–140: A letter within a letter; Oliver Goldsmith, *The Citizen of the World*, in *Persian and Chinese Letters*, Universal Classics Library, Washington – London 1901; published in 1762, pp. 360–364: The story of Catharina; pp. 382–385: The story of the princess and her two daughters.

[8] Cf. Van Roosbroeck, *Persian Letters Before Montesquieu*, pp. 22 ff., 40, 41 ff.; and Newell Richard Bush, *The Marquis d'Argens and his Philosophical Correspondence*, Ann Arbor 1953, p. 52. Once the foreign observer has become a literary convention, one notes an attempt on the part of the editor-publisher to authenticate his use of the foreign observer figure. Lyttelton, in his introduction 'To the Bookseller', in *Letters from a Persian*, p. v, writes; "I am aware that some People may suspect that the Character of a *Persian* is *Fictitious*, as many such Counterfeits have appear'd both in France and England. But whoever reads them with Attention, will be convinc'd, that they are certainly the Work of a perfect Stranger. The Observations are so *Foreign* and *out of the Way*, such *remote Hints* and *imperfect Notions* are taken up, *our present Happy Condition* is in all Respect *so ill understood*, that it is hardly possible any *Englishman* shou'd be the Author."

cited in both works as cruel, and Spanish religious institutions as extremely intolerant. This is referred to as a conclusive proof of affinity by some scholars. Euchel, however, certainly did not have to resort to *Lettres Persanes* for information on the cruelty of the Inquisition and on Spanish intolerance; nor, for that matter, did he necessarily draw from Montesquieu his clichés about the Spanish character. This material is readily available in the epistolary writings,[9] to say nothing of works of other kinds available to Euchel.

Again, both writers depict their oriental protagonists as prompted to undertake their respective European journeys by their desire to acquire knowledge, and to probe the strange customs of Europe. As a result of their encounters with an alien culture and religion, both Usbek and Meshulam are made to voice doubts concerning their own religious practices. "I have doubts", Usbek writes to the "servant of the prophets", "I must trace them down". Thus the dependence of Euchel's work on Montesquieu's is alleged.[10] Significantly, however, the urge for knowledge and voicing of scepticism are in no way unique to *Lettres Persanes*, or to *The Letters of Meshulam*. They abound in the epistolary literature which I studied, such as the *Turkish Spy*, *The Jewish Spy* and *The Citizen of the World*.[11]

---

[9] *Lettres Persanes*, lxxviii, pp. 258–263; *'Igrot Meshulam*, p. 174. The cliché of the Spaniards being extremely proud is used in other writings. See, for example, Marana, *The Second Volume of Letters Writ by a Turkish Spy*, 18th edn., London 1707, book III, letter xxvi, p. 244: "The *Spaniards*, are the Proudest People in the World"; and *The Jewish Spy*, I, xxxvii, p. 279. The treatment by both Montesquieu and Euchel of the Inquisition is cited by Sha'anan (*'Iyunim*, p. 78) and Neiman ('A Hebrew Imitation', p. 166) as linking the two authors.
The intolerance and cruelty of the Inquisition in the Vatican and in Spain are highlighted in many such writings. See, for example, Defoe, *A Continuation of Letters*, pp. 6, 19, 56, 271; *The Jewish Spy*, I, p. 56 ("That Inquisition which thirsteth after the Blood of *Israel*"), p. 176.

[10] *Lettres Persanes*, xvii, p. 93; on his desire to acquire knowledge see letter i, p. 54. In *'Igrot Meshulam* see p. 39 (his goal: acquisition of knowledge, and learning other peoples' cultures, customs and opinions), and pp. 40, 44, 45 (Meshulam's scepticism). Cf. Paulina Kra, 'The Invisible Chain of the *Lettres Persanes*', *Studies on Voltaire and the Eighteenth Century*, xxiii, Geneva 1963, pp. 23–24. The desire to acquire knowledge is cited by Sha'anan (*'Iyunim*, p. 77) and Neiman ('A Hebrew Imitation', p. 164) as a proof of resemblance of the French and Hebrew works.

[11] While the mission of the "spy" in the spy series (such as *The Turkish Spy*, and *A Continuation of Letters*) is understandably the acquisition of knowledge, the foreign observer stories have it, too. See, for example, Lyttelton, *Letters from a Persian*, pp. 1–2: Selim writes to Mirza that since Usbek (of *Lettres Persanes*) had not provided them with a first-hand report on England, he has "an ardent Desire to know the rest" of the places; he is thus going on this trip so "that I might be able to gratify thy Thirst of Knowledge". Similarly, Aaron Monceca, in *The Jewish Spy*, is "being resolved to see every Thing with my own Eyes" (vol. I, p. 29). And Lien Chi Altangi, in his first letter, advises his correspondent: "I begin to learn somewhat of their manners and customs" (*The Citizen of the World*, i, p. 295). As to the special interest of the foreign observer in "manners and customs" see note 55 below.
Scepticism develops gradually by foreign observers as they begin to realise the relativity of all religions. Upon comparing religious dogmas and practices with their own, they discern some positive aspects of the foreign religion as well as some negative aspects of their own religious principles and practices. One necessary step in the road to scepticism is the realisation on the part of the observer that each religion claims it alone possesses truth, and that believers of all other religions are destined to damnation. Thus the Turkish spy finds some positive aspects in Christianity: some precepts in Christianity, if truly observed, are no less holy than those in Islam. "As for me," he writes, "I begin really to think, That there may be *Saints* amongst the *Christians*, as there are amongst *Us*." Following that, he dwells on the relative nature of religious truth: "They have one *Article* that puzzles me. They affirm, There is but one Truth, so that we

God's love for humanity and the corollary obligation on the part of men to love one another are also recurrent themes in both works, cited as proof of affinity. Yet these are not uniquely Montesquieu's ideas, nor Euchel's, for they are to be found in other Enlightenment writings.[12] That the ordinances of religion ought to be of benefit to all mankind is also stressed in both works. However, this notion, too, is to be found in the writings of the Enlightenment.[13]

The figure of the ultra-orthodox Moslem Mulla may be thought to be paralleled by that of Meshulam's grandfather. Their religious mentality is very much alike, and their manner of proving the authenticity of given Islamic and Jewish

---

are lost, if we are not *Christians*, or they are damned, if they are not *Mahometans*" (*The Turkish Spy*, vol. I, book I, letter xi, p. 27). In *The Jewish Spy*, however, it appears that the Jewish writers are possessed by scepticism from the outset, and it did not result directly from their travels and from their experience in comparative religion.

[12]*Letters Persanes*, xlvi, pp. 464–466; lxix, pp. 239–242; '*Igrot Meshulam*, pp. 48–49. Cf. Neiman's allegation of resemblance of the two works on account of the similarity in discussion of "the ideal of 'love for fellow man' " ('A Hebrew Imitation', p. 167). In the Enlightenment literature, see, for example, the five principles of Natural Religion in Herbert of Cherbury, *The Antient Religion of the Gentiles*, London 1705, pp. 3–4, and cf. Charles Blount's version in his *Religio Laici*, London 1683, pp. 49–50; J. J. Rousseau, 'Profession de Foi du Vicaire Savoyard', *Émile*, *Oeuvres Complètes de J. J. Rousseau*, I, Paris 1852, pp. 590–591.

These notions are to be found also in the epistolary literature. See, for example, the Turkish spy's characterisation of Islam as love, and his rejecting the Christian damnation of the non-believers, in Defoe's *A Continuation of Letters*, p. 21. The Chinese writer characterises the "Divine Being" as held by the Persians as "wise and just, and such as all those ought to have who don't suffer themselves to be blinded either by Prejudices, or by Sophistry of their own forming" (Marquis d'Argens, *Chinese Letters*, London 1741, p. 196). The Jewish writer depicts God's attributes as goodness and justice (*The Jewish Spy*, I, letter xxxvi, p. 263). Worship, according to him, was handed down for man's happiness and not for his destruction; it is inconceivable that God should create men in order that they may be damned (pp. 268–269).

[13]*Lettres Persanes*, xlvi, pp. 464–466; lxix, pp. 239–242; '*Igrot Meshulam*, p. 48. In addition to the sources cited in note 11, see also Matthew Tindal, *Christianity as Old as the Creation*, London 1730, pp. 31–49.

The Turkish spy writes to Bedredin, "Superiour of the Convent of Dervises": "But dost thou not believe, thou, who art a *Dervis*, the most illuminated, That a Man, of what Religion soever he be, provided he be a good Man, may be happy after his Death? Tell me, I pray thee, thy Opinion herein; it is a Point very important to be decided" (*Turkish Spy*, vol. I, book I, letter xi, p. 27). Aaron Monceca writes to Isaac Onis, "a Rabbi at Constantinople", regarding the ceremonies: "Ceremonies ought to be observed when it may be done without risking one's Life, and the Lives of a thousand Innocents; but when there is such evident Danger impending, the Use thereof may be suspended. It is not the same Thing as to the Substance of Religion, from which nothing can nor ought to excuse us" (*The Jewish Spy*, I, letter xxiv, pp. 175–176). He further writes that precepts were abolished in the past so as to facilitate the survival of the Jews. Thus Spanish Jews, namely, the Marranos, who are not observing circumcision, "at this Day", fearing for their safety, are justified (p. 176).

It should be pointed out that Meshulam, too, is very appreciative of the Marranos in their desire to adhere to the fundamentals of Judaism, while discarding the precepts the observance of which may endanger their lives. In his sympathy for the Marranos, and his emphasis on "the worship of the heart which is fundamental" ('*Igrot Meshulam*, p. 44), Euchel comes close to the views expressed in *The Jewish Spy* underlying which are some tenets of Judaism and deism. The similarity between deism and Judaism is being stressed in *The Jewish Spy* (vol. I, pp. 27–28; and cf. the Index, Letter D, "Deists of France", no pagination, where the idea is put forth overtly: "*Deists of France*, skilfully painted under the character of *Jews*"). For more discussion of the Marranos see also p. 28. The similarity between *The Jewish Spy* and '*Igrot Meshulam* points to a common source, i.e., the Jewish code.

ordinances and laws, respectively, is very similar.[14] But as such techniques are generally adopted by authors when, in satire, they present the figures of orthodox persons in a pseudo-authentic way, or make use of their religious naïveté,[15] the dependence of the one work upon the other is not conclusively established.

The two protagonists' similar interest in history, and more importantly their special interest in historical processes, while points of resemblance, are not necessarily evidence of influence, as asserted, since the same features are found in other works as well.[16] Again, although the protagonists of both works pass through Smyrna[17] and Livorno (Leghorn), many other locales do not correspond in the two works.

Thus, although there are various similarities between *Lettres Persanes* and *'Igrot Meshulam*, these similarities are superficial only. In addition, the cited similarities abound in epistolary literature written both before and after Montesquieu. Some of the items are found also in Enlightenment literature of other kinds. It follows, then, that we have found no convincing evidence of influence by the French upon the Hebrew work in terms of ideas and topics treated.

C. Our third category consists of themes which, though found in both *Lettres Persanes* and *'Igrot Meshulam*, are accorded antithetical treatment in these works. This material, like that of the other categories, is also to be found in other writings of the period.

While women's freedom is satirised by the French writer, Euchel is full of praise for the social role of European women, and for the degree of freedom they have won. In spite of the obvious dissimilarities in this topic, advocates of affinity bring it as support for their contention.[18] Understandably, Euchel's purpose in such praise is to suggest that the Jewish people adopt this new attitude towards women and thus modernise Jewish social life. As a *Maskil*, his aim is to reform Jewish life, to model its society, religion and culture on the lines of their European counterparts.

---

[14]*Lettres Persanes*, xvi, pp. 91–92; xviii, pp. 95–97; xxxix, pp. 150–152; *'Igrot Meshulam*, pp. 46–47. See also note 64 below.

[15]See, for example, the *Turkish Spy*, vol. I, book I, letter ix, pp. 17–20; and *A Continuation of Letters*, p. 3.

[16]*Lettres Persanes*, cxxxvi, pp. 422–424; *'Igrot Meshulam*, pp. 81–83, 171–172. Sha'anan (*'Iyunim*, p. 79) stresses some similarity in the protagonists' interest in history books. An interest in contemporary historical trends is indeed very much the business of the "spy". See, for instance, in *A Continuation of Letters*, a description of the fall of the English king (pp. 12–17) and the war between France and Germany (pp. 22–27). There is, however, also an interest in past history: the history of the Arab nation and its culture (pp. 126–131). The Jewish spy, discussing the writing of history, criticises several history books (*The Jewish Spy*, I, pp. 286), and mentions sources that may be used for the writing of history (p. 285).

[17]Both Sha'anan (*'Iyunim*, pp. 77–78; *Hasifrut Ha'ivrit*, I, p. 76) and Neiman ('A Hebrew Imitation', p. 168) emphasise the resemblance in locale between Montesquieu and Euchel. Similarity in locale is found also in the studied epistolary literature. Aaron Monceca, too, passes through Smyrna (*The Jewish Spy*, I, p. 13). See also note 44 below.

[18]*Lettres Persanes*, xxvi, pp. 115–118; xxxviii, pp. 147–149; lii, pp. 186–188; *'Igrot Meshulam*, pp. 84–85, 175. The discussion of European women, while differently treated by Montesquieu and Euchel, is nevertheless mentioned by Sha'anan (*'Iyunim*, p. 78; *Hasifrut Ha'ivrit*, I, p. 76) and by Neiman ('A Hebrew Imitation', p. 168) as correlating the French and the Hebrew works.

Significantly, the topic of women is dealt with in the epistolary literature – such as the *Chinese Letters* and *The Jewish Spy* – in various ways.[19] In terms of this topic then, there is no real similarity between *Lettres Persanes* and *'Igrot Meshulam*.

Again, unlike the Persians who seem to ridicule French literature and French libraries, Meshulam is depicted as appreciative of Western literature and libraries. This interest in libraries and in literature is cited as a convincing similarity between Montesquieu and Euchel, although each treats the subject matter differently. Yet an interest in libraries and literature is in no way unique to Montesquieu; it is found elsewhere in the epistolary literature, for example, in *The Jewish Spy*.[20] In order to understand Euchel's motives, one must bear in mind the state of Hebrew literature at the time and the lack of public libraries devoted to Judaica. Nor is it surprising that when Meshulam compares Arabic poetry, and the Hebrew poetry which is modelled upon Arabic poetry, with Italian poetry and its translation into Hebrew, he finds the latter worthy of much praise.[21] To Euchel, European literature is the model for Hebrew literature to adopt.

Both works pay much attention to customs and social practices. However, while Montesquieu's intention is to satirise them, Euchel extols such customs, which he hoped to introduce into Judaism. Similarly, the French writer is critical of religious ceremonies whereas Euchel is highly respectful of them. We must add, however, that an interest in European customs and practices on the part of the foreign observer is at the core of all such writings, such as *The Turkish Spy*, *Letters from a Persian* and *The Jewish Spy*.[22]

Of a different kind are Usbek's comments regarding the benefits to the state from the citizens who profess a minority religion. These people, according to his way of thinking, hope to advance socially and materially, and thus they are quite beneficial to the state.[23] Behind this notion is the theory that religious

---

[19] Cf. Weitzman's introduction to his edition of the *Turkish Spy*, p. xii. Women, in general, become an object of the foreign observer's interest. The Chinese depicts their customs, costumes and make-up (*Chinese Letters*, pp. 7–10). He is able to compare the liberty given to women by the Europeans with the strict attitude of the Persians toward their women only to conclude that the Chinese treat their women moderately (p. 98). To the Jewish writer in *The Jewish Spy*, Jewish women are the example of chastity unlike Christian, European women (vol. I, pp. 3–5). He describes, tongue in cheek, the liberty of women in Italy – which Euchel praises so much (see note 18) – as follows: "This Liberty which the Women have at *Genoa*, renders Society amiable and charming. There is not a City in Italy where a Traveller and a Foreigner may pass their Time more agreeably" (letter xxxiv, p. 251).

I do not know whether Euchel read or used *The Jewish Spy*. He could have read the German translation, by Friedrich Nicolai, *Jüdische Briefe*, which was published in Berlin in 1764–1766. Whatever his sources were, he clearly utilised the material in a way that served his purpose, namely, advocating the liberation of Jewish women.

[20] *Lettres Persanes*, cxxxiii–cxxxvii, pp. 414–427; '*Igrot Meshulam*, pp. 44, 46, 174. Cf. *The Jewish Spy*, I, letter xiii, pp. 85–92 (public libraries in Paris); and criticism of literature (pp. 255–262). The influence of Montesquieu on Euchel regarding Meshulam's visit to a library is cited by Sha'anan ('*Iyunim*, p. 79; *Hasifrut Ha'ivrit*, I, p. 77; 'The Letters of Meshullam as Symptom', p. 363) and by Neiman 'A Hebrew Imitation', p. 169); Sha'anan also adds Meshulam's interest in "literary subjects" as another likeness between Montesquieu and Euchel.

[21] '*Igrot Meshulam*, pp. 176, 245–249. Cf. A critical appreciation of a Turkish poet, Achmet Chelibi, as "extravagant" and "monstrous" in *The Jewish Spy*, I, p. 192.

[22] See note 11 above, and note 55 below.

[23] *Lettres Persanes*, lxxxv, pp. 278–281.

pluralism and religious tolerance are actually beneficial to the state. Euchel also cites the material ambitions of members of a minority group, but does so in order to wage an all-out attack on the conceited Jews of his time.[24] As we shall see, he does this in the course of an historical analysis of the rise and fall of Spanish Jewry. Euchel thus reverses the treatment of a topic found also in *Lettres Persanes*. In this instance he turns an approved attitude into a disapproved one. And this technique serves his purpose very well indeed. As in the other cases, European Enlightenment literature in general stresses the idea of religious pluralism and religious tolerance.[25]

Another change is found in the use made of questions. Usbek addresses various questions in his letters to his correspondents in Persia, and he receives answers to his questions. These questions are intended to arouse interest, to create expectations and tension, and to form some continuity in the novel.[26] Meshulam, however, asks rhetorical questions for which he receives no answers. Perhaps Euchel planned to have these questions answered in subsequent letters that were not published, or which may never have been written. As they now appear, these questions are purely rhetorical: they are intended to allude to Euchel's views on important matters on which he did not dare to express his opinion openly.

The nature of the questions is manifested in the following example: "I did not know," Meshulam writes, "whether these things were truthful (correct), for according to my thinking the success (happiness) of the Israelites is in the observance of the *mitzvot* (religious commandments) alone, and if it were possible to have well-being and to be happy without observance of the *mitzvot* would not Socrates the Greek and Zoroaster the Hindu have as much well-being and be as happy as any Israelite? – Let me know, my brother, your view in this investigation."[27]

Meshulam is here asking one of the most important questions concerning the Jews in the modern age: Is it possible for the Jew to be happy and complete without observance of the religious commandments? In other words, how would

---

[24]*Igrot Meshulam*, pp. 81–83, 172–173.

[25]On the necessity of religious pluralism, see Voltaire, *Letters Concerning the English Nation*, London 1733, letter vi, 'On the Presbyterians', p. 45: "If one religion only were allowed in England, the government would very possibly become arbitrary; if there were but two, the people wou'd cut one another's throats; but as there are such a multitude, they all live happy and in peace." The Index has it clearly stated: "*Religions*, (Plurality of) these very necessary, and of Advantage to the Happiness and Prosperity of the English" (unpaginated). Yet no one should suspect Voltaire of acknowledging religious tolerance in England. In effect, letter v, 'On the Church of England', spells it out: "England is properly the country of sectarists [. . .] *Nevertheless*, tho' every one is permitted to serve God in whatever mode or fashion he thinks proper, yet their true religion, that in which a man makes his fortune, is the sect of Episcoparians or Churchmen, call'd the Church of *England* [. . .] No person can possess an employment either in *England* or *Ireland*, unless he be rank'd among the faithful" (pp. 34–35).

Harcourt Brown points out that the first quotation from Voltaire (p. 45) was written originally in English; see his article 'The Composition of the *Letters Concerning the English Nation*', *The Age of the Enlightenment*, Studies Presented to T. Besterman, St. Andrews University Publications No. LVII, Edinburgh 1967, p. 22.

[26]*Lettres Persanes*, xvi, pp. 91–92; xviii, pp. 95–97.

[27]*Igrot Meshulam*, p. 44.

a Jew retain his identity as a Jew while attempting to adopt the non-religious aspects of European culture? Considering Euchel's other writings and the *Weltanschauung* of Hebrew Enlightenment, I believe that Euchel's intention is to point out that indeed a non-observant Jew could be as happy as any one else.[28] Finally, it may be pointed out that the technique of the rhetorical question is used frequently in epistolary literature.[29]

D. Our fourth category includes themes which, though common to both works, have a uniquely Jewish slant in Euchel's. In most such cases Euchel attaches a meaningful Jewish touch, or a Jewish colouring, to the matter in hand. In both works, for example, the oriental protagonists are aware of European clothes, and are sensitive about their own strange attire. They conclude that although their exotic attire serves as a topic of conversation, it constitutes in effect a hindrance to their attempt to learn the truth about Europe.[30] Euchel goes further: the changing of clothes is seen as a symbolic act which transcends the meaning given it in the French work or in such a story as *The Turkish Spy*.[31] Meshulam, changing his oriental dress, is taking the first step in the adoption of European culture. Whether or not one is permitted by Jewish law to adopt European dress is a focal point of discussion among the protagonists representing the various segments of Judaism in the *Letters of Meshulam*.[32]

---

[28] See my article on Euchel cited in note 1.

[29] The technique of the question is frequently used in the epistolary literature. The Turkish spy asks questions (see the question in quotation, note 13 above), yet we have only his letters as no replies were incorporated in the book. Rhetorical questions are often used in *The Jewish Spy* in the manner employed by Meshulam. Aaron Monceca asks Isaac Onis: "What thinkest thou, dear *Isaac*, to see so much Confusion and Disorder in the Manners and Customs of the *Nazarenes*?" (*The Jewish Spy*, I, letter i, p. 3). Onis does not answer this question directly, however, he does relate his own impressions from his first visit to Europe (letter ix, pp. 60–66).

In the same vein, Monceca resorts to rhetorical questions as he relates a "discovery" he has made in Paris: "I have a crabbed Question to propose to thee, and desire thee to communicate it to other Rabbies of thy Acquaintance, that I may know both their Sentiments and thine. I have discovered a vast number of *Jews* at *Paris*, who do not believe they are *Jews*, or know any thing at all of the Matter. Thou wilt think, perhaps, that I only jest, yet nothing is more true [. . .] I know not how we can refuse them the Title of *Jews*. They believe a God, who created the World, who rewards the Good, and punishes the Bad. What more do we believe? Is not that the Whole of our Religion, except a few Ceremonies that have been enjoined us by our Doctors and Priests?" (*The Jewish Spy*, I, letter iv, pp. 27–28). As in the previous case, Onis does not answer his questions. They are indeed rhetorical questions.

[30] *Lettres Persanes*, xxx, pp. 128–129.

[31] *The Turkish Spy*, vol. I, book I, letter i, p. 2. The "spy", of necessity, must change his clothes so as to appear an ordinary citizen of the country. Monceca, too, wishes to appear European in his attire, thus – he writes – "I have left off my *Levant* Robe for a close-bodied Coat [. . .] I would fain have kept on my old Habit, but was obliged to dress my self after the *French* Manner, or expect to be stared at by all the Eyes of Paris" (*The Jewish Spy*, I, letter ii, pp. 9–10). Although Monceca is not attaching any importance to the change of clothes, as does Meshulam, he does make an interesting analogy between the clothes fashion and religious fashion (pp. 10–12).

[32] '*Igrot Meshulam*, pp. 40–41, 43. Meshulam's grandfather opposes the change of his Arabic clothes to European ones while his father favours the change. Out of respect to his grandfather, Meshulam does not change his clothes until after he departed from him. The grandfather believes that a Jew must not change "the customs of his fathers [forefathers?]." However, Meshulam voices his opinion that there is no divine law concerning the custom of wearing a particular dress. Following the advice of his father, he changes his oriental clothes. See my study of Euchel, cited in note 1, for a full discussion of the subject and its meaning.

A comparative treatment of Christian and Moslem religious ceremonies is used to underline the preference accorded by Montesquieu to the original source of all religions, namely, natural religion.[33] It was his hope, as it was the hope of the deists among the European thinkers of the Enlightenment, that natural religion should gain ground and eventually occupy the place of the existing revealed religions. The treatment of this theme by the Hebrew author serves another purpose. His purpose is to point out that foreign elements penetrated into Judaism in the past, and to show that precedents exist for changing Jewish religious law.[34] Describing the Catholic worship in Spain as very similar to the Jewish worship, Meshulam writes: "Most of their prayers are the songs of David from the Book of Psalms translated into their language. (. . .) and I saw them observing customs like the customs of Israel: they pray *tefilat hashkavah* (the prayer for the dead), and light candles for the souls of the dead." And he concludes in the rhetorical manner noted above: "I did not know whether they had seen and followed the custom of Israel, or whether those customs came to us while we were in exile among them; for I do not know whether there is any mention of these customs in either the Jerusalem or the Babylonian Talmud. Let me know your view in this matter."[35] Meshulam is here implying that some Jewish customs are not Jewish at all in their origin, but indeed constitute a direct borrowing from Christianity.[36]

The Jewish perspective which Euchel lends to these themes makes it rather difficult, if not impossible, to trace their origin exclusively to *Lettres Persanes*. Indeed, various other epistolary writings treat religious themes in somewhat like manner.[37]

The various religious practices and ordinances described in both works are, of course, seen from the Jewish point of view in the Hebrew work. Prayers are found in *Lettres Persanes* as well as in *The Letters of Meshulam*.[38] It is only natural that the prayers in the Hebrew work should be the Jewish prayers. In the same vein, the pseudo-Islamic sermonising, found in the French work, has its parallel in the old-school, orthodox homilies of traditional Judaism, as represented by Meshulam's grandfather.[39] Similarly, discussion of the achievement of happiness

---

[33]*Lettres Persanes*, xxxv, pp. 138–140.

[34]*'Igrot Meshulam*, p. 45. An analysis of Euchel's text is found in my study cited in note 1.

[35]*'Igrot Meshulam*, p. 45. Cf. Friedlander's article, cited in note 2 above, p. 112.

[36]See my study of Euchel, cited in note 1, part two, pp. 64–65, notes 125–128 and their related text.

[37]A common literary convention seems to prevail in these writings. It consists of the writer's ostensible discovery that those professing another religion as well as their customs are virtually identical with their counterparts in the writer's own religion. For the foreign observer it is indeed a discovery; however, this device is employed in such a way as to convey the message of the discovery to the reader. In addition to the objectives discussed above in the text (Montesquieu's and Euchel's), this technique adds a twist of irony to the story. See note 26 above for such a use in *The Jewish Spy*, I, letter iv, pp. 27–28.
It should be pointed out that mourning and burial customs are featured in the *Chinese Letters*, pp. 305–314.
Unlike the glorifying tone of Meshulam in describing the church, Aaron Monceca draws a grotesque caricature of a church and the worship therein (*The Jewish Spy*, I, pp. 29–32).

[38]*Lettres Persanes*, xlvi, pp. 164–166; *'Igrot Meshulam*, p. 41.

[39]*Lettres Persanes*, xxxix, pp. 150–152, Hagi Ibbi's letter to Ben Josué, a Jew converted to Islam. In *'Igrot Meshulam* the grandfather, Mordechai, employs the traditional homilies in his pre-

in *Lettres Persanes* is, in *The Letters of Meshulam*, connected with the observance of the Jewish commandments.[40]

Finally, the Troglodyte story, narrated at length in Montesquieu's fiction, has its apparent Jewish counterpart in '*Igrot Meshulam* in the story of the Jews in Spain.[41] As in the other examples discussed in this category, the similarities between the Troglodyte story and the story of the rise and fall of Spanish Jewry are too broad and general to warrant the conclusion that Euchel's work is here indebted to Montesquieu.

E. There is yet a fifth category which is comprised of dissimilarities in related aspects of the two works. Paradoxically, we may note that, like most of the similarities discussed above, these dissimilarities are peripheral and external. But if they are in effect too trivial to prove that there is no connection between the two epistolary works, they certainly cannot prove that there was a direct borrowing from Montesquieu, as suggested by some students of Euchel's work.

As we shall presently observe, Euchel's interests were not those of Montesquieu, nor did he have the same literary and social objectives. Euchel obviously had no intention of writing as voluminous a work as Montesquieu's. In the introduction to the *Letters of Meshulam* mention is made of twelve letters only.[42] It is unfortunate that even this number of letters was not published; for the Hebrew work comprises just six letters. It stands to reason that Euchel had to confine his writing to a limited number of issues and subjects. His scope, then, is limited at the outset. Naturally, one expects a limitation in the number of protagonists and locales. Instead of three protagonists travelling in Europe, as is the case in *Lettres Persanes*, Euchel has only one, Meshulam. Although both protagonists originated in the Orient, Usbek comes from Persia whereas Meshulam comes from Syria.[43] Not only is their place of origin different, but,

---

sentation of his spiritual will to Meshulam (pp. 46–47). See my analysis of his letter in the study cited in note 1. Cf. the Mullah's reply to Usbek's request for religious guidance as interpreted by Paulina Kra, in 'Religion in Montesquieu's *Lettres persanes*', *Studies on Voltaire and the Eighteenth Century*, LXXII, Geneva 1970, pp. 55–63.

[40] *Lettres Persanes*, x, p. 75; '*Igrot Meshulam*, p. 44. See note 39 above and its related text. Cf. Sha'anan's 'The Letters of Meshullam as Symptom', pp. 362, 367, regarding Euchel's yearning for mundane happiness.

[41] *Lettres Persanes*, xi–xiv, pp. 76–88. The story of the rise and fall of Spanish Jewry ('*Igrot Meshulam*, pp. 81–83) is directly and openly critical of the conceit of the Jews in Spain, in contrast to the ostensible praise of the virtues of the Troglodytes by Montesquieu. I have elaborated on the Jewish theme in my study on Euchel cited in note 1. On two interpretations of the Troglodytes story as allegory, see Allessandro S. Crisafulli, 'Montesquieu's Story of the Troglodytes: Its Background, Meaning, and Significance', *Publications of the Modern Language Association of America*, LVIII (1943), pp. 372–392; Kra, 'Religion in Montesquieu's *Lettres persanes*', *loc. cit.*, pp. 40–55.

[42] '*Igrot Meshulam*, p. 39. In his introduction, which is addressed to the editors of the journal and the members of the society of the *Maskilim*, the editor–publisher writes that he was submitting twelve letters for publication. He expresses his willingness to send them the rest of the letters which he still possessed. Sha'anan suspects that Euchel originally intended to compose a comprehensive work similar to those in the genre ('The Letters of Meshullam as Symptom', p. 369).

[43] From Ḥaleb, or Aleppo, which was known for its well-established Jewish community. The fact that both protagonists come to Europe from the Orient is cited as parallel by Sha'anan ('*Iyunim*, p. 77; *Hasifrut Ha'ivrit*, I, p. 76) and Neiman ('A Hebrew Imitation', p. 164).

so is the main locale where the story takes place. The centre of activities in *Lettres Persanes* is Paris, whereas the Hebrew work has nothing to do with France, the French or with Paris. Instead, the *mise-en-scène* is Madrid; the people described are the Spaniards, who are contrasted with the Italians. The Spanish locale was selected by Euchel for the purpose of calling attention to the Marrano Jews and their predicament in Spain. *Lettres Persanes*, it is true, does have excerpts from letters coming from Spain and describes the Spaniards and their customs and institutions, but this material is not centrally germane to the French work as are the comparable references to Spanish material in Euchel's work.[44]

The alleged indebtedness of Euchel to Montesquieu involves the notion that Euchel aimed at imitating *Lettres Persanes*, even that perhaps *The Letters of Meshulam* is to be considered a "free translation" of the former work. Some deviations from the original French work are explained as a misunderstanding of the original irony and satire on Euchel's part.[45]

Careful comparison of the two works shows that most of the items used to prove resemblance are no more than external, superficial and peripheral similarities. I have found no internal, profound or meaningful resemblance. These superficial similarities have here been shown to offer no conclusive evidence of borrowing, for the same similarities are found elsewhere in the epistolary literature of the period.

We may suppose, therefore, that Euchel was familiar in a general way with *Lettres Persanes*, as he was probably familiar with some other writings of the epistolary genre.[46] Euchel, as a student of Kant, and as a Hebrew enlightener *par excellence*, was certainly versed in the Enlightenment literature of that century. As a matter of fact, we know from his *Haskalah* writings that he definitely was abreast of the Enlightenment issues of the time. Some of his topics and ideas

---

[44]*Lettres Persanes*, letter lxxviii, pp. 258–263; *'Igrot Meshulam*, p. 174. Sha'anan maintains that Rica visited Spain, and that Meshulam, in the Hebrew work, comes to Spain "in his footsteps", thus alluding to a direct borrowing by Euchel from Montesquieu (*'Iyunim*, p. 78; *Hasifrut Ha'ivrit*, I, p. 77). However, Rica does not pay a visit to Spain; he only cites from a letter which he received from a Frenchman who had visited in Spain (letter lxxviii).

A positive depiction of the Italians (as contrasted with the Spaniards, see note 9) is not unique to the Hebrew work. *The Jewish Spy*, for example, portrays the Genoese as "industrious, addicted to commerce" (vol. I, letter xxviii, p. 205). Meshulam writes that they "are diligent in every trade and commerce" (*'Igrot Meshulam*, p. 174). *The Jewish Spy* further depicts the Genoese as "very polite" people, who "receive Persons that are recommended to them with very great Respect" (vol. I, letter xxxiv, p. 251). Meshulam depicts the Italians in general as follows: "They are modest and they welcome each person in accordance with his honour" (p. 174). These similarities, however, are not conclusive even in a limited sense, for *The Jewish Spy* contrasts the Genoese with the people of Rome who are portrayed as lazy and insolent . . . (vol. I, letter xxviii, pp. 204–205).

[45]*Hasifrut Ha'ivrit*, I, p. 76.

[46]Sha'anan believes that Euchel was "an indubitable student of Montesquieu" (*'Iyunim*, p. 75). In his early study, Sha'anan states that Euchel has undoubtedly read the *Lettres Persanes*, although he was familiar with German imitations as well (*ibid.*, p. 77). However, in his last study, Sha'anan raises the possibility that Euchel had not read Montesquieu in the original ('The Letters of Meshullam as Symptom', p. 355). Neiman, on the other hand, is definitely sure that "There can be no doubt that Euchel read the *Lettres Persanes* in the original" ('A Hebrew Imitation', p. 164). No documentation is given though.

were adopted by Euchel from general writings produced during the period of the Enlightenment.

In so far as *Lettres Persanes* and *'Igrot Meshulam* are similar, this fact perhaps indicates some common ideology of the Enlightenment.

One should note, however, the fundamental difference between the two works, for they do not have the same literary goal. Although both are satiric works, they do not share the same object of satire. Moreover, the object of satire in the one is the subject of glorification in the other. Not only did Euchel gear his satire to the problems and predicament of Jewish society, but he directed his satire at the Jewish reality in Europe, and aimed its arrows at targets which are not identical with those of his French counterpart.

A better insight as to the essential difference between these works may be gained by finding the overall satiric concept, or guiding principle, in the two writings. Montesquieu bases his satire on the presupposition that the exotic oriental culture is much superior to the corrupted European culture. Euchel, on the other hand, has an antithetical presupposition. According to him, Meshulam's culture, the culture of the Orient, is a reflection of the Jewish culture, which, in his view, is inferior to European culture. The latter is considered by Euchel and by the other *Maskilim* as more advanced and enlightened.[47] European culture and civilisation ought to be adopted by Jewish society, according to this point of view of the Hebrew *Haskalah*. Its adoption would advance the Jewish cause, and the Jews would thus make progress in their integration into European society. This basic difference between the two writers dictated their differing approach to the subject-matter.

It should be emphasised that this difference in satiric concept sets Euchel's *'Igrot Meshulam* apart from most other epistolary writings; as a literary phenomenon it is unique and outstanding.

Clearly, then, we must look elsewhere than to *Lettres Persanes* for a more meaningful and significant interpretation of *'Igrot Meshulam*. Such an interpretation can be gained, I believe, by a more thorough exploration of Euchel's other writings.

Students of Euchel's epistolary writing have thus far failed to examine *The Letters of Meshulam* against the background of Euchel's other Hebraic works. It is especially surprising that no attention has been paid to a similar epistolary work published by the Hebrew author in 1785, which certainly should be compared with *The Letters of Meshulam*. In that year Euchel published in *Hame'asef* a series of authentic letters, which were entitled *The Letters of Isaac Euchel*, and were addressed to his student Michal Friedländer. These letters were written on the occasion of Euchel's documented voyage to Copenhagen in 1784.[48] Although

---

[47]Expressions of the superiority of European culture abound in the writings of the early *Maskilim* in Germany, especially in their journal, *Hame'asef*. For one such example, see my article 'The First Call of A Hebrew *Maskil* to Convene A Rabbinic Assembly for Religious Reforms', *Tarbiz*, XLII, No. 3–4 (April–September 1973), pp. 484–491 [Hebrew; English summary, p. xiii]. It should be noted that both Sha'anan and Neiman, in their respective studies, arrive at the same conclusion.

[48]*'Igrot Yitzhaq Eichel* [*The Letters of Isaac Euchel*], *Hame'asef*, II (1785), pp. 116–121, 137–142

the two epistolary works by Euchel are essentially quite different, there appears to be a close relationship between the authentic letters and the fictional story whose epistolary form is a literary technique, and which was published a few years afterwards. It is safe to assume that if the European epistolary writings mentioned above did exert some influence on Euchel, such influence was interwoven with his personal experience during those travels, as given expression in his letters to Michal Friedländer.

Although the epistolary form is already in use in the first volume of *Hame'asef*, the letters consist mainly of articles which naturally do not exhibit the literary characteristics of the epistolary genre.[49] Euchel was actually the first author in modern Hebrew literature to have utilised the epistolary technique to treat a given subject through a series of letters, or one letter divided into various sections. It is only in Euchel's attempts that we note the impact of the epistolary novel which prevailed in European literature at the time.[50] The epistolary techniques in *The Letters of Isaac Euchel* are rather limited. It is one letter (though it is divided into sections) which is sent one way only, namely, from Euchel to his student. The author failed to publish a continuation of the first letter. His second attempt, in the form of *The Letters of Meshulam*, constitutes an important development in the genre. In it there are a number of letters, written by different people who have different views from one another. These views, as expressed by the respective writers, are presented in contrasting fashion in the best tradition of the genre.[51] The epistolary techniques were further developed in the Hebrew literature of the nineteenth century. They are manifested in a full-fledged epistolary novel such as *The Revealer of Secrets* by Joseph Perl, or the partially epistolary novel, *The Hypocrite*, by Abraham Mapu.[52]

(cited henceforth '*Igrot Isaac Euchel*). These letters were republished by Adam Martinet, *Tif'eret Yisra'el* [The Glory of Israel], Bamberg 1837, pp. 59–69; by Shmuel Yosef Fuenn, *Sofrei Yisra'el* [The Writers of Israel], Vilna 1871, pp. 134–137; and by myself, *Mavo Lasifrut Ha'ivrit Hahadashah Bame'ot Ha-18 Veha-19, Meqorot* [Introduction to Modern Hebrew Literature in the 18th and 19th Centuries, Texts], Jerusalem 1972, pp. 23–24, 26–27. On Euchel's trip and documents related to it, see H. Vogelstein, 'Handschriftliches zu Isaak Abraham Euchels Biographie', *Beiträge zur Geschichte der deutschen Juden*, Leipzig 1916, pp. 221–231.

Both Sha'anan and Neiman, and for that matter all students of Euchel, are oblivious to the relation between '*Igrot Isaac Euchel* and '*Igrot Meshulam*.

[49]*Hame'asef*, IV (1788), pp. 17–31 (Hebrew grammar); *Hame'asef*, II (1785), pp. 154–155, 169–174, 178–187 (Halachah, religious legal matters). Cf. the use of the epistolary form in non-fictional works in the second half of the eighteenth century in England, Frank Gees Black, *The Epistolary Novel in the Late Eighteenth Century*, Eugene, Oregon 1940, pp. 3–4.

[50]See the appendices in Black's *The Epistolary Novel*, listing the epistolary fiction from 1740 to 1840, and the charts (p. 174); and Martha Pike Conant, *The Oriental Tale in England in the Eighteenth Century*, New York 1908, pp. 155–199, on the epistolary satire.

[51]The letter of Meshulam's father ('*Igrot Meshulam*, pp. 47–50), is so structured as to contrast and contradict the fundamental principles as presented by the grandfather (pp. 46–47). See my study, cited in note 1, part two, pp. 59–61, notes 111–115 and the related text.

[52]Joseph Perl, *Megaleh Temirin* [Revealer of Secrets], Wien 1819; Abraham Mapu, '*Ayit Zavo'a* [The Hypocrite, or: The Painted Vulture], Vilna 1869. Cf. Shmuel Werses, *Sipur Veshorsho*, pp. 9–12, 18–21; David Patterson, 'Epistolary Elements in the Novels of Abraham Mapu', *Annual of the Leeds University Oriental Society*, IV (1964), pp. 132–149; Patterson, 'Epistolary Elements in the Hebrew Novels of the Period of Enlightenment', *Annual of the Leeds University Oriental Society*, V (1963–1965), pp. 86–99.

There are a number of aspects which the two works have in common. Both are travelogues in the form of letters. In this respect they are unique in *Hame'asef*. Both works pay attention to customs and practices prevalent in European society, exhibiting them mostly from an admirer's point of view.[53] Both works intend to point out the highly advanced and enlightened stand of European society *vis-à-vis* the alleged inferiority of Jewish society.[54] The same terminology regarding "customs" and "opinion" is used in the same context in both *The Letters of Isaac Euchel* and *The Letters of Meshulam*.[55] Prayer occupies an important place in both; it also plays a vital role in the plot of the story and in its ideology. The narrator–protagonist is portrayed in both works as a true believer who occasionally finds it necessary to pray to his god.[56]

[53] Although Meshulam is critical of the Spaniards in general, he is full of admiration of their manner of worship (*'Igrot Meshulam*, p. 45). The apex of glorification of Europe is found in his description of the Italians (p. 174). Interestingly and significantly, the positive and glorified attitude towards the Italians has its reflection in Meshulam's similar depiction of Italian Jews (pp. 173, 174) and Italian Hebrew literature (pp. 245–249). Similarly the negative attitude towards the Spaniards has its reflection in the generally negative attitude towards the historical Spanish Jewry, excluding the Marranos (pp. 81–83, 171–173). The generally positive attitude towards Europe is discerned in Meshulam's tone of presentation of certain institutions (libraries, p. 174) and customs (women's liberation, p. 175).
In his non-fictional letters, Euchel writes that upon arrival in a city, it is his goal "to pay attention to the characteristics of every city [. . .] and situation of the people that dwells in it, and above all, [to pay attention] to our brethren the children of Israel that dwell there, [to] their situation [predicament] and characteristics, [and to note] whether they are well [goodness is their share; they are happy] or not, [and] whether they have begun to tend [shepherd, or: be associated with] the gardens of wisdom, or they refrained [their hands became weakened] from touching it [=wisdom]" (*'Igrot Isaac Euchel*, p. 118). The phrase "whether they have begun to tend the gardens of wisdom" is indeed indicative of his point of view regarding the state of his contemporary Jewry in its adoption of Western culture and secular education and knowledge (=Ḥochmah, wisdom).

[54] The editor-publisher prefaces the letters by referring to the state of the Jews being in *Galut*, exile ("he [God] lowered the glory of Israel to the dust" – *'Igrot Meshulam*, p. 38), while praising the enlightenment activities of the *Maskilim* through their journal, *Hame'asef*. His utilitarian goal is clearly stressed in the preface. For Euchel's attitude towards Jewish society in his non-fictional letters, see note 53.

[55] The terms *nimusim* (customs) and *de'ot* (opinions) are associated in *'Igrot Isaac Euchel* (p. 118) and in *'Igrot Meshulam* (p. 40). Underlying the concepts in the two works is the notion of the relativity of customs and opinions. The fictional work goes one step further to stress the non-divine nature of these customs and opinions, and their dependence on time and place (pp. 40–41). The term *techunah* (characteristic) also appears in the same context in both (*'Igrot Isaac Euchel*, p. 118; *'Igrot Meshulam*, p. 39).
A cursory check on the use of terms in some of the studied works reveals some instances where "customs" and "opinions" do appear together as the principal interest of the given author. Lyttelton, in his introduction to *Letters from a Persian*, p. vi, writes about "their own admir'd Customs, and favourite Opinions". Aaron Monceca, in *The Jewish Spy*, writes about "opinions" and "Manners" in one sentence (vol. I, letter ii, p. 13). However, it seems that the accepted terms are "Manners" and "Customs" which are more frequently used. See, for example, in the *Chinese Letters*, letter ii, p. 7; v, p. 25. In *The Jewish Spy*, I: letter i, p. 3; iii, p. 24 (by Monceca); ix, p. 60 (by Isaac Onis).
By contrast, Usbek undertook the trip as a result of his desire for "knowledge" ("savoir" – letter i), namely, his desire to become educated in Western sciences ("sciences de l'Occident" – letter viii). Usbek uses the term "customs" ("coutumes" – letter xxiii) and Rica employs the terms "European usages and customs" ("moeurs et [. . .] coutumes européennes" – letter xxiv).

[56] *'Igrot Isaac Euchel*, pp. 119–121 (two out of 12 pages); *'Igrot Meshulam*, pp. 41, 44, 45.

The two epistolary writings manifest a considerable interest in the translation of poetry into Hebrew. The first deals with a translation into incorrect, sloppy Hebrew of a German poem, while the second offers an exemplary translation by the Hebrew poet Ephraim Luzzatto of Metastasio's poetry. The latter further discusses the qualities of Italian poetry in comparison with oriental poetry.[57]

Both works have the same didactic, educational, preaching tone. This tone is quite natural to *The Letters of Isaac Euchel* where Euchel plays his role as a teacher. His intention, clearly stated, is to prove that one is able to express oneself on all subjects through the medium of the Hebrew language.[58] In the fictional work the use of the didactic tone is more complicated as it involves discovery of the author's covert point of view and the deciphering of the irony in the grandfather's letter.[59] Meshulam's rhetorical questions, too, are didactic in tone, as his questions are directed at the reader as well as at his correspondent. Meshulam's moralistic preaching to his correspondent is intended also for his reader.

As an author, Euchel uses the figure of his narrator to exhibit his presence as an educator. This feature is expressed in both works through the educational footnotes. Unlike most footnotes in the satirical epistolary genre which in many cases serve for satirical purposes, the notes here are serious, didactic and educational.[60]

In both works Euchel is seen to possess a unique technique of description, or point of view. The narrator is made to observe the landscape from a central point, his own; he describes the scenery on his right and on his left.[61]

---

[57] '*Igrot Isaac Euchel*, pp. 140–142, a discussion of translation of a poem by Haller and of the translator occupies over two pages of this 12-page work. '*Igrot Meshulam* devotes almost four pages (out of some 27), more than a full letter, or chapter, to Italian poetry and its excellent translation into Hebrew. As an example of poetry under the influence of the oriental-Arabic poetry he cites a poem by the Jewish poet Samuel Ibn Adiya. See also note 21 above.

[58] '*Igrot Isaac Euchel*, pp. 117–118.

[59] See my study cited in note 1, part two, pp. 59–61, notes 111–115 and their related text.

[60] On the use of footnotes for satirical purpose by the Hebrew writer Perl, see Werses, *Sipur Veshorsho*, pp. 27–28. For the use of notes by the Hebrew author Erter, see my paper 'Narrative Techniques of Isaac Erter's Satire "Gilul Nefesh" ', read at the Sixth World Congress for Jewish Studies, Jerusalem 1973; published as 'Erter's Narrative Methods in the Satire "Gilgul Nefesh".' *Biqoret Ufarshanut*, XI–XII (January 1978), pp. 135–136 [Hebrew]. It should be stressed that the footnotes in *Lettres Persanes* are not intended for satirical purpose. Cf. Robert F. O'Reilly, 'The Structure and Meaning of the *Lettres Persanes*', *Studies on Voltaire and the Eighteenth Century*, LXVII, Geneva 1969, pp. 95–96. Some of the footnotes are intended to highlight the role of the fictional translator who is mentioned in the introduction. Neither are the notes in *The Jewish Spy* of a satirical nature; they are learned and serious.

Although the first footnote in the Hebrew work is signed 'divrei Hame'asfim', [the words of the editors of *Hame'asef*] (p. 39), and similarly the first footnote in each new instalment (pp. 172, 246), are so signed, I tend to think that Euchel himself, a former editor of the journal, and a frequent contributor afterwards, provided the footnotes himself, and used the customary editorial signature. At least one such footnote (p. 40, note***) plays an important role in deciphering the point of view of the editor–publisher regarding the central, thematic problem of changing one's customs in a foreign environment.

[61] '*Igrot Isaac Euchel*, p. 119: "On my right is the big, wide river [...] and on my left fertilised fields." '*Igrot Meshulam*, p. 42: "We passed the Grecian lands [countries] which are on our right, and the lands of the African part on our left." The latter is especially an artificial point of view indicative of the use of a map rather than an actual seafaring near the Greek islands; for one does not see the African continent while travelling near the coast of Greece.

There is further an identical date – the Hebrew month '*Iyar* – in the first letters of both works.[62] Some unique seafaring terminology appears likewise in both.[63]

The protagonists of the two epistolary writings may be related to one another. Michal, Euchel's student in the first letters, appears in the image of Meshulam, the fictional figure who is out to look for wisdom and truth. Isaac Euchel (abbreviation, in Hebrew, is A.A.), the central, active protagonist of the first letters, turns out to be 'Uriyah Ha'Eshtemo'i (Hebrew abbreviation: also A.A.).[64]

The identification of the protagonists in the two Hebrew works leads us to conclude that these works are more than merely closely related. It appears that *The Letters of Meshulam* in effect continues *The Letters of Isaac Euchel* in a fictional manner. The authentic letters and Euchel's European trip apparently stimulated the author to follow up the letters discontinued in 1785. Five years later Euchel decided to publish the second series of letters. The passing years brought several changes in the function of the authentic key figures as transformed in the fictional letters. Michal, in the guise of Meshulam, is now going to seek wisdom on his own. He can no longer rely on his teacher for that. True, he does listen to the advice given to him by the teacher–father – Euchel, in his literary character of 'Uriyah; he still continues to receive his letters, he acts in accordance with his father's advice, and he considers his father an example to be followed in religious and social matters. Yet Meshulam now must experience in himself and by himself; he must face reality by himself, and he must cope with his own problems so as to find his own truth. The identical dates in the beginning of the first letters in the two works are perhaps a testimony that Meshulam follows in Euchel's footsteps.

The fictional names in *The Letters of Meshulam* are significant. *Meshulam* derives from the Hebrew root meaning "to be whole", or "to be integral", and perhaps indicates one who is looking for his "wholeness".[65] '*Uriyah*, meaning "the light", or "the fire of the Lord", represents the enlightened, though with a traditional orientation.[66] 'Uriyah's letter exhibits many views expressed pre-

---

[62] '*Igrot Isaac Euchel*, p. 116; '*Igrot Meshulam*, pp. 39, 43.

[63] '*Igrot Isaac Euchel*, p. 120; '*Igrot Meshulam*, p. 40: "Rav haḥovel vechol malaḥav" [the captain and all his sailors].

[64] Isaac Euchel used to sign all his books and articles in Hebrew and in Yiddish not by the Hebrew name *Yizḥaq*, but by its Yiddish equivalent '*Izeq* (whose first letter is the Hebrew Aleph). It is only in the title of the non-fictional letters that his name appears as *Yizḥaq* Eichel. Thus the abbreviation A.A. [Hebrew: Alef. Alef.] corresponds. 'Uriyah, in Hebrew, begins also with an Alef. Similarly, it may be supposed that the abbreviation of the grandfather's name, *M*ordechai Ha-*E*shtemo'i, may echo that of the mullah, *M*ehemet *A*li (*Lettres Persanes*, xvi, p. 94).

On an attempt to identify the protagonists of *Lettres Persanes* and consider it as a contemporary allegory, see J. L. Carr, 'The Secret Chain of the *Lettres Persanes*', *Studies on Voltaire and the Eighteenth Century*, LV, Geneva 1967, pp. 333–344. Cf. note 41 above.

[65] ShLM. See Friedlander's article, cited above in note 2, p. 108, note 9.

[66] 'Or Yah, or 'Ur Yah. The grandfather, Mordechai, may be the representation of Mordechai Haẓadiq, the righteous, after the book of Esther. See Ch. Szmeruk, 'The Name Mordecai-Marcus – Literary Metamorphosis of a Social Ideal', *Tarbiẓ*, XXIX (1960), pp. 76–98 [Hebrew; English summary, p. v–vi]. See also Friedlander's above-mentioned article, note 8 and related text.

viously by Moses Mendelssohn, the eminent guide of Hebrew *Haskalah*. In the light of Euchel's biography of Mendelssohn, one may conclude that Euchel created in the figure of 'Uriyah a composite both of himself and of Mendelssohn.[67]

To sum up, then, Euchel could have been influenced by *Lettres Persanes* as well as by other such epistolary writings. Yet this influence more probably reached *The Letters of Meshulam* through the medium of his own experience as first expressed in the authentic, non-fictional *Letters of Isaac Euchel* – hence the differences in literary formulation and in the ideological objectives of the two authors. There is something uniquely Hebraic in Euchel's work in his Haskalah point of view and in his treatment of vital problems that were the focal point of Jewish reality at that time. Euchel's field of vision is not as wide, as inclusively European, as was Montesquieu's. His work is concentrated on the Jewish and Hebraic aspects of the European milieu.

Thus, while Montesquieu treats the total range of European literature, though with some obvious limitations, Euchel deals only with poetry and its translation into Hebrew. The French author discusses various aspects of world history, whereas the Hebrew author has in mind Jewish history in Spain. It should be pointed out that Euchel's historical analysis is far from purely academic; it is not intended to be an irrelevant hypothesis on far-fetched historical issues. More searching analysis of his discussion of the rise and fall of Spanish Jewry would yield significant insight into Euchel's views on the German Jewry of his day.[68] The limitation of his field of vision, compared to that of Montesquieu, is necessitated by the narrower scope of Euchel's work.

In conclusion: *The Letters of Meshulam* perhaps owes some features of its form and some of its topics to *The Persian Letters* and similar epistolary writings; but failure to compare *The Letters of Meshulam* with *The Letters of Isaac Euchel* deprives the work of its significance as an artistic piece of literature.

[67] See my article cited in note 1, part two, p. 62, note 120 and its related text.
[68] *Ibid.*, p. 66, note 129 and related text. Neiman seems to project the same view as to Euchel's intentions (in his article, p. 167).

Emancipation and Assimilation

The Forgotten Connection
Women and Jews in the Conflict between Enlightenment and Romanticism

BY JULIUS CARLEBACH

There is a refreshing tendency in the more recent literature on Jewish emancipation to resist the particularistic approach of many earlier studies[1] which tend to view the history of Jewish emancipation as a rather special, not to say unique phenomenon. Even where modern historiography endeavours to place Jewish destiny in a "context" of universal or, more especially, European social and economic history, this can and has been done without relinquishing an occasional tendency to treat events as uniquely relating to Jews.[2] It can be demonstrated that Jewish history sometimes has a catalytic effect on its environment and in this paper I would like to look at the origins of Jewish emancipation in conjunction with the beginnings of the movement for the emancipation of women.* There are a number of reasons why the history of the women's movement should provide a useful comparison to that of the Jews. First, they are movements which manifest themselves at about the same time, i.e., in the last quarter of the eighteenth century and this is not, as we will show, an accidental factor.[3] Secondly, both women and Jews have been, and to some extent still are subjects of intense discussions to elicit their natures and "essences" (*Wesen*). The question of whether or not they represent biological (sex-race) or social (role) categories, or whether they possess other innately determined characteristics has occupied many writers and still continues to do so.[4] Thirdly, following on from this, emancipation for both categories has been preceded by long and extensive debates on whether – and if so – how women and Jews should be educated. That is to say, should they be educated to develop their minds and personalities

---

*The author is greatly indebted to Professor Ernest Krauss of the Institute for the Study of Religious and Ethnic Minorities in the University of Bar Ilan for providing the facilities and peace to write this paper during the summer of 1978. An earlier version of the paper was presented to the Graduate-Faculty Seminar in Sociology in the University of Sussex in March 1978.

[1] See, for example, the work of Reinhard Rürup esp. 'Jewish Emancipation and Bourgeois Society', in *LBI Year Book XIV* (1969), pp. 67–91.

[2] Salo W. Baron 'Newer Approaches to Jewish Emancipation', in *Diogenes* (1960) 29, pp. 56–81.

[3] There is a very extensive literature on Jewish emancipation, e.g., M. A. Meyer, *The Origins of the Modern Jew*, Detroit 1967; H. M. Graupe, *Die Entstehung des modernen Judentums*, Hamburg 1969; Jacob Katz, *Out of the Ghetto*, Cambridge, Mass. 1973. On women, serious historical studies are not so numerous, cf. Lily Braun, *Die Frauenfrage. Ihre geschichtliche Entwicklung und wirtschaftliche Seite*, Leipzig 1901; Marianne Weber, *Ehefrau und Mutter in der Rechtsentwicklung*, Tübingen 1907; Jacob Bouten, *Mary Wollstencroft and the Beginnings of Female Emancipation in France and England*, Philadelphia 1975 (1922). None of these link Jewish and women's emancipation in any way.

[4] E.g. S. Goldberg, *The Inevitability of Patriarchy*, London 1977.

or should they be trained to maximise their role performance.[5] Fourth, the respective histories of the two groups in their endeavours to achieve emancipation show many similarities with encouraging progress alternating with periods of regression and reaction. Fifth, resistance to emancipation by no means always comes from external opponents of the two groups. Inasmuch as emancipation is bound to raise questions of identity and social function, change or the likelihood of change has often produced fierce objections from within each group. Sixth, the two groups again appear alike in that both managed to secure for themselves a great deal of recognition, support and influence by circumventing arbitrary social barriers and by generating "contradictions" between their social performances and public definitions. One need only think of the great influence exercised by, say, Madame de Staël, or the impact of Jews like Moses Mendelssohn or the Rothschilds. In England this was perhaps even more marked. While women like Mary Carpenter were directly responsible for a great deal of social legislation,[6] Moses Montefiore was appointed High Sheriff of Kent (1837) long before Jews (or indeed women) were admitted to parliament or even to universities. Like Mendelssohn, Montefiore was often cited as an example in debates in Germany.[7] Seventh, a pervasive ambivalence towards both groups can often be shown to be present in influential personalities, when they attempt to give expression simultaneously to lofty principles and base prejudices. From Voltaire and Diderot to Treitschke and beyond him, an unmistakable hostility based at best on a deep conservatism, but more often on outright enmity, can be seen readily enough. There are also some who have taken it upon themselves to defend both groups, like for example, August Bebel. Eighth, women and Jews have often been linked by antisemitic writers who have alleged that Jews wanted to destroy the virtue and innocence of Christian women. Such an argument is likely to arise in situations in which women share disenfranchised status with other groups (for instance American Negroes), not least because association between disadvantaged groups may lead to an accelerated disintegration of an existing social order. Thus, the Berlin Salons of the late eighteenth – early nineteenth centuries could be viewed in this way. Sexually and religiously disadvantaged women meeting with a politically impotent intelligentsia, help each other towards a deeper consciousness of their irrational positions and a better understanding of the conditions determining their situation. Hence they aspired to be and hoped to be seen as living refutations of accepted causes of their inferior statuses.

The ninth point of similarity between the two groups is concerned with the fate they have shared over many centuries of being reduced to dependant status. In pre-industrial Europe, women and Jews had to secure their positions by total dependencies. In the case of women, social position, class, wealth and education were governed by and reflected the class, wealth and status of father and husband. This gave some scope for gaining personal advantage, albeit an

[5] J. J. Rousseau's *Émile*, Paris and Amsterdam 1762, is a classic of this genre. For Jews Naphtaly Herz Wessely's *Divrei Shalom Ve-E-meth* (Words of Peace and Truth), 1782, might be cited.
[6] Cf. Julius Carlebach, *Caring for Children in Trouble*, London 1970.
[7] E.g., in the 7th Rhein Landtag of 1843.

haphazard one. Jews in the Holy Roman Empire were tied since 1236, either directly to the imperial crown, or indirectly, through the Emperor, to the ruling nobility or clergy. Although only a minute number of Jews achieved positions of wealth and influence, the economic performance of the few gave protection and limited security to the Jewish population.[8] By the end of the eighteenth century, Jews no longer enjoyed either a monopoly or a dominance in trade and finance, but their total dependence on ruling élites continued and provided the protection without which they were liable to be expelled at will.

Women and Jews share the dubious distinction, together with French Huguenots, Jesuits and Freemasons,[9] of having been attacked for being "a state within a state". About women the accusation was made, somewhat sourly, by Montesquieu, who thought that certain aristocratic ladies exercised undue influence over government ministers. In the case of Jews, it was popularised and justified by Fichte[10] as a serious obstacle to Jewish emancipation, though S. W. Baron has described it as fair comment for the pre-emancipation period when Jews enjoyed a degree of internal autonomy or "self-government" which justified a description of a state within a state.[11]

Attempts have been made to link the position of women in society with those of other "minority" groups, notably slaves and Negroes.[12] An elaborate recent study of women and Jews as "deviants" is Hans Mayer's *Aussenseiter*.[13] Mayer projects a pessimistic image of the effects of the Enlightenment by using subsequent events (i.e., the Hitler era) as its consequence and as the focus of what has to be explained. This tends, at times, to lead to the presentation of variable literary expressions as representative of historical periods and thereby obscures connected sequences in the history of ideas. This attempt to establish the failure of the Enlightenment by an erudite analysis of women, Jews and homosexuals in literature does not establish a justification for the concept of deviance in relation to women and Jews. It appears to be inappropriate because in placing these two groups on the margins of society the centrality of their respective roles in the evolution of the post-feudal era is lost.

Finally it is important to consider that the advent of "bourgeois" society forced a reappraisal of the traditional positions of women and Jews into the

---

[8]For a lively and detailed description see Hilde Spiel, *Fanny von Arnstein oder die Emanzipation*, Frankfurt a. Main 1962.
[9]J. Katz, 'A State within a State. The History of an anti-semitic Slogan', in *Israel Academy of Science and Humanities* – 4:3 (1969). In this meticulously researched paper Katz does not mention that one of the earliest applications of this slogan was made by Montesquieu about women in 1731. Cf. Montesquieu, *Lettres Persanes*, Amsterdam 1731, p. 83ff.
[10]See the discussion of Fichte below.
[11]Baron, *op. cit.*, p. 69.
[12]Helen Mayer Hacker, 'Women as a Minority Group', in *Social Forces*, 30 (1951). Hacker uses discrimination as the link-variable, but it is difficult to see how half of any given population can be regarded as a minority, unless C. G. Jung's interesting approach is applied. He also discussed women striving for emancipation as a minority in that they would be mainly middle-class, urban dwellers. Peasant women, he argued, are and always were the same. Cf. *Die Frau in Europa*, Zürich 1929, p. 9.
[13]Hans Mayer, *Aussenseiter*, Frankfurt a. Main 1975. See also Ernst Simon's interesting critique of Mayer, 'Drei gescheiterte Emanzipationen', in *Bulletin des Leo Baeck Instituts*, XV (1976), No. 52.

arena of public debate. Before we turn our attention to aspects of that debate, we might look briefly at the meaning of the now so common and widely used concept of "bourgeois" society.

I

There may be a grudging recognition that "the bourgeoisie has played a highly revolutionary role in history"[14] but Marx and Engels, in the *Communist Manifesto* of 1848 stereotyped and denigrated a multifaceted, dynamic, creative and pervasive social, economic and cultural phenomenon and reduced it to a temporary and morally sterile manifestation which, it was claimed, threatened to engulf civilised society. An indiscriminate mixture of English industrialism, French politics and German intellectualism, an arbitrary conglomerate of historical periods and national differences, enabled them to construct a social "reality" in which complex interactions were reduced to simplistic causal relationships, in which "ought" and "is" were readily interchangeable and in which the particular was presented as the inevitable harbinger of the universal. The result has been a general confusion in which innocuous developments acquire sinister and pejorative meanings. To be bourgeois becomes synonymous with being capitalists, although there is no objective basis for such an assumption which would survive systematic analysis only as an apodictic pronouncement to the faithful.[15] To understand the origins of the emancipation of women and Jews which have their roots in the advent of a *Bürgertum* one must dispel some of the misconceptions imposed on events, concepts and sequences by the Marx–Engels heritage. The difficulty of such a task lies not only in the influence Marx and Engels have come to exercise on so much of what has been said and written, it is also compounded by the fact that the English language has no adequate equivalents for *Bürger*, and *Bürgertum*[16] – complex and indispensable terms for our deliberations.

In order to place women and Jews in a socially comprehensible context, we might look at three important factors concerning the *Bürger*, their origins, types and characteristics. While there is broad agreement on these factors, the historical period with which we are concerned is too long and some of the issues too obscure for definitive statements. Sombart has described two possible origins of both the term and the concept *Bürger*. The first is the emergence of a group of people in fourteenth-century Florence who evolve a set of "virtues" to guide their conduct in business,[17] the second he described as merchants in Genoa who

[14] 'Manifest der Kommunistischen Partei', 1948, in *Marx–Engels Werke* (*MEW*), vol. 4 (East) Berlin 1959, p. 464.
[15] The confusion generated by Marx and Engels creates difficulties even for those who are ideologically committed to Marxism. Thus the editions of the *MEW* have to add an explanatory note to the Manifesto (preface, p. XV) to explain why middle class – *besitzende Klasse* and bourgeoisie are used interchangeably. The East Berlin edition of *Heines Werke* has to explain why *citoyen* – i.e., *Bürger* is used by Heine in *contrast* to bourgeois (cf. vol. 4, 1968, p. 344, n. 241).
[16] Cf. Eda Sagarra, *A Social History of Germany 1648–1914*, London 1977, p. 253.
[17] Werner Sombart, *Der Bourgeois. Zur Geistesgeschichte des modernen Wirtschaftsmenschen*, München–Leipzig 1913, pp. 135 and 195. I have used this book extensively. Although Max Weber re-

built castles (*Burgen*) for themselves during the pre-capitalist period. Bergier, in a more recent analysis described the origins of the bourgeois or burgher as town-dwellers who were active as merchants, officials, artisans, lawyers and men of letters who were granted certain rights conferred upon them by charter and who thus enjoyed real privileges, unlike the peasants.[18] This account is of particular interest because it suggests that inasmuch as Jews were also mainly town-dwellers with rights and restrictions defined by charter, they might be said to have been "burghers" irrespective of any occupation or other status.[19]

If there is some choice in deciding on the origins of *Bürger*, types of *Bürgertum* are even more prolific. Sombart has made an interesting distinction between an "old-type bourgeois", one of whose chief characteristics incidentally is *Bürgerlichkeit*. This old type lasted until the end of the eighteenth century (and is therefore of special significance for us) and its outstanding feature was that it used trade as a means to an end in a period where "the measure of all things is man".[20] The modern *Wirtschaftsmensch* (i.e., the new type of economic man) emerged in the nineteenth century and for him on the other hand not the needs of men but the needs of business must always take priority. Profit and business are the primary concerns.[21] Bergier lists four types of bourgeois – rentiers, a conservative group who live on income from property, learned professions, mainly law and public administration, the big merchants and bankers concentrated in the main in Europe's major cities, London, Paris, Amsterdam and Frankfurt a. Main, and a fourth and largest group – artisans and shopkeepers. Between them these groups do not form a "bourgeoisie" in the Marxist sense, i.e., they are not, as yet, a social class. The learned professions and the big merchants tend to wield political power and thus represent a ruling élite while the main source of the industrial bourgeoisie, the group that Marx really had in mind was drawn mainly from artisans and shopkeepers.[22] Sagarra draws attention to a classification which is perhaps the most important for us. In Germany we find references to an "arbeitenden Mittelstand" (working middle class) and there is also reference to the fact that in the eighteenth century the artisan craftsman "was virtually identifiable with the notion of burgher".[23] The German middle class was a *Bildungs- und Besitzbürgertum* which derived its status mainly from education and

---

regarded it as "by far the weakest" of Sombart's major works (*Religions-Soziologie*, vol. I, p. 27, n. 2) it is full of interesting ideas. It is less forced than his *Die Juden und das Wirtschaftsleben*, Leipzig 1911, though even here Sombart makes constant reference to Jewish dominance in trade, yet every specific example he quotes concerns non-Jewish practitioners.

[18] J. F. Bergier, 'The Industrial Bourgeoisie and the Rise of the Working Class 1700–1914', in C. M. Cipolla (ed.), *The Industrial Revolution* (Fontana Economic History of Europe, vol. 3), p. 399.

[19] Even restrictions constitute a social definition of a group. Perhaps we should emphasise that we are not here concerned with contemporary theories of social stratification nor with sources of social inequality, but with roots of inner-directed sources of life-styles which may well extend across traditional class-based boundaries.

[20] Sombart, *Der Bourgeois*, p. 194.

[21] Bergier, *op. cit.*, pp. 217–218.

[22] *Ibid.*, pp. 401–403.

[23] Sagarra, *op. cit.*, pp. 67 and 69.

which, until the 1850s was relatively poor.[24] There is also reference to the German *Kleinbürger*, an important group which played a significant part in upholding social order and which was most susceptible to the consequences of change and unrest.[25] Brunschwig has drawn attention to the large numbers of poor and vagrants in big cities, notably in Berlin, where he estimated two-thirds of the population consisted of a poor "working class" which was not, however, an industrial proletariat.[26]

Another consequence of the Marx–Engels insistence on a simple dichotomy between a bourgeoisie and a proletariat is the excessive preoccupation, in much of the subsequent literature, linking *Bürgertum* and *Bürgerlichkeit* with the emergence of capitalism. In spite of the greater probability that capitalism as a concept was coined in response to socialism and that the industrial bourgeoisie emerged as a class to make a common stand against the working class,[27] and notwithstanding the reality that the industrial bourgeoisie was created by the industrial revolution rather than the other way round,[28] from Max Weber and Werner Sombart to the present day there remains the fascination to discover the character traits which mark out the bourgeois, the spirit which might have moved him, the influences which might have guided him. Sombart, the most assiduous researcher in the field thought that notably in Italy, Scotland and America, sets of "virtues" (*Tugenden*) developed which marked out the *Bürger*, not by his legal or social status but by his own definitions of values and principles governing all human and above everything, commercial relationships. Daniel Defoe is frequently cited,[29] and so are others, but for Sombart the greatest of them all, the "Fleisch gewordene Bürgerprinzip"[30] is Benjamin Franklin, the man who coined the maxim that "Time is money" and whose motto was "Industry and Frugality".[31] Franklin listed thirteen virtues which created an appropriate ethos for the advent of modernity and which eventually took hold of Europe.[32] These virtues are broadly those enumerated by Max Weber[33] as the "Protestant Ethic" and by others as dominant Puritan values, i.e., work, frugality, usefulness, sexual morality and benevolence.[34] However, inasmuch as these virtues are concerned with personal and domestic relationships as much as with business and work relationships, their effectiveness and impact extend far beyond economic fields. In Marxist theory this would be seen as sequential, i.e.,

---

[24] *Ibid.*, p. 254. This is also the view of W. Dilthey, *Das Erlebnis und die Dichtung*, 8th ed., Leipzig–Berlin 1922 who described this group as "mässig begütert", p. 290.

[25] *Ibid.*, p. 253. Sombart, *Der Bourgeois*, p. 23, described the main interest of this group as "sichere Ruhe".

[26] Henri Brunschwig, *Enlightenment and Romanticism in Eighteenth-Century Prussia*, Chicago–London 1974 (1947), pp. 111–115.

[27] Bergier, *op. cit.*, p. 418.

[28] *Ibid.*, p. 414.

[29] E.g. Daniel Defoe, *An Essay on Projects*, 1697, and *The Complete English Tradesman*, 5th edn., 1745.

[30] Sombart, *Der Bourgeois*, p. 136.

[31] *Ibid.*, p. 152.

[32] *Ibid.*, pp. 153–159.

[33] In his famous *The Protestant Ethic and the Spirit of Capitalism*, London 1930.

[34] Cf. Hellmut O. Pappe, 'Enlightenment', in *Dictionary of the History of Ideas*, 4 vols. New York 1973. See vol. 2, pp. 89–100, esp. p. 94.

social relations as "superstructures" of economic relations but there is no evidence to show these "virtues" to have appeared sequentially, since they were as important in Protestant Germany in the eighteenth century where commercial development was continually constrained by excessive controls of enlightened despotism, where industrial development was virtually absent and where education – *Bildung* – was a more reliable indicator of social status than for example in England, yet *Bürger* values were the dominant norms. Neither the early industrialists[35] nor the merchants had much of an education, but in Prussia at the end of the eighteenth century they did educate their children, especially their sons.[36] In the absence of any real career outlets except for the civil service and the church, a disproportion of able young men became officials and clergymen and secured and reinforced that *Bildungsbürgertum* which came to dominate thought, art and culture in Germany. This *Bürgertum* was concerned more with ideas and relationships than with economic development. While many of the social processes of this period did indeed move along the same paths as in England and France, notably the disintegration of feudal remnants of estates, corporations and guilds, in Germany the process was slower and perhaps never entirely successful.[37]

II

Precisely because the ethos of *Bürgerlichkeit* extended into the domain of private relationships and personal beliefs it was inevitable that attitudes to women and Jews should be under constant discussion and the need for change, at least in theory, constantly reviewed. If not the only categories, women and Jews were of greater interest than others because the range of their functions often extended beyond their sharply defined roles. Women were deeply and at times prominently involved in innovatory and commercial activities in the seventeenth century,[38] while Jewish women almost certainly participated in commercial activities as far back as the thirteenth century,[39] but the general trend for the rising *Bürgertum* was to establish the home as the central and sole domain of women. Because the woman was expected to create a warm, effective and supportive base from which her husband could operate in society and to ensure the proper training of the young, her role was increasingly restricted to and within the home, meaning here as opposed to the household which was usually also a workplace. There was also an expectation that she would adhere to the same essential virtues by which the husband was to be governed in his perfor-

---

[35]Bergier, *op. cit.*, p. 415.
[36]Brunschwig, *op. cit.*; see his chapter on the Middle Class.
[37]Fritz Stern, 'The Integration of Jews in Nineteenth-Century Germany', in *LBI Year Book XX* (1975), pp. 79–83, esp. p. 81.
[38]Sombart, *Der Bourgeois*, p. 59.
[39]Cf. Julius Carlebach, 'Deutsche Juden und der Säkularisierungsprozess in der Erziehung', in *Das Judentum in der Deutschen Umwelt 1800–1850. Studien zur Frühgeschichte der Emanzipation*, herausgegeben von Hans Liebeschütz und Arnold Paucker, Tübingen 1977 (Schriftenreihe wissenschaftlicher Abhandlungen des Leo Baeck Instituts 35), p. 82, n. 64.

mance of worldly duties.[40] Campe, writing about the same time as Benjamin Franklin compiled a list of "virtues" a woman should cultivate, which is very similar to that cited by Sombart from Franklin.[41] A glance at the two lists in juxtaposition is instructive:

CAMPE	FRANKLIN
Attention	Moderation – In food and drink.
Order	Silence – Speak only to some purpose
Cleanliness	Order – A time and place for everything
Industry	Determination – do what you should do
Thrift	Frugality – do not waste money
Domestic skills	Industry – do not waste time
Well-being	Honesty – do not deceive
Honour	Justice – do not harm others
Domestic peace	Control of feeling – do not take offence
Happiness of husband	Cleanliness – body, clothes, house
	Calmness – do not fuss over trivialities
	Modesty – sex only for children or health
	Humanity – like Jesus or Socrates

The woman is here clearly perceived as the centre of the home which becomes the primary social institution of *Bürgertum*. It should be noted, however, that in this conception there is no awareness of any possible variation related to class structure and social need. The *bürgerliche* woman does not work outside the home primarily because she *should* not be active outside the home. The new middle class was thus rejecting the lifestyle of aristocratic ladies as well as the partial domesticity of the lower orders. In a remarkable passage of his analysis of *Bürgertum*, Sombart introduces an improbable concept which we ought to mention here not because of its intrinsic worth, but because it is certainly, though perhaps intuitively, drawn from historical events of the last quarter of the eighteenth century. Just as in his discussion of Jews Sombart eventually poses the question whether Jewish characteristics are innate[42] so in his *Der Bourgeois* Sombart poses the question whether there is a "born" *Bürger*.[43] His deliberations lead him to contrast the *Bürger* with what he has called the *Unbürger* – the difference between these two is the difference between erotic and *bürgerliche* nature. The *Unbürger* is governed by his love life, the *Bürger* by his rationality.[44] This means the following opposites:

UNBÜRGER	*BÜRGER*
Subjective personal values	Objective material values
Genussmensch	*Pflichtmensch*
Individualist	Hard
Personality	Materialist
Aesthetic	Ethical
Living	Ordering
Observing	Educating
Thinking	Instructing
Colourful	Colourless

---

[40]Sombart, *Der Bourgeois*, p. 147. See also W. H. Bruford, *Germany in the Eighteenth Century. The Social Background of the Literary Revival*, Cambridge 1971, p. 224, and Ulrich Herrmann, 'Erziehung und Schulunterricht für Mädchen im 18. Jahrhundert', in *Wolfenbütteler Studien zur Aufklärung*, Band III, Wolfenbüttel 1976, pp. 101–127.

[41]Quoted by Herrmann, *op. cit.*, p. 108 from 'Fatherly Advice to my Daughter' (1789).

[42]For a fuller discussion see the section on Sombart in Julius Carlebach, *Karl Marx and the Radical Critique of Judaism*, London 1978, pp. 227–233.

[43]Sombart, *Der Bourgeois*, p. 259.

[44]*Ibid.*, p. 263.

Improbable as Sombart's schema may appear it does enable us to view the *Bürger* concept independently of sexual division and, as we shall see it has implications for the emancipation of women in conflict with the tenets of Romanticism.

Unlike women, Jews have been highlighted all too frequently in relation to their *Bürgerlichkeit* and their position in civil society and much of the relevant literature has been and continues to be discussed at length. Our concern here is quite specifically with the image of the Jew as the "bourgeois par excellence",[45] at least in Europe. The most famous name associated with this image is once again Karl Marx who regarded Jews as the embodiment of civil society. There is an element of truth in Marx's assertion, but he arrived at it by equating Jews with trade, which produced a highly distorted picture and led to a wholly untenable identification of Jews with capitalism by many of Marx's followers and by men like Sombart,[46] who simply ignore the following important factors: Firstly, that Marx was only concerned with the nature of "civil society" when he wrote about Jews and had not yet begun to explore the concept of capitalism,[47] secondly, that Jews in Germany did not form part of an industrial bourgeoisie until the second half of the nineteenth century (i.e., after Marx had written about them),[48] thirdly, that Jews were as likely to be prominent in socialism as they were in capitalism,[49] and fourthly, that Jews managed to adapt to pre-capitalist Europe economically as well as, and at times better than they did to capitalist Europe.[50] Accordingly there is no *prima facie* case for assuming a special confluence between Jews and capitalism other than as a favourite accusation of their opponents.[51] On the other hand there does appear to be a convergence between the traditional Jewish ethos and life-style and what emerged in eighteenth-century Germany as a *Bildungs- und Besitzbürgertum*. If to give but one example we take the enumeration of "virtues" set up by Benjamin Franklin (as set out above) which typified the *Bürger* ethos we have discussed and compare it with the most widely read rabbinic guide on social conduct then we see that the "virtues" stipulated in *Pirkei Avoth* (*Ethics of the Fathers*), a text read regularly by Jews over the ages and dating back to around the second century C.E., are almost identical. Notable differences concern firstly constant references

---

[45] Fritz Stern, *loc. cit.*, p. 81.

[46] Carlebach, *op. cit.*; for a detailed analysis of Marx's views.

[47] As discussed by Marx – cf. T. B. Bottomore (ed.) *Karl Marx. Early Writings*, London 1963.

[48] Cf. Monika Richarz, 'Jewish Social Mobility in Germany during the Time of Emancipation (1790–1871)', in *LBI Year Book XX* (1975), pp. 69–77, esp. p. 74.

[49] Reinhard Rürup, 'Emancipation and Crisis. The "Jewish Question" in Germany 1850–1890', in *LBI Year Book XX* (1975), pp. 13–25, esp. p. 22, is therefore right in refuting Sombart's association of Jews and capitalism, but unconvincing when he says that capitalism (as opposed to what?) has no reason to discriminate against Jews. See 'Emanzipation und Krise. Zur Geschichte der "Judenfrage" in Deutschland vor 1890', in *Juden im Wilhelminischen Deutschland 1890–1914*. Ein Sammelband herausgegeben von Werner E. Mosse unter Mitwirkung von Arnold Paucker, Tübingen 1976 (Schriftenreihe wissenschaftlicher Abhandlungen des Leo Baeck Instituts 33), pp. 1–56, esp. p. 4.

[50] Baron, *op. cit.*, pp. 66 and 77.

[51] At best J. Lestschinsky's description of Jews as "Anhängsel der kapitalistischen Wirtschaft" might be appropriate, though, as he noted pessimistically, it means that Jews will be the first to be jettisoned in times of crisis. See *Das Wirtschaftliche Schicksal des Deutschen Judentums*, Berlin 1932, p. 8.

to study and learning and injunctions to concern oneself with the welfare of the community, both occurring in the *Ethics of the Fathers*, but absent in Franklin's inventory. In fact Franklin's rules are more specifically inner-directed and self-centred than traditional Jewish sources which additionally lay great stress on social and communal relationships.[52] What we are arguing here is that the corpus of Jewish religious tradition certainly from post-biblical times contains the basic norms and values which eventually became the universally accepted ideology of West-European *Bürgerlichkeit*.

If we now turn our attention to the social and economic changes taking place during the period under discussion we find that a number of well-documented features of Jewish life in Europe combine to facilitate their adaptation to the industrial era. Thus, rapid increases in population led to a growing demand for food and Jews were advantageously placed to provide links between town and country. Their relatively wide distribution over small conurbations, concentration in trade, preference for cash transactions, their insecure status and the resulting willingness to gamble on high profit by buying risky stock (especially in contrast to the peasant's preference for stability and certainty), their persistent aspirations towards personal and social betterment and their lack of commitment to any established social order,[53] all now became assets. Hobsbawm offered seven reasons for Jewish readiness for "bourgeois" society.[54] They were a minority, mainly urban, well adapted to urban living, mainly literate, not involved with agriculture, mainly concerned with commerce or the professions and, largely as a result of their insecure position, always willing to consider new ideas and situations. Similarly, Monika Richarz[55] has pointed out that Jews were more rapidly urbanised than other sections of the population, tried to avoid employment as industrial workers because they preferred to be self-employed and were ever on the lookout for advancement. This latter characteristic had also been noted by Ruppin who argued that Jewish artisans tended to use their trade as a means, not as an end. They always aspired to being independent, enjoyed taking a chance whether by gambling, investing in perishable goods or on the stock exchange.[56]

What emerges from this very brief review is that if we look at the situation of Jews at the end of the eighteenth century in Germany we note that (*a*) they were, as they always had been, singularly well attuned to the *Bürger* ethos which was rapidly becoming the ruling ethos of German society.[57] (*b*) social and economic changes taking place in the wider society were particularly favourable for the advancement of existing Jewish skills and attributes. In other words German

---

[52]Even so, it is precisely the Jews who are always accused of an excessive "egoism" and self-interest, particularly by the radical philosophers of the nineteenth century. See Carlebach, *op. cit.*

[53]Cf. Wilhelm Treue, *Wirtschaft, Gesellschaft und Technik vom 16. bis zum 18. Jahrhundert*, Dtv 1974. See also Sagarra, *op. cit.*

[54]E. J. Hobsbawm, *The Age of Revolution in Europe 1789–1848*, London 1977 (1962), pp. 240–241.

[55]Richarz, *loc. cit.*, pp. 75–76.

[56]Arthur Ruppin, *Die Juden der Gegenwart*, 3rd edn., Berlin 1918, p. 61.

[57]This does not, of course, exclude the persistence of strong conservative (and usually also anti-Jewish) elements in Germany as suggested by Fritz Stern in *The Politics of Cultural Despair*, New York 1965 (1961), p. 8.

and Jewish ideologies of "the good life" converged to a point where both sides could see that greater integration or cooperation might be of mutual benefit.

Reference has already been made to a widely held view[58] that Jews were well-adapted to urban living or were more rapidly urbanised than other sections of the population. What might be the reason for this proclivity for urban living? The answer may well lie in the inherent "contradiction" between the philosophical ideal of individualism, then emerging as the greater good, and the harsh realities of economic survival in haphazardly growing cities. To recall Brunschwig's description of the plight of the poor in Berlin the population of the city was growing as a result of an influx of landless peasants, craftsmen deprived of their living by competition from industrial manufacturers and untrained youngsters now in oversupply as domestic servants. To the *Bürger* of Berlin, in conflict with discontented journeymen, faced with increasing vandalism and often in fear for life and property, these new elements of the population were a threat and a danger. Workhouses were put up but these were expensive and represented concentrations of potential danger.[59] The Jews, on the other hand, came to the city and would set up communal institutions catering not only for religious needs but also for social, cultural and educational requirements. If they did not spontaneously provide for their own, they could be made to do so, but this would be unlikely to be necessary, since communal care and cohesion was an integral part of the Jewish *Bürger* ethos.[60]

In discussing Jewish *Bürgerlichkeit* and perceptions of them, we are obviously not able to support such interpretations by demonstrating clearly enunciated views and attitudes, not least because these were not, as yet, issues of which most of the populace were consciously aware. Some contemporary documents can, however, be interpreted to illustrate points already made. Jakob Lestschinsky has reproduced a remarkable example of a document which, to our mind illustrates our contentions, though he himself offers a very different interpretation.[61] In 1800 a group of 25 Jewish families in Dettensee lived in three houses owned and assigned to them by a petty duke who himself resided in Switzerland. They addressed a petition to him in which they sought permission to build their own houses, expand the community to 40–50 families and to be relieved of some of the restrictions imposed on them. Lestschinsky described the petition as "dreadful evidence" of an "undignified existence". He abhorred the pleading, the begging, the flattery, subservience and sense of inferiority all of which he felt were clearly displayed in the petition. A different reading might, however, be more accurate. The first impression conveyed by the document is one that entirely supports Ismar Schorsch's view that the Jews often "couched

---

[58]Richarz, *loc. cit.*, Hobsbawm, *op. cit.*
[59]Brunschwig, *op. cit.*, pp. 111–117.
[60]Lestschinsky has briefly referred to the importance of this factor in an analysis of Polish Jews. See 'Jews in the Cities of the Polish Republic', in *YIVO Annual of Jewish Social Science*, vol. I, New York 1946, pp. 156–177, esp. pp. 159–160.
[61]The document is a petition from Jews in Dettensee (Schwarzwald) presented in 1800 and published by H. Bach in the *Israelitisches Gemeindeblatt*, Mannheim 15th August 1930, and reproduced by Lestschinsky in *Das Wirtschaftliche Schicksal des Deutschen Judentums*, pp. 19–20. For the full text of the petition see the Appendix.

a defiant posture in the most conciliatory terms".[62] Our petition is really quite insolent. Consider such phrases as "We do not want to speak of . . ." and then doing so, or "We will be silent about" and not being so. Or asides that a "noble friend of mankind" would "dissolve into tears" if he saw "his brothers" live in worse conditions than criminals. A tortuously worded sentence hides an unmistakable challenge. If the noble lord doubted the truth of their statements he should come and see for himself. The petitioners are sure that their insecure status "is only a formality" but would nevertheless appreciate a firm declaration concerning their own and their children's rights of residence.

A second, remarkable feature of the document is the clever way in which it underlines the essential *Bürgerlichkeit*, the commitment to middle-class values, of Jews living in appalling circumstances. They want to live decently, healthily, with appropriate separate quarters for men and women, master and servants, to be able to protect moral standards, care for the sick, uphold law and order and have security. A careful reading of the petition will show that no less than nine of Franklin's thirteen principles are fortuitously embedded there. The document also emphasises the Jews' determination to look after themselves. They want to build their own houses, make provisions for their children, widows and orphans and the like and expand their occupational activities. These points were not and indeed could not have been stated as explicitly as we have done but the document does suggest that Jews incorporated social respectability as an integral part of the negotiating process between themselves and their environment, between ruler and his subjects, between the arrogant exercise of power and their acknowledged but unwillingly tolerated dependant status.

III

Just as there is no real equivalent for *Bürgerlichkeit* in the English language, so there is no precise equivalent for another great concept of our period – *Menschlichkeit*. This is not really surprising for the concepts of German Enlightenment tend to emerge from extended contemplation and all-embracing reflection. While in England a dynamic *Bürgertum* was practically exploring the implications of its growing political power and in France, a steady growth of civil discontent led to a revolution which called for rapid decisions, in Germany the sustained control of enlightened despotism left little alternative to sophisticated rumination on vital issues. While English pragmatism eschewed commitment to theoretical principles and opted for spontaneous action, French deliberation disliked actions which seemed to have only pragmatic justification. German thinkers could afford to go deeper and further than their West European counterparts, for there was little likelihood that their systematic assaults on the state and the position of the individual within it would lead to anything other than a counter-argument. *Menschlichkeit*, perhaps best explained as the celebration of the universality and rationality of humanity, the theoretically uncon-

---

[62]Ismar Schorsch, *On the History of the Political Judgment of the Jew*, The Leo Baeck Memorial Lecture, 20, New York 1976, p. 13.

ditional equality and accordingly the rights and freedoms of and for all, this was the revolutionary contribution which a "classless" *Bürgertum* aspired to. There was, however, an implicit assumption that the *Mensch* or *homme* who was to be the beneficiary of the new era would be Christian and male. If he was not, then clearly an Aristotelian test of equality would have to be applied, that is to say, all human beings are equal unless reasons for unequal treatment can be shown to be justified. Hence it was both logical and necessary that the questions of women and Jews should be considered. This is not to say that either one or both categories were discussed systematically or even in the light of emerging Enlightenment concepts. In France Rousseau derived an inferior position for women from his naturalism[63] and expressed himself only casually on the subject of Jews. The Encyclopaedists (with one notable exception) were generally hostile and contemptuous towards both groups. Hertzberg has gone so far as to claim that: "Modern, secular anti-semitism was fashioned not as a reaction to the Enlightenment and the Revolution, but within the Enlightenment and Revolution themselves."[64] In Germany, the question of the position of women was not immediately part of the general debate. Lessing's determination to assert the principle of *Menschlichkeit* was first directed against the dominant theology of his day – it was natural therefore that inasmuch as he intended to challenge the hegemony of church theology as part of the political establishment, he should have concentrated his attention on questions of social class and religious toleration.[65]

With Lessing we have reached a sequence of personal relationships and events which will enable us to review the origins of the movements for the emancipation of women and Jews, though henceforth we will have to reverse the order we have followed so far because, historically, representations concerning the Jews preceded those for women. We will also attempt to show that the opposition to Jews and women had its roots in the demands for their emancipation. It is well known that Lessing's *Nathan der Weise* (1779), the first assertion of the *Menschlichkeit* of the Jew in Germany, owed much of its inspiration to his friendship with Moses Mendelssohn. Although it is now established that Lessing derived his Nathan from a figure in Boccaccio's *Decameron* it remains true that, as Altmann, put it, "Nathan without Mendelssohn would have been like Hamlet without the Prince of Denmark".[66] In that same year, 1779, François Hell published an attack on the Jews of Alsace, in which, among a rash of accusations, he described them as being a "state within a state", an accursed and criminal people.[67] Through their most distinguished member, Herz Cerf-

---

[63] Cf. the final section 'Sophy or Woman' in *Émile* (Everyman's edn. transl. by Barbara Foxley), London 1969 (1762).

[64] Arthur Hertzberg, *The French Enlightenment and the Jews*, Philadelphia 1968, p. 7.

[65] See for example W. Dilthey's essay on Lessing in *Das Erlebnis und die Dichtung, op. cit.*, and Elise Dosenheimer's *Das Deutsche Soziale Drama von Lessing bis Sternheim*, Konstanz 1949.

[66] Alexander Altmann, *Moses Mendelssohn. A Biographical Study*, London 1973, esp. pp. 569–582. Dilthey, *op. cit.*, mentions Boccaccio but not Mendelssohn.

[67] *Observations d'un Alsacien sur l'Affaire présente des Juifs d'Alsace*, Frankfurt a. Main 1779. See Altman, *op. cit.*, p. 449 ff., Katz, 'A State within a State', *loc. cit.*, p. 38, noted that Hell was the first to use the "state within a state" accusation about Jews, albeit in a very special sense. He also mentions Dohm but does not refer to the connection between Hell and Dohm via Mendels-

berr, the Jews of Alsace appealed to Mendelssohn for help. Mendelssohn in his turn, asked another friend, Christian Wilhelm von Dohm to help draft a 'Memoire' in reply to Hell. Though friendly with Mendelssohn, Dohm did not particularly like the Jews, but was a firm advocate of *Menschlichkeit*, which he regarded as synonymous with "true politics". However, as a result of his preparatory study for the 'Memoire' Dohm became interested in the subject of the Jews and like Max Weber he planned to make an extensive study of Jewish history, thought and culture from original sources.

Dohm combined political realism, a sense of absolute justice and an undogmatic deism. He showed considerable ability as a political economist and was particularly interested in the nature and characteristics of the then forcefully emerging *bürgerliche* society.

A combination of pressure of work and the magnitude of a project to study the history, thought and culture of the Jews from original sources, persuaded Dohm to abandon such an ambitious task in favour of a more immediate course of action. Instead, he decided to examine the position of Jews in his own time and in 1781 he published his famous *Über die bürgerliche Verbesserung der Juden*. Mention has already been made of Dohm's total commitment to the idea of *Menschlichkeit*, a humanitarian concept strongly shared at that time by scholars and civil servants.[68] There are those who see Dohm's effort as a tribute to Mendelssohn,[69] those who see him as pure altruist who wanted to generate social conditions in which Jews could enjoy the full benefits both of their religion and of citizenship in a host society,[70] those who see him as a calculating civil servant projecting his own assessment of state-interest[71] and finally an extreme view implying a Machiavellian calculation in which Jews are seen as an obstacle to universal equality and in which Dohm's plan for emancipation is a device to eliminate the Jewish presence.[72] On balance it is most likely that parts of all these separate views contributed to Dohm's thinking, though his primary mode of analysis also reflected the main geo-political considerations of Frederick II and his Civil Service. In 1768 Frederick II argued in his 'Political Testament' that "the first and truest principle which holds good everywhere is that the strength of a state consists in the number of its subjects."[73] Accordingly Frederick divided large peasant holdings into many small-holdings, he offered great incentives, especially to German-speaking, foreign colonists, paid their travel costs and provided farms and stock to give them a start. The notion of increasing the size of the population thus became a rationally derived and deliberate principle of social policy, even if in practice it was largely counterproductive.

---

sohn. Dohm (see below) refers twice to Hell's essay in his book *Über die bürgerliche Verbesserung der Juden*, Berlin–Stettin, pp. 60–61 (note) and p. 80, 2nd rev. edition.

[68]Dilthey, *op. cit.*, pp. 134–135.

[69]E.g., Altmann, *op. cit.*

[70]E.g., Willy Cohn, 'Christian Wilhelm von Dohm', in *Historia Judaica*, 13:2 (1951), pp. 101–108.

[71]E.g., Schorsch, *op. cit.*, p. 12.

[72]Gerson D. Cohen, 'German Jewry as a Mirror of Modernity', in *LBI Year Book XX* (1975), pp. IX–XXXI, esp. p. XV.

[73]Quoted by Brunschwig, *op. cit.*, p. 101.

While the indigenous peasantry, though essential to Prussia was grossly exploited by an all too frequently irresponsible aristocracy, so that peasants and skilled craftsmen emigrated to the Crimea or America, less stable foreign settlers received incentives to settle in Prussia. It appears very likely that the highly developed civil service – including Dohm – was unaware of the disfunctional processes in rural areas, because real increases in population did take place in towns, not only or even mainly from rural drift but as a result of a decreasing death rate. Yet the middle classes had neither the freedom of the market place nor the opportunities for entrepreneurship to create a sound economic base for themselves or to ensure their own security by providing employment and incomes for the growing unskilled and untrained labour force in the towns.

For all that, Dohm based his argument on the reasoning of Frederick II and argued that all states in Europe needed more population, that all of them were taking active steps to increase their populations, yet most states always made an exception of one class of people, the Jews. He set out in some detail the restrictions and discriminations Jews were subjected to and asked why states should thus deprive themselves of more population, and Jews of all rights, when the general trend was towards more liberal conditions for all. To answer this, he began by looking at the moral content of Judaism, starting with the law of Moses and explaining the evolution of the Jewish people and their religion. He agreed that Jews had developed a strong exclusivity to ensure their survival, but concluded that "all religious systems destroy the bonds that unite mankind [because] all religions deny rights to those who differ from them – if this is a natural consequence of all beliefs, then it cannot be a reason for withholding civil rights from adherents of one particular belief."[74] Furthermore, Dohm argued, "religious differences are not the only ones in civil society. There are social classes, guilds, countrymen and townsmen, soldiers and civilians, scholars and lay-people. Even within the religions there are sects and denominations." The task of the state is to allow all these categories to function, to prevent them from turning competition and action into dislike and discrimination, to enclose them in the greater harmony of the state. It should allow them to cherish their differences but ensure that each one is first and foremost a citizen.[75]

Dohm's first principle then is, that it is possible to be different but equal. His second principle is expressed in a famous phrase "The Jew is a human being more than he is a Jew." That is to say, whatever grounds may be put forward to justify the ill-treatment of a Jew, what matters is that he will respond as a human being. If he is hated, he will hate, if he is oppressed he will seek revenge. Dohm accepted that in their dealings with the Gentiles Jews were often corrupt and dishonest, but insisted that if they were, it was not because they were Jews, but because of the way in which Jews were treated. Any other human group, living under the same conditions, would react in like manner. To prove his point Dohm used historical evidence. Even after the destruction of Jewish political independence in 70 C.E. Jews were respected and respectable citizens

---

[74]Dohm, *op. cit.*, p. 24. In connection with this résumé of Dohm's treatise see also the analysis of H. D. Schmidt, 'The Terms of Emancipation', in *LBI Year Book I* (1956), pp. 28–33.
[75]Dohm, *op. cit.*, pp. 27–28.

of the Roman Empire. It was only with the rise of Christianity that they were systematically excluded from all areas of social and civil life, except in trade which was assigned to them because the Christians despised it. This argument led Dohm to an interesting analysis of the relationship between occupation and character. He was not concerned as he emphasised, with assigning blame, but in establishing cause and effect. Trade, through its intrinsic characteristics had an adverse effect on character. Jews had been compelled for centuries to engage exclusively in trade. As a result every Jewish child learned undesirable practices from its parents which influence character – it follows that trade corrupts Jews *not* that Jews corrupt trade. It further follows that by relieving Jews from having to engage in trade their original good character would be restored. Dohm advocated complete and immediate equal rights, full access to secular education and to all occupations albeit with some limitations on access to public offices. At the same time he insisted on the right of the Jews to extend any prescribed syllabus for secular education by adding whatever religious education they wanted for their children.

Dohm proved to be an acute observer and a lively analyst. While some of his insights concerning Jews were very probably gleaned from discussions with Moses Mendelssohn, others of a more general nature are reminiscent of a de Tocqueville,[76] or even the social analyses of Bruno Bauer and Karl Marx.[77] He has interesting comments on the strength of the Jewish family,[78] regards the "corruption" of the Jews as beyond doubt, even though he stressed that it was a consequence of their history,[79] and went so far as to suggest that this corruption was produced in the course of child rearing that is to say, an evolutionary sequence in which Jews chose dishonest trading methods in response to oppression and then transmitted these to their children as a *sine qua non* of survival.[80] Dohm was clearly in disagreement with Mendelssohn on the right of religious authorities to exclude members of the community for short periods or permanently – a principle to which Mendelssohn was strongly opposed while Dohm defended it with equal vigour.[81] Two further points are of particular interest. First, Dohm fully recognised that the traditional Jewish approach to education was inimical to any future assimilation or even integration. Accordingly he strongly advocated the displacement of non-allocative religious education in favour of a specific occupationally orientated (i.e., vocational) education.[82] Secondly, Dohm might be said to have anticipated the Jewish Reform Movement by his correct analysis of the likely effect of the introduction of civil rights on traditional Judaism. He argued that the state should make it its business to inform itself about Jews and weaken their isolation by fostering a general enlightenment and a general morality independent of all religion which would heighten the

---

[76]E.g. *L'ancien régime et la révolution*, 1856.
[77]E.g. Dohm's comments on the position of Jews in Poland. *op. cit.*, pp. 87–89.
[78]*Ibid.*, pp. 7 and 103.
[79]*Ibid.*, pp. 34 and 40.
[80]*Ibid.*, p. 117.
[81]*Ibid.*, p. 133.
[82]*Ibid.*, p. 129. For a fuller discussion of this issue see my essay in *Juden in der Deutschen Umwelt*, *op. cit.*

sensitivity of all. The resultant "civil contentment" in an orderly state and the enjoyment of long-withheld freedoms would disperse "religious rigidity". This is precisely what the rabbinic objections to the emancipation processes were about.[83]

The final part of Dohm's book dealt with objections which had been or might be put forward to his advocacy on behalf of the Jews. He would first state the objection in the form of a question or counter-argument and then "reply" to it.[84]

Dohm was a pioneer. He was the first person in Germany to present a reasoned case for granting Jews civil rights, for incorporating Jews into *Bürger* society, then emerging as the new social order, and by implication, for discarding traditional and feudal categories through which human beings were grouped and confined from birth, to fixed roles, rights, privileges and obligations in the body-politic. Instead he defended a system in which each man would progress through his own volition to achieve and acquire according to his abilities and efforts. The publication of Dohm's treatise did not lead to any immediate action but henceforth the problem was open. If it was not solved neither was it possible ever again to set it aside or to ignore the force of Dohm's argument. His work was to have yet another effect – though for Dohm probably entirely unexpected – it led directly to an application of his mode of analysis, his reasoning and his conclusions to the question of the emancipation of women. Before we turn our attention to that other civil servant who followed in the footsteps of Dohm on behalf of women, we will have to rehearse briefly the social background of the most radical, most challenging and most completely forgotten contribution to the evolution of human rights.

IV

Enlightenment was about reason and *Bürgertum* was about virtues. Enlightenment challenged all authority, *Bürgertum* aspired to be authority. Enlightenment could contemplate the idea of anarchy secure in the belief that reason would prevail, *Bürgertum* was bent on order and looked askance at anything which might disturb the tranquillity of virtuous living. As yet the lower social classes had no place in political processes and aberrant aristocracy was useful, even in its excesses, as a fearful example of the costliness of vice. Debating the position of Jews was gratifying and wholesome, not least because it enabled the citizenry to bear witness to good Samaritanism while relying on an articulate and aggressive clergy, drawn from the ranks of the middle classes, to defend and uphold a dominant Christianity and its faithful adherents – the *Bürger* of Germany.[85] Women presented an altogether different problem, even though the original debate may have started from the same premises as that about the Jews, namely

[83]Dohm, *op. cit.*, p. 28.
[84]*Ibid.*, from p. 140.
[85]An excellent example is Friedrich Schleiermacher, the suave, broadminded friend of Jews (or better, Jewishness) who, for all that, disdainfully rejected Judaism as "the distasteful manifestation of a mechanical movement from which life and spirit have long since departed". *Über die Religion* (Kröner), Leipzig n.d. [1799], p. 209.

that all human beings are equal, that all human beings have reason and that all human beings have rights. Our period is still the era of absolutism and enlightened despotism, an era in which the king was absolute master in the state and man was absolute master in the house, always despot, only occasionally enlightened.[86] A change in the position of women would affect every home, every family, every marital relationship. If it was inevitable that Enlightenment would raise the question of the status of women, it was equally inevitable that *Bürgertum* would somehow obliterate it. It happened in France, it happened in England and it happened in Germany. And for all the differences in social, economic and cultural conditions in these countries, it happened at the same time, though not as responses to the same challenges.

In France it was the women of the aristocracy whose behaviour outraged the people and helped to stoke the fires which led to the Revolution.[87] Memoirs of the period describe the activities of upper-class ladies, their grace, frivolity, insensitivity and sentimentality. With the advent of the Revolution, a swell of protests arose side by side with the process of demoralisation. The National Assembly in France was bombarded with pamphlets, leaflets and petitions from women[88] demanding formal recognition of the right to education for girls. Talleyrand's verdict, delivered in 1791 is of considerable interest. He argued that education for girls should be limited because it raised the question whether women were citizens. He accepted that it must seem contradictory to the ideals of the Revolution to give women less than full equality, to exclude half the human race from constitutional benefits, but, he argued, it must be considered that the purpose of all state institutions was the greatest happiness of the greatest number and the exclusion of women from full rights was a means to increase the happiness of both sexes, therefore it must be accepted. Since it was the objective of education to raise boys to citizenship, and nature had destined women to be confined to the home to rear children, and since defiance of nature could only lead to unhappiness, education for boys and girls could not be equal.

With that statement, the women of France and their contribution to the Revolution had been written off. Mary Wollstencroft and Theodor Hippel were still to reply to it, but the only substantive French call for the emancipation of women made by Jean Antoin Condorcet (1743–1794) was as effectively eliminated as he himself was to be a couple of years later. Condorcet, a mathematician and the last of the Encyclopaedists published his article *Sur l'Admission des Femmes au Droit de Cité* in 1790, perhaps the first reasoned argument to be issued in that period. In it he insisted that the principle of equality established by the Revolution had been damaged because half the human race had been denied

---

[86] Theobald Ziegler, *Die geistigen und sozialen Strömungen des neunzehnten Jahrhunderts*, Berlin 1899, p. 561.

[87] According to August Bebel, *Die Frau und der Sozialismus*, Berlin–Bonn–Bad Godesberg 1977, (1881), pp. 87–92, and Franz Mehring, *Zur Preussischen Geschichte vom Mittelalter bis Jena*, Berlin 1930, p. 242, aristocratic women in Prussia behaved in much the same way as those in France, but they may have been biased or have exaggerated.

[88] It is difficult to understand why a present day feminist should have written off French feminists of the period of the Revolution as "female hooligans" and "men's women". Cf. Constance Rover, *Love, Morals and the Feminists*, London 1970, p. 12.

the right to share in the legislative process. To justify this it would be necessary to show not only that natural law for women differed from that for men, but also that women were incapable of carrying out civic duties. Since a woman is as human as a man, she must have the same natural law, for either there is no such thing as natural law, or it applies to every human being irrespective of sex, religion or race. Condorcet rejected the argument based on the physical differences of the sexes. He could not see why pregnancy or any other temporary physical disabilities should prevent women from exercising their civil rights any more than a sick man was prevented from doing so. If it is argued that women have not contributed anything to science or shown signs of genius, then the answer must be that civil rights have never been linked with intelligence. Even if claims of inferior education or inferior powers of judgment are put forward, they do not constitute an argument for denying women political rights, for if they did, a free constitution would be impossible and all government would have to be confined to a small body of able and educated men. If there were legitimate complaints about shortcomings in women, they would be likely to be the consequences of their social conditions. There were some objections said to be based on practical grounds – that women would have too much influence on men – as if open influence were not preferable to a secret one – that women would neglect home and children – yet no one has expressed fears that men going to work would neglect their families. In any event many women do not have small children and voting takes up much less time than most leisure activities. Such practical arguments had always been used to justify tyranny. Condorcet argued his case on grounds of reason and justice but found no response in France.

In England, Mary Wollstencroft's *Vindication*[89] was a direct response to the self-indulgent prescription for the education of girls by Rousseau, the exclusiveness of Thomas Paine's *Rights of Man* and the casual arrogance with which Talleyrand, to whom her book is in fact dedicated, dismissed equal education – and with it equal rights for women – in the French National Assembly. Accordingly, she concentrated on the question of education, entirely agreed that the women of her day were not ready for full civil rights, that as a result of the treatment they had received at the hands of men over the ages they were corrupt, sly and deceitful, but that with full and equal education, they would prove to be fully equal to the burdens and duties of citizenship and, more importantly, of motherhood. Mary Wollstencroft was a rebellious rather than a radical person. Her book is full of political asides on many issues, but shows little awareness of the problems of girls of the lower classes. Her analysis was well received and her main thesis was widely accepted. The book was translated immediately into both French and German (1793).

Writing almost simultaneously with Mary Wollstencroft, Theodor Gottlieb von Hippel (1741–1796) published his contribution to the "woman-question" in the same year in which Christian Gotthilf Salzmann's translation of Mary Wollstencroft's *Vindication* appeared. Hippel's essay *Über die bürgerliche Verbes-*

---

[89] *A Vindication of the Rights of Women*, London 1792. The book is well-known and has been analysed too often recently to warrant detailed discussion here.

*serung der Weiber*⁹⁰ was written because he felt that "although women carried the banner of the French Revolution it did not change their position".⁹¹ There can be no doubt that the real inspiration of and model for his work was Dohm's *Über die bürgerliche Verbesserung der Juden*. There is no reference to Dohm by name, but apart from one direct reference there are arguments, comments and replications of modes of analysis which establish the relationship between the two essays. To begin with there is the title itself. Hippel also posed a question: "In our own time the civil improvement of Jews has been strongly advocated – should a real people of God deserve less attention than a so-called one?"⁹² Dohm's book might be considered to have been effective, at least in the sense that it led to civil rights for Jews in France. Hippel therefore criticised the new French constitution for according civil rights to a tiny minority while ignoring the rights of half the nation.⁹³ Dohm had centred his argument on Prussia's need for population but mere numbers, countered Hippel, were of no use to a state. It needs the right type of *Kolonisten*⁹⁴ and what better solution to the population problem than giving the other sex the rights which would make them part of the people. Dohm had made a point of showing how the Jews could aspire to no more than a tolerated position as *Schutzjuden*. Women, Hippel argued, because they had no civil rights, were not citizens but merely *Schutzverwandte*.⁹⁵ Dohm demonstrated how Jews gradually became the object of discriminatory legislation in Roman law and how this was transmitted to the rest of Europe. Hippel demonstrated the same process concerning women.⁹⁶ "The Jew" Dohm had asserted, "is a human being more than he is a Jew."⁹⁷ "Where freedom is suppressed," wrote Hippel, "nothing that is and is called human can flourish,"⁹⁸ and he called on men to "let those whom God created as humans – be human." Dohm explained how the "evil done to Jews is used as a justification for doing it." Hippel too argued that in the case of women "Man creates needs and then asserts that it is precisely those needs which make male dominance essential."⁹⁹

There are many more indications that Hippel was familiar with Dohm's work and that he intended his essay to be a companion call for another oppressed category in society, but enough has been mentioned to substantiate the relationship.¹⁰⁰

Theodor Gottlieb von Hippel was born in East Prussia and began his studies

---

⁹⁰First published 1793, though Herrmann, *op. cit.*, gives its publication year as 1792. A new edition was issued recently by Syndikat of Frankfurt a. Main 1977 which is the text I have used; p. 123 of that edition makes it clear that Hippel wrote early in 1792.
⁹¹Hippel, *op. cit.*, p. 107.
⁹²*Ibid.*, pp. 20–21.
⁹³*Ibid.*, p. 121.
⁹⁴Hippel took the somewhat unusual term "Kolonisten" directly from Dohm.
⁹⁵Hippel, *op. cit.*, p. 66.
⁹⁶*Ibid.*, pp. 82–86.
⁹⁷Dohm, *op. cit.*, p. 28.
⁹⁸Hippel, *op. cit.*, pp. 81 and 131.
⁹⁹Dohm, *op. cit.*, p. 34; Hippel, *op. cit.*, p. 69.
¹⁰⁰I am not aware of any previous attempt to link the two essays.

at Königsberg University at the age of 16.[101] In 1780 he was appointed Mayor and Chief of Police of Königsberg and in 1786 he was promoted to the rank of *Geheimer Kriegsrat* and President of the city of Königsberg. He was the uncle of a famous nephew of the same name who made his reputation as the author of a call to Prussia, *An mein Volk*.[102]

Hippel's essay was not well received when it was published, in fact it was so radical and so far ahead of its time that even a century later, a strong feminist movement in Germany did not really know how to handle such an absolute demand for total equality and preferred the more innocuous and moderate tract by John Stuart Mill. Nevertheless Hippel ought to be regarded as a major influence on the evolution of thought in Germany, if not directly through his published work then through his personal associations with men like Kant, Hamann, Jean Paul and at least indirectly through Fichte.[103]

Hippel introduced his essay with a short chapter designed to read like an address to a national assembly (presumably as a reply to Talleyrand). He reminded his readers that human beings were able to control their destinies to a considerable extent, because "when nature began to fashion man, she left most of the process in our own hands, so as to share with us the honour of creation".[104] At the time he was writing he felt that too much was being changed without being improved. Many women found their situation intolerable – they did not object to being women but to the way in which they were treated. It was not his intention to lead women from slavery, only to encourage them to achieve their own freedom. Nor was he calling on women to become manly, he merely wanted every man and woman to have the right to develop his or her true self.

Hippel deliberately avoided any discussion of sexual issues in order to stress that his primary concern was the presentation of the case for women as human beings. Hence he began with a question in his next chapter: "Are there differences between men and women apart from sex?" He regarded women (represented by the Biblical Eve) as having led men (Adam) not to sin but to reason, Eve "broke the chains of instinct which suppressed reason",[105] and thereby initiated "the first revolution" successfully. Given such a role, it followed for Hippel that "Nature, in creating the sexes, did not intend to establish a real difference between them, least of all to favour one at the expense of the other ... (What might have induced nature to honour and glorify half its greatest creation and neglect and deny the other half ... ?)"[106]

Like Dohm in the case of Jews, Hippel conceded that constant oppression had destroyed women's sense of freedom and their faith in themselves, but this would last only as long as women continued to be oppressed. The law, he noted, which hypocritically restricted the civil rights of women, ostensibly in their own interests and to compensate for their supposed weakness quickly forgot about

---

[101]Cf. Theodor Hönes, *Theodor Gottlieb von Hippel. Die Persönlichkeit und die Werke in ihrem Zusammenhang*, Bonn 1910.
[102]Theodor Bach, *Theodor Gottlieb von Hippel. Der Verfasser des Aufrufs 'An mein Volk'*, Breslau 1863.
[103]Cf. Bach, *op. cit.*, p. 6.
[104]Hippel, *op. cit.*, p. 16.
[105]*Ibid.*, p. 24.
[106]*Ibid.*, p. 26.

weakness when it came to questions of crime and punishment. Here both sexes were treated with complete equality. So too, when it comes to sin the church does not distinguish between men and women." Justice has had her blindfold removed because the law denies women rights of person and property but holds them fully accountable for all laws pertaining to the state and the ruler."[107] If men claim superiority over women, how did this come about? To answer this question, Hippel presented an elaborate evolutionary-anthropological account of the history of mankind,[108] in which he credited women with inventing the storage of food (the second revolution) and animal husbandry. Man, thus freed to develop his physical strength and his powers as hunter and fighter took advantage of this. "Thus woman came to command domestic animals and before she knew what had happened she had become one herself."[109] Hippel concluded that the superiority of men is a result of evolutionary circumstances and not evidence of greater mental powers. There was no reason to suppose that, if women were to be given freedom they would abuse it and if they did, they will have been enticed to it by men.[110] On the question of modesty (*Schamhaftigkeit*) a concept destined to be of great importance in subsequent years,[111] Hippel was equally uncompromising. If modesty is a virtue, he argued, then it resides in marriage, and if it is not practised by both sexes it is no more than a pretentious game.

Hippel was led to speculate on why men on the one hand assign so much importance to their occupations whilst denying women the right to choose theirs. "When will the choice of occupation cease to be the royal prerogative of men?"[112] In a particularly interesting passage, Hippel anticipated events when he suggested that men of the upper classes "would face a war" from their enlightened women and anticipated Marx when he argued that among the lower classes differences between the sexes were little more than a biological reality. Socially they shared the same fate.[113] A direct result of the continued oppression of women was their greater appetite for revolution. While men prefer that to which they are accustomed, women prefer that which is new.[114] The largest section of Hippel's essay is devoted to 'Suggestions for Improvement'. The demand is for emancipation,[115] because "The time is gone when women could be persuaded that as minors they are better off ... any freedom is better than the most comfortable slavery."[116] Women had rights and Hippel proclaimed

---

[107]*Ibid.*, p. 47.
[108]This was very much in the tradition of Enlightenment, cf. Pappe, *op. cit.*, p. 93.
[109]Hippel, *op. cit.*, p. 60.
[110]*Ibid.*, p. 92.
[111]Fichte made it a central factor of femininity, see below.
[112]Hippel, *op. cit.*, p. 105.
[113]This was one of the main arguments of the 'Communist Manifesto' of 1848. *MEW*, 4, Berlin 1959, p. 469.
[114]Hippel, *op. cit.*, p. 112.
[115]According to J. Katz, the term "emancipation" was not used in a Jewish context until the 1830s. Hippel used it here in 1792 (*op. cit.*, p. 119) see also J. Katz 'The Term "Jewish Emancipation": Its Origin and historical Impact', in A. Altmann (ed.), *Studies in Nineteenth-Century Jewish Intellectual History*, London 1965.
[116]Hippel, *op. cit.*, p. 119.

these in mock defiance of an imaginary tradition-bound, male-dominated French National Assembly. "Why should a woman not be a person?" If, according to the Bible, women are "bones of our bones, flesh of our flesh, why not citizens like us?"[117] "Why the difference in the education of the two sexes" when both have the same origins, are made of the same substance and are destined to share the same fate.[118] The only acceptable solution would be for "Honour, rights and rewards to become consequences of personal achievement, not sex-bound privileges, and to allow women to become persons and citizens."[119] Like Dohm, Hippel set up his own objections to his arguments in order to anticipate and reject criticism which might be made against him. Some of these "defences" certainly are pungent and to the point and have a remarkably modern ring. If, for example, it is objected that women cannot be given freedom because their task is to educate their children Hippel replied, "Is it only the duty of women, do not the children belong to the father too and should he not share in rearing them?"[120] His final dramatic statement sums up his long argument. "Only a denial of reason can suppress the truth that that which is equally human is equally rational."[121]

There can be little doubt that of all the material written about women from the French Revolution to the emergence of "Women's Liberation" in the 1960s, none has remained more topical and more radical than Hippel's appeal for equal rights for women. As has been suggested, it is most likely that its very radicalism explains the almost total lack of response from any generation to Hippel's exercise. For all generations except the present one Hippel went too far, and for the present generation his arguments are now self-evident, and Hippel suspected that he might be ignored.[122] In their different ways, the call for the emancipation of Jews and its derivative, the call for the emancipation of women, both failed. Why should this have been so?

V

By the end of the eighteenth century Enlightenment had given way to Romanticism, the emancipation of women was almost forgotten until women themselves made it an issue after the Revolution of 1848 and opposition to the emancipation of Jews had gathered so much momentum that by 1815 it had been effectively halted. Although discussions about Jews continued unabated, with increasing participation from Jews themselves, they remained a tolerated element in Germany until 1869.

Among the more striking features of the Romanticism which descended upon

---

[117] *Ibid.*, p. 131.
[118] *Ibid.*, p. 132.
[119] *Ibid.*, p. 143.
[120] *Ibid.*, p. 218.
[121] *Ibid.*, p. 248.
[122] *Ibid.*, pp. 250–252. After this volume had gone to press, Wayne State University Press announced the first English version of Hippel's essay by T. F. Sellner: *On Improving the Status of Women*, Detroit 1979.

Western Europe was firstly that it should have affected countries as diverse economically and industrially as England, France and Germany. Secondly that women and Jews who, in some measure were victims of Romanticism, should also have participated in its spread[123] and thirdly, that in the framework into which we have placed our discussion, Romanticism represents the victory of *Bürgerlichkeit* over Enlightenment's more broadly conceived *Menschlichkeit*. The rationality proclaimed by Enlightenment was absolute and universal, but *Bürgertum* intent on virtue rather than reason chose to give its rationality a purely instrumental dimension, enough to further economic interests but without undermining the social order. In Germany the advent of Romanticism appears almost like a conspiracy against women. Philosophers and theologians, writers and artists, combined to create a new climate, a new feminine ideal.[124] Education was decried, virtue elevated, motherhood was sanctified and the home sentimentalised. The family was projected as nothing less than a miniature state – and just as God presided over the universe and the King over the fatherland, so the father presided over the home, a place of order, of security – and of *Gemütlichkeit*. *Gemüt* was the new key to happiness – women, said Schleiermacher, were "the most perceptive readers of worthwhile literature because they still used their imagination. Nothing can be grasped by intelligence (*Verstand*) only that which is internalised through the emotions (*das Gemüterfasste*) becomes truly one's own."[125] The tone was the key – nothing as crude as the French Civil Code of 1804 which firmly restored the patriarchal father to his former glory – there was a wooing of womanhood. The calculated absence of Eros in the sober debates of Enlightenment was displaced by a tacit, if appropriately modest, consent to pleasure – just so long as it was pleasure celebrated in the home. After the battle of Jena the revitalised housewife becomes a *Deutsche Frau*. To her lover she is not just woman, but German womanhood. The model for this ideal is Queen Louise, the woman who is at once housewife and queen, mother and princess. She suffers for and on behalf of her beloved country and her early death fosters a legend. Novalis gives the legend the image of housewifeliness. Duty, for women and girls is the faithful execution of menial tasks with the dignity of a queen, the absolute submission to man the master, the expression of love through self-denial. Kleist's *Kätchen von Heilbronn* is prototypical of all that is woman and German. Her image fuses with that of the late queen – the obedient maid in the home, the spiritual freedom of servile and adoring love, the mystique of majesty and fatherland.[126] As Eichendorff would have it – a girl's soul is not created for herself but solely for her lover. The recompense is coined by Börne who confirmed that, "The female is citizen in the Kingdom of love." Perhaps the greatest irony was the passionate devotion with

---

[123]The most vivid examples are the Berlin Salons where Goethe was idolised and Schleiermacher lionised.

[124]Philosophers are discussed below, for writers and artists see for example Ernst Heilborn, *Zwischen zwei Revolutionen. Der Geist der Schinkelzeit 1789–1848*, Berlin 1927, esp. pp. 136–144; Ziegler, *op. cit.*, pp. 560–567; and Michael Mitterauer und Reinhard Sieder, *Vom Patriarchat zur Partnerschaft. Zum Strukturwandel der Familie*, München 1977, esp. p. 40.

[125]Quoted by Heilborn, *op. cit.*, p. 137.

[126]Ziegler, *op. cit.*, p. 565.

which Jewish women of the upper social strata dedicated themselves to the spread of romantic idealism while their men withdrew into the more sober world of enlightened rationality.[127]

Implicit in the highly emotional presentation of true femininity is a rejection of the enlightened approach to a socio-political equality of the sexes and the renewed quest for a deeper and ennobling analysis of the essence of womanhood. In this sense, the search for revitalised yet conservative enrichment of traditional values is a repetition of earlier and simultaneous attempts to find an appropriate solution to the vexed problem of the rationally incontrovertible claims for Jewish emancipation. In his dispute with Moses Mendelssohn, Johann Georg Hamann made the supremacy of faith his central argument and justification for rejecting the Jews, though he claimed to have a deep respect for Judaism and to be motivated solely by his determination to penetrate to the essence of things.[128] Although, as we shall see, it was Fichte who was to provide the intellectual justification for the exclusion of Jews and women from the corpus politicus, Jews themselves contributed towards subsequent delays in realising their emancipation. This is well illustrated by the famous incident of the letter to Teller which David Friedländer published in 1799[129] and which offered a partial acceptance of Christianity by Jews in return for full civil rights.[130] The "semi-Christian" envisaged by Friedländer had all the characteristics of the subservient woman – both were the dreams, the visions and the victims of a romantic, all-engulfing *Bürgertum*.

It would seem reasonable to argue that the emancipation question for women and Jews had its first phase in the final quarter of the eighteenth century, that it was inspired and initiated by Enlightenment and that it was brought to an abrupt end by Romanticism. We might also note here that the second phase had quite a different character in that the Jewish question was politicised by fierce oppositions from both left and right (i.e., "Christian State" and materialistic conceptions)[131] while for the *Frauenfrage* sharply delineated class differences created separate and internally opposed movements pursuing independent goals in their quest for solutions.[132]

---

[127]Cf. Michael A. Meyer, *The Origins of the Modern Jew. Jewish Identity and European Culture in Germany 1749–1824*, Detroit 1967, pp. 86–90.
[128]For details of the dispute see Altmann's Biography of Mendelssohn, *op. cit.* and Rengstorf's masterly chapter in K. H. Rengstorf und S. von Kortzfleisch (eds.), *Kirche und Synagoge. Handbuch zur Geschichte von Christen und Juden*, Stuttgart 1970, vol. II, esp. p. 160 – W. Dantine's chapter is also highly relevant. Hamann was an important member of the circle around Kant to which Hippel also belonged.
[129]Rengstorf und von Kortzfleisch, *op. cit.*, pp. 161–163.
[130]Cf. I. Jost (who knew Friedländer and had discussed the "letter" with him) described it as an attempt "die Herstellung eines vom Glauben nicht weiter bedingten *Menschenthums* zu erreichen" in *Geschichte des Judenthums und seiner Sekten*, Pt. III, Leipzig 1859, p. 318. See also M. A. Meyer, *op. cit.*, pp. 75–76.
[131]I have discussed the second phase in some detail in *Karl Marx and the Radical Critique of Judaism*.
[132]Cf. Georg Schwägler, *Soziologie der Familie. Ursprung und Entwicklung*, 2nd edn., Tübingen 1975, pp. 77–81. It will be apparent that in looking at women and Jews I have come to a two-phase conception like Simon Dubnow, *Weltgeschichte des Jüdischen Volkes*, Berlin 1928, vol. 8, pp. 69–73, but that Dubnow's phases have a narrower structure because they deal only with Jewish emancipation.

It would also be reasonable to argue that in each case there was deeply felt concern, that women and Jews would isolate themselves or remain isolated unless they were either emancipated or brought under absolute control. Jews, to a considerable extent always had been "a state within a state", certainly in so far as they had operated internal communal infrastructures which carried substantial degrees of autonomy. For women there was an assumption that in ancient days women lived and worked in groups,[133] and Montesquieu, as we have seen, accused them of being "a state within a state". The idea that women would and could separate themselves also occurs as late as 1848 when Marx and Engels made contrasting bourgeois and proletarian *Weibergemeinschaften* an important element in their discussion.[134] We might speculate that this fear may have played a part in determining the hostile attitude of the French National Assembly towards half the population of France – its women, when it is recalled that a similar fear relating to Jews was clearly expressed in the famous incident on 23rd December 1789 when Deputy Clermont-Tonnerre told the Assembly: "To the Jews as a nation we must deny everything, to the Jews as individuals everything is to be granted . . . we cannot have a nation within a nation . . ."[135] This was an echo of women as a state within a state as Montesquieu described them. It may well be that the fear of women united as a group deprived them of their rights in France. That fear was greatly muted in relation to the Jews, because, as the speaker said, if the Jews want to be a group, let them leave France – he could hardly have issued such a challenge to women.

A third conclusion we might draw from our review is that our period becomes more comprehensible if we accept that Enlightenment and *Bürgertum* were not simply simultaneous or sequential cultural manifestations but opposed to each other and in continuous conflict whenever and wherever they converged in social or cultural situations. No figure illustrates this better, no thinker did more to help Romanticism overcome the sobriety of Enlightenment and it may be reasonable to suggest that few thinkers, before Marx, appealed so strongly to the people, as did Johann Gottlieb Fichte. As a philosopher Fichte was wholly committed to the ethical individualism of German idealist philosophy. He was an admirer of Kant, and a staunch opponent of the somewhat naïve naturalism of Rousseau. Before we consider the method by which Fichte enabled his countrymen to reject the emancipation of women and Jews, we might briefly consider his particular style, which inspired great confidence as a *Wissenschaftslehre* and was therefore regarded as entirely "objective". It also had great charm and a disarming dignity – so much so that even a shrewd feminist like Marianne Weber could not conceal an unmistakable admiration for the man who convinced Germany that marriage was and had to be an act of absolute surrender of the woman to her husband.[136] Whenever Fichte made a harsh judgment he managed to add a kindly comment or to confuse his detractors, by stressing high moral or other qualities of those he denigrated. He must have appealed strongly

---

[133]Hippel, *op. cit.*, p. 44.
[134]*MEW, op. cit.*, vol. 4, pp. 478–479.
[135]Dubnow, *op. cit.*, p. 94.
[136]Marianne Weber, *op. cit.*; she is probably the most knowledgeable analyst of Fichte's work among German feminists.

to the *Bürger* of his period because his "science" is riddled with moral axioms which in turn are cleverly elevated *Bürger* virtues. At any rate Fichte displayed an assiduously cultivated ambivalence towards controversial subjects and can still be interpreted in very different ways. Jacob Katz for example, in commenting on Fichte's famous passage on Judaism as "a state within a state" clearly sees Fichte as "imbued with the traditional antisemitic attitudes"[137] and claimed that Fichte depicted the Jews "as a dangerous sub-group incurably corrupt and corrupting".[138] This may well be the way in which Fichte was read and used, but it is not what he wrote. His comments about Jews are in fact full of contradictions, but in addition to his hostile comments, he also, like Dohm, emphasised that the Jew was human and had to have human rights, though he denied them civil rights because he regarded Jewishness as an inherent characteristic, which made it impossible for the Jew to accept the virtues and ideas of German *Bürgertum*. Further, Fichte's comments on Jews should be set against his comments on that other "fearful state" the military. The method is identical. Soldiers are described as "raw semi-barbarians", ignorant, violent and a menace to decent citizens. A footnote then praises the manliness, decisiveness, courage and sociability of the educated officer corps for whom Fichte expressed his sincerest admiration.[139]

The same principle underlies Fichte's analysis of marriage and the position of women though this is treated much more comprehensively and with considerable perspicacity. It is likely that Fichte's starting point was the abstract and dispassionate analysis of Kant.[140] Kant stipulated a *Geschlechtsgemeinschaft*. The problem, as defined by him lies in the nature of the relationship between man and wife and in the way they use each other in their sexual association. For Kant there are three basic principles here. First that marriage is fundamentally a sexual association, second that marriage is an *a priori* condition for human sexual relations and third that men and women have equally strong and equally valid claims on each other based on their identical sex drives.[141] Nevertheless Kant regarded it as proper and self-evident that the law should regard man as the master and require the woman to obey him because the man is the source of the couple's property and the common interests of both require him to assume a commanding posture, a duty arising directly from the unity and equality of the couple.[142]

---

[137]J. Katz, 'A State within a State', *loc. cit.*, p. 45. Perhaps Katz felt some distaste for Fichte, since he appears to have misunderstood an important sentence. Where Fichte wrote "daß dieser Staat auf den Hass des ganzen menschlichen Geschlechts aufgebaut ist . . ." Katz has "The hatred of the Jew *by* the entire human race . . ." (my emphasis). Cf. J. G. Fichte, *Beitrag zur Berichtigung der Urteile des Publikums über die französische Revolution*, Hamburg 1973 (1793), p. 114 and J. Katz, *loc. cit.*, p. 44.

[138]*Ibid.*, p. 45.

[139]Fichte, *Beitrag, op. cit.*, pp. 116–117. That is why Fichte offered two drastic alternatives for Jews. Either they would have to be given "new heads devoid of any Jewish ideas" or their homeland would have to be restored to them so that they could live there independently. *Ibid.*, p. 115.

[140]Immanuel Kant, *Metaphysik der Sitten*, Hamburg 1966 (1922), probably written 1785 first publ. 1797, pp. 92–95 and 190–191.

[141]*Ibid.*, p. 191.

[142]*Ibid.*, pp. 93–94.

Fichte's analysis is very much more elaborate and, in the context of his period, more reassuring. Beginning with the same premises as Kant he argued that both in nature and in reason marriage is an end in itself (*Selbstzweck*).[143] In its natural dimension it is the obvious method of satisfying sexual needs (with the production of children only as a possible consequence, not a primary purpose) and at the moral level (*sittlich*), it is the only rational method of satisfying sexual needs which will also, at the same time ennoble the participants. Man and woman are complete equals as moral beings in that they possess reason and ethical freedom though there are physical differences which affect their relationship, especially in that the male is active while the female is passive (*leidend*).

Only woman has an innate capacity for love, in man it is an acquired trait, and through it woman is restored to equality with man even at natural level. In "giving herself" to the man she loves, she protects her human dignity even though the act reduces her to an object, because her submission has been elevated into a freely offered sacrifice to the beloved man and is not regarded by her as a result of her own desires. Woman renounces her rights (including of course all political rights) and all her property to be with the man she loves. None of this can, in any way, be enforced by the husband. In doing so he would seriously impair her freedom, her own imperative wish and will. On the contrary, the man can only respond to his wife's act of submission with "magnanimity" (*Grossmut*).[144] Through her love he will learn to love, through her selfless devotion, each will want to relinquish his personality to allow that of the other to be supreme.[145]

Having thus established that the natural and moral purpose of marriage is realised by the complete subjection of the woman, it follows that the state can cease to regard her, judicially, as a person. Through marriage she becomes identical with her husband, who in turn becomes her legal guardian and representative. He takes all that is hers into legal ownership. He has a public and a private life. She has only a private and domestic life. The question of civil rights does not therefore arise. The woman enjoys civil rights through her husband and even expresses her political views by discussing questions with her husband who would give voice to them in the public sphere.

Fichte thus transmuted the authoritarianism of the patriarchal family, the self-satisfied convictions of *Bürgertum*, the dreams of artists and the fantasies of immature adolescents into a "scientifically" grounded theory of human relations. In an additional section[146] he now, rather smugly, demolished the claims of "a few women and some of their self-appointed advocates" (*unberufene Schutzredner*), that women had no civil rights.[147] As usual Fichte began by asserting that the question whether the woman had equal rights in the state can only be regarded as superfluous. To raise the question meant to question whether women *per se* were the equals of men and that, to him, was never in doubt. Only

---

[143] J. G. Fichte, *Grundlage des Naturrechts nach Prinzipien der Wissenschaftslehre*, Hamburg 1960 (1796), p. 298 ff.
[144] *Ibid.*, p. 307.
[145] *Ibid.*, p. 308.
[146] *Ibid.*, pp. 339–349.
[147] The structure of Fichte's argument here strongly suggests that he was replying to Hippel.

the extent to which women might want to exercise their civil rights could be an issue. A woman is either under the control of her father – in which case her legal position is no different from that of a young man. Or, she is married, in which case, as Fichte had already shown at length, she would not want to exercise civil rights other than through her husband and could not do so without losing her dignity. The only women who would claim a right to civil rights would be those who were not content with having their civil rights publicised through their husbands, but who additionally, want it known that they have exercised them, i.e., those "seeking fame in life and after their death".[148] In doing so women relinquish the attractive modesty of womanhood for a contemptible vanity. Nevertheless Fichte saw no problem, if a woman exercised her civil rights publicly if her husband, for one reason or another, was unable to do so himself, and he followed a biblical prescription that widows and divorced women had a proper claim to share civil rights and to exercise them in the same way as a man.[149] Fichte also demolished three central issues raised by Hippel and also by Mary Wollstencroft. First, that if women had "always" or for a very long time, been subjected by men then this was not an act of oppression but evidence of a need for such a relationship, secondly that women had never been deprived of education as a form of culture, but only of vocational training for roles they could not occupy anyway and thirdly, that women could not be eligible for public office because of their innate tendency to love which disqualified them from giving complete loyalty to both a husband and an office.

At this point Fichte's argument was conducted at the same level as that on Jews. His particular style of stressing the rights of those he is reducing to subservience or rejection combined the right note for a Germany longing for the secure values of the Middle Ages and fearful and suspicious of the irreversible changes which the modern world was threatening. Fichte thus became the man who enabled Germany to cling to its traditions and values and still regard itself as being thoroughly modern because its values were "scientific".

We have suggested that the opening phase of the emancipation of Jews in Germany in the last quarter of the eighteenth century could be usefully explored if we stipulate that German *Bürgertum* as yet untouched by the industrial revolution which changed England, and influenced intellectually but not practically by the political revolution in France, was an incoherent movement, which in the main was opposed to and in conflict with Enlightenment. That the simultaneous, if hitherto unconnected onset of the emancipation of Jews and women was regarded as a part of the same social process and that the collapse of both movements at the end of the century marked the complete, if temporary, victory of German *Bürgertum*. Symbolically we might describe our analysis as being exemplified and indeed encapsulated by two literary events which shattered the internal cohesion of German *Bürgertum*. In 1779 our era opened with the publication of Lessing's *Nathan der Weise* which caused a furore because

---

[148] *Ibid.*, p. 342.
[149] A woman's vows can be nullified by her father if she is single or by her husband if she is married, but if she is a widow or divorced her vows must stand. Cf. *Numbers* 30:2–17, esp. 10

it conveyed the message that the Jew was human and entitled to be regarded as an equal. This was resolved by a gradual assumption that it was only *a* Jew, Moses Mendelssohn, who should be seen in this way and who was entirely accepted accordingly. In 1799 Friedrich Schlegel caused a scandal with the publication of *Lucinde*, a novel which was to herald a new relationship between men and women, but which was shrugged off eventually as the unpleasant revelation of the improper adventures of just one woman – the daughter of the self-same Mendelssohn, who was for long remembered mainly as an unfaithful wife.[150] There must have been much satisfaction in the realisation that with *Lucinde* the essential unsuitability of both women and Jews to be accepted as equal citizens, received unexpected but wholly convincing justification.

[150]The fact that it was Mendelssohn's adulterous daughter who was the central figure of *Lucinde*, is well illustrated by Heine who viciously attacked the novel as "unzüchtige Nichtigkeit" and "liederlich romantisch". On at least three occasions he referred to the personal histories of the main figures in the most contemptuous terms. See *Heines Werke*, Berlin–Weimar 1968, vol. 4, pp. 236, 237, 239 and vol. 5, p. 328.

APPENDIX

Petition of the Jews of Dettensee

"Hochwürdiger Reichsfürst, Gnädiger Fürst und Herr!
Euer Hochfürstliche Gnaden wollen sich gnädigst zu erinnern geruhen, daß unsere Judenschaft in drei Herrschafts-Gebäuden zusammen zu leben angewiesen sind; so wie dies nun für ehemalige Zeiten uns zureichend war, so ist es jetzt für nun bestehende 25 starke Familien kaum möglich, denn nun reicht bei mehreren Familien der Platz kaum zu Lagerstätten für die Nacht hin. Wir wollen nicht davon reden, wie traurig es ist, wenn eine ganze Haushaltung in zwei kleinen Gemächern (mehr hat keines von uns) ihr Leben das ganze Jahr hindurch zubringen soll. Wir schweigen davon, welchen Nachteil diese Lebensart für die Gesundheit haben muß, und führen nur dies an, daß in kleinen Wohnungen bereits zwei Familien eingepropft sind; daß in all unseren Wohnungen Vater, Mutter, Kinder und Gesind meist auf einem Haufen schlafen, daß diese durch die Notwendigkeit gedrungen sind, alle Sittlichkeit zu vergessen und sich ohne Unterschied des Geschlechts vor- und nebeneinander anzukleiden; treffen solche Gemächer dann noch Krankheiten oder Wochenbetter, so ist das Elend noch größer und gewiß oft namenlos. Könnte der edle Menschenfreund, der das Elend seiner Brüder aufsucht, um es zu erleichtern, in einem solchen Zustand öfters in unseren Wohnungen bleiben, gewiß, daß Mitleiden würde ihm Thränen lösen, wenn er sehen müßte, daß viele von uns eingekerkte Menschen, die um ihrer Verbrechen willen in Gefängnissen schmachten, um ihren Zustand zu beneiden haben. Sollte Ew. Hochfürstlichen Gnaden an der Wahrheit dieser Erzählungen zweifeln, so lassen sich Höchstdieselbe durch gnädigste Anordnung eines Augenscheines huldreichst zu dem Elend der leidenden Menschheit herab, und Ew. Hochfürstliche Gnaden werden Gewißheit erhalten, daß unser Zustand so traurig ist, als er weit und breit bei Menschen nicht angetroffen wird . . .

Der zweite Punkt unserer untertänigsten Vorstellung geht dahin, daß der uns erteilte Schutz für die Zukunft auch auf unsere Kinder dergestalt wirksam sein möge, daß wir dieselbe bei erlangtem volljährigem Alter untereinander verheiraten dürfen.

So hart es uns ist, mit unserer ganzen Familie in ein paar Gemächern eingepropft zu sein, ebenso drückend und niederschlagend ist der Gedanke, auch nicht die geringste Hoffnung zu haben, diese Familie los zu werden. Daß die Erschwerung der Heiraten den nachteiligen Einfluß auf die Sittlichkeit habe, ist in der Erfahrung zu sehr gegründet, als daß wir solche zu entwickeln erst nötig hätten.

Wie glücklich würde uns daher die Erlaubnis machen, daß sich unsere Kinder, sofern keine wichtige Abhaltungsgründe dagegen wären, alle untereinander und so auch die Witfrauen ungehindert verheiraten dürfen. Einmal haben wir gezeigt, daß die Judenschaft zu Dettensee weder der gnädigsten Herrschaft noch den übrigen Bürgern zum Nachteil seien, wie könnte dies durch Ausbreitung derselben gescheheń? Fünfundzwanzig auf einem kleinen Haufen lebende äußerst starke Familien, die sich selber zur Last sind, können gewiß weniger Gutes wirken und sind jedermann mehr zum Ärgernis und zur Last als 40 kleine Familien, die ungehindert ihre Tätigkeit auszuüben imstande sind; wo 25 Familien darum bestehen können, weil sie von auswärtigem Gewerbe leben, da können unter den nämlichen Bedingungen auch 50 leben.

Man wende nicht ein, daß die kleinen Familien wieder größer werden und sich so immer stärker multiplizieren, denn würde man nach diesem System bei Bevölkerungs-Berechnungen verfahren, so hätte man längst nicht nur die Juden, sondern die halbe Christenheit von den Traualtären zurückweisen müssen.

Die Welt steht viele tausend Jahre, und immer hat auf ihr die Menschheit Platz gefunden. Diesen Platz wird sie in künftigen Jahrtausenden ebenso bequem noch finden, und immer wird gewiß ein jeder Ort in jedem Land Judenschaft mit Christenheit im gleichen Verhältnis sehen.

Was demnach die allbekannte Großmut und Menschenliebe Ew. Hochfürstlichen Gnaden uns nicht versagen werden, dies wagen wir nun in aller Untertänigkeit zu bitten, daß nämlich unseren Kindern und Witfrauen unter den nötigen Bestimmungen für die Zukunft die Heiraten gnädigst gestattet werden. Endlich können wir nicht umhin, auch dies noch anzuführen, daß es uns äußerst hart fällt, bei Erlangung unseres Schutzes so ganz nicht auch nur für den kommenden Tag gesichert zu sein: indem unseren Schutzbriefen, und zwar erst in neueren Zeiten, die Klausel einverleibt wird, daß der einmal erteilte Schutz mit oder ohne Ursache entzogen werden könne. Wir sind zwar von den erhabenen Gesinnungen Ew. Hochfürstlichen Gnaden zu sehr überzeugt, als daß wir das letzte befürchten sollten, doch können wir in tiefster Untertänigkeit den Wunsch nicht unterdrücken, daß um der Folgezeit willen, für das Vergangene und für die Zukunft gedachte Klausel, die wahrscheinlich bisher nur als Form angesehen wurde, hochgeneigtest erlassen werden möchte."

The Religious Reform Controversy in the Berlin Jewish Community, 1814–1823

BY MICHAEL A. MEYER

In November 1815 an innocent advertisement for a recently published small volume appeared in a Berlin newspaper. It offered for sale a *Sermon on the Holiday of Rejoicing in the Law Held in a New Private Temple in Berlin* by Isaak Levin Auerbach.[1] This laconic notice came to the attention of the Prussian monarch Frederick William III who thereby learned for the first time of the modern religious services which had been conducted for about half a year in the house of Israel Jacobson. The King demanded his officials provide him with an explanation since such private gatherings were not to be tolerated.[2] It was thus a chance incident – and not, as commonly assumed, orthodox complaints[3] – which sparked a controversy that was to last for eight years. It would set reformers against traditionalists in a prolonged struggle to win the approval of Prussian ministers and of the King for their point of view. In the end, the traditionalists would win a complete victory.

Over a century ago Ludwig Geiger presented what is still the most extensive account of this controversy in his *History of the Jews in Berlin*.[4] Although Geiger based his description on a number of archival documents, there is much unpublished material which Geiger either did not see or chose to ignore. On the basis of this new evidence it is possible to construct an account both fuller and in certain points quite different from that of Geiger. Specifically, it is possible to shed considerable new light on the attitudes of the Prussian ministers involved and on the political manoeuvres employed by the two factions in the Jewish community. The documents also enable us to analyse the motives – the hopes and the fears – of both reformers and traditionalists.

When Israel Jacobson came to Berlin in 1814 he found a community which for two years had been disputing over religious and educational reform but as yet had reached no decisions. The Prussian Edict of Emancipation had called forth David Friedländer's radical reform proposal[5] and led to the formation of a commission, composed of two representatives each from Berlin, Potsdam, Königsberg and Breslau, which was to formulate a plan for the reorganisation

---
[1]*Predigt am Freudenfeste der Tora gehalten in einem Privat-Tempel zu Berlin*, Berlin 1815.
[2]Albrecht to Schuckmann, 29th November 1815, Moritz Stern Collection, P17/548, Central Archives for the History of the Jewish People (CAHJP), Jerusalem. Except as otherwise indicated, all archival sources used for this study are to be found in the Stern Collection in File P17/548 or in File P17/580, and in some instances in both.
[3]David Philipson, *The Reform Movement in Judaism*, rev. edn., New York 1931, pp. 23–24; Israel Zinberg, *A History of Jewish Literature*, trans. Bernard Martin, IX, Cincinnati 1976, p. 244.
[4]*Geschichte der Juden in Berlin*, Berlin 1871, I, pp. 165–168; II, pp. 210–234.
[5]*Über die durch die neue Organisation der Judenschaften in den Preussischen Staaten nothwendig gewordene Umbildung*, Berlin 1912.

of religious and educational institutions. But the Prussian War of Liberation prevented the commission from doing its work. It also became apparent that most of Berlin Jewry did not favour extreme reform. In the elections to the commission, in January 1813, the two candidates proposed by the elders of the community, David Friedländer and Ruben Samuel Gumpertz, were both soundly defeated, while victory went to the conservative Solomon Veit and to the community rabbi Meyer Simon Weyl.[6] The following year, Veit was likewise elected to the Council of Elders, which governed the community, along with the moderate reformers Gumpertz and Jacob Herz Beer.[7] But the status of Jewish religious life following emancipation remained undetermined, a lack of definition which encouraged both sides to hope for the victory of their contradictory positions.

The initial factionalisation of the community on a specific issue of religious worship occurred in 1814. In the summer of that year the *Gesellschaft der Freunde*, a fraternal and benevolent society composed mostly of Jewish *Maskilim* but including also some Christians, requested use of the Berlin community synagogue in order to hold a religious observance of the forthcoming Prussian peace celebration.[8] It was to consist of a sermon and the singing in German of selected appropriate psalms. The elders promptly gave their assent. But when they communicated their decision to the wardens of the synagogue (*Synagogenvorsteher*), who throughout this period were orthodox Jews, the immediate result was a petition calling upon them to rescind the permission. The petitioners objected to any use of the synagogue by individuals who would not feel bound by Jewish tradition. They argued that such an imposition could lead to a rift in the community and threatened that it might cause individuals to withhold contributions to its charitable institutions. The elders now turned to the Berlin rabbinate for its opinion. But the rabbis' reply left no doubt about their feelings. Like the petitioners, they resented this intrusion of an exclusive private organisation, whose members were not traditional Jews, into their domain. Specifically, they prohibited the proposed sitting together of men and women during the celebration, the giving of a sermon by someone who was not a fully observant Jew (and hence might say something contradictory to Jewish tradition), and the use of female voices in a choir. As for the prayers in German, that was a matter which could only be decided after consulting the most prominent rabbis in Prussia; meanwhile they prohibited it categorically. The result was that the *Gesellschaft der Freunde* chose to conduct the celebration in its own meeting hall. The significance of the incident lies not in its specific outcome, but in making clear to that faction of the community which had actively favoured worship reforms, especially since the Emancipation Edict of 1812, that they could not without severe opposition gain their ends through the public institution of the community synagogue. The logical recourse, therefore, was the establishment of private services intended only for those who shared the desire

---

[6]*Gemeindeblatt der jüdischen Gemeinde zu Berlin*, 9th August (1912), pp. 103–106.
[7]Berlin Collection, KGe2/129, CAHJP.
[8]The documents relating to this matter are all in the Stern Collection, P17/467. Cf. Ludwig Lesser, *Chronik der Gesellschaft der Freunde in Berlin*, Berlin 1842, p. 57.

Reform Controversy

for new forms of Jewish worship. Their conscious intent was to create a model which could be expected eventually to be adopted by the community as a whole.[9]

Although the Prussian Jewry Regulation of 1750 severely limited the holding of services outside the synagogue, there were in fact thirteen such *minyanim* in Berlin in 1815.[10] Jacobson thus had ample precedent for the private "temple" which he created in his home in the spring of 1815, a few months after settling in the Prussian capital.[11] Notwithstanding the commonly held view,[12] there is no evidence that the orthodox complained to the government or to the elders regarding these services. On the contrary, it seems likely that they were relieved at the opportunity to deflect reforming activity away from the synagogue. It was the government, prompted by the King himself, which interfered. The local police were ordered to inquire of Jacobson regarding the nature of his services. The one-time head of the Westphalian Consistory responded with a general description and a defence on three grounds: the community synagogue did not provide inspiration, the services at his home were entirely in keeping with Jewish practice, and there were other such private gatherings already in existence. He sent along copies of the prayers and songs, a special prayer for the welfare of the King, and – ironically – the sermon by Auerbach which had directed the King's attention to the matter in the first place.

Within the government the Minister of the Interior Friedrich von Schuckmann, as the responsible official, presented a carefully considered recommendation to the counsellor of the King.[13] Despite hostility and contempt for Jacobson and his effort, Schuckmann none the less at this stage suggested toleration. His reasoning was as follows: if the services were to be closed, irresistible reformatory pressure would be focused on the synagogue itself which would also thereby achieve greater importance. With anticipated orthodox opposition, the reformers would then be driven to more extreme measures. They would found a new sect composed in reality of "mere naturalists initially retaining a Mosaic mask". After a while they would drop the mask, along with burdensome circumcision, creating a non-denominational society "to which a number [of Christians] would convert out of selfish interest in order to establish business and family relations with wealthy Jews". He therefore recommended taking as little notice of the Jacobson services as possible. Enthusiasm for the services would, it was hoped, cool rapidly while the better educated and wealthy would continue to seek the baptism that would make their children – though not themselves – into honest Christians.

Schuckmann's views did not persuade Frederick William III. On 9th December 1815 he ordered all private Jewish religious gatherings in Berlin to be closed, since they necessarily led to separatism. Only in the synagogue would

---

[9]This is stated explicitly in elders to Altenstein, 19th January 1818, Berlin Collection, KGe2/81.
[10]*Ibid.*, KGe2/10.
[11]The only published eye-witness account of the services from this year is contained in *Sulamith*, 4:2 (1815), pp. 66–70. An account of the services conducted later in the home of Jacob Herz Beer was published most recently by Nahum N. Glatzer, 'On an Unpublished Letter of Isaak Markus Jost', in *LBI Year Book XXII* (1977), pp. 129–137.
[12]E.g., Philipson, *op. cit.*, (with wrong date), pp. 23–24.
[13]See Appendix, I.

Jewish worship be tolerated. Insisting that the Jewry Regulation of 1750 was still valid in such matters even after 1812, the King was not swayed by considerations of religious freedom. Quite the contrary, he was concerned that the slightest toleration of diversity among Jews might encourage similar sectarian moves among Christians – a tendency which he, like his predecessor, considered most dangerous.[14]

Shortly before the prohibition, Jacob Herz Beer, a wealthy banker and an elder of the community, had at considerable expense to himself instituted similar services, open to all, in the more spacious quarters of his home. When informed of the King's order, he appealed both to the liberal chancellor, Hardenberg, and to the King himself to reverse the decision. His letters refer to the impossibility of initiating a German service in the community synagogue without offending the consciences of those for whom the exclusive use of Hebrew was an essential of their faith. Those who did not know Hebrew had been put in the position of either attending no service at all or one that was incomprehensible to them. They sought a "refuge" outside the synagogue. Apparently having previously reached an agreement with Jacobson, he requested that at least one German service (that in his home) be permitted in Berlin. His efforts proved fruitless. Though Hardenberg was sympathetic, Frederick William was not.[15] The temple at Beer's home was closed by the police.

It was only during the next stage, once the reformers had been forced back into the public realm, that the orthodox began to play a politically active role. On the basis of a passage in the King's letter to Hardenberg which left open the possibility of using German in the synagogue itself, Schuckmann – either on his own initiative or at someone's prompting – "ordered" the elders to institute German there if in fact the majority of the community, including women and children, no longer knew Hebrew. Now, apparently for the first time, the traditionalists were spurred into action, requesting the elders immediately to seek reversal of the order and threatening independent action in case of refusal.

The elders, though their majority was favourable to reform, were not eager to impose a wholly German service on the entire community (in fact the services in the private temples had remained mostly in Hebrew). They sought desperately for some device which would enable the continuation of two different services, the traditional one in the synagogue and that with organ, German sermon and some German prayers in the home of Elder Beer.

They hit upon two possibilities which they tried in sequence. The first was to argue before Schuckmann that it was their duty to provide for the religious needs of the entire community, but the existing 100-year-old synagogue could not hold even half its members. They suggested, therefore, that services be held

---

[14]Already in 1788, during the reign of Frederick William II, an edict on religion specified that "no conventicles harmful to the Christian religion and the state be held under the name of religious gatherings. By such means all manner of disruptive people and new teachers would seek to gain followers and proselytes, thereby seriously abusing tolerance." See Leopold Auerbach, *Das Judenthum und seine Bekenner in Preussen und in den anderen deutschen Bundesstaaten*, Berlin 1890, p. 282 n.

[15]The King's memorandum to Hardenberg of 28th January 1816 is printed in Geiger, *op. cit.*, II, pp. 219–220.

both in the synagogue and in another location in Spandauer Street (Beer's house), where fortuitously a room was already suitably arranged. Nothing was said about the character of the services in either location or why they had just now become aware of this alleged paucity of space. They sought transparently to restore the *status quo ante*, which in all likelihood would also have satisfied the orthodox. But the King called their bluff; he would allow only one service. If the present synagogue was too small, he wrote to Schuckmann, let them build a larger one in its place. The King's response embarrassed the elders, who had no intention of undertaking a major building project, especially as few members regularly attended the traditional services in the synagogue and there was no apparent compromise form of worship which would attract both factions. They therefore resorted to a second device. What would exist at 72 Spandauer Street would not be a place of worship at all, but exclusively a place of spiritual edification (*Erbauungs-Anstalt*) where on Sabbaths and Jewish holidays edifying discourses would be held in the German language. Not surprisingly, the Prussian authorities were no more favourably inclined to this proposal than to the previous one.

By the autumn of 1816 the advocates of German services were pressing for implementation of Schuckmann's order, the only path left open to them. In response, the elders, seeking as always to preserve harmony in the community, put forward a new proposal: in the synagogue itself a German service would be held *after* the Hebrew one. This would have the additional advantage of solving the alleged space problem. The proposal was to be explored by a commission of ten, to which the elders appointed five modernists and five traditionalists. After two meetings, the commission reached the expected deadlock. The reformers claimed they had received the sanction of "several Godfearing and learned rabbis"[16] and pressed for consecutive services. The orthodox members of the commission replied cleverly that two services meant two sects. In a concession that was no concession at all they volunteered to submit the matter of using German to "a consistory of seven authorised rabbis" serving in Prussia provided that the other side would agree in advance to abide by their decision. Obviously the pro-German faction would not take so unpromising a gamble.

Following the failure of the commission, the elders proceeded immediately with yet another strategy. It was discovered that the community synagogue was in need of extensive repairs. In order to insure full participation in the levy to finance the work, the elders, on 27th January 1817, claimed to the government that it was necessary to rebuild the synagogue in such a way that a second room (*ein Anbau*) be added so that the Hebrew and German services could take place simultaneously. They submitted a drawing and asked for official per-

---

[16]The reference is in the protocol of the second session, 12th January 1817. It must refer to responsa other than those collected in *Nogah Hatzedek*, Dessau 1818. The latter were not composed before the autumn of 1817. Most likely these were oral opinions. However, Michael Silber has called my attention to the possibility that they might have been thinking of the rabbinic justification given to the reforms instituted in Westphalia by Menahem Mendel Steinhardt in his *Divre Igeret*, Rödelheim 1812.

mission. Amazingly, the King – possibly unaware of the intent of the addition – gave his approval to the building project.

The elders were now able to persuade the Berlin police (carefully avoiding resort to any higher authority) to allow them to hold public services in three[17] separate locations while the synagogue was being rebuilt. One of the three was, of course, the home of Jacob Herz Beer. Thus in August 1817, after an interruption of more than a year and a half, the German–Hebrew services once again took place. In September the young Eduard Kley, who had been a teacher in Beer's home, conducted a confirmation there for two Jewish girls whom he had taught. This ceremony – which was the first confirmation of Jewish girls anywhere – almost proved to be a fatal error. In a remarkable repetition of what had happened two years earlier, the King's attention was once again, apparently by chance, directed to the reformers when he read an article in a St. Petersburg newspaper. The article reported the confirmation, noting that it was held according to a new rite approved by the King himself! In a blistering letter to Schuckmann, on 29th October 1817, Frederick William demanded to know immediately who was responsible for this blatant contravention of his will. Only after being assured of the temporary nature of the arrangement and the distorted character of the newspaper report[18] did the King on 12th December 1817 give his permission for the services to continue, provided that the work on the community synagogue be completed by the following summer. From that time on, he insisted, "the religious services of the Jews will be held nowhere else in Berlin but in this synagogue, and according to the traditional rite without the admixture of arbitrary innovations".[19] This language of the King soon became known to the orthodox who made ample use of it in the confusing struggle which now ensued.

The elders, without Solomon Veit who at this point withdrew himself from their decisions on religious matters and joined the orthodox faction,[20] decided to request the creation of a government commission which would examine the prayers, catechisations and sermons of the Beer temple. They were hopeful that it would give them official sanction. Only once they had received such approval would it make sense to them to proceed with constructing the addition to the synagogue.

[17]It is thus necessary to correct Simon Bernfeld, *Toldot Hareformatzion Hadatit Beyisrael*, Cracow 1900, p. 89, who thought that the orthodox had no choice but to attend services in the Beer temple at this time. On the same page Bernfeld also errs in believing that David Friedländer was an elder at this time. In fact Friedländer was not only no longer a leader of the community, but he soon became disenchanted with the Beer services which he regarded as too timid. See 'Et Rejsebrev fra I. N. Mannheimer', *Tidsskrift for Jødisk Historie og Literatur*, I (1917–1919), pp. 296–297. Finally, it is also erroneous to suggest that the government ministers were inclined toward the reformers. Hardenberg, who had no immediate jurisdiction over these matters, was the only significant minister who was favourably disposed to the reform circle. He had died by the time of the definitive decision in 1823.

[18]The elders were at pains to point out that, contrary to the report, the rite was not a new one, that Jewish confirmation ceremonies had in fact been held in other places, and that there had been no claim of receiving the approval of the King.

[19]The King's permission is printed in Geiger, *op. cit.*, II, p. 221.

[20]His substitute was Liebermann Schlesinger, like Beer a banker and a proponent of the German services.

It was not the services in Beer's home but the prospect of a permanently divided synagogue which now, for the first time, stirred the orthodox to present their case to the government. On 12th January 1818 a group of nine traditional Jews, led by the Royal Directorial Agent Gottschalk Helfft and including the five orthodox members of the deadlocked commission appointed by the elders, wrote a letter of complaint to Minister of the Interior von Schuckmann. They accused their opponents in terms which they knew would be the most damaging: the worship of the reformers was "in respect both to language and essence altered according to their own discretion"; they were guilty of making "arbitrary changes" and of "sectarian spirit". Seeking to bypass the elders, the petitioners asked Schuckmann to seek the King's approval for their previously proposed rabbinic referendum. The elders, however, sought to foil their intent. In a lengthy survey of Jewish religious and intellectual development,[21] which was sent to Karl von Altenstein, the man who had just been appointed to head the newly created Ministry of Religion, they traced the process of Jewish enlightenment, the decline of rabbinic influence, and the rise of German cultural identification. They insisted that the German services were a necessity for the growing number, especially of women and children, who did not know Hebrew. Contrary to rumour, the Beer services were not sectarian. The services in the new addition to the synagogue, which would be based on them, would differ only in that some of the prayers would be in German, there would be organ accompaniment and a German speech. They admitted candidly that some members of the community regarded certain Jewish doctrines and prayers as inappropriate for the present age and therefore favoured selectivity. But their private opinions would not be allowed to influence collective decisions. The elders again requested the appointment of a government commission, asking permission to postpone work on the addition until it completed its deliberations.

In the spring and summer of 1818 an atmosphere of utter confusion reigned in which elders and orthodox each tried to press their case with the various government bodies that possessed some jurisdiction in Jewish affairs. In June, Altenstein finally created an investigative commission, but it produced no authoritative report.[22] Although the elders completed the necessary structural repairs to the synagogue, they refused to redecorate the interior, claiming that the nature of the interior arrangements was dependent on whether there would be a second sanctuary or not, and the King had allowed an *Anbau*. But the latter depended on a government decision with regard to the legitimacy of the German services, and this kept being postponed. Meanwhile the orthodox, resting their case on the King's order to complete the remodelling rapidly, demanded immediate completion of the original sanctuary.

When the elders continued to delay the interior arrangements, the orthodox first offered to advance funds, then complained to Altenstein, and in midsummer, claiming to represent the community, they sent a memorandum to the

[21] See above, note 9.
[22] For the work of the commission see Geiger, *op. cit.*, II, pp. 223–228. Its preliminary report, dated 25th November 1818, included the views presented to it by both sides. As it is unpublished and of considerable interest, an excerpt has been included as Appendix, II.

King himself.²³ Although their by-passing the elders and the two relevant ministries to address the monarch directly resulted in a severe government reprimand,²⁴ the traditionalists did manage to obtain a prohibition of the *Anbau*. They did not get a new order to complete the interior arrangements, though they were informed that it was permitted. Since the elders now preferred to leave things as they were, everything remained stalled awaiting a final decision on the permissibility of a separate service or the unlikely prospect of agreement with regard to a single compromise service acceptable to both sides. Meanwhile, as the months continued to pass without a resolution and the services in the Beer house attracted ever larger numbers,²⁵ the traditionalists resorted to an extreme measure. In May 1819 they began on their own to rebuild the interior of the synagogue and by June they were holding services in the half-completed sanctuary.²⁶ The elders quickly obtained an injunction to stop the work of the carpenters. Not only did they regard such action as an attack on their authority, but they must also have realised that once the synagogue was rebuilt in the old fashion, without special arrangements for a speaker's pulpit and organ, and once traditional services were regularly held there again, it would be much harder to institute changes. On 28th June the orthodox sent a long memorandum to the chancellor in which they claimed to represent more than 250 heads of families.²⁷ Echoing the language of the King, they referred to their opponents repeatedly as innovators (*Neuerer*) and pointed out the deleterious *political* effects of sects and divisions. Startlingly they concluded that whoever was not satisfied to be a traditional Jew "has the option to become a Christian".

Though their protestations were in vain and despite a court order against them, Helfft and his associates continued to have work done on the interior of the synagogue and services continued to be held there. By the end of 1819 a temporary *modus vivendi* seems to have been achieved: those favouring a traditional service would continue to pray in the not quite completed synagogue while the proponents of a modernised service could, for the time being, continue under community auspices to worship in the home of Jacob Beer.

This truce lasted for more than three years. But during that period developments occurred in Prussia which were distinctly unfavourable to Jewish religious reform. The early Jewish proponents of social and religious integration believed that they were not alone in desiring the creation of new forms of

---

[23] Interestingly, in this letter of 30th July 1818, the orthodox refer twice to the community synagogue as a "temple". The letter includes the signatures of Rabbi Weyl and of Elder Solomon Veit.

[24] Order of Prussian Administration in Berlin, 10th November 1818.

[25] Geiger, *op. cit.*, II, p. 221 and Appendix, II.

[26] Berlin Collection, KGe2/81. Veit objected to this illegal move but continued to favour the cause of the traditionalists.

[27] It is not possible to be certain about which faction was the larger. The figure of more than 250 heads of families would seem to be the approximate equivalent of the 245 family heads given for the reformers in Appendix, II. But only the latter document gives other categories as well. A newspaper account quoted in a document of 14th January 1820 (Stern Collection, P17/454) speaks of the opposition to the reform group as only "slightly more than half" its size. In any case, with the exception of their radical wing, the reformers in Berlin were not a distinct minority. See also below, note 34.

Jewish expression more appropriate to the age; they thought that Christians, as well, desired a lessening of religious differences and closer contact between Jews and Gentiles. They were proud of introducing ceremonies like confirmation and readily invited prominent Gentiles to attend. It was, therefore, hard for them to understand that such public display of Jewish modernity could arouse ire rather than appreciation. Yet such was clearly the case in the circle of the King. In 1821 Frederick William issued an order prohibiting Christian clergy and public officials from attending Jewish ceremonies lest such participation appear to detract from the status of Christianity and lead to an undesired rapprochement with Judaism. When none the less three Christian preachers attended a Jewish confirmation ceremony in Landsberg on the Warthe, held in February 1822, they were severely called to account once a newspaper report brought the incident to the King's attention. The King was generally displeased by the publicity received by such ceremonies, which attracted public interest on account of their novelty. His minister, Altenstein, had to see to it that in the future the censor would allow only Christian ceremonies to be reported in the press.[28] In 1822 Jews were also excluded from the higher ranks in the army and barred from educational and academic positions in Prussia. In February of that year the King gave his approval to the newly created Berlin "Society for the Propagation of Christianity among the Jews".[29] Minister of the Interior Schuckmann praised its work as "the only true religious improvement of the Jews" and wrote to its president, von Witzleben, that reform of the Jewish service made Jews "even more dangerous to civil society than they were before".[30] In fact it was Witzleben – and once again not the orthodox – who redirected Schuckmann's attention to the services in Beer's home and thus set in motion the process which would lead to the final and complete suppression of any but wholly traditional Jewish worship in Berlin.

In this atmosphere and out of their shared mistrust of the reformers, Schuckmann and Altenstein now decided to ignore the government's own investigation into the permissibility of religious reform and to proceed on the basis of the King's will. This was interpreted by Altenstein to exclude a separate location, even within the same building, the use of an organ, the giving of sermons, or any change whatever in the existing liturgy. Only the possibility of using the German language remained open.[31] The elders were told there could be only one sanctuary and its interior arrangements had to be completed promptly so that services at Beer's house could cease. A petition to the elders, signed by 151 proponents of reform headed by Joseph Mendelssohn, was passed on to

[28]Ismar Freund Collection, P2/D.M./4, CAHJP. This file contains the typescript of a short, apparently unpublished study of the Landsberg incident which incorporates archival material.
[29]Documentary material on the society in Ludwig von Rönne and Heinrich Simon, *Die früheren und gegenwärtigen Verhältnisse der Juden in den sämmtlichen Landestheilen des Preussischen Staates*, Breslau 1843, pp. 109–114.
[30]See Appendix, III. The order referred to in Schuckmann's letter requests the police to investigate an anonymous newspaper report (sent to him by Witzleben) that indicates services are being held in Beer's home. In the interim Schuckmann had apparently forgotten about the – albeit temporary – permission to hold these services given by the King in December 1817.
[31]Altenstein to Schuckmann, 10th February 1823.

Altenstein but, of course, rejected. By September 1823 the Beer temple was closed.[32] The only possibility which still remained open was a renewal of the earlier proposal for some mutually agreed upon compromise within the single sanctuary of the synagogue. But that required the approval of the rabbi and Weyl proved to be wholly unyielding. When the elders[33] appointed a committee of interested individuals to consult with him regarding the possibility of having a few German prayers and an edifying talk following the wholly traditional Hebrew service, Weyl refused even to meet with them. He did not hide his fear that "this modern service would in the course of time displace the true service in the original language",[34] i.e., the worshippers would increasingly come only for the added German portion. Weyl knew that the King's expressed will and the spirit of the times were on his side and therefore, from his position of strength, he could afford to reject even the mildest concession. He saw himself as the "spiritual authority" (*geistlicher Vorstand*) of the community with exclusive right to decide in matters of religion. But when the elders thereupon took their case to Schuckmann, they received a favourable response.

The Interior Minister's apparently surprising attitude is not difficult to explain. In a rescript issued only a few months earlier, on 14th March 1823, he had given his sanction to a memorandum on the role of the rabbi which Elder Gumpertz had furnished orally to the government commission in 1820. According to Gumpertz, the rabbi was merely a consultant in matters of Jewish practice, a "Kauscherwächter" without independent authority or the functions of Christian clergy.[35] No less than Gumpertz, Schuckmann was desirous of minimising the authority and respect of the rabbis. He therefore ruled that the elders, and not Weyl, possessed the authority to determine synagogue ritual

---

[32]Schuckmann to Berlin Police, 2nd September 1823.

[33]Veit had reassociated himself with his colleagues on religious matters. Like them, he favoured the supplementary German prayers and sermon, but he opposed the preachers selected because they were not reliably orthodox.

[34]Weyl to elders, 12th August 1823. Weyl's fears proved to be well grounded. After the German services in the community synagogue had already been prohibited, a Christian writer in Berlin reported in the Supplement to the Augsburg *Allgemeine Zeitung*, No. 25, (1824), p. 102 that in a community of 700 families, less than seventy individuals had attended the traditional services. Of these, scarcely twenty knew enough Hebrew and Aramaic to understand all the prayers. By contrast, more than 1,600 persons attended the German hymns and sermon, including a large proportion of women. Even if this writer, who favoured the use of German in the Jewish service as a step towards conversion to Christianity, exaggerated the figures greatly, there can be little doubt that at this stage the overwhelming majority of the Berlin community – whether out of religious motivation or out of curiosity – preferred to participate in the German edification.

[35]Printed in Wilhelm Freund, *Zur Judenfrage in Deutschland*, I (1843), pp. 213–216. Cf. Appendix, II. In the memorandum Gumpertz claims that Weyl remained *Vice-Ober-Land-Rabbiner* because he was not deemed worthy of the full title enjoyed by his predecessors. Gumpertz's anti-rabbinic sentiments were no doubt part of the reason for Weyl's mistrust of the elders. As there was no official document specifying the duties of the rabbis, so there was none delineating the duties of the elders. In 1817 Weyl was asked by the Berlin police authorities to present an outline of the latter for the guidance of newly elected elders in Frankfurt a. d. Oder. He noted that in synagogue matters the elders were responsible to "uphold the traditional ordinances". See Rönne and Simon, *op. cit.*, pp. 144–145, pp. 146–148 and cf. Auerbach, *op. cit.*, pp. 294–296.

Reform Controversy 149

within the limits imposed by the government – and these, according to his interpretation, did not preclude "an edification" following the traditional service.[36]

On this basis the elders decided to proceed despite Weyl's opposition. They appointed Isaak Levin Auerbach and Isaak Noah Mannheimer to give the sermons and they set a date for the first "devotion" (*Andachtsübung*). This spurred the orthodox to renewed action. They gathered 112 signatures and on 13th September channelled their protest to the Ministry of Religion. Weyl could expect that Altenstein, who had earlier turned to him for authoritative opinions in Jewish matters,[37] would be sympathetic. He appealed to the minister as his ecclesiastical superior to sustain the rabbi's authority as spiritual head of the Jewish community. Sermons, to his mind, were superfluous. But if they were to be given, he insisted on his prerogative to choose the preacher.[38]

For the moment Altenstein remained silent. On Saturday morning, 25th October 1823, for the first time, the traditional service in the community synagogue was followed by a German devotion. In their complaint to Altenstein the orthodox described it as a nearly two-hour long German sermon given by the preacher Auerbach, who was attired in an ecclesiastical robe. Before and after the sermon, and whenever a biblical verse was mentioned, an appropriate hymn was sung in German by a choir of boys from the Jewish Free School wearing short black mantles.[39]

This report had the desired effect on the Minister of Religion. Almost immediately he wrote to Schuckmann criticising him for ignoring the rabbinate and for granting his permission to the elders. The King would certainly regard what happened on 25th October in the category of "innovations". External changes were bound to lead to doctrinal ones, even to the creation of a new sect. Above all he resented Schuckmann's trespassing on his domain.[40] On the same

---

[36]2nd September 1823. This document is printed in Gabriel Riesser, *Gesammelte Schriften*, III, Frankfurt a. Main–Leipzig 1867, pp. 138–139.

[37]See Horst Fischer, *Judentum, Staat und Heer in Preussen im frühen 19. Jahrhundert. Zur Geschichte der staatlichen Judenpolitik*, Tübingen 1968 (Schriftenreihe wissenschaftlicher Abhandlungen des Leo Baeck Instituts 20), p. 107.

[38]Weyl to Altenstein, 16th September and 22nd October 1823. By this time the orthodox Isaac Bernays had begun to give German sermons in the community synagogue in Hamburg, and it is likely that this example influenced Weyl not to object categorically to German sermons.

[39]Unterthänigstes Pro Memoria, 28th October 1823, Stern Collection, P17/454; on the composition of the choir: Berlin Collection, KGe2/81.

[40]Altenstein to Schuckmann, 30th October 1823. Jurisdiction in Jewish *religious* matters did in fact by law belong to the Ministry of Religion. See Rönne and Simon, *op. cit.*, p. 89; Auerbach, *op. cit.*, p. 289 n. Unlike Altenstein, Schuckmann seems to have been a bureaucrat interested only in political considerations, an "arch-philistine" (as Stein once called him) with little appreciation for matters of the spirit. In Schuckmann's view, any independent popular movement represented a potential threat to the absolute authority of the state. For this evaluation of the Minister of the Interior see Ernst Müsebeck, *Das Preussische Kultusministerium vor hundert Jahren*, Stuttgart–Berlin 1918, pp. 125, 151–152. Yet despite their differing attitudes to religion and their personal rivalry, Altenstein and Schuckmann were fundamentally in agreement with regard to the dangers of Jewish religious reform and the need to prevent any change that would reduce the pressures for conversion. In a memorandum which he prepared in the spring of

day he composed a reply to Weyl but had to indicate that he could not give him a decision without first conferring with Schuckmann. It was at that point that the representatives of the orthodox decided to turn to their most reliable ally. On 2nd November 1823 they wrote directly to the King, painting for him a vivid spectre of morally and religiously suspect preachers and of elders bent on arbitrary innovation, sectarianism and schism. The result was all they could have hoped for. The King's well-known order to Schuckmann of 9th December 1823 even used almost precisely the same unambiguous language which the orthodox had proposed to him: the services would be held "without the slightest innovation in language, ceremonies, prayers or hymns, wholly according to established custom". Frederick William would not tolerate a new Jewish sect in Prussia.

The reformers had been outmanoeuvred. Their "non-service" in the synagogue, which had taken place for only two months,[41] was now unconditionally prohibited. In an obviously unsuccessful belated appeal to the King they wrote that they felt at the edge of an abyss: how would they now raise their children religiously? They were simply left dangling. Their children did not know Hebrew and had probably imbibed their parents' contempt for the disorderly, unaesthetic and to them uninspiring worship. The Beer services had provided some relation to Judaism, however tenuous. That link was now dissolved.

Throughout the reign of Frederick William III Prussian officials continued to abide scrupulously by the King's will,[42] denying the Jews both recognition and religious freedom. After 1826, a few of those who sought a modern service were able to participate with their children in worship held at the newly

---

1819 regarding the relation of his ministry to the state bureaucracy as a whole, Altenstein included the following paragraph on the Jews:

Die Juden

Sie beabsichtigen zum Teil, vorzüglich hier [in Berlin], mannigfaltige Veränderungen ihres Gottesdienstes. Ein Gottesdienst in deutscher Sprache wird ihnen nicht versagt werden können, da man ihnen den Gebrauch der deutschen Sprache im bürgerlichen Leben zur Pflicht gemacht hat. Ein Aufgeben des Ritualgesetzes und der Sittengesetze, die sie gleichfalls beabsichtigen, und wodurch sie sich das Lästige des Judentums zu erleichtern suchen, ist bedenklich und erfordert genaue Prüfung. Diese ist veranlasst. Der Übergang zur christlichen Kirche wird dadurch nicht erleichtert, sondern erschwert. Dieser Übergang würde leicht bei einiger Strenge in den bürgerlichen Verhältnissen und einigen Anstalten, auf die Überzeugung einzuwirken, zu bewirken sein, und es mag sich auch noch so viel dagegen sagen lassen, so wird solcher doch immer einer grössern Verbreitung eines halben und vornehmen Judentums vorzuziehen sein. Dieser Übertritt wird in den ersten Generationen den Christen durch ihre Vermischung mit solchen nachteilig werden, allein es ist doch ein minderes Übel. Das Resultat der Prüfung ihrer Glaubensveränderung wird Veranlassung geben, diesem Gegenstand näher zu treten. Vorerst ist als Vorbereitung zu jeder andern Massregel nötig, dass sie mit Ernst in den bestehenden Schranken aller Art gehalten werden.

The entire memorandum is published in *ibid.*, pp. 279–293.

[41] The prohibition was conveyed to the elders on 26th December 1823. I have found no documentary basis for Zunz's assertion in *Die gottesdienstlichen Vorträge der Juden*, Berlin 1832, p. 476, that they continued until 3rd March 1824.

[42] See Rönne and Simon, *op. cit.*, p. 94.

opened Jewish community school. The synagogue itself remained unchanged. As Gabriel Riesser expressed it: Judaism was left to suffocate in its tightly closed shell and those Jews estranged from established practice were driven to seek spiritual nourishment in the lap of the Christian church.[43]

[43]Riesser, *op. cit.*, III, p. 154. A missionary's report from Berlin, dating from the period immediately following the closing of the temple, includes the following caution: "Observe then well, that we must not allow the Jews, under the appearance of an approximation on their part, to hold a peculiar deistical worship. It is not till after the shutting up of this new temple, which had existed nine years, that the want of a more satisfactory religion shews itself so strongly." See *Eighteenth Report of the London Society for Promoting Christianity Amongst the Jews*, London 1826, p. 64.

APPENDIX

The three documents which follow are all from the Moritz Stern Collection, P17/548, in the Central Archives for the History of the Jewish People. Thanks are extended to the Archives for permission to publish them. The transcriptions are faithful to the handwritten copies in the collection, which were made from originals in the Prussian State Archives. Spelling and punctuation have not been altered, even where there are inconsistencies. The date on the third document was added by a later hand.

I

Da mir von einem hiesigen Privattempel der Juden bis zu der neuerlichen Ankündigung einer so genannten Predigt, die in demselben gehalten sein sollte, nie etwas bekannt geworden war, so habe ich auf Ewr. Hochwohlgeboren geehrtes Schreiben vom 29ten v. M. von dem Polizei-Praesidenten Le Coq Bericht darüber erfordert und ermangle nicht, diesen Bericht anliegend ergebenst mitzutheilen.

Ewr. Hochwohlgebornen werden daraus ersehen, dass eigentlich nur von einem Zimmer in der Mieths Wohnung des ehemaligen westphälischen jüdischen Consistorial Praesidenten Jacobson die Rede ist, welche die jüdische Eitelkeit, von der der reiche halbgelehrte Jacobson vorzüglich besessen ist, einen Tempel nennt, um sich wichtig zu machen. Da das Landrecht II Th. 11 Tit. §22–23 den geduldeten Religionsgesellschaften die freye Ausübung ihres Privat Gottesdienstes sowohl in dazu bestimmten Gebäuden als in Privat Wohnungen verstattet, so bin ich der Meinung, dass hiervon keine Notiz weiter zu nehmen sey und die Versammlungen der Juden zum Gottesdienste keinesweges mit Zwang in die Synagoge zu weisen sind. Der Cultus zu der Synagoge würde dadurch gewissermassen zu einem öffentlichen gestempelt und das Bestreben der Juden sich als eine mit gleichen Rechten im Staate der christlichen gegenüberstehende Religionspartei zu betrachten, erhielt dadurch neue Nahrung, so wie der Drang der so genannten Aufgeklärten unter ihnen auf Reform ihres Cultus von Staats wegen, wovon das Juden Edict spricht, wozu ich aber, wie ich gestehen muss, kein Vertrauen habe und woran ich deshalb aus inniger Ueberzeugung nicht rühren mag. Die gewisse Folge wäre, dass mit dem Geschrei über den Gewissens–Zwang von den alten Juden eine neue Secte, eigentlich blosse Naturalisten, anfangs mit Beibehaltung einer mosaischen Maske ausschiede. Das wäre nicht wohl zu hindern, den sie würde behaupten, ihre Dogmen wären das wahre gereinigte Judenthum, und wer soll von Staats wegen darüber entscheiden? Stände die neue Secte vom Staate als geduldet anerkannt nun erst da, so würde sie die mosaische Maske mit der lästigen Beschneidung wohl bald ablegen und wir hätten eine Gemeinde von Theophilanthropen, zu der mancher aus Eigennutz, um mit den reichen Juden in Geschäfts– und Familien Verbindung zu treten, und mancher aus neuerungssüchtiger Geckerei übertreten dürfte; und so ärgerlich dies Sr. Majestät und jedem vernünftigen Christen sein würde, so sähe ich doch nicht ab, wie man es mit Bestand der Gesetze und der Gewissensfreiheit hindern wollte. Darum glaube ich, dass man von dem religiösen Treiben der Juden, so lange es nicht gegen Gesetze anstösst, so wenig als möglich Notiz nehmen muss. Dann verfehlt die Absicht der Eitlen, die Aufsehen erregen, den Messias einer neuen Secte spielen, hier wie Jacobson jüdische Consistorial Praesidenten werden möchten, ihren Zweck, und sie werden der unbelohnten Ausgaben und Mühe für einen unbedeutenden häuslichen Kreis bald müde werden. Die Gebildeteren und Wohlhabenden werden ferner wie bisher sich häufig taufen lassen und zwar grössesten Theils schlechte Christen sein, ihre Kinder aber durch die Erziehung und Verbindung mit andern Familien, wie die Erfahrung lehrt, ganz rechtliche Menschen werden und selbst in dieser Abkunft einen Sporn dazu haben, damit man ihnen solche nicht vorwerfe.

        Berlin den 2ten Dezember 1815
                Schuckmann

An des Königlichen Geheimen Cabinets Raths Herrn Albrecht Hochwohlgebornen.

II

Bericht des Oberpräsidenten von Heydebreck über das Resultat der commissorischen Untersuchung vom 25ten November 1818.

... Die respectiven Forderungen und Erklärungen der neuen Gemeinde oder, wie sie lieber genannt sein will, der für den Gottesdienst in deutscher Sprache stimmenden Gemeinde, welche 435 selbstständige Personen, nämlich 245 Familienväter, 162 unverheirathete Männer, 16 Wittwen und 12 Jungfrauen zählt, beziehen sich auf folgende Gegenstände.

1) Sie verlangen im Allgemeinen eine angemessene und dem Zwecke zusagende Einrichtung des jüdischen Gottesdienstes. Ueberzeugt, dass dieser Zweck nicht erreicht werden kann, wenn der Gottesdienst wie bisher ausschliesslich in hebräischer Sprache, die dem bei weitem grössten Theile der Gemeindeglieder und besonders den jungen Personen und dem weiblichen Geschlechte durchaus fremd ist, gehalten und weder in der Regel durch Predigt lehrreich und erbaulich, noch durch einen geordneten Gesang erwecklich gemacht wird, geht ihr Wunsch dahin: 1) dass die Mehrzahl der in der Synagoge zu sprechenden Gebete in deutscher Sprache abgefasst 2) der Gesang durch Begleitung einer Orgel geregelt und 3) durch Predigten für gehörige Belehrung der Gemeindeglieder gesorgt und zu allen diesen Einrichtungen die erforderliche Erlaubniss ausgewirkt werde.

2) Sie erklären, dass sie im Fall der Gewährung dieser Wünsche deshalb keinesweges als von der mosaischen Religion ausgeschieden angesehen werden, vielmehr sich ferner als Bekenner derselben erachten, und durch ihre Anträge nur bezweckt haben wollten, was keiner Religionsparthei zu versagen sei, nämlich, den Cultus von allem Unzweckmässigen zu reinigen, und ihn wahrhaft nützlich für Verstand und Herz zu machen.

3) Sie äussern ferner, es liege so wenig in ihren Wünschen, sich von denjenigen ihrer hiesigen Glaubensgenossen, die nicht mit ihnen gleiche Ansicht theilen, zu trennen, dass sie vielmehr aufrichtigst gegenseitige Annäherung begehrten, gern unter vorausgesetzter Bewilligung obiger Punkte sich in einer und derselben Synagoge mit ihnen versammeln wollten und nur wenn der andre Theil der Gemeinde sich unnachgiebig bewiese und demselben vorzugsweise der Gebrauch der alten Synagoge eingeräumt werden sollte, alsdann auf ihren frühern Antrag, sich in einer besondern Synagoge zu versammeln und zu dem Ende den ihnen durch die Königl. Kabinetsordre vom 3ten März 1817 zugestandenen Anbau zu bewirken, zurückkommen müssten.

4) Sie erklären sich auch mit den Commissorien darüber völlig einverstanden, dass eine Synagogen-Commission, über deren Zusammensetzung das Nähere

noch vorbehalten bleibe, sowohl behufs der nähern Anordnung des ganzen Cultus, als auch um über die Beobachtung und Aufrechthaltung des einmal Festgesetzten zu wachen, eingesetzt und dieselbe verpflichtet werden müsse, das Resultat ihrer diesfalsigen Verhandlungen der Landesbehörde zur Genehmigung und Bestätigung einzureichen.

5) Was sodann den Rabbi der Gemeinde betrifft, so verpflichten sie sich zwar darauf Bedacht zu nehmen, dass er an seinen Einkünften nichts verliere, erklären jedoch zugleich ihn nur als Schriftkundigen und Rathgeber für die, welche in Fällen des Ceremonialgesetzes oder in andern Gewissensangelegenheiten ihre Zuflucht zu ihm nehmen wollten, ansehn zu können, verlangten aber, da seine, wie aller zeitherigen Rabbinen-Bildung, dieselben nicht eigne, durch Predigten und in hochdeutscher Sprache zu belehren und zu erbauen, für jetzt und bis dahin, wo sie den religiösen Bedürfnissen zusagende Rabbinen fänden, noch neben ihm eigentliche Prediger anstellen zu dürfen, die sie indessen hinsichts ihrer Kenntnisse einer Prüfung unterwerfen und für welche sie demnächst feststehende Gehalte ausmitteln wollten.

6) Endlich erklären sie, sofort als sie in dieser Angelegenheit zu einem bestimmten und ihren Wünschen entsprechenden Resultat gekommen sein würden, ihre Aufmerksamkeit auch auf das Schulwesen der Gemeinde zu richten und namentlich für Feststellung der jüdischen Freischule Sorge zu tragen.

Die Erklärung der alt-gläubigen Gemeindeglieder, von welchen wegen Langsamkeit ihrer Repräsentanten die Verzeichnisse noch nicht beigebracht sind, lautet im Allgemeinen dahin: dass jede Abänderung in Religionssachen nicht nur eine Störung sei, sondern auch zu neuen Abänderungen führe, welche ins Unendliche fortliefen, so dass sich gar nicht bestimmen lasse, was endlich daraus werden mögte, dass auch Conventionen und gerichtliche Festsetzungen dieser Willkührlichkeit nicht abhelfen könnten, da selbst ein Gebrauch, der einige tausend Jahr fortgedauert habe, jetzt abgeändert werden solle. Sie müssen daher wünschen, dass der Gottesdienst ihrer Väter unverändert beibehalten und namentlich, dass bei demselben der hebräischen Sprache und zwar beim Gebete sowohl als überall wie bisher ihre Stelle ausschliesslich gelassen werde, zumal eine so grosse Unkunde derselben, wie sie behauptet werde, nicht statt finde, sie vielmehr noch von Mehreren studiert und verstanden werde und auch der weibliche Theil der Gemeinde, wenn freilich mit ihr nicht bekannt, doch durch die Sorge der Familienväter unterrichtet worden sei.

Was die Orgel betreffe, so hielten sie solche keinesweges für unentbehrlich, den Gebrauch derselben in der Synagoge vielmehr für störend und gesetzwidrig. Gegen die Predigten wäre nichts zu erinnern, vorausgesetzt dass sie von geprüften sowohl gesetz- als schriftkundigen Gelehrten gehalten würden, die sich zugleich durch einen unsträflichen Wandel auszeichneten.

Sollte indessen in der bisherigen Art des Gottesdienstes etwas geändert werden, so dürfte dies nicht ohne Zustimmung des Rabbiners oder vielmehr nicht ohne Zusammenberufung einer aus mehreren der vorzüglichsten Rabbiner des preussischen Staats bestehenden Synode geschehen...

   Berlin den 25ten November 1818
             v. Heydebreck

An des Königl. Geheimen Staats-Ministers Herrn Freiherrn v. Altenstein Excellenz hier.

III

[13.4.1822]

An des Herrn General-Major und General Adjutant Herrn v. Witzleben Hochwohlgeboren.

Auf Ew. geehrtes Schreiben vom 12ten d. M. habe ich die abschriftlich anliegende Verfügung an das hiesige Polizei-Präsidium erlassen, da die Anzeige sehr wahrscheinlich ist. Ich habe mich hiezu verbunden geachtet sowohl aus Pflicht zur Aufrechthaltung der Königl. Bestimmungen als weil auch nach meiner Ueberzeugung die vielbelobte Veredlung des Israelitischen Cultus nicht blos eine Seifenblase jüdischer Eitelkeit ist, sondern die Juden der bürgerlichen Gesellschaft noch gefährlicher macht als sie vorher waren. Den es bedarf wohl keines Beweises, dass dieser israelitische Deismus die gewinsüchtigen Leidenschaften dieses Volkes noch weniger im Zaume halten würde, als alttestamentarischer Glaube.

Von der andern Scite wäre nicht dafür zu stehen, ob sich im Antagonismus gegen pietistische Sectirerei nicht sogenante Christen an diesen Deismus, wenn seine Duldung ausgesprochen werde, anschliessen mögten, zumahl wenn Heirathsspeculationen auf Töchter solcher reichen Deisten hinzuträten.

So lange die Juden, wenn sie nicht Christen werden, in Beziehung gegen den Staat Juden bleiben müssen, hat das Ministerium des Innern gegen solche jüdische Speculationsproselyten das gesetzliche Mittel, dass ihm die Reception der Juden im Staate ausschliesslich zusteht.

Nachdem es in einigen vorgekommenen Fällen diese Befugnis ernstlich geübt und solche neue Juden aus dem Lande vertrieben hat, sind solche Speculationen nicht weiter vorgekommen.

Bei Ew. Theilnahme an der einzigen wahrhaften religiösen Verbesserung der Juden habe ich gerne diese Gelegenheit genommen, mich darüber zu erklären, warum ich von je her ein Widersacher jener blos scheinbaren Verbesserung gewesen bin.

Ich bitte, die Versicherung meiner vollkomsten Hochachtung anzunehmen.

Schuckmann

Language Behaviour and Assimilation
The Situation of the Jews in Northern Germany in the First Half of the Nineteenth Century

BY PETER FREIMARK

> "... sondern ihre Sprache ... verrathet sie".
> Johann Jacob Schudt, *Jüdische Merckwürdigkeiten*, II. Teil, p. 291

Language and society is a topic that has attracted ever increasing attention in recent years, as witnessed by the remarkable growth of sociolinguistics – above all in the U.S.A. and Britain – and by the way in which research in this field has established itself as a new discipline in its own right, independent of general linguistics. Historical dialectology also added new insights, which have enriched our knowledge of linguistic change in the past.

To begin with, however, the initiative came undoubtedly from the socio-linguists, who departed from the established lines of research and broke fresh ground.[1] The last ten years have brought a truly overwhelming spate of new publications,[2] mostly concerned with empirical observations of the correlation between language and social strata or groups. Two topics of particular interest within this general field are the circumstances in which language acts as a social barrier and investigations into the language and linguistic behaviour of social minorities.

The sociology of language, on the other hand, has some leeway to make up in this field.[3] The same still applies to historiography, although the latest trend

---

[1] Cf. Joshua A. Fishman (ed.), *Readings in the Sociology of Language*, The Hague–Paris 1968, p. 7: "Linguistics, particularly American linguistics during at least the first half of this century, has been primarily a 'formal discipline', almost along the lines of abstract mathematics. It has concentrated on the analysis of language structure. Thus, language 'per se', in the form of a corpus of sounds and smaller or larger units of meaning, has been examined for its patterns, as if it were something that existed above and beyond its users and its uses. Psychologising and sociologising have not only been ignored (as leading in 'exolinguistic' directions) but have been attacked in former years by the most distinguished American linguists as dangerous and misleading pursuits. In contrast to the mainstream of American linguistics, linguists with strong sociocultural interests have represented a smaller parallel tradition, usually under the rubric of 'anthropological linguistics'."

[2] A good survey is presented by Norbert Dittmar, *Soziolinguistik. Exemplarische und kritische Darstellung ihrer Theorie, Empirie und Anwendung. Mit kommentierter Bibliographie*, Frankfurt a. Main 1973. English version: *Sociolinguistics. A Critical Survey of Theory and Applications*, transl. by Peter Sand, Pieter A. M. Seuren and Kevin Whiteley, London 1976.

[3] Cf. T. Luckmann, 'Soziologie der Sprache', in R. König (ed.), *Handbuch der empirischen Sozialforschung*, vol. 2, Stuttgart 1969, p. 1074: "It hardly needs stressing that as regards the problems of relations between vocational structure, economic role patterns and linguistic repertoires or styles ('jargon'), the study of the sociology of language is approaching largely uncharted territory."

shows an increasing interest in the historical study of problems that have been primarily the concern of social scientists, problems relating to the structure of human action and behaviour. The new trend – variously described as a tendency to 'anthropologise history",[4] or to embark on a "history of mentalities" [5] – clearly indicates the growing readiness of the science of history to face interdisciplinary problems and adopt new approaches.

It is proposed in this study to present some recent insights in the field of the history of language and the language behaviour of the Jews in Germany during the first half of the nineteenth century. It is an investigation conceived in the modern spirit of interdisciplinary contacts, so that a coherent picture will emerge from the combined findings of workers in the fields of general history, history of education, history of language and sociolinguistics. A brief first part outlines the linguistic situation in Germany in the eighteenth and early nineteenth centuries against the general historical background. The second part investigates the linguistic "peculiarities" of the Jews in Germany during the relevant period, giving special attention to the conditions in Northern Germany and to the position of Anton Rée. The concluding third part confronts the results thus obtained with current sociolinguistic views. It should be made clear from the outset that in embarking on this study, the author was largely guided by an endeavour to find out how much substance there was in the supposed Jewish "peculiarities" and to consider the problem in the context of developments and tendencies in the non-Jewish outside world.

I

The linguistic situation in Germany towards the end of the eighteenth century can be sketched in rough outline as follows: In the course of the seventeenth and eighteenth centuries Latin had lost ground steadily as the language of science and learning, and French had largely been displaced as the language of the Courts. Concomitantly, modern High German increasingly assumed the role of a common and superordinate or "high" language. After the ground had been prepared by the grammarians – notably Schottel, Gottsched and Adelung – this language was widely disseminated and came to be generally accepted through the works of the German classics.[6] It was the enlightened middle class which espoused the evolving high language, to begin with as a written language, and much more slowly and gradually as a spoken, colloquial language. The

---

[4]Cf. W. Lepenies, 'Geschichte und Anthropologie. Zur wissenschaftlichen Einschätzung eines aktuellen Disziplinenkontakts', in *Geschichte und Gesellschaft*, 1 (1975), pp. 330 ff.; *idem*, 'Probleme einer historischen Anthropologie', in Reinhard Rürup (ed.), *Historische Sozialwissenschaft*, Göttingen 1977, pp. 126–159. See also T. Nipperdey, 'Die anthropologische Dimension der Geschichtswissenschaft', in G. Schulz (ed.), *Geschichte heute. Positionen, Tendenzen, Probleme*, Göttingen 1973, pp. 225–255, reprinted in T. Nipperdey, *Gesellschaft, Kultur, Theorie. Gesammelte Aufsätze zur neueren Geschichte*, Göttingen 1976, pp. 33–58.

[5]W. Lepenies, *Melancholie und Gesellschaft*, Frankfurt a. Main ² 1972. Of basic importance for our approach: N. Elias, *Über den Zustand der Zivilisation. Soziogenetische und psychogenetische Untersuchungen*, 2 vols., Frankfurt a. Main ²1977.

[6]Cf. A. Bach, *Geschichte der deutschen Sprache*, Heidelberg ⁹1970, p. 352.

high language coexisted with a multitude of dialects or local vernaculars spoken mostly by the lower strata, the "plebs". Around 1800, however, the appraisal of those dialects underwent a profound change. Whereas the earlier grammarians, Gottsched among them, had looked upon the dialects as distortions of the common language, as language "corrupted" by the uneducated lower strata of the people, the new historical philology which came into being in the early years of the nineteenth century discovered the source of the common language in the dialects.[7] Jacob Grimm's *Deutsche Grammatik* of 1819 no longer started with the formulation of "laws" governing the use of language but studied the language as it actually was.[8] This led to a fundamental change in the scientific approach to dialects. In the seventeenth and eighteenth centuries some dialect material had been recorded, but the scholarly study of German dialects only began with J. A. Schmeller's book on Bavarian dialects, *Die Mundarten Bayerns grammatisch dargestellt*, published in 1821, at a time when the Romantics' view of language and Wilhelm von Humboldt's idea of language as a living organism began to be widely accepted. A thorough investigation of all German dialects, however, was left to the "Young Grammarian School" of the 1870s when, notably as a result of the work of A. Leskien (1876), the validity of the laws of sound shift had been rigorously established.[9]

The growth and dissemination of the high language is intimately connected with, and effectively reinforced by, developments in the field of literature. Thus, one of the effects of the middle-class striving for emancipation, based largely on the educational reform programmes of the Enlightenment, was the emergence of a literary market in which the free writer and poet, increasingly independent of patronage by the courts and the nobility, could hold his own.[10] Although, according to Schenda,[11] the reading public in the eighteenth century comprised little more than ten per cent of the adult population, the output of books, literary magazines and pamphlets was constantly increasing. A new "middle-class public" emerged,[12] as witnessed most clearly by the literary *salons* and the reading circles, which turned the reading of works of literature into a social event, while private reading was promoted at the same time by reference and lending libraries.[13] The linguistic vehicle used by the literary works of that period was the German high language, which by the end of the

[7]Cf. C. M. Schirmunski, *Deutsche Mundartkunde. Vergleichende Laut- und Formenlehre der deutschen Mundarten*, Berlin 1962, p. 57. On the problem of dialects, see W. Henzen, *Schriftsprache und Mundarten. Ein Überblick über ihr Verhältnis und ihre Zwischenstufen im Deutschen*, Berne ²1954, pp. 12 ff.
[8]Henzen, *op. cit.*, p. 156.
[9]*Ibid.*, p. 159.
[10]Cf. H. Kiesel and P. Münch, *Gesellschaft und Literatur im 18. Jahrhundert. Voraussetzungen und Entstehung des literarischen Marktes in Deutschland*, Munich 1977, pp. 77–104. See also A. Martino, 'Barockpoesie, Publikum und Verbürgerlichung der literarischen Intelligenz', in *Internationales Archiv für Sozialgeschichte der deutschen Literatur*, 1 (1976), pp. 132–135.
[11]R. Schenda, *Volk ohne Buch. Studien zur Sozialgeschichte der populären Lesestoffe 1770–1910*, Munich ²1977, p. 443. Schenda estimates the potential reading public in Central Europe in 1770 at about 15 per cent of the adult population, rising in 1800 to 25 per cent, and by 1830 to 40 per cent (p. 440).
[12]J. Habermas, *Strukturwandel der Öffentlichkeit*, Neuwied–Berlin ⁴1969, pp. 102–116.
[13]Cf. Kiesel and Münch, *op. cit.*, p. 178.

eighteenth century had reached a stage of relative stability. The tendency towards unification – hence the term *Einheitssprache*, unified language – finally prevailed in the second half of the eighteenth century. This development, culminating in the great works of the German classics, has been graphically described by E. A. Blackall.[14]

The emergence of the unified common language and the penetration of elements of that common language into regional speech was of great significance for the further development of the German language. The common language came to be accepted as a norm to which dialects and colloquial speech[15] had to be subordinated.[16] At a time of an awakening German national consciousness, use of the common language became a mark of belonging to the German nation.[17]

The historical background against which those linguistic developments proceeded is well known. As far as the Jews in Germany were concerned, the trend has been summed up by terms such as exodus from the ghetto, tolerance, emancipation, assimilation – terms which spotlight the fundamental process of transformation affecting the Jewish minority. Yet this process cannot be adequately understood unless it is seen in the context of the changes taking place in the society at large. The modern Jewish question is a question enquiring into the position of the Jews in modern society.[18] In the context of the assimilation endeavours promoted by certain Jewish circles – at first chiefly the *Maskilim*, supporters of the Jewish Enlightenment, and the Court Jews – the problem of language was bound to come to the fore, since language was one of the most conspicuous marks of distinction setting Jews and non-Jews apart.

While it is true that there were Jews who mastered the German language as

---

[14] E. A. Blackall, *The Emergence of German as a Literary Language 1700–1775*, Cambridge 1959. German translation: *Die Entwicklung des Deutschen zur Literatursprache*, with an appendix on new research results 1955–1964 by D. Kimpel, Stuttgart 1966.

[15] On the relationship between written language, colloquial language and dialects, cf. Henzen, *op. cit.*, pp. 19–25.

[16] Cf. M. M. Guchmann, *Der Weg zur deutschen Nationalsprache*, part 2, [East] Berlin 1969, p. 189.

[17] The connection between the emerging German national consciousness and the development of a common German language has been pointed out before. See for instance Hans Kohn, *The Idea of Nationalism*, New York 1946; H. L. Koppelmann, *Nation, Sprache und Nationalismus*, Leyden 1956. For German-Jewish history, cf. George L. Mosse, *Germans and Jews. The Right, the Left and the Search for a 'Third Force' in Pre-Nazi Germany*, London 1971, pp. 9 f. For corresponding relations in the Middle Ages, cf. R. Jakobson, 'The Beginnings of National Self-determination in Europe', in *The Review of Politics*, 6 (1945), pp. 29–42, reprinted in Fishman, *op. cit.*, pp. 585–597. See also K. W. Deutsch, 'The Trend of European Nationalism. The Language Aspect', in *American Political Science Review*, 36 (1942), pp. 533–541, reprinted in Fishman, *op. cit.*, pp. 598–606. It will suffice in this connection to recall the origins and dissemination of Modern Hebrew (Ivrit).

[18] Cf. Reinhard Rürup, 'Judenemanzipation und bürgerliche Gesellschaft in Deutschland', in *Emanzipation und Antisemitismus (Kritische Studien zur Geschichtswissenschaft No. 15)*, Göttingen 1975, pp. 11–36; the English version, 'Jewish Emancipation and Bourgeois Society', in *LBI Year Book XIV* (1969), pp. 67–91. The essay appeared for the first time in E. Schulin (ed.), *Gedenkschrift für Martin Göhring. Studien zur europäischen Geschichte*, Wiesbaden 1968, pp. 174–199. For contemporary discussions of the situation of the Jews in the eighteenth century, see Jacob Toury, 'Die Behandlung jüdischer Problematik in der Tagesliteratur der Aufklärung (bis 1783)', in *Jahrbuch des Instituts für Deutsche Geschichte*, V, Tel-Aviv 1976, pp. 13–47.

early as the eighteenth century,[19] we cannot ignore the fact that Yiddish was the colloquial language of the vast majority. In addition to the Hebrew and Yiddish documents of that period, there appears an increasing number of documents using the German language, though written in Hebrew characters.[20] It is not surprising then, that many official pronouncements,[21] including, in particular, the Prussian Emancipation Edict of 11th March 1812,[22] should have stipulated the use of German in commercial transactions, private treaties, etc.

The role of language as an instrument of differentiation is confirmed in a large number of autobiographical narratives[23] for a period extending well into the twentieth century.[24] Perhaps even more important is the fact that in the German literature of the eighteenth and nineteenth centuries – including both prose fiction and stage plays – Jews are commonly characterised by their use of "jargon" or other linguistic habits felt to be odd and alien by the majority. Here, of course, an exception must be made for the drama of the Enlightenment which, in accordance with its tenets, presented the Jews in a positive light, in glaring contrast to the traditional typology. In those plays, the Jewish heroes mostly speak a pure high German.[25] It is noteworthy, however, that in the common run of plays, Jews using "jargon" are portrayed as negative characters, usually belonging to the lower strata.[26] This role of jargon as a mark of status occurs equally in plays by Jewish authors, among them S. Höchheimer.[27]

[19]On the knowledge of German in the eighteenth and first half of the nineteenth century, cf. A. Shohet, *Beginnings of the Haskalah among German Jewry* (in Hebrew), Jerusalem 1960, pp. 58–63; J. Toury, 'Deutsche Juden im Vormärz', in *Bulletin des Leo Baeck Instituts*, VIII (1965), No. 29, pp. 75 ff.; Steven M. Lowenstein, 'The Pace of Modernisation of German Jewry in the Nineteenth Century', in *LBI Year Book XXI* (1976), pp. 44 ff.

[20]For an example of the former, cf. H. M. Graupe (ed.), *Die Statuten der drei Gemeinden Altona, Hamburg und Wandsbek* (Hamburger Beiträge zur Geschichte der deutschen Juden, Bd. 3), part 1, Hamburg 1973, p. 47; for the latter, cf. Isaak Wetzlar's *Libes Briv* and M. Mendelssohn's *Frometbriefe*.

[21]Three examples from Northern Germany: Rescript of the Danish King Christian VII, dated 29th July 1796, requiring the judgments of the Altona Rabbinical Court to be given in the High German language, quoted in G. Marwedel (ed.), *Die Privilegien der Juden in Altona* (Hamburger Beiträge zur Geschichte der deutschen Juden, Bd. 5), Hamburg 1976, pp. 349 f.; 'Entwurf zu einer Verordnung für die Herzogthümer Schleswig und Holstein, die Verhältnisse der mosaischen Glaubensgenossen betreffend', *Allgemeine Zeitung des Judenthums*, No. 34 (22nd August 1840); 'Gesetz betreffend die Verhältnisse der Juden im Herzogtum Holstein vom 14. Juli 1863', in Marwedel, *op. cit.*, p. 413.

[22]Cf. J. Freund, *Die Emanzipation der Juden in Preußen*, vol. 2, Berlin 1912, p. 455.

[23]Cf. Monica Richarz (ed.), *Jüdisches Leben in Deutschland. Selbstzeugnisse zur Sozialgeschichte 1780–1871*, Stuttgart 1976, Veröffentlichung des Leo Baeck Instituts, sub index 'Judendeutsch'; Ingrid Belke (ed.) *Moritz Lazarus und Heymann Steinthal. Die Begründer der Völkerpsychologie in ihren Briefen*, Tübingen 1971 (Schriftenreihe wissenschaftlicher Abhandlungen des Leo Baeck Instituts 21), pp. 375 ff.

[24]See, e.g., Gershom Scholem, 'Von Berlin nach Jerusalem. Jugenderinnerungen', in *Neue Rundschau*, 87 (1976), pp. 544, 547 f. An extended version was published under the same title as a book, Frankfurt a. Main 1977, pp. 36 ff.

[25]Cf. H. G. Klemm, 'Der Topos vom guten Juden. Beobachtungen zur Bühnenfigur des Juden in den Dramen Schröders, Ifflands und Kotzebues', in *Theokratia*, II (1970–72), Leyden 1973, pp. 340–371.

[26]Cf. H. Jenzsch, *Jüdische Figuren in deutschen Bühnentexten des 18. Jahrhunderts*, doctoral thesis, Hamburg 1974, p. 173.

[27]*Der Spiegel für Israeliten. Ein Gegenstück zu der Posse "Unser Verkehr"*, Nuremberg 1817.

Here, language is used as a mark of differentiation for educational purposes. It is quite another thing when Jews in general are characterised by "their" language, as was predominantly the case in the serious literature as well as in popular novels and newspaper cartoons in the nineteenth century, often under the influence of antisemitic convictions.[28]

There is another sphere in which the profound significance of linguistic behaviour for the relationship between the Jewish minority and the majority society is clearly manifested. Beginning in the early years of the eighteenth century, a growing number of publications appeared in which Christian authors dealt with the "Judaeo–German" language (*Jüdisch–deutsch* or *Judendeutsch*). To begin with, this literature presented chiefly studies of idiom, prompted by missionary intentions. But towards the end of the eighteenth century and afterwards there is an increasing tendency in such publications to explore the supposed mysteries of the "Jewish commercial and business language".[29] Continuing on that tack, the next step is to declare *Judendeutsch*[30] to be virtually identical with the jargon of crooks and robbers.[31] A characteristic example of this type of reasoning was provided by A. F. Thiele at the beginning of the 1840s:

> "The Jewish crooks differ from their Christian fellow crooks ... both as regards the character of their criminal activity and their thieves' jargon. Whereas the terminology of the Christian crooks varies from province to province, so that frequently communication between them becomes difficult, the Jewish jargon is the same throughout Germany".[32]

Thiele's book was published at a time when organised criminal bands had been largely eliminated,[33] so that crooks and thieves worked, as a rule, individually.

---

[28]This tendency is implied, e.g., in Gustav Freytag's *Soll und Haben*. For instances of cartoons, see E. Fuchs, *Die Juden in der Karikatur*, Munich 1921. On the linguistic situation in both Jewish and antisemitic jokes, cf. most recently L. Röhrich, *Der Witz. Figuren, Formen, Funktionen*, Stuttgart 1977, pp. 275–285. Antisemitic novels of the twentieth century – e.g., A. Dinter's *Die Sünde wider das Blut* – are using the same method. On group-specific linguistic peculiarities in Northern Germany in the nineteenth century, cf. H.-D. Loose, 'Zur Funktion des Niederdeutschen in den Karikaturen der Hamburger Zeitung "Reform"', in *Zeitschrift des Vereins für Hamburgische Geschichte*, 60 (1974), p. 189. A selection from the cartoons, drawn by Christian Förster, was subsequently published as *Hamburger Bilderbogen*. The fourth issue is headed 'Unsere Lait', Hamburg n.d. The captions are written in the Jewish variant of High German (*jüdelnd*). Enduring interest in publications with a German-Jewish accent on the part of a Jewish reading public is documented as late as the middle of the nineteenth century. See for instance *Bilder aus de Neischtad. Scenen aus dem Leben von unse Lait, dargeschtellt von Schlomche Beer*, Hamburg 1843, or *Galanter Fremdenführer mit Adressen dorch Hamborgs Schaine Gegenden*, by Daniel Meschores, Hamburg 1855. See also H. Denkler, 'Flugblätter in "jüdischdeutschem" Dialekt aus dem revolutionären Berlin 1848/49', in *Jahrbuch des Instituts für Deutsche Geschichte*, VI, Tel-Aviv 1977, pp. 215–257.
[29]Cf. the survey given by F. C. B. Avé-Lallemant in *Das Deutsche Gaunerthum in seiner socialpolitischen, literarischen und linguistischen Ausbildung zu seinem heutigen Bestande*, vol. 3, pp. 230–240.
[30]Terms such as *Judendeutsch* or *Jüdisch-deutsch* appear in the sources quoted. In our text the term Yiddish (*Jiddisch*) is used, which is the designation now generally used by philologists for the "Western Yiddish" of the German Jews.
[31]Avé-Lallemant, *op. cit.*, vol. 3, p. 46.
[32]A. F. Thiele, *Die jüdischen Gauner in Deutschland, ihre Taktik, ihre Eigenthümlichkeiten und ihre Sprache, nebst ausführlichen Nachrichten über die in Deutschland und an dessen Grenzen sich aufhaltenden berüchtigsten jüdischen Gauner*, Berlin ²1842, p. 199. The work was positively reviewed in *Orient* of 5th February 1842. The second volume of the work appeared in Berlin in 1843.
[33]Cf. C. Küther, *Räuber und Gauner in Deutschland. Das organisierte Bandenwesen im 18. und frühen*

Language and Assimilation

Distinction on religious grounds thus seems to indicate an anti-Jewish bias on the part of the author, unless he was merely repeating old clichés. Twenty years later Avé-Lallemant showed greater discernment in dealing with this problem. Anticipating objections to his procedure of "considering the German-Jewish language in the middle of an investigation of thieves' cant", he argued that even in the middle of the nineteenth century the concepts of "Jew" and "crook" were being regarded as identical and that there was talk of a "Jewish fraternity of crooks" and a "Jewish thieves' cant". Accordingly, he thought it opportune to "dissociate and separate the different substances as in a critical chemical process".[34]

Faced with an increasingly negative reaction to Yiddish on the part of the non-Jewish outside world in the first half of the nineteenth century, Jewish circles bent on assimilation endeavoured to remove that stumbling block. The chances of success were favourable for two reasons: in the first place, more and more Jews were prepared to shed old speech habits, and the use of German became more widespread from generation to generation. In the second place, there was a general tendency in the society at large to replace dialects by the high language, a trend actively supported and encouraged by philologists and educationists. At a time when philology had reached a dominant position as the "cultural discipline *par excellence*"[35] and language teaching had assumed an unprecedented importance,[36] such endeavours of linguistic acculturation could scarcely fail.

II

Contempt for local vernaculars is eloquently expressed in a travel journal of 1789, recording in a fastidious style impressions of a visit to Hamburg, where the traveller is partly amused, but even more pained by the Low German dialect coming from the lips of ladies and gentlemen he met even at "excellent *auberges*" or at the stock exchange, where "I thought a thousand times: Oh: *si tacuisses!*"

---

19. *Jahrhundert* (Kritische Studien zur Geschichtswissenschaft, Bd. 20), Göttingen 1976. According to Küther, "by the time around 1800, at any rate, it was hardly possible to draw a neat dividing line between purely Jewish bands and their German neighbours" (p. 155, note 59).

[34]Avé-Lallemant, *op. cit.*, vol. 3, p. XI.

[35]R. Vierhaus, 'Bildung', in O. Brunner, W. Conze, R. Koselleck (eds.), *Geschichtliche Grundbegriffe. Historisches Lexikon zur politisch-sozialen Sprache in Deutschland*, vol. 1, Stuttgart 1972, p. 536. See also H. Gipper and P. Schmitter, 'Sprachwissenschaft und Sprachphilosophie im Zeitalter der Romantik', in *Current Trends in Linguistics*, vol. 13 (Historiography of Linguistics), The Hague–Paris 1975, pp. 481–606. Of particular interest for the North German region are the remarks by a man who at the time taught at the *Israelitische Freischule* in Hamburg, Immanuel Wohlwill, in an article, 'Bemerkungen über Sprache und Sprachunterricht, als Beförderungsmittel der allgemeinen Bildung', in *Sulamith*, vol. 7 [1825], No. 1, pp. 25–42.

[36]Cf. G. Jäger, 'Humanismus und Realismus. Schulorganisation und Sprachunterricht 1770–1840', in *Internationales Archiv für Sozialgeschichte der deutschen Literatur*, 1 (1976), pp. 146–159.

He would have liked people of good standing to adopt "the more refined Upper Saxon or High German speech".[37]

Fifteen years later an anonymous author reported in a magazine article upon the situation of the Jews in Hamburg and Altona. The article, which indicates a very positive attitude on the part of the author, contains the following passage:

> "Viewed from every possible angle, I find it entirely incomprehensible why our Jews in their large majority should persist to obstinately in speaking the language of the country in which they have their homes, the language that has become their mother-tongue in a mutilated form that is most offensive to the ear. Even when they speak the correct language without any alien admixture, they do it with an accent that is no less unpleasant than the mutilation of language itself, and which is commonly called the Jewish dialect . . . In these days when on the whole so little weight is attached to differences of religion, that language, which is so conspicuously disagreeable, is one of the main disturbers of the peace. It is not only the German whose ear is offended by the discordant sounds of that speech. The same applies to any non-Jewish person, and herein lies the proof that this language is truly objectionable and an outrage against universal public taste, which surely means against *genuine good* taste. And taste, once offended, is implacable: it inevitably takes revenge by mockery and ridicule."[38]

---

[37]"Will man den ächten Genius der rechten derben provinziellen Sprache in Hamburg kennen lernen, so darf man nur auf den vornehmsten Victualienmarkt (Hoppenmaark wird er hier genennt) oder auch an die Börse (naa de Beurs) gehen. Ich hatte oft Mühe, auf letzterer die Erschütterung meines Zwerchfelles zu unterdrücken, wenn ich den feinsten Süßling, dessen äußere Eleganz meine Aufmerksamkeit auf sich zog, sein Jargon langsam und zerrend aus dem Munde herauspoltern hörte. O! si tacuisses! dachte ich tausendmal. Selbst in angesehenern Familiengesellschaften und in den vorzüglichen Auberges trifst Du häufig mehrere Damen und Herren, die sich durchaus nicht zu der feinern obersächsischen oder hochdeutschen Mundart bequemen wollen, und die einem mit ihrem starken Plattdeutschen die Ohren überfüllen."

Niedersachsen (In seinem neuesten politischen, civilen und literarischen Zustande). Ein in der Lüneburger Haide gefundenes merkwürdiges Reisejournal. Herausgegeben von Quintus Aemilius Publicola, 3 vols., (fictitious place of publication, "Rome") 1789, vol. 1, pp. 176 f. (reprinted Hamburg 1975). The anonymous author was Johann Hermann Stoever. For a biographical note, see R. Graewe in *Stader Jahrbuch*, 1963, pp. 129–143. Here, the two distinct uses of the term "low" should be noted. *Low German* (the group of dialects of Western and Northern Germany) is contrasted with the *Upper German* dialects of the South. Either of them can be contrasted as a "low", subordinate variant with *High German*.

[38]"Von jeder Seite betrachtet, ist es mir in der That unbegreiflich, warum unsre Juden in der bei weitem grössern Zahl, noch immer so fest dabei beharren, die Sprache des Landes, in welchem sie einheimisch geworden sind, die für sie Muttersprache geworden ist, verstümmelt, und zwar für das Ohr äußerst unangenehm verstümmelt, zu sprechen; und selbst, wenn sie dieselbe auch ohne fremde Beimischung und rein sprechen, es in einem Ton thun, der abermals so unangenehm als die Verstümmelung der Sprache selbst ist, und den man gemeiniglich den jüdischen Dialekt nennt . . . In unsern Zeiten, da man im Durchschnitt wirklich nur noch sehr wenig aus der Verschiedenheit der Religion macht, ist in der That jene, auf eine so unangenehme Art sich auszeichnende Sprache eine der Hauptfriedenstöhrerinnen. Nicht nur das Ohr des Deutschen, nein, das Ohr jedes andern Nichtjuden empfindet das außerordentlich Mißtönende derselben; und das ist ein Beweis, daß sie es wirklich sey und daß sie dem allgemeinen, das heißt ja wohl so viel als, dem *wahren guten* Geschmak anstößig seyn müsse; und der beleidigte Geschmak ist unversöhnlich; er rächt sich unausbleiblich durch Spott und Lächerlichmachen."

'Über den Zustand unserer Judenschaft', in Hamburg und Altona. Ein Journal zur Geschichte der Zeit, der Sitten und des Geschmaks, 3 (1804), No. 6, pp. 291–308; No. 8, pp. 129–142. The quoted passage is on p. 134. About 6,400 Jews lived in Hamburg around 1800, thus forming the largest Jewish community in Germany. Cf. H. Krohn, *Die Juden in Hamburg 1800–1850. Ihre soziale und politische Entwicklung während der Emanzipationszeit*, Frankfurt a. Main 1967, p. 9.

Language and Assimilation 165

The two travellers' comments strikingly illuminate the linguistic and social conditions prevailing in Hamburg at the turn of the eighteenth century. The debate on language, dialect and jargon was by no means confined to the Jewish minority, but concerned to no less a degree the society at large. Yet there are noteworthy differences in the appraisals of the two authors: whereas Stoever, for all his censoriousness, was inclined to dismiss the oddities of Low German with a superior smile, the anonymous author, writing in the best tradition of the Enlightenment, sounded a distinct note of reproach. It must be added, however, that the editorial attitude of the magazine was one of greater detachment. A footnote of the publisher, appended on the next page, said:

"Is the discordant character of the Jewish–German dialect really as evident as the author assumes? Accent is a matter of habit."[39]

The prevalence of Yiddish continued to be the subject of comment in the nineteenth century,[40] but to assess their significance it is necessary to consider these criticisms in the context of the contemporary discussions on the respective roles of high language and dialect. During the eighteenth and well into the nineteenth century, mastery of High German was by no means to be taken for granted in Northern Germany, even in middle-class circles.[41] As Stoever's journal makes clear, *Plattdeutsch*, the Low German dialect, was still predominant, even in the towns. Yet, in the fields of administration and education – in that order – High German had gained substantial ground in the sixteenth and seventeenth centuries.[42] As early as 1650, Lübeck, Hamburg and Bremen had adopted High German as the language of official transactions and negotiations and of school instruction; nevertheless, Low German maintained its position as the medium of everyday intercourse, so that as late as 1765 the Bremen city fathers saw themselves compelled to issue a rigorous ban on the use of Low German at school.[43] In Hamburg the civic oath was administered in the Low German dialect until 1845.[44]

From the 1830s onward, the gradual displacement of the Low German vernacular by High German was accompanied by a debate which at times was

---

[39]"Über den Zustand . . .', *loc. cit.*, p. 135.
[40]Cf. *Allgemeine Zeitung des Judenthums* of 26th September 1837: "News from Hamburg . . . To the stranger, the poorer classes of the Jews make themselves conspicuous by their jargon which, as in most large communities, they speak with an almost complete lack of inhibition. But the intermediate sections, too, and in part even the higher classes have retained some habits that set them apart and which they might well have dropped long ago, especially as they have nothing to do with religious observances." *Der Orient* of 24th January 1843: "The *Israelitische Freischule* in Hamburg . . . One should not underrate the difficulties confronting a teacher who has to instruct a large number of pupils from the poorer classes. We are aware of the horribly corrupt jargon spoken in their homes. The pupil must learn to forget a lot, before the teacher can break through and begin to make welcome progress. But should it be necessary for the teacher to have to fight the same shortcomings in the higher forms?"
[41]Cf. R. Engelsing, *Analphabetentum und Lektüre*, Stuttgart 1973, p. 77 f.
[42]Cf. A. Gabrielsson, *Das Eindringen der hochdeutschen Sprache in die Schulen Niederdeutschlands im 16. und 17. Jahrhundert*, doctoral thesis, Hamburg 1933.
[43]*Ibid.*, p. 39.
[44]Cf. J. Bolland, 'Die Sprache des Gesetzgebers in Hamburg', in *Zeitschrift des Vereins für Hamburgische Geschichte*, 60 (1974), p. 152.

conducted with some vehemence. To begin with, it was the champions of High German who carried the day. In a pamphlet published in 1834 in Hamburg, Ludolf Wienbarg, one of the spokesmen of the literary movement known as *Das Junge Deutschland*, argued in favour of "extirpating" the Low German language which, he thought, militated against the spreading of education and culture.[45] Wienbarg's demand for the extirpation of Low German as a language "inimical to education and intellectual activity",[46] bears some resemblance to some modern sociolinguistic propositions postulating "compensatory language education" so as to remove social language barriers. On the other hand, the role the High language is destined to play as a "common language of all Germans",[47] though mentioned by Wienbarg, is not of primary importance in his scheme.

A similar line of reasoning can be found in a pamphlet by A. Seitz, published in 1840. Seitz, himself a teacher, drew attention to the "disadvantages accruing for the educational progress of *Gymnasium* pupils from the exclusive use of *Plattdeutsch* as a colloquial language", and demanded that "the High German language must become the mother tongue of every German".[48] He went on to point out – as many of his colleagues would point out today – that "of two children similarly gifted and of the same age, the one speaking High German will always be further advanced in his intellectual development than the one speaking *Plattdeutsch*".[49]

Yet another publication in the same vein came from the Jewish physician J. Goldschmidt, who in a lecture published in 1846, described *Plattdeutsch* as "a great obstacle to any kind of education and culture".[50]

Such was the background against which in 1844 Anton Rée's book on "the language conditions of contemporary Jews, in the interest of the present age

---

[45] Ludolf Wienbarg, *Soll die plattdeutsche Sprache gepflegt oder ausgerottet werden? Gegen Ersteres und für Letzteres*, Hamburg 1834. He writes on p. 10: "Plattdeutsch has long since become too narrow for the intellectual level of our age. It stopped growing in the sixteenth century; it cannot absorb and reproduce the intellectual and material advances of civilisation, and thus condemns the vast majority of the people in Northern Germany, who still use it for everyday communication, to a state of tutelage, brutishness and intellectual vacuity, in glaring and outrageous contrast to the condition of the educated."

[46] *Ibid.*, p. 11.

[47] *Ibid.*, p. 8.

[48] A. Seitz, *Über die Nachteile welche aus dem Gebrauche der plattdeutschen Sprache als ausschließlicher Umgangssprache für die Bildung der Gymnasialschüler hervorgehen. Rede, gehalten bei Gelegenheit eines Schulexamens*, Norden 1840, p. 10.

[49] *Ibid.*, p. 12.

[50] J. Goldschmidt, *Über das Plattdeutsche als ein großes Hemmnis jeder Bildung*, Oldenburg 1846. Reference to this work is made in K. Schulte Kemminghausen, *Mundart und Hochsprache in Norddeutschland*, Neumünster 1939, p. 66. Schulte Kemminghausen deals with the debates between the advocates of Low and High German. In outlining Wienbarg's position and also in some other places, the author shows a marked antisemitic tendency. Naming Heine and Börne as the foremost representatives of the *Junge Deutschland*, he attributed the acceptance by Wienbarg and others of the ideas of the Enlightenment to Jewish influence. He credited Wienbarg with some national feeling, but censured him for an "utter lack of any feeling for the domains of emotion and will in the human make-up" (p. 68). A new appreciation of Low German, notably as a literary language, came later in the nineteenth century, beginning in the 1850s, promoted above all by the collections of Low German poetry by Klaus Groth, *Quickborn*, 1852, and the literary work of Fritz Reuter.

Language and Assimilation

and with special regard for popular education" was published.[51] In the context of the general debate on the role of High German, this book was the most important comment from Jewish quarters, focusing attention in particular on the Jewish aspects of the wider problem. Rée's work has been the subject of earlier studies, which linked his views with critical statements about Yiddish from Heinrich Graetz and others and proceeded to examine his demands from an exclusively Jewish angle.[52] Here, in contrast, it is proposed to draw on new local sources and to point to certain features – hitherto overlooked – that are common to the case made by Rée and arguments put forward by non-Jewish champions of the cause of High German.

Anton Rée was born in Hamburg on 9th November 1815 and died in the same town on 13th January 1891. After graduating at Kiel University in 1837 as a doctor of philosophy, in the following year he took a teaching post at the *Israelitische Freischule* in Hamburg, a Jewish educational institution founded in 1815. In spring 1848 he succeeded Eduard Kley as head of the school, a post he retained till he died. In addition to his work as an educationist, he engaged actively in politics as a member of the Hamburg Constituent Assembly of 1848, of the Hamburg City Assembly (*Bürgerschaft*) 1859–1871, of the Constituent Diet of the North German Confederacy (1867) and of the *Reichstag* (1881–1884). A staunch liberal, he made a name for himself in particular as a protagonist of the general primary school.[53]

Before entering into a discussion of Rée's propositions, it will be well to give a brief sketch of the position of the German language as a subject of instruction at the Jewish schools in Hamburg during the period in question, for it is only in this context that the motivation and the value of his approach can be clearly appreciated.

At the *Freischule*, the German language was from the outset treated as a subject of special importance.[54] Even before the school's foundation, in 1814, E. Michaelis, who later became head of the school, wrote in a memorandum:

> "General instruction in the second form should be combined by the teacher with instruction in the German language according to a primer, but more along practical than theor-

---

[51] Anton Rée, *Die Sprachverhältnisse der heutigen Juden, im Interesse der Gegenwart und mit besonderer Rücksicht auf Volkserziehung*, Hamburg November/December 1844.
[52] For a survey, see H. Beem, 'Yiddish in Holland. Linguistic and Sociolinguistic Notes', in *The Field of Yiddish. Studies in Yiddish Language, Folklore and Literature* [1], New York 1954, p. 123; and most recently Julius Carlebach, 'Deutsche Juden und der Säkularisierungsprozess in der Erziehung. Kritische Bemerkungen zu einem Problemkreis der jüdischen Emanzipation', in *Das Judentum in der Deutschen Umwelt 1800–1850. Studien zur Frühgeschichte der Emanzipation*, herausgegeben von Hans Liebeschütz und Arnold Paucker, Tübingen 1977 (Schriftenreihe wissenschaftlicher Abhandlungen des Leo Baeck Instituts 35), p. 71. On Rée, cf. Toury, '"Deutsche Juden" im Vormärz', loc. cit., p. 76.
[53] Cf. J. Feiner, *Dr. Anton Rée, ein Kämpfer für Fortschritt und Recht*, Hamburg 1906. For Rée's political convictions – which are outside the scope of this study – see M. Zimmermann, *Hamburgischer Patriotismus und deutscher Nationalismus. Die Emanzipation der Juden in Hamburg 1830–1865* (Hamburger Beiträge zur Geschichte der deutschen Juden, Bd. 6), Hamburg 1979, p. 109 ff.
[54] For the school's history up to 1891, cf. E. Müller, *Geschichte der Stiftungsschule von 1815 zu Hamburg. Festschrift zum 100 jährigen Bestehen der Schule*, Hamburg n.d. [1915]. On p. 21, Müller points out that the Portuguese Jews in Hamburg spoke *plattdeutsch*, "whereas the German Jews, even in the *plattdeutsche* language region, spoke a corrupt High German dialect".

etical lines. The aim of instruction in the mother tongue is that the children should be able to speak as faultlessly as possible, with a pure accent; and that they should be able to spell correctly . . . to copy written material and write down texts learnt by heart or dictated to them."

Regarding the subject of calligraphy, the memorandum said: "At this school, the children will be taught only to write the Gothic and Latin scripts."[55] In the Bill on the *Israelitische Freischule* in Hamburg, published in Altona in 1820, Clause 3 demands the "extinction of all peculiarities in custom, language and behaviour", and Clause 22 lays down:

> "In all three forms, primacy before all other subjects of instruction shall be accorded to the German mother tongue, which at all times should be considered the most important subject at this school, so that a clear and pure language, free of all alien elements, shall spread from here."

The statutes of the school, as revised in 1850, do not refer to particular subjects or syllabuses. However, a supplement to the statutes, signed by the Praeses of the school, Ferdinand Beit states:

> "Compared with other subjects, in all classes a great deal of time is devoted to the mother tongue, which in our case appears to be doubly justified, as we have to combat a peculiar dialect spoken by many of our boys."[56]

The *Freischule* was not alone in its endeavour. At the *Talmud-Tora-Schule*, founded in 1805, Chaham Isaak Bernays introduced in 1822 a reform of the syllabus, with instruction in the German language included for the first time. This school went to the length of appointing a Christian teacher, so as to make sure, as Bernays put it at the time,

> "that the accent of a complete stranger should counteract the careless dialect, and that the presence of a stranger should impose certain constraints on the conduct of the boys, with beneficial effects on discipline".[57]

Such endeavours, however, did not interfere with the principle of maintaining separate Jewish schools. The issue was concisely summed up in an article in

---

[55] Staatsarchiv Hamburg, Bestand Jüdische Gemeinden 535a.
[56] Staatsarchiv Hamburg, Staats- und Privatschulen, Israelitische Freischule, 11 A 4. For the first few years after 1816, the lists of pupils of the *Freischule* also contain the school reports, but as time went on, less and less information was recorded. There are, however, occasional entries referring to a pupil's "Jewish" or "Hebrew" accent. See Staatsarchiv Hamburg, Staats- und Privatschulen, Israelitische Freischule I C 1–3.
[57] J. Goldschmidt, *Geschichte der Talmud Tora-Realschule in Hamburg. Festschrift zur Hundertjahrfeier der Anstalt 1805–1905*, Hamburg n.d. [1905], pp. 57 f. See also the memoir of Bernays in M. M. Haarbleicher, *Zwei Epochen aus der Geschichte der Deutsch-Israelitischen Gemeinde in Hamburg*, Hamburg 1867, pp. 248 ff. The orthodox Rabbi Ettlinger also appointed Christian teachers at his private school in Altona, according to M. Eliav, *Jewish Education in Germany in the Period of Enlightenment and Emancipation* (in Hebrew), Jerusalem 1960, p. 235. Interesting material, including remarks on German language instruction, can be found in a list of Jewish private schools and schools for the poor, compiled in 1829 on the initiative of Senator Abendroth (Staatsarchiv Hamburg, Bestand Jüdische Gemeinden 532). At that time there were five schools for the poor, attended by 311 boys and 163 girls, as well as seventeen private schools attended by 236 boys and 134 girls. The *Talmud Tora-Schule* numbered 181 pupils, the *Freischule* 130. Another report on Jewish schools in Hamburg in the first half of the nineteenth century in E. Zimmermann (ed.), 'Erinnerungen des Hamburger Bibliothekars Meyer Isler (1807–1888)', in *Zeitschrift des Vereins für Hamburgische Geschichte*, 47 (1961), in particular pp. 48–52.

Orient of 2nd January 1841, which posed the question: "Are Jewish institutions of education needed, and what should they be like if they are to answer their purpose?" In answering this question, the magazine said:

> "The objection that Jewish children would be placed in a better position to learn to get rid of peculiarities of speech and gesture if they were attending Christian schools cannot be dismissed out of hand. Even though well-educated Jewish teachers have an important contribution to make to that end, daily intercourse with Christian children is undoubtedly far more effective. But such considerations are of no significance and carry no weight at all when a truly vital concern, the upholding of the religion, is at stake."

The shift of emphasis in the teaching of German was equally pronounced in the case of a school for poor Jewish girls, the *Unterrichts-Anstalt für arme israelitische Mädchen*, founded in 1798. According to the statutes of 1825, instruction in needlework was deemed no less important than "scholarly study", with "reading of Hebrew and German" ranking third among the "scholarly subjects". The revised version of the statutes, dated 8th September 1851, relegated needlework to eighth place out of nine subjects, while German became a subject in its own right, a position which it retained after a further revision of the statutes in 1859. The same trend affected instruction in "Judaeo-German writing": to begin with, under the 1825 statutes, a separate subject, it rates in 1851 only a passing mention in a note appended to the section on "Calligraphy in the Gothic and Latin script", which says: "Reading Hebrew in the final year, provided it is clear that there is a felt want for this subject." The restriction is made yet more explicit in the 1859 statutes, which stipulate: "Judaeo-German writing will be taught in optional lessons to those children whose parents wish them to receive this instruction."[58] At the *Freischule*, a petition by a group of parents, requesting that instruction in the senior forms should include Judaeo-German writing – "a minor skill, yet for the lack of which many former pupils got into difficulties when, after leaving school, they took up work in offices" – was rejected by the governors at their meeting on 17th October 1825 on the grounds that it was "not in keeping with the primary object and needs of a general secondary school (*Bürgerschule*)".[59]

Now to Anton Rée and his "language relations". The salient points of this programmatic essay are the demand that "the civic position of the Jew must be bettered",[60] and the statement that "apart from the possible envy of Christian

---

[58]Staatsarchiv Hamburg, Bestand Jüdische Gemeinden 536a.

[59]Staatsarchiv Hamburg, Staats- und Privatschulen, Israelitische Freischule, II A 9, protocol of 17th October 1825. In David Friedländer's primer – *Lesebuch für Jüdische Kinder*, Berlin 1779; new edition by M. Stern, Soncino Gesellschaft, Berlin 1927 – the children are introduced at the beginning to the German (Gothic letters), Latin and "Jewish" alphabets. Heymann Steinthal wrote about his schooldays at a Jewish school in Anhalt between 1830 and 1840: "The bottom form wrote only *Jüdisch*, the middle form alternately *Jüdisch* and German, the upper form only German and Latin." (Belke (ed.), *op. cit.*, p. 382.) *Der Orient* of 21st November 1843 wrote: "So long as our parents and grandparents are not entirely familiar with the German written language, it is necessary to continue to cultivate the Judaeo-German script." The issue continued for a long time to be topical, as can be seen from comments in the *Allgemeine Zeitung des Judenthums* of 23rd June and 8th September 1868. Avé-Lallemant noted in 1862 that the use of that script was still "incredibly widespread" (*op. cit.*, vol. 3, p. 256; vol. 3 was published in 1862).

[60]Rée, *op. cit.*, p. 20.

competitors and the disabilities imposed by the law of the land, the greatest obstacle to the prospering of the Jewish artisan and worker is his peculiar speech".[61] Nor is that the worst handicap imposed by the dialect on its speakers, for:

> "its corroding and empoisoning effects are yet more manifest in social life, where the baneful influence is not left to work itself out in the future but can be seen to have acted in the past and to be acting in the present".[62]

According to Rée, the continuing use of the dialect was inspired by "old Jewish" attitudes. With some passion he exclaimed:

> "I do love the past, which is unforgettable and as close to my heart as are my own father and mother, and I look upon it with the eyes of a grateful and reverent child. But at the same time I must listen also to the demand of the present and the call of the future, and I must leave the parental home: indeed, I must find a new home and give myself to my new life so as to become *one* flesh and *one* blood with it. Ancient Jewish life be blessed by me and honoured. Yet for me and for my future it is a thing of the *past*. It has fulfilled its purpose and is no longer equal to the new unfolding prospects which I am driven by an ethical imperative to pursue. It must give way to the new fatherland."[63]

The unavoidable conclusion for Rée is that for the sake of "social reconciliation" the Jews must get rid of the "special dialect" *in all classes*.[64] This, in his view, can be achieved only:

> "by the right approach to the *young generation*, that is to say by either abolishing the existing separate educational institutions, or by ensuring that they will act decisively against anything conducive to isolation".[65]

A comparison of Rée's remarks with the publications of Wienbarg and Seitz shows that some of the arguments used by the three authors in favour of the elimination of dialect are identical. All three point out that dialect impedes the dissemination of culture and learning and appeal to teachers and schools to remedy that shortcoming by intensified efforts to promote the High German language. Rée emphasises this demand by suggesting the abolition of separate Jewish schools and the establishment of general primary schools for all.[66] The relationship between nationality and language is similarly noted by all three authors,[67] although Rée attaches more importance to this argument than the others, since he has to deal with the problem of a Jewish nationality.[68] In arguing the same case, Wienbarg and Seitz even used the same words. To Wienbarg the High German language was "the mighty bond (*Band*) uniting North and South",[69] while Seitz described the common language as a "bond tying the members of a nation most solidly and enduringly together as links

---

[61]*Ibid.*, p. 36.
[62]*Ibid.*, pp. 39 f.
[63]*Ibid.*, pp. 55 f.
[64]*Ibid.*, p. 123.
[65]*Ibid.*, p. 133.
[66]*Ibid.*, pp. 125 ff.
[67]*Ibid.*, p. 119; Wienbarg, *op. cit.*, p. 18; Seitz, *op. cit.*, p. 9.
[68]Rée, *op. cit.*, pp. 53 ff., 131 ff.
[69]Wienbarg, *op. cit.*, p. 8.

in a chain".[70] A similar terminology, incidentally, was used by Friedrich Hebbel in a critical essay on Wienbarg's pamphlet, referring to the "only bond still knitting together the German tribes".[71] Not surprisingly, both Wienbarg and Hebbel invoked Martin Luther's name in this context. Finally, it may be noted that all three authors – Wienbarg, Seitz and Rée – looked upon the family as the citadel of dialect, in Wienbarg's words the "custodian of the most intimate and affectionate relationships".[72] This observation is borne out by more recent findings concerning familial socialisation and language behaviour.

The idea that a dialect speaker invites mockery and ridicule was emphasised as early as 1804 by the above-mentioned anonymous author's comments on the Jews of Hamburg. The same point was made frequently in the subsequent years. It is mentioned both by Seitz[73] and Rée,[74] and also – to record just one more instance – by a memorandum of the supreme Jewish authority in the Grand Duchy of Baden, the *Großherzoglich Badische Oberrath der Israeliten* at Karlsruhe in 1834.[75] The related problem of the discrediting of a social minority through its deviating speech is undoubtedly the central issue for Rée, in clear contrast to Wienbarg and Seitz, for whom the most vital concern is the dissemination of culture and knowledge among the lower classes. In Wienbarg's case this was not mere theory, for, on his own evidence, he felt driven to write his pamphlet by specific instances of social injustice, "by several shameful trials in which the Eutin judiciary arraigned a number of hapless, desperate and destitute agricultural labourers, who virtually had no roof over their heads . . . nearly all of whom were unable to speak the High German language and thus were as good as defenceless, utterly helpless victims of arbitrary power".[76] With his demand for more "popular education" he followed the best traditions of the Enlightenment. Rée also supported this demand, and, judged by today's standards, he made out a better case by drawing the relevant conclusions from an analysis of the problem, whereas Wienbarg argued on the moral plane and gave little attention to the social implications. Rée, on the other hand, contrived in an impressive manner to demonstrate the import of specific language behaviour and its dependence on social conditions. Speakers of the dialect, he noted, were placed at a disadvantage by no means confined to earning opportunities and social relations, an iniquitous state of affairs that must be remedied. He found that "the degree to which the dialect is dominant in individual cases depends on the social status of the individual and on the kind of people with whom he has regular contacts and with whom he lives, as determined by birth, kinship, education, occupation and intercourse, since our language is largely fashioned by our environment and even the individual endowed with the gifts

---

[70]Seitz, *op. cit.*, p. 9.
[71]Friedrich Hebbel, 'Vom Büchertisch' (1858), in *Sämtliche Werke*, edited by R. M. Werner, Berlin 1901 ff., vol. 12, p. 114.
[72]Wienbarg, *op. cit.*, p. 27.
[73]Seitz, *op. cit.*, p. 7.
[74]Rée, *op. cit.*, p. 40.
[75]J. Toury, *Der Eintritt der Juden ins deutsche Bürgertum. Eine Dokumentation*, Tel Aviv 1972, pp. 312 f. See also K. Streckfuss, *Über das Verhältniß der Juden zu dem christlichen Staate*, Halle 1833, p. 24.
[76]L. Wienbarg, *Ästhetische Feldzüge*, ed. by W. Dietze, Berlin–Weimar 1964, p. XVI.

of a genius will be only imitative in this field, to begin with".⁷⁷ Accordingly he demands the social betterment of the Jews and indeed their social integration, for "only then will the evil we are fighting be rooted out completely".⁷⁸

It is his lucid analysis of the links between language behaviour and social structure which lend Rée's work such a strikingly modern note as an outstanding early example of the sociolinguistic approach. Admittedly, Rée was influenced by the contemporary debate on high language and dialect; moreover, most of his practical suggestions for remedying the situation would appear old-fashioned and antiquated today.⁷⁹ Such weaknesses were exposed at the time by the *Allgemeine Zeitung des Judenthums*, which in 1845 devoted a series of articles in five consecutive issues to a detailed review of the book. The paper accused Rée of being "impractical" and of forgetting the role of the home – that is to say, the family – beside that of the school in his fight against the dialect.⁸⁰ Yet the decisive point was missed by the reviewer when he complained that the work was hard to understand and that its style was "precious, in the Goethian tradition, which makes it too cumbersome for the modern reading public, otherwise very correct and intelligent".⁸¹ A review in *Hamburgischer Correspondent* showed greater understanding by pointing out that the author "arrives at the non-partisan result that the peculiar traits of the Jews of today, interpreted by the opponents of emancipation as attributes of nationality, go no further than peculiarities of language".⁸²

III

The debates on the linguistic situation conducted in Northern Germany acquire special interest in the light of the fact that German became the dominant spoken as well as written language of the Jews virtually throughout the German-speaking regions within the span of a few generations.⁸³ In keeping with the view of Max Weinreich, who stressed the need "to contribute to a greater general awareness of the language factor in Jewish cultural history",⁸⁴ it is proposed

---

⁷⁷Rée, *op. cit.*, p. 88.
⁷⁸*Ibid.*, p. 24. The subject appears to have been a novel one for the contemporary Jewish public. The notice announcing the work in *Der Orient* of 17th December 1844 said that the work was "dealing with a subject never treated before, a *res intacta*: in brief, the habit of *mauscheln*".
⁷⁹This applies, for instance, to his remarks on the anatomical peculiarities of the Jews' vocal organs (p. 77). This line of reasoning, incidentally, was retained much later by H. Loewe in *Die Sprachen der Juden*, Cologne 1911, p. 77, and by the Hungarian linguist E. Schwartz, as reported by M. Weinreich, 'Roshe-prokim vegn mayrevdikn yidish', in Yudl Mark (ed.), *Yuda A. Yofe-Bukh*, New York 1958, p. 185.
⁸⁰*Allgemeine Zeitung des Judenthums*, 10th, 17th and 24th February, and 3rd and 10th March 1845.
⁸¹*Ibid.*, 10th February.
⁸²*Hamburgischer Correspondent*, 25th December 1844.
⁸³Cf. the important remarks by P. Gay, 'Begegnung mit der Moderne. Deutsche Juden in der deutschen Kultur', in *Juden im Wilhelminischen Deutschland 1890–1914*, Ein Sammelband herausgegeben von Werner Mosse unter Mitwirkung von Arnold Paucker, Tübingen 1976 (Schriftenreihe wissenschaftlicher Abhandlungen des Leo Baeck Instituts 35), p. 255.
⁸⁴M. Weinreich, 'Yiddishkayt and Yiddish. On the Impact of Religion on Language in Ashkenazic Jewry', in Fishman, *op. cit.*, p. 383. This paper was first published in *Mordecai M. Kaplan Jubilee Volume*, New York 1953, pp. 481–514.

here to review that development in a wider context and to arrive at a deeper understanding in terms of modern sociolinguistic findings.

The abandonment of Yiddish and its gradual replacement by German marked a decisive change in a linguistic situation that had endured for centuries. Hebrew as the language of religion, combined with Yiddish as intra-group colloquial language had for a long time formed the basis for the religious life and social intercourse of Ashkenazic Jewry, with a profound formative effect on awareness and mentality.[85] That does not mean that the two languages and the two spheres of life were neatly separated by a clear line of demarcation. M. Mieses in the second decade of this century[86] and Max Weinreich more recently[87] have pointed to the strong influence of the religious factor in the development of Yiddish, clearly apparent in the adoption of many Hebrew words. Conversely, late medieval Hebrew shows the influence of idiomatic peculiarities characteristic of Yiddish, so that a special Ashkenazic brand of Hebrew came into being. Weinreich has made the interesting suggestion that the opposition of "sacred versus profane" should be replaced by a distinction between "language of recording and oral language";[88] yet, the increasing literary use of Yiddish during the post-medieval period indicates the problems inherent in any scheme of rigorous functional division.

From the angle of the history of language, the gradual adoption of German brought about two significant changes:

1. In step with the advance of German as the medium of written and oral communication among the Jews in Germany, the role of Yiddish and Hebrew declined, not only among the liberal Jewish bourgeoisie, but even in orthodox circles.[89] These linguistic changes impeded contacts with East European Jewry. Thus, the emergence of a separate identity of German Jewry is not due solely to religious and socio-economic differences, but also to a considerable extent to linguistic change. The loosening of ties with the Jews of Eastern Europe was further accentuated by the fact that there the opposite trend prevailed in the nineteenth century, with Yiddish developing – in sociolinguistic terms – into a "complete language".[90]

2. No less important than the adoption of the German language was the fact that Yiddish lost its standing as a language in its own right, both among the Jews and in society at large. It came to be despised as "bad, corrupt German" or "jargon".[91] It is true that that process of disparagement was already under

[85]This observation is based on the well known Sapir–Whorf hypothesis according to which the world picture of a speech community is determined by the structure of its language. See for instance J. B. Carroll (ed.), *Language, Thought and Reality*, Cambridge (Mass.) 1956.
[86]M. Mieses, *Die Entstehungsursache der jüdischen Dialekte*, Wien 1915.
[87]Weinreich, 'Yiddishkayt . . .', *loc. cit.*
[88]*Ibid.*, p. 411.
[89]This aspect is treated in depth by M. Weinreich, *Geshikhte fun der yidishn shprakh*, New York 1973, vol. 1, pp. 251–320, with a comprehensive bibliography in vol. 3, pp. 295–297. In vol. 1, p. 287, Weinreich recalls that Yiddish had no place in the programme of Neo-Orthodoxy.
[90]H. Kloss, *Die Entwicklung neuer germanischer Kultursprachen von 1800 bis 1950*, Munich 1952, pp. 40 ff., and his paper '*Abstand* languages and *Ausbau* languages', *Anthropological Linguistics*, 9 (1967), pp. 29–41. These concepts have been fully accepted by modern sociolinguistics.
[91]Weinreich, *Geshikhte . . .*, *op. cit.*, vol. 1, p. 286.

way in the seventeenth and eighteenth centuries,[92] but it was intensified in the nineteenth century,[93] at the very time when the German dialects had largely lost their negative image, having become subjects of serious study according to modern scholarly criteria. In view of the constant influx of East European Jews into Germany during that period, the arguments about Yiddish – mocked as jargon and *mauscheln* – never ceased. Terms of abuse such as *Mauscheljude* confronted the assimilated Jewish bourgeoisie with its own supposed linguistic past, and it reacted with uncertainty, mockery, aversion and fear.[94]

Both above statements can be taken to a deeper level of understanding by proceeding from the historiolinguistic to the sociolinguistic approach. There are some fundamental sociolinguistic insights, gained by a large number of empirical investigations, which enable us to consider the relationship between language behaviour and social structure from an historical point of of view. It is taken for granted here that the two entities are linked by a certain relationship, although the precise nature of that relationship is still a controversial point among sociolinguists.[95]

Ad 1: The linguistic situation of the Jews in Germany until the early years of the nineteenth century – like that of the East European Jews well into the twentieth century – was characterised by the simultaneous prevalence of bilingualism and diglossia,[96] with the H(igh) Variant assigned to Hebrew, the L(ow) Variant to Yiddish.[97] The further development of Yiddish was significantly influenced by the German language, looked upon as a model, as evi-

[92] German Jews were said to be conspicuous for their "ridiculous pronunciation", "corrupt German" and "queer accent", according to Johann Jacob Schudt, *Jüdische Merckwürdigkeiten*, Frankfurt–Leipzig 1714, part 2, p. 291: "Es haben aber die Teutsche Juden eine sonderliche lächerliche Aussprache/verderbtes Teutsch und wunderlichen accent, daß man sie von Teutschen Christen gar leicht unterscheiden kan."

[93] As Note 91. The survival of Yiddish was also noted by I. M. Jost in his entry 'Judenteutsch, Jüdisch-Teutsch', in *Allgemeine Encyclopädie der Wissenschaften und Künste* (Ersch-Gruber), section 2, part 27, Leipzig 1850, pp. 322 ff. On p. 322 he offers his definition: "Judenteutsch, Jüdisch-Teutsch, ein Jargon . . . der den teutschen Juden . . . bis ins gegenwärtige Jahrhundert herein eigenthümlich war und ungeachtet der überall jetzt obsiegenden Muttersprache [!] noch immer nicht gänzlich gewichen ist."

[94] A situation aptly characterised by Franz Kafka in his 'Talk on the Yiddish language', in which he told his audience to their faces: ". . . some of you are so scared of the jargon that one can almost see the fear in your faces . . . Yet, fear of the jargon, fear tinged with an element of revulsion, can be understood, if one wants to understand." (F. Kafka, 'Rede über die Jiddische Sprache', in *Hochzeitsvorbereitungen auf dem Lande und andere Prosa aus dem Nachlaß*, Frankfurt a. Main 1953, p. 422.) For the context, cf. H. Binder, *Kafka-Kommentar zu den Romanen, Rezensionen, Aphorismen und zum Brief an den Vater*, Munich 1976, pp. 387–404.

[95] Cf. N. Dittmar, *op. cit.*, pp. 290–295; Engl. version, pp. 235–239.

[96] R. T. Bell, *Sociolinguistics. Goals, Approaches and Problems*, London 1976, p. 135: "Bilingualism, then, is the result of the use of more than one code by an individual or a society. Diglossia is the result of the valuation of such functional divisions and hence bilingualism and diglossia can occur separately or together in a speech community." See also K. Rein, 'Religiöse Sprachinseln täuferischen Ursprungs in den Vereinigten Staaten von Amerika', in *Zeitschrift für Dialektologie und Linguistik*, Beihefte, Neue Folge, No. 15, Wiesbaden 1977, pp. 27 ff.

[97] Cf. J. A. Fishman, *The Sociology of Language. An Interdisciplinary Social Science Approach to Language in Society*, Rowley (Mass.), 1972, p. 95. (Also in J. A. Fishman (ed.), *Advances in the Sociology of Language*, The Hague–Paris 1971, vol. 1, pp. 217–404, and in *Current Trends in Linguistics*, vol. 12 (3), The Hague–Paris 1974, pp. 1629–1784.)

denced notably in the "Germanisation" of spelling.[98] The gradual transition manifest in the texts of the eighteenth century in the German-speaking regions – the emergence of a "High German literature in Hebrew script", as Mieses put it [99] – has not so far been studied in scholarly detail. Apart from the important influence of the Enlightenment,[100] the tendency towards adopting the German language was reinforced by the recognition that German was a national language the use of which should establish the speaker's credentials as a member of that nation.[101] But the ever-growing readiness for acculturation, apparent in the trend of linguistic change, led to profound changes in the German Jews' sense of identity.

Ad 2: In the scientific classification of *Germanistik*, Yiddish figures as a *Nebensprache* or *Nahsprache* (a secondary or kindred language) in relation to German.[102] That is why in a sociolinguistic analysis the well-known explanatory models illuminating the relation between high language and dialect [103] or the various linguistic codes existing within a society [104] are here only of limited relevance, although interesting conclusions could be drawn concerning minority languages and the relative status-ranking of various social groups.[105] More important in this context is the problem of behaviour towards language or, more precisely, the problem of the external and self-evaluation of a speech community.[106] This is one of the foremost fields of recent sociolinguistic research, closely connected with the problems of language maintenance and language shift. It is not possible within the scope of this study to outline tentative explanations in terms of behavioural implementation and cognitive aspect, which have so far been put forward.[107] On the other hand, recent findings on the uniformity of social

---

[98] J. A. Fishman, 'The Phenomenological and Linguistic Pilgrimage of Yiddish: Some Examples of Functional and Structural Pidginisation and Depidginisation', in J. A. Fishman (ed.), *Advances in the Creation and Revision of Writing Systems*, The Hague–Paris 1977, p. 301. First published in *Kansas Journal of Sociology*, 10:2 (Autumn 1973).
[99] M. Mieses, *Die Gesetze der Schriftgeschichte. Konfession und Schrift im Leben der Völker*, Wien–Leipzig 1919, pp. 121 ff.
[100] Fully treated by I. E. Barzilay, 'The Jew in the Literature of the Enlightenment', in *Jewish Social Studies*, 18 (1956), pp. 243–261, in particular p. 255, citing an interesting statement about "jargon" by M. Grégoire.
[101] Cf. the literature cited in Note 17; also E. Haugen, 'Dialect, Language and Nation', in J. B. Pride and J. Helmes (eds.), *Sociolinguistics*, Harmondsworth 1972, pp. 97–111, first published in *American Anthropologist*, 68 (1966), pp. 922–935.
[102] A. Bach, *op. cit.*, p. 35; W. Henzen, *op. cit.*, p. 25. For the origin of the concept, cf. S. A. Birnbaum, 'Institutum Ascenezicum', in *LBI Year Book XVII* (1972), p. 244, note 4.
[103] For the German language region, cf. U. Ammon, *Dialekt und Einheitssprache in ihrer sozialen Verflechtung*, Weinheim–Basle 1973. Also important *International Journal of the Sociology of Language*, No. 9 ('The Social Dimension of Dialectology'), The Hague–Paris 1976.
[104] Basil Bernstein's comprehensive contributions to the study of the social barrier effect of languages are of relevance here. It must be noted, however, that his results have been increasingly modified and amended of late (cf. N. Dittmar, *op. cit.*, pp. 1–126; Engl. version, pp. 1–101).
[105] Cf. U. Oevermann, *Sprache und soziale Herkunft. Ein Beitrag zur Analyse schichtenspezifischer Sozialisationsprozesse und ihrer Bedeutung für den Schulerfolg*, Frankfurt a. Main ²1972, p. 25.
[106] Cf. Fishman, *The Sociology of Language, op. cit.*, pp. 140 ff.
[107] *Ibid.*, pp. 143–149.

attitudes to languages[108] and on the prestige attached to various languages[109] are soundly established results with a direct bearing on our topic. In this context it can be said that to some extent in the eighteenth, and more decisively in the nineteenth century, Yiddish became within the German-speaking regions a sociolect[110] that branded those speaking it with a mark of shame. This was in striking contrast to the developments in the non-Jewish sphere. The concurrent efforts to assure the dominance of the standard language over the dialects in Northern Germany were only partially successful. In the rural areas in particular the dialect has continued, to this day, to hold its own as a medium of communication. Owing to the low prestige rating of the dialect, the vernacular speakers were made to look ridiculous and subjected to discrimination, but there was never any doubt about their belonging to the German speech community. Speakers of Yiddish, on the other hand were assigned to a social minority characterised by religion, social status and, not least, by their speech.

The adoption of the German standard language by the Jewish minority accompanied – and to some extent was instrumental in bringing about – a profound social transformation, especially in the second half of the nineteenth century, when growing numbers of Jews rose into the middle classes and maintained their position. This vertical mobility went hand in hand with the linguistic changes described in the foregoing. It also led occasionally to hypercorrect use of language,[111] a sociolinguistic phenomenon not confined to Jews. Similar instances have been observed in the course of recent empirical studies, which found that it is above all the lower middle class which tends to react in a linguistically hyper-correct manner.[112]

A fundamentally new attitude to Yiddish evolved in the closing decades of the nineteenth and the first decades of the twentieth century. Certain Jewish circles turned to Yiddish as the language of East European Jewry. They made it the subject of scholarly study and came to recognise it as the well-spring of a rich

---

[108]William Labov, 'The Study of Language in its Social Context', in J. A. Fishman (ed.), *Advances in the Sociology of Language*, The Hague–Paris 1971, vol. 1, p. 202: "One basic principle emerges: that social attitudes towards language are extremely uniform throughout a speech community." First published in *Studium Generale*, 1970, pp. 30–87.

[109]Fishman, *The Sociology of Language*, op. cit., p. 132: "The more prestigious language displaces the less prestigious language." T. Luckmann, loc. cit., p. 1066: "Certain analogies can be discerned here with the differential prestige and the institutionally predetermined structuring of situations of use – inclusive of certain socio-psychological implications, such as the question of identification – which reveal the relations between high language, dialect, slang and vocational jargon in speech communities that have a minority status within a given society, and whose members have reached different stages in the process of acculturation." See also N. Elias, op. cit., vol. 1, pp. 149 f.

[110]Sociolect has been defined as "language behaviour of social groups, which on the strength of a few of its peculiarities is branded as inferior by other groups and interpreted as a symbol of social contempt". (*Handbuch der Linguistik. Allgemeine und angewandte Sprachwissenschaft*, Munich 1975, p. 389.)

[111]*Handbuch der Linguistik*, pp. 405 f.: "Social mobility within the stratified structure of a society is reflected in the hypercorrect use of language by certain groups. The different language variants are typical of values and norms specifically attached to certain strata. Social stratification is a motive force in the process of language shift."

[112]Fishman, *The Sociology of Language*, op. cit., pp. 65 f.

culture and literature.¹¹³ It must be noted, however, that these endeavours took place against the background of an altered political situation, directly or indirectly influenced by the rise of modern political antisemitism. When it turned out that even after linguistic and social acculturation the desired German-Jewish co-existence continued to be beset by severe strains and stresses, Jews found the way back to their own language, though not in order to speak it,¹¹⁴ but to find new bearings and a sense of security in their own past. It had become manifest that the changes in language behaviour postulated by educationists and language reformers in the first half of the nineteenth century had failed to secure the hoped-for social integration. Socioeconomic and religious factors as well as age-old mental stereotypes and prejudices had proved stronger.

¹¹³Cf. Birnbaum, *loc. cit.*, p. 243; F. Goldmann, 'Die Sprache der Ostjuden', in *Jahrbuch für jüdische Geschichte und Literatur*, 19 (1916), pp. 135–164, in particular p. 151, where the following interesting comparison is made: "These brief and sketchy surveys of the various fields will at least have shown that there can be no question of a corrupt or disfigured language and that Yiddish may claim the same respect and consideration as any other German dialect. One should not, of course, confuse Yiddish with the offensive *Gemauschel* with which the humorous journals brainlessly and witlessly fill their columns. Yiddish is no more nor less a corrupt language than, say, the language of Fritz Reuter, or Gerhart Hauptmann's Silesian dialect." See further Robert Weltsch in his 'Nachwort' to *Juden im Wilhelminischen Deutschland, op. cit.*, pp. 694 f., and Emanuel S. Goldsmith, *Architects of Yiddishism at the Beginning of the Twentieth Century. A Study in Jewish Cultural History*, London 1976.

¹¹⁴Zionism chose a different road with the revival of Hebrew.

The Yiddish Written Word in Nineteenth-Century Germany

BY STEVEN M. LOWENSTEIN

The translation of the Pentateuch into High German by Moses Mendelssohn in 1778–1783, marked a milestone in the transition from Yiddish to German as the written language of German Jewry, but it did not result in an overnight changeover in the writing and reading habits of German Jews.[1] In fact, the transition was an extremely long and complex process with numerous intermediate stages. The popular written language of pre-Emancipation German Jews was Yiddish, but it was quite different from modern East European Yiddish. An example from a typical literary text from the early eighteenth-century Germany shows the difference quite clearly:

> "Ich habi disus an gifangin bs'd [besiyato dischmayo] zu schreibin nach den Tot vun eier vrummin Vatir das es mir ist giwesin likzas lenachas ruach, wenn mir die malcholism i Gidankin seinen gikumin un' vun schwari Deiges . . . also ich menichi Leilo schlof los zu gibracht also ich oft baleilo auf gistandin un' die schlof losin Schoes dar mit zu gibracht . . ."[2]

Generally the Yiddish texts were composed in a literary language which was a compromise between the spoken dialects of Eastern and Western Europe. In

---

[1] I would like to thank Dr. David Roskies for his help and advice with this essay.
[2] In modern Yiddish this passage would read approximately as follows: "Ich hob dos ongehoiben zu schreiben bs'd nochn Toit vun eier vrummen Voter as es sol sein far mir a bisl lenachas ruach wenn die melancholische Gedanken seinen gekummen zu mir un die schwere Deiges . . . Asoi arum, hob ich a Teil Necht nit gekennt schlofen, asoi bin ich oft ufgestannen in der Nacht un sich varnummen mit dem in die Schoes wos ich hob nit gekennt schlofen . . ." (The quote is from David Kaufmann's original edition of the memoirs of Glückel of Hameln, p. 3.)

The transcription used in this article is neither the commonly accepted YIVO transcription nor a scientific phonetic transcription. Rather, I have purposely based the transcription on German spelling rules wherever possible. I have done this so that differences between German and Yiddish appear only when there is an actual linguistic difference in the text so that no differences appear merely because of the style of transcription. In High German texts in Hebrew script where Umlauts were not used in the text, they have been supplied in my transcription; I did not follow this procedure for texts which were clearly Yiddish but even there German spelling rules were used for better comparison. (Thus I transcribed *vun, kummen, spielen, Sorg*, rather than *fun, kumen, shpiln, zorg* as required by the YIVO transcription rules.)

Most Yiddish books in seventeenth- and eighteenth-century Europe were printed in Western Europe, especially in Amsterdam, Prague and the German towns of Sulzbach, Dyhernfurth, Wilhermsdorf, Offenbach and Frankfurt a. d. Oder. These books were intended for sale in both Eastern and Western Europe. Depending on the genre of the work the literary language would be influenced more by Hebrew or by German. Communal record books, for example, were written in a special mixture of Yiddish and Hebrew while secular romances or translations of German *Volksbücher* were written in a style very close to German.

For a survey of early Yiddish literature see: Chone Shmeruk, 'Di alt-yidishe literatur (ire onheybn un primere kontaktn)', *Pinkes far der Forshung fun der yidisher Literatur un presse*, New York 1975, pp. 138–218.

the late eighteenth century[3] some German Jews began the transition to High German, by writing German in Hebrew script. Mendelssohn's translation was the most famous instance of this type of writing. In actuality writing of High German in Hebrew letters (sometimes called *Jüdisch-deutsch*) was not a completely uniform transitional stage. Writers of *Jüdisch-deutsch* differed in their spelling systems, their insertion of Hebrew words in their German texts, and in the degree of their knowledge of all the rules of German grammar.[4] When "High German" texts in Hebrew script contain many Hebrew words or commit numerous lapses in grammar, it becomes difficult to distinguish them from Yiddish texts. In fact, there was a continuum of forms from "pure" Yiddish to "pure" German in Hebrew script, and it is not always clear to which category a particular text should be assigned.

As German Jews moved towards using German as their language of literary expression, a change took place in those texts which continued to be written in Yiddish. The very purpose of writing Yiddish came to be viewed by many as the reproduction of as accurate as possible a picture of the speech of the "uneducated" Jew, and the idea of a standardised literary Yiddish was looked upon more and more as a contradiction in terms. For this reason many Yiddish texts written in Germany after 1780 abandoned the old rules of literary Yiddish and reproduced local Yiddish dialects as phonetically as possible. Yiddish dialect writing could be produced either in Hebrew script or in Latin (or Gothic) letters. Although the dialect forms behind both types of text were essentially the same, the Hebrew-script writings often served a different purpose and addressed a different audience than did the Latin-letter Yiddish dialect texts.

It is significant that each of the four types of Yiddish or transitional writing styles found in nineteenth-century Germany – old literary Yiddish, High German in Hebrew script (*Jüdisch-deutsch*), Yiddish dialect in Hebrew script and Yiddish dialect in German scripts – served different audiences, flourished in different periods and tended to concentrate in different genres.

Works continued to be published in old literary Yiddish in Germany until the late 1830s. Often this fact can be established only by a direct perusal of surviving volumes from this period, since a number of factors obscure the Yiddish nature of the published works. Besides the fact that German-Jewish bibliographers[5] indiscriminately refer to Yiddish and German works in Hebrew script as

---

[3]Max Weinreich, *Geshikhte fun der yidisher Shprakh*, New York 1973, vol. 3, pp. 292–294; Herbert Paper, 'An early example of Standard German in Hebrew Characters', in *Field of Yiddish*, 1 (1954), pp. 143–146. Paper deals with a text first published in 1765 which is described by Steinschneider as one of the earliest printed German works in Hebrew letters.

[4]While some writers were so scrupulous in avoiding Hebrew words that they even translated Hebrew proper names into German (e.g., Salomo instead of Schlomo), others inserted whole Hebrew phrases into sentences that were otherwise pure German. Some orthographic systems in *Jüdisch-deutsch* did not distinguish between *i* and *ü* or between *ö* and *e* while others actually placed Umlauts over Hebrew letters. All spelling systems of *Jüdisch-deutsch* were based subconsciously on the old Yiddish spelling systems (e.g., Vav yud for au) with suitable modifications.

[5]See, e.g., Leopold Löwenstein, *Die hebräischen Druckereien in Fürth*, vol. 3 of *Zur Geschichte der Juden in Fürth*, Frankfurt a. Main 1909–1913; Magnus Weinberg, *Die hebräischen Druckereien in Sulzbach* (1669–1851), Frankfurt a. Main 1904–1930, as well as Steinschneider's classical article, 'Jüdisch-deutsche Literatur', *Serapeum* (1848–1849).

"*Jüdisch-deutsch*", there is the even more significant fact that the printers tried to hide the fact that books were written in literary Yiddish by providing them with High German title pages and introductions. In some cases the printer's German was faulty,[6] but in others they were more or less successful. One can contrast the title page of the Sulzbach *Tse'ena Ure'ena* (Women's Bible paraphrase) of 1836 which is in High German with the intermixture of some Hebrew words:

> "Ein lehrreiches Sefer von grosem Nützen sowohl für das männliche – als auch weibliche Geschlecht, welche an Schabbos we Yom Tov ihre Ruhestunden in religiöser Andacht zuzubringen suchen, finden darin hinlänglichen Unterhalt, und können viele wissenschaftliche und für jedermann beinahe nöthige Gegenstände daraus erlernen. Um damit nun jeder selbst auch der unbemittelte Mann dieses (in frühern Zeiten so theure) Sefer besitzen kann, haben wir uns entschlossen es nochmals zu drucken und zwar mit weit schönerem Papier und besserer Hanocho als es bis jetzt erschienen ist..."

with the completely Yiddish beginning of the work itself:

> "An erschten Tag beschaft Hk'bh [hakodosch boruch hu] Himmel un' Erd un' die Erd war wist un' leer finster auf den ab grund un' der (kise hakowod) vun Hk'bh der is gestanden in Liften iber die Wasser. Un' warum hot die Torah an gehoben mit der (Beys). Es lernt uns wie is ein (Beys) hot drei Seiten die zu sein un' die vierte Want is offen aso is auch die Welt..."[7]

The books printed in literary Yiddish in early nineteenth-century Germany were all reprints of earlier works. In many, probably in most, cases there was little change from earlier editions. The reprinted works covered some of the religious and entertainment repertoire of traditional Yiddish literature: prayer-book translations, women's prayerbooks (*Techinos*), *Tse'ena Ure'ena*, collections of customs (*Minhogim*), and a few translations of German *Volksbücher*. Although the printers did not feel there was enough of a market for new works in literary Yiddish, they did find enough readers to merit reprinting some of the traditional

---

[6] The printer of the Yom Kippur *machsor* (prayer book) translation in Offenbach in 1812 evidently attempted to provide the book with a High German title page, but the result was the following:

"Kawonas Hapaytan, welcher sehr nötig und nützlich ist, weiln durch diesen ein jeder verstehn kann den Inhalt von jeden Piut, was der Ikkur mekawen hatefilo ist. Weiln bischas hatefilo es die Zeit nicht zulässt den ganzen Deutsch von jeden Piut durch zu sehn, und durch diese kurze Erleuterung, versteht ein jeder den Inhalt..."

The body of the book vacillates between German and Yiddish forms (e.g., *wir* and *mir* 'we', *sind* and *sein* '(they) are').

[7] There are a few errors in the German of the title page. The body of the book is virtually unchanged from eighteenth-century editions.

Translation of the title page: "An educational book of great use both for the male and female sex, who desire to occupy their hours of leisure on Sabbath and Holidays in religious meditation; they find in it sufficient entertainment and can learn many scholarly things almost useful for everyone. And so that even the man without any financial resources can now own this (formerly so expensive) book, we have decided to reprint it with much better paper and better discount(?) than previously."

Translation of the Yiddish passage: "On the first day the Holy One Blessed be He created heaven and earth. And the earth was desolate and empty, darkness over the abyss and the throne of the Holy One Blessed be He stood in the air over the waters. And why does the Torah begin with the letter *beys*? To teach us that just as a *beys* has three sides which are closed and the fourth wall is open, so too is the world..."

favourites. The last known literary Yiddish book in Germany was the Sulzbach *Tse'ena Ure'ena* of 1836. Although the book was no longer printed in Yiddish thereafter, it long continued to enjoy remarkable popularity among German Jews.[8]

Though no new works in literary Yiddish were printed after 1800, they continued to be written at least during the first decade or two of the nineteenth century. One humorous work written during the Continental Blockade of Napoleonic Europe satirises the high price of coffee in twenty-two acrostic stanzas. The first stanza of this 'Schehn neies Kaffeelied verfasst auf die Teihrung des Kaffe in Teitschland im Jahr 1808 benigun Tiher Rabbi Jischmoel' reads as follows:

> "*A*chenu beys jisroel was werin mir jetzund an fangin,
> mir kennen kein Gnad mehr bei unser Weiber erlangin.
> Mir haben den Kaffee Abschied musen gebin.
> Jetzund tuhn unser Weiber in eitel Machlokes lebin.
> Wann nuhr Scholom kummt balt bei Zeit
> dass der Kaffee kann wieder werin an gebreit
> Hen, das ist ja gahr nicht schehn.
> Kein Weib will in Tewilo gehn."[9]

Other extant literary Yiddish writings from early nineteenth-century Germany in addition to this poem include an account by Ber Ullmann of the mass

---

[8] Two anecdotes from my own personal experience may serve to illustrate the remarkable persistence of use of the *Tse'ena Ure'ena*.

My grandmother, born in Ermershausen, Northern Bavaria in 1888, once told me how she had regularly read the *Tse'ena Ure'ena* to the other Jewish women of her village. Before the reading she had to practise reading the Yiddish text which was difficult to read especially because of such archaic words as *neiert* "rather" and *klomar* "that is to say".

Even more remarkable is an incident involving a man of about the same age who was born in Edelfingen, Württemberg. In the late 1960s (!) I found out that this man, who lived in the Washington Heights section of New York City (the chief German-Jewish neighbourhood), owned a copy of the 1789 Sulzbach *Tse'ena Ure'ena*. After I visited him, he agreed to lend me the volume so that I could study it, but only on the condition that I return it before Friday, since he read from it every Sabbath.

[9] The original handwritten copy of the poem is in the Susanne Meyer collection in the Archives of the New York Leo Baeck Institute. The family who possessed the copy came from Rheinhessen and the Rhine Palatinate.

Translation:
"O brothers, house of Israel what can we begin now;
we can no longer find grace with our wives.
We had to bid farewell to coffee
Now our wives live in pure disharmony.
If only peace would soon come,
so that coffee could be prepared again.
O, it is really not very nice
No woman will go to the ritual bath"*

*Required by religious law each month before marital relations are permitted.

This poem is similar to the many topical "historische Lieder" which appeared in the Yiddish language in seventeenth- and eighteenth-century Europe. The 'coffee poem' is set to the tune of a very serious Yom Kippur poem about the martyrdom of ten Talmudic sages. To a certain extent it parodies the original, a practice also found in some of the earlier "historische Lieder". On the genre of satiric "historische Lieder" in pre-nineteenth-century Yiddish see Chone Shmeruk, 'Hashir al hasrefa l'Eliahu Bachur', *Kovetz al Yad*, new series, vol. 6 (1966), pp. 343–368.

arrest of Jews in the communities of Pfersee, Kriegshaber and Steppach near Augsburg in 1803 as well as some communal record books and innumerable private account books and private letters.[10]

All the works in "literary Yiddish" have one thing in common – Yiddish is used because it is the natural or most convenient means of communication, not merely for effect. The opposite is generally true of Yiddish dialect literature. Most of those who wrote in this type of language knew standard German quite well, but chose to write Yiddish dialect for a specific purpose.

It is interesting that almost every extant Yiddish dialect work in Hebrew letters from Germany after 1780 is written in the form of a drama or dialogue. Almost all are comedies – some written with a satiric–didactic purpose, others merely for entertainment. The two best known of the Yiddish dialect plays, Isaac Abraham Euchel's *Reb Henoch oder wos thut men dermit* (c. 1784) and Aron Halle Wolfssohn's *Leichtsinn und Frömmelei* (Breslau 1796),[11] are both pro-Enlightenment satires written partly in High German and partly in Northeast German Yiddish dialect by two leading disciples of Moses Mendelssohn.* In Wolfssohn's play the ignorant older generation as well as the villainous Talmud tutor Reb Josephche speak in thick Yiddish: when the father catches the supposedly "saintly" Josephche flirting with his maid, Josephche pretends to repent:

> "'Boruch hamokom boruch hu! Das ihr kummt! Ir saht mahn Gauel. Ki hizalto nafschi mimowes es ragli midechi!'
> Reb Henoch: 'Wohs soll dehs beteiten?'
> Reb Josephche: 'Wohs? Lieber Reb Henoch! Moh Enosch ki siskerenu! Wohs is der Mensch! E Tipe Srucho, en Nischt, e gor Nischt! Wehrt ihr dau nit kummen, Ribauno schel Aulem wohs wehr aus mir gworren!'"

while the young as well as the Enlightened hero Markus speak perfect High German:

> "In diesem verworfenen Hause, dem Aufenthalt aller Wollust und Schwelgerei, die Tochter meiner Schwester! In diesem Grabe der Unschuld, vielleicht schon selbst eine Gemordete? O das sind deine Früchte blinder Religions-Eifer."[12]

*On Euchel see the essay by Moshe Pelli in this volume of the Year Book – Ed.

[10] A copy of the original Yiddish version is found in the Leo Baeck Institute, New York. An English translation was printed privately in New York 1928 under the title *Chronicle of Ber Bernhard Ullmann 1803* translated by Carl J. Ullmann.

[11] An exception to the rule that Hebrew letter dialect works were all dramas is the poem 'Des Chasens Klole' a parody on Uhland's 'Des Sängers Fluch'. The manuscript of the poem is found in the Lise Meitner collection in the Archives of the New York Leo Baeck Institute and probably comes from Moravia.

For biographical sketches of Euchel and Wolfssohn see *Encyclopedia Judaica*, Jerusalem 1971, vol. 6, pp. 956–957, vol. 16, p. 617 and *Jüdisches Lexikon*, Berlin 1928, vol. II, p. 541. Both men were editors of the pioneering Hebrew periodical *Hame'asef*. Euchel wrote the first biography of Moses Mendelssohn in Hebrew. Euchel's play was reprinted in *Arkhiv far der Geshikhte fun yidishn Teater un Drame*, Vilna 1930, pp. 85–146 and Wolfssohn's in Zalmen Reisen's, *Fun Mendelson biz Mendele*, Warsaw 1923, pp. 37–68. Reb Josephche's Yiddish is more tinged with Polish Yiddish dialect, than the Yiddish of the other Yiddish-speaking characters (e.g., Reb Henoch).

[12] Translation:

> "'Praised be the Lord! That you are here. You are my redeemer!
> For you saved my soul from death, my leg from falling [Psalm 116, 8]!'
> Reb Henoch: 'What is the meaning of this?'

Many of the other authors of Yiddish dialect dramas followed Euchel and Wolfssohn's example, not only in using Yiddish dialect for comic and satiric purposes, but also in having different characters speak in different dialects. In Joseph Herz's Purim play *Esther oder die belohnte Tugend* (Fürth 1827), characters speak either Franconian Yiddish, High German or a comic mixture of the two. The anonymous *Als der Sof is gut, is alles gut*[13] uses literary Yiddish, Polish Yiddish and a parodied form of South German Yiddish for different characters.[14] A. L. Rosenthal's *Die Hochzeit zu Grobsdorf* (1822)[15] carefully distinguishes between the Hessian German dialect of non-Jewish characters and of Jews speaking with them:

> "Jokev: 'Jo eich will dirsch sah (sagen). Wann eich däi Geschenke fir meich kennt behahn, dann kehm eich araus; däi Geschenke krieh ober die junge Loie (Leute).'
> Bauer: 'So so, ha ha! Däi kräisste nit! Dann seist dou ahch ahn ormer Schelm. Wahste wohs? Es wern doch ach villecht sibern (silbernen) Leffin geschenkt? Sich wahste wohs du dann taust? Pratezirter ah Poor aweck.'"

and the Hessian Yiddish spoken by most of the Jewish characters:

> Reb Josephche: 'What? Dear Reb Henoch. What is man that you should remember him [Psalm 8, 5]! What is man! A filthy drop, a nothing. Absolutely nothing! If you wouldn't have come now, O Lord of the Universe, what would have become of me.'"
> Translation of the German passage:
> "In this contemptible house, the home of all lust and debauchery, the daughter of my sister. In this grave of all innocence, perhaps already killed? O, these are your fruits, blind religious zeal."

---

[13]Herz's play, *Esther oder die belohnte Tugend* was reprinted in a new edition in 1855. The play is the subject of a recently published study and critical edition by Robert M. Copeland and Nathan Susskind, *The Language of Herz' Esther*, Tuscaloosa, University of Alabama Press 1976.

Als der Sof is gut is alles gut was published for the first time by Leib Fuks in Paris in 1955. The manuscript was found in Amsterdam in 1946 and the play is known to have been performed in Amsterdam probably for Purim 1798. Fuks assumes the play was written in Holland, but Max Weinreich in his article, 'A shprakh-dokument fun arum 1800', *Yidishe Shprakh*, 7 (1957) pp. 16–52, argued that internal evidence points to a German origin.

[14]The hero Reb Lippman speaks literary Yiddish: "Schweig still! Genug, genug! Was kummt dou dervun araus mit die Machlokes? Das leid ich nit länger in mein Haus und bifrat vun solche schlechte Menschen wie ihr seit und genug! Ihr Leit kummt dernoch wiederum Get zu gebin und jetzt geits derweil fort . . ."

Reb Yoksch, a Polish Jew who has abandoned his wife speaks in his native dialect: "Dobre Notz; a lieben harzigen scheinen guten nobend. Boruch haschem as ech die sechije hob zi sehn aach gesind. Ech lebin, a aschkenasischer Kotzen un a feine Berje un le'ejle minhon takisch a gut jidil oched, das hot schoint legamre gor kein Schatz, ubifrat meint ihr ech hob och leben schoin vun aach in Poilin gehert . . ."

The South German cantor from "Fingerloch" mixes up *b*'s and *p*'s, *t*'s and *d*'s etc. and speaks like this:

"Ssie had mich in alles mei Firtschawt werricht
ten leiter gein Frau hab ich jetzt nicht
ssie had alles ketohe nach mei Fille
Tieses had a fenig mei Ssorg getohe schdille.
Ich hap niemals etfas schlechds an ihr keschbihrt
aber leiter jetzt is ssie turch ten Schuft forden werwihrt."

[15]The original handwritten manuscript is in the Max Weinreich Collection of the YIVO Institute for Jewish Research in New York. Act one was published by me in *YIVO Bleter*, 45, 1975, pp. 57–84, along with a modern Yiddish translation. The remainder of the play has never been published.

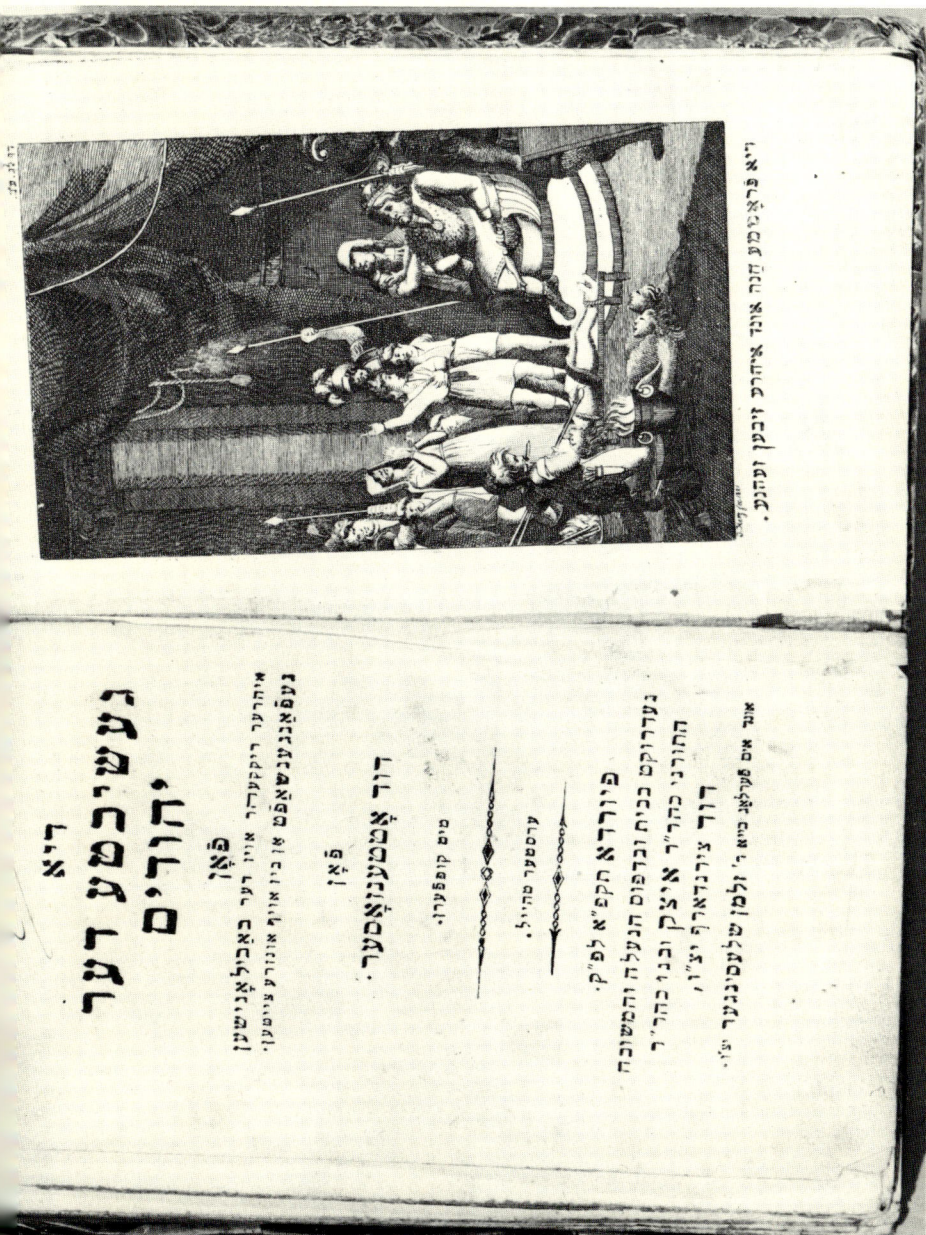

Title-page and frontispiece of *Die Geschichte der Jehudim* by
David Ottensoser, Fürth 1821

From the Archives of the Leo Baeck Institute, New York

Poster in Yiddish dialect, issued during the Revolution of 1848, satirising government policies

"Sich, sou maches die Männer. Erscht lafese sich die Bah stumb biss sie ahm hon, dernauch worfese ahm alles vor. Er hot doch voraus gewisst was ich hon – was brauch er mir alleweil newich noch mei Bettel vor der Thir zu worfen? Ah Masel, dass kahner derbei wor . . ."¹⁶

Although the authors of Yiddish dialect plays in Hebrew letters usually did not use Yiddish as their own natural language of discourse, they did intend their works for audiences that still had an intimate knowledge of both Yiddish and traditional Jewish culture. This type of literature differed considerably from the surviving literary Yiddish works. The genres represented were totally different. The dialect literature took an anti-traditional point of view in many cases, while the literary Yiddish works remained totally within the traditional framework. All the dialect literature was newly written while most of the literary Yiddish works were mere reprints of older works. In fact the Yiddish dialect literature in Hebrew script forms one of the transitional phases between Old Yiddish and Modern German as the literary language of German Jews. Through it Enlightenment writers and others were able to reach an audience still very knowledgeable about the tradition with their non-traditional message.

Yiddish dialect writing in Latin or German script did not differ much in actual language from dialect writing in Hebrew script, but it tended to have a different social purpose and often a different audience. While the Hebrew letter productions were naturally intended for an exclusively Jewish audience which was quite knowledgeable about Jewish lore, the Latin letter texts were sometimes addressed to non-Jewish readers, and almost always to a readership with far less Jewish knowledge than the audience for Hebrew-letter writings. The last known Hebrew letter dialect piece was written in 1827 (though it was reprinted in 1855),¹⁷ but Latin letter materials in Yiddish dialect continued to appear at a much later date. There is less uniformity among the Latin letter writings than among their Hebrew letter counterparts.

One of the types of Latin-letter Yiddish dialect literature, and probably the earliest, was written by non-Jews and intended mainly for non-Jewish readers or listeners. Some of these works were clearly antisemitic, such as the infamous comedy by Karl Borromäus Sessa *Unser Verkehr*, the hit of the 1815 season.¹⁸ The crude stories and poems written in Franconian Yiddish by Friedrich Freiherr von Holzschuher under the pseudonym "Itzig Veitel Stern" are somewhat more accurate linguistically but just as anti-Jewish. The titles themselves (*Gedichter*,

---

¹⁶Translation of the Hessian German passage:

"Jokev: 'Yes. I will tell you. If I could keep the presents for myself, then I'd come out all right; but the young couple will get the presents.'

Peasant: 'So, so, ha, ha. You won't get them! Then you, too, are a poor rascal. You know what? Maybe some silver spoons will be given as a present? Look, you know what to do then? Sneak a few away.'"

Translation of the Hessian Yiddish passage:

"See that's how men act. First they run their feet off till they get one [a wife], afterwards they blame everything on them. He knew beforehand what I have – why does he have to throw my poverty at my door all the time? It's lucky that no one was here."

¹⁷Joseph Herz's *Esther oder die belohnte Tugend*.

¹⁸See, e.g., Simon Dubnow, *Weltgeschichte des Jüdischen Volkes*, Berlin 1929, vol. 9, p. 17, for a description of the effect the play had on Jewish standing, as well as about the Jews' fight against it.

Perobeln unn Schnoukes fer unnere Leut; *Die linke Massematten der houchlöbliche Jüdenschaft*; and *Das Schabbes-Gärtle vun unnere Leut* etc.) are mocking enough. An example from one of the less crude poems gives an idea of Stern's language:

"Was is der Mensch?
Eppes e rores philosouphisches Gedicht, viel hauch unn tief.

Was is der Mensch?
E Schatten is der Mensch.
Er lahft unn handelt spiet unn früh:
Er is aweck, mer wahss net wie.
Meschores, wie der Kehr unn Srore,
Die Ische, Kalle unn der Isch:
Heut sinn se routh ass wie e Fisch
Unn morring sinn se schoh kapore
Sou is der Mensch
E Schatten is der Mensch . . ."[19]

Yiddish dialect written for a non-Jewish audience but without the antisemitic animus of Sessa or "Stern" is found in a series of posters printed in Berlin during the Revolution of 1848 which comment on the political events of the day.[20] The use of imitations of Yiddish by antisemitic writers continued to be a practice even much later, though the authenticity of the imitations was reduced as Yiddish receded more and more as an actively spoken language.

By the second half of the nineteenth century most German Jews probably no longer read or spoke Yiddish. It was in this period that Yiddish dialect writing for a Jewish audience in Latin letters became popular. With the exception of the works of the Alsatian Jewish writer Meyer Woog who wrote in an area where the Yiddish language was still very much alive,[21] the writers of Yiddish dialect

---

[19]Holzschuher wrote mainly in the 1830s. He was born in Nürnberg in 1796 and died in 1861. One of his satires directed specifically against emancipation was entitled: *Die Manzipaziuhn der houchlöbliche kieniglich bayerische Jüdenschaft. En Edress an die houchvehrliche Harren Landständ, ousgestodirt vun Schächter Eisig Schmuhl unn drükken gelosst vun Itzig Feitel Stern*, Ansbach 1834. All of "Itzig Veitel Stern's" stories are set in the small towns around Nuremberg.

Translation of the poem:
"What is Man?
Such a wonderful philosophical poem. Very high and deep

What is man?
Man is but a shadow
He runs and trades early and late
He is gone, no one knows how.
Servant like nobleman and prince
Woman, bride and man.
Today they are red just like a fish
and tomorrow they've already croaked.
Thus is man
Man is but a shadow."

[20]K. Spalding, 'The Idiom of a Revolution, 1848', *Modern Languages Review*, 4 (1949), pp. 60–74. Examples of these posters can be found in the Archives of the New York Leo Baeck Institute.

[21]Woog was a native of Hegenheim, Alsace and died in 1905. Some of his poems and plays (e.g., *Merkwerdigi Chidduschim aus'm Elsass*, Basel 1879, *Deforim Beteilim Leeri Keilim*, etc.) are preserved in the New York Public Library.

Of somewhat different nature are the handwritten and typed Jewish dialect poems in the Baer–Oppenheimer family collection in the Archives of the New York Leo Baeck Institute.

in Latin letters were writing for audiences without a really intimate knowledge of Yiddish. For this reason Yiddish dialect was used either as a specifically humorous device, or as a means of evoking a life-style treated as already dead.

Some writers used Yiddish dialect specifically to preserve dead folklore for posterity. Perhaps the earliest such work is Abraham Tendlau's *Sprichwörter und Redensarten deutsch-jüdischer Vorzeit* (the title itself is significant) printed in Frankfurt a. Main in 1860. Several individuals in various parts of Germany transcribed conversations of older Jews around the same period. It is interesting that these transcriptions were not printed or retranscribed until the first years of the twentieth century when there was a renewal of interest in Jewish folklore.[22] This revival of interest in Western Yiddish, also indicated by the founding of Max Grunwald's *Jahrbuch für jüdische Volkskunde* and the reprinting of Tendlau's book in abridged form in the 1930s, was, however, greatly overshadowed by the interest in East European Jewish life which developed in Germany in the early twentieth century under the influence of Martin Buber, Hermann Struck and others.

The humour of the Latin-letter Yiddish dialect works differed from those in Hebrew letters in that the main joke in the Latin-letter texts was the language itself. The earlier texts certainly satirised traditional life and played with language, but never made Yiddish itself and the malapropisms of its speakers the central point. A whole series of pamphlets entitled *Gedichte und Scherze in jüdischer Mundart* was issued in Berlin beginning in the 1860s. The series, written for a Jewish audience, mocks Yiddish and its speakers while appealing to the nostalgia of its readers. The authors use such pseudonyms as Nathan Tulpenthal, Eduard Hermann Schaute, Reb Moser Graggler and Jeinkew Medinegeier. A good example of the level of these popular pamphlets is the beginning of the first in the series *Schmonzes Berjonzes*:

> "Veitel Heimann's Reisebriefe aus Leipzig und Berlin an seine Gattin Esther in Inowraclaw: . . .
> Gebenschtes Estherleben!
> Dein lieben Brief hob ich schon bekummen nechten [gestern] in die Früh. Wie geschwind dos geiht, früher is e Brief vun Inowraclaw nach Leipzig verzehn Tog unterwegs gewesen, jetzt geiht er mit'n Lokomotivcher ein Tog. Dos is aber noch gor nischt, wenn

---

These poems, some stemming from the twentieth century, deal satirically with a number of topics. Written in Bruchsal, Baden, they seem to reflect a more lively knowledge of Yiddish dialect than most of the printed joke books. Among the items in the collection is a poem 'Das Alphabet von 1934', an anti-Nazi satire in High German with the admixture of large numbers of Yiddish expressions.

[22]One such work is the memoirs of Aron Hirsch Heymann (born Strausberg near Berlin 1802 – died Berlin 1880) containing numerous anecdotes in the Yiddish of Brandenburg which was privately printed in 1909. (See Monika Richarz [Hrsg.], *Jüdisches Leben in Deutschland. Selbstzeugnisse zur Sozialgeschichte 1780–1871*, Stuttgart 1976, Veröffentlichung des Leo Baeck Instituts, pp. 213–235). There were also the dialogues published by Sigmar Mehring in 1912 and 1913 from his father's papers; the first of these reproduced a conversation of two Jewish soldiers in 1813; the second was entitled 'Wolf und Itzig zur Einholung des Königs in Breslau im November 1861'. Monologues in the Yiddish dialect of Liedolsheim, North Baden which were originally copied down in the 1850s were retranscribed by the local historian Berthold Rosenthal in the early twentieth century under the title *Gespräche mit Onkel Jokef*.

man ehm schickt mit'n Telegraf, kümmt er noch e halbe Scho [Stunde] früher, eh' man hot ihn geschrieben. Heisst'n Geschäft! . . ."[23]

This text already shows signs that the author knew High German better than the dialect he was reproducing. Books of Jewish humour continued to be written even in the twentieth century, but with less and less authenticity of the dialect.[24]

A number of more serious German-Jewish writers used elements of Yiddish dialect in their High German novels about traditional or old-fashioned Jewish life. In their works the Yiddish element is rarely used mockingly or humorously, but rather to evoke the traditional surroundings or to depict the characters more accurately. One of the earliest writers of this type of work was Aron Bernstein (1812–1884) whose novels *Mendel Gibbor* and *Vögele der Maggid* describe Jewish life in the small towns of West Prussia. In the works of some writers (for instance in Georg Hermann's *Jettchen Gebert* and *Henriette Jacoby* only a few elements of the old Jewish dialect are to be found. In others, for instance Jakob Wassermann's *Die Juden von Zirndorf*,[25] the dialect appears almost full-strength in the speech of certain characters. It is interesting that the works of a writer like Jacob Picard who himself knew the Yiddish dialect of Southern Baden from home, use very little dialect in his evocative collection of rural Jewish stories, *Der Gezeichnete*.[26]

Writing High German in Hebrew script which began some time during the eighteenth century underwent an even greater change in function during the nineteenth century than did writing in Yiddish dialect. In the time of Mendelssohn and his disciples, *Jüdisch-deutsch* was one of the means used by the *Maskilim* (followers of the Enlightenment) to spread their ideas among the Jews. The Bible translation by Mendelssohn in Hebrew letters and other works by David Friedländer, Herz Homberg and others, were intended to wean the German-Jewish masses away from Yiddish, their usual language of speech and reading, and to teach them German. The *Jüdisch-deutsch* of Mendelssohn's translation and similar texts was very difficult for the ordinary German Jews and one of the chief objections to it by the rabbis was that the reader would waste too much time trying to understand the difficult German. A copy of Mendelssohn's translation

[23]Translation:

Veitel Heimann's travel letters from Leipzig and Berlin to his wife Esther in Inowraclaw:

"Blessed Esther darling.

I received your dear letter already yesterday morning. How quickly it goes. In the old days a letter from Inowraclaw to Leipzig was en route for fourteen days. Now it goes with the little locomotives in one day. But that's nothing. If you send it with the telegraph it will arrive a half hour before you write it. Some business."

[24]Examples of such books are: Chaim Jossel, *Schabbes Schmus, Schmonzes Berjonzes*, Berlin–Leipzig 1907; *Meisses und Schnohkes*, Leipzig–Berlin n.d., and Paul Nikolaus, *Jüdische Miniaturen*, Hannover–Leipzig 1924–1925.

[25]*Mendel Gibbor* was first published in 1858–1859; *Vögele der Maggid*, in the same years. *Jettchen Gebert*, 1907, *Henriette Jacoby*, 1908 – both novels are set in Berlin. *Die Juden von Zirndorf*, Munich 1897 is set in Franconia.

[26]In his autobiographical article 'Childhood in the Village', in *LBI Year Book IV* (1959), pp. 273–293, Picard makes specific mention of the Jewish dialect of his hometown Wangen am Bodensee. *Der Gezeichnete* was published in English translation by the Jewish Publications Society in 1956 under the title *The Marked One*.

of the Psalms printed in Offenbach in 1804–1805 gives clear confirmation of the assumption that most Jews had difficulty with the language. The edition contains a lengthy glossary of difficult words. Among the words which had to be explained were such ordinary words as "Unfall", "Busse", "Gruft", "Heiden", "Wut", "Tyrann" and "Thron".

The *Maskilim* continued to write in *Jüdisch-deutsch* in the early nineteenth century, though their aim may no longer have been specifically to wean the Jews away from Yiddish. A number of educational works were written in High German in Hebrew script. Among these were several on historical subjects including Aron Wolfssohn's *David der Besieger des Goliath* and David Ottensoser's *Die Geschichte der Jehudim* (Fürth 1821–1825).[27] *Jüdisch-deutsch* was often an official subject of instruction in the Jewish schools set up under Enlightenment auspices in the late eighteenth and in the early nineteenth century as well as in many other public and private Jewish schools in the early nineteenth century. A number of textbooks were dedicated in whole or in part to the teaching of this subject. The earliest such textbook was David Friedländer's *Lesebuch für jüdische Kinder* (Berlin 1779) which included a *Jüdisch-deutsch* section, and probably the latest was published in Fürth in 1859.[28]

As High German became more and more accepted by German Jews, Enlightenment and Reform leaders changed their attitude towards *Jüdisch-deutsch*. Since it was no longer a vehicle for the gradual transition to standard German, they felt that it no longer served any purpose. The number of hours of instruction in reading and writing *Jüdisch-deutsch* were reduced and in many cases abolished. However, there are extant examples of school exercises in *Jüdisch-deutsch* from Württemberg in the 1880s.[29]

As the "liberals" dropped the use of German in Hebrew script, the conservatives adopted it. Almost all printed works in *Jüdisch-deutsch* after 1830 are traditionally religious in nature. In many ways High German in Hebrew letters began to perform the function formerly performed by literary Yiddish. By 1842 the Fürth printers were issuing their formerly Yiddish women's prayerbook (*Techinos*) in *Jüdisch-deutsch*. Prayerbook and Bible translations, cemetery prayerbooks and other religious works continued to be printed throughout the mid-nineteenth century in *Jüdisch-deutsch*; one very late *Jüdisch-deutsch* work was published in 1879 in Rödelheim.[30]

[27]Wolfssohn's play, first published in 1802, was reprinted in Fürth in 1815. Ottensoser's book was a history of the Jews since the Babylonian Exile. The list of pre-subscribers (*Prenumeranten*) found at the beginning of the book, lists a large number of names almost all from Bavaria.

[28]Much information on the teaching of *Jüdisch-deutsch* in German-Jewish schools is found in Mordechai Eliav, *Hachinuch Hayehudi beGermaniya bizman Hahaskala ve-haEmantsipatsiya*, Jerusalem 1961, especially pp. 84, 102–3, 113, 134, 137, 192, 200, 224, 237, 272–77, 294. *Jüdisch-deutsch* textbooks included C. Rehfuss' *Loschon Jehudis oder vollständige jüdisch-deutsche Fibel*, Frankfurt a. Main 1833 (reported in Max Weinreich, *Geshikhte fun der yidisher shprakh*, vol. 3, p. 294) and *Sammlung von Novellen, Legenden und Parabeln ... zur Unterhaltung für Erwachsene und die reifere Jugend sowohl hauptsächlich zur Übung im hebräisch-deutsch lesen*, Fürth 1859, see Leopold Löwenstein, *op. cit.*, p. 105.

[29]Eliav, *op. cit.*, pp. as above. The school exercise books from Laupheim, Württemberg are to be found in the YIVO Archives.

[30]A copy of Jehoschua Heschel Miro's, *Techinos*, Rödelheim 1879, is to be found in the YIVO Library.

Besides reprints or reworkings of older works there were a number of new religious guidebooks written by German Orthodox rabbis during the nineteenth century. At least one of these works, *Amiro Lebeys Jaakov*, a guide to the traditional duties of women, written by Seligmann Baer Bamberger, the rabbi of Würzburg, enjoyed remarkable popularity.[31] Its first edition of 5,000 copies in *Jüdisch-deutsch* printed in Fürth in 1858 was sold out and required a second (Fürth, 1864) and a third edition (Frankfurt a. Main 1870). This fact is evidence that *Jüdisch-deutsch* was still a practical means of communication in the third quarter of the nineteenth century, at least in Orthodox circles. Certainly Rabbi Bamberger's intention was to communicate certain information about religious law, not particularly to encourage the use of *Jüdisch-deutsch*.

Writing of letters in *Jüdisch-deutsch* was a widespread practice in nineteenth-century German-Jewish families and there are many such letters extant. In some cases the Hebrew script served cryptic purposes (since even a message on a postcard could not be read by an inquisitive postman) but mainly they were used simply for intimate family correspondence, especially by parents writing to their children.[32]

Relatively little is known about the reading audience of the various types of Yiddish and *Jüdisch-deutsch* circulating in nineteenth-century Germany. Some writers, acting on the assumption that Yiddish became extinct in Germany shortly after the printing of Mendelssohn's Bible translation, have assumed that the works published in literary Yiddish in early nineteenth-century Germany were intended exclusively for export to Eastern Europe. It is true that the East European market had been very important to German-Jewish printers in the eighteenth century, but there is evidence that this was less true after 1800. In that year the Austrian government forbade the importation of Hebrew and Yiddish books printed outside the kingdom. In addition Hebrew and Yiddish printers in Eastern Europe became ever more active.[33] The fact that some printers of Yiddish remained in business till the middle of the century despite the decline of the East European market, would seem to indicate that they were still finding readers in Germany. The practice of printing High German introductions to Yiddish works likewise indicates an attempt to appeal to a German-Jewish audience.

A bit more direct evidence that some Jews were still reading literary Yiddish works is the Hessian Yiddish dialect play *Die Hochzeit zu Grobsdorf* mentioned above.[34] Before her marriage the bride's father advises her on how to conduct

---

[31] The preface to the second edition of Bamberger's book mentions that the first edition of 5,000 had been sold out. (See also Leopold Löwenstein, *op. cit.*, p. 108). Another newly written guide in *Jüdisch-deutsch* printed in Germany was Jacob Weil's *Sefer Toras Schabbos*, Karlsruhe 1839, which deals with the traditional Sabbath regulations.

[32] *Jüdisch-deutsch* was also used for business purposes (especially for business secrets). The Rothschild family continued to use this form of correspondence for quite some time during the nineteenth century.

[33] Magnus Weinberg, *op. cit.*, (1904) pp. 93–96. On Hebrew and Yiddish printing in Eastern Europe see Aron Freimann, *A Gazetteer of Hebrew Printing*, New York 1946; *Encyclopedia Judaica*, vol. 13, pp. 1110–1112.

[34] See p. 184 above.

herself and among other things urges she refrain from reading "treyfe deitsche" books with these words:

> "Los dich nor vun treyfe deitsche boseler Laiene. Mer hon im jerresche ahch scheyne Sforim. Laien am Schabbes Nauchmittag hibsch im Ze'eno Ure'eno, dernauch den Eilespiegel, Schilteborger Narrn, Wormser Nissim, den Moschol Hakadmone, den Minhogim un dou gebts noch gar viel jerresche Sforim umbeschrieh . . ."[35]

Despite the satire in the passage, this does seem to indicate that at least old-tradition Jews still read a wide range of Yiddish books in 1822.

There is some further evidence about the readership of *Jüdisch-deutsch* works. Ottensoser's *Geschichte der Jehudim* had hundreds of Bavarian Jewish subscribers. Bamberger's *Amiro Lebeys Jaakov* sold out an edition of 5,000 copies and went into a third edition. Although the evidence about a substantial *Jüdisch-deutsch* reading public is no proof of a similar public for Yiddish, one can assume that at least the dialect literature appealed to a home-grown audience. The series of *Gedichte und Scherze in jüdischer Mundart* contained over twenty pamphlets and many of the pamphlets sold several editions.[36]

There has been no discussion here of the survival of Yiddish in spoken form in Germany, though there is a fair amount of literature on the subject. It is now quite widely recognised that habits of speech did not change overnight with Mendelssohn's Bible translation, and that various remnants of Yiddish speech survived until very late in Germany. In certain circles there were survivals even into the twentieth century, and in Southern Baden, Alsace and Switzerland, spoken Yiddish dialects were still lively enough to be recorded in the 1960s.[37] The written forms of Yiddish which survived obviously depended on an audience of persons who spoke, or at least recognised, Yiddish or Yiddish-tinged German. But written Yiddish went one step further; for it not only required the familiarity with some form of Yiddish, but also the consciousness that, for some reason (even if negative), this form of speech was worth recording in writing. It is undoubtedly true that the social and literary functions performed by Yiddish and *Jüdisch-deutsch* in nineteenth-century Germany were limited. While humour, practical religious law and nostalgia might sometimes be expressed in *Jüdisch-deutsch* or Yiddish, the great polemical subjects of the day – Emancipation, religious reform, antisemitism – not to speak of economic, political or tragic literary matters, were never seriously discussed in the Hebrew letter texts.

---

[35]Translation: "Keep away from non-kosher, impure German reading. We have nice books in Jewish too. Read the Tse'ena Ure'ena nicely every Sabbath afternoon, afterwards [read] Eulenspiegel, Schildburger Narren, Miracles of Worms, the Early Legends, the book of Customs and then there are still many more Jewish books, thank goodness . . ."

[36]See, e.g., Max Weinreich, 'Roshe-prokim vegn mayrevdikn yidish', *Yuda A. Yofe Bukh*, New York 1958, p. 182. The copy of volume one of the series held in the Library of the New York Leo Baeck Institute states that it is the "Fünfte Auflage". Weinreich mentions another volume which reached a seventh edition.

[37]See, e.g., Weinreich, 'Roshe-prokim', *loc. cit.*, pp. 160, 177; Steven Lowenstein, 'Results of Atlas Investigations among Jews of Germany, *Field of Yiddish*, 3(1969), pp. 16–35; Richard Zuckerman, 'Alsace: an Outpost of Western Yiddish', *Field of Yiddish*, 3(1969), pp. 36–57; Florence Guggenheim-Grünberg, 'Überreste westjiddischer Dialekte in der Schweiz, im Elsass, und in Süddeutschland', *For Max Weinreich on his seventieth birthday*, The Hague 1964, pp. 72–81; Guggenheim-Grünberg, *Surbtaler Jiddisch, Schweizer Dialekte in Text und Ton*, Heft 4, Frauenfeld 1966.

Many genres which were common in modern East European Yiddish (e.g., lyrical poetry, printed Yiddish sermons, newspapers, scientific textbooks) were absent in nineteenth-century Germany.

Yet despite the limitation in function and audience, the very existence of writing in Yiddish or *Jüdisch-deutsch* indicates a realm of expression often directed specifically to the less educated Jew which has been previously unrecognised. Even at a relatively late date, German was not the only means of expression for the ordinary German Jew.

Autobiography and Genealogy

The Memoirs of B. L. Monasch of Krotoschin

BY PETER FRAENKEL

Baer Loew Monasch (1801–1876) was a printer and publisher of Jewish books at Krotoschin (Krotoszyn) in the Province of Posen (Poznań). Apart from daily and festival prayer-books he published such works as the Jerusalem Talmud – the first reprinting since 1609 – the entire Torah in eighteen volumes with Rashi and Onkelos and German as well as Judaeo-German or *Jüdisch-deutsch** translation by Fürstenthal and the *Sohar*. He and his successor also printed the *Monatsschrift für die Geschichte und Wissenschaft des Judentums*, which was then edited by his son-in-law Heinrich Graetz.

The memoirs were started in 1855 while Monasch was on jury duty at the nearby town of Ostrowo (Ostrów Wielkopolski) and added to, periodically, until 1871. They were hand-written in German but contained quotations and book titles in Hebrew. The original was, in 1932, in the hands of a grandson, Dr. Berthold Monasch of Leipzig. Another grandson, Dr. Martin Goldschmidt of Breslau then had copies typed, partly for the benefit of Rabbi Louis Lewin, who wished to write a monograph to commemorate the 100th anniversary of the founding of the printing works. Publication proved difficult in 1933 and Lewin eventually confined himself to an article.[1] One of the typed copies of the memoirs has come down to the translator – a grandson of Goldschmidt's. The original – traced only while this article was in the press – is in the hands of Mrs. E. M. Kaufman, née Monasch, of Melbourne.

The following excerpts are taken from a manuscript of some 18,000 words. It has not been previously published in print, though excerpts of this English translation have been broadcast by the British Broadcasting Corporation and excerpts from the German original by Bayerischer Rundfunk.[2]

The memoirs provide an insight into the life and living standards of Jews in nineteenth-century Prussian Poland – a life of poverty, insecurity and painfully slow capital creation. Monasch relates that selling books at country fairs proved too strenuous for his delicate constitution, implying that he had to carry his own wares, probably on his back. He relates, without considering it particularly remarkable, that seven members of his family slept in one room. During his most active period as a publisher he complains that he could not afford a new pair of trousers. The fire of 1827, according to this account, reduced the richest families in Krotoschin to penury in one night.

---

*For a discussion of the question of the linguistic classification of these "Yiddish" texts see the essay by Steven M. Lowenstein, 'The Yiddish Written Word in Nineteenth-Century Germany', in this volume of the Year Book – Ed.
[1]Louis Lewin, 'Gründung der Krotoschiner Buchdruckerei im Jahre 1833', *Monatsschrift für die Geschichte und Wissenschaft des Judentums*, 1933, p. 464.
[2]'A General's Grandfather', BBC Radio 3, 1st February 1977. 'Aus den Memoiren meines Ur-ur-grossvaters', B.R. 22nd October 1977.

The community among whom he laboured appears to have been made up of small craftsmen. Jewish occupations listed among the Prussian statistics for 1837 are: tobacco-blender, tailor, locksmith, dyer, tanner, baker, saddler, cap-maker, barber, butcher, furrier, carpenter, glove-maker, miller, biscuit-baker, haberdasher and printer. Remarkably, the list includes only one occupation of middleman or retailer – that of haberdasher. Even here the term used – *Posamentierer* – may still be understood in the old sense of maker of lace and gold braid. Of course, we cannot be certain that the list is complete or accurate.

As factory industries developed in Germany proper, many of these professions became obsolete. The Province of Poznań – already affected adversely by the partition of the Polish market – became even more of a backwater. This explains the exodus of both Jews and Germans which resulted in the failure of the Germanisation policy of the Prussian administration.

Krotoschin had had a comparatively large Jewish population since the fifteenth century. In 1840 there were 2,203 Jews – 32 per cent of the total population. By 1871 – though the town had grown slightly – the Jewish community had shrunk to 1,149 or 18 per cent. By 1895 their number was 300 or 7 per cent. This exodus overseas and to Germany-proper helps to explain the precarious finances of a printer and publisher of Jewish books and his need to seek markets further west, in Breslau (Wroclaw) and east, in "Congress-Poland" and Russia – which he describes. His successor and son-in-law Hermann Goldschmidt turned increasingly towards German printing and brought out the *Krotoschiner Kreisblatt*.

Monasch explains that the memoirs are written for his descendants "as a legacy and for their emulation". However, at least in part, his motive appears to have been to justify his financial failures and to show himself a man of probity. As he sets down in an entry in October 1855, despite his heavy work-load he is determined to continue with the memoirs because "the fear that a speedy death might overtake me will not leave me alone" and because "in this, my favourite task, I find consolation for all the misfortunes, humiliations, sufferings and misjudgments I have had to endure".

As his motto he chose the saying of King Friedrich Wilhelm III "Meine Zeit in Unruhe – meine Hoffnung in Gott."

The Memoirs

I was born in Krotoschin in the year 1801, so I am now 54 years of age. My father, who was also born in Krotoschin, was a school-master, widely respected for his learning. My mother came from Breslau and was revered for her good nature. She bore thirteen children of whom three – two brothers and one sister – survive. Until my twelfth year I was an only child, all the others having died in infancy, and since I was a delicate and sickly child, my parents pampered me . . .

Since I displayed a clear and nimble mind, my parents decided to make a rabbi of me. My father instructed me in Biblical and Rabbinic writings and taught me to read and write German. Talmudic studies, however, I had to do with another teacher. I did not care much for these, because the lessons strained my memory and because I had to take them outside our home.

Besides, there were at that time great movements of French and Russian troops through Krotoschin and my school-fellows managed to persuade me, rather than to spend my time studying the Talmud, to come out and hear the military bands, to see the colourful uniforms of the soldiers and their smart marching – all of which were novelties for us.[3]

My parents came to recognise that their wish that I should become a rabbi was unlikely to be fulfilled, since I displayed more of a bent towards manual skills than towards scholarly pursuits.

Now my father was not only a teacher but also a bookbinder, a trade he practised every night after teaching. Despite my father's objections I insisted on helping him with binding and on staying up late to help him with his work.

One day, when I had reached my fourteenth year, my father said to me: "Since you show no inclination towards study, I would like you to become a painter . . ." I wept and said: "I don't want to be a painter. You yourself have always said to me that it is written in the Talmud that one should let one's son learn a trade that is both clean and not too strenuous. But painting is not a clean trade – the master-painter is filthy from head to foot. What's more, it must be very strenuous to carry those large vats about. I would rather remain a bookbinder."

"I would not mind," replied my father, "if you could be a skilled bookbinder like the one at Militsch.[4] But he is a Gentile and will not teach you because he'll fear competition."

My father only did the cheaper binding. He did not know how to do gold-tooling and other such art-work.

One day my father said to me: "Let us travel to Militsch and see whether we can come to an arrangement with the master-binder." He did manage to arrange with Master Drebs that I should be apprenticed for a year, but that I should have my board and lodging with a Jew. My master was to receive fifteen Marks in two instalments.

[3] Monasch appears to refer to Napoleon's Russian campaign of 1812. He was eleven at the time.
[4] Militsch (Milicz) is a small town fifteen miles from Krotoschin on the way to Breslau (Wroclaw).

My master soon showed himself well satisfied with my work. I only needed to be shown a thing once and I went away and did it correctly. But Master Drebs kept the more elaborate secrets of the trade to himself. Since these were the very things I wanted to learn, I noted everything I saw him do carefully.

My master traded in school and prayer-books and used to go and sell these at country fairs. After I had been apprenticed to him some three months, he chanced to travel to the annual fair at Pleschen. He left a dozen schoolbooks for me to work on during his absence. At the time I did not realise that schoolbooks should be finished simply. I longed to undertake my master's sort of work, so I decided to finish each of the books in its own individual style and to try out the tricks of the trade that I had picked up . . . I worked hard on my twelve books and finished them in four days – each more beautiful than the other. On the fifth afternoon my master came back and I was as if struck by lightning when he pronounced my work totally unsatisfactory. He was furious, shook me by the shoulders, beat his wife for not watching me and ordered me home to go and fetch the money that the school-books had cost him . . .

(Eight days later) a letter came from my master demanding the money for the books but never once referring to my return to Militsch. My father . . . said: "You are not to go back, since he does not even ask for you." I was in despair and it took all the persuasive talents of my mother, brother and sister to stop me from running back to my master on foot.

Later, when I grew older, I discovered that my parents were not really in a position to pay for my board and lodging and that my dismissal was not altogether unwelcome as it freed them from a great financial burden.

Once again I busied myself with my father's work . . . Following my instructions, my father bought paring knives, stamps and fillets and some letter-stamps for titles, but he could not buy any more than that . . .

After my sixteenth birthday, when my reason had developed, I became dissatisfied with staying at home and constantly pestered my parents to let me go back to my master at Militsch or to another at Breslau or at least to buy some more equipment. The last my parents probably could not afford to do. At that time a family friend who lived at Borek came for a visit. He said to my father: "Listen, I'll tell you what: Reb Jekew the bookbinder at Borek has died. And you know what a good bookbinder he was. Perhaps the widow will sell you the tools. What good are they to her now? If you like your son can travel to Borek with me and see what can be arranged."

My father agreed and gave me a Thaler for the journey . . . The widow at Borek received me well, but . . . said she still had a lot of work left over from before her husband's death. If I would finish off this work, she would sell me the tools and, on top of that, split the earnings for the work with me. In my innocence I agreed at once and started to work the following day. What I did not know was that the cunning woman only went out then and got in the work . . . (Eventually) my parents came to terms with her and I was delighted to receive a good and complete set of tools.

In these two years the outside world did not impinge upon me at all. I worked all day and, if there was too much work, my father helped. Every night

I had to take lessons with him in Biblical studies, the Mishnah and the Ethics of the Fathers, as well as reading, writing and arithmetic.

My father took all my earnings, but gave me money whenever I had to travel to Breslau to purchase materials. I never went there without bringing back some new tool or other. My father did not approve of these purchases. He said, "You ought to save up for some fine clothes. Clothes make the man."

For my nineteenth birthday I received a smart new suit and a red cotton dressing-gown.

Some time later the district court needed a file binder. A court-messenger reported this to my father and advised him to go to the chief magistrate and to apply for this post on my behalf. The magistrate looked me up and down and said I seemed too small to take on such a job. My father, however, assured him that I was a capable lad and begged him to try me out. So the following day I went, very timidly, to the law courts and worked there for a trial period of one month. The gentlemen of the court soon grew fond of me as I worked quickly and competently. I came to be accepted and was promised a monthly salary of three Marks which my father was to collect and in return for which I was expected to spend two to three hours at the court every morning.

I did my work regularly and to the satisfaction of the gentlemen of the court and thus not only became acquainted with some of them so that they entrusted their bookbinding to me, but I also acquired some semblance of education and some pride and came to be respected among my friends as if I were a genuine civil servant.

Gradually my home life changed. I no longer participated regularly in my father's nightly study sessions. I remained out with friends and on many an evening returned late. In the morning I got up later than had been my custom and I often went about my work with my head uncovered. This greatly upset my good, devout father. He often took me to task for my behaviour and complained that my entire character appeared to have changed and that I was no longer the good son I had once been. He endeavoured to guide me back to the old path by drawing my companions towards himself. He prevailed upon them to come to the house and to keep me company while I worked. He taught me to play Solo-whist and arranged card-parties for Saturday evening, and so I started to remain at home again, but I did not continue with the nightly study sessions. My father therefore decided to try and accustom me to German rather than to Hebrew writings. He brought me useful books, which I found to my liking. I conceived the idea of joining the lending library which the Postal Secretary Hallschaur then ran. My father agreed to this provided I showed him every book I brought home. Finding these books both edifying and entertaining, I read assiduously and my parents were once again content with me and with this arrangement.

At that time there lived in Krotoschin a colporteur or itinerant bookseller named Klose who sold prayer, school and song-books. He bound the ordinary books himself, but gave the finer work to me. I earned good money from him and we came to be on very friendly terms. Klose and his wife hawked their books around country fairs, coming back every two or three months to stock up again. In the beginning he always paid me before he went on his tours, but later – as he gave me more work and larger amounts were involved – he settled up whenever he returned from his travels. Occasionally he remained a few Thalers in arrears. On one occasion he remained away longer than usual. When he came back after eleven weeks he explained that he had been laid up ill for five weeks and could not afford to take delivery of the books waiting for him unless I could give him fifty Marks' credit. However, he placed an even larger order than before, saying that due to his illness he had not managed to visit certain areas. Since Klose now owed me fifty Marks and new orders needed to be worked on, I found myself eighty Marks short for the purchase of new books and materials. One of my friends offered to obtain a loan for me, and in this way I managed to complete the order. But imagine our shock as more and more time elapsed and Klose did not return. I found myself swindled and defrauded of my hard-earned savings and was poor again.

This was the first such blow, sustained in my nineteenth year. Since then a red thread of misfortune winds through my entire life, so that whenever I have come to something, somehow or other I have been deprived of it again.

I languished and fell into a serious brain-fever which racked me for six whole weeks. When I rallied a little, my father came up to my room, as he was wont to do, sat by my bed and spoke. "My son," he said, "thanks be to God, you have been saved and will soon rise again from your bed. However, you have saddened me greatly for I now realise that you grieve so much over money lost that you become seriously ill. You do not trust God to provide for you. You have some learning. You know the story of Job. I am much aggrieved that you love money more than God. Now resolve to mend your ways and you will see that God will never desert you."

After a few months I had saved another thirty Thalers which I lent to a friend. One morning this friend came to bring back the money, but since it was time for me to go to the law-courts to do my filing, I did not have time to hand the money to my mother to look after, but merely put it in the drawer of my work-table and locked the room . . . When I came back I discovered that the thirty Thalers were no longer in my drawer. The money must have been stolen by some eavesdropper, and to this day I do not know what happened. I wept bitterly concerning this second misfortune, finding myself impoverished once again. My mother persuaded me to visit a fortune-teller who laid her cards and said: "You have had great harm done to you. One of your best friends has done this damage to you. Beware of good friends. Great fortune and great misfortune are ahead of you. Your good heart will cause you much annoyance and misfortune."

My father was very annoyed that my mother had taken me to a fortune-teller, saying that we had done very wrong because . . .[5] is forbidden to a Jew.

At that time the Dyhernfurth press completed the printing of the Talmud.[6]

---

[5] Gap in typescript – original Hebrew not transcribed.
[6] The renowned Hebrew printing press at Dyhernfurth (now Brzeg Dolny) in Silesia had been in operation since 1689.

There were many subscribers for this great work and I received a lot of binding work, so that I soon forgot my losses and worked with great zeal to improve my position and to satisfy my customers. Now the bookbinder Weisleder received no work from Jews, and since he knew that the binding of the Talmud gave me a lot of work, he grew envious and tried to undermine me. He denounced me to the authorities in Posen, saying that I was only twenty-one and not a masterbinder. Thereupon the authorities forbade me to carry on my trade. My father, however, appealed saying that he was the master and I the apprentice, and so the prohibition was revoked.

One summer's evening in my twenty-second year . . . I presumed to pay a first visit to this girl . . .[7] I do not know how it happened, but I ventured to pay a second and third visit and noted that her parents did not seem to disapprove of these calls . . .

I spent sleepless nights! I was constantly drawn towards this beautiful girl and on one of my frequent visits – I don't know how it came about – we declared our mutual love to one another, sealed it with the first fiery kiss of love and agreed to get married.

That night the most rapturous images floated before my eyes. I tossed on my bed and could hardly wait for dawn to announce my good fortune to my parents. In the morning I bashfully told my mother of the developments of the previous evening. She was delighted and kissed me. Shortly after I had confided the secret to her, my father came up to my room and declared himself well satisfied with my choice, but requested that I cease my visiting until matters could be arranged between the parents and I could be publicly announced a bridegroom.

The following evening, however, I found I simply could not comply with my father's wishes and went and visited my beloved as before. I told her of my emotions and how I had spent the previous night and that I had confided in my mother. She admitted that matters were much the same with her and that she, too, had not been able to keep the secret from her parents.

Our respective mothers had a common friend who acted as go-between and a few days later we celebrated our engagement. Our wedding, however, was postponed for a year.

I loved my bride ardently, with all the youthful fire of first love and – although in later years my wife very frequently wronged me and accused me of matters of which I had no inkling, thereby giving rise to much domestic discord and often making my life a misery – I can affirm that my love for her has neither become extinguished, nor has it cooled even to this day, in my fifty-fifth year.

We celebrated our wedding in the year 1823 . . .

For my household I only bought cheap furniture and furnished my rooms simply. I worked industriously and eagerly and never frittered away a minute. If I had no book-binding to do, I made hat-boxes, just to keep busy and to augment my income. I accumulated a small supply of prayer, song and schoolbooks, mirrors, brief-cases, handbags and other fancy-goods fashionable at the

[7]Mathilde Wiener. For the origin of the Wiener family see Maxa Nordau, letter in *Jewish Chronicle*, 25th February 1977, p. 22.

time and with these I travelled to fairs, like Drebs, my old master and Klose the man who had defrauded me. However, I soon had to admit that my physique would not stand the exertions of these strenuous tours, so I was compelled to give this up again.

Nine months after our wedding, my wife presented me with a daughter whom we named Julia, now Mrs. Behrend. My wife's first confinement was very difficult and painful. Both her breasts became sore and she could not suckle the child. A wet-nurse had to be engaged for the infant, a surgeon for the mother. Only after three months did the breasts heal and then the mother endeavoured to suckle the child. After much effort she accomplished this, to the surprise of our friends and her own great joy.

In 1826 my wife gave birth to a second daughter, whom we named Maria after her two grandmothers. It is she who is now married to Dr. Graetz in Breslau. My wife again suffered much illness on the birth of our second child and our domestic expenses, despite our withdrawn style of life, increased, so that I started to think about starting some side-line business again.[8] I considered establishing a lithographic printing press but since I did not have the necessary capital I had to arm myself with patience. In my spare time I carved a model of a lithographic press and of a printing press from wood. In this way I prepared myself for starting one or other of these businesses. On my frequent trips to Breslau I made acquaintances in various printing firms and picked up many of the tricks of the trade.

On the evening of Friday, 1st August 1827 a conflagration broke out in this town . . . There had been fires in Krotoschin before . . . As soon as I heard the noise I rushed to the site of the fire to help with salvaging and extinguishing the flames, as I had done on earlier occasions. Within half an hour, however, I realised that this fire was bigger than all previous ones and that it was quite impossible to put it out. I ran home and only just managed to enter with great difficulty. I found that my wife and sister had already packed a few clothes and some small tools and were about to carry off the children. We saved nothing except a few featherbeds, one suitcase full of clothes and a chest of small tools. Most of the Jewish inhabitants suffered similarly. The wealthiest people in town were turned into paupers and beggars in that unfortunate night. 160 houses and their contents were destroyed within three hours.

We carried our children and our few possessions to the house of a friend, the carpenter Moldenschauer in Kalisch Street and spent several days there, disconsolate and perplexed, with almost no food and clothing. After a few days I rented a room in Kozminer Street and, although space was very confined, moved in with my wife's parents and her brothers.

The question now: what to do? where to turn? how to make a living without tools, without household utensils? But the precept "Where need is greatest, God is nearest" still holds true. Shortly before the fire a customer, Herr von Blan-

---

[8]Earlier unsuccessful attempts at diversification related in the memoirs were to establish a grrocery, a bookshop and a paper-dyeing shop.

kowski, commissioner for the ducal estates at Dobersize,[9] had asked me to come to the duke's château to bind his files of invoices and vouchers. He promised to pay well for this. The news that Krotoschin had been levelled spread rapidly in the neighbourhood and Herr von Blankowski sent me a friendly and comforting letter requesting that, true to my promise, I travel to Dobersize in the messenger's cart. I travelled there with an apprentice, but without boots, having lost mine in the conflagration, and worked at the château for eight days. This work required practically no tools. Herr von Blankowski paid me very generously and made me a gift of some new boots and some groceries, before sending me home in his cart.

These first good earnings after our disaster gave me renewed courage. My customers among the court officials supported me generously with money, so that a fortnight after the fire I managed to travel to Breslau to buy new tools and materials and to start my bindery again. I acquired more customers than ever before, had a lot of work which paid better than previously and so I decided to build a new house.

What little money we had did not even suffice to pay the workmen and we were forced to incur debt upon debt so as to complete even a single-storey building and to be able to move in.[10] I lodged ceaseless complaints with the royal authorities in Posen that, although I had been one of the first to commence rebuilding, I had not received any subsidy from the royal coffers.[11] The local authorities now decided that I deserved favourable consideration and one week after the birth of my son I received forty Marks as a reconstruction grant.

A long time before, while on one of my visits to Kalisch, I had arranged for the local lithographer there to issue me with a certificate of apprenticeship. The moment I received my forty Marks I speedily travelled to Breslau and there assembled the equipment for a lithographic workshop – even if only a primitive one. After much effort I received a licence from the royal authorities. I engaged a lithographer in Breslau and thus succeeded, at long last, in establishing a lithographic press.

---

[9] Probably the Duke of Thurn and Taxis who was also Duke of Krotoschin.
[10] Among numerous debts enumerated by Monasch, one for 300 Marks from an uncle of his wife's in Kalisch (Kalisz) in Congress-Poland was to have serious consequences.
[11] The King of Prussia had offered compensation – Monasch refers to it curiously as *Feuerkostengeld*. However, the authorities insisted that the money be used for the construction of *massiv* or solid buildings. The authorities looked upon the percentage of solidly built dwellings as an index of economic development and collected detailed statistics on house-construction. In 1805, for example, the Prussian commissioners complain that in the Province of Poznań brick or stone-built houses with tiled or metal roofs were rare, timber construction with thatch or shingle covering frequent. In 1816 only one house in twenty-six was *massiv*, a much lower proportion than in any other province of Prussia.

The drive to encourage better building standards was one of many designed to bring the lands annexed in 1798 up to the standard of the rest of Prussia. Efforts were made, for example, to raise the standards of education and skill among the large Jewish population, which Prussian surveys showed to have been low. They were compelled to establish communal schools and exhorted to diversify their occupations. Regarding the latter, results were slow. Gentile masters were often reluctant to take on Jewish apprentices and the dietary laws made it difficult for Jews to accept apprenticeships.

My exertions bore fruit. I received sizeable commissions for my lithographic press from offices and law-courts in this town and in the surrounding area. However, I had to pay four Marks a week to the lithographer and to guarantee him one year's employment. He therefore ate up most of the week's takings. Now due to the great fire, my brother had not been able to finish his apprenticeship as a horn-turner. Since he showed great talent as a lithographer I sent him to Breslau to learn the trade and promised that if he would come and work for me, I would pay him fifteen Pfennigs a week for the first year after his return, one Mark for the second and 2 Marks for the third, plus free board and lodging throughout. Our father approved of this arrangement, through which I hoped to improve my income.

Round about midsummer's day 1830 I gave the lithographer notice, having employed him longer than a year and having thus met my obligation to him. I instructed my brother to come back from Breslau and to enter my business.

I made some small alterations to our house, extending the room that my parents-in-law had occupied. In this room there now lived, or rather slept, my two older girls, my brother and sister, my two brothers-in-law and my mother-in-law. The good relations among them gave me satisfaction. We lived very simply and I worked hard at my two businesses, since it was my endeavour to free myself from debt . . .

Five days before Easter 1831, my good father died, in his fifty-fourth year, having been ill only four days. Before departing this life he blessed his children and mine. His blessing to me was in the words that King David spoke to his son Solomon: "Mayest thou prosper in all that thou doest, and whithersoever thou turnest thyself." And he added: "You must promise to care for your sister, that she may come under the chuppah and to support your brother."

A few hours later he passed away amidst deep mourning.

1831 was, for me, a year full of both joys and sorrows. But listen, dear reader, and judge whether God's finger did not stretch forth to extend it's special protection over me!

Twelve days after the death of my beloved father, my wife presented me with a second son, whom we naturally named Louis, after my father.[12] The joy in the young son helped to still some of the pain of my father's death.

My household was growing and despite all my industry I could not manage to pay off the heavy debts on my house. It will not surprise anyone that several of my creditors grew impatient and sued me.

I confided my troubles to a good customer of mine, the magistrate Herr Müller. He advised me to appeal to the court for a respite and to prove that I would be able to pay my debts within three years. If my creditors did not lodge any objections, I would be granted a moratorium. I availed myself of this advice. However, among my debts I did not list the 300 Marks I owed the uncle in Kalisch. For one, I assumed he would not press me and, for two, I hoped to

---

[12] Louis was to emigrate to Australia and, in his turn, to father a son who became General Sir John Monash, G.C.M.G., K.C.B., Grand Officier Légion d'Honneur etc., commander of the Australian division in France in 1918.

pay him before any of the other creditors. But around that time revolution broke out in Poland.[13]

Many youngsters, afraid of being called up, came over the border to await the outcome. Among those who came here was the son of my wife's uncle. This young scoundrel apparently received reports of my court action in some spitefully distorted form, quarrelled with us and proceeded to press me in my sorest spot by briefing a lawyer, Herr Brachvogel, to file an objection to the moratorium on behalf of his father. Following his malicious reports home, he received documents and powers-of-attorney to proceed against me without giving quarter – whereby my house would undoubtedly have come under the hammer. I was summoned, charged with falsification and requested to explain why I had suppressed a creditor. The only thing I could say in my own defence was that the uncle had made me a gift of the money – a rather poor defence, I must admit.

At that time cholera raged in Poland and over here all sanitary measures were taken to prevent the spread of this terrible disease . . .

At this point my wife and I had to appear in court and Herr Brachvogel, presenting his documents and powers of attorney, hounded me so that I did not know which way to turn and had to stand before the court like some miserable sinner.

In my terrible state of dejection, embarrassment and perplexity, God gave me a fortunate idea. It was as if He Himself had put the right words into my mouth. I spoke up bravely, requesting Herr Müller to be so good as to let me see my opponent's documents and powers-of-attorney. This was done and after I had leafed through them for a little while, I began to speak with courage in the presence of all:

"Gentlemen," I said, "I stand by my assertion that my uncle made me a gift of 300 Marks for the building of my house and I contest the authenticity of the letters, documents and powers-of-attorney presented here. Moreover, I assert that all these papers are forgeries, not sent over from Kalisch as my opponent alleges. And I wish to prove my charges thus: These papers carry neither postal nor sanitary office stamp. Gentlemen, you are no doubt aware that cholera is raging in Kalisch!"

The judges stared at me as if turned to stone. Herr Müller seized the papers, flung them into the furthest corner of the court-room and turned to Herr Brachvogel: "You have brought an investigation upon yourself," he said. "How dare you present to this court unfumigated and unstamped papers from a focus of infectious disease? Defend yourself. Prove where you obtained these papers from and whether they are genuine or not."

Herr Brachvogel looked annihilated. Unable to utter a single word in reply, he could only beg for an adjournment. To me Herr Müller said: "The investigation will be instituted at once, but since there are no other objections, you will get your moratorium."

But God's mercy was even greater that year. The revolution in Poland brought large numbers of Prussian troops to town. Staff headquarters for all the military

[13]November 1830.

in the area were established in Krotoschin, also arms dumps and hospitals. As a result I was given so much work for my lithographic press that I had to order a second one and in a short while earned so much that I could repay 150 Marks to the uncle in Kalisch in three instalments, which gave me great joy. The remaining 150 Marks I only managed to pay off several years later.

In 1832, after the suppression of the Polish revolution and the withdrawal of Prussian troops, my business gradually returned to its slow old ways. I worked very industriously at my two enterprises. No offer of work was ever too petty for me. In 1832, a chemist by the name of Ackermann established himself in Krotoschin. He asked me whether I would undertake to label his jars, pots and bottles for him, using black ink upon yellow labels. I accepted and we agreed upon a payment of one Pfennig per piece. I promised my brother a bonus over and above his usual wages and the two of us spent several weeks in Herr Ackermann's abode. Despite this we did not neglect our regular occupations. When all the labelling was done, my total bill came to fifty Thalers.

The year 1833 was one of the most remarkable of my life. In that year the government introduced its Reform of the State of the Jews. The new law decreed that the Jews in the Grand Duchy were to be classified either as "naturalised" or as "tolerated or certificated".[14] The naturalised were granted rights equal to those of Christian citizens. I was among those who received the patent of naturalisation.

At the same time the administration of the Jewish congregations was regulated by royal decree. The members of each corporation were made to elect 15 representatives and an executive committee of four. I was among the first elected representatives and in those days it was a great honour to be chosen to sit around the green table. I can flatter myself that my proposals for the improvement of the state of my community were always approved with greater alacrity than those of other members.[15] Each representative was elected for a term of three years. Until 1849 I was re-elected every term. After 1849 I joined the executive committee.

Our synagogue, which had been destroyed in the great fire of 1827, was to have been rebuilt in 1829. In fact, the executive of the period managed to have the outer walls erected, up to first-floor level. However, as a result of the reforms of 1833, the rebuilding of the synagogue was interrupted, the settlement of other community affairs demanding much time and effort. For twelve whole years, until 1841, the unfinished walls stood exposed to wind and weather and were very nearly ruined as a result. In 1841 the representatives at last agreed to rebuild the synagogue and to raise money by selling shares. The shares offered to

[14]Under the regulations of 1st June 1833 only the wealthier and better-educated Jews in the Grand Duchy – subsequently Province – of Poznań qualified for naturalisation. Even these, in fact, did not enjoy full equality. Posts in the civil service and army, for example, remained closed to them. At the same time a similar two-tier system was proposed for the more westerly areas of Prussia. There, however, the Jew had – under the Napoleonic reforms – enjoyed more extensive rights and the new regulations were considered retrograde. Led by the Rothschilds, the Jews in the West succeeded in having that legislation dropped. In Prussian Poland, however, the 1833 regulations were welcomed.

[15]The following details of community affairs are taken from an appendix to the memoirs, written in 1865.

members were valued at sixty, forty-five and twenty-five Marks and each shareholder was to receive two synagogue-places, a man's and a woman's, which he could use freely until such times as the shares were redeemed from the income of the synagogue. The seats were arranged in three classes, corresponding to the value of the shares. In addition, each shareholder was to pay an annual Kanen of three, two or one Thaler to the community chest, depending on his class.

Thus the synagogue came to be built and was solemnly inaugurated in 1845. I had been elected a member of the building-committee but since the other members cared little for this work, or nothing at all, I alone had to shoulder the colossal task of supervising and directing this large enterprise. My duties caused me much vexation, but nevertheless I brought the building to completion, in return for which I have the satisfaction of knowing that I have secured a house of God for my community.[16]

In 1829 the corporation executive rebuilt the old community and schoolhouse, the earlier one having also been destroyed in the fire. This had, however, been reconstructed so shoddily that in 1846 the police closed it because of its state of dilapidation. A new one could not be built straight away as funds were short, and so rooms had to be rented at great expense. As soon as I joined the executive I introduced a proposal that a new school and community house be erected and I succeeded in having the present splendid building soundly constructed at little expense to the community.

Between the years 1845 and 1851, i.e., for seven years, the shareholders had not paid the Kanen-monies and I made the calculation that these amounted to some 1,700 Thalers. However, since the community members were of the opinion that the synagogue seats for which they had taken up shares were their property and that they need not pay Kanen-monies, I proposed asking the government for permission to offer the synagogue-places for auction to the highest bidder.

We – that is the corporation committee – proved to the government that the auction would not only bring in a capital of 12,000–15,000 Thalers, with which we could pay off old debts, but that if the Kanen-monies were deducted when redeeming the shares, enough would remain to build a new school and community house.

We requested the authorities' permission for our financial proposals and also to cut down the century-old pine-trees on the cemetery so as to use the timber for the construction of the school and community-house. The government approved all our requests and empowered us to sell off the synagogue places. The agitation caused among the public in consequence was very great and some malevolent members of the congregation, jealous of our success with the authorities, ran down our building-site. They reported to the government that there had already been a school-house on this spot, which had fallen into a state of decay and had had to be closed. They requested the government to have the school built somewhere else. But to do this a new plot would have had to be bought and our funds did not suffice for this.

---

[16]The Krotoschin synagogue was – according to information given to the translator by the town clerk – destroyed during the German occupation of the 1940s. The cemetery where Monasch was eventually buried was turned into a park at the same time.

The government sent a commissioner to Krotoschin to investigate the matter and to suggest to the community executive that we purchase a new building site and offering a government loan for this purpose. I persuaded my committee not to give in, and to insist on the old site. The commissioner had the site surveyed and found it to be good. He had the members of the congregation assembled in the synagogue to hear their views.

Our opponents yelled, "A new site!" Our friends yelled, "The old site!" The commissioner then put the question to us: "Gentlemen, for what reason do you insist upon the old site? A new one might well be healthier for a school and more advantageous." I stepped forward and requested permission to speak: "Herr Commissarius," I said, "we insist on the old site because all religious denominations have their schools close to their churches, for school and church must go hand in hand. Our old site is near our church. The new one cannot be."

"A well-founded reason," said the commissioner. "Gentlemen, I bid you adieu. I have no business here. You have a good committee who will undoubtedly do their best for the community."

Our opponents had to go home with long faces and we built our large and well-appointed community and school-house on the old site.

After this I endeavoured to have a rabbi appointed for the community, but since I failed with this proposal and it caused me much bother and misunderstanding, I voluntarily resigned in 1852, the law dispensing me from holding office because I still had six under-age children. Since that time I have refused all office.

It was around June 1833, while I was busy with my bookbinding, that a young man called on me and introduced himself as a printer from Warsaw. He informed me that he hoped to establish a printing press in town and that he had already had discussions with the local authority. I had to hide my inner agitation from this stranger, but as soon as he left I hurried to the local authority and in the presence of district secretary Kusche, who was a good friend of mine, told the district commissioner [17] what I had just heard and informed him that I had myself intended to establish a book printing press to go with my lithographic press. Herr Kusche spoke up for me and persuaded the district commissioner to turn down the stranger's application at once. I was requested to submit my testimonials and to apply for a licence as a printer of books. I immediately travelled to Dyhernfurth to see the brothers Warschauer who had taken over the Jewish printing press there.[18] Because of their bad management they had nearly brought it to its last legs.

I paid them thirty Marks and received from them a testimonial of apprenticeship as proof of my competence. I then applied to the Krotoschin district office and received a licence.

I was very short of capital so I had a wooden printing press constructed locally and bought only very few varieties of type in Breslau. Upon my advertisement, a locally reputed teacher, Herr Kaselitz, requested me to publish his

[17] *Landrat*.
[18] See note 6 above.

Monasch of Krotoschin

grammar and we drew up a contract. His book was to include many lithographic drawings. We soon managed to complete this little volume.

In accordance with our contract I was to supply quantities of the book to Herr Kaselitz upon cash payment. Unfortunately a similar grammar, and probably a better one, had been published just previously in Leipzig and as a result only very few of Herr Kaselitz's could be sold and all the rest were so much scrap paper. I could scarcely recover one-sixth of my costs.

My second little German volume did not fare much better. A certain Eichborn from Posen had obtained permission from the authorities to have the new laws regarding the Jewish communities printed in both German and Judaeo-German writing and to have them sold to the Jewish public. He wanted to have the work printed at his own expense.[19] I travelled to Posen and believing Herr Eichborn to be a very fine, learned gentleman, signed a contract with him. This time I was to deliver all 3,000 copies. Upon delivery I was to have one-quarter of my money in cash, the rest in three bills of exchange redeemable at two-monthly intervals. I did indeed receive one-quarter in cash, but when the first bill fell due there was no money to meet it and it was the same with the second and third and I came to discover that I had been defrauded.

But Almighty God did not desert me. Rabbi Jaffe of Zduny requested me to print a Hebrew work for him. For this I needed Hebrew type, but I did not let this discourage me. I drew up a contract, but having paid dearly for experience, insisted upon payment in the course of the printing and Rabbi Jaffe complied with this very promptly and punctually.

My typesetter had told me that the former owner of the Dyhernfurth press, Herr David Sklower, now in Breslau, still had some Hebrew type, so I journeyed there and bought this from him, paying part in cash and the remainder by means of bills of exchange.[20]

Not only did I not get into any financial embarrassment with this Hebrew book, but I had pleasure in the work and obtained an entirely new concept of printing work.

But providence was even kinder to me. Hardly had I completed the work for Rabbi Jaffe that Rabbi Urbach from Lenschütz in Poland, the father of the Ostrowo rabbi,[21] commissioned a major work of 120 sheets under the same conditions as Rabbi Jaffe's. This work brought me good luck and some repute. I worked an entire year at it and it enabled me to set up a proper Hebrew printing press.

I now gave notice to my typesetter, for he was a great debauchee. My brother and I had learnt sufficient from him, and between the two of us we set up and printed a third, smaller work for Rabbi Spyro of Tscharnikau. This too proved

---

[19]W. J. Eichborn, *Sammlung der die neue Organisation des Judenwesens im Grossherzogthum Posen betreffenden Gesetze, Instruktionen Rescripte usw. in deutscher und zugleich in hebräischer Schrift*, Posen 1834.

[20]Monasch must have had some Hebrew type for the Judaeo-German part of the previous work. He appears to have bought a rabbinic type. The new Hebrew work was a talmudic interpretation: *Beth Minhas* by Rabbi R. Mordechai Michael Jaffe.

[21]Rabbi M. Urbach.

lucrative. These three Hebrew, or rather rabbinic works were printed in the old rabbinic type I had bought from Sklower in Breslau.

As before, I carried on bookbinding with my own hands. In addition I often lent a hand with both printing and lithography. It was my sole pleasure to be fully occupied and to be able to work myself thoroughly tired. I knew of no pleasures save only to work for and care for my loved ones and to be constantly with them, allowing myself none of the amusements and distractions that many other men and fathers of families cannot deny themselves. In leisure hours and on holy days it was my sole delight to sit at home and to study Hebrew or German books.

My ever-forward-striving spirit soon convinced me that I could not rely upon having printing orders at all times. If I wanted to get on in life I would have to do business in different ways. In Posen I had met a certain Sussman, a bookseller, who strongly urged me to set up my own Jewish publishing firm. In particular he advised me to publish the German translation of the Five Books of Moses by Dr. Johlson, which had appeared recently, together with the original Hebrew text and a Judaeo-German translation. It was to be assumed that this might be a lucrative business since no such work had appeared for some time. I took note of his suggestion, but could not tell him of my straightened circumstances. I did, however, discuss the suggestion with my family and it found their approval.

The few varieties of type I had acquired in Breslau were worn and quite inadequate for the printing of a Pentateuch. The type-foundries in Breslau had no Hebrew type, but my enquiries showed that I could obtain both Hebrew type and matrices from the firm of Dressler & Rostfingerlin in Frankfurt a. Main. Since I could not ask this firm for credit, I placed an order for the five most essential matrices and arranged for these to be sent to a business house in Breslau, from whom I undertook to redeem them for cash.

I did not have enough money to buy even the most essential bits of equipment, so I was compelled to have recourse to an expedient: I asked the Andersch press in Frankfurt, who used the same Hebrew type as I had on order, to print 2,000 sample sheets of the Pentateuch following my own design and prescript. I distributed these sheets together with a subscription-form which I printed myself, requesting an advance of ten Pfennigs per subscriber. This expedient produced excellent results. I immediately received over 1,200 orders from near and far and got over 400 Marks in cash into my hands.

My success encouraged me. The matrices arrived a few weeks later and I gave them to a type-foundry where I had a little credit and had the Hebrew type cast. I took on two assistant compositors and several boys and soon managed to complete the first fascicle of the Pentateuch.[22]

---

[22] Most of Monasch's bigger works were published in fascicles or sections which subscribers collected and had bound once the work was completed. This Pentateuch contained the Rashi commentary, the Aramaic of Onkelos and the German translation of Johlson revised by R. Fürstenthal which was printed in German and *Jüdisch-deutsch*. For a list of Monasch's publications see the article by Akiba Baruch Posner, 'The Printing Press of Monasch in Krotoschin' (in Hebrew), in *Arescheth*, vol. I, Jerusalem 1949, pp. 260–278.

Eventually I was to have twenty-five different sorts of Hebrew type, four printing presses and thirty-six people in my employ, yet I never succeeded in having a constant reserve of fifty Thalers in cash, materials and wages swallowing up so much money. My wages bill alone came to as much as fifty Marks a month.

As soon as I had brought out a few segments of the Johlson Pentateuch and had managed to improve my financial circumstances a little, I proceeded to marry off my sister. This cost me 400 Thalers, but in this way I fulfilled the last request of my late father.

Just as a rose, at the end of summer, blooms in all its glory, so stood my printing enterprise at the end of this period (1836–1842). I regard this as the summer of my life. Like the gardener I eschewed no labours to bring my plant to flower and to fruition. No work was too hard for me, no work too humble. I feared neither frost nor the summer's heat. I neglected nothing. But pray do not believe, my dear ones, that I ever rewarded myself for my labours or that I ever permitted myself indulgence in any pleasures as compensation.

My expanding business demanded so much of my time that I could not participate personally in the education and training of my children, especially my sons. I sent them to the local high school and for two years kept a resident tutor whose task it was to instruct them in religion, Jewish learning and Hebrew. He received free board and lodging and sixty Marks a year from me. However, since my sons showed little inclination towards Jewish scholarship, I gave the tutor notice, though I continued sending them to high school. Of Louis I thought he might become a scholar so I sent him to the high school in Glogau, which cost me 200 Thalers a year. But since this expenditure was too great a burden, I brought him back after a year and put him into the local high school.

My children grew and my household expenses likewise. As my business expanded, so did my financial troubles and my worries. Ever more money was tied up in credit and I myself often had to borrow money at high rates of interest so as to meet my commitments . . .

In the year 1840 a new source of business opened up for me. Jewish booksellers in Cracow ordered large quantities of books marketable in Poland and the Austrian territories.[23] Cracow was then a free city so that books could be sent there free of customs duty. From Cracow they were smuggled into the neighbouring territories.

My daughters grew apace and since experience shows that one should marry off a girl in the flower of her youth – "Strike while the iron is hot", as the saying has it – I started thinking about a match for my eldest daughter Julie. In 1841, while on a business-trip, I got to know a young man, a qualified bookdealer

[23]Nowhere does Monasch say what works were exclusively marketable in the East. Only once is a book printed for Cracow referred to by name – the *Sohar* – the main work of the Kabbala. Further west this work was viewed with incomprehension and disapproval. Son-in-law Graetz writes scathingly of the false and misguided enthusiasm of the Hassidim and of the *Lügenbuch* of the Kabbala. It therefore is not improbable that Monasch is embarrassed about the books he is exporting and avoids listing them.

called Behrend at Wollstein. Since I liked him, I asked a friend to suggest a match with my daughter to him.

My little Julie was seventeen at the time of her engagement, so it is not surprising that the child agreed readily to everything asked of her and acted according to her parents' wishes. The marriage cost me 2,000 Marks, including the dowry of 1,200. At Christmas 1842 I had the pleasure of seeing my eldest daughter married to Herr Behrend . . .[24]

I agreed to take them into my business at Krotoschin . . . However, this fatherly deed brought about the autumn and winter of my life. My son-in-law did not concern himself in the least with the practical work but, alas, made only too full a use of his right to have a say in the management. This gave rise to much unpleasantness.

My business in Jewish books now received a slick, businesslike veneer, but the old solidity was lost. Living in amity with one's business associates, not being in too much of a hurry, being satisfied with what God gives . . . all these were lost. The business was brought in line with the German book trade. I had long held that this could not be done with Jewish books. For example, I did not think one should concern oneself with retail prices. Books published only recently now had to be reprinted repeatedly. To be able to sell, a commercial traveller had to be engaged. Such a change in the pattern of business, compared with the slow but solid old ways, required far more capital than we had at our disposal.

Before my son-in-law joined the firm Fürstenthal, who had earned a lot of money from me with his translations from the Hebrew, persuaded me to let him re-translate the old Hebrew work *Menorat ha-Ma'or*[25] and to publish it by subscription. I had brought out two fascicles of the work, but since it had no success I wanted to suspend publication of further instalments. My son-in-law, however, insisted on continuing and in the course of the three years of our partnership, twelve fascicles of the work appeared, although we did not even recover a third of the production costs. There remain three more sections to complete this work. Our commercial traveller looked for new customers and quick sales, but was not concerned whether these were steady and reliable customers or not. We lost much money because he sold the first fascicles of sets to unreliable customers who did not take up subsequent ones so that we were left with incomplete sets. Many bad debtors had to be taken to court, but we recovered little money. Despite my tremendous efforts during this period, I could never even manage to buy myself a new pair of trousers.

I determined to endure patiently and to fulfil all my obligations under our three-year partnership agreement. My sole concern was to see my second daughter well married and God did indeed help me to accomplish this. His mercy is great and incomprehensible: before an illness even appears, the cure is already in sight! Good matches for my second daughter were proposed to me

---

[24] Benzion Behrend was the translator, from Hebrew into German, of a number of works subsequently printed by Monasch and the author of a number of articles of biblical interpretation published between 1870 and 1873 in the *Monatsschrift*. He was the co-founder of a *Verein für Wahrung jüdischer Interessen* which, at the time of the 1848 Revolution, demanded the cancellation of the old blood-debts imposed upon Jewish communities.

[25] *The Light of Wisdom.*

from various quarters. When I suggested one of these to Marie, she replied quite boldly: "Dear father, I could never marry a man whose level of education is below that of my brother-in-law Behrend." I was taken aback by this answer and said: "If this were your firm resolve, you would have to marry a man with a doctorate! And you know I cannot afford that." "One can never know," she replied. "Do try. I'm sure you'll find." It now dawned on me what she was getting at: I talked it over with my wife and we then entrusted my son-in-law Behrend with starting negotiations for a match between Dr. Heinrich Graetz and Marie. We had met Herr Graetz at my elder daughter's engagement party. He was a childhood friend of Behrend's and a relative of his. At that time he was a house-tutor in Ostrowo. He became a family friend and visited us frequently and my second daughter found favour in his eyes. In the meantime he had acquired a doctorate and was now living in Breslau.

After a short while Marie and Dr. Graetz became engaged. The engagement was celebrated in the summer of 1845, but since Dr. Graetz had until then not found a suitable position, the wedding was not celebrated until 1850, i.e., five years later. I agreed to give a dowry of 1,000 Marks in cash, to buy a library worth 500 Marks and to pay fifteen Marks a month for his support, so long as he did not have proper employment. However hard these commitments were for me, I have never regretted incurring them and every day I pray to God that he may bestow upon me such good and happy matches for my other daughters. For three years I fulfilled the commitment undertaken towards Dr. Graetz, although I found it extremely difficult. When, later, I was no longer able to do so – neither to pay the fifteen Marks a month nor to give the promised dowry of 1,000 – Dr. Graetz nevertheless fulfilled his part and treated me so *nobly* that I shall be eternally grateful to him.[26]

At the end of 1845 the Cracow business unfortunately came to an end. As an aftermath of the Polish revolution, the free city status of Cracow ceased and the town was incorporated into Austrian Galicia. The import of Hebrew books into Cracow was no longer permitted and all orders came to an end. I was left with many volumes only marketable in Cracow. These were extra copies of books I had printed on my own account while fulfilling commissioned orders from Cracow. I did not know what to do with these and it is not surprising that I was in a deep state of gloom.

I came to realise that with this new state of affairs, the firm could not support two families, so I resolved not to keep up the partnership beyond the period of our three-year contract. I explained this to my son-in-law Behrend and gave him notice. But since I wanted to improve the state of the business and to give my son-in-law a way of earning a living, I suggested that he take my large stocks – worth over 10,000 Marks – at a discount of 50 per cent, move to Breslau

---

[26]Graetz himself relates in his diary his deep love for Marie Monasch, but expresses himself less kindly about his father-in-law to-be: "A thousand complications . . . first of all the Old Man who first thought of *la gloire* and subsequently of getting away cheaply . . . Behrend . . . who did not want so much cash drawn from the business . . ." (P.F.'s translation). Heinrich Graetz, *Tagebuch und Briefe*, Herausgegeben und mit Anmerkungen versehen von Reuven Michael, Tübingen 1977 (Schriftenreihe wissenschaftlicher Abhandlungen des Leo Baeck Instituts 34), p. 143.

and open a Jewish bookshop there. I offered him a 50 per cent partnership in this shop. Had my son-in-law listened to my advice and my well-meant proposal, we would both have become rich men and I would have been able to launch many more fine publications upon the world.

I myself could not have started such a bookshop in Breslau because I had a family of ten children and it would have cost far too much – what with the high cost of tuition and the grand style of living there. It would also have been much more difficult to marry off so many girls there.

Early in 1847 the price of provisions rose, so that I could hardly find any buyers for my modest new publications and could not even recover a twentieth of my costs.

On my travels I had learnt that many Polish and Russian Jews visited Königsberg[27] and Memel[28] regularly and purchased Jewish books there to take back to their countries.

In May 1847 I therefore packed up 5,000 Marks' worth of unbroken sets of volumes, hired two carts and undertook the journey to Königsberg. I took my eldest son Isidor, who was then apprenticed to a lithographer at Ohlau in Silesia, along with me. The journey took us fourteen days[29] and cost over 200 Marks.

It was my misfortune that the price of provisions rose ever higher and when I got to Königsberg rye had reached ten Marks a quart. I tried my hardest to sell my wares in Königsberg. I offered them to many rich Polish and Russian Jews, but everywhere I received the same answer: that in these days people would rather buy bread than books. With the greatest of difficulty I managed to sell enough for our own subsistence in Königsberg.

After three weeks of this I decided to risk the journey to Memel by steamship. It was a journey that ought to have taken nine hours. The first three miles were on land, in a coach provided by the steamship company. There were some sixty of us. When we reached the Kurische Haff we had to seat ourselves upon a lighter so as to reach the steamship which waited far out in the water. To our misfortune a great storm arose and, despite all the efforts of the oarsmen, our lighter threatened to turn over. The further we penetrated into the water, the greater grew the danger of our overturning and being buried in the sea. The cries, the prayers, the terror of the people on the lighter were heartbreaking. When the men on the steamship perceived our danger, they shot a coil of rope towards us. Luckily our oarsmen managed to catch this and to fix it to a hook on the lighter. This was our salvation! The steamship men speedily pulled in the rope and in this way we managed to get aboard. Several of us had to be carried on to the vessel half dead and stiff from the water that had splashed all over us.

In Memel I discussed my problem with an old business acquaintance who was the rabbi and ritual slaughterer there. He advised me that there was only one man in town who could afford to do a deal in these times of want . . .

[27] Now Kaliningrad.
[28] Now Klaipeda.
[29] A distance of 250 miles.

My friend conducted me to a Herr Freidenthal, a very rich and kind man ... He said he was willing to assist me, either by buying my stocks outright or by selling them for me on a commission basis. I was not prepared to agree to a commission deal since it would not have helped me out of my immediate predicament, so I sold him some 4,000 Marks worth of books for 1,200.

You can imagine how depressed I was when I got back home, but fate had yet harder trials in store for me.

Just then the congregation asked me to lead the prayers at the festivals of New Year and the Day of Atonement because they did not employ a cantor that year, 1847. In previous years I had frequently discharged this honorary office, so I could not very well refuse. I carried out my duties conscientiously and shook out my grief and sorrow-filled heart before God in prayer. Probably the recitation of the prayers affected my weakened nerves. A few days after the Day of Atonement I fell into a nerve and gastric fever which kept me in bed for two months. My recovery was in doubt and my wife also fell ill, probably with the grief of losing me, so that two doctors were needed to attend to us. My wife recovered first and when I eventually rose up from my sickbed, my ruin was complete.

The first volume of the Pentateuch, which I was publishing afresh, was completed but, although I wrote to all my customers and told them of my penury, I only gathered in very little money and could not continue with the work without support. I approached Behrend and suggested he join me in this project and agreed to his harsh conditions only to complete the publication and to be able to face the world as an honest man. I was permitted to draw eight Marks a week for the support of my family from the Pentateuch project but my son-in-law took sole control of the publication. Other work done in the print-shop remained my own.

Patiently, but with a heavy heart, I worked with my four assistants, even though I was now in a subordinate position. It was a very constrained life on my small income and we had meagre fare. I was hardly able to satisfy the most essential requirements of my multitudinous family. Monies did not come in and several debtors who owed me large sums went bankrupt. As a result I could not satisfy my creditors and was forced to declare myself insolvent. In this bad situation my wife advised me to apply to the municipality for a licence for a tavern. I believed that my conduct hitherto had earned me the confidence of the authorities.

These rejected my petition. Repeated entreaties met with repeated refusals and the only course remaining to me was to petition the ministry. But I received no reply from Berlin for a very long time.

Then came the memorable year 1848. On 18th March general revolution broke out. At the first sign my son-in-law, whose subordinate I now was, suspended printing, paid off my four assistants and ceased the weekly payments of eight Marks to me, never bothering to ask how his parents-in-law with their ten dependent children were to get a living. I was in dire distress and did not know where to find dry bread. But God saw my need and did not desert me.

During the six months of revolution my son Isidor and I did the work demanded by those times: we printed proclamations, posters, voters' rolls, ballot papers, speeches and so on. Several times I was woken up in the middle of the night and asked to do rush work required in the morning. My labours, during this period, were so well paid that I managed to live without the eight Marks from Behrend and even saved a modest sum.

By now I had sent several reminders regarding my tavern to the ministry without receiving any reply, so in September 1848 I undertook a journey to Berlin, which I could only afford because of my modest savings.

Our local *Landrat* Baur[30] – who was then our deputy in the National Assembly – knew my situation well. He interceded on my behalf, introduced me to the minister and gave me a ticket for the No. 1 gallery of the National Assembly. I was received by the Minister, Herr von Bonin,[31] and by his permanent secretary von Pomeresche on the second day of Rosh Hashonoh. The minister permitted me to put my case, which I did amidst tears. He treated me very kindly and referred me to Herr von Pomeresche. The latter asked me whether it would be possible to start an inn in my house. I replied: "If it has to be, yes."

"Well," replied Herr von Pomeresche, "you go back home and make an application for an inn to your local authority." A fortnight later I had the consent!

In the beginning the tavern did so well that it looked as if I might soon be able to give up my printing presses altogether. But gradually the hubbub slackened off. I myself was no longer required to help very much with the tavern, my wife and daughter managing it by themselves. I found I could go back to my printing and work diligently at this, to my great joy. I employed a few assistants again and several apprentices. The revolution was quelled gradually and my son-in-law ordered work to start again, which meant I drew eight Marks a week.

On 1st October 1850 I succeeded in celebrating the wedding of my daughter Marie to Dr. Heinrich Graetz.

The Pentateuch project was completed in 1850 and my cousin Moritz in Breslau bought up all the complete sets, paying part in cash, part with bills of exchange for 1,600 Marks, half of which should have been due to me. My son-in-law did, however, not hand these over to me since he wanted to use them to settle with my creditors. But though my creditors were pressing for payment my son-in-law did nothing to settle with them. They threatened me with imprisonment for debt. At this point my cousin Moritz from Breslau[32] appeared as a saving angel and announced that he had decided to have all my earlier publications reprinted gradually and to re-issue them at his own expense. He ordered 2,000 *Machsorim* at once, offered me a large advance and agreed to settle with

---

[30]A liberal who threw in his lot with the Polish party. See Aron Heppner und Isaak Herzberg, *Aus Vergangenheit und Gegenwart der Juden und jüdischen Gemeinden in den Posener Landen*, Koschmin/Bromberg 1909.

[31]Minister of Finance in the short-lived Pfuël administration, 21st September–16th October 1848. Von Bonin was offered but declined the premiership after Ernst von Pfuël.

[32]Bookseller. The title-page of many of B. L. Monasch's later publications contains the legend: *Zu haben in Breslau bei M. Monasch Carlstrasse No. 27 Fechtschule*.

Hagadah auf Peßach

nebst

Einleitung

über Bestimmung und Gesetze des Festes

genannt

Ateres Z'wi.

Mit Kommentar von **Abudrham.**

Und deutscher Uebersetzung.

Krotoschin, Druck und Verlag von B. L. Monasch & Sohn.
1844.

Title-page of Passover Hagadah printed in 1844
by B. L. Monasch

From the Archives of the Leo Baeck Institute, New York

my two inconsiderate creditors. He kept his word, bought my debt off the creditors at 50 per cent and later demanded not a penny more from me.

After the wedding my second son-in-law, Dr. Graetz, and his wife moved to Lundenburg in Austria where he had been offered employment. It was therefore the duty of one of the parents to visit the young couple and at Eastertide 1851 I undertook the journey. Naturally I was received with love and I count the days that I spent with my children at Lundenburg among the best of my life, as I count these children as the brightest jewel of my parental crown. They have first place in my heart: my daughter because she has turned out in my own image, just as I had hoped. She is revered and loved everywhere for her virtue and will make me immortal. My son-in-law shares first place in my heart not only because he is a famous and learned man, but because he has become like a true son to me. He has treated me with indescribable generosity and has honoured me as a father in a manner which must certainly be difficult to find in the smart young world of today.

In 1851 my wife bore her last child, a weak little girl whom we named Helene after her aunt. However, the following year this weak child died of the cholera. This last issue of my wife's unfortunately cost her her health. Her nerves were weakened severely and she could not suckle the child so a wet-nurse had to be engaged. Her nervous debility became so acute that it developed into a form of mental illness which lasted for nearly two years. Although it never deteriorated sufficiently to make her certifiable, my own life became greatly embittered by her imaginings and delusions. In the twenty-nine years of our married life I had succeeded, by means of love, in softening the small traces of the usual failings of the female sex that I discovered in her: the susceptibility to flattery and glitter, the tendency to disputatiousness, covetousness, obstinacy, vanity, jealousy and egoism. Now, all of a sudden, all these passions awoke in my beloved wife as a result of her illness. The worst of the evil passions was jealousy, but since I felt justifiably and deeply aggrieved by all reproaches, much unpleasant dissension arose which always ended in a great outpouring of the heart and bitter weeping and greatly disturbed my domestic peace and bliss.

I consulted a doctor who assured me that this was due to the change of the female condition and that many women suffer grievously with this. Matters would change and improve with time, he said . . . He advised me to send her away from home for a longer period so as to free her from all domestic cares. Around that time my son-in-law Dr. Graetz moved from Lundenburg to Berlin, so I hastened to try and persuade my wife to visit him and his wife there.

The walks and excursions and the air of Berlin had a beneficial effect upon my wife's nerves. So had the love of her children who afforded her all possible diversions and entertainments. After seven weeks she came back home, hale and hearty, and not even the slightest trace of her former mental illness has remained. Peace and happiness returned to my house and I count the second summer of my life from that year and consider myself the happiest of fathers of families.

1853 was one of the most remarkable years of my life. My son Louis decided to restore the family fortunes by emigrating to Melbourne in Australia, but to come back after five years. He took advantage of his mother's presence in Berlin to wrest her blessing from her. Louis' employer showed great confidence in him and offered him 2,000 Marks' worth of goods on credit to take along to Australia. He further agreed to engage Louis' younger brother, Julius, in his place. I was flattered by the confidence shown in my sons and my own objections faded away.

In the year 1853 my son-in-law, Dr. Graetz, was appointed permanent first professor at the Jewish Theological Seminary (the Frankel Foundation) in Breslau. My son-in-law Behrend bought himself a beautiful solidly built house.

My cousin Moritz Monasch in Breslau kept his word and placed regular orders so that my printing presses were uninterruptedly busy. I also received large orders from Poland so that in 1853 I could realise my long-cherished plan and buy a high-speed press for 1,800 Marks.[33]

Ostrowo, 19th April 1860

I cannot forbear to mention that my third son-in-law caused me great heartache. He asked me for an endorsement for a bill of exchange for 459 Marks. I am always willing to serve my children, even be it with the blood of my heart. Suspecting nothing, I signed. When the due-date came I found myself obliged to pay even though I could not afford it, so that there should be no blot upon my family. It cost me much sorrow and many long hours of labour to make up for this loss. The only reason I do not bear Nathan any grudge is because he treats my Charlotte well, especially as she had been previously engaged to a man from Ostrowo and this match was dissolved. I will not bother to relate the circumstances in detail, but they caused me much humiliation, sorrow and misery at the time.

Ostrowo, 6th July 1863

In 1860 Julius invited me to visit him in Berlin and to inspect his business. I am ever ready to comply with the requests of my children, provided only these are morally befitting and within my powers. I paid him a five-day visit and when I enquired about the state of the business I received very satisfactory answers, both from Julius himself and from his apprentices. Since I am unacquainted with the drapery trade I could not convince myself personally. A few months later Julius wrote to us that a good match had been proposed to him from Stettin with a dowry of 3,000 Thalers. I gave my enthusiastic approval to the match as it was a good family and an attractive, sensible girl.

Six months later I, my wife, Isidor and Rosa attended a wedding at Stettin so brilliant that we only wished to live to see our other children celebrate such splendid weddings.

Four months later I received a letter from Berlin, not by the hand of my son but by that of one of his apprentices, which asked me to hasten there by the first

---

[33] At this point the memoirs, written in 1855, come to an end, but are added to at irregular intervals until 1871.

coach. Something, it said, had occurred which could only be communicated on the spot. Imagine our shock! We thought Julius seriously ill or even dead and I set out at once. But in Berlin I discovered, to my dismay, that Julius was bankrupt and in the debtors' prison.

Herr Lewy Manasse[34] had also been summoned to Berlin and when we met he asked: "Dear Papa, did you know that Julius was in such a bad way?" I, who am frank and honest in all things, could answer: "No, I knew nothing of this. Don't you remember, when we first met in Stettin I asked you whether you had assured yourself regarding my son's affairs. I myself could not judge. But you said you had and it did me good to hear this from you." "Yes, dear Papa," he said, "you are a good and honest man. But your son has behaved not only like a scoundrel but like a fool as well. There is not even 20 per cent left to arrange a settlement with the creditors."

Herr Manasse and his sister Frau Benjamin demanded that Julius's wife should leave her husband and return with them to their mother in Stettin. My Emilie, however, remained steadfast and replied: "No, I will not leave my husband. What would become of him when he comes out of prison and does not find me here? Do you want me to drive him to become dissolute and immoral on top of all his misery and misfortune? No, I will not leave my husband. If that should be my fate, I will work with him and share bread and water with him, but I will not leave him. You would do better to give him all your help, so that he can work his way up again. He is a good man, only he has a false sense of shame and would not confide his misfortune to anyone."

To hear these words from my daughter-in-law was balm for my wounded heart. I grew doubly fond of her and decided to endure all my misfortunes patiently for her sake.[35]

14th July 1863

One great joy accompanied the misery of the year I have related. After ten years absence my son Louis from Melbourne arrived in Krotoschin on the eve of Passover and spent a fortnight with us. His arrival seemed like a ray of hope that I might be permitted to live my last years happily and free of worry.

After the holidays I asked Louis to accompany me to the cemetery to visit the graves of his grandparents and of his sister Hanchen. I was pleased when Louis agreed at once and without contradiction. On the way I told him about the critical state of my finances and explained to him how I came to get so deeply into debt. Louis was indignant that I had not written to him years before as he would then have sent me financial assistance which would have prevented my getting ever deeper into debt.

Louis now undertook to free me from the burden of my debts and to make me an allowance of at least 1,000 Thalers a year. My heavy heart danced with joy, to have such a good son. But . . . in Breslau he confided the results of our conversation to my family there, no doubt with the best of intentions. I was

[34] Brother of Julius's wife.
[35] Several other sons and sons-in-law suffered financial disasters which Monasch describes. In two cases he himself lost money as a result.

summoned to Breslau at once – no doubt also with the best of intentions – and my family demanded nothing less than that I declare myself bankrupt. Thereafter they would come to an arrangement with my creditors and free me of my burden of debts in one blow.

I thank God that he has granted me both patience and integrity. I told my children that I would on no account agree to this. Much as it hurt, I would rather forgo all of Louis' assistance and preferred to die bowed down with debts and cares, rather than to live free of these but as a blackguard, having dealt unjustly with other men. Bathed in tears I travelled home. I refused to be comforted until I received a letter from Louis from Berlin in which he assuaged my pain and reassured me that he would not go back on his word and would secure an old age free of worry for me.

Krotoschin, 2nd October 1865

Two years and three months have elapsed. I have lived through such heartbreak and misfortune that my physical powers have greatly diminished and my hair has turned grey.

Louis, during his visit here in Europe, married Berta Manasse from Stettin, the sister of his brother Julius' wife, Emilie, and she went to Melbourne with him.

Now Louis' visit and the rumours that he was very rich[36] and had made great purchases of goods in Europe for export to Australia had the effect that I lost all my credit. People were convinced that my son had left me a lot of money. They assumed that no rich son comes from Australia without leaving his parents ample financial aid. I found that I could no longer cover my old debts by means of new bills of exchange and in this way hide my bad situation. This had been my practice for years, only so as to remain in honour and an honest man. Our worries affected my wife greatly and one day she said: "Let us sell our house and reduce our debts. If Louis then sends us help, we will marry off our girls. As for the remaining debts, with hard work you will be able to pay them off gradually." It was hard for me to sell my hardearned house to strangers, but I saw that my wife was right. We now managed to pay off three-quarters of our debts and I did believe this would restore people's trust in me, but this was not to be. People turned away from me as if I were a swindler and I lost all my credit.

All these events had so deleterious an effect upon the health and spirits of my dear, ailing wife – she could not overcome the pain of it – that two days after the Jewish New Year, 1864, she fell ill and died four days later. My wife has now passed to a better world and has left all our sorrows, now doubly heavy, for me alone to bear.

Since July I remain alone in Krotoschin with my daughter Rosa and must bear my sorrows, worries and pain by myself.[37]

Oh Lord, my God! With contrite heart and bowed-down in spirit I pray to

---

[36] Louis became the owner of the general store at Jerilderies, in the outback, 200 miles north of Melbourne. This was the settlement that Ned Kelly captured some years later.

[37] Of his ten children only two remained in the Province of Poznań – the others migrating to Breslau, Berlin, Australia and the U.S.A. See will.

you most fervently: Have mercy upon me. Free me from my sufferings. Do not make me live through any more years as filled with misery and suffering as the two just past. Grant me the mercy to see my daughter Rosa married and to hear from my five children overseas that things go better for them there than they did here. My God, I have never transgressed your laws, never done ill to any man, never been quarrelsome or disputatious. I have never insulted my fellow men by word or look. Have I not worked faithfully and honestly for my family ever since I got married, laboured with love and devotion? Grant me your mercy, oh Lord, to live my last years in your service free of sorrow and of debts. And when it behoves you to call me to be received unto my fathers, let it be in honour and as an honest man. Amen.

24th October 1865

It is my desire that the firm I founded with such great sacrifices should remain with my descendants and in my family name If this proves impossible and the firm must pass into the hands of strangers, I require that my name, at least, should be retained and on the title-page of my publications it should always say "Formerly B. L. Monasch in Krotoschin."

Marienbadt, 26th May 1870

In the last five years God has heard my prayers and extended his mercy to me so that my long-nourished hope of coming to this spa has now been realised.

In December 1867 a match for my daughter Rosa was proposed to me. The match was quite welcome since the young man is a qualified typesetter and printer and was hoping to marry into a firm such as mine. In January 1868 the young man came from Danzig to Krotoschin, the young people liked each other and an engagement came about. We celebrated the wedding of my daughter Rosa to the typesetter Hermann Goldschmidt from Danzig at the residence of my son-in-law Professor Dr. Heinrich Graetz in Breslau. For her dowry – since I had no liquid assets – I made my daughter Rosa sole heir of my printing works and all my household goods, but retained the usufruct for life. I also took her husband into the firm as a partner.

Providence was even kinder to me and freed my old age from worry. My children in Australia . . . asked me to accept a monthly allowance of twenty Thalers so that I would no longer have to work. I accepted this offer and now receive £3 sterling punctually every month and live comfortably and abundantly off this and need no longer be tied to the business.

My son-in-law Dr. Graetz also invited me to retire from the business and to come and live with him in Breslau. My doctors, however, advise me not to remain idle as this would shorten the span of my life. What is more, I still have a few small debts to settle, for I wish to owe nothing, except only my soul to God. I have therefore decided to remain in Krotoschin with my daughter Rosa and to carry on working until I am totally incapacitated, though no longer as strenuously as before.

As a result of this decision I have managed to travel to Marienbadt for my health and to take the waters here. It is only now, in my sixty-ninth year, that I have at last managed to see a health resort, to enjoy the wholesome air and to partake of the well-waters. I have made many pleasant acquaintanceships and it is my wish and prayer that every good man might be able to free himself from the cares of home and business for a month and travel to this place, to Marienbadt.

Marienbadt, 17th June 1871

On the 7th of this month I celebrated my seventieth birthday in the circle of my family in Krotoschin.

This year my children made me a birthday present of 100 Thalers to enable me to take the waters here and so, God be praised, I did not have to borrow anything. Thanks to my Australian children I have succeeded in paying off all my debts honestly and now owe nothing to any man and only my soul to God.[38]

---

[38] There are no further diary entries. Monasch died five years later, in 1876, and was buried in Krotoschin.

APPENDIX

Last Will of B. L. Monasch of Krotoschin

I have ten children, five male, five female, and their names, in age order are as follows:

1. JULIE, Mrs. Behrend, here.
2. MARIA, Mrs. Graetz, in Breslau.
3. ISIDOR, married in Breslau.
4. LOUIS, married in Melbourne.
5. CHARLOTTE, Mrs. Goldschmidt, Newark, N.J., America.
6. JULIUS, married in Melbourne.
7. ROSA, unmarried, here.
8. ULLRIKE, unmarried, Melbourne.
9. MAX, unmarried in Melbourne.
10. ADOLPH, ditto, in Breslau.

My property consists of my extensive printing works, my household goods, three places (two for men, one for a woman) in the local Synagogue and my Jewish publications. These consist of:

1. The entire Bible, i.e., the twenty-four books of the Holy Writ with Hebrew texts, Hebrew commentary and German translation by Fürstenthal, eighteen volumes.
2. The Five Books of Moses with German translation by Johlsohn, five volumes.
3. The Five Books of Moses with German translation by Salomon, five volumes.
4. The Festival Prayers of the Jews with German translation by Fürstenthal & Cunov, five volumes.
5. Atonement Prayers of the Jews with German translation by Fürstenthal, in three different rites: as in Poland, Posen and Prague.
6. Purim Prayers, translation and commentary by Fürstenthal.
7. Mourning Prayers for the Fast of the 9th of Ab (the Destruction of Jerusalem) translation by Fürstenthal.
8. Prayers for the Cemetery with German translation by Fürstenthal.
9. Daily Prayers for the Entire Year, with German translation by B[ehrend?].

All these publications have Hebrew texts and German translations printed with both German and Hebrew letters and all have been translated at my own expense and have been through a number of editions.

My property, as listed above, has a value of at least 5,000 Thalers and if death should overtake me before I have seen my daughter Rosa married, I nominate her sole heir. However, I place upon her the obligation to

   a) pay all my existing debts, so that no one shall say anything against me, and
   b) to make over to her brother, my youngest son Adolph, one-fifth part of the net sum.

If, however, my daughter Rosa should be married at the time of my decease, and I have made no other stipulations, my son Adolph should get his one-fifth of the net sum while the other nine children shall have the remaining four-fifths divided amongst them in equal shares.

                                                  B. L. Monasch
                                                24th October 1865

The Ephraim Family and their Descendants (II)

BY DOLF MICHAELIS

In the first part of this study of the Ephraim family[1] we followed their fate from 1695, the year Nathan Heine Ephraim moved from Altona to Berlin, till the end of the eighteenth century. There he founded a firm which for three generations played a part as financiers, minting concessionaires and political agents of the kings of Prussia. They belonged to the small clan of privileged Court Jews at a time when the bulk of their brethren suffered under a variety of restrictive laws and regulations. The turn of the century brought with it a change in the civic situation of the German Jews under the influence of the ideas of the French Revolution and the decrees of the temporary Napoleonic regime, culminating in the reforms of Chancellor von Hardenberg which marked the beginning of the emancipation of the Jews in Prussia. The fourth generation of the Ephraim family was therefore a generation confronted with novel conditions which brought them face to face with the Christian world from which they had hitherto been separated by legal restrictions and barriers of a culture alien to the Jews, who up to then had lived in a closed society with a way of life and languages of their own. We shall in this part of the story try to see how those of the following generations came to grips with the new situation. As we know, some of them left the Jewish fold and intermarried. Others have remained faithful to the religion of their fathers to this day.

Prussia's utter defeat in 1806/1807 brought with it decisive changes in its internal politics. Freiherr vom Stein and Fürst von Hardenberg initiated far-reaching reforms aimed at releasing the citizen from the bondage of state direction and the restrictions on private initiative. Parallel to these reforms various drafts of the new laws concerning the Jews of Prussia were prepared by ministerial committees from 1806 until eventually the Stein edict of emancipation in 1812 was approved by King Frederick William III, which cancelled the existing restrictive laws and recognised the Jews as citizens of the state.

Two basic lines of Christian opposition to emancipation, however, emerged: the one argued that even a secular society was basically Christian and that, therefore, there was no place for Jews as equals, the other claimed that Jewish religion, morality, tradition and mentality all set Jewry apart and made its assimilation into non-Jewish society undesirable and illusory.[2]

Yet there were other Protestant leaders who were proponents of reformist ideas and followers of the new Romantic movement and they also exercised great influence on some of the younger generation of the privileged Berlin Jewish families. Probst Teller and the young theologian Friedrich Schleier-

---

[1]'The Ephraim Family', in *LBI Year Book XXI* (1976), pp. 201–228.
[2]Dora Sussmann, 'The Katz dimension of Jewish history', in *Scopus*, The Hebrew University, Jerusalem, vol. 27, No. 2 (1973), p. 30.

macher were leading figures in this movement. Both had close contacts with Jewish intellectuals and foremost among these were Jewesses who, like Rahel Levin, later the wife of the diplomat and writer Varnhagen van Ense, Henriette Herz and other members of well-known Berlin Jewish families, searched for ways of release from the bondage of Jewish orthodoxy which to their way of thinking was an outmoded form of religion. Conversion to Christianity was for them not a mere formality or a means to achieve equality, but an answer to their spiritual needs which traditional Judaism no longer supplied. As Schleiermacher observed, they were educated and affluent persons, well versed in all worldly things, who wished to acquire rights and be accepted as citizens.[3] For the Romantics religion meant the Christian religion, and for those now seeking in religion an escape from rationalism, the Jewish religion seemed an unpromising heaven.[4] In the minds of those about to convert their decision also paved the way into a wider world.

It would, however, be erroneous to take the descendants of Moses Mendelssohn or the intellectual Jewesses of Berlin as typical for Prussian Jewry. They were a minority representing only a small segment of the community. The majority remained either observant Jews or became followers of the new trend of Liberal Judaism. The result of this development was the disappearance of almost all leading Jewish families of the "Salon" period from Jewish life between 1810 and 1830.[5]

To those who adopted Christianity and married into Gentile titled families belonged two daughters of Aron and Rösel Mayer (née Ephraim), i.e., granddaughters of the famous "Münzentrepreneur" Nathan Veitel Heine Ephraim. The elder of the two was Sara Sophie Leopoldine Wilhelmine, who was born in Berlin in 1760 and died in Oranienburg (near Berlin) in 1828. She married at the early age of fifteen Jacob Wolff, an elderly businessman in Berlin. It was a marriage forced on her by her parents and her married life was very unhappy. After ten years Sara became a widow, and in 1797 she married Ferdinand Dietrich Wilhelm Baron von Grotthus. Grotthus came from Livonia, was a gentleman farmer who, after the loss of his capital through war and misfortune, was, until his death, postmaster in the little town of Oranienburg. Goethe knew him and mentioned him as the "adventurous Grotthus" in his *Campagne in Frankreich*. Sara lived all her life in close contact and great friendship with her younger sister Marianne who died before her in 1814. Sara and Marianne had strong intellectual interests which brought them into contact with the great thinkers, writers and poets of their time. Their marriage into the nobility opened for them the doors of the houses of the Christian bourgeoisie and of high society. Like Rahel Levin-Varnhagen von Ense, Henriette Herz in Berlin and Fanny von Arnstein, daughter of the Berlin banker Daniel Itzig, Frau von Fliess (daughter of a rabbi), they were leading figures in the world of the

---

[3] Quoted in Sussmann, *loc. cit.*
[4] Cf. Jacob Katz, *Out of the Ghetto*, Cambridge, Mass. 1973, p. 120.
[5] Adolf Leschnitzer, 'Geschichte der deutschen Juden vom Zeitalter der Emanzipation bis 1933', in Franz Böhm and Walter Dirks (eds.), *Judentum, Schicksal, Wesen und Gegenwart*, vol. 1, Wiesbaden 1965, pp. 257–258.

intellectual Berlin and Vienna Salons. Here were the meeting-places of the young élite of the Jewesses who had become, so to say, "salon- und kulturfähig". Friedrich Schleiermacher writes in a letter in August 1798:

> "It is only natural that young scientists and socialites visit the great Jewish homes, they are by far the richest bourgeois families, almost the only ones who keep open house where one meets people from many countries . . ."[6]

Heinrich von Kleist, the patriotic Prussian writer and poet, writes to his sister in February 1801:

> "I am seldom in society. I would prefer Jewish society if they were not so ostentatious with their education. I made the acquaintance of a Jew named Cohen whom I found most interesting . . ."[7]

Karl August Varnhagen von Ense, the husband of Rahel Levin, has left us a pen-portrait of the two sisters Sara and Marianne. The older, Sara:

> "vereinigte lebhaften Geist und außerordentliche Herzensgüte, die schönste Bildung, Kenntnis fremder Sprachen und Litteraturen, Geschmack in Künsten und alles sonstige Wissen und Können, welches für gesellschaftlichen Glanz und häusliches Wohlbehagen geeignet ist."[8]

After this glowing praise of her good-heartedness, her intellectual prowess, knowledge of languages and literature, he mentions that in her youth Lessing and Herder belonged to her admirers. Marianne is described by Varnhagen as more beautiful and attractive than her sister Sara. She was less good-hearted but was endowed with sharp intelligence. Marianne was not given to long-term planning and cared only for the present. The saying "après moi le déluge" which she used to quote lost its harshness through her charm and her cheerfulness. One of Marianne's first admirers was Count Christian Bernstorff, a Danish diplomat in Berlin (1791-1794) who reluctantly gave up the idea of marrying her because of the resistance of his father, the Danish minister Andreas Christian Bernstorff. In 1797 Marianne married Prince Heinrich XIV of Reuss, a well-educated elderly man who served for many years in Berlin as Austrian ambassador to the Court of Prussia. Marianne did not live in her husband's house in spite of being legally married to him. After Prince Reuss's death in 1799 she would have been entitled to the status of a Princess of Reuss, but her princely relatives persuaded her to renounce the title, and she took the name "von Eybenberg". The family compensated her with an annuity which enabled her to live comfortably in Vienna. There she became a well-known hostess. Her salon emulated those of Fanny von Arnstein and Cecilie von Eskeles, daughters of wealthy Jewish Berlin merchants married to bankers in Vienna. Marianne von Eybenberg could, of course, not compete in terms of riches with financiers' families who were members of the Austrian moneyed élite, founders of banks and issuing houses for government loans. However, Marianne's charm and her intellect attracted men and women of rank and reputation, among them the

---

[6]Franz Kobler (ed.), *Juden und Judentum in deutschen Briefen aus drei Jahrhunderten*, Wien 1935, p. 146.
[7]*Ibid.*, p. 147.
[8]*Denkwürdigkeiten und Vermischte Schriften*, vol. 4, Mannheim 1838, pp. 215–225.

Princesses of Kurland, the princely families de Ligne and de Clary and others who preferred her company to that of the Arnsteins and Eskeles. Prince Louis Ferdinand of Prussia (1772–1806), a nephew of Frederick the Great, knew Marianne from his visits to Vienna.[9]

A decisive event in the lives of both sisters was their meeting with Goethe in Karlsbad, which he had visited almost every year since 1795. We know of the friendly relations which developed between Goethe and Marianne and Sara from the numerous letters they exchanged. Goethe corresponded with them, with interruptions, from 1795, when they became acquainted, until 1824. Varnhagen von Ense was the first to publish some of these letters as an appendix to the chapter 'Frau von Grotthus und Frau von Eybenberg' in his collection of essays.[10] Ludwig Geiger comments in great detail on a larger collection of this correspondence in *Goethe-Jahrbuch XIV*. We know the full text of twenty-one letters written by Marianne von Eybenberg to Goethe from 1795 till 1810, twenty-two letters from Goethe to Marianne from 1796 till 1810, twelve letters from Sara von Grotthus to Goethe from 1796 till 1825, and twenty-one letters from Goethe to Sara from 1797 till 1825. Some of them are letters in answer to others which are lost. Goethe was quite taken by the charm and vivacity of Marianne. Friederike Christiane Brun, whose poetry inspired Goethe's friend Zelter to set some of it to music, writes in her diary on Goethe's meeting with Marianne in her house: "Marianne, die holde Seele, geht ihm ans Herz."[11] Marianne's letter to Goethe dated Berlin, 22nd February 1795 indicated the beginning of a cordial and very friendly relationship. Marianne recalls the happy hours in Karlsbad and she expresses her confidence of their meeting there again. After mentioning her acquaintance with the Prince de Ligne and their having met in Töplitz she concludes her letter:

"Adieu, guter Goethe (den Geheimen Rat habe ich mir sehr gerne von Ihnen wegräsonnieren lassen); also immer guter lieber Goethe, dabey bleibt es, von nun an bis in Ewigkeit, Amen."[12]

Varnhagen writes on Goethe's feeling for Marianne that in the beginning of their relationship he fell in love with her, an emotion which later gave way to an attitude of respectful attentiveness. Goethe mentions Marianne several times to his friends. In summer 1797 he writes to Schiller:

"Auch ist die berühmte Marianne Meyer hier. Es ist schade, daß sie nicht einige Tage früher kam. Ich hätte doch gewünscht, daß Sie dieses sonderbare Wesen hätten kennenlernen."[13]

---

[9] Rahel an Brinckmann Ende Mai 1800 Berlin: "Prinz Louis, den finde ich gründlich liebenswürdig. Er hat mich gefragt, ob er mich öfter besuchen dürfte, und ich nahm ihm das Versprechen ab. Solche Bekanntschaft soll er noch nicht genossen haben. Ordentliche Dachstubenweissheiten wird er hören. Bis jezt kannte er nur Marianne, aber die ist getauft und Prinzess und Frau von Eybenberg: was will das sagen." Rahel Varnhagen, *Im Umgang mit ihren Freunden. Briefe 1793–1833*, München 1967.
[10] *Denkwürdigkeiten und Vermischte Schriften*, vol. 4, p. 215 ff.
[11] Johannes Urzidil, *Goethe in Böhmen*, Zürich 1962, p. 29.
[12] *Goethe-Jahrbuch XIV*, Frankfurt a. Main 1893, p. 28 (Ludwig Geiger's comments on the correspondence are on pp. 95–127).
[13] Quoted by Varnhagen von Ense, *op. cit.*, p. 298.

Marianne was not the only woman of Jewish origin whom Goethe met during his travels in Bohemia and Austria. David Veit writes that Goethe met Rahel Levin, and he quotes Goethe's describing her as "ein Mädchen von außerordentlichem Verstande, die immer denkt, und von Empfindungen – wo findet man das! es ist etwas Seltenes."[14] Through Marianne Goethe also met Cecilie von Eskeles (née Itzig) and Eleonore von Fliess (née Eskeles), both well known in Viennese society. He gave readings of his poems and other writings in their house. Goethe's friend Riemer remarks in this regard how sensitive Jewish women are:

> "Jüdische Frauen besitzen die Gabe, ein sensibles Publikum zu sein, öfters in noch liebenswürdiger Gestalt ... Goethe trug seine ersten dichterischen Erzeugnisse ihnen gerne vor, wie ich dieses aus eigener Miterfahrung an Frau von Eybenberg, von Grothus, von Eskeles, Fliess u.a.m. bestätigen kann."[15]

When Riemer wrote these lines he did not take notice of the fact that some of these listeners to Goethe's lyric poetry had married out of their faith and no longer considered themselves as Jews. For him they simply remained Jewish women, an attitude which largely prevailed throughout the span of German-Jewish history. The Jewesses whom Riemer mentions belonged to a generation which fervently tried to absorb as quickly as possible the culture of the Western world and for a certain Jewish élite in the salons of Berlin and Vienna this new world was represented by Lessing and Goethe. Rahel Levin, and the sisters Marianne and Sara knew Goethe's writings and were at times fervent partisans at war with certain anti-Goethe circles in the Berlin of the 1790s.[16] George Steiner remarks on this phenomenon, in an essay on the part played by Central European Jewry in Western culture, that

> "an almost axiomatic sense of Goethe's transcendent nature, of the incredible rightness and humanity of his art, colours the entire European Jewish enlightenment and continues to mark its few survivors."[17]

The "Jewish question" appears but seldom in the early correspondence with Goethe. We know only of the letters written by the two sisters to Goethe where such concerns are mentioned, but we do not know whether Goethe reacted as not all his letters have been preserved. Marianne writes on 11th December 1795 about her sister Sara who was severely ill. At that time Sara had a serious nervous breakdown and Marianne believes that her sister is tormented by religious problems:

> "Unter anderen Torheiten spielt die Religion eine Rolle, oder vielmehr die Religionen; denn bald ist die christliche, bald die jüdische die hervorherrschende und alleinseligmachende."[18]

The background to Marianne's remark seems to be a reference to her sister's

---

[14]Urzidil, op. cit., p. 63.
[15]Ibid.
[16]See Ludwig Geiger in Goethe-Jahrbuch XIV, Anmerkungen des Herausgebers zu dem Briefwechsel Goethes mit Marianne von Eybenberg und Sara Grothus, p. 99.
[17]George Steiner, Language and Science, London 1967, p. 171.
[18]Goethe-Jahrbuch XIV, p. 29.

unhappy marriage to the elderly Jacob Wolff. Sara's letter to Goethe of 20th March 1797 mentions that time of her life:

> "Ich zu 15 Jahren durch Moses [i.e., Mendelssohn] Gewalt und der Mutter Zwang an einen Elenden verheiratet wurde, der meine Existenz zehn Jahre durch zur Höllenqual machte und mich um allen körperlichen Reiz und ferner Geistesausbildung brachte, bis mein geliebter Erlöser erschien."[19]

The first part of the letter explains the reason for Sara's harsh judgment of Mendelssohn. For at the age of thirteen a young man fell in love with her and he sent her Goethe's *Werther's Leiden* which Sara returned to him

> "nachdem ich ihn verschlungen hatte, und schickte ihm mit tausend unterstrichenen Stellen und einem sehr glühenden Billet zurück."[20]

This letter never reached her young lover because her father intercepted it.

Moses Mendelssohn, who was at that time Sara's tutor, remonstrated with her and asked her whether she had forgotten God and religion, and he threw the book out of the window. Her grief over her beloved father's attitude, Mendelssohn's "Gemeinheit" and her love for the young man whom she never saw again combined to make her ill. Lessing, another friend of the family, saw her shortly afterwards and brought her another copy of *Werther*, saying to her: "Only later on will you know what a genius Goethe is."[21] Sara goes on to say that she knew that Lessing and Mendelssohn quarrelled over this affair. Sara's change of religious beliefs became the subject of a controversy within the ranks of the *Kurmärkische Konsistorium* (a Protestant authority). They reprimanded the Prediger Stein when he confirmed the baptism of Sara based on a written declaration only without any religious preparation or examination of her knowledge. The file's main subject is called: 'Der Vorgang mit den beiden getauften und zu ihrem alten Glauben wieder zurückgekehrten Juden, Geschwister Aron Mayer'.[22] According to this document Sara declared that only under pressure from her parents did she return to the Jewish faith, but that she retained her belief in Christianity. Marianne, the younger sister, seems not to have taken the religious problem too seriously and she writes to Goethe on this subject in a lighter vein. On 28th February 1797 she reports to him of a play-reading in Hanover: Lessing's *Nathan der Weise* was the subject of this evening's reading. Marianne thinks that none of the participants were aware of what Lessing really wanted to convey in his play. Marianne's attention was drawn to an elderly lady, a "Ministerin", who did not seem to understand why a book with a Jew as a leading figure was chosen to be read in distinguished society, and apparently had no inkling that Marianne too was a daughter of Zion:

> "Gar zu gern hätte ich es ihr gesagt. Sie sah mich immer an, wenn eine Stelle kam, die ihr als Christin nicht behagte, als wollte sie sagen: Was soll das hier? Habe ich recht gehört?"[23]

[19] *Ibid.*, p. 53.
[20] *Ibid.*, p. 51.
[21] *Ibid.*, p. 52.
[22] Ludwig Geiger, 'Vor Hundert Jahren', in *Zeitschrift für die Geschichte der Juden in Deutschland*, 1889, p. 225.
[23] *Goethe-Jahrbuch XIV*, p. 34.

The Ephraim Family

Marianne's observation was very much to the point, for Christian society was shocked by Lessing's plea for religious tolerance and his portrayal of Nathan, the Jew, as a noble character full of wisdom, a sage and merchant like Lessing's friend, Moses Mendelssohn.

Marianne and her sister wrote to Goethe about life in Vienna where they had made their salons a centre of social and intellectual life and told him of the regular readings of his poems within the circle of their friends. The families of Prince de Ligne and Prince de Clary and Kurland were among their guests. Goethe in his letter of 9th February 1797 to Sara von Grotthus thanks her for her interest in his writings and says he appreciates her understanding reception. He promises her another epic poem and hopes that it will enjoy a favourable reception in her circle.

> "Da ein Schriftsteller sich muss gefallen lassen, daß so manches wunderlich genug genommen und beurteilt wird, so findet er sich freilich sehr getröstet, wenn seine Arbeit einmal bei einem gebildeten Individuo als Naturprodukt wirkt . . . Bald sehen Sie wieder ein episches Gedicht von mir, dem ich eine so gute Aufnahme auch in Ihrem Cirkel wünsche."[24]

Goethe did not forget the happy time he had spent with Marianne in Karlsbad in 1795. Ten years later he writes to her: "Be assured that I often remember the good days on the shores of the Töpel when we enjoyed happy hours which cannot be relived."[25] When they met again in 1808 in Karlsbad Goethe talked to her about his work on the *Wahlverwandtschaften*. Marianne was of course proud that Goethe was attracted to her not only by her charm but also because he liked her in the role of good listener. He continued his correspondence with her and on 16th June 1809 he tells her that the second part of the novel was nearing completion ("Der Roman, den Sie durch Ihre Teilnahme so sehr gefärbt haben, ist nun bald völlig abgedruckt").[26] They met again in Karlsbad in 1810. It was to be their last meeting. Marianne went there for treatment for a "liebenswürdige Krankheit", not knowing that her illness was very serious. She never returned to Karlsbad and died in Vienna on 26th June 1812. For Goethe too it was a critical time when he had hidden fears that approaching old age might rob him of his virility. In his novel *Der Mann von 50 Jahren*[27] he touches on this problem. Goethe was then in his early sixties, Marianne not yet forty. We meet Marianne in this novel, for Goethe draws a pen-portrait of her.

> "Sie ist eine junge Witwe, Erbin eines alten reichen, vor kurzem verstorbenen Mannes, unabhängig und höchst wert es zu sein, von Vielen umgeben, von ebenso Vielen geliebt, von ebenso Vielen umworben . . . Doch wenn ich mich nicht sehr trüge, mir von Herzen angehörig."[28]

He not only praises her charm but he also knows of her weaknesses, her vanity and her craving for undivided attention.

> "Die Art dieser jungen verführerischen Witwe ist mir nicht unbekannt, weiblichen

---

[24] Varnhagen von Ense, *op. cit.*, pp. 224–225.
[25] Urzidil, *op. cit.*, p. 140.
[26] *Ibid.*, pp. 141–142.
[27] Goethe worked on this novel in 1803, took it up again in 1807 and eventually it became a chapter in *Wilhelm Meisters Wanderjahre*.
[28] *Wilhelm Meisters Wanderjahre*, vol. 2, chapter 3, Zürich 1961, pp. 198 ff.

> Umgang scheint sie abzulehnen und nur eine Frau um sich zu haben, die ihr keinen Eintrag tut, ihr schmeichelt sie noch mit Worten und geschickter Behandlung der Aufmerksamkeit zu empfehlen ... Ich denke nichts Übles von dieser schönen Frau. Sie scheint anständig und behutsam genug, aber eine solche lüsterne Eitelkeit opfert den Umständen auch wohl etwas auf ..."[29]

There is also mention of another Jew whom Goethe encountered who interested him sufficiently to consider introducing him in one of his novels – and someone with the name of Ephraim as it happened. On 28th October 1782 he writes to Charlotte von Stein on his meeting "with the Jew Ephraim" and that he would like to portray a Jew in one of his novels:

> "Meiner L. einen guten Morgen zu sagen hat mich allerley, zuletzt der Jude abgehalten. Von ihm zu erzählen, wird mir ein Spaß sein. Bald habe ich das Bedeutende der Judenheit zusammen und habe große Lust, in meinem Roman auch einen Juden anzubringen ..."[30]

Goethe met in Bohemian spas several Jews, among them Simon Edler von Lämel and David Veit, a physician, philosopher and a great admirer of his. Was it perhaps the meeting with Ephraim which influenced Goethe to characterise Jews as follows?

> "Jüdisches Wesen: Energie, der Grund von allen unmittelbaren Zwecken. Keiner, auch nur der kleinste, geringste Jude, der nicht entscheidendes Bestreben verriete, und zwar ein irdisches, augenblickliches. – Judensprache hat etwas Pathetisches."[31]

Marianne and Sara's correspondence with Goethe did not only deal with literary matters and expressions of friendship. Several letters disclose that Marianne acted for Goethe also as a go-between with sellers of Greek coins and precious stones.[32]

The Bohemian spas were fruitful meeting-places for leading figures of the time. Thinkers and writers mingled with men in politics and the aristocracy of Europe. It was at Töplitz that the two sisters made the acquaintance of the Prince de Ligne, then a man in his sixties. A Frenchman by culture and an Austrian by residence, a man at home in many countries, well received at the courts of Europe, Charles Joseph Prince de Ligne was born in 1735, the son of an ancient family of noblemen at Hainault on the borders of France and the Low Countries. He was a true son of the European aristocracy. Frequently residing at Paris, Brussels, and in later years Vienna, his travels and military duties led him to Germany, Poland and Russia. De Ligne strikes a cosmopolitan note when he writes in his memoirs:[33]

> "Il a toujours été de mode de me bien traiter partout. J'ai six or sept patries: Empire, Flandre, France, Autriche, Pologne, Russie, et presque Hongrie, car on est obligé d'y donner d'indigénat à ceux qui font la guerre aux Turques."

---

[29] *Ibid.*, p. 211.
[30] *Goethe's Briefe an Frau v. Stein*, Leipzig 1925, p. 187. Ludwig Geiger indeed assumes that Goethe refers in fact here to Benjamin Veitel Ephraim and that the idea was to mention him in his *Wilhelm Meister*.
[31] *Maximen und Reflexionen*, Goethe's Werke, vol. 12, Wegner–Hamburg 1953, p. 187.
[32] See Goethe's letter to Marianne of 25th April 1803, in *Goethes Sämmtliche Werke*, Propyläen Ausgabe, München 1914, vol. 15, p. 27; also vol. 16, p. 326 (letter of 26th April 1805) and vol. 19, p. 92 (letter of 22nd August 1808).
[33] Quoted in Marthe Oulié, *Le Prince de Ligne*, Paris 1926, p. 4.

EPHRAIM MARCUS EPHRAIM
(1716–1776)

From the Collection of Mrs. Rudolf Wittkower, New Jersey
Photo by courtesy of Werner Wittkower, Tel-Aviv

ISAAC JACOB GANS

JACOB EPHRAIM/DUFRESNE

From the Collection of Mrs. Rudolf Wittkower, New Jersey
Photos by courtesy of Werner Wittkower, Tel-Aviv

Portrait drawing of Ida Stern and her four children

From the Collection of Eva Michaelis-Stern, Jerusalem

De Ligne fled Vienna when Napoleon's forces were approaching the town during the second occupation of Austria in May 1809. He found refuge in Pest at a boarding-house of a Jewish Sephardic family. It was not the first time that de Ligne had had contact with Jewish people. In Vienna he had frequented the salons of the rich Jewish bankers and in the Bohemian spas he had met Marianne von Eybenberg and Sara von Grotthus. De Ligne made no secret of his liking for Jewish society: "Ils préfèrent encore cette compagnie intelligente de moins à la fadeur des autres."[34]

We find traces of de Ligne's connections with Jews elsewhere in his autobiographical writings. As an old man he met Casanova, then librarian at the castle of Dux in Bohemia. At his request he provided Casanova with letters of recommendation to Jewish bankers in Berlin. We do not know their name but it seems not impossible that it was the family Ephraim, of whom de Ligne knew because of the friendship with Marianne von Eybenberg and Sara von Grotthus. We know of his relations with the two sisters already from Marianne's letter to Goethe of 22nd February 1795 where she mentions de Ligne.

> "... 10 Tage nach Ihnen ging ich nach Töplitz, wo ich etwas über 3 Wochen blieb; dort existierte ich viel mit dem Prince de Ligne, Sie kennen diesen gelanten schönen Geist, den der Ruf so partheiisch in seine Protection genommen, er ist liebenswürdig und gewiss nicht ohne Talente, aber nach dem was ich von ihm gehört, ehe ich ihn sah, dürfte ich mehr erwarten, als ich fand, nächstens schicke ich Ihnen einige Sachen von ihm, ein Envoy, ein Gedicht gegen der Hofnung und was er Sara im Fächer und mir im St. Buch geschrieben."[35]

De Ligne was attracted to the two sisters, like others before him, by their charm, their intellect, and also by their admiration for Goethe and his circle. He knew of course of their Jewish origin. This was no hindrance for him. On the contrary, it may even have been an added reason for strengthening the bond of friendship. The Prince de Ligne was a Catholic, but he did not hide his criticism of the Church as an established institution. We do not know when he began to be interested in the Jewish problem. His letters to the Countess Cosel in winter 1761 disclose that through her he got his first lesson in the mysteries and ceremonies of the Jewish religion. He then visited the eighty-year old aristocrat who had lived for forty-eight years in enforced seclusion in the old castle of Stolpe. She was a proselyte devoted to the Jewish faith. De Ligne quotes her as saying to him:

> "Every week those dispersed all over the world gather in order to listen to the sayings of the prophets. I have lived in this castle for half a century, but in prayer I am united with all the others ... I give you one of our bibles. Keep it in my memory."[36]

He not only kept the bible in her memory, but we know that his contacts with

---

[34] Quoted in Oulié, *op. cit.*, p. 153. On his opinions on Jewish bankers de Ligne writes in *Lettres de Fedor à Alphonsine*:

"On fréquente de plus en plus les Juifs, surtout les banquiers, à cause de leurs fêtes magnifiques. On *s'amuse parfois* à leur faire peur avec les autodafés, mais si on ne les traite pas encore en égaux, du moins admire t'on leur culture et leurs connaissances souvent cabalistiques." Oulié, *op. cit.*, p. 53.

[35] *Goethe-Jahrbuch XIV*, p. 27.

[36] Kobler, *op. cit.*, p. 115.

Jews on a personal level and his travels in Eastern Europe made him keenly aware of the existence of the Jews as a religious and national entity.

Christian Dohm's and Lessing's writings in Germany and Count Mirabeau's book on Moses Mendelssohn and his appeal to Frederick William II for an improvement in the social and civic status of the Jews were signposts for a change to come in the attitude of the Christian world towards the Jews. The Prince de Ligne added a new dimension to these liberal tendencies when in his *Mémoirs sur les Juifs* he not only castigated the powers that be – Church and Government – for their part in keeping the Jews in their downtrodden condition but also asked, like Dohm, Lessing and Mirabeau before him, both for better opportunities for Jews in their countries of residence and repatriation to the Holy Land for their sake and the benefit of the country. De Ligne wrote his exposé in 1798.

He did not publish it until 1801 when he sent it to Sara von Grotthus, whom he calls "a perfect woman and his tender friend". In his letter of dedication he tells her that she is

> "a daughter of a nation whose old genealogical tree makes a test of forefathers superfluous... Accept from me the defence of your people... Our scientists have not invented for the Jews doubtful genealogical tables. But among the Christians there are many more Cains than among the Jews... Unfortunately, we have no Solomon and no Joshua for in every battle have I not said to myself: 'Please, God, let the sun disappear.'"[37]

After his introductory remarks showing his respect and high regard for the people of the Old Testament he does not mince words in describing the terrible conditions under which the Jews of his time are forced to live. (He mentions especially Poland and Bohemia where they had to wear yellow markings and special hats.) After an unmerciful description of the outward appearance of the Jews he blames the authorities for their degradation, due to the unending deprivations and difficult living conditions amid narrow lanes without sun and air. He then praises the Jews for their strict moral code, the chastity of their women. "Did anyone ever meet a Jewess in a House of Shame?", he asks. "Jews are never drunk, they are obedient and faithful subjects of the princes."[38]

There are Jewish districts in all European capitals and from now on they should be rebuilt with proper drainage systems. The Jews should wear picturesque oriental clothes and be employed in arts and crafts according to their leanings. They will then become a useful and healthy part of the population. De Ligne seems to be doubtful of his success in convincing his fellow-Christians and he, therefore, advocates an alternative solution:

> "If the Christians however have neither the ability nor the good intentions to liberate the Jews from their present conditions, the sovereign of Turkey should be persuaded to return them the Kingdom of Judah."

This would also benefit the Turks in many ways, because the Jews could be their political advisers with the consent of a wise sovereign.

[37] *Ibid.*, p. 171 and Prince de Ligne, *Neue Briefe*, ed. Viktor Klarwill, Wien 1924, pp. 186–187.
[38] *Mémoires et Mélanges Historiques par le Prince de Ligne*, II, Paris 1827, pp. 35–36.

The Ephraim Family

"Ils prendraient place au Divan: il ne faudrait pour cela q'un empereur musulman ou un grand-visir un peu raisonnable pour y consentir."[39]

They will replace unreliable Greeks and will bring trade and commerce to the cities of the Levant. They would also make the desert bloom again; they would found industry and crafts, and:

"Jerusalem petit trou horrible à présent, qui fait mal au coeur aux pauvres diables de pélerins redeviendrait une capitale superbe."[40]

While de Ligne propagates the return of the Jews to Judaea, he at the same time advises the European governments to make good use of their abilities and give them equal opportunities with the Christians. The Jews would then cease to be bedraggled pedlars and petty traders. "Let them be soldiers. Why shouldn't they be just as brave as their forefathers under the command of Joshua, Gideon, or Abner?" he asks. "There is no reason," he writes, "why Jews could not be good farmers and craftsmen."

"Ils seront, au moins dans ce monde ci heureux, utiles, et cesseront d'être le plus vilain peuple de la terre."[41]

It is certainly not a manifesto written with the purpose of political action like Herzl's *Judenstaat*. As far as we know, there was no reaction to this remarkable document of a well-wishing old-world gentleman and humanitarian dreamer. The way in which he dedicated this work to Sara von Grotthus, a daughter of the Jewish nation, is indeed most moving.

Sara and Marianne had five brothers – Moritz Meyer, Carl, August, Heyman and Veitel. We have information on only one of them, Veitel and his descendants, who remained Jewish. Other Ephraims, as was the case with the Mendelssohns or the Itzigs, followed the trend of the time and married into Christian society. Careers previously closed to them were possible for those who relinquished their faith. Some acted from conviction, for others it was a "formality" which the state demanded as a condition for their acceptance into certain professions or government positions. Eduard Gans, who later on became a leading legal authority and a professor at Berlin University, was typical of those who saw baptism as a merely imposed formality. He expressed his views on this in a forthright way when he said to Felix Eberty (a descendant of the Ephraim family and himself a professor at the Berlin University) after his conversion in 1825:

"If the state is so narrow-minded that it permits me to serve it to the best of my ability on condition that I profess a creed I do not believe in then I shall bow to its wishes."[42]

We have mentioned the prominent part played by certain Jewish families and especially by women in intellectual circles in Berlin at the end of the

---

[39] *Ibid.*, p. 41.
[40] *Ibid.*, p. 41.
[41] *Ibid.*, p. 49.
[42] Felix Eberty, *Jugenderinnerungen eines alten Berliners*, Berlin 1925, p. 313.

eighteenth century. In spite of their privileged position as Court Jews, they too suffered from limitations in their civic status – Daniel Itzig's full citizenship rights were an exemption. On the other hand they developed increasingly close contacts with the leading spirits of their time. This created a tension which for some of them became in time unbearable. Attracted by a wave of intellectual freedom, the ideas of early German Romanticism and protest against the stiff orthodoxy of their parents, they yearned to enter Christian society.

Alexander and Wilhelm von Humboldt became close friends of the children of Moses Mendelssohn. The Schlegels, Schleiermacher, Gentz and Johannes von Müller were frequent guests of the Berlin Jewish salons. On first view it seems strange that just the aristocracy and not the bourgeoisie was attracted to the Jewish salons. Karl Hillebrand in his essay 'Die Juden und die neuen Ideen' concludes that the Jews turned to the aristocracy because they did not share the narrow prejudices of the bourgeoisie. The younger members of aristocratic families fled from the boredom and stiffness of their own society, Hillebrand writes, to the pretty and graceful Jewesses whose parents had given them a good education.[43] Letters written at the time by eminent members of Christian society illustrate the situation. Schleiermacher writes to his sister on 23rd March 1799:

> "... eine Frau eigentlich zur Freundin zu haben ist schon übler, und dass die Herz [Henriette Herz] gerade eine Jüdin ist, gereicht gewiss vielen zum Anstoss; aber das ist eben eins von den jämmerlichen Vorurteilen ..."[44]

Friedrich von Gentz in a letter from Vienna in 1802 praises the hospitality of the Jews:

> "... das Arnsteinersche Haus [Franziska v. Arnstein, daughter of Daniel Itzig] ist die grösste ... Resource aller hier ankommenden Fremden ... Wie wohl war mir, als ich hier auf einem Punkte ausser Ihrer liebenswürdigen Freundin Henriette und Ihrer trefflichen Mutter auch noch Mad. Levi, die ich immer liebte und schätzte, Mad. Ephraim, die ich – zu meiner ewigen Schande gesagt – nie eines Blickes würdigte, und in der ich eine der interessantesten Frauen finde ... Frau von Eybenberg, die hier mein Trost, meine Freundin, meine Stütze ist ..."[45]

The beginning of social integration made itself felt in those families who met the best of the enlightened Christian society of the time. A high percentage had been baptised. Some of them did so only after the death of their parents. Dorothea Mendelssohn, after her separation from her first husband Simon Veit, hesitated a long time before she married Friedrich Schlegel for "she would have stuck a dagger in her mother's heart".[46] Only two of Moses Mendelssohn's children remained Jewish. The incidence of conversion was more marked in the case of families in Northern Germany and especially in Berlin, for these Jews were concentrated in the cities and their occupational and social status was

---

[43] Karl Hillebrand, *Unbekannte Essays. Die Berliner Gesellschaft in den Jahren 1789 bis 1815. Das Judentum und die neuen Ideen*, Bern 1955, pp. 15–16. The first version of Karl Hillebrand's Essays was published in French in *Revue Des Deux Mondes*, Paris (March, May, November 1870).
[44] Kobler, *op. cit.*, p. 145.
[45] *Ibid.*, pp. 147–148.
[46] Felix Gilbert, *Bankiers, Künstler und Gelehrte. Unveröffentlichte Briefe der Familie Mendelssohn aus dem 19. Jahrhundert*, Tübingen 1975 (Schriftenreihe wissenschaftlicher Abhandlungen des Leo Baeck Instituts 31), p. XXI.

different from that of Jews in Southern Germany who resided mainly in small rural communities.

Sophie Jeanette, the daughter of Benjamin Veitel Ephraim, like her sister Elke Angelika a cousin of Sara von Grotthus and Marianne von Eybenberg, was born in Amsterdam in 1764. She married Israel Stieglitz of Arolsen in 1798. His father was Hirsch Stieglitz, a *Kammeragent* of the Prince of Waldeck.[47] Israel Stieglitz had been a friend of Wilhelm v. Humboldt since his student days at the medical faculty of Göttingen. In 1800 Israel Stieglitz converted and took the name of Johann. In 1802 he became *Hof- und Leibarzt* to the court of Waldeck.[48] He died in Hanover in 1843. His brother Ludwig Johann was married to Amelie Gottschalk. He founded the St. Petersburg banking firm of Stieglitz & Co. who became financiers and builders of Russian railways.[49]

Ludwig Stieglitz was born in 1778 in Arolsen and settled in St. Petersburg. He became a court banker to the Russian Czar and was granted the title of Baron. The descendants of the Stieglitz family continued to play a part in Russian society and were high officials and officers in the Russian army and navy. Bodo Freiherr von Meydell, a descendant who lives in Germany, wrote a history of the family tracing their origin to their Jewish forefathers including the Ephraims. In contrast to other Christian descendants of the Ephraims who hid their Jewish ancestry[50] he stressed in his book that he wanted to repay an ancient debt because his family had concealed the truth of their descent and heritage from him and others.[51]

Rosette Rösel Ephraim, a daughter of Zacharias Veitel Ephraim (1734–1779), married in 1777 Heymann Josef Fraenkel, like his brothers Benjamin, Hirsch and Michael, a banker. The Fraenkels were a well-known Berlin Jewish family whose sons and grandsons succeeded in their banking business. One of them, Samuel Fraenkel (born 1773) went in 1800 to Warsaw where he was active in placing Russian and Polish debentures in the European market. In 1806 he converted and took the name of Samuel Anton. The Fraenkels were closely connected in their banking business with the Mendelssohns. The founder of the banking business of Mendelssohn was Joseph, the eldest son of Moses Mendelssohn. He was born in 1770 and after an apprenticeship with Itzig and Co. (Daniel Itzig was a business associate of Ephraim in the minting of Prussian coins) he became independent in 1795 in premises in Spandauer Strasse, at that time a predominantly Jewish quarter. After a partnership with Moses Friedländer, a son of David Friedländer and an Elder of the Jewish community, he took his younger brother Abraham as a partner.[52] J. & A. Mendelssohn

---

[47] Jacob Jacobson, *Jüdische Trauungen in Berlin 1759–1813*, Berlin 1968, p. 349.

[48] He was also the family doctor of the Meyerbeers. See Giacomo Meyerbeer's letters to his wife Minna, in Giacomo Meyerbeer, *Briefwechsel und Tagebücher*, II, pp. 228–229. See also pp. 294, 316.

[49] Kurt Grunwald, 'Europe's Railways and Jewish Enterprise. German Jews as Pioneers of Railway Promotion', in *LBI Year Book XII* (1967), pp. 163–209.

[50] Professor Georg Ebers does not mention the name of his father, Meyer Moses Ephraim, in his *Die Geschichte meines Lebens*, Berlin 1893.

[51] Bodo Freiherr v. Meydell, *Die Stieglitz, Ihre Vorfahren und Nachkommen*, Neustadt a. d. Aich 1967.

[52] On the bankers Fraenkel and the beginning of the banking house of Mendelssohn see Hugo Rachel and Paul Wallich in *Berliner Grosskaufleute und Kapitalisten*, III, Berlin 1967, p. 112 ff.

opened their business in Poststrasse 16, the "Palais Ephraim" which at that time was occupied by various business firms and store rooms. They moved in 1815 to Jägerstrasse 51 where it existed from 1827 under the name of Mendelssohn & Co. until its forced liquidation in 1939. (The last senior partner was Franz von Mendelssohn, who inherited the title granted to his father by Emperor Frederick III in 1888.)[53] Josef Maximilian Fraenkel was from 1806 a non-active partner of the Mendelssohns. When Abraham Mendelssohn retired in 1821, his younger brother Alexander became a partner of the firm; he conducted its business under the name of Mendelssohn & Fraenkel until 1827 when Fraenkel too retired. Josef M. Fraenkel lived as a gentleman of leisure until 1857. His three daughters married into the Prussian nobility.

Heymann Joseph Fraenkel (1784–1814), the husband of Rosette Ephraim, did not enter a partnership with the Mendelssohns but he was connected with them in many joint transactions, above all in the placing of government loans and issues. From 1803 onwards he was a member of the Berlin Stock Exchange Commission. Fraenkel's son Zacharias Fraenkel Veitel Ephraim, born in 1781, who changed his name in 1812 to Wilhelm Zacharias Friebe, took over his father's banking business at an early age.

We have reason to believe that the main activity of the Fraenkels, the Mendelssohns and other private bankers who started as money changers was the participation in short and medium term loans to state and provincial institutions. From the beginning of the nineteenth century they also sold to the private clientele debentures issued by these institutions. We have to remember that the system of state finance through the issue of debentures to the public started in Prussia much later than in other European countries with well-developed capital markets like Amsterdam or London. The first Prussian state debentures One Million Gulden were issued in 1792/1793 and guaranteed by King Frederick William II. The origin of the Berlin Stock Exchange goes back to 1761 when merchants and bankers met in the morning hours to deal in bills and local and foreign currencies. The first company which issued shares was the *Königliche Seehandlung* founded by King Frederick II. The first debentures were issued by agricultural credit institutions – *Provinzial Landschafts Kreditanstalten*. The debentures were quoted for the first time in a *Berliner Amtlicher Kurszettel vom 9. August 1805* issued by special permission and signed by ten *Vereidete Makler* (sworn in brokers), according to their names, most of them Jews.[54] Most of the members of the new Stock Exchange Committee were also Jews, among them Heymann Josef Fraenkel and David Ephraim.[55] This was quite remarkable for, while Jews were known to deal in bills, coins and goods in the

---

[53] On the banking history of Mendelssohn & Co. in the nineteenth and twentieth centuries see Wilhelm Treue, 'Das Bankhaus Mendelssohn', in *Mendelssohn Studien*, Berlin 1972, p. 30 ff.

[54] See copy of the list of quotations attached, printed in S. Spangenthal, *Die Geschichte der Berliner Börse*, Berlin 1903.

[55] Rachel/Wallich, *op. cit.*, p. 543. David Ephraim (1762–1835) was later involved in loan transactions with members of the Austrian aristocracy who owed him large sums of money. Consequently he was unable to meet his obligations to other parties. He then transferred his residence to Vienna where he became a Catholic and took the name of Johann Andreas Schmidt.

market,[56] here for the first time they acted by official appointment at a time when they did not yet enjoy citizens' rights.

The first decade of the nineteenth century saw the most severe national crisis Prussia had known since the Seven Years War. The decline reached its lowest point in 1806 at the defeat of Jena and Auerstadt. Great parts of Prussia including the capital city Berlin were occupied by the armies of Napoleon. The brokers who signed the first list of quotations in 1805 wrote on 28th October 1806 that because of the presence of the French Imperial army in Berlin, the arrival of the Emperor Napoleon and the interruption of postal services it was decided not to fix quotations.[57]

A burden to be borne by the residents of Berlin was the contribution demanded by the French occupying power in 1807. The *Königliche Bank* and the *Königliche Seehandlung* had fled with their liquid assets to Königsberg. They returned to Berlin only in 1809. It fell to the private bankers of Berlin to raise funds and to provide intermediate finance until more or less normal conditions should again prevail. Only bankers with sufficient backing in the country and abroad could undertake this enormous task. Of the four banking firms concerned in it two were Jewish-owned, namely Sal. Moses Erben and Liebmann Meyer Wulff, the last one being related to the Ephraims. The daughter of Liebmann Wulff had married Veitel Heine Ephraim, who in 1816 assumed the name of Viktor Ebers. The finances of Prussia were of course in a sorry state following wars and contributions to be paid to France. Income from taxes was insufficient to cover current needs and Chancellor von Hardenberg had recourse to any means to make ends meet. Short-term loans were a stop gap and the dates on which they were due had more often than not to be prolonged, and the long-term loans raised with bankers and merchants were in reality forced loans.

The number of Jewish residents in Berlin in the first decade of the nineteenth century was approximately 3,300 of a total population of 170,000.[58] Of the Jews eligible as permanent residents of Berlin 190 were merchants. The rest were small traders and pedlars.[59] Significant for the part played by Jews in the raising of funds for state purposes are the figures quoted in a list of participants and contributions to government loans from 1812 to 1815. Almost half of a total of 3,250,000 Thalers were contributed by Jewish bankers and merchants. At the top of the list we find Liebmann Meyer Wulff, and among the big contributors Zacharias Fraenkel Veitel Ephraim (later named Friebe) and Veitel Heimann Ephraim (Ebers).

A list of well-to-do residents of Berlin, headed by the Christian bankers Gebr. Schickler with one million Thalers, mentions among Jewish bankers and merchants Zacharias Fraenkel Friebe with 250,000 Thalers and Veitel Ephraim,

---

[56]*Ibid.*, p. 536: "Die Judenmäkler haben solches zu allen Zeiten betrieben, gegenwärtig wohl am stärksten, gestalt das ganze Publikum wie bekannt, nach diesem Wesen sich in der Juden Diskretion befindet." Aus Stadtarchiv Berlin, Innungssachen Mäkler I, 3rd May 1761.
[57]Spangenthal, *op. cit.*, p. 21.
[58]On Jewish population statistics in Berlin see Herbert Seeliger, 'Origin and Growth of the Berlin Community', in *LBI Year Book III* (1958), pp. 159–168.
[59]On Jews in trade and professions, see Stefi Wenzel, *Jüdische Bürger und kommunale Selbstverwaltung in Preussischen Städten*, Berlin 1967, pp. 27 ff.; Rachel/Wallich, *op. cit.*, p. 294 ff.

Unter den Linden, with 200,000 Thalers. The estimates of personal wealth, their high contributions and participation in government loans indicate that by the beginning of the nineteenth century some Jews in Berlin beyond the very small circle of Court Jews of earlier times had reached positions of affluence and influence in financial affairs. Their large participation in state loans also means that they must already have had a Christian clientele for otherwise they would not have had the placing power for these loans. Alexander von Humboldt is a case in point. The Humboldts had been clients of the Mendelssohns for decades, from the time of the partnership with the Fraenkels.[60] The connections of the Jewish bankers with financial institutions of the Prussian state, which began at the time of their "voluntary" participation in the state loans, became even closer after the defeat of Napoleon, when some of them acted as transfer agents for the French reparation payments to Prussia.[61] Hardenberg in a letter to the Prussian *chargé d'affaires* in Paris in 1819 refers to Joseph Mendelssohn as "unser dort anwesender Bankquier". These transactions involved very considerable sums. Wilhelm Treue mentions the sum of 199 million French Francs handled between 1815 and 1821 by the Mendelssohns, Rothschilds, Gontard and Fraenkel-Friebe.[62] Of the many descendants of the Ephraims who married out of the faith, Zacharias Fraenkel Friebe's three daughters married into families of the Prussian Aristocracy. Bertha Friebe married Freiherr Franz von Thielmann, the son of a Prussian general. Wilhelmine Friebe married Wilhelm Adolf Gerth. After 1853 the family name was with the King's consent Tortilowicz von Batocki-Friebe.

The Batockies were army officers and high government officials. The son of the first title holder was President of the Prussian province of East Prussia and honorary professor at the University of Königsberg. It is most likely that the name Friebe was added to the family name Batocki because of a clause in the "family trust", in Prussian law called *Fideikommiss*. Very often the founder of such trusts made the utilisation of the income from the trust capital conditional on the addition of the founder's name to those of his descendants. Veitel Heimann Ephraim (1776–1832), a great-grandson of Nathan Veitel Ephraim, the Court Jew of Frederic II, changed his name in 1816 to Viktor Ebers. His son Wulff took the name Paul Ebers. His daughter Henriette (Mirel, Minette) married a son of Mendel Oppenheim, who in 1827 became Moritz von Oppenfeld. His younger daughter, Johanna Franziska (1808–1878), married Frédéric

---

[60]Hanns G. Reissner, 'A. v. Humboldt und die Familie J. Mendelssohn', in *Mendelssohn Studien*, II, Berlin 1975, p. 141 ff.

[61]The way Prussian governments made use of the services of Jewish bankers was commented upon by Colonel de Stoffel, a French diplomat in his letter of October 1868 to Louis Napoleon: ". . . It is noteworthy that nearly all Prussian governments of the last 100 years have employed a Jew (already at the time of Sieyès) as a more or less occult instrument. Without being precisely an intriguer Bleichröder aspires to play a role and to take the place of his precursors among whom the Jew Ephraim shines in first place . . ." Quoted by Fritz Stern, in *Gold and Iron. Bismarck, Bleichröder and the Building of the German Empire*, London 1977, p. 118; On Sieyès' French emissary in Berlin in 1791 and Benjamin Ephraim, see my essay 'The Ephraim Family', in *LBI Year Book XXI* (1976), p. 225.

[62]Treue, *loc. cit.*, p. 36.

The Ephraim Family

Adrian Graf von Limburg-Stirum (1804–1874), a Dutch aristocrat. In order to comply with the conditions of the trust and legally bear the title *Fideikommissherr auf Eberspark*, Friedrich Wilhelm Graf von Limburg-Stirum (1835–1912) was granted permission in 1867 by William I of Prussia to add to his name "genannt Ebers". He was the son of Johanna Franziska Ebers and the grandson of Veitel Heimann Ephraim Ebers. Eberspark was a large country estate and castle in the Prussian province of Poznań situated between Bromberg and Schneidermühl (now Poland). The same permission was given to his son Friedrich Wilhelm Richard Paul (born 1871) by Emperor William II in 1913.[63] The Jewish ancestry of the Grafen von Limburg-Stirum was of course well known to the German Emperor. It led him to an unrestrained outbreak against the count in 1899. At that time the Conservatives in the *Reichstag* under the leadership of Graf von Limburg-Stirum were in opposition to a project supported by the *Kaiser* for a network of canals in West Germany (Dortmund–Rhein). In a telegram to the Chancellor von Bülow he wrote:

> "Krasse Dummheit ist mit bösem Willen gepaart, durch einen Judenjungen ausgenutzt. Ich bin entschlossen, die Partei durch schwere gesellschaftliche Strafen meinen Zorn fühlen zu lassen, Keine Auflösung, worauf Zentrum und Freisinn gehofft. Aber Ausschluss der Limburger und Genossen aus der Gesellschaft."[64]

And in a telegram of September 1899 he added:

> "Die traditionellen Stützen von Thron und Altar, die von jeher vom Königlichen Hause verzogen worden sind, haben sich gegen den Herrn gewandt, und das unter Führung des Judenabkömmlings Limburg . . ."[65]

Bülow writes that Limburg-Stirum, the leader of the Conservatives, was the son of a Dutch aristocrat and a Jewess. He quotes Bismarck's opinion that the pairing of a German stallion and a semitic mare sometimes produces good results. Bülow thinks that this is so in the case of Graf Stirum, because he inherited from his father seriousness and staying power and from his mother's side a sharp and clear intelligence. Bülow is surprised by the *Kaiser*'s outburst against the count's Jewish descent for, in his opinion, the *Kaiser* was not an antisemite[66] and he mentions in this connection many Jewish friends of the *Kaiser* – Albert Ballin, Emil Rathenau, Eduard Arnhold, Paul von Schwabach and others.[67] William II's instability and his emotional vacillations are of course well known. They were evident also in the case of his personal relationships with Jews.[68]

---

[63]'Die Berliner Familie Ephraim – Ebers und ihre gräflichen Nachfolger', in *Mitteilungen der Gesellschaft für Jüdische Familienforschung*, I, Berlin November 1924. See also *Gothaisches Genealogisches Taschenbuch der Gräflichen Häuser*, Gotha 1914, p. 550 ff.

[64]Bernhard Fürst von Bülow, *Denkwürdigkeiten*, Bd. I, Berlin 1930, p. 296 ff.

[65]*Ibid.*

[66]On William II and his ambivalent attitude to the Jews see Lamar Cecil, 'Wilhelm II und die Juden', in *Juden im Wilhelminischen Deutschland 1890–1914*. Ein Sammelband herausgegeben von Werner E. Mosse unter Mitwirkung von Arnold Paucker, Tübingen 1976 (Schriftenreihe wissenschaftlicher Abhandlungen des Leo Baeck Instituts 33).

[67]Bülow, *op. cit.*, p. 297.

[68]In this connection this author recollects an incident he witnessed personally in 1933 at the bank Gebr. Arnhold–S. Bleichröder. It was in the beginning of April when Paul von Schwabach showed him a silver-framed photo of the *Kaiser* which had just arrived at the bank. It was signed William II I.R. – "meinem lieben v. Schwabach zum 1. April 1933". On that date, the

The brother of Veitel Heimann Ephraim, since 1816 Viktor Ebers, whose aristocratic descendants we have just mentioned, had a younger brother Moses Heimann Ephraim (1781–1852), from 1812 named Martin Ebers. His granddaughter married August Freiherr von Brandenstein. His grandson was Georg Moritz Ebers (1837–1898), an Egyptologist, a professor at the University of Leipzig and a pupil of Richard Lepsius. He travelled extensively in Egypt and Palestine. In addition to his scientific publications he wrote on the Near East and also historical novels which were very popular at the time.[69] In his autobiography Hegel, Schleiermacher, Christian Rauch and Alexander von Humboldt are mentioned as friends of the family. He refrains, however, from touching on his Jewish origin.[70] Eduard Meyer, Professor of Ancient History at the University of Berlin, wrote a long appreciation of Ebers in 1899.[71] On the very first page he discloses the Jewish lineage of Georg Ebers, stating that his family originates from that of the well-known Ephraim "under Frederick the Great" whose descendants separated into the families of Ebers and Eberty, and observes that Georg Ebers's "forefathers belonged to the numerous Jewish families of Berlin, which as early as the end of the eighteenth century had reached a position of public esteem and considerable wealth". He also touches on the social aspect in remarking that the family freed itself from the narrow confines of inherited traditions. They converted and married into Prussian and Saxon aristocratic families. Their homes were, like those of the Mendelssohns, Hitzigs and Beers, the centre of the literary and artistic life of Berlin.

We meet the same attitude to his Jewish origin in the autobiography of Felix Eberty (1812–1884), Professor of Law at the University of Breslau.[72] He vividly describes life and people in Berlin during the first half of the nineteenth century and the portraits of members of his family and of the people he met in his parents' house are penned with a loving sense of humour. But he never gives us to understand that they were Jews or of Jewish origin. Varnhagen and the poet Chamisso were his father's friends from childhood. A poem by Chamisso dedicated to his father is printed in the book. It is signed "Souvenir d'Adelbert Chamisso, May 1804". The business partner of his father, Heimann Joseph Ephraim (1784–1856), was Jacob Herz Beer who made his fortune in sugar refineries. The Beers' house was a centre of musical life where actors, musicians and writers met. One of his three sons was the famous composer Giacomo Meyerbeer (1791–1864), whose original family name was Jakob Liebmann Meyer Beer, Liebmann after his grandfather, the Berlin banker and *Judenältester*

Boykottag organised by the Nazis, William II remembered the Jewish ancestry of his friends, the Schwabachs, whom Bülow mentions in his memoirs. The present author has no doubt that William chose the date quite intentionally and the Schwabachs understood it as a gesture of sympathy.

[69] *Durch Gosen zum Sinai*, Leipzig 1872; *Palästina in Wort und Bild*, Stuttgart 1883/1884; *Ägypten in Wort und Bild*, Stuttgart 1879; *Eine Ägyptische Königstochter*, Stuttgart 1875.

[70] *Die Geschichte meines Lebens vom Kinde bis zum Manne*, Stuttgart 1893.

[71] Eduard Meyer, *Kleine Schriften. Zur Geschichtstheorie und zur wirtschaftlichen und politischen Geschichte des Altertums*, Halle 1910, 'Georg Ebers', pp. 505–524. The article was previously published in *Biographisches Jahrbuch und Deutscher Nekrolog*, Bd. 3, 1899.

[72] *Jugenderinnerungen eines alten Berliners*, 1876, published Berlin 1925.

Liebmann Meyer Wulff. On his mother's side he was a cousin of Johanna Franziska, Henriette (Minette) and Paul Wulff Ebers whom we have mentioned previously. Unlike his cousins, Meyerbeer remained in the Jewish fold. From 1830 onwards he lived and worked most of the time in Paris, but remained closely attached to his family in Germany and kept in contact with them by correspondence and visits.[73] His strong Jewish feelings expressed themselves in a letter of condolence to his mother Amalia Malka on 30th August 1812 when, on the occasion of his grandfather Liebmann Meyer Wulff's death, he vows that he will always be faithful to his grandfather's religion.[74] Meyerbeer's successes brought him admiration and honours. But he also had to suffer humiliations and hatred because of his race. Yet he kept the solemn promise to his mother and he remained a Jew until his last day. His three daughters, however, converted and married Christians.

When Eduard Meyer wrote that Jewish families, the Ebers, the Ebertys, Mendelssohns and others, freed themselves from their inherited tradition, he meant of course Jewish orthodoxy. There were, however, other descendants of the Ephraim family who did not choose conversion and some of them were to be found among the leaders of the Jewish Reform movement. Others again became scholars who made a name for themselves in the natural sciences and humanities.

One branch of the family which remained Jewish is that of Marcus Heine Ephraim (1692–1768). He was a brother of Veitel Heine Ephraim, the famous court banker of King Frederic II, and for some time his brother's partner. His son Ephraim Marcus Ephraim (1716–1776) did not continue the business of his father and uncle. The son of Ephraim Marcus Ephraim, named Joachim Heimann Marcus Ephraim (1748–1812), married Fredche Gans, daughter of Isaac Jacob Gans (who died in 1798). The Gans family of Celle–Hannover was known already in the seventeenth century as court factors and well-to-do merchants. The father of Isaac Jacob Gans was Salomon Nathan Gans, married to Jente Hameln of the family of the famous Glückel von Hameln (1646–1719). The Gans family is mentioned in her memoirs.[75]

Joachim Marcus Ephraim had four sons and two daughters. The descendants of two of his sons, namely Ephraim Heine Ephraim and Jacob Ephraim, are still alive. Ephraim Heine Ephraim married Ester Manasse and had a daughter Friederike (1833–1919), who married Lesser Lowitz and whose grandchildren live in Israel, Germany and Australia. The marriage contract of Friederike Ephraim stipulated a bridal gift of 1,500 Thalers, a sum of money granted to her by the *Gans'sche Stiftung*, the *Witwe Heimann Zacharias Ephraimsche Stiftung*,[76] the *Nauensche Stiftung* and the *Ephraim Veitel Stiftung*. Some if not all of these family

[73]Meyerbeer, *op. cit.*, II, pp. 217, 235, 249.
[74]The letter is published in the catalogue *Exposition Meyerbeer, Salle Bermann, Bibliothèque Nationale et Universitaire Jerusalem*, December 1964, p. 8. The original is in the collection of the *Institut für Musik-forschung*, Berlin–Jerusalem.
[75]*Denkwürdigkeiten der Glückel von Hameln*, Berlin 1913, p. 43 ff.
[76]A handwritten translation of the original Hebrew document outlining the rules of this fund, dated 10th January 1802, is in the Central Archives for the History of the Jewish people, P 17/665.

trusts from which female descendants of the family received bridal gifts were in existence until 1933.[77] These funds are among the oldest of their kind.

The brother of Ephraim Heine Ephraim, Jacob Ephraim, renamed Dufresne in 1812, was a volunteer in the Prussian army during the Napoleonic wars. His portrait is in the possession of Mrs. Rudolf Wittkower, New York. His daughter Cecilie (1836–1913) was married to Isidor Wittkower. Her grandson was the eminent art historian Rudolf Wittkower (1901–1975), known for his fundamental studies on Italian classical art. He was a member of the Warburg Institute, London, Professor at Columbia University and member of many learned institutions. His brother Werner Wittkower[78] (born 1908) is a leading architect in Israel. He designed many public buildings, among them the Museum Haaretz in Tel-Aviv.

The middle of the nineteenth century, with the gradual civic emancipation of Prussian Jewry, their entry into some of the professions and occupations hitherto closed to them and their daily contact with Christian society, previously confined to a thin layer of the Jewish community, was a time of severe religious crisis caused to no small degree by this development. There was a growing opposition to traditional orthodoxy with its unbending demand for a strict adherence to the laws of the Torah. But there was at the same time also resistance to those who wanted to sever all links with the Jewish community. Finally a fight was waged against religious indifference with its attendant danger of Judaism becoming no more than an empty shell. The Reform movement was in the forefront of this battle for a renewal and survival of Judaism. The spiritual leader of the movement in Berlin and the chief organiser of its *Genossenschaft für Reform im Judentum*, founded in 1845, was Sigismund Stern (1812–1867).

Sigismund Stern, born in Karge, a small town in the Province of Poznań, was educated by his father in the Jewish traditional way. After leaving the *Joachimsthalsche Gymnasium* he studied at Berlin University under Hegel, Schlegel and Schleiermacher. His doctoral thesis at the University of Halle in 1834 was on *Vorläufige Grundlegung einer Sprachphilosophie* and in 1835 he became headmaster of the "Jostsche Institut", a Jewish boys' school. In 1836 he married Ida Fürstenberg, a great-granddaughter of Veitel Meyer, the son of Rösel Ephraim. Next to his teaching profession his great interest was in literature and linguistics. In 1840 he published a *Lehrbuch der allgemeinen Grammatik*. His research on numerals in various languages was based on a thorough knowledge of Semitic and Far Eastern languages.[79] Even as a student Stern had been a member of a literary club in Berlin, the *Sonntagsverein im Tunnel über der Spree*. Writers, actors and high government officials were among its members. (Theodor Fontane, a lifelong member, wrote extensively on the club.)[80] Stern, whose pen name there was "Der punische Sterngucker", contributed many poems on historical subjects, and for years also edited the club's weekly publication.

[77] I am indebted for the information on this branch of the family to Else Wallach, Jerusalem and Elly Münzer, München, grand-daughters of Friderike Ephraim.
[78] To whom I am indebted for the information on this branch of the family.
[79] Arthur Galliner, *Sigismund Stern. Der Reformer und der Pädagoge*, Frankfurt a. Main 1930, p. 20.
[80] Theodor Fontane, *Gesammelte Schriften*, Zweite Reihe, Vierter Band, Berlin 1925, p. 174.

The Ephraim Family

His experience as headmaster of the Jewish boys' school opened his eyes to the problems of the Jewish Community of Berlin. Only ten per cent of the Jewish children were sent to Jewish schools because of indifference or prejudice against Jewish teachers. In his lectures in 1844–1845 on the task of the community he dealt with this problem and with the position of Jewry in the Christian state, demanding the state recognition of the Jewish religion and equal rights for a "deutsch-jüdische Kirche" with the Christian religious institutions,[81] which in his view followed logically from the emancipation edict of 1812. At the same time he called on his co-religionists in an *Aufruf an unsere deutschen Glaubensbrüder*, written by himself, Aron Bernstein (whose pen name was Rebenstein) and J. Simion, to join in a movement for the renewal of Jewish life and reform of the Jewish religion.[82] This was the prelude to the formation of the Reform community in Berlin, which in 1850 became the *Berliner Reformgemeinde* with its own Temple which existed from 1854 until its destruction in the *Kristallnacht* in 1938. In 1847 the Reform movement started to publish its own monthly *Reformzeitung. Organ für den Fortschritt im Judentum*. Stern used the journal as a platform for propagating his views on religious and political issues. From January 1847 onwards his articles set the tone of the journal. Most of them are addressed to the Jews on matters of reform, reorganisation of the community and education. Other articles deal with political issues, mainly the continuing inequalities suffered by Prussian Jewry. In his ideas on religious reform and renewal, Stern, while recognising the important role of Orthodoxy in the past, was of the opinion that full integration in the life of modern society and the state was not possible within the halachic rules. The "deutsch-jüdische Kirche" and its adherents should, like the German Protestants, be an integral part of the state and not, like the Catholics, seek its centre of gravity outside the country.[83]

Stern's credo that the Mosaic laws were conceived as a constitution for a Jewish state and that the Jews are Germans of Jewish faith and not nationality was for him the logical outcome of his proposals for a complete change in the ceremonial tradition and prayers. The dedication of the Reform Synagogue in Berlin on 10th September 1854 was to be the crowning act of his activities in Berlin. With a heavy heart his colleagues on the board of the Reform movement allowed him to follow the call of the Philanthropin in Frankfurt, which since 1804 had developed into a full-scale educational institution for Jewish boys and girls under the leadership of Michael Hess and Isaak Markus Jost. Stern became headmaster of the school in 1855, warmly recommended by Gabriel Riesser, Abraham Geiger, and Moritz Veit, like Stern fighters for emancipation and religious revival. For Stern it was a fundamental change in his life. In Frankfurt he became again the educator in a school which served the community as a whole.[84] Next to his educational activities he retained, as many of his lectures

---

[81]*Die Aufgabe des Judentums und der Juden in der Gegenwart*, 2nd edn., Berlin 1853 (the book was based on his lectures).

[82]S. Stern, *Geschichte des Judentums von Moses Mendelssohn bis auf die Gegenwart*, Frankfurt a. Main 1857, p. 290 ff.; also in Caesar Seligmann, *Geschichte der Jüdischen Reformbewegung*, Frankfurt a. Main 1922, p. 120 ff.

[83]Stern, *Die Aufgabe des Judentums . . .*, op. cit., p. 147 ff.

[84]On Stern's aims as the head of the Philanthropin see Arthur Galliner, 'The Philanthropin in

and books witness, a keen interest in contemporary history and politics. The violent upheavals of 1848, the discussions on German unification were for him more than mere subjects of scientific research and he dealt with them in his *Geschichte des deutschen Volkes*[85] and *Habsburg und Hohenzollern. Österreich und Preussen in ihrem Verhältniss zu Deutschland und zu den Interessen der deutschen Nation.*[86] His *Stein und sein Zeitalter* was at the time acclaimed as a work of great importance. Stern's work in Frankfurt was cut short by his untimely death in 1867.

His daughter Clara married Dr. Marcus Kalisch (1825–1885), a Hebrew scholar born in Treptow, Pommerania, who settled in London. He was secretary to the Chief Rabbi Dr. N. M. Adler until 1853, and also tutor to the children and nieces of Baron Lionel Rothschild. One of his pupils wrote in her memoirs:

> "Dr. Kalisch married the daughter of Rabbi Stern of Frankfort and we speedily made friends with that lady and have always retained a warm interest in their family, particularly in the very talented and energetic daughter Constance Hoster, well known as an authority in foreign languages . . ."[87]

The grandson of Sigismund Stern was William Stern (1871–1938), professor at the universities of Breslau and Hamburg and, after his expulsion from Hamburg in 1933, at Duke University, North Carolina. He was a pioneer in Child Psychology and intelligence tests. His life and work was described by his daughter Eva Michaelis-Stern in an earlier Year Book.[88] His scientific archive was fully catalogued by his son Günther Stern-Anders, himself a philosopher and writer.

In an allusion to the views of his grandfather, Sigismund, William Stern once wrote to his daughter:

> "The biography of your great-grandfather will disclose to you one of the hidden sources of your deep interest in Jewish affairs. Faced with other problems he aimed at other targets, but he in common with you strove to pave the way to save Jewry from stagnation and lethargy."

Written three years before the catastrophe befell German Jewry in 1933, this is a truly moving testimonial by this descendant of the Ephraims, a man who, like most of his generation, witnessed the collapse of his world, a representative of the generation which believed in the solution of the Jewish problem through progress, liberalism and the ideals of humanism.

Frankfurt. Its educational and cultural Significance for German Jewry', in *LBI Year Book III* (1958), p. 180 f.

[85] Berlin 1850.

[86] Berlin 1860.

[87] Lady Constance Battersea, in *Reminiscences*, London 1922, p. 29 ff. See also Lucy Cohen in *Lady de Rothschild and her daughters, 1821–1901*, London 1935, p. 79 ff.

[88] 'William Stern 1871–1938. The Man and his Achievements', in *LBI Year Book XVII* (1972), pp. 143–154.

The Gernsheims of Worms

BY HELMUT GERNSHEIM

The founder of the Gernsheim family came to Germany as a refugee from Spain following the expulsion of the Jews from that country in 1492. Nothing is known about him, not even his name; merely the fact that this Sefardic Jew settled in the little township of Gernsheim on the Rhine from which he took his new name. This was three centuries before the edict, issued by Napoleon in March 1808, made it compulsory for Jews living in the annexed Rhine territories to take surnames.

Two well-known fifteenth-century printers were born in Gernsheim: Peter Schoeffler, collaborator of Johann Gensfleisch alias Gutenberg in Mainz, and Johann Manthen, printer and publisher in Venice. What attracted my ancestor to Gernsheim, and which trade he occupied there, is shrouded in mystery. Half a century later, Salomon Gernsheim, presumably his son, moved to nearby Worms on the left bank of the Rhine, where he died in 1620. His tombstone in the old Jewish cemetery marks the first of our line. The last Gernsheim in Worms, Dr. med. Friedrich Gernsheim committed suicide with his wife on 29th July 1938 in order to escape a worse fate at the hands of the Nazis. Thus we can look back on 400 years of family genealogy and history.

The majority of the Gernsheims were in the leather business, either as tanners or dealers of hides, making Worms an important trade centre. A great-great-grandson of Salomon Gernsheim founded in 1768 the oldest leather firm in Germany. He is Michael Gernsheim (*c.* 1705–1792), better known as the last *Judenbischof* (episcopus judaeorum), an honorary office he occupied for thirty-four years. As the elected head of the Jewish community he was responsible for its autonomous administration and jurisdiction, assisted by a twelve-member council or *Judenrat*. The title *Judenbischof* had been created in 1090 by the German King and Holy Roman Emperor Heinrich IV (1066–1106) in connection with certain privileges the Jews of Worms received from him in return for their (financial) support for his invasion of Italy.[1] They were: autonomy in administration and jurisdiction within the community, free movement within the kingdom, choice of trade, freedom from taxes and guarantees as to their property. In any infringement of these the *Judenbischof* had the right of appeal to the king.[2] In contradistinction to his Christian counterpart he had no religi-

---

[1] The Jewish community of Worms was perhaps 1,500 strong by the middle of the eleventh century. It was one of the oldest and largest, and also wealthiest along the Rhine. Otherwise it would have been impossible for it to make a sizeable financial contribution to the King meriting such generous privileges. The synagogue built in 1034 (of which nothing remains) is a further indication of the size and wealth of the Jewish community of Worms at that time, for it was the first in Germany, and was after Toledo the oldest in Europe.

[2] Already six years after the granting of the privileges the king was powerless to prevent 800 Jews of Worms being butchered by the first crusade before it set out on its mission. In the plague of 1349, for which the Jews were made responsible, the community was completely wiped out by

ous function. In fact, a rabbi could not be elected to this position; only a lay member of the council to which the rabbi usually belonged. The *Judenbischof* had to be a businessman of exemplary integrity and be possessed of considerable wealth to be able to assist the less fortunate members of the community. He was elected for life.[3] The Bishop of Worms had to be notified of the election. When satisfied by his own independent enquiries as to the quality of the chosen man he was installed as *Judenbischof* in a special swearing-in ceremony in the Bishop's palace. Michael Gernsheim was elected in 1758, sworn-in in March of the following year, and held office until his death on 20th September 1792. He was the last *episcopus judaeorum* not only in Worms, but anywhere.[4] A contemporary pastel portrait in the possession of the family shows him in his colourful striped Bishop's robes and wearing the Doge-like pointed cap.

In 1848 Michael's grandson Salomon Gernsheim bought from the Pistorius family their patrician mansion dating from 1690. It was one of the first and finest houses erected after the devastation of the town by General Melac, Commander of Louis XIV's army, the previous year, for the then mayor of the town, Wirnhirn. In the middle of the eighteenth century two functional side-wings were added enclosing a courtyard leading to a fairly large garden extending to the Dominikstrasse. At the same time the façade and front rooms along the busy Kämmererstrasse were redecorated in the fashionable rococo style. The upper story contained the elegant drawing and music rooms, the entire ground floor serving as a showroom of "S. Gernsheim & Söhne". One side-wing contained the offices and store-rooms of the firm, the other the living quarters. Around the turn of the nineteenth century the building was placed under protection as an ancient monument (*Denkmalschutz*).

The strict division of business, home and entertainment in the horseshoe-shaped building was still adhered to up to my grandmother's death in December 1923. However, during the French occupation of Worms after the First World War, the reception and music rooms in the front-wing – which were rarely used after the introduction of the electric trams had made the narrow Kämmererstrasse the noisiest shopping street in Worms – were occupied by two high-ranking French officers with whom my grandmother was on good footing. (The first Frenchman to requisition the then mayoral residence of Pistorius was the still uncrowned Emperor Napoleon I with Josephine while on an inspection tour of the French Army on the Rhine in 1804.)[5]

---

mass suicide. By 1800 the community in Worms had risen again to about 400, or roughly one-tenth of the 4,768 strong population.

[3] Following the example of Worms, the Christian authorities of certain other Rhineland episcopal towns, such as Cologne, Mainz and Speyer later bestowed the title *Judenbischof* also on the elected heads of their Jewish communities, probably with similar responsibilities of community rule.

[4] In 1792 the French took possession of Worms, and in March 1793 all privileges which the Jewish community had ever received from the Emperor, from the City of Worms (a free town of the Empire) and from the Bishop of Worms (each granted in return for extortionate payments) were cancelled. This also meant the abolition of the office of the *Judenbischof* and his functions.

[5] *Wormser Zeitung*, 5th September 1926.

MICHAEL GERNSHEIM

Last Judenbischof and founder of
Germany's oldest leather firm

FRIEDRICH GERNSHEIM

WILHELM GERNSHEIM

From the Collection of Helmut Gernsheim, Lugano

The courtyard of the horseshoe-shaped Gernsheim house in Worms, 1888/1889

From the Collection of Helmut Gernsheim, Lugano

Michael Gernsheim, the founder of the wholesale business, had stocked every kind of hide required for the most diverse manufacturing branches. Under his son and grandson the firm "S. Gernsheim & Söhne" gradually rose to the leading position in Germany in the wholesale and export trade, and became one of the chief suppliers to the army. As army contractors, the family amassed a considerable fortune, particularly in the 1870–1871 war with France, after which a branch of the firm was opened in Strassburg. My grandfather having died rather young in 1888 his eldest son, then just twenty, inherited the firm and left it in the hands of an experienced uncle of his. On his death the following year he took two associates into the firm, none of his younger brothers having shown any inclination to enter the family business after finishing the *Gymnasium*. With their help my uncle succeeded in steering the firm through the First World War and the crazy time of inflation, when each new hide cost several times as much as the previous one sold. Yet after the death of his partners, and not having a male heir himself, my uncle decided in, November 1928, to put the firm into liquidation.[6]

The house in the Kämmererstrasse 40 had already been sold in 1924 by the heirs of the estate to the Chamber of Commerce. From 1st January 1925 until its total destruction by bombs in 1945 this old patrician mansion served as "Das Haus des Handwerks" (House of the Guilds). "S. Gernsheim & Söhne" remained, however, installed in the side-wing it had occupied since 1848, until the dissolution of the firm on 21st November 1928. It marked the end of an epoch for Worms, for the leather trade and for one branch of the Gernsheim family whose fortune had been based on it.[7]

While the majority of the male Gernsheim descendants of the *Judenbischof* were in the leather trade, other branches had gone into the grocery or wine trade. (A relation, Alfred Langenbach, was owner of the Liebfrauenkirche vineyard in Worms from which the original and genuine "Liebfraumilch" hock is produced.) A few became rabbis and medical practitioners. After the emancipation of the Jews there also emerged some notable bankers, jurists, analytical chemists, musicians, composers, and historians. Almost without exception they settled after their studies in larger cities offering greater opportunities, notably Frankfurt, Mannheim, Berlin, Munich, and New York.

With few exceptions the Gernsheims were a hardy tribe known for their longevity. An astonishingly high number reached the patriarchal age of eighty to ninety years, and even more. A daughter of the *Judenbischof*, Regina Gernsheim, born in 1754, lived a hundred years and thirty days. Michael Gernsheim, founder-partner of the celebrated New York bankers Kuhn, Loeb & Co., reached the age of ninety-five. At ninety-two he completed a translation of Dante's *Divine Comedy* into English, and even one year prior to his death in 1933, cello playing was still part of his daily routine.[8] Rabbi Michael Gernsheim who died in 1749 in his eightieth year, is praised on the inscription on his

---

[6] *Wormser Zeitung*, 2nd December 1928, 'Das Ende einer alten Wormser Firma'.
[7] *Wormser Zeitung*, 5th September 1926, 'Die Entstehungsgeschichte des Hauses des Handwerks'.
[8] Dr. Guggenheim, 'Alte Jüdische Familien in Worms', *C.V.-Zeitung*, XIII, No. 22 (31st May 1934).

tombstone as "Prince and Leader, conversant not only in the Torah, but in all sciences, particularly in astronomy".

Captain Josef Gernsheim (1850–1912), later owner of a tanning factory, made history in the Franco-Prussian war. At the battle of Gravelotte, in August 1870, Josef, then a lad of twenty, was decorated for distinguished service and raised to the rank of captain, a quite unheard-of distinction at a time when Jews were barred from becoming officers in the German army. In 1912 he was buried with military honours. During the First World War the attitude of the army to Jews changed somewhat and another relation, Dr Eugen Gernsheim (1880–1966), entered the war as a cavalry captain and was discharged with the rank of major. Yet despite his distinguished record of military service he was dismissed in 1935 from his position as *Landgerichtsdirektor* of Berlin (president of the Berlin district court). He was forced by the Gestapo during the Second World War into a labour corps, serving first as a factory worker and later in a railway repair gang. He also spent two terms in a concentration camp, but was each time released. In June 1945 he was installed as judge in a lower court in Berlin, three years later re-installed in his pre-war position, and in January 1953 made President of the Senate, with the right to remain in office for an additional nine years, to compensate for the years he had been deprived of under the Nazis.

Up to the 1920s several Gernsheims retained strong ties with cultural life in their home town. For the 400th anniversary of the *Gymnasium* in 1927 my uncle Dr Alfred Gernsheim (1870–1931) undertook to write the *Festschrift*.[9] Prof. Friedrich Gernsheim (1839–1916) gave several concerts in Worms, the last in 1912. Today the largely forgotten composer and conductor is honoured by a street named after him. In 1966 Worms staged a Gernsheim Festival to commemorate the first half-century of his death. It had been planned for his 75th birthday, when the First World War intervened.

Friedrich, the son of a doctor, was born on 17th July 1839. Both his parents were highly musical, particularly so his mother who came from the very gifted Kaulla family in Augsburg. She was an excellent pianist and was often accompanied by her husband playing the flute. Very early the child displayed an exceptional talent for memorising the music he had heard and an ability in noting it down. His piano and violin teachers in Worms and Frankfurt considered the nine-year-old Friedrich a prodigy destined for a musical career. On 5th May 1850 he made his début in a concert in Frankfurt in the four-fold capacity of piano and violin soloist, and conductor of an overture composed by himself. An enthusiastic reception led his mother to take him on a concert tour to Karlsruhe, Strassburg, Basle, Mannheim and Cologne. Everywhere Fritz was hailed as "the little Mozart" becoming the talk of the town. A lithograph was published of him in 1852 holding the conductor's baton. Charlotte Kestner in Basle (daughter of Goethe's Lotte in Weimar) wrote excitedly to a friend: "My motive for writing is Fritz Gernsheim of Worms, a most lovable genius of

[9] Dr. Alfred Gernsheim, *Das Gymnasium zu Worms 1803–1813. Aus Anlass der 400-Jahrfeier des Gymnasiums nach den Quellen zusammengestellt*, Worms 1927.

ten and a half in music as in mentality . . . I don't like to voice the opinion of the masses in such a matter, but Fritz is irresistible for everyone."[10] In May 1852 Friedrich's exceptional talent opened to him the Leipzig conservatory. He was their youngest student. For two years such celebrated musicians as Ferdinand David (violin), Ignaz Moscheles (piano), Moritz Hauptmann (composition) and Julius Rietz, conductor of the famous Gewandhaus concerts were his teachers. They were unanimous in prophesying a brilliant future for him.

After further concerts in Worms, Strassburg and Nancy with works by Mendelssohn (piano concerto), Sivori (violin), Blumenthal, and his own as soloist, conductor and composer, the fifteen-year-old Friedrich was considered ready to absorb and profit from the unparalleled opportunities Paris, the musical centre of the world, had to offer. He gave recitals in the Salon of the Princess Troubetzkoi and found admiring crowds in several concerts at the "Salle Herz". At the same time he continued to study composition at the conservatoire, formed a life-long friendship with Camille Saint-Saëns, and was befriended by the sixty-five-year-old Rossini at whose receptions he heard and admired the greatest pianists of the time: Franz Liszt and Anton Rubinstein. In 1859/60 he attended the complete series of concert performances of Wagner's operas, conducted by the composer with the intention of preparing the French public for the première of his revised *Tannhäuser* at the opera in March 1861. Wagner's music opened a new world of sound to Friedrich. He was electrified by it, and for a time became an ardent Wagnerite. Yet in later years his enthusiasm waned, perhaps because Gernsheim was by nature a romantic coming under the influence of Brahms, perhaps on account of the deep-rooted antagonism against Wagner which he found in the rather conservative official circles he served for fifty years of his life. As late as 1900 he said to a friend: "To show admiration for Wagner here (the Royal Academy of Music in Berlin) is considered a crime."

The five years' stay in Paris was a valuable maturing stage for Gernsheim's future. Having decided against a career as soloist, to devote his time to composing and conducting, an opening occurred in this direction just as he was preparing to leave Paris in the spring of 1861. Hermann Levi, another Wagnerite with whom he had become friendly in Paris, decided to vacate his position as musical director of Saarbrücken for a better post in Rotterdam, and introduced Gernsheim as his successor. Saarbrücken was a good start for a musician of twenty-two, but very provincial and dull after five years spent in the glittering French metropolis. Gernsheim managed to hold on for four years, but was greatly relieved when Ferdinand Hiller, the "music pope of the Rhineland", offered him a teaching position at the Cologne conservatory. Here Engelbert Humperdinck became one of his pupils. Soon afterwards Gernsheim was also offered the direction of the Municipal orchestra and of the Choral Society, placing him in an important position in the musical life of Cologne and giving him much greater opportunities and experience than he had enjoyed at Saarbrücken. Training the choir to a high standard was no mean task, but this also

---

[10]The letter in German is quoted in full by Karl Holl in his biography of *Friedrich Gernsheim*, Leipzig 1928, p. 13–14.

stimulated his creative powers to compose several choral works (*Salamis, Roman Funeral, Nordic Summernight, Germania*) with the pleasure of getting them performed under his own direction. Apart from performances of Bach cantatas and works by Mendelssohn and Schumann Gernsheim became known for his lively support of his young contemporaries, notably Bruch, Gade and Brahms, in whose compositions he felt a certain affinity with his own.

The most outstanding event of his nine years' activity in Cologne was doubtless the first complete performance of Brahms' *German Requiem* on 10th November 1870 in memory of the dead of the late war with France. His superb rendering of this great work left a deep impression and marked an historic occasion. Brahms could unfortunately not be present at the performance, but he was deeply moved and sent Gernsheim the following letter from Vienna.

> Dear Mr. Gernsheim, Nov. 70
>
> You can imagine what great pleasure and honour it is for me to have my Requiem performed in commemoration of those who gave their lives at this great time. The thought moves me so deeply that I am unable to speak about it.
>
> I would have been present in Cologne, if my [financial] situation at this moment had made it somehow possible, and were I not soon to expect your visit the paper would be surprised how long a letter I could write.
>
> For today then only a few requests. I would like to have a keepsake of your performance and hope you can still get me a programme. Further, if you have an opportunity and find it proper, would you please express my thanks to the various bodies who have taken such painstaking trouble with my work. Naturally, you will have to make the longest speech to yourself! For it is thanks to you, above all, that the performance no doubt turned out decidedly better than my work is, unfortunately. Lastly, my kindest regards to our common acquaintances, above all to your mother and our maestro Hiller, and so forth to bankers and colleagues . . .
>
> We will soon meet here – so once more my hearty and sincere thanks.
>
> Yours Joh. Brahms.

Gernsheim, on whom the *Requiem* had left an unforgettable impression when Brahms had played to him extracts from the score two years previously while spending the summer in Bonn, repeated the performance on two further occasions in March and April 1871.

Meanwhile, in December 1870, Gernsheim had gone to Vienna at the instigation of Brahms to play his (Gernsheim's) piano concerto with the Vienna Philharmonic Society. It had already been received with acclamation in Basle, Cologne and Paris, each time with the composer as soloist. Gernsheim stayed for nearly a month, enjoying the sights of the Austrian capital under the expert guidance of his friend, his senior by six years. In the evenings, when not going to concerts or the opera together, they played their latest compositions to each other.

In 1872 the Duke of Coburg conferred on Gernsheim the title of Professor. In the winter of 1873/4 the thirty-five-year-old composer was offered the position of conductor at the new opera house in Cologne, in addition to his other duties as director of the Municipal orchestra and choir.

Gernsheim's experience in this new field was of comparatively brief duration, for in June 1874 he left Cologne to become director of the "Society for the Advancement of Music" in Rotterdam. His new duties placed him in charge of the orchestra, the choir and the opera – the only opera house in Holland to perform in German – as well as of the conservatory. One can hardly imagine how one man could carry out so many responsibilities in those days and yet find time to compose and travel. This position made him the leading authority on music in Holland, and Rotterdam became his home for the next sixteen years. It proved to be a very fruitful period for the country he served and for his own creative work. He was delighted by the high standards his predecessors had set, and the complete freedom of activity he enjoyed. It left him sufficient time for his numerous engagements as conductor and pianist of his own works, as guest conductor at the *Deutsche Oper* in Berlin, and for the writing of three symphonies, a violin concerto, a number of choral works, chamber and vocal music. In Berlin his performances of *Fidelio, Don Juan, Faust* and *Tannhäuser* were considered outstanding, though the latter gave rise to a speculation that Gernsheim was about to join the Wagner camp. This hope was, unfortunately, not fulfilled, despite efforts by Levi and von Bülow; yet how strong the antagonism to Wagner was in official circles can be gauged from the fact that even the (unfounded) rumour almost cost him the Berlin appointment a few years later.

Brahms paid several visits to Rotterdam, either as soloist in his piano concerto, or to hear one of his or his friend's new works performed. As time went on Friedrich's compositions became decidedly more Brahmsian in character, with staccato bars. Both were followers of the "classic-romantic" tradition, and their minds and methods lyric. In a like manner both composers refused to be drawn into the Wagner controversy. His spiritual affinity with Brahms was so marked that it earned him the designation of "the Dutch Brahms".

Into the Rotterdam period falls Gernsheim's marriage in 1877 to Helene Herrnsheim of Karlsruhe whom he had known from childhood, and the death of his mother, who after her husband's death in 1872 had rejoined Friedrich on his musical wanderings and remained a faithful companion until her death in 1889.

The following year Gernsheim became director of the Stern conservatory in Berlin and its teacher in composition. When these positions had been offered him ten years previously he understandably did not wish to give up his much wider field of influence in Rotterdam. However, now he felt ready to return to Germany, the additional appointment as artistic director of the famous Stern Choral Society tipping the scale. For the latter election Hans von Bülow had recommended him as "the right man in the right place". During the next fourteen years his performances of the greatest choral works in the repertoire, from Bach's *B minor Mass* to Verdi's *Requiem*, and including Handel, Haydn, Mozart, Beethoven, Mendelssohn, Schumann, Berlioz, Brahms, Bruch and Humperdinck became annual events of the metropolis, looked forward to with eager expectation. For a better understanding of Verdi's unfamiliar work – Gernsheim gave the first performance of the *Requiem* in Germany – he published a small handbook with musical annotations.[11]

For his nomination as a member of the Royal Academy of Music in 1892 he

[11]Prof. Friedrich Gernsheim, *Der Musikführer zu G. Verdi's Messa da Requiem*, Frankfurt a. Main, n.d.

had to write a cantata. He surprised everyone with a massive choral work for full orchestra *Hymn after the words of the Holy Scripture* which had its first performance the following year on the Kaiser's birthday. In September of the same year he conducted his *Hymn to Apollo*, written for the 50th anniversary of the Vienna Choral Society, at the *Hofburg* in the presence of the Emperor Franz Joseph and the Court. For the inauguration of the Kaiser Wilhelm Memorial Church in Berlin in November 1895, Gernsheim chose the rarely heard *Paulus Oratorio* by Mendelssohn. Collaboration of the Stern choir at a performance of Mahler's great *Resurrection* Symphony brought the two composers into close touch. Though their compositions were too different for either to feel more than polite interest in the other, Mahler performed Gernsheim's third symphony in Hamburg and was present at the first performance of his fourth with the Berlin Philharmonic under Nikisch. Gernsheim, on the other hand, was impressed by Mahler's song cycle *Des Knaben Wunderhorn*.

After Brahms's death Max Bruch, Professor of composition at the Berlin Academy, remained Gernsheim's main music friend. For twenty-five years they exchanged opinions and tried out their new compositions on each other. A large correspondence, now at the Jewish National Library in Jerusalem, bears witness to this friendship.

Having given up his teaching appointment at the Stern conservatory in 1897 with the intention of devoting more time to composition, Gernsheim was in 1901 placed in charge of the Masterschool for Composition at the Royal Academy. This was a life appointment entailing light duties and carrying a handsome stipend which enabled him to relinquish soon afterwards his directorship of the Stern choir. The last years, from 1902 to 1915, were a very productive period in which he wrote a fourth symphony, a cello concerto, the second violin concerto (which had a great success under Henri Marteau in Hamburg), a German *Te Deum* for orchestra and mixed choir, a trio, two quartets (which Joachim took up for his concerts), a tone poem and two song cycles, set to poems by O. J. Bierbaum and Ricarda Huch respectively. These late works are free from the influence of Brahms, and Gernsheim's biographer Karl Holl considers them his best and most mature works.

Despite the threats of war Dortmund kept to its arrangement for a two-day Gernsheim Festival to celebrate his 75th birthday in July 1914. The Royal Academy in Berlin honoured him with the election to Vice-President. It marked the zenith of his career, but he set greater store by his recognition as a composer. In October of the following year he was thrown into the abyss of distress by the tragic death of his elder and favourite daughter who was only twenty-one years old. This terrible shock began to affect his health, and eventually led to his own death on 10th September 1916. An *In Memoriam* for string orchestra, organ and voice was his last completed work. His wife Helene followed him eleven years later to the cemetery in Berlin-Weissensee. Friedrich Gernsheim's second daughter, the actress Clara Pick-Gernsheim died in Tel-Aviv in 1974, a grand old lady of eighty-eight.

Friedrich Gernsheim's opus comprises ninety-two main works, twenty-five youthful compositions (prior to 1861) and twenty unnumbered works. Among the former are four symphonies, two violin concertos, a piano concerto, a cello concerto, a large number of choral works with orchestra, quartets, sonatas for violin or piano, and songs. They are rarely performed nowadays outside Israel, but this does not mean that his work may not be rediscovered one day, as Mahler and Bruckner, Albinoni and Vivaldi were in our day. After the Second World War Mrs. Pick-Gernsheim obtained from the Berlin Academy of Music a stack of her father's printed music sheets that were found in a basement. This she presented to the National Library in Jerusalem on the 50th anniversary of his death, adding her own collection of MS scores and piano arrangements, pictures and documents and nearly 500 autograph letters from composers, conductors and soloists, 315 of them by Max Bruch.

According to his daughter Friedrich Gernsheim was small of stature with strong oriental features. On the rostrum he was like a general directing the orchestra with vigour and complete self-assurance. His conducting was admired for the objective adherence to the composer's directions. He would have been shocked by the subjective interpretations that became fashionable with Toscanini. His biographer considers that his genius found its finest expression in his inspired compositions which are polished in form, showing an amazing inventiveness of ideas and melodies. Unable to put forward any personal opinion, having only once heard a *Fantasy and Fugue for Organ*, a late work (op. 76) which I would have ascribed to Reger without knowing the programme, I prefer to quote, as a probably fair summary of Gernsheim's achievements, a contemporary English critic.[12]

> "Gernsheim's numerous works display the most solid worth, even though the academic quality is present at times. Of his four symphonies, the first and last are most frequently given. For mixed chorus and orchestra he has composed several great works, the *Nordische Sommernacht* (Nordic Summernight, op. 21), and *Der Nornen Wiegenlied* (Lullaby of the Norns, op. 65) being among these. Of his male choruses, also with orchestra, such works as *Salamis* (op. 10) and the medieval *Waechterlied* (op. 7) are in the repertoire of every German male choir. There are many worthy examples of chamber music by him, also a violin concerto (the 2nd, op. 86) that won a Boston success under Paur."

Wilhelm Gernsheim, born in Mannheim on 15th January 1899, is another composer in the family – though descended from a different branch in Worms. In 1880 his father Ludwig had founded there with a partner the private bank of "Gernsheim & Wachenheim" which flourished until his death in 1930. His mother Martha Laudon had been a soprano opera singer in her native Hamburg and later in Mannheim, and it is doubtless from her that Wilhelm Gernsheim inherited his musical talent. It was for her voice that he began to write little poems and set them to music from the age of nine. He studied at the *Musikhochschule* in his home town, making his first concert appearance, in April 1919, with Schumann's toccata and a ballad by Chopin. On completion of his studies he published three song cycles of which his *Japanese Miniatures* and *Arabian Nights* enjoyed considerable success with Austrian and German singers up to 1932. He also wrote a *Trio*, first heard in Heidelberg in 1923, and a *Rondo* for violin and chamber orchestra which had its first performance in Mannheim in

---

[12]Arthur Elsen, *Modern Composers of Europe*, London 1909, p. 51.

1927. A comic opera, *Der Goldene Topf*, after a story by E. T. A. Hoffmann, remained unfinished. It was as a lyrical song writer that Gernsheim's talent was most evident, and in these his spiritual affinity with the masters in this genre, Schubert and Schumann, was unmistakable, as a critic pointed out in 1928.[13]

His first major work, a mystic song drama *Der Ackermann und der Tod* for which he adapted and set to music a work written by Johann von Saaz about 1400, was completed in 1934. His work having been banned by the Nazis the previous year from being publicly performed or published, it was printed under the pseudonym "W. F. Laudon" (his mother's maiden name) which he then adopted. Written for mixed choir and orchestra, a boys' choir, organ, cembalo and solo voice parts this dramatic work lasting two hours had its first performance in the Martin Church, Basle, on 5th May 1935. Its setting to polyphonic baroque church music seemed most apt for the timelessness of the theme: the eternal enigma of death. Despite the traditional form and harmony the musical expression was free from pastiche, and Laudon's mystic drama found a strong echo in the Basle press.[14] Yet instead of turning this excellent reception of his work to his advantage by seeking an opportunity for a continuation of his musical career in exile, however precarious, Gernsheim made the cardinal mistake of returning to Germany to study for a profession that would secure him later a living abroad.

This mistake cost him fifteen of his best years, and when he eventually found himself free to return to his beloved music he was an ill man and too old to adapt himself to the life and language of a foreign country. But I am anticipating the order of events. With his musical career wrecked by the Nazi régime Gernsheim studied dental medicine in Heidelberg. As a "half-Jew" he was not barred from the university, and despite his intense dislike for dentistry it was as Dr. med. dent. that he hoped to find peace of mind when he settled in a Yugoslav resort. With the German occupation of that country in 1941 his idyllic life came to an unexpected and sudden end. He was sent back to Germany and put to work in a military hospital until the end of the war.

By 1947 Gernsheim seems to have picked up the old threads again, for we find him in charge of the musical direction of an opera concert in Heidelberg with scenes from Bizet's *Carmen* and himself at the piano. In May 1948 his mystic drama *Der Ackermann und der Tod* was well received at its first performance in Germany, at Christ Church, Heidelberg – this time under his own name. Yet despite these propitious beginnings he was determined to leave Germany, and eventually in 1950 he obtained permission from the Swedish Government to settle in Gothenburg. Here he became a member of the Music-Pedagogical Society, and soon afterwards obtained a position as a part-time teacher for piano and the theory of music at the Margarete Music school. His free time was entirely devoted to composing. Gernsheim's Swedish opus comprises over two hundred songs, a *Concerto grosso* for full orchestra, and a Suite *O Menschenherz, was ist dein Glück?* This Suite, written for string quartet, cembalo, flute and alto

---
[13]Dr. Karl Anton, 'Willi Gernsheim', *Rheinische Musik-und Theater Zeitung*, XXIX, No. 23/24 (16th June 1928).
[14]*Basler Nachrichten* and the *National Zeitung*, on 6th May 1935; *Basler Volksblatt* on 7th May 1935.

voice was first performed in Mannheim in 1958. Most of the other works were first heard in concerts in Gothenburg and Stockholm.

After the opening of my exhibition at the Gothenburg Art Museum in April 1956 I was surprised when Wilhelm announced himself as my "cousin". We had never heard of each other before, but publicity sometimes does wonders. We spent many a day in each other's company, my wife and I listening for hours to extracts from various compositions Wilhelm played for us on the piano or cembalo. A great admirer of eighteenth- and early nineteenth-century music, it is perhaps not surprising that his own writing retained some of the period flavour, and this restricted performances to select audiences. What had struck Swiss critics in 1935 as a novelty and considered as "an audacious flight from our restless time into a period of tranquillity fitting the text" was a form of expression that seemed strange in a contemporary composer, although the outstanding lyrical qualities of Wilhelm Gernsheim's music were never disputed. Ten years later the nostalgia for a bygone time was reawakened, but in 1956 few listeners had the taste for it. My cousin was aware of this too, but he had neither the inclination nor the strength to live up to contemporary expectations. He himself was essentially a dreamer living in the past.

In Gothenburg Wilhelm Gernsheim felt like a fish out of water. The translation of his German song texts, poems by Bethge, Claudius, Lenau, Bierbaum and himself, or from *Des Knaben Wunderhorn* etc. into an unfamiliar foreign idiom was in itself an irksome task. Unable to meet the costs of a music printer he and his future wife Karin printed off scores on a duplicating machine. The sheets were then bound and numbered for presentation.

Wilhelm Gernsheim died in 1975 in his seventy-seventh year. The allegory of the ploughman and death was his own philosophy of life: all happiness is transitory and all earthly things unimportant, or "What shall it profit a man, if he shall gain the whole world and lose his own soul?" His music was his soul, and for the pleasure he gained from it Wilhelm was willing to forfeit renown and honours.

Germany and Palestine

The Esra Verein and Jewish Colonisation in Palestine

BY JEHUDA REINHARZ

Following the murder of Czar Alexander II on 1st March 1881, a reactionary government under Alexander III came to power in Russia. Shortly after the new Czar's accession to the throne, a wave of pogroms spread throughout Southern Russia during the summer months, destroying dozens of Jewish communities. The official reactionary policy of the new régime condoned the pogroms and instituted the "May Laws" of 1882 limiting Russian Jews to the contracted "Pale of Settlement". The persecution of the Jews continued under the reign of Nikolai II (1894–1917), during which ruthless pogroms and expulsions persisted with government approval.[1]

The pogroms of 1881 became a turning point in Jewish history, shattering forever the hope of real emancipation in Eastern Europe. The largest emigration and population transfer in Jewish history followed, during which most of the emigrés went to the United States. This large-scale movement also affected Germany and German Jewry. From the turn of the century until the First World War, Germany shared a border with Russia. Because of its geographical proximity and access to the sea, Germany became the transit country for Eastern European Jews travelling to the United States, many of whom chose to settle in Germany for a variety of personal reasons. During these years, therefore, the number of Eastern European Jews in Germany increased dramatically. The philanthropic organisations of Western Jewry, particularly German-Jewish organisations, undertook to help these Eastern European Jews primarily by organising and directing the emigration to America and other countries.[2]

The Russian pogroms had a great impact on segments of German Jewry and helped shape their attitude towards the settlement of Palestine. Throughout the nineteenth century efforts to rebuild and settle Palestine or to help its Jewish inhabitants came from orthodox circles whose motivations were religious and philanthropic. Following the pogroms and the reawakening of national feelings among Eastern European Jewry, an increasing number of German Jews talked about the settlement of Palestine within a Jewish national context. Plans for rebuilding Palestine became more concrete and associations which promoted

---

*The author would like to express his gratitude to Dr. Michael Heymann for his comments on an earlier draft of this article.
[1]Simon Dubnow, *History of the Jews in Russia and Poland*, Philadelphia 1918, II, pp. 243 ff. See also *Ha-Zefirah*, No. 135 (19th June/1st July 1891), pp. 548 ff.
[2]Shalom Adler-Rudel, *Ostjuden in Deutschland 1880–1940. Zugleich eine Geschichte der Organisationen, die sie betreuten*, Tübingen 1959 (Schriftenreihe wissenschaftlicher Abhandlungen des Leo Baeck Instituts 1), p. 6. See also Zosa Szajkowski, 'The European Attitude to East European Jewish Immigration (1881–1893)', in *Publications of the American Jewish Historical Society*, XLI, No. 2 (December 1951).

such ideas were no longer confined to the orthodox. The main problem of these new associations was the raising of adequate funds to execute their ideas.[3]

The first German association with this purpose, the *B'nai B'rith* of Kattowitz, was founded in 1882 by Selig Freuthal and Moritz Moses. This fifty-member association was linked to similar societies in Russia, Romania and Austria and published a 'Monatsbericht'. Towards the end of 1882 the *B'nai B'rith* began publishing *Der Colonist* which in 1883 became a weekly subtitled 'Zeitschrift für Beförderung der Emigration der Juden aus den Ländern in denen ihre Menschenrechte nicht geschützt sind'. *Der Colonist* was German Jewry's first organ devoted wholly to matters concerning Palestine.[4] In early 1884 Professor Hermann Schapira of Heidelberg established the *Zion* organisation whose main purpose was "the dissemination of knowedge of Hebrew history, language and literature amongst Jews . . . the fulfilment of the idea of colonisation amongst Jews".[5] Response to *Zion* was meagre and so were its accomplishments.

At the initiative of the *B'nai B'rith* a conference was convened in Kattowitz in November 1884 of all *Hovevei Zion* associations in Eastern and Western Europe concerned with the settlement of Palestine. These organisations elected an executive committee headed by Leon Pinsker. As a direct result of this conference the *Ahavass Zijon* organisation was founded in Hamburg in May 1885.[6] Pinsker had a staunch supporter in Germany in the person of Rabbi Isaak Rülf of Memel who for twenty years had been a member of the *Israelitischer Verein zur Kolonisation von Palästina*. Under the impact of Pinsker's *Autoemanzipation, ein Mahnruf an seine Stammesgenossen von einem russischen Juden* (1882), Rülf published his *Aruchas Bas-Ami, Israel's Heilung* which demanded a return to Palestine.[7]

Pinsker's pamphlet appeared at the time that scores of *Hovevei Zion* societies emerged spontaneously and simultaneously in the Russian Empire and in Romania. The most important material achievement of the *Hibbat Zion* movement was the establishment in the 1880s and 1890s of the first farming settlements in Palestine.[8] Initiated by the *Bilu*, a group of Jewish students from

---

[3] Mordechai Eliav, *Ahavat Zion v'Anshei Hod, Yehudei Germania v'Yishuv Erez Israel ba-Meah ha-19*, Tel-Aviv 1970, pp. 355–356.

[4] For the *B'nai B'rith*'s first public proclamation and statutes, as well as the *Monatsberichte* see Central Archives for the History of the Jewish People (CAHJP), GA Beuthen, S97/20. See also Israel Klausner '*Ha-Agudah B'nai B'rith b'Kattowitz*', *Sefer ha-Yovel mugash likhvod Dr. N. M. Gelber* (edited by Israel Klausner, Raphael Mahler and Dov Sadan), Tel-Aviv 1962; and Jacob Toury, '*Ha-Gilayon ha-Rishon shel Haluz Kitvei Ha-Et shel Hovevei Zion ba-Lashon ha-Germanit*', in *Hazionut*, III, Tel-Aviv 1973.

[5] Alter Druyanov, *Ktavim le-Toldot Hibbat Zion v'Yishuv Erez Israel*, I, Tel-Aviv 1925, pp. 206–211. Interestingly, the statutes of the *Zion* were originally written in Hebrew. They clearly state that in case of any doubt, the original Hebrew version was to be regarded as authoritative.

[6] Central Zionist Archives (CZA), A 147/23/2.

[7] Reuwen Michael, 'Israels Heilung. Isaak Rülf und die Anfänge des Zionismus in Deutschland', in *Bulletin des Leo Baeck Instituts*, VI (1963), No. 22, pp. 126 ff.; Mordechai Eliav, 'Zur Vorgeschichte der jüdischen Nationalbewegung in Deutschland', in *Bulletin des Leo Baeck Instituts*, XII (1969), No. 48.

[8] On the background and origin of the *Hibbat Zion* movement see David Vital, *The Origins of Zionism*, Oxford 1975, parts one and two. There were earlier attempts at colonisation by the so-called "Old *Yishuv*" – notably in Petah Tikva in 1878 – but this and other attempts failed. Thus the new arrivals from Russia and Romania found an urban Jewish population of only

Russian high schools and universities who wanted to lay the foundations for the renaissance of the Jewish people in *Erez Israel*, they were joined by other pioneers, some of whom had modest savings. All of these settlers were imbued with idealism and hope that soon a mass immigration would follow in their wake which would help rebuild the land.[9]

In 1882 the settlers from Russia and later from Romania founded Rishon le-Zion in the South, Zikhron Ya'akov near Haifa and Rosh Pina in the Upper Galilee. In 1883 immigrants from Poland founded Yesud ha-Ma'ala near Lake Huleh and others restored Petah Tikva north of Jaffa.[10] Despite their enthusiasm, the immigrants were unprepared for the task at hand, possessing neither sufficient material resources, physical stamina, nor adequate agricultural knowledge to make the colonies economically viable. In addition, they were exposed to malaria, Bedouin raids, harsh climate and the constant difficulties imposed by the Ottoman régime. The endangered settlements were saved only by the financial generosity of Baron Edmond de Rothschild of Paris.[11]

At the same time the Czarist régime in Russia promoted the oppressive measures against Jews to the level of public policy. The cumulative consequence of numerous restrictions against Jews, culminating in their expulsion from Moscow in 1891–1892 gave rise to a renewed mass immigration. Paradoxically, this exodus was aided by Russia's legalisation of the *Hovevei Zion*'s central arm, the "Odessa Committee" (1890), which had formerly been an illegal organisation but which was now seen to aid Russia's aim of ridding itself of the Jews. By 1914 two million Jews are estimated to have left Russia, some of whom founded new settlements in Palestine: Hadera (1890), Rehovot (1890), Mishmar Ha-Yarden (1890), Bnei Yehuda (1891), Ein Zeitim (1891), Meir Shefeya (1891), Moza (1894), Hartuv (1895), Beer Tuvia (1896), Metula (1896), Mahanayim (1899) and the Sejera Training Farm (1899). Thus, by 1900 there were twenty-two Jewish rural settlements widely dispersed throughout Palestine on 76,000 acres with a total Jewish rural population of 5,210 managing 705 farms.[12]

These were modest but important gains. When the First Zionist Congress convened in Basle in 1897, fifteen years had elapsed since the beginning of modern Jewish settlements in Palestine. Theodor Herzl and the World Zionist

---

24,000 and a rural Jewish population of some 480 people, as well as the agricultural school Mikveh Israel founded in 1870 by Charles Netter on behalf of the *Alliance Israélite Universelle*.

[9]See Israel Klausner, *Be-Hitorer Am*, Jerusalem 1962, and Alex Bein, *Toldot ha-Hityashvut ha-Zionit* (fourth edition), Ramat Gan 1970.

[10]Israel Klausner, *Mi-Kattowitz ad Basle*, Jerusalem 1965, I, II; and *Hibbat Zion be-Romania*, Jerusalem 1958.

[11]See Israel Margalith, *Le Baron Edmond de Rothschild et la colonisation juive en Palestine, 1882–1889*, Paris 1957. It is estimated that the total amount invested by Baron Edmond de Rothschild in the Jewish settlements in Palestine was £5·6 millions, of which £1·6 million was invested between 1883–1889. During the same period (1882–1889) the total investment of all *Hovevei Zion* societies in Russia, Romania and Central and Western Europe was about £87,000. See Bein, *Toldot*, p. 10, note 1.

[12]David Gurevich and Aaron Gertz, *Ha-Hityashvut ha-haklait ha-Ivrit be-Erez Israel*, Jerusalem 1938, p. 31 and Abraham Revusky, *Jews in Palestine*, London 1938, pp. 10–12. See also Willy Bambus, *Die jüdischen Ackerbaukolonien in Palästina und ihre Geschichte*, Berlin 1895, in CZA, A142/34; Willy Bambus, *Palästina in der Gegenwart*, Berlin [1891].

Organization were greatly influenced by the achievements of these early settlements. Those founded between 1882 and 1900 undoubtedly created the model and framework for all subsequent colonisation.

In the final months of 1883 a small group of young men in Berlin held several preparatory meetings to establish a new organisation. One of the earliest records states that the group's purpose was the "dissemination of knowledge of Jewish history and literature". But this common denominator among the group's interests was soon recognised as ancillary at best. Their true interest was encouragement of Jewish settlement in Palestine. Unlike other German organisations with this interest, the members of the new group were neither important rabbis nor even orthodox in many cases. The founding members' positive approach to the Jewish community in Palestine might have been influenced by Rabbi Esriel Hildesheimer. Their chief impetus, however, was news of the establishment of *Hovevei Zion* groups in Eastern Europe and the plight of pogrom victims, some of whom had found refuge in Palestine. Moreeover, German Jewry's lack of understanding and sympathy for colonisation was disheartening to these seven relatively unknown and inexperienced men who decided to establish a large association with branches throughout Germany and possibly even abroad. Funds for the colonists and colonisation in Palestine would be collected by this broad membership. The purpose was not to imitate the *Halukkah* system – the organised collection of funds in the Diaspora for distribution among the needy – but rather the opposite, i.e., to help Jewish farmers in Palestine become self-sufficient and independent of *Halukkah*. The association was formally established in Berlin on 26th January 1884 with the rather modest name: *Esra, Sammelbüchse für Palästina*.[13]

In its first public circular, dated *circa* March 1884, the *Esra* stated:

> "Though the famed Jewish beneficence has been particularly grand toward Palestine and though ample donations have been flowing to Palestine since time immemorial, they have all fallen far short of even adequately supporting our many brethren who live there condemned to a life of involuntary idleness and poverty. Need and sickness rage among Palestinian Jewry to the delight of missionaries who cast their nets among our starving brethren and promote an unbelievable trade in souls.
>
> "In view of the fact that until now the mode of assistance has been a planless squandering of funds and energy and has only resulted in missionaries viewing the Holy Land as a fertile hunting ground and its half-starved Jewish inhabitants as their prey; in view of the fact that farming in Palestine is blessed with an auriferous soil and is currently the only reliable source of income; in the conviction finally, that with methodical, rational management, the millions spent for support of the poor could be easily used for the purchase of land in Palestine which could be inhabited by capable and willing Jewish farmers, many associations were formed in Russia and Romania, which during their three-year existence have established eight colonies (Mikveh Israel,[14] Rishon le-Zion, Rosh Pina, Yesud Hamaala, Samarin,[15] Ekron and Gedera)[16] with a population of 2,000!

[13]*Die Jüdische Presse*, Nos. 15/16 (9th April 1884), p. 160. The seven men who established the *Esra* were: Behrmann, J. Cohn, Dr. H. Hirschfeld, Max Karfunkel, H. Norwitzky, Isaak Turoff and Weinreich. Eliav, in 'Zur Vorgeschichte' lists different names. It seems that he lists the members of the first executive committee who were not all among the founders of the *Esra*.
[14]Not established by the *Hovevei Zion*. See previous paragraphs.
[15]Zikhron Ya'akov.
[16]In fact, only seven settlements are listed here.

"Should we German Jews dissociate ourselves completely from these new endeavours of unforeseen consequences? Our continuously persecuted and oppressed, impoverished and starving brethren in Russia still find the time for great creations. Should we German Jews, who under a just and impartial government enjoy the full protection of the law, look on idly? Should the Russian Jews shame us, we, who since the days of Mendelssohn have taken over the intellectual leadership of Jewry?

"The undersigned Central-Comité, which has inscribed on its banner the support of Jewish farmers in Palestine as well as the battle against missionary activities there, turns to you, you men and women in Jewry in whose breasts a warm Jewish heart still beats for the welfare of your brethren, with the request to join everywhere the local committees, which in co-ordination with the central committee in Berlin will seek to achieve the noble goal; and no-one whose heart harks back to the magnificent past of his people will shun our request and evade doing his duty in support of our goal."[17]

During its early years *Esra* probably chose to emphasise the battle against missionary activities directed toward the Jews of Palestine so as to gain the financial support of German Jewry for the organisation. The defeat of missionary activities, however, never became the *Esra*'s main concern. Clearly, colonisation was the major objective of the founders.[18] Initially, the statutes stipulated that no more than one third of the funds not used for propaganda could be used in Palestine while the rest was earmarked for organisational interests in Germany. These initial restrictions on expenditure in Palestine were quickly rescinded.[19]

The main office of the *Esra* was located in Berlin and headed by the journalist Max Karfunkel and his deputy, Dr. H. Hirschfeld.[20] The executive committee consisted of nine members including a chairman, a treasurer, and all the founding members.[21] Membership was open to adult men and women who paid minimum yearly dues of 50 Pfg.[22] The association established a network throughout Germany. Active *Esra* members who were able to recruit ten new members were given the honorary title *Gabbe*; those successful in recruiting one hundred new members were honoured with the title *Obergabbe*. As part of its efforts to increase membership, the *Esra* also distributed medals: a silver Star of David to the *Gabbe* category and a golden one to the *Obergabbe* group.[23]

---

[17] *Esra, Sammelbüchse für Palästina*, 'Aufruf!', Berlin 1884. The appeal ended with the Talmudic prescriptions: *Vehamosif yosifu lo min hashamayim*. (*Tractate Beitza* 16:A) and *Israel rahmanim bnei rahmanim hem!* (*Tractate Kiddushin* 4:A) *The Encyclopaedia Judaica*, Jerusalem 1973, VI, p. 895, erroneously lists the date of the circular as being end of 1886.

[18] The first paragraph of the statutes of 1884 mentions both the battle against missionary activities and the colonisation in Palestine as the twin aims of the *Esra*: "Der Verein hat den Zweck, die jüdischen Kolonien in Palästina zu unterstützen, sowie den Missionsbestrebungen daselbst entgegenzukommen". Later statutes did not mention missionary activities at all. See, e.g., 'Statut des Vereins Esra' [1900?]; CZA, A1/2/2/6.

[19] See 'Statut des Vereins Esra', under 'Verwendung des Vereinsvermögens'; CZA, A1/2/2/6.

[20] *Esra, Sammelbüchse für Palästina*, No. 2 (23rd February 1885), p. 4 and *Die Jüdische Presse*, Nos. 15/16 (9th April 1884), p. 160. The members of the first executive committee were: Max Karfunkel, Dr. H. Hirschfeld, Max Hirschfeld, H. Norwitzky, Adolf Sandheim and Louis Lazarus.

[21] In fact, the number of members of the executive committee varied greatly, at times consisting of only four members and at other times reaching fifteen or more.

[22] The *Festschrift zum fünfundzwanzigjährigen Jubiläum des Esra*, Berlin 1909, p. 2, indicates that the membership dues were 50 Pfg. It was doubled to one Mark in 1886, see *Jeschurun*, No. 19 (13th May 1886).

[23] *Festschrift*, pp. 2–3.

Exactly one year after the establishment of the *Esra*, on 26th January 1885, the *Esra* commenced publication of a periodical under the editorship of Max Hirschfeld with a title identical to that of the association – *Esra, Sammelbüchse für Palästina*.²⁴ Membership figures for the association climbed quickly: on 28th April 1884 the *Esra* executive committee reported over 1,500 members;²⁵ less than a month later, on 18th May 1884 it reported 2,350 members;²⁶ and during the first general membership meeting which took place in January 1885, the leadership of the *Esra* reported over 3,000 registered members.²⁷ Among the first to join was Hirsch Hildesheimer, the son of Rabbi Esriel Hildesheimer and the editor of *Die Jüdische Presse*, who brought with him others from the orthodox camp. The income from these members, however, was very disappointing: 1,331 Mark in 1884 which dwindled to 894 Mark the following year.²⁸ The first sums of money (300 Mark) to be sent to Palestine were transferred through Rabbi Adolf Salvendi, who was active in the association *Esrat Nidachim*.²⁹ This method of transfer of funds was unusual and did not comply with the *Esra*'s statutes which required direct involvement of the association in Palestine. Hildesheimer's request for larger sums for *Esrat Nidachim* was rejected on the grounds that *Esra* wished to collect larger sums of money before disbursing them. The minutes of the meeting at which this matter was discussed indicate that although the membership was unsure precisely how funds should be expended, they firmly rejected any method resembling *Halukkah*. They argued that by having access to large sums of money Jewish farmers would become self-sufficient and thus immune to the pressure of missionaries.³⁰

By mid-1885 the *Esra* had members in eighty-three German cities and in twenty-nine cities abroad.³¹ Nevertheless, its meagre income prevented the carrying out of meaningful activities. The low morale of the organisation was compounded by the lack of a strong, prestigious leadership. The officers elected during the first general meeting (e.g., Hirsch Hildesheimer and Dr. Gustav Karpeles) declined re-election for various reasons, and thus the unknown Dr. H. Hirschfeld succeeded Max Karfunkel as president of the *Esra* on 2nd February 1885.³² These circumstances resulted in the continued decline of membership and income.

Hirschfeld and his associates recognised the necessity of reorganising to reverse the organisation's downhill trend. Membership dues were increased

---

²⁴This publication had a circulation of 500–1,000 copies. It ceased publication by mid-1885. See *Jeschurun*, No. 19 (13th May 1886).
²⁵*Der Israelit*, No. 36 (5th May 1884), p. 603.
²⁶*Ibid.*, No. 41 (22nd May 1884), p. 692.
²⁷*Esra, Sammelbüchse für Palästina*, No. 2 (23rd February 1885), p. 5 and Nos. 3/4 (3rd April 1885). See also *Der Israelit*, No. 13 (16th February 1885), pp. 218–219.
²⁸*Festschrift*, p. 9.
²⁹It seems that 150 Mark were sent in 1884 and 150 Mark in 1885. The full name of the association with which Salvendi was connected was *Esrat Nidachim le-Tiferet Moshe ve-Yehudit* established in 1883 in Palestine for the purpose of helping Palestinian Jews find work and acquire skills in various crafts. See *Der Israelit*, No. 41 (22nd May 1884), p. 692; and No. 13 (16th February 1885), pp. 218–219 as well as Eliav, *Ahavat Zion*, pp. 305–308.
³⁰*Esra, Sammelbüchse für Palästina*, No. 2 (23rd February 1885), p. 6 and No. 5 (24th April 1885).
³¹*Ibid.*
³²*Ibid.*, Nos. 3/4 (3rd April 1885), p. 12.

from 50 Pfg. to one Mark and publication of the *Esra, Sammelbüchse für Palästina* was discontinued to conserve funds. At the end of January 1886 after the second general membership meeting, the statutes were revised to reflect *Esra*'s focus on activities devoted to the colonisation of Palestine.[33] With this change, *Esra* saw itself as a parallel organisation to the *Hovevei Zion* in Russia.[34] An office was established in Berlin with a small full-time staff to handle the voluminous correspondence, solicit funds and increase membership. The strategy was to create local committees in those cities containing large concentrations of members such as Berlin, Hamburg, and Kattowitz, where Moritz Moses, a cofounder of *B'nai B'rith* became head of the *Esra* as well. In February 1886 the *Esra* began directly supporting Jewish colonies in Palestine by sending 1,000 Mark to Yesud ha-Ma'ala. The *Esra*'s support for this colony continued for many years.[35]

The impact of the *Esra*'s reorganisation did not immediately affect its income which in 1886 amounted only to 1,500 Mark.[36] Of greater significance was Willy Bambus's joining of the local committee in Berlin soon after its establishment in June 1886. Bambus also joined the *Esra*'s executive committee and was the driving force behind all its activities until his death in 1904. Bambus's complete dedication to the idea of practical colonisation in Palestine had a pervasive influence on the *Esra*.[37] Another important milestone in the organisation's development was the establishment of the monthly *Serubabel* beginning in September 1886.[38] The founder of this publication was the Russian-born Albert Katz, while Bambus was its publisher and moving spirit.[39] Members of the editorial board included Isaak Turoff, a founder and future secretary of the *Esra*, and Ferdinand Wolff, a leader in the *Ahavass Zijon* of Hamburg. During its two years of existence – until July 1888 – the *Serubabel* functioned as the main organ of the widely dispersed *Hovevei Zion* groups in Western and Eastern Europe whose activities it tried to coordinate. The columns of *Serubabel* were devoted to matters of colonisation, reports on *Hovevei Zion* groups throughout Europe, and refutation of arguments against colonisation in Palestine or the existence of Jewish national feeling. For these reasons the *Serubabel* devoted

---

[33]At this meeting Adolf Sandheim was elected president of the *Esra*.
[34]*Beilage zur Jüdischen Presse*, No. 19 (13th May 1886); *Der Israelit*, No. 39 (17th May 1886), p. 670; *Jeschurun*, No. 19 (13th May 1886), pp. 293–294.
[35]*Jahres-Bericht der* (sic!) *Vereins Esra pro 1886*, Berlin 1887: *Serubabel*, No. 3 (11th March 1887). The funds were sent to Palestine through Hirsch Hildesheimer.
[36]*Festschrift*, p. 9. See also the sceptical attitude of the orthodox *Jeschurun* toward the reorganisation efforts: *Jeschurun*, No. 19 (13th May 1886), pp. 293–294.
[37]Willy Bambus (1862–1904), author and editor, was born in Berlin. He came from an assimilated family and turned later to orthodoxy. In 1889–1891 he edited the *Jüdisches Volksblatt* in Vienna. One of the founders of the *Verein für Geschichte und Literatur* in Berlin (1892) and of *Jung Israel*: he was owner and editor of *Zion* in Berlin from 1897. Later he also became active in the *Hilfsverein der deutschen Juden* of which he became secretary.
[38]The first issue of *Serubabel*, subtitled: *Organ für die Interessen des jüdischen Volkes*, appeared on 29th September 1886.
[39]See letter of Willy Bambus to Leon Pinsker of 12th November 1886 notifying him of the establishment of a newspaper, in Alter Druyanov, *Ktavim*, III, pp. 864–865. See also Jehuda Louis Weinberg, *Aus der Frühzeit des Zionismus*, Jerusalem 1946, p. 85.

much space to news about the *Esra* and was perceived therefore by some individuals as an official organ of the association.[40]

Although the *Esra* gained national and even international recognition among *Hovevei Zion* groups, its income and membership did not increase. The election of a wealthy banker, Max Itzig, to the presidency of the association in 1887, saw the income remaining constant at 1,500 Mark, rising to almost 2,000 Mark in 1888 and dropping again to 1,300 Mark the following year Thus, for all practical purposes the association was at a standstill for several years, its activities in Palestine being limited to continued support for Yesud ha-Ma'ala.[41] In 1889 when Hirsch Hildesheimer joined the *Esra*'s executive committee, his paper, *Die Jüdische Presse*, instead of the defunct *Serubabel*, became its chief public supporter.[42] In the eyes of many the *Esra* was henceforth identified with Hildesheimer's circle.

During the late 1880s and early 1890s Jewish colonisation in Palestine and Jewish national ideas in Germany were on the increase. The first consciously nationalist group in Germany was the *Russischer Jüdischer Wissenschaftlicher Verein* founded in December 1888. Its charter members were twelve Russian-Jewish students joined by Heinrich Loewe of Wanzleben, who sought to alleviate the plight of Jewish refugees passing through Germany.[43] A counterpart to the Russian association was established by Heinrich Loewe in May 1892 in Berlin. Under the name *Jung Israel* it sought to attract German Jews to its ranks. As the *Hovevei Zion* movement in Germany gained momentum, its centre of activities was moved from Vienna to Berlin. After the folding of the *Selbst-Emancipation* because of renewed financial difficulties in 1893, it was transferred to Berlin under the name *Jüdische Volkszeitung, früher Selbst-Emancipation*. This new organ and the *Jung Israel* became the focal points of Jewish national activity in Germany.[44]

Despite the efforts of its approximately twenty members, the *Jung Israel* was seen as too radical to attract German-born Jews of the middle class to its

---

[40]See, e.g., *Serubabel*, No. 2 (1st November 1886), and No. 3 (1st December 1886). In the latter issue the editors felt constrained to publish the following note: "Es ist . . . in weiten Kreisen die Ansicht vebreitet, unsere Zeitung 'Serubabel' werde im Auftrage des Central-Comités des Vereins Esra herausgegeben. Diese Meinung ist eine irrthümliche. Obwohl der eventuelle Reingewinn von unserem Blatte für Colonisationszwecke verwendet werden soll, so wird der 'Serubabel' doch vollständig mit *Privatmitteln* herausgegeben. Der Verein Esra wird freilich von uns nach Kräften unterstützt, aber nur weil die Ziele des Esra sich zum grossen Theil mit den Unserigen decken. Aus demselben Grunde werden wir auch alle andere Palästinavereine bereitwillig unterstützen, denn der 'Serubabel' ist ein Organ für die Interessen des jüdischen Volkes, nicht für die eines einzigen Palästinavereines."

[41]*Festschrift*, p. 8.

[42]Eliav, *Ahavat Zion*, p. 310.

[43]See the statutes of the Verein in CZA, A126/12/1; See also *Selbst-Emancipation*, No. 3 (2nd February 1891), and *Selbst-Emancipation*, No. 22 (16th November 1891). In May of 1888 was founded the association Lemaan Zion, see Druyanov, *Ktavim*, I, pp. 611–613 and *Die Jüdische Presse* (May 1888). *Lemaan Zion* was founded at the initiative of Rabbi Esriel Hildesheimer; it encouraged self-sufficiency among Palestinian Jewry and also fought against missionary activities.

[44]For the early history of German Zionism see Jehuda Reinharz, *Fatherland or Promised Land. The Dilemma of the German Jew 1893–1914*, Ann Arbor 1975, pp. 90 ff.

ranks.⁴⁵ As a result, the indefatigable Heinrich Loewe, Max Bodenheimer and Max Oppenheimer founded in 1893 the *Jüdische Humanitätsgesellschaft* with a vague Jewish self-awareness programme. The vague name and programme was successful in attracting academic youth⁴⁶ and on 4th July 1895 the *Humanitätsgesellschaft* merged with *Jung Israel* to form the *Vereinigung jüdischer Studierender*,⁴⁷ which changed its name around 1900 to *Verein jüdischer Studenten an der Universität Berlin*. The *Verein jüdischer Studenten* sympathised with the emerging Zionist movement and can be recognised therefore as the forerunner of the *Kartell jüdischer Verbindungen*.⁴⁸

Early in 1891 Max Bodenheimer, a young lawyer from Cologne, published the pamphlet *Wohin mit den russischen Juden? Syrien ein Zufluchtsort der russischen Juden*,⁴⁹ which advocated the settlement of Syria and Palestine by Eastern European Jews for their protection and social and economic rehabilitation in occupations such as farming and crafts. The many copies of Bodenheimer's brochure created links with other *Hovevei Zion* groups in Germany and abroad. When in July 1891 the initiative came to convene in Paris a conference of all *Hovevei Zion*, Bodenheimer published 'Zionisten aller Länder vereinigt Euch!' in the Hamburg *Menorah*.⁵⁰

The generally increased German-Jewish interest in and awareness of Jewish nationalism and colonisation in Palestine that Bodenheimer and other *Hovevei Zion* groups promoted, also contributed to an increase in the *Esra*'s membership and income. From the 1890s on, the income of the *Esra* climbed steadily until it reached over 16,000 Mark per year in 1899, enabling the *Esra* to increase its contributions to the colonies in Palestine from below 10,000 Mark in combined disbursements between 1884 and 1891 to a five-fold increase between 1892 to 1899, reaching nearly 45,000 Mark.⁵¹ In order to emphasise its close ties to Palestine and other *Hovevei Zion* groups, the *Esra* changed its name in 1891 to *Esra, Verein zur Unterstützung ackerbautreibender Juden in Palästina und Syrien*.⁵² Despite these accomplishments the *Esra* recognised its inability to establish its own settlements in Palestine. Thus, throughout its history the *Esra* aided settlements founded by other institutions or associations whose funds had been depleted. Under the leadership of president Moritz Dorn, elected in 1892,

⁴⁵Among the members were, besides Heinrich Loewe, his brother Richard (who was also active in the *Esra*), Selig Soskin, Theodor Zlocisti, Osias Thon, Markus Ehrenpreis, David Neumark, Max Jungmann and Willy Bambus. See Max Jungmann, *Erinnerungen eines Zionisten*, Jerusalem 1959, pp. 18–19. Most of the members hailed from Galicia. Loewe was probably the only German-born member.

⁴⁶*Jüdische Volkszeitung*, No. 2 (9th January 1894).

⁴⁷*Zion*, No. 6 (20th July 1895), p. 178.

⁴⁸See Jehuda Reinharz, 'The Origin and Development of the *Bund Jüdischer Corporationen*', in *The Wiener Library Bulletin*, XXX (1977), New Series, Nos. 43/44, pp. 2–7.

⁴⁹In the same year Isaak Turoff of the *Esra* published under the pseudonym Paul Dimidow, the less well-known brochure *Wo Hinaus? Mahnung an die Westeuropäischen Juden*.

⁵⁰*Die Menorah* (4th September 1891); CZA, A15/I/4.

⁵¹*Festschrift*, p. 8. Income between 1884–1891 was close to 15,000 Mark and between 1892–1899 close to 72,000 Mark.

⁵²*Jahres-Bericht des Vereins Esra pro 1891*, Berlin 1891; Weinberg, *Aus der Frühzeit*, p. 96. By 1890 Heinrich Loewe and Leo Motzkin had become members of the *Esra*. See *Selbst-Emancipation*, No. 5 (2nd March 1891), p. 5.

and aided by Willy Bambus, Hirsch Hildesheimer, Jehuda Holzmann and Isaak Turoff, all funds of the *Esra* excluding necessary expenditures in Germany, were used exclusively to assist Jewish colonies in Palestine. Between 1891 and the later protection by Baron Edmond de Rothschild the *Esra* supported Petah Tikva as well as Mishmar Hayarden.[53]

During 1891 also the *Esra* attempted the ambitious project of dispatching Hirsch Hildesheimer and Rabbi Samuel Mohiliwer to Paris to persuade the *Alliance Israélite Universelle* and the Jewish Colonisation Association to support Jewish settlement in Palestine. Their mission was successful. The *Alliance* officially recognised the importance of Jewish farmers settling Palestine. In 1894 the *Alliance* permitted its president, Narcisse Leven, who also headed the ICA, to head a new roof-organisation called the *Comité Central des Hobébê Sion*,[54] which by 1897 embraced all the established *Hovevei Zion* groups in Russia, Germany, England and the United States as well as new groups in Scandinavian countries, Switzerland and Galicia. To a large extent this roof-organisation influenced the ICA's increasing involvement in Palestine. Moreover, the *Comité Central* established the colony of Beer Tuvia in Southern Palestine as a model colony, and received 16,000 Mark from the *Esra* for its support.[55]

Spurred by an increasing membership, which in 1895 included 2,166 individuals in 261 German communities,[56] the *Esra* made a policy exception and single-handedly settled five families near Rehovot.[57] The *Esra* also assisted the Galician *Ahavat Zion* in settling Mahanayim and Moza and continued to support Mishmar Hayarden.[58] Just as important was the *Esra*'s aid, beginning in 1896, in the export and sale of Palestinian wines and other produce which the organisation also displayed at the Berlin Exhibition of Trade and Industry, and later in Breslau, Hamburg, Cologne and Frankfurt a. Main. The success of the Palestinian exhibition led to the establishment in 1897 of the *Import-Gesellschaft Palästina G.m.b.H.* which tried – though only with minimal success – to bolster the fledgling economy of the Palestinian *Yishuv*.[59]

In January 1896 Theodor Herzl published a summary of his views in *The*

---

[53] *Jahres-Bericht pro 1891*, p. 3. As of 1891 the *Esra* also appointed Louis Unger as its representative in Jerusalem; it seems, though, that this arrangement did not last very long.

[54] Other leaders of the new association included Grand Rabbin Zadoc Kahn and Émile Meyerson, the director of the ICA for Russia and Palestine.

[55] CZA, A2/82; *Fünfunddreissig Jahre Verein Esra*, Berlin 1919, pp. 9–10; *Festschrift*, p. 5 and Klausner, *Mi-Kattowitz ad Basle*, II, pp. 247 ff.

[56] *Bericht des Esra Verein pro 1894 und 1895*, Berlin 1896.

[57] This suburb of Rehovot was called *Esra* and is still known as Shkhunat Esra.

[58] *Festschrift*, pp. 5–6; *Die Jüdische Presse*, Nos. 14/15 (5th April 1895), and *Zion*, Nos. 4/5 (17th May 1896), p. 148. On the other hand see the position of the *Jüdische Volkszeitung*, No. 28 (10th July 1894) which criticised the *Esra* for not spending enough funds on advertising its goals and the virtues of colonisation. In fact, on 31st March 1895, the *Esra* did establish an *Agitationskommission*. See *Zion*, Nos. 3/4 (15th May 1895), p. 115.

[59] Circular of the *Esra* of January 1897 in CZA, A1/2/2/6. Willy Bambus travelled to Palestine for the first time in 1895 in the company of Heinrich Loewe and was the driving force behind the Palestinian exhibition in Germany. See: Willy Bambus, 'Meine Reise nach Palästina', in *Erste Beilage zur Jüdischen Presse*, Nos. 42–52 (1895). The company established by Bambus had a branch in Paris and one in Hamburg; See: CZA, A28/7.

Jewish Chronicle,⁶⁰ and a month later his *Der Judenstaat* appeared. In their memoirs of the period, members of both the Russian and German *Hovevei Zion* groups in Germany described their excited reception of Herzl's plans,⁶¹ but in many cases his political plans for the attainment of Palestine were not favourably received. To Herzl the projected Zionist movement symbolised the "embodiment of the sovereign will of the Jews, as a kind of provisional government in exile",⁶² and he called for Jewish settlement in Palestine under international guarantees. Many German *Hovevei Zion* groups who had worked for the same end rejected Herzl's political approach as unrealistic and a threat to their civic and political positions within Germany.⁶³ Herzl's *Judenstaat* divided these groups into those who joined his political Zionism movement⁶⁴ and those who preferred practical settlement rather than political solutions.

Herzl's basic tenet was that Palestine should be secured for the Jews by means of an internationally guaranteed charter. He therefore opposed as "infiltration" all colonisation projects prior to the legal acquisition of the Jewish people's right to settle in Palestine. Between 1896 and 1910 Herzl's ideas shaped the ideology of the first generation of German Zionists. Max Bodenheimer and other early members of *Hovevei Zion* groups supporting settlement, rallied around Herzl's strict opposition to "infiltration" without adopting all his policies. Regarded as the only person capable of uniting the scattered and ineffective *Hovevei Zion* groups, Herzl's leadership was sought and other projects of the *Hovevei Zion* were temporarily postponed.⁶⁵

From the start the *Esra* viewed Herzl's plans with suspicion expressed in the ideology formulated by the rather ambivalent Hirsch Hildesheimer and Willy Bambus.⁶⁶ As the ranking leaders in the German *Hovevei Zion* movement, their support was sought by Herzl and his associates. By the mid-1890s the *Esra* had become the largest *Hovevei Zion* and the only colonisation association in Germany.⁶⁷ Hildesheimer considered Herzl's plans unrealistic and bordering on fantasy, inviting a comparison between Herzl and Sabbatai Zvi.⁶⁸ Hildesheimer and Bambus represented the views of the *Esra*'s general membership that colonisation of Palestine must continue house by house and settlement by settlement regardless of concurrent diplomatic manoeuvres.

By November 1896 Herzl had decided to convene a Zionist congress. On 24th January 1897 Willy Bambus and Theodor Zlocisti wrote to Herzl suggesting a meeting to find a means by which the dissenting Berliners and Herzl

---

⁶⁰Theodor Herzl, 'A Solution of the Jewish Question', in *The Jewish Chronicle* (17th January 1896), pp. 12–13.
⁶¹See, e.g., Max Bodenheimer, *So Wurde Israel*, Frankfurt a. Main 1958, p. 65; Chaim Weizmann, *Trial and Error*, New York 1949, p. 43; Elias Auerbach, *Pionier der Verwirklichung* Stuttgart 1969, Veröffentlichung des Leo Baeck Instituts, p. 79.
⁶²Ben Halpern, *The Idea of the Jewish State* (2nd edition), Cambridge 1969, p. 84.
⁶³Sammy Gronemann, *Zikhronot shel Yekke*, Tel-Aviv 1945, p. 121.
⁶⁴See, e.g., Rülf's enthusiastic letter to Herzl of 3rd June 1896; CZA, NA1/(1–3).
⁶⁵Bodenheimer, *So Wurde Israel*, p. 69.
⁶⁶See the first reaction to Herzl's article in *The Jewish Chronicle* in *Zion*, No. 1 (30th January 1896), p. 11.
⁶⁷*Zion*, No. 11 (29th December 1895), p. 334.
⁶⁸Bodenheimer, *So Wurde Israel*, p. 69.

might cooperate. Specifically, they suggested the funding of an agrarian bank in Palestine and the transformation of the publication *Zion* into a multi-lingual organ. In his reply of 26th January 1897 Herzl too stressed his desire for cooperation. Although his response to the bank and newspaper suggestions was cautious, he stated that "there can be really nothing more than shades of difference in our opinions".[69] Bambus and his associates, probably aware of Herzl's plans to convene a congress, hoped to draw him towards their own views.

The meeting occurred in Vienna on 6th–7th March 1897 attended by Willy Bambus, accompanied by Nathan Birnbaum, Moritz Moses and Osias Thon. Among the others present were Markus M. Ehrenpreis, Abraham Salz, Leon Kellner and others with Herzl presiding.[70] The first day of the conference was devoted to discussions about a newspaper, and resulted in an agreement to establish a daily newspaper contingent on raising the necessary funds. The second day resulted in the decision to convene a Zionist congress on 25th August in Munich.[71] All invitations to the congress would be signed by Herzl assisted by an organising committee. Herzl was empowered to determine the content of the invitations.

The smooth, conflict-free meetings proved deceptive.[72] There seems to have been a serious misunderstanding concerning the implications of the decisions agreed upon by the participants. Each party mistook the friendliness of the meetings for substantive concurrence whereas in fact, neither party had yielded much. For example, Bambus wanted two congresses, one "internal" and the other "external" so that major issues and sensitive questions could be discussed privately. Herzl, on the other hand, understood "two congresses" to mean a single congress with both public and private sessions.[73] Bambus was also displeased with what he considered the compromising word "Zionist" and preferred the name "Conference of pro-Palestine societies" for the planned congress. Herzl rejected this suggestion as unacceptable for the public forum to discuss "The Jewish Question". Despite these differences during the two-day March meeting, Bambus and Herzl parted amicably. In fact, Herzl's sense of Bambus's agreement probably encouraged him to continue with his preparations for a congress.

The differences in opinion, however, were bound to lead to a clash. When Herzl published his preliminary congress announcement in early April 1897,

---

[69] Alex Bein, *Theodore Herzl*, Philadelphia 1962, pp. 215–216. See also Herzl to Bambus, 26th January 1897 in *Igrot Herzl* (ed. Alex Bein et al.), Jerusalem 1957–1958, II, No. 182, p. 196.
[70] For the protocol of the discussions see CZA, Z1/34. See also Herzl's entries in his diaries, *The Complete Diaries of Theodor Herzl* (edited by Raphael Patai and translated by Harry Zohn), New York 1966, II, pp. 518–520.
[71] Later changed to 29th August 1897 in Basle in the wake of the opposition to the congress which developed in Germany. See Reinharz, *Fatherland*, pp. 173 ff.
[72] Herzl was definitely impressed by Bambus's personality: . . . "a quiet, clear-thinking organiser . . . With Bambus I discussed important points and I learned interesting things from him . . . With Willy Bambus I established good rapport . . ." and optimistically: "One thing is already clear, Bambus and I are going to do all the work. The others are going to watch." *Diaries*, II, pp. 519–520.
[73] Protokoll; CZA, Z1/34. See also Vital, *The Origins*, p. 331.

mincing no words as to his intentions, a storm of protest erupted among the Munich Jewish community and other German-Jewish organisations and individuals. The executive committee of the *Esra* also protested and Bambus began to dissociate himself from Herzl's plans. On 22nd April 1897 he wrote to Herzl that Zionism was still "das rothe Tuch, vor dem sich alle fürchten". "Not much can be done about this state of affairs, especially not with the constant insistence on the word 'Zionism'." Bambus proposed two alternatives: replace the idea of convening a radical Zionist congress with a congress that will deal only with organisational questions; convene separate "internal" Zionist and "external" Palestinian congresses. At the same time Bambus informed Herzl of the statement he had sent to the newspapers opposing Herzl's position.[74] On the same day the following notice appeared in the *Laubhütte*, *Allgemeine Zeitung des Judentums* and *Der Israelit*:

> Deliberations are currently taking place on the convening of a large Congress devoted to general Jewish problems such as the emigration of the Russian Jews, etc. Whether it will be a Zionist Congress, according to the suggestions put forward by Dr. Herzl, or, following proposals made by others, a conference of the Palestine associations, or whether it will take a still different form, cannot be determined as yet, for the entire affair is definitely in the stage of preliminary discussion. This invalidates all inferences based on Dr. Herzl's plan.[75]

Hirsch Hildesheimer followed suit with a sharp renunciation, dissociating himself from Herzl's plans, and Bambus withdrew from the organising committee of the congress. It thus became clear that Berlin would not become the centre of Germany's fledgling Zionist organisation because of the constant disagreements between Bambus, Adolf Friedemann and Heinrich Loewe who basically supported Herzl's plans.[76] On 11th May 1897 Herzl asked Bodenheimer to assume leadership of the pro-Zionist *Hovevei Zion* groups in Germany.[77] Bodenheimer was only too glad to comply with Herzl's wish. A year earlier he had founded the *National-Jüdische Vereinigung in Köln* with the help of David Wolffsohn and others. The first *Delegiertentag* of the German Zionists took place in Bingen on 11th July 1897 where the organisation changed its name to *National-Jüdische Vereinigung für Deutschland*. The organisational procedures were completed during two meetings on 28th August 1897 in Basle, and on 31st October in Frankfurt a. Main where the organisation adopted the name *Zionistische Vereinigung für Deutschland*.[78] One can speculate whether Berlin would have become the centre of Zionist activity in Germany had Bambus (more prominent at that time than Bodenheimer) rallied to Herzl's camp.

---

[74]See Bambus's letter in Henriette Hannah Bodenheimer, *Toldot Tokhnit Basle*, Jerusalem 1947, p. 27 and Henriette Hannah Bodenheimer (ed.), *Im Anfang der Bewegung*, Frankfurt a. Main 1965, p. 34, note 9. See also Herzl's reaction in *Diaries*, II, p. 538. In a letter to Herzl dated 20th May 1897 Bodenheimer informed him that he had had a visit from Bambus who claimed that at Vienna he had been under the impression that an agreement had been reached to convene two congresses; *Im Anfang*, p. 39.

[75]*Diaries*, II, pp. 543–544.

[76]Loewe resigned from the *Esra*'s executive committee already in March 1896; *Zion*, (30th March 1896), p. 99; Bodenheimer, *So Wurde Israel*, p. 75.

[77]Bodenheimer, *Im Anfang*, pp. 36–38.

[78]See CZA, A1/VI/2/20; A15/II/13; W/147/1, and A/1/2/2/6. See also Reinharz, *Fatherland*, pp. 100–102.

As matters developed, Cologne remained the official headquarters of the ZVfD until 1910.

After some hesitation, Bambus decided to attend the First Zionist Congress, which was held in Basle on 29th–31st August 1897. He even prepared a list of suggested delegates from Germany for the Congress.[79] A likely rationale for Bambus's participation was his calculation that having failed to prevent the Congress from convening, he might salvage whatever remained.[80] At the Congress he was able to defend the *Comité Central des Hobébê Sion* and practical work in Palestine.[81] The Congressional deliberations, however, did not alter Bambus's or his *Esra* colleagues' views concerning colonisation in Palestine. Shortly after the Congress, on 11th October 1897, Bambus became sole owner of the *Zion* and used its pages to support the ideas of the *Esra* and attack political Zionism much to the chagrin of German Zionists.[82] Nevertheless, many considered Bambus a Zionist supporter, even if he disagreed with the particular methods of political Zionism. Bodenheimer continued to seek his consultation in unifying the various splinter groups of Berlin and his support for the Cologne central office. Bodenheimer even suggested converting the *Zion* into the official mouthpiece of German and world Zionism. Clearly the small and weak ZVfD could not easily dispense with the services of so prominent a personality as Bambus, nor could it afford to alienate the *Esra*.[83]

Bambus was a delegate to the Second Zionist Congress held in Basle on 28th–31st August 1898. In the opening address of the Congress, Herzl called on the Zionists to "conquer the communities" of the Diaspora and to challenge the assimilationists' self-appointed role as spokesmen of the Jewish people. At this Congress the foundations of the Jewish Colonial Trust were laid. One of the highlights of the sessions, however, was Leo Motzkin's report on the new and old *Yishuv*. Impressed by Motzkin at the First Zionist Congress, Herzl invited him to attend the meetings preparing the Second Congress which took place on 23rd–25th April 1898 in Vienna. At those meetings a debate arose as to the viability of practical work in Palestine. To resolve the issue it was decided to send someone to Palestine to prepare a report for the Second Zionist Congress. Herzl's request that Motzkin undertake this mission was fulfilled.[84]

[79]CZA, Z1/35. Herzl was highly incensed at the idea that Bambus might attend: "Bambus is said to have the intention of coming to Basle. He won't get a membership card . . ." *Diaries*, II, p. 574. And later: "Since I was not in the hall during the debate on colonisation, Bambus ventured on to the platform and sneaked himself on to some committee. I let the bastard go . . . because in the meantime the Congress had taken such a turn toward greatness, that I did not want to spoil the impression any more with these annoyances." *Diaries*, II, p. 585.

[80]Bein, *Theodore Herzl*, p. 227.

[81]*Protokoll des I. Zionistenkongresses in Basel vom 29. bis 31. August 1897*, Prague 1911, pp. 204–206.

[82]*Zion* (Ende Oktober 1897), p. 261. Bambus also attacked political Zionism in articles in the *Allgemeine Zeitung des Judentums* and *Die Jüdische Presse*. See Heinrich Loewe's polemic against Bambus in *Die Welt*, No. 26 (26th November 1897), p. 12 and Bodenheimer to Bambus, 13th September 1897; CZA, A48/60.

[83]CZA, A48/60. Bambus even appeared at Zionist debates with the *Centralverein* and other German-Jewish organisations where he defended the Zionist cause in public. See *Zion* (Ende November 1897), pp. 277–283. Bambus was also instrumental in founding the *Berliner Zionistische Vereinigung* in December 1897; See *Zion*, No. 1 (Ende Januar 1898), p. 27.

[84]Alex Bein, *Sefer Motzkin*, Jerusalem 1939, p. 53, who cites *Haolam*, No. 9 (4th November 1937).

The Esra Verein

After nine weeks of travel and investigation in Palestine Motzkin reported to the Second Zionist Congress in a frank, critical evaluation of the achievements of colonisation in Palestine. Using statistical data, he showed the colonists' economic progress, but he also described the moral failure of the colonists' dependence on the corrupt administration of the Baron Edmond de Rothschild. His assessment of the condition of Jews dependent on the *Halukkah* was that these funds were completely inadequate and that the opportunity to work the land would be welcomed by the colonists. Motzkin concluded that given the present conditions, immigration ("infiltration") to Palestine must cease until the appropriate legal requirements (charter) had been obtained. Those Jews already in Palestine should be aided through agricultural and industrial projects administered by the Jewish Colonial Trust.[85]

Motzkin's report was a direct attack on the methods and achievements of the *Esra* and similar organisations and provoked a vehement protest from Bambus who claimed that since Turkish restrictions applied only to mass immigration and not individuals, colonisation was not illegal.[86] The Baron's administration, he stated, was generally not corrupt. Finally, Bambus charged his former *Esra* associate with presenting a distorted, one-sided picture of conditions in Palestine leading to untrustworthy conclusions. The valid conclusion, Bambus claimed, was to continue colonisation efforts with the support and buttress of new industrial and vocational incentives.[87] After the Congress Bambus continued his counter-attack in a separate pamphlet and other publications using a sharper tone and *ad hominem* arguments.[88]

The Second Zionist Congress was the last attended by Bambus and marked his retirement from Zionist affairs. In September 1898 he informed Bodenheimer of his resignation as a *Vertrauensmann* of the ZVfD in Berlin.[89] The bitter debates on the methods of colonisation begun at the Second Zionist Congress and the sharp attacks against the *Esra*'s goals produced a schism between the Zionist Organization and the colonisation associations.[90] When the ZVfD offered Bambus a mandate for the Third Zionist Congress he re-

---

[85] *Stenographisches Protokoll der Verhandlungen des II. Zionisten-Congress gehalten zu Basel vom 28. bis 31. August 1898*, Vienna 1898, pp. 99–127.

[86] Bambus was prepared for the debate on colonisation since he knew of Motzkin's trip to Palestine. See letter of Bambus to a friend in London, 6th June 1898; CZA, A2/82. (Doc. I in Appendix.)

[87] Bambus's speech was followed by a debate in which Motzkin and Loewe countered his charges while others supported his point of view. *Stenographisches Protokoll . . . des II. Zionisten-Congress*, pp. 179–197.

[88] Willy Bambus, *Herr Motzkin und die Wahrheit über die Kolonisation Palästinas*, Berlin 1898. This was answered by Motzkin, 'Eine Erwiderung', in *Die Welt*, No. 44 (4th November 1898), p. 7; No. 45 (11th November 1898), p. 89 and No. 52 (30th December 1898), p. 6. See also *Die Welt*, No. 43 (28th October 1898), p. 11 and Willy Bambus, 'Zionismus contra Kolonisation', in *Zion*, No. 8 (Ende August 1898), pp. 14–16.

[89] See letters to Bambus by Fabius Schach and Max Bodenheimer, 27th September 1898 and 5th October 1898; CZA, A28/13/2.

[90] Interestingly, Bambus continued to maintain good relations with Ahad Ha'Am and invited the latter to join him on his 1899 trip to Palestine. Ahad Ha'Am declined only because of the recent death of his father and the ensuing financial problems. See Ahad Ha'Am to Willy Bambus, May 1899; CZA, A28/13/3.

jected the offer, stating that in his view the current leadership of the World Zionist Organization was "detrimental to our cause . . . I am therefore forced to fight this leadership".[91] After their brief attempt to accommodate political Zionism, Bambus and the *Esra* leadership reconcentrated their efforts on Jewish colonisation in Palestine, or as Hirsch Hildenheimer put it, *Kleinkolonisation*.[92]

By 1898 the *Esra* had 4,000 members in 265 *Gemeinden*.[93] The association spread throughout Germany including some of the orthodox strongholds where it attracted rabbis and leaders of the orthodox community.[94] By 1899 the income of the association rose to over 16,000 Mark.[95] Concurrently far-reaching events were transpiring in Palestine. In 1898 the Baron Edmond de Rothschild fired Scheid, his chief inspector for the Palestinian colonies, and the next year he transferred the administration of these projects to the Jewish Colonization Association. Reacting to these new developments, the *Esra* initiated a conference in Frankfurt a. Main of *Hovevei Zion* societies from Germany, Russia, England, Galicia, France and Denmark. The conference (27th–28th March 1900),[96] which also drew delegates from the *Alliance Israélite Universelle* and *Kolel Hod*, decided to promote industry in the Palestinian cities of Jerusalem, Safed, Jaffa, Tiberias and Hebron in order to replace charity with work opportunities for immigrants and to support religious education in Palestine.[97]

Little action resulted from these decisions. Many of the small colonisation groups in the West were already in the process of amalgamation with local Zionist groups or disintegrated of their own accord. The *Esra*, on the other hand, continued its activities in Palestine. From 1900 on it supported the settlers of Bnei Yehuda, east of Lake Kineret,[98] as well as the tiny *Esra* colony near Rehovot, Beer Tuvia and Mahanayim. The *Esra* also tried to consolidate the scattered German *Hovevei Zion* groups into a colonisation umbrella organisation through the publication of its *Mittheilungen*.[99] The *Esra* continued to convene meetings of societies and groups interested in colonisation and other practical work in Palestine. At one such conference in 1903 the *Esra* reiterated its objectives: the acquisition of land in Palestine and the promotion of agriculture and industry within a systematic plan. These twin aims were to be achieved through the establishment of new associations outside Palestine which would share their resources and intensive propaganda.[100]

[91]CZA, A15/VII/36.
[92]*Zion*, Nos. 1/2 (Ende März 1899), p. 41.
[93]*Bericht des Esra pro 1896, 1897 und 1898*, Berlin 1899, p. 3.
[94]*Bericht des Esra pro 1900, 1901, 1902 und 1903*. Berlin 1904; CAHJP TD/162.
[95]*Festschrift*, p. 9.
[96]Not 1899 as stated erroneously by Eliav, *Ahavat Zion*, p. 311 and Israel Klausner in *Encyclopedia of Zionism and Israel*, I, p. 304. Both apparently rely on *Festschrift*, p. 7.
[97]Circular of the *Comité Central des Hobébé Sion*, 1st March 1900; CZA, A2/82. See also *Mittheilungen des Verein Esra* (15th November 1902), pp. 3–5; CZA, A1/2/2/6.
[98]Bericht des Esra pro 1900, 1901, 1902 und 1903, Berlin 1904, CAHJP, TD/162 and *Mittheilungen des Verein Esra* (15th November 1902), pp. 2–3; CZA, A1/2/2/6. See also 'Sitzung des Central Comités des Esra, Berlin, den 9/12, 1902', CZA, A12/21.
[99]See the first issue *Mittheilungen des Verein Esra* (1st April 1902); CZA, A1/2/2/6.
[100]Resolution of the conference which met in Berlin on 19th October 1903, *Mittheilungen des Esra Vereins* (1st November 1903); CZA, A1/2/2/6. See also Bambus to Meyerson, 20th October

The pogroms in Kishinev (1903) and Homel (1905) strengthened the *Esra*'s resolve to settle Eastern European refugees as farmers in Palestine. The association consulted with experts, such as Aaron Aaronson and S. D. Levontin as to where these refugees ought to be settled.[101] In 1906 Boris Schatz established the Bezalel school in Jerusalem as a centre of the *Yishuv*'s cultural life. From its inception the *Esra* supported the school's craft industries with funds and sales outlets for the weaving, needlework, metalwork and wood and ivory carvings produced by Bezalel students.[102] When the Hebrew Teachers' Seminary in Jerusalem was founded in May 1904 by the *Hilfsverein der deutschen Juden*, the *Esra* supported a number of its students.[103] Similarly, it supported the Kiryat Sefer Agricultural School founded by Israel Belkind. In sum, during the period between 1900 and 1908 the *Esra* expanded its activities beyond agricultural projects and invested nearly 62,000 Mark in the colonies, individual farmers and various educational institutions in Palestine.[104]

The most significant achievement of the *Esra* in the pre-First World War years was the settlement of some 1,500 Yemenite Jews in Palestine. Important waves of Yemenite-Jewish immigration to Palestine began in 1882, corresponding to the *Bilu Aliyah* from Russia. Originating in urban population centres in Yemen, the settlers came primarily to Jerusalem and secondarily to Jaffa. The second Yemenite mass immigration began in 1908 and was composed of villagers from northern Yemen who turned to agricultural work in and around the existing Jewish colonies in Judea and the Galilee. They adapted well to the harsh conditions in Palestine, earning a reputation as hard-working and reliable farm hands.[105]

The *Esra* began to take an interest in the Yemenite Jews as potential agricultural workers and settlers soon after the second wave of immigration. On 11th January 1909, Professor Leopold Landau, a member of the executive committee of the *Esra*, wrote on its behalf to S. D. Levontin, director of the Anglo-Palestine Company in Jaffa, stating that the *Esra* was interested in building homes for agricultural workers in the colonies. The *Esra*'s expectation was that these hired hands would eventually save enough funds to be able to acquire their own parcels of land and repay the *Esra* for the cost of building their homes. This project also required that the veteran settlers provide the

---

1903; CZA, A28/7. The conference was also tied to the struggle of some of the practical Zionists (Alfred Nossig) against Herzl, which intensified in the wake of the Uganda issue. See *Ost und West*, November 1903, columns 787–792.

[101]For a while Aaron Aaronson served as a main unofficial adviser to the *Esra* on matters of colonisation. Later S. D. Levontin of the Anglo-Palestine Company was also called upon for advice. See the protocols of the *Esra* for 1903–1905: CZA, A12/21.

[102]*Bericht des Esra pro 1904 und 1905*, Berlin 1906, pp. 6–7. See also 'Protokoll der Sitzung des C. C. des Esra vom 13. März', 1906; CZA, A12/21.

[103]Bambus was a key figure in the *Hilfsverein* and helped the establishment of the Teachers' Seminary. See Moshe Rinott, *Hevrat ha-Esra le-Yehudei Germania*, Jerusalem 1971, pp. 109 ff. See also 'Protokoll der Sitzung des C. C. des Esra vom 4. Oktober 1905'; CZA, A12/21 and 'Protokoll der Sitzung des C. C. des Esra 4.12.1910'; CZA, A12/21.

[104]*Festschrift*, p. 9.

[105]Pinhas Kafra, *Mini Teiman uvi-Shaarayim, Rehovot-Shivim Shanah, 1907–1977*, Rehovot 1978.

necessary land. Furthermore the association insisted that these agricultural workers be carefully chosen to ensure maximum success and minimum friction. The *Esra* suggested that Yemenites were most suitable for this project but stipulated that the Anglo-Palestine Company act as creditor and guarantor for the loans and help select the best candidates. Levontin's advice was also sought for the location of the prospective settlers.[106]

On 15th February 1909, Levontin replied that the Anglo-Palestine Company was prepared to guarantee the *Esra*'s loan for the building of workers' homes. He suggested housing ten Yemenite families near Rehovot and building homes in Kfar Sabba for long-term workers in Palestine who desired to become independent farmers. Levontin promised that the Anglo-Palestine Company would guarantee the prompt repayment of at least 80 per cent of all loans within an eighteen year period.[107] From the *Esra*'s point of view, this rate of return was favourable, considering the circumstances in Palestine. Frequently, the *Esra* had complained that moneys lent to workers or colonies were never repaid. Thus Levontin's reply was encouraging and prompted the *Esra* to begin negotiating the details of the arrangement. In time, the ZVfD also became involved as a broker between various Zionist institutions in Palestine and the *Esra*. With the help of the ZVfD, the permanent employment of the Yemenite Jews settled by the *Esra* was guaranteed. On 10th May 1911 the *Esra* formally entered an agreement to provide a loan of 10,000 Frs. to settle Yemenite Jews in the colonies.[108]

The cooperation of the Anglo-Palestine Company made it convenient and safe for the *Esra* to make this loan. As a result the *Esra* expanded its loans to build houses for Yemenites in Petah Tikva, Rishon le-Zion, Zikhron Ya'akov and Hadera.[109] In Hadera the association also helped in the financing of a water pipeline and a fully equipped medical clinic headed by Dr. Brünn.[110] The settlement of Yemenite Jews proceeded smoothly. A special envoy in Aden selected immigrants who expressed willingness to work the land and helped defray their travel costs. Through this process, approximately 90 per cent of the Yemenites who committed themselves to settle in the colonies, did so. By April 1912 more than two hundred Yemenites were settled in the various colonies with the combined assistance of the *Esra*, the Anglo-Palestine Company, the Jewish National Fund and other Zionist institutions.[111] By June 1912, 650 Yemenites were successfully resettled,[112] and by 1914, 1,500 Yemenites had come to Palestine as a result of the initiative of the *Esra*. These immigrants included 500 adult workers representing 15 per cent of all Jews engaged in agriculture in Palestine.[113] The Yemenites proved to be excellent workers and

[106]CZA, Z3/1638. (See Doc. II in Appendix.)
[107]*Ibid.*
[108]'Protokoll der Sitzung des C. C. des Esra am 10. Mai 1911'; CZA, A12/21.
[109]See *Bericht über die Tätigkeit des Esra für die Jahre 1910, 1911 und 1912*, Berlin 1913, p. 19.
[110]'Protokoll der Sitzung des C. C. des Esra vom 15. Februar 1911', and 'Protokoll der Sitzung des C. C. des Esra vom 15. Juni 1911'; CZA, A12/21.
[111]See Report of the Anglo-Palestine Company (?) of 17th April 1912; CZA, Z3/1638.
[112]*Jüdische Rundschau*, No. 22 (31st May 1912), p. 201 and No. 23 (7th June 1912), p. 208.
[113]*Fünfunddreissig Jahre Verein Esra*, pp. 16, 20; *Bericht des Esra pro 1913*, Berlin 1914.

eye-witness accounts of the period indicate that their tenacious work habits and commitment to the soil did much to boost the morale of other settlers.

The resettlement of the Yemenites was brought to a halt in August 1914 with the outbreak of the First World War. This world crisis brought new challenges and tasks for the *Esra*. The *Yishuv* was in a precarious position as a result of the blockade by the Allied fleet, the denial of access to Western markets, and the impending economic paralysis. Even the flow of the *Halukkah* money ceased. Meanwhile Djemal Pasha, the Turkish governor of Palestine, indiscriminately arrested the leaders of the *Yishuv*. Many voluntarily left, while others such as Arthur Ruppin, were forcibly expelled. As a result of this political and economic upheaval, the Jewish community in Palestine was demoralised, the settlements were unable to market their produce and agricultural workers were for the most part unemployed and often starving.[114] To alleviate the conditions in the *Yishuv*, the ZVfD, the *Esra* and a number of other German-Jewish organisations founded the *Hilfswerk für Palästina* in March/April 1915.[115] But the funds of these groups were insufficient to sustain the *Yishuv* during the war.

On 2nd November 1915, Otto Warburg, a long-time member of the *Esra*'s executive committee and president of the World Zionist Organization (1911–1920), wrote to Moritz Dorn, the president of the *Esra*, describing the plight of the *Yishuv*. He suggested that the *Esra* send funds particularly to help unemployed workers.[116] The *Esra* responded immediately by sending 10,000 Mark which were well spent in colonies in Judea, Samaria and the Galilee.[117] Early in 1916 the *Esra* sent another 5,000 Mark.[118] On 13th February 1917, Arthur Ruppin wrote to the *Esra* from Constantinople soliciting additional funds for the *Yishuv*. Apparently this last request was not approved. (See Doc. IV in Appendix.)

Following the Balfour Declaration of 1917 and the San Remo decisions of April 1920 whereby the Supreme Council of the Entente Powers granted England mandatory authority over Palestine, the World Zionist Organization undertook large-scale immigration.[119] In this context the activities of the *Esra* became ever more marginal considering the much larger funds raised for the *Yishuv* by the *Keren Hayessod* and other Zionist enterprises and projects.[120] Nevertheless, the *Esra* did not disband but hoped to continue assisting the colonisation of Palestine aside from the activities of the World Zionist Organization.[121] The devaluation

[114]For intercession of the ZVfD on behalf of the *Yishuv* see Bodenheimer to Mahmud Mukhtar, 27th August 1914; CZA, A142/95; ZVfD to Auswärtiges Amt, 4th October 1916; CZA, A142/47/2. See also Isaiah Friedman, *Germany, Turkey, and Zionism 1897–1918*, Oxford 1977.
[115]CZA, A15/VII/28.
[116]Warburg to Dorn, 2nd November 1915; CZA, Z3/1638. (See Doc. III in Appendix.)
[117]Thon to Dorn, 31st December 1915; CZA, Z3/1638.
[118]See Thon to Warburg and Dorn, 3rd February 1916, Warburg to Dorn, 3rd March 1916; CZA, Z3/1638.
[119]The Third *Aliyah* began early in 1919 with a small group that arrived via Siberia and Japan. The immigration gathered momentum in the following years.
[120]For example, the Palestine Restoration Fund (*Keren Hageulah*) sent £983,000 in 1918–1919 for the activities of the Zionist Commission in Palestine. See Jehuda Reinharz, 'Introduction' to *The Letters and Papers of Chaim Weizmann*, IX, Jerusalem/New Brunswick, 1977, p. XXII.
[121]*The Encyclopaedia Judaica*, VI, p. 896 erroneously states that the *Esra* "disappeared in the early 1920s".

of the German Mark, however, compounded the problems of the *Esra* and seriously hampered its activities. At the suggestion of Arthur Ruppin, its resources were redirected to training German–Jewish men and women in agriculture and crafts which could be useful in Palestine.[122] Clearly, the organisation had lost its influence and importance. Attempts to revive the local chapters were minimally successful.[123] An attempt to create in 1925 a *Palästina–Heimstätten–Gesellschaft Esra* which would build in Palestine homes for professionals as well as old-age homes also failed.[124] Membership continued to dwindle and by 1932 the activities of the *Esra* were curtailed to a minimum. The association had all but ceased to exist.[125]

Zionist historiography has tended to depict the *Esra* as an insignificant philanthropic organisation which accomplished very little even in its specialised area of colonisation in Palestine.[126] From its inception in 1884 until its slow demise by 1932, the *Esra* spent over 300,000 Mark for various purposes in Palestine:[127] these included loans to colonies, the building of homes, individual grants and loans for multiple purposes, the establishment of educational, cultural and professional institutions, clinics, etc. Within the context of the needs of the *Yishuv*, this contribution was minor. However, the *Esra* undertook these activities when few diaspora institutions or individuals were interested or capable of this work. The help extended by the *Esra* often came at crucial junctures in the history of those being helped. The funds expended in Palestine were therefore more than financial assistance, they also helped maintain the colonists' morale.

Without the *Esra*'s assistance several farms and perhaps even colonies might have been unable to survive difficult periods. The *Esra* was the first, and for many years the sole German organisation which seriously supported multiple projects in Palestine. The *Esra* can be considered, therefore, the most knowledgeable German institution concerning conditions in Palestine. Its periodic reports frequently contained first-hand detailed accounts about the land and the Jewish settlements. Bambus, Turoff and other officers of the *Esra* undertook numerous trips to Palestine and maintained close contact with the settlers. Thus the *Esra* served as a storehouse of information to *Hovevei Zion* groups and the ZVfD By virtue of its close association with Palestine, the *Esra* served both as a financial and an organisational guide for all projects undertaken in Palestine. Moreover, since its activities stemmed from national motivations, the *Esra*

---

[122]Ruppin to *Esra*, 11th December 1919; CZA, Z3/1638. (See Doc. V in Appendix.) See also *Der Gedanke des Esra*, [1920]; CZA, A1/2/2/6.

[123]Arthur Hantke, 'Notiz über die ZVfD', 28th December 1924; CZA, KH2/1781.

[124]See: *Das neue Programm des Kolonisationsvereins Esra*; CZA, A1/2/2/6.

[125]See: 'Sitzungsberichte vom Dienstag, dem 24. Mai 1932'; CZA, A132/6. At this point, the Berlin local chapter which had always been the largest in Germany, had only 170 members.

[126]Typical of this attitude is Richard Lichtheim, *Die Geschichte des deutschen Zionismus*, Jerusalem 1954, p. 101. Lichtheim is probably correct about the figure of 115,000 Mark spent by the *Esra* in Palestine to support the colonies from 1884 to 1909, but he did not take into account the period immediately following.

[127]This is an estimate, since we do not have exact figures for all fifty years of the *Esra*'s existence, but it can be seen as a minimum figure. In 1912–1913 alone the *Esra* appropriated more than 100,000 Mark for colonisation. See *Bericht des Esra für die Jahre 1910, 1911 und 1912*, p. 5.

OTTO WARBURG

By courtesy of the Jewish National and University Library, Jerusalem

HIRSCH HILDESHEIMER

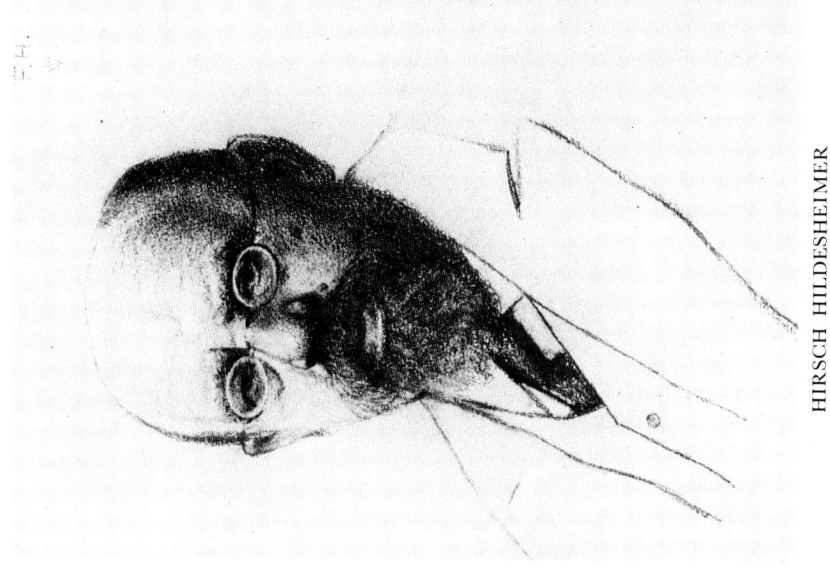

WILLY BAMBUS

contributed significantly to the awakening of Jewish national feelings in Germany.

Throughout its existence, the *Esra* opposed the system of *Halukkah* on moral and practical grounds urging that Jewish settlers be aided in becoming self-reliant. For fifty years the *Esra* provided loans without interest rather than charity, even if the loans were infrequently repaid. Though it shied away from Herzl's political Zionism, for all practical purposes the *Esra* was a Zionist association. Without forging a synthesis between practical and political Zionism, its ideology was closer to the Russian *Hovevei Zion* and Zionists than to Western European, particularly German Zionism which, by the turn of the century, had become primarily "philanthropic". Before the First World War the *Esra* did more to promote agricultural, industrial and cultural development in Palestine than did the ZVfD, which did not support directly a single colony or project in Palestine.

Soon after the turn of the century, practical Zionism gained momentum and was crystallised in the "synthetic" Zionism of the Tenth Congress in Basle. By 1911 political Zionism as the single direction of the movement, had been discredited in many Zionist quarters. Instead, practical-synthetic Zionism was seen as the rational way to achieve Zionist goals. This practical trend took form as early as 1908 with the establishment in Jaffa of the *Palästina Amt* under the directorship of Arthur Ruppin. Such trends within the World Zionist Organization were in keeping with the aims and ideology of the younger generation of German Zionists.[128] After Herzl's death many ZVfD members wanted to cooperate and coordinate their work with the *Esra*. The ZVfD leadership recommended that its members join the *Esra*[129] so that Zionist members could move the *Esra* to endorse the Zionist platform.[130] The Zionists also acknowledged that the *Esra* was an organisation with practical accomplishments in Palestine to its credit. In 1910, for example, the income of the *Esra* and of the ZVfD was almost identical (18,000 Mark). While the ZVfD spent its funds on propaganda, organisation, newspaper, office staff, etc., the *Esra* spent most of its income in Palestine.[131] It was natural, therefore, for prominent Zionists such as Otto Warburg, Hans Gideon Heymann and others to join the *Esra* and assume positions of leadership, particularly on the executive committee.[132] In a complementary fashion, the *Jüdische Rundschau* began to publish regularly reports of the

---

[128]See Reinharz, *Fatherland*, pp. 144 ff.
[129]'Protokoll der Sitzung des Centralcomités vom 27. August 1906 in Cöln'; CZA, A142/47/1.
[130]'Protokoll der 2. Plenarsitzung des Zentralkomitees vom 25. Mai 1911'; CZA, Z2/410 and 'Protokoll der Zweiten Sitzung des Geschäftsführenden Ausschusses vom 11. Oktober 1910'; CZA, Z2/1409.
[131]For comparisons of the budgets see: *Bericht über die Tätigkeit des Esra für die Jahre 1910, 1911 und 1912*, p. 33, and 'Unsere Finanzen', 2nd November 1910; CZA, Z2/1409. One should note, however, that this comparison in income and expenditure relates only to the *official* budget of the ZVfD, and not to all the funds contributed for various colonisation projects by German Zionists. After all, German Zionists contributed directly to the upbuilding of Palestine through contributions to the Jewish National Fund, participation in the various agricultural organisations created by Otto Warburg and the purchasing of shares in the Jewish Colonial Trust.
[132]'Bericht von Adolf Friedemann–Protokoll der Plenarsitzung des Zentralkomitees vom 26.12.1910; CZA, Z2/409 and A15/V11/23.

Esra's activities to save the association the expense of mailing separate news bulletins.

In conclusion, although the *Esra* did not particularly emphasise a national ideology, it should be considered one of the first and continuing expressions of Jewish nationalism among German Jewry.

APPENDIX

I

Letter of Willy Bambus to a Friend in London

Berlin, 6. Juni 1898.

Sehr geehrter Herr Doktor,

Sie würden mich sehr verbinden, wenn Sie mir möglichst bald eine Mitteilung darüber zukommen lassen würden, wie man in unsern Freundeskreisen in London über den zweiten Baseler Kongress und die Stellungnahme auf demselben denkt. Es ist ganz unzweifelhaft, dass die Kolonisationsfrage den eigentlichen Streitpunkt bilden wird und wir Freunde der Kolonisation haben allen Grund bei Zeiten uns zu entscheiden, in welcher Richtung wir thätig sein wollen. Mir persönlich erschien nach unsern deutschen Verhältnissen als das allerbedenklichste die Verquickung zwischen der Kolonisation und dem Judenstaat. Unser Verein Esra hat sich deswegen auch der zionistischen Partei nicht angeschlossen und wird dies unter keinen Umständen thun. Seine Mitglieder sind zu neun Zehntel Gegner des Judenstaates und der Name Herzl wird nun leider einmal bei uns als gleichbedeutend mit dem Judenstaat angesehen.

Ich übersende Ihnen eine Nummer des Zion, in der Sie die Berliner Beschlüsse bezüglich einer Reihe von initiativen Anträgen zum Kongress finden.

Ich bitte sehr darum, dass Sie mir möglichst umgehend Mitteilung machen, welchen Standpunkt Sie und Ihre Freunde in London zu diesen Vorschlägen einnehmen.

Wird Ihr Verein sich offiziell am Baseler Kongress beteiligen, resp. haben Sie in London viel Schekelzahler und steht schon etwas über die Delegiertenwahl fest?

Ich wäre nicht abgeneigt bei der Wichtigkeit, die ich diesen Dingen beilege, Ende des Monats persönlich nach London zu kommen, sofern Sie glauben, dass meine Reise dorthin irgend einen Zweck haben könnte. Da ich anfangs Juli nach Karlsbad gehe, kann ich reisen nur in den letzten Tagen dieses Monats oder in den ersten Tagen des Juli.

Endlich bitte ich mir freundlichst den letzten Konsulatsbericht des englischen Konsuls in Jerusalem zu beschaffen, den ich trotz Bestellung bei Ihrer Buchhandlung, bisher nicht erhalten konnte. Auch Ihr "Palästina" ist mir zu meinem lebhaften Bedauern diesmal nicht zugekommen.

Mit der nochmaligen Bitte um möglichst baldige und ausführliche Antwort, zeichne

Hochachtungsvoll und ergebenst
W. Bambus

Source: CZA, A2/82.

II

Letter of Esra to Anglo-Palestine Co.

Central-Comité des Vereins "Esra", Berlin

Berlin N.W., den 11/1/09
Luisenstrasse 12.

An die
Anglo-Palestine Co.
z.H. des Herrn S.D. Levontin,
Jaffa.

Hochgeehrter Herr Director!

Wie Ihnen vor einiger Zeit bereits von privater Seite geschrieben wurde, ist bei uns Geneigtheit vorhanden, in jüdischen Kolonien Palästinas uns bei Errichtung von Arbeiterwohnungen zu beteiligen.

Unbedingte Voraussetzung dafür ist die Gewissheit, dass die so angesiedelten Taglöhner in der betreffenden Kolonie zu auskömmlichen Löhnen dauernd beschäftigt werden und dass nicht etwa die Kolonisten die Löhne der durch den Besitz von Haus u. Hof an die Scholle gefesselten Arbeiter nachträglich willkürlich herabsetzen. Andererseits muss auch Sicherheit dafür vorhanden sein, dass die Arbeiter nicht durch Trägheit oder durch ungebührliches Verhalten ihrerseits Anlass zur Unzufriedenheit u. Streitigkeiten geben. Solche Zustände, wie sie zum Bedauern aller Zionsfreunde 1906 in Petach-Tikwah geherrscht haben, müssen unter allen Umständen vermieden werden. In dieser Beziehung müssen Garantien geschaffen werden.

In zweiter Reihe müssen wir darauf bedacht sein, dass die anzusiedelnden Taglöhner die Kosten Ihrer Installierung schliesslich selber tragen, das heisst, sie allmählich wieder erstatten. Da wir jedoch aus Erfahrung wissen, dass die Leute in den Kolonien erhaltene Darlehen sehr ungern zurückzahlen, müsste diese Rückzahlung von zahlungsfähiger u. zahlungswilliger Seite uns garantiert werden.

Schliesslich erachten wir es als selbstverständliche Voraussetzung, dass recht billig gewirtschaftet wird und mit möglichst wenig Geld, möglichst viele und doch gute Arbeiterwohnungen erbaut werden.

Wie allen diesen Postulaten genügt werden soll, vermögen wir freilich von hier aus nicht zu entscheiden. Sie, die an Ort u. Stelle sind und Land und Leute genau kennen, werden uns darüber beste Auskunft geben können. Unsere im Nachstehenden dargelegten Ansichten werden daher durch Beantwortung der am Schlusse dieses Briefes gestellten Fragen möglicherweise modifiziert werden.

Wir halten es ferner in erster Reihe für notwendig, dass die Kolonisten, denen die Ansiedlung von jüdischen Arbeitern in ihrer Mitte moralisch und materiell doch in erster Reihe zu gute kommen wird, durch Hergabe von erforderlichem Grund u. Boden auch ihrerseits zum Gelingen des Unternehmens beitragen. Auch hätten sie in der Folge für pünktliche Zahlungen der festgesetzten Mieten aufzukommen. Aus dem Betrag dieser Mieten sollen in erster Reihe unsere Vorschüsse und alsdann der noch näher zu bestimmende Preis für Grund u. Boden etc. nachträglich bezahlt werden.

Durch solche Beteiligung u. Bürgschaft der Kolonisten wäre auch die Gefahr, dass diese später willkürlich die Löhne der angesiedelten Arbeiter herabdrücken könnten, wesentlich gemildert. Wer eventuell für eine leerstehende Wohnung die Miete aus eigener Tasche bezahlen müsste, wird sich, zweimal überlegen, mit dem Wohnungsinhaber Streit zu beginnen und ih vielleicht so zum Verlassen der Wohnung zu nötigen.

Gegen die Möglichkeit, dass die Arbeiter ihrerseits Veranlassung zu Zwistigkeiten geben könnten, müsste man sich durch sorgfältige Auswahl der anzusiedelnden Taglöhner zu schützen suchen. Allein schon aus diesem Grunde würden wir gerne unter den anzusiedelnden Arbeitern einen erheblichen Prozentsatz Jemenyten sehen. Sie sind überdies anspruchsloser als europäische Juden und würden sich mit einem wesentlich bescheideneren u. daher billigeren Wohnhause begnügen.

Um möglichen Missverständnissen aus dem Wege zu gehen, wollen wir unsere Wünsche an der Hand eines Beispieles präzisieren: Angenommenenfalls, wir hätten uns entschlossen, in der Kolonie X. Arbeiterwohnungen zu bauen. Wir würden Sie dann zunächst bitten, die Grundbesitzer dieser Kolonie zu veranlassen, sich zu einer Baugenossenschaft zusammen zu tun, welche in allen Geldsachen *Ihnen* haftbar wäre. Dieselbe hätte dann uns für jeden anzusiedelnden Arbeiter etwa 25 Dunam Land zu überweisen, dessen Preis genau so wie die Kosten der Gebäude von dem Ertrage der Mieten zu zahlen wäre. Von den Mieten werden zunächst wir und alsdann die Genossenschaft befriedigt. Für die pünktliche Zahlung dieser Mieten hätte die Genossenschaft zu bürgen. Sie könnte es auch ohne alles Risiko tun, da ihre Mitglieder zugleich die Arbeitgeber der Angesiedelten sind.

Ferner wäre unter Ihrer Aufsicht zur Auswahl der anzusiedelnden Arbeiter zu schreiten, wobei Sie darauf bedacht sein müssen, dass diese nebst bereits erprobten europäischen Landarbeitern auch aus jemenytischen Juden bestehen, die sich zur Landarbeit voraussichtlich sehr wohl eignen werden.

Sind die Voraussetzungen durch Sie geschaffen, so wollen wir Ihnen einen Credit eröffnen, den Sie unter Mitwirkung eines von uns zu ernennenden Vertrauensmannes ausschliesslich zu dem oben bezeichneten Zwecke, das heisst zur Ansässigmachung jüdischer Landarbeiter in der Kolonie X . . . zu verwenden hätten. Für die pünktliche Rückzahlung der von uns durch Sie verausgabten Gelder hätten *Sie* sich uns gegenüber zu verbürgen.

Selbstredend würde es Ihnen freistehen, von den angesiedelten Arbeitern resp. von der Genossenschaft ausser dem Betrag zur Rückzahlung der für sie gemachten Auslagen noch einen kleinen Extrabetrag als Provision für Ihre Mühewaltung u. Ihr Risiko der Garantieleistung uns gegenüber zu verlangen.

Nach obigen Darlegungen bitten wir Sie, uns nachstehende Fragen recht präzise beantworten zu wollen:

1. In welcher Kolonie sollten zuerst Arbeiterwohnungen errichtet werden?
2. sind Sie in her Lage, die Grundbesitzer der betreffenden Kolonie zu veranlassen, sich an dem Unternehmen durch Hergabe von Grund u. Boden etc zu beteiligen?
3. halten Sie es für ausführbar, dass man eine Anzahl Jemenyten als landwirtschaftliche Taglöhner ansiedelt?
4. würden Sie uns gegenüber die Garantie für die pünktliche Rückzahlung der von uns zum Bau von Arbeiterwohnungen an Sie überwiesenen Summen übernehmen?
5. welche Garantie würden Sie uns für ein zukünftiges gutes Einvernehmen zwischen Arbeigebern u. Arbeitnehmern in der betreffenden Kolonie vorschlagen?

6. was würde uns unter Berücksichtigung aller vorgeschlagenen Modalitäten die Installierung eines jüdischen Arbeiters durch Sie ungefähr kosten?

Nochmals hervorheben möchten wir, dass wir diese Transactionen nicht selbstständig vorzunehmen wünschen, sondern dass wir Ihnen gegen entsprechende Provision die Durchführung überlassen, während wir selbst bereit sind, Ihnen für diese Zwecke ein entsprechendes Kapital zur Verfügung zu stellen.

Wir würden überdies die Ansiedelung von kleinen u. wenig kinderreichen Familien als Arbeiter bevorzugen, in der Voraussetzung, dass diese dann schliesslich sich zu kleinen Bauern emporarbeiten können u. werden. Die Unterbringung von unverheirateten Arbeitern in Massenquartierung erscheint uns wegen der Streitigkeiten, die in Massenquartierungen leicht entstehen, bedenklich, und diese einzelnen Arbeiter müssen alsdann auch ausziehen, sobald sie sich verheiraten.

In der Hoffnung, dass mit Ihrer freundlichen Hilfe unser Vorhaben sich bald verwirklichen wird, sehen wir Ihrer baldigen Antwort entgegen und zeichnen

mit vorzüglicher Hochachtung
(gezeichnet) im Auftrage des Subcomités
Prof. Dr. L. Landau
Geheimer Medicinal Rat.

Source: CZA, Z3/1638.

III

Letter of Professor Otto Warburg to Verein Esra

Professor Dr. Otto Warburg
  Berlin W. 15
    Uhlandstrasse 175

den 2. November 1915

  An den
    Verein "Esra"
    z. Hd. d. Herrn Moritz Dorn
      Berlin N.W.
    Luisenplatz 8

Sehr geehrte Herren!

Ich will Ihnen nachstehend einiges aus den letzten Berichten mitteilen, die wir aus Palästina erhalten haben. Sie werden daraus entnehmen, dass die Lage der Kolonien eine ausserordentlich ernste ist, und dass insbesondere die Lage der Landarbeiter zu den schwersten Bedenken Anlass gibt. Besonders charakteristisch ist folgende Stelle aus einem Brief des Herrn Oettinger vom 24. September 1915 an das Hauptbureau des Jüdischen Nationalfonds, Haag: "Die Arbeiter, vor allem in Judäa, leiden von Arbeitslosigkeit. In erster Linie in Pethach Tikwah gibt es eine verhältnismässig bedeutende Zahl von jüdischen Arbeitern (nahezu 300), die zumeist arbeitslos bleiben. Die Arbeiter in Judäa leiden überall mehr als die Kolonisten infolge der Tatsache, dass die Orangengärten und Weinberge in diesem Jahre keine Ernten gaben, und dass die Mandeln sich sehr schwierig verkaufen lassen. Viele Arbeiter gehen barfuss, weil sie kein Geld haben, um das unbrauchbar gewordene Schuhwerk durch neues zu ersetzen. Es versteht sich von selbst, dass die Arbeiter sich noch seltener als die Kolonisten den Luxus einer Lampenbeleuchtung oder das Trinken von gezuckertem Tee erlauben können. In unseren Farmen haben diese Umstände begonnen, in einer immer härteren Weise fühlbar zu werden."

Nach einem anderen Bericht, den wir erhalten haben, befinden sich selbst in Galiläa, dessen Lage doch sowohl im allgemeinen, als auch besonders jetzt während des Krieges verhältnismässig besser ist als die von Judäa, über 100 jüdische Arbeitslose aus dem landwirtschaftlichen Beruf und wie in Judäa ist die Zahl ständig im Wachsen begriffen. Die Gründe für diese immer zunehmende Arbeitslosigkeit sind darin zu suchen, dass infolge der allgemeinen Geldnot im Lande, insbesondere wegen des Ausbleibens der notwendigen Hilfsgelder sowie wegen der Petroleumnot die Kolonisten nicht imstande sind, ihre Wirtschaft im vollen Umfang aufrecht zu erhalten, sie sehen sich infolgedessen vielfach genötigt, einen Teil der Arbeiter zu entlassen.

Ich bin deshalb der Ueberzeugung, dass es unbedingt erforderlich ist, durch neue Geldsendungen nach Palästina, der Notlage der jüdischen Arbeiter abzuhelfen. Meiner Ansicht nach ist es gerade Sache des Esra, hier einzuspringen, selbst auf den Fall hin, dass es nötig sein sollte, hierfür einige der Papiere zu beleihen. Es handelt sich nicht um Ausgaben, sondern nur um Darlehen für Arbeiten auf den Pflanzungen, die doch gemacht werden müssen und die auch mit Bestimmtheit ersetzt werden, wenn die Besitzer der Pflanzungen, fast alles Russen, wieder Geld schicken dürfen, was ihnen ja jetzt als feindlichen Ausländern verboten ist.

Ich ersuche Sie daher, den Vorstand des Vereins zu einer Sitzung einzuberufen.

Mit vorzüglicher Hochachtung und
ganz ergebenst
Prof Warburg

Source: CZA, Z3/1638.

IV

Letter of Dr. Arthur Ruppin to Verein Esra

Hotel Pera Palace
Konstantinopel, 13.2.17.

Sehr geehrte Herren!

Ich erlaube mir von Konstantinopel aus, wo ich mich z. Zt. aufhalte, mitzuteilen, dass die Not der palästinensischen Kolonisten mit dem Fortdauern des Krieges progressiv wächst. Besonders gilt dies von den judäischen Pflanzungskolonien, denen nun schon die dritte Ernte an Orangen, Wein und Mandeln durch die Unmöglichkeit der Ausfuhr zum grossen Teil verloren geht, oder als unverkäufliche Ware (Wein) die Keller füllt. Noch mehr als die Kolonisten leiden die Arbeiter in diesen Kolonien, weil es für sie keine Arbeit gibt. Die Kolonisten möchten sie gern beschäftigen, aber woher das Geld zur Bezahlung des Arbeitslohnes nehmen?

In dieser Sachlage wende ich mich an Sie mit der Anfrage, ob Sie zu den Summen, die Sie in dieser kritischen Zeit bereits für die palästinensischen Kolonien aufgewandt haben, noch weitere Summen hinzufügen könnten. Ihre früheren Summen haben viel zur Linderung der Not beigetragen. Wir haben sie grösstenteils als Darlehen an sichere Kolonisten oder Gesellschaften zwecks Beschäftigung von Arbeitern gegeben. Wir haben dadurch dem Kolonisten und dem Arbeiter geholfen: den ersteren zur Instandhaltung seiner Pflanzung, dem anderen zur Erlangung von Arbeitsgelegenheit.

Können und wollen Sie uns in diesem segensreichen Werk weiter unterstützen?

Hochachtungsvoll
gez: Dr. Ruppin.

Source: CZA, Z3/1638.

V

Letter of Dr. Arthur Ruppin to Verein Esra

11. Dezbr. 1919

Verein
    "Esra", per Adr. Herrn Dorn
               Berlin N.W.6.
               Luisenplatz 8.

Dr. Ru/H

Sehr geehrte Herren!

Ihr Herr Turoff war kürzlich bei mir und teilte mir mit, dass Sie Ihre Arbeit in Palästina gern wieder aufnehmen möchten und Sie beabsichtigen, zu diesem Zwecke von der Anglo Palestine Co einen Kredit von Frs 100 000 aufzunehmen.

Ich kann von hier aus nicht ermessen, ob es der A.P.C. im Augenblick möglich ist, bereits langfristige Kredite zu geben. Aber sogar wenn sie diesen Kredit bewilligte, können Sie nach meiner Ansicht damit kaum etwas anfangen. Die Arbeitslöhne und die Kosten für Materialien sind in Palästina so gestiegen, dass Sie mit einem Betrage von 100 000 Frs kaum für 10 Familien eine landwirtschaftliche Existenz, wozu ich den Bau eines Häuschens, die Anschaffung von Inventar und das erste Aufbrechen des Bodens, sowie den ersten Lebensunterhalt des Ansiedlers rechne, bestreiten können. Mir scheint also, dass eine irgendwie nennenswerte Tätigkeit Ihres Vereins in Palästina, wenn Sie sich auf einen Kredit von nur 100 000 Frs stützen, unmöglich ist.

Auf der anderen Seite ist es noch viel weniger möglich, mit den Jahreseinnahmen, die Ihr Verein in deutscher Währung erhält, in Palästina Kolonisation zu treiben. Die deutsche Währung ist ja zur Zeit, wie Sie wissen, so entwertet, dass 100 000 Mk. nur einem Betrag von etwa 10 000 Schweizer Frs entsprechen, d. h. knapp zur Ansiedlung *einer* Familie ausreichen.

Unter diesen Umständen scheint es mir klar zu sein, dass Ihr Verein, so lange die Entwertung der deutschen Valuta anhält, gut tun wird, die Arbeit in Palästina selbst zu unterbrechen und in dieser Zwischenzeit die vorbereitende Tätigkeit in Deutschland für Palästina auf sein Programm zu setzen. Nur wenn Sie sich dazu entschliessen, die Gelder, die Ihnen in deutscher Währung zufliessen, auch in Deutschland in deutscher Währung auszugeben, haben Sie die Möglichkeit, in dieser Zwischenzeit etwas Erspriessliches für Palästina zu leisten. Als das Nächstliegende, was Sie demgemäss in Ihr Programm aufnehmen könnten, würde ich Ihnen die landwirtschaftliche (eventl. auch die handwerkerliche) Ausbildung von jungen Leuten für Palästina vorschlagen. Es gibt, wie

Sie wohl wissen, unter den Blauweiss-Verbänden eine starke Strömung dafür, dass die jungen Leute hier in Deutschland die Landwirtschaft erlernen, damit sie in Palästina schon mit gewissen landwirtschaftlichen Erfahrungen ankommen. In letzter Zeit haben sich Gruppen dieser jungen Leute mit Hilfe der Mittel, die ihnen von ihren Eltern oder von dritter Seite zur Verfügung gestellt worden sind, landwirtschaftliche Güter gekauft resp. gepachtet.

Ich könnte mir vorstellen, dass Sie diese Bestrebungen durch Gewährung von Hypotheken auf die gekauften Güter oder durch Zuschüsse zu den Betriebskosten fördern können. Wenn Sie auf diese Weise mit der Jugend, soweit sie sich für den landwirtschaftlichen Beruf in Palästina vorbereiten will, in Kontakt treten, so würden Sie wahrscheinlich auch für Ihren Verein neue Menschen und wertvolle Kräfte gewinnen und überhaupt für Ihre Tätigkeit und Propaganda ein neues und weiteres Feld erobern können.

Wenn Sie diese meine Anregung weiter verfolgen wollen, so stelle ich Ihnen anheim, sich mit Herrn Referendar Walter Moses in Verbindung zu setzen, der als Leiter des Jüdischen Arbeitsamtes (Berlin N. 24, Monbijouplatz 1) bisher bereits die landwirtschaftliche Ausbildung der jüdischen Jugend gefördert hat.

In ausgezeichneter Hochachtung
Dr. Ruppin

Source: CZA, Z3/1638.

The Hilfsverein der deutschen Juden, the German Foreign Ministry and the Controversy with the Zionists, 1901–1918

BY ISAIAH FRIEDMAN

The visit of Kaiser Wilhelm II to Constantinople and Jerusalem in the autumn of 1898 ushered in a new era in German foreign policy in the East. The idea of *Drang nach Osten* was not new. It had been propounded since the middle of the nineteenth century by a number of German thinkers, economists and strategists but it was not until Wilhelm II dismissed Chancellor Otto von Bismarck that pro-Turkish orientation became the cornerstone of German foreign policy. In this context the Jews were not overlooked.*

On the eve of Wilhelm II's departure it appeared that the Emperor might declare his protection of Jewish immigration and colonisation in Palestine. Guided by his friend and mentor, Count zu Eulenburg, the Kaiser arrived at the conclusion that Turkey would benefit economically from Jewish settlement in Palestine, while Germany would gain a firm foothold in the Orient, simultaneously easing the solution of the Jewish problem.[1] However, the Sultan strongly objected to the scheme and as a result Wilhelm lost his enthusiasm. At the *Auswärtiges Amt* it was evident that only by developing an attitude of sympathetic disinterestedness towards Turkey and by avoiding any policy which might be objectionable to her, might such intricate negotiations as the Anatolian and Baghdad railway projects be conducted successfully. It was imperative for Germany to steer clear of any scheme with a political complexion, such as Zionism was.

Yet whatever motives compelled German diplomacy to dissociate itself from Zionism, interest in the Jewish settlement in Palestine continued. "If we are willing to see a Jewish settlement in Palestine," wrote Dr. Hans von Miquel, the Counsellor at the German Embassy in Constantinople, "we are concerned with those Jews who refuse to participate in the Zionist movement and who can be useful to us because of their knowledge of the German language".[2] Like the French, the Germans were quick to grasp the importance of their language as

---

*This is an expanded version of the subject as I dealt with it in my book, *Germany, Turkey and Zionism, 1897–1918*, Oxford University Press 1977. I should like to thank the American Council of Learned Societies for a Travelling Grant to the Bonn and Jerusalem Archives.
[1] I. Friedman, *Germany . . . and Zionism*, pp. 65–68. On Wilhelm II's attitude to Jews see Lamar Cecil, 'Wilhelm II. und die Juden', in *Juden im Wilhelminischen Deutschland 1890–1914*. Ein Sammelband herausgegeben von Werner E. Mosse unter Mitwirkung von Arnold Paucker, Tübingen 1976 (Schriftenreihe wissenschaftlicher Abhandlungen des Leo Baeck Instituts 33), pp. 313–347.
[2] *Auswärtiges Amt Akten, Türkei*, Nr. 195, *Juden in Türkei* K 692/K 176325–9 (hereafter referred to briefly as *Türkei* 195 and the coding K 692 is omitted), von Miquel to Bethmann Hollweg, 26th July 1911, dis. no. 202.

a medium which could ease peaceful economic and cultural penetration, and in the process, the Jews were singled out as the most suitable agents for its dissemination.

Von Miquel had particularly in mind the *Hilfsverein der deutschen Juden*. This organisation was founded on 28th May 1901 in Berlin in the presence of delegates from all over the country, representing a wide spectrum of German Jews prominent in politics, finance, industry, science and journalism. It was a distinguished gathering. The nature of the newly founded body was philanthropic. Its aim was to promote the welfare of its co-religionists in Eastern Europe and the Near East by rendering both spiritual and economic assistance.[3] Unlike the *Centralverein deutscher Staatsbürger jüdischen Glaubens* (founded in 1893) and the *Verband der Deutschen Juden* (founded in 1904), which were primarily concerned with the internal problems of German Jewry, the *Hilfsverein* was the first German-Jewish organisation to undertake the care and assistance of Jewish communities outside Germany. In this respect it modelled itself on the pattern of the *Alliance Israélite Universelle*, founded in 1860 in Paris, but while the *Alliance* was French-orientated, the *Hilfsverein* endeavoured to serve both Jewish and German interests. German Jews were profoundly patriotic. They were also the most cultured and sophisticated among their co-religionists in Western Europe. Their liberation from *Alliance* domination was therefore long overdue. It is worth remembering that British Jews seceded from the *Alliance Israélite Universelle* in 1871, when the Anglo-Jewish Association was founded, and that Austrian Jews did so two years later.[4]

The *Hilfsverein* was headed by James Simon and Dr. Paul Nathan, leading figures of German Jewry; the first acted as President and the latter as Director. The first President Eugen Landau, a leading financier in Berlin and Honorary Consul-General of Spain, had resigned after about six months of service, and was succeeded by Simon, the cotton magnate, a distinguished philanthropist and a personal friend of the Kaiser. His name added weight to the Association, but it was Nathan, its Director, far better versed in Jewish affairs, who was recognised as its "guiding genius". He was for over twenty years – from 1884 to 1907 – editor of the *Nation*, the most influential liberal organ, and played a conspicuous role in the Radical-Liberal party of Friedrich Naumann. From 1899 to 1919 he was a member of the City Council of Berlin but his real ambition lay in national politics. However, civic equality notwithstanding, his faith proved a serious handicap and he was not elected to the *Reichstag*. Bitterly disappointed and concerned with the rise of political antisemitism, he decided to dedicate the rest of his life to Jewish affairs.[5]

[3]*Erster Geschäftsbericht des Hilfsverein der deutschen Juden*, 1901–2, Berlin 1903; *Festschrift zum 25-jährigen Bestehens des Hilfsvereins*, Berlin 1926, pp. 5–7; Jacob Toury, *Die politischen Orientierungen der Juden in Deutschland. Von Jena bis Weimar*, Tübingen 1966 (Schriftenreihe wissenschaftlicher Abhandlungen des Leo Baeck Instituts 15), p. 239.

[4]See: Z. Szajkowski, 'Conflicts in the Alliance Israélite Universelle and the Founding of the Anglo-Jewish Association, the Vienna Allianz, and the Hilfsverein', in *Jewish Social Studies*, vol. 19 (1957).

[5]See: Ernst Feder, *Politik und Humanität. Paul Nathan, ein Lebensbild*, Berlin 1929; idem, 'Paul Nathan and his Work for East European and Palestinian Jewry', in *Historia Judaica*, April 1952;

The Kaiser's trip to the East fired Nathan's imagination. As a Liberal he was a strong opponent of Germany's colonial policy[6] but this had nothing to do with promoting German influence in Turkey. Following his own trip to Asia Minor, Nathan made the following remark:

> "European civilisation is destined to play a significant role in this part of the world. German know-how and diligence are contributing conspicuously towards Turkey's development . . . particularly noticeable is railway-building, and as a result, the general standard of living will be raised . . ."[7]

But it was primarily the prospect of extensive activity among the Jewish community in Turkey, in Palestine in particular, that made Nathan so enthusiastic. On 21st September 1898, on the eve of the Kaiser's departure for the East, he wrote to the *Auswärtiges Amt* requesting its approval of *Der deutsche Schulverein für die Juden des Orients*. The letter was not sent directly to the Foreign Ministry but to his friend, Arthur von Huhn, the Berlin correspondent of the *Kölnische Zeitung*. Von Huhn maintained close relations with Bernhard von Bülow, the Foreign Minister, and was highly thought of at the Ministry.[8] Nathan pointed out that hitherto education had been monopolised by the *Alliance Israélite*, which was linked with French cultural policy, but German Jews could no longer acquiesce in this state of affairs. Now that German industry and trade had acquired a strong foothold in Turkey, the *Alliance*'s predominance was no longer justifiable. Second, unlike their Spanish co-religionists, who traditionally looked to France for inspiration and support, Polish and Russian Jews, whose immigration to Turkey was increasing, showed a marked preference for the German language and commerce. This, Nathan maintained, would give the *Schulverein* a good opportunity to serve not only Jewish interests but to further German influence as well. However, there was little chance that the scheme would be viable unless the German Government protected it. Without such protection the projected educational institutions would be subject to the arbitrary rule of the Turkish authorities. The request was in line with the customary procedure followed by German institutions of a humanitarian and patriotic nature which were active in the Ottoman Empire.[9]

It was with good reason that Nathan asked for protection. The Ottoman administration was corrupt and ineffective. Officials were free to act on their own accord, regardless of authority and law; even the native Moslems were treated harshly and arbitrarily. Non-Moslems, Jews in particular, were exposed to even greater risks. In this respect, protection proved a source of succour. The

---

idem, 'Paul Nathan, the Man and his Work', in *LBI Year Book III* (1958); see also the remarks by Robert Weltsch in *ibid.*, Introduction, p. XII. A worthy biography of Paul Nathan has still to be written.

[6]See, e.g., Nathan's article in the *Nation*, vol. VII (1889–1890), p. 615.

[7]*Nation*, vol. VIII (1890–1891), p. 557.

[8]Friedman, *Germany . . . and Zionism*, pp. 88–89; Bernhard von Bülow, *Denkwürdigkeiten*, Berlin 1930, vol. III, p. 73. Von Huhn served as a go-between for Nathan also on another occasion (*ibid.*, vol. I, p. 469; Feder, *op. cit.*, p. 103).

[9]*Türkei* 195, K 175925–7, Nathan to Huhn, 21st September 1898 (received by A.A. on 24th September 1898).

Treaty rights under the system of Capitulations accorded to foreign Powers an extraordinary status. They could use force whenever their subjects or protégés were maltreated, but in most cases a mere warning from a Consul had a sobering effect on the local authorities. Moreover, individuals or institutions which were protected were not subject to Ottoman jurisdiction; they were exempt from taxation and military service. Protected schools were administered independently of the Ottoman Ministry of Education.[10]

Nathan's project was referred to Marschall von Bieberstein, the German Ambassador in Constantinople. Inexplicably it took him nearly two years to forward it to Friedrich Rosen, the Consul-General in Jerusalem. The latter doubted whether the *Schulverein*'s activities would yield any direct political advantage to Germany, because the majority of the orthodox Jews in Palestine were concerned primarily with religious affairs, whereas the liberal ones were mainly Zionists. None the less, he thought that the introduction of German would check the spread of French and the population in the East would realise that European learning was not necessarily synonymous with the French language. Moreover, it would be useful in easing the relations between the Consulate and the *Ashkenazi* Jews in Jerusalem who spoke a "German-Jewish dialect", *Yiddish*. Marschall, who earlier had misgivings about the application of Nathan's project to Ottoman Jews, who were predominantly *Sephardim*, accepted Rosen's arguments and recommended it to Berlin.[11]

Several months later, Nathan was assured by Baron von Richthofen, the State Secretary, that the German Consulate in Palestine would support the *Schulverein* establishments "so long as they were managed by Germans, or bore decisive German features". The Minister was, however, less responsive to Nathan's plea to intercede with the Porte for the removal of the restrictions on Jewish immigration and land purchase. He also cautioned Nathan to be more discreet in his pronouncements if he wished to avoid arousing the suspicions of the Turkish Government because in the meantime "the term *Schulverein* has gradually acquired a [German] chauvinistic flavour".[12]

Subsequently the Association changed its name to *Hilfsverein der deutschen Juden* and embarked upon the organisation of a network of Jewish schools in Turkey. On 9th December 1903, James Simon told the Foreign Ministry that the *Hilfsverein* intended to found a Teachers' Seminary in Jerusalem; since it would train teachers to use German as the language of instruction and since financial support would come from German sources, he thought that the institution deserved the *Reich*'s protection. Edmund Schmidt, the newly appointed Consul-General in Jerusalem, evinced no objection to the idea, though "under

---

[10]On the system of Capitulations and Turkey's attitude towards the Jewish settlement in Palestine during the nineteenth century see Friedman, *Germany . . . and Zionism*, pp. 30–49.

[11]*Türkei* 195, K 176006–13, Marschall to Chancellor Hohenlohe-Schillingsfürst, 30th August 1900, dis. no. 123, citing also Rosen's dispatch of 9th August. German Consular reports are found at the Israel State Archives and reproduced in Mordechai Eliav, *Die Juden Palästinas in der deutschen Politik. Dokumente aus dem Archiv des deutschen Konsulats in Jerusalem, 1842–1914*, Tel-Aviv 1973. For Rosen's dispatch see pp. 257–259. There is also a translation in Hebrew in a separate volume accompanied by notes.

[12]*Türkei* 195, K 176019–22, A.A. note, 5th May 1901 and a marginal annotation.

the understanding that the institution will bear a decisive German character".[13]

As no positive response was forthcoming from Berlin, Ephraim Cohn-Reiss, the Director of the *Hilfsverein*'s schools, resubmitted the application,[14] but it was not before 1913 that the Consulate granted the protection, though on a non-official basis. The delay was not due to ill-will, or lack of confidence. Von Kiderlen-Wächter, the new Foreign Minister, held Nathan in high esteem and regarded him as "a man of tested German convictions". In August 1907, before Nathan's trip to Turkey, he recommended Nathan warmly to the Embassy in Constantinople and the consular authorities.[15]

Nathan's stay in Constantinople coincided with the Young Turk Revolution of July 1908 which took the Wilhelmstrasse entirely by surprise. Marschall was at that time on vacation, both the dragoman and the Counsellor of the Embassy were out of the city; and Paul Weitz, the Constantinople correspondent of the *Frankfurter Zeitung* and an expert on Turkish affairs, was also away. The Revolution was a serious blow for Germany. She seemed to have lost the favoured position which she enjoyed under the Hamidean régime, but Kiderlen-Wächter was not perturbed. He referred to the revolutionaries as "dreamers . . . and enthusiasts", who were neither "numerous, [nor] . . . dangerous".[16] Nathan, it appears, shared this cavalier attitude. Soon after the Revolution he approached a number of prominent Jewish personalities in Constantinople, Salonica, Jerusalem and Jaffa and asked them to induce the Jewish population in the Ottoman Empire to join moderate Moslem elements who endeavoured to reform the political system of Turkey and who rejected all "Utopian experiments . . . On the basis of profound knowledge of the atmosphere within the Jewish communities in the Orient, it may be safely assumed", he assured the *Auswärtiges Amt*, "that the *Hilfsverein*'s advice will be accepted, all the more so since the Oriental Jews were imbued with conservative concepts". He intimated that, during the forthcoming elections for the *Haham Bashi*, the Chief Rabbi of Turkey, the *Hilfsverein* would send Dr. Bernhard Kahn, its Secretary-General, to Turkey in order to influence Ottoman Jews to vote along the lines compatible with the *Auswärtiges Amt* interests.[17]

---

[13]Eliav, *Dokumente* . . . , *op. cit.*, pp. 263–267, Simon and F. Rathenau to A.A., 9th December 1903; Schmidt to the Embassy, 21st April 1903. The Teachers' Seminary opened on 5th May 1905.
[14]*Ibid.*, pp. 291–292, Cohn to Schmidt, 27th March 1908.
[15]*Türkei* 195, K 176144–5, Kiderlen-Wächter to Marschall, and to Consulates, 5th August 1907, dis. nos. 682, 243 and marginal annotations.
[16]*Die Grosse Politik der Europäischen Kabinette 1871–1914*, Berlin 1927, vol. XXV-2, Nr. 8875, Kiderlen-Wächter to Bülow, 10th July 1908. On Paul Weitz see Friedman, *Germany . . . and Zionism*, pp. 49, 259, 333.
[17]*Türkei* 195, K 176207–9, Nathan to A.A., 6th August 1908. The memorandum was written following a conversation between James Simon and Dr. Stemrich. This interesting document tends to contradict the view prevalent in British circles at that time that the Young Turk Revolution was inspired by "a world revolutionary conspiracy of Freemasons and Jews". The late Professor R. W. Seton-Watson, in his book *The Rise of Nationality in the Balkans*, London 1917, maintained that "Financial aid [to the Young Turks] came from wealthy . . . Jews of Salonica, and from the capitalists, international and semi-international of Vienna, Budapest [and] Berlin . . ." (*ibid.*, p. 135). See also Leonard Stein, *The Balfour Declaration*, London 1961, pp. 37–40; Isaiah Friedman, *The Question of Palestine, 1914–1918: British–*

Dr. Stemrich, the Under Secretary of State, was impressed with the *Hilfsverein*'s "meritorious efforts" and told Marschall that, according to information received from its prominent members, the candidature of Nahoum Effendi was unsuitable because he was philo-French and known as a supporter of the Young Turks. Stemrich added that the deposition of Rabbi E. M. Panizel, the Chief Rabbi in Jerusalem, who maintained close relations with the *Hilfsverein*, confirmed the fears of German Jews about Nahoum's proclivities. The Embassy should therefore not favour his candidature for the post of Chief Rabbi of Turkey.[18] However, in spite of the Embassy's assistance, the *Hilfsverein* was unsuccessful in its efforts to prevent both Nahoum's election and influence Ottoman Jewry. The latter hailed the Young Turk Revolution and remained implicitly loyal to the new régime.[19]

Although Nathan's attempt to interfere in Turkish politics proved unsuccessful, his educational enterprise was of lasting importance. He laid the foundation of an extensive network of schools in Palestine, from kindergartens to a Teachers' Training College which, unlike the *Alliance Israélite* schools, employed pedagogic methods. Instructors were competent and Ephraim Cohn-Reiss, the *Hilfsverein*'s educational director, was known as an efficient administrator. Nathan was also responsible for the introduction of Hebrew as a medium of instruction, in the belief that it would serve as a unifying factor for the polyglot composition of the *Yishuv*. Scientific subjects, however, were taught in German. From its inception until the outbreak of war the total investment in the enterprise amounted to 106,500 francs, and during the war an additional sum of 70,000 francs was spent on maintenance.[20]

Though the motives for introducing Hebrew as a language of instruction were pedagogical rather than national, the Zionists fully appreciated the *Hilfsverein*'s activities. Short of financial resources sufficient to maintain an independent schools' system, they willingly cooperated. This harmonious relationship paved the way for a partnership in a more ambitious project, the foundation of a Technical College in Haifa,[21] Nathan's brainchild. With Dr. Shmarya Levin, a member of the Zionist Executive, he managed to prevail upon Kalman Wissotzky, a Russian tea magnate, to make a large financial contribution; while Levin himself interested Jacob Schiff, a celebrated Jewish financier and philan-

---

Jewish–Arab Relations, London 1973, pp. 54–55. It is worth noting that Prof. Seton-Watson was a friend of the Jews, *ibid.*, p. 242.

[18] *Türkei* 195, K 176218–9, Stemrich to Marschall, 30th November 1908, dis. no. 1885.

[19] Friedman, *Germany . . . and Zionism*, pp. 141–148.

[20] Richard Lichtheim, *Rückkehr. Lebenserinnerungen aus der Frühzeit des deutschen Zionismus*, Stuttgart 1970, Veröffentlichung des Leo Baeck Instituts, pp. 132, 170; Ephraim Cohn-Reiss, *M'Zichronoth Ish Yerushalaim* [Memoirs], vol. II, Jerusalem 1933, 1936, pp. 282–283. It appears that Cohn-Reiss was the first teacher to introduce Hebrew as the language of instruction in Palestine. The experiment was made at the Boys' School founded by von Lämel, subsequently taken over by the *Hilfsverein*, *ibid.*, pp. 145–148. For a more detailed study of the *Hilfsverein*'s educational institutions see Moshe Rinot, *Hevrat Haezra L'Yehudey Germania*, Jerusalem 1971, pp. 69–163.

[21] *Jüdisches Institut für technische Erziehung in Palästina*. On its early development see Cohn-Reiss, *op. cit.*, II, p. 256–258 and *passim*; *Toldoth Hatechnion B'reshito, 1908–1925* [The Early History of the Technion], Haifa 1953.

thropist in New York in the project who also gave a sizeable donation. Both Wissotzky and Schiff were represented on the board of the preparatory committee over which James Simon presided; the *Hilfsverein* members were in a majority. Three Zionists, Ahad Ha'am, Dr. Yehiel Tschlenow and Shmarya Levin also joined the board, though strictly in their private capacity. It was understood that the language of instruction for scientific subjects in the College would be German,[22] but Simon went further by assuring the Foreign Ministry that it would help to promote *Deutschtum* in the East. He made it clear, however, that the College would be exclusively an educational and non-political institution; it would be open to both Jewish and non-Jewish students and render valuable service to Turkey.[23]

The foundation of a Technical College in Turkey had been mooted in the Wilhelmstrasse for some time and the *Hilfsverein*'s proposal was therefore well received. When Simon asked the State Secretary for his support he found a ready ear. An intercession with the Porte was required in order to obtain from the Turkish Government the permit for building and exemption from import duties for various materials and instruments. Promptly, the State Secretary asked Marschall to assist the *Hilfsverein*'s representative "to the best of his ability" since the enterprise promised to further German interests.[24] But Marschall had a different approach. He did not wish to make the Institute subject to the Ottoman Education Law and recommended that they should follow the common practice used when founding foreign schools – a principle which he had advocated in March 1903 and with which the Ministry had concurred; the *Hilfsverein* should shelve its application and open the Institute without Ottoman authorisation, leaving the settlement of difficulties to subsequent negotiations between the Embassy and the Porte.[25] Thus, in spite of his assurances that "Germany alone desired ... to keep [Turkey] intact [and] ... increase her strength",[26] Marschall missed no opportunity of asserting Germany's rights under the system of Capitulations.

Simon was astonished at Marschall's method and Nathan dashed to Constantinople but there Marschall reiterated his advice: "Bauen sie ruhig, ich werde Sie schützen." But these tactics did not work. The Turks reacted so vehemently, prohibiting the building of the Technical College, that even intervention by the German Consulate proved useless. Frustrated, Simon and Nathan

---

[22] The above is based on the following sources: *Im Kampf um die hebräische Sprache*, hrsg. vom Zionistischen Actions-Comité, Berlin 1914, pp. 9–15; Jacob Thon, 'Jewish Schools in Palestine', in *Zionist Work in Palestine*, ed. Israel Cohen, New York 1912, pp. 87–88; Selig Brodetski, 'Cultural Work in Palestine', in *Zionism and the Jewish Future*, ed. Harry Sacher, London 1916, pp. 171–189; Israel Cohen, *The German Attack on the Hebrew Schools in Palestine*, London 1918, pp. 6–7; *Palestine during the War*, Report presented to the Twelfth Zionist Congress, London 1921, p. 8.

[23] *Türkei* 195, K 176225–8, Simon to Kiderlen-Wächter, 21st September 1909; K 176234–5, same to Zimmermann, 25th October 1909; K 176283–6, same and Nathan to A.A., 25th January 1911.

[24] *Ibid.*, K 176225–8, Simon to St. Sec., 21st September 1909; St. Sec. to Marschall, 26th September 1909.

[25] *Ibid.*, K 176243–5, Marschall to A.A., 18th November 1909, dis. no. 342.

[26] G. P. Gooch, *Before the War, Studies in Diplomacy*, vol. 1, London 1930, p. 191.

appealed to the Foreign Ministry anew, on the grounds that the College would benefit Turkey too and would assist in her reconstruction.[27]

The Ministry lost no time in instructing the Consulate to support the building of the Technical College. It strongly urged Marschall "to repel the Turkish encroachment . . . [and] . . . intercede with all necessary weight for the interest of the endangered institution".[28] Marschall's démarche followed and the Porte was requested to advise the Governor of Haifa "to refrain from making difficulties". However, the Turkish Government remained adamant: unless a formal application for a permit was submitted, no building would be tolerated. Marschall pleading ignorance, complained that the Board of the College had failed to submit such an application, only to be corrected by the Ministry that if the latter had abstained hitherto from applying, "it was due to His Excellency's former point of view in this matter".[29]

The *Hilfsverein* leaders swiftly complied with the required formalities and subsequently the Porte granted the desired permit.[30]

On 18th April 1912, when the foundation stone of the College was laid, Loytved-Hardegg, the Vice-Consul in Haifa, attended the ceremony, and this was taken as a hint that it was under German protection.[31] He thought it would play a significant role in meeting the need for engineers and technicians in Turkey, which was likely to increase as soon as various projects for the construction of roads, railways, ports, powerhouses and irrigation got under way.

The event gave the Vice-Consul an opportunity to reappraise Germany's attitude towards Zionism.

> "Is it not natural that the Jews, influenced by the awakening of national movements and stimulated by the general drive of colonisation, have become more conscious of their own racial and religious distinctiveness?"

Judging from the achievements in colonisation and the strong idealist motivation, Zionism in all likelihood "would bring about the solution of the Jewish problem and the cultural renaissance of the Jewish people".

Loytved-Hardegg did not accept the Zionists unreservedly, but in his view they deserved more respect than the "assimilationists". He believed that the Zionists, because of their idealism, were likely to gain greater influence over Jewry in general, and in the Technical College in particular. As a result of their efforts, Hebrew had been transformed from a written to a spoken language and

---

[27] *Türkei* 195, K 176283–6 and encl. K 176287–8, Simon and Nathan to Marschall, and to A.A., 25th January 1911.
[28] *Ibid.*, K 176282, A.A. to Consulate, 26th January 1911; K 176289–90, A.A. to Marschall, 30th January 1911, dis. no. 74.
[29] *Ibid.*, K 176291, Marschall to Chancellor Bethmann Hollweg, 8th February 1911, dis. no. 354; K 176293, same to same, 4th March 1911; dis. no. 644; K 176302, A.A. to Marschall, 17th March 1911.
[30] *Ibid.*, K 176331, Marschall to Bethmann Hollweg, 2nd January 1912, dis. no. 26; K 176332, Zimmermann to Simon, 10th January 1912.
[31] *Ibid.*, K 176230–302, Correspondence between A.A. and the Embassy, September 1909–March 1911. This confirms the statement made by Chaim Weizmann in his *Trial and Error*, London 1949, p. 143 which invalidates Dr. O. K. Rabinowicz's criticism of Weizmann in *Fifty Years of Zionism*, London 1952, p. 90.

eventually would become "the living national language of all Jews". It is worth noting that, unlike subsequent developments, the revival of Hebrew did not worry the Vice-Consul unduly. So long as Yiddish remained the dominant medium of communication among Jews, and so long as they showed a marked preference for German *Kultur* and merchandise, he thought that German interests would not be impaired. Considering the prevalent mood among Palestinian Jews, the *Hilfsverein* leaders would be well advised to pay more attention to Zionist wishes and take heed of Jewish national aspirations.[32]

To Nathan (who received a copy of Loytved-Hardegg's report) this advice was unacceptable. Ideologically, he insisted, the *Hilfsverein* and the Zionists were worlds apart and, in view of Turkish hostility to the Zionists, too close an identification with them might bring the *Hilfsverein* as well into disfavour with the Turkish Government.

Loytved-Hardegg replied that in this case ideological differences were of little consequence since the consensus of Moslem and Christian population in Palestine was that all Jewish enterprises in Palestine served the cause of Zionism anyhow. He was aware of his duty to protect the *Technikum* but if he thought it desirable for the *Hilfsverein* to come closer to the Zionist point of view, it was because of his conviction that Zionism, growing in importance and influence, was likely to capture the majority of Jews one day. The *Technikum* too would be conquered for the Zionists from within by Jewish students coming from Russia, where their admission to universities was restricted. As for *Deutschtum*, the *Technikum* was important only in so far as it served to spread knowledge of the German language and science, but personally he regarded this institution primarily as "a purely Jewish undertaking".[33]

This exposé and particularly the last statement, which elicited no objection from the Foreign Ministry, shows that the Zionist apprehensions from 1913 to 1914 that the *Technikum* "was to become a German institution" were greatly exaggerated.[34] Equally there was no proof that "secret pressure [was] exercised by the German Government with a view to making the Jewish schools nurseries of Prussian *Kultur*".[35] More likely it was the *Hilfsverein* representatives themselves who "repeatedly pointing to the Jews as a link between Germany and the Orient, praising the projected *Technikum* in Haifa as a stronghold for *Deutschtum* in the Holy Land . . . fed the Zionists' suspicions that Jewish colonisation was to be subordinated to German political aspirations". This was the conclusion of Dr. Heinrich Brode, the Consul in Jaffa, when reviewing the episode about

[32] *Türkei* 195, K 176334–9, Loytved-Hardegg to A.A. 18th April 1912, dis. J no. 1063/no. 54.
[33] *Ibid.*, K 176345–51, Nathan to Simon, 18th June 1912 (a copy was sent to Loytved-Hardegg); K 176357–62, Loytved-Hardegg to A.A., 10th July 1912, dis. J no. 1707/no. 89.
[34] In his article 'The Orientation of the Zionist Executive's Policy on the Eve of the First World War' [Hebrew] in *Zion*, Jerusalem 1957, Dr. P. A. Alsberg concludes that "There is no doubt that the German Foreign Ministry hoped that the *Technikum* would become a German institution", and that the German Vice-Consul in Haifa "exerted his influence in favour of its adopting a German character" (p. 166). On the other hand he assumes that "no secret negotiations" between the German Foreign Ministry and the *Hilfsverein* took place. The article is a chapter of an unpublished doctoral dissertation (Hebrew University 1957), based on Zionist material.
[35] Israel Cohen, *The German Attack . . .*, pp. 18–19; *idem*, *Travels in Jewry*, London 1952, p. 27; Foreign Office Handbook, *Zionism*, X, No. 162, London 1920, p. 44.

two years later.³⁶ At the time, the Palestinian Zionists took the *Hilfsverein*'s pronouncements as the thin end of the wedge, assuming them to have been inspired by the Wilhelmstrasse, but documentary evidence shows that this impression was mistaken. Neither Berlin nor the Consulate in Palestine nourished any intention of pushing German *Kultur* at the expense of Hebrew education.

Brode in his annual trade report for 1912, described Zionist colonisation in most glowing terms; as did celebrated German agricultural experts when visiting Palestine. In the Wilhelmstrasse too, the climate seemed to become more favourable and it was for the first time that the Germans – and the Turks independently of them – discovered in Zionism certain advantages.³⁷

However, by mid-1913 the Consulate in Palestine reverted to its earlier position, insisting that after all it was safer to support the *Hilfsverein*. Loytved-Hardegg in particular was worried by the rapid revival of Hebrew, which was bound to affect the status of German. Already in the Grammar Schools in Jerusalem and Jaffa (not under the *Hilfsverein*'s supervision) German had been downgraded to an optional foreign language together with English and French. He regretted this restriction since he regarded the Jews as "the most suitable mediators between West and East . . . and exceedingly competent to introduce Western civilisation into the underdeveloped East". Loytved-Hardegg was not clear about the policy being considered at the Wilhelmstrasse but, should the *Reich* Government favour an agreement with the Zionists, he thought the moment most propitious; German had not yet been completely displaced and the Zionists were still not in a position to behave too independently. He suggested that, in return for German protection, scholarships and assistance offered by German universities, the Zionists should agree that German became the first compulsory language in their schools, "with full respect for the particular needs of Hebrew".

While this report was being written, Dr. Alfons Finkelstein, the newly appointed Director of the Technical College, called on the Vice-Consul. Learning from his visitor that the *Hilfsverein* intended to introduce German as the language of instruction in the Grammar School affiliated to the *Technikum*, he realised that such a move might constitute an important precedent for other grammar schools in the country. He suggested that the Foreign Ministry should "prevent the Zionists from increasing their influence over the *Hilfsverein*", and "tighten cooperation with those Jews who were loyal to Germany".³⁸

Edmund Schmidt, the Consul-General in Jerusalem, went to greater lengths. Under the erroneous impression that the Hebrew *Gymnasium* in Jerusalem had placed itself under French protection, he suggested that Berlin should declare that the *Hilfsverein* schools were under German protection. This, he hoped, would also restrain the "radical Zionists from Hebraising the *Hilfsverein* schools". More disquieting was the news that the French Consulate had taken under its protection 7,000 Moroccan Jews in Palestine with a speed and zeal

---

³⁶*Türkei* 195, K 177300–46, "Memorandum . . ." encl. to dis. no. 76/1278, Brode to Bethmann Hollweg, 26th August 1915.
³⁷Friedman, *Germany . . . and Zionism*, pp. 161–167.
³⁸*Türkei* 195, K 176407–14, Loytved-Hardegg to A.A., 9th May 1913, dis. J. no. 1280/no. 58.

that astonished even the Jews themselves. Schmidt now suspected that the French desired to extend their sphere of interest from Syria to Palestine as well.[39]

What made the Consulate change its tune? First, as is evident from documents just quoted, it was feared that German would lose its privileged position. This apprehension was not without justification. Both the labour circles of the second *aliyah*[40] and the Teachers' Union demanded that Hebrew should be the exclusive language of instruction, even in the *Hilfsverein* schools; they would not tolerate a bilingual co-existence. The *Hapoel Hatzair*, the Labour's organ, since its inception had untiringly attacked the *Hilfsverein* for its super-patriotic stance and for dissemination of German "against the wishes of parents and students", and to the detriment of the Hebrew national education. Cohn-Reiss was vilified most unscrupulously.[41]

The sharpening of the Franco-German rivalry in the Levant on the eve of the First World War, was another factor that caused the Consulate to modify its position. French influence was always strong among Ottoman Jewry. The schools of the *Alliance Israélite Universelle* preceded those of the *Hilfsverein* by at least two decades, and the election of Haim Nahoum Effendi in 1908 to the position of Chief Rabbi of Turkey, despite opposition from the *Hilfsverein* and the German Embassy, was a considerable triumph for the francophiles.[42] In April 1911, at the instigation of the French Embassy in Constantinople, all the foreign missions requested the Porte to rescind restrictions on land purchase in Syria and Palestine by foreign Jews,[43] and in December 1912 the French Ambassador made an unprecedented move when telling the Chief Rabbi that France was ready to watch over the interests of Jews in the East and meet their requests. Freiherr von Wangenheim, the newly appointed German Ambassador in Constantinople, suspected that France aspired to assume an overall protectorate of Jews in the East and advised Berlin to do everything possible to thwart it. He wired Berlin: "I am convinced that a certain amount of intervention on our part on behalf of the Jews would be economically, politically and culturally advantageous to us."[44]

Dr. Arthur Zimmermann, the Under-Secretary of State, accepted Wangen-

---

[39] *Ibid.*, K 176437–9, Wangenheim to A.A., 30th June 1913, citing Schmidt's dispatches of 15th, 17th June. Denied recognition by the Ottoman Government (since the majority of teachers and students were foreign nationals) the *Gymnasium* decided to invite the protection of one of the European Powers. This would have entitled its graduates to enter universities abroad and by the same token would have made the Porte recognise it. It appears that the Quai d'Orsay was seriously interested in the deal, provided French was introduced as a compulsory subject, but this seemed to the *Gymnasium* too high a price and they did not proceed with the matter. Israel Klausner, 'Episodes in the History of the Hebrew Gymnasium in Jerusalem', in *Sefer Hayovel shel Hagymnasya Haivrit* (Hebrew), Jerusalem 1960, pp. 49–55. Unlike the *Technikum*, the *Hilfsverein* schools were not under German protection.

[40] On which see Friedman, *Germany . . . and Zionism*, pp. 134–137 and the sources quoted therein.

[41] Rinot, *op. cit.*, pp. 170–179.

[42] *Türkei* 195, K 176218–9, Stemrich to Marschall, 30th November 1908, dis. no. 1885. A biographical note on Nahoum appears in *Modern Turkey*, ed. Ed. Mears, New York 1924, p. 86; an obituary in the *Jewish Chronicle* and *The Times*, 18th November 1960.

[43] *The British Consulate in Jerusalem in relation to the Jews of Palestine, 1838–1914*, Documents ed. by A. M. Hyamson, London 1941, vol. II, Lowther to Grey, 24th April 1911, p. 577.

[44] *Türkei* 195, K 176393–4, Wangenheim to A.A., 4th January 1913, tel. no. 5.

heim's advice and commented: "The *Hilfsverein* under the leadership of James Simon would doubtless be prepared to counter the *Alliance Israélite* aspirations". He thought, however, that the *Auswärtiges Amt* should wait until Simon himself took the initiative in this matter.[45] Simon could be relied upon. The French Consul in Salonica hardly disguised his annoyance when reporting on "the *Hilfsverein*'s Germanising tendencies".[46]

Thus, any French success prompted the Germans to a counter-move and in such an atmosphere it was only those who conformed who could be trusted. The fact that the Palestinian Zionists did not launch a campaign against the *Alliance* schools[47] similar to that which they had against the *Hilfsverein*'s, coupled with rumours that the Hebrew Grammar School in Jerusalem had placed itself under French protection, tended to magnify the German Consulate's suspicions.

It is against this background that one can appreciate why the Consulate attached such importance to the decision of the Board of the Technical College on the question of language of instruction. The issue was controversial. While the *Hilfsverein* representatives favoured German, ostensibly on pedagogical grounds, claiming that Hebrew was not yet sufficiently developed for teaching technology and science, the Zionists, who were in a minority, pointed to the successful experience in the Hebrew gymnasia of Jerusalem and Jaffa and pressed that Hebrew be accepted in principle to replace German some time in the future. To resolve the deadlock, they suggested a compromise: exclusive use of Hebrew in the preparatory Grammar School affiliated to the College, and in the College itself one scientific subject to be taught experimentally in Hebrew. The *Hilfsverein* rejected this proposal.

The Zionists had an additional reason for pressing their demands. As members of an international organisation, they were unwilling and unable to identify themselves with one bloc of Powers exclusively.[48] They realised that "any European language used as a vehicle for instruction must imprint on the school a one-sided political character to the detriment of Palestinian Jewry",[49] and therefore endeavoured to keep the schools free from the influence of the contending Powers. It was in these terms that Shmarya Levin appealed to Nathan before the crucial meeting of the Board on 26th October 1913, emphasising that only Hebrew could provide the Technical College with a semblance of neutrality. But this was the last thing that interested Nathan. His reference to pedagogical considerations, which spoke in favour of German,[50] was hardly likely to convince the Palestinian Zionist who maintained that education was "a national matter".[51] Whatever the merits of this argument, it ignored the fact that the Zionist members on the *Technikum* Board were in a minority and could not claim

[45]*Ibid.*, Zimmermann's marginal annotation on K 176394.
[46]*Ibid.*, K 176324, Dr. J. (?) to *Hilfsverein*, Constantinople, 24th February 1911.
[47]In fact, they objected equally to instruction in French but for tactical reasons refrained from waging war on two fronts simultaneously.
[48]Lichtheim, *op. cit.*, pp. 230–232.
[49]*Im Kampf um die hebräische Sprache, op. cit.*, pp. 26–27.
[50]Cohn-Reiss, *op. cit.*, pp. 176–179; Alsberg, *loc. cit.*, p. 167.
[51]*Im Kampf um die hebräische Sprache, op. cit.*, p. 62.

an exclusive right to draft its programme. Moreover, the original agreement, to which all parties had committed themselves, stipulated that scientific subjects were to be taught in German. Ahad Ha'am, the prudent philosopher, repeatedly warned his fellow Zionists that, with the paucity of Hebrew textbooks and the inadequacy of Hebrew terminology, as well as the absence of experienced staff to teach scientific subjects in that language, a speedy conversion of the *Technikum* into a Hebrew institution was both impractical and unfair. The change was tantamount to a breach of the agreement with the *Hilfsverein*; it had never been discussed among the Zionists themselves; the claim was absolutely new. He was prepared to fight for the predominance of Hebrew in the affiliated Grammar School but, unlike the school, the Technical College was not an educational but a professional institution. It was concerned with training skilled engineers and technicians. "That was what *all* of us thought at that time . . . noisy propaganda in favour of Hebrew and 'Hebrew only' smacks of demagogy, in which I shall not take part."[52]

In an effort to bridge the gap Ahad Ha'am attempted to convince Nathan of the necessity of introducing Hebrew into the *Technikum* gradually. He pointed to the successful experiment of teaching scientific subjects in that language in the grammar schools of Jerusalem and Jaffa. That the University of Berlin accorded them recognition showed that their standard was not adversely affected by the experiment. Moreover, it was politically desirable to refute the contention of the Entente that Jewish enterprises in Palestine were subordinated to German interests in the East. Nathan, however, remained unmoved. Ahad Ha'am gained the impression that his correspondent's counter-arguments merely camouflaged the real motives, the nature of which he was not in a position to divulge. He suspected that Nathan's inflexibility was determined by some secret agreement between the German Government and the *Hilfsverein*.[53]

Shmarya Levin went even further. On 23rd November 1913 he reported to the Zionist Executive on the meeting of the Board of the *Technikum* and quoted statements made by the *Hilfsverein*'s representatives. According to him James Simon declared that the *Reich* Government had demanded that German should be the only language of instruction in the Technical College and the affiliated Grammar School; that the Under-Secretary of State, Zimmermann expected the Board to adopt a decision along these lines; and that in a negative case Germany's protection of the institution might cease.[54]

This statement attributed to Simon does not appear in the minutes of the Board's meeting. If Simon did make it, he might have used it merely for

---

[52] *Ig'groth Ahad Ha'am* [letters], Jerusalem–Berlin 1924, vol. V, Ahad Ha'am to Joseph Klausner, 25th May 1913, p. 53; to Sh. Levin, 27th May, 10th, 19th June, pp. 56–57, 62–68; to M. Ben-Hillel Hacohen, 15th June, 25th November, pp. 64–65, p. 119–20; to M. M. Ussishkin, 8th August, pp. 75–76; to Druyanov, 23rd December 1913, p. 136, Article 4 of the Agreement committed its signatories to maintain the *Technikum* merely as 'a Jewish institution'. As Ahad Ha'am rightly pointed out, no mention was made of its Hebrew, let alone Zionist character, because the founders were eager to find a common denominator among all parties concerned.
[53] *Ibid.*, to Nathan, 28th September, 19th October 1913, pp. 81–82, 98–99; to Moshe Smilansky, 18th November 1913, pp. 113–116.
[54] Central Zionist Archives (hereafter CZA), Z 3/444, meeting on 23rd November 1913.

tactical reasons to soften his opponents' position but it should not be taken as proof of its veracity.

It remains now for us to examine whether or not the German Government did exert pressure on the *Hilfsverein* as was widely believed by the Zionists at that time.[55] As mentioned already, it was only after Finkelstein's visit that Loytved-Hardegg advised Berlin to support the *Hilfsverein*.[56] Early in August, fearing that the Board's decision might have wider repercussions on the use of German in the East, he wrote to the Foreign Ministry again. Should the *Hilfsverein*'s position be adopted, all Jewish and non-Jewish grammar schools would be impelled to give greater scope to German in their curricula. On the other hand, once the Zionists were successful in conquering the Grammar School, they would win over the *Technikum* easily later; only humanistic subjects and religion should be taught in Hebrew. He believed that such a solution would be acceptable to the Board and advised that "in the realm of science any political controversy between the national and non-national Jews should be avoided".[57]

Usually Zimmermann preferred not to interfere[58] but in this case, when transmitting a copy of the Vice-Consul's dispatch to the *Hilfsverein* leaders, he contented himself with a cryptic observation that it was "worthy of serious consideration". Whether Zimmermann's remark could be termed as "pressure" is a matter of opinion. Whatever the case, the *Hilfsverein* hardly needed any prodding. The stand taken by the *Auswärtiges Amt* was fully consistent with their own.[59] Their patriotism was sincere, as was their belief that German was so much more suited to instruction in scientific subjects than was Hebrew. Besides, what made their attitude so stiff was their deeply ingrained suspicion that the Zionists were using Hebrew merely as a stalking horse to undermine their hegemony on the Board of the Technical College. The art of compromise was never Nathan's forte and at the opening of the Board's meeting, on 25th October 1913, he declared that he would regard rejection of his programme as a vote of no confidence and would resign. This rigid stand prejudiced the proceedings from the outset and excluded any possibility of discussion, let alone compromise. The Zionist members found themselves in an untenable position. They doubted Nathan's sincerity, suspecting that pedagogical arguments camouflaged his intention to establish German at the expense of Hebrew. After their counter-proposal was rejected, they consulted the Zionist Executive and subsequently resigned from the Board. The Russian members of the Board (representing the Wissotsky family), notwithstanding their sympathy for Hebrew, were reluctant to endanger the College's future and voted for Nathan's motion, which recommended that scientific and technical subjects were to be taught in German, but

---

[55]Professor Rinot, who also studied the question, arrived at the conclusion that Germany did pressurise the *Hilfsverein* leaders, Rinot, *op. cit.*, pp. 37, 191, but all the evidence adduced in his study is proof to the contrary.

[56]See above, p. 300.

[57]*Türkei* 195, K 176453-7, Loytved-Hardegg to Bethmann Hollweg, 8th August 1913, dis. J. no. 2026 no. 100.

[58]See above, p. 302.

[59]It is worth noting that on previous occasions whenever Nathan disagreed with the Consulate, he did not hesitate to press his own views (see above, p. 299).

the humanistic ones in Hebrew, "in accordance with the Jewish character of the *Technikum*". In the absence of the American delegates, Nathan's motion gained a majority of 7 to 3[60] but, as events proved, it was a Pyrrhic victory.

Loytved-Hardegg applauded the Board's resolution as an "astute move". It amounted to the unofficial introduction of German as "the *de facto* language of instruction", enhancing thereby its standing in other schools as well. He rejoiced at the Zionists' failure,[61] but his jubilation was premature. Both the German Consulate and the *Hilfsverein* underestimated the depth of feeling and the vigour with which national Jewry in Palestine were prepared to fight for what they regarded as their cultural independence. To them the Board's decision was a menace to Hebrew. Stirring demonstrations were held all over the country which precipitated a bitter quarrel, the *Sprachenkampf*, that went beyond cultural considerations. It led ultimately to the rift between the *Hilfsverein* and the Zionists and involved the German Consulate as well. Yet, contrary to the generally held view, the evidence shows that the Consulate was not inimical to Hebrew, but when the controversy came into the open, it could not remain indifferent and turned against the Zionists.

Was the conflict inevitable? Our evidence suggests that however disparate their concepts were, neither the *Hilfsverein* nor the Zionist Organization desired it. Professor Otto Warburg, the Chairman of the Zionist Organization, continued to serve on the *Hilfsverein* Committee,[62] and Dr. Weizmann, at the XI Zionist Congress, held in Vienna in September 1913, publicly expressed his fears that the premature introduction of Hebrew into the Technical College might adversely affect the quality of teaching. The same doubts were felt by Dr. Yechiel Tschlenow, a Russian Zionist leader and a member of the Institute's Board. In an appreciative reference to the *Hilfsverein*'s work, he went so far as to state that its educational programme was compatible with "the national aim". Shmarya Levin thought differently. At the same Congress he declared that upon the Zionist Organization lay "an unconditional obligation to concentrate in its hands the total cultural work in Palestine", and to exclude those bodies "which lacked that banner".[63] Nathan took offence, all the more so since it was the *Hilfsverein*, as he had declared a year earlier at its general assembly, that had first grasped the importance of organising the Jewish communities in the East, and especially of educating youth. It was unthinkable to him that this primacy, gained by heavy investment and pioneering work, should now be lost. As he later confided to Loytved-Hardegg, the Zionist claims jeopardised the very independence of the *Hilfsverein*'s activity, and he was determined to resist them.[64]

[60]CZA, Z 3/443, Tschlenow's report of the meeting of the Zionist Executive, 23rd November 1913; Alsberg, *loc. cit.*, p. 168.
[61]*Türkei* 195, K 176462–4, Loytved-Hardegg to Bethmann Hollweg, 10th November 1913, dis. J. no. 2758/no. 147.
[62]Richard Lichtheim, *Die Geschichte des deutschen Zionismus*, Jerusalem 1954, p. 171.
[63]*Stenographisches Protokoll der Verhandlungen des XI. Zionisten-Kongresses in Wien*, September 1913, pp. 307–308; Nathan, *op. cit.*, pp. 12–13, citing *Die Welt*, 3rd September 1913. The discrepancy between the statement made by Weizmann and the XI Congress and that referred to in *Trial and Error* was pointed out by Rabinowicz, *Fifty Years of Zionism*, pp. 85–97.
[64]*Türkei* 195, K 176357–62, Loytved-Hardegg to A.A., 10th July 1912, dis. no. 1707/89; K 176606–7, 29th December 1913, dis. no. 3186/166.

Even so, Nathan regarded the "Palestinian *Exaltados*", the Teachers' Union, whom the Zionist Executive in Berlin was "too weak" to restrain, as chiefly responsible for the *Sprachenkampf*. But the teachers too had grievances; those in the *Hilfsverein* schools saw that since 1911 the progress of Hebrew had been held back in favour of German and for this, during the Teachers' Union conference in August 1913, they blamed chiefly Ephraim Cohn-Reiss, suspecting that he had submitted to "secret pressure exercised by the German Government".[65]

In his memoirs Cohn rejected the charge that he was a willing instrument in the "germanising of the *Yishuv*"; in rural areas, where graduates of the *Hilfsverein* schools were not as a rule expected to pursue a higher education, German was excluded from the curriculum. Moreover, unlike France, Germany was interested in the dissemination of German only in so far as it enhanced her commercial prospects in the East, and for this very reason was inclined at first (i.e., in 1912–1913), to come to terms with the Zionists.[66] In saying so Cohn was undoubtedly correct, and it was certainly due to him that Hebrew was introduced into the *Hilfsverein*'s schools. But it was also true, as he had himself admitted, that in 1913 he rejected the teachers' proposal to accelerate the process of Hebraisation in his schools. In Brode's opinion, Cohn bore the prime responsibility for arousing Zionist suspicions, though indiscriminate condemnation of the *Hilfsverein* as "betrayers of the national cause" was unjustifiable.[67]

If Cohn-Reiss infuriated the teachers, Dr. Finkelstein by his frequent indiscretions managed to bring the Hebrew protagonists to the boil. While still in Germany he was appointed the Director of the *Technikum* and after arriving in Palestine he persisted in claiming that the College was "a German institution".[68] Had it not been for the tense atmosphere, the resignation of the Zionist representatives on the Board of the *Technikum* would have passed without any serious repercussions; but in the circumstances, the episode served as the final blow which sparked off the Teachers' Union struggle against "the complete suppression of Hebrew". Animated protest meetings were held all over the country and a strike was declared in the *Hilfsverein* schools. Yet, whatever the merits of the teachers' struggle and that of their followers, the form into which it degenerated brought no honour to their cause.

The German Consulate was incensed. Following the resolutions adopted at the Zionist mass meeting in Haifa,[69] Loytved-Hardegg noted:

> "The time will come when these doctrinaire and radical demonstrators will be grateful to [the Board] for having prudently considered in their resolutions practical needs, having in mind, in the first place, efficient and well-educated Jews and not Hebrew-speaking chauvinists . . . So long as the Jews are not firmly rooted in Palestine, it will be short-sighted even from the Zionist point of view to press Hebrew into the foreground at the expense of the efficiency of Jewish education. Hebrew would in any case develop automatically, and those who protest overlook the fact that by excessive encouragement

---

[65] Nathan, *op. cit.*, 54–55; *Im Kampf* . . . , pp. 16–18; Lichtheim, *Rückkehr*, p. 133; Cohen, *The Attack* . . . , pp. 8–10.
[66] Cohn-Reiss, *op. cit.*, pp. 148, 168, 179, 208.
[67] *Türkei* 195, K 177336–7, Memorandum by Brode, 26th August 1915, see note 36.
[68] CZA, A 20/58 (Sh. Levin's papers), Levin to Nathan, 6th July 1913.
[69] *Im Kampf* . . . , pp. 26–30.

of a Jewish national language, they magnify the suspicions of the Arabs and weaken Jewry by this internal struggle . . . ' '[70]

Edmund Schmidt, the Consul-General, accused the Zionists of attempting to suppress German in order to impose Hebrew as the sole language of instruction in the *Technikum* and force the *Hilfsverein* out of their schools. The fact that no comparable action had been taken against instruction in French in the schools of the *Alliance Israélite Universelle* was proof that the entire campaign was directed against Germany alone. It was satisfactory that Cohn-Reiss had not yielded to the teachers' demands, and he expected that Nathan, on his forthcoming visit to Palestine, would be able to stand up to his opponents.[71] But when Nathan arrived, accompanied by Dr. Bernhard Kahn, the *Hilfsverein*'s Secretary-General, he failed "to pacify excited public opinion". He dismissed the agitation of the advocates of Hebrew as "Zionist propaganda"; the fact that the Orthodox sympathised with the *Hilfsverein* gave him reason to believe that the strike lacked general support. This was not a sound conclusion for although the Orthodox viewed the revival of Hebrew as profanation of the holy language, they were equally opposed to the modern education of the *Hilfsverein* schools. Nathan remained adamant, and when Dr. Mossinsohn, Director of the Tel-Aviv Hebrew *Gymnasium*, attempted to negotiate, he found him inaccessible. Influenced by Cohn-Reiss, the *Hilfsverein* leaders were determined not to yield an inch. Compromise solutions were rejected and it was decided to dismiss those teachers who declined to teach according to the syllabus.[72]

This complicated matters still further. A demonstration was held on 10th December in front of the Lämel School in Jerusalem, and when some excited people in the crowd began smashing windows, Cohn-Reiss called for the German Consul and the Ottoman police. Upon their arrival he dismissed those teachers who, in any case, had been scheduled for dismissal on that day. However, much to Schmidt and Cohn's consternation, the teachers were followed by their students. This was interpreted by the Zionist press as evidence that it was the police who had expelled the teachers under Cohn's orders in the presence of the German Consul. In his report to the Foreign Ministry Schmidt vigorously denied this allegation. He had responded to Cohn's request reluctantly, and it was only because the disruption of the school seemed imminent that he felt obliged to be present and thereby indicate that it was under German protection. He dismissed Zionist press reports as "tendentious exaggerations" and "systematic incitement". The police had been called "only to disperse the demonstrators; the Zionist charge that in *Hilfsverein*'s schools, Hebrew could no longer find a place was without foundation. Nor did the pro-Hebrew movement command

---

[70] *Türkei* 195, K 176485–7, Loytved-Hardegg to A.A., 17th November 1913, dis. no. 2837/152.
[71] *Ibid.*, K 176490–1, Schmidt to Wangenheim, 24th November 1913. In fact the Teachers' Union intended to undertake a similar campaign in the *Alliance* schools but the Zionist Executive stopped them, Alsberg, *loc. cit.*, p. 170.
[72] The above is based on the following sources: *Die Welt* (January 1914); Cohen, *The Attack* . . . , pp. 15–16; Nathan, *op. cit.*, pp. 12, 34–51; Alsberg, *loc. cit.*, p. 168; *Türkei* 195, K 176592–602, Brode to A.A., 30th December 1913, dis. no. 115/2010; K 176536, Schmidt to Wangenheim, 16th December 1913, dis. no. 2635. However, according to Cohn-Reiss, Nathan refused to negotiate with the teachers so long as they continued to strike, *op. cit.*, II, pp. 186–189.

general support; only the Zionist settlements and particularly the intelligentsia backed it. Yet, despite his annoyance, Schmidt urged the *Hilfsverein* not to precipitate a complete rupture with their partners and considered that undue emphasis on the German character of their schools was undesirable.[73]

Brode described the Hebrew protagonists in Jaffa/Tel-Aviv as "anarchist agitators" and "terrorists" imbued with revolutionary socialist doctrines; they were undermining the civilising influence of German Jews and causing concern to the Orthodox. He had refrained from interfering in this internal Jewish conflict, lest it might "add fuel to the fire unnecessarily"; but, in contrast to Schmidt, he realised that the Hebrew movement was "not directed against *Deutschtum* as such", but only against the *Hilfsverein*.[74]

Loytved-Hardegg was also annoyed. None the less he appreciated that for the Zionists the revival of Hebrew was "one of the main prerequisites in the achievement of their aim. It served them as a means for the unification of the Jewish people, separated by multilingualism, and as a manifestation of their distinct character. It represented their 'national existential minimum'." Much as he wished the *Hilfsverein* to emerge victorious, he feared that in the last resort it would be the Zionists who would gain the upper hand. Should they succeed in winning over the non-German members of the *Technikum*'s Board, the *Hilfsverein* would have to surrender. Reconciliation was therefore the soundest solution, particularly as the controversy did not turn on matters of principle but only on the efficacy of Hebrew as a medium of instruction for scientific and technical subjects; and on this narrower question an agreement was likely to be reached[75]

In Berlin, Dr. Hans von Rosenberg, the Head of the Eastern Department of the Ministry, made no secret of his sympathies. Interviewed by Dr. Rosenbaum, editor of the *Hamburger Israelitisches Familienblatt* (issue of 1st January 1914), he professed his confidence in the leaders of the *Hilfsverein*, both as "good Germans and good Jews". He was convinced that their stand with regard to the language of tuition at the *Technikum* was dictated not by political motives but solely out of regard to Jewish interests. The German Government on its part had no desire to subordinate Jewish institutions of learning to political aims. The only purpose in cultivating German was to facilitate commercial and cultural relations consonant with the well-being of Palestine Jewry. With all due respect for its religious and historical importance, Hebrew "can hardly be expected to serve as more than a language for internal communication". The policy of the *Hilfsverein* therefore made sense. None the less, as far as the *Sprachenkampf* was concerned,

---

[73]*Türkei* 195, K 176536–43, K 176584–6, Schmidt to Wangenheim, 16th, 30th December 1913; K 176548, same to A.A., 30th December, tel. no. 11. Schmidt, however, was unable to explain the presence of the police outside the Girls' School, although no demonstrations took place there. For Nathan's account see *op. cit.*, pp. 18–19, and for the Zionist version *Die Welt* (December 1913; January 1914); *Im Kampf...*, pp. 37–46; Cohen, *The Attack...*, pp. 15–16. That of Cohn-Reiss's, *op. cit.*, II, pp. 190–194, is not very reliable.

[74]*Türkei* 195, K 176478–94, K 176592–602, Brode to A.A., 24th November, 30th December 1913, dis. nos. 100/1754, 115/2010.

[75]*Ibid.*, K 176605–16, Loytved-Hardegg to A.A., 29th December 1913, dis. no. 3186/166.

unless individual German nationals or institutions under German protection were attacked, his Ministry would remain strictly neutral.

Nathan was not satisfied. With his return to Berlin the campaign intensified. In January 1914 his pamphlet *Palästina und palästinenischer Zionismus* appeared and the influential *Frankfurter Zeitung*, which backed him consistently, opened its pages to him. In its issue of 4th February 1914 he complained bitterly of "the scandalous terrorist scenes" in Palestine; the *Hilfsverein*'s goal was to educate an élite which, while mastering Hebrew for daily use, would, through the medium of a European language, be brought into contact with modern trends in science and technology. Just as the *Alliance Israélite* and the Anglo-Jewish Association showed preference for French or English, it was natural for the *Hilfsverein* to favour German. A promising beginning had been disrupted by the Zionist political ambitions. In a country with such a diverse population as Palestine, "it was particularly dangerous to kindle the torch of exaggerated chauvinism . . . it might destroy the cultural oasis, tended with such care".

The Zionists replied in a pamphlet *Im Kampf um die hebräische Sprache* and, judging from the generous response and the number of voluntary contributions for the Hebrew Schools' Fund, it was clear that their arguments were gradually gaining ground. Shmarya Levin was particularly successful in enlisting the help of American Jewry. But it was not until the meeting of the *Technikum*'s Board, on 24th Feburary 1914, that the *Hilfsverein* was decisively defeated. During that meeting the American and Russian members of the Board sided with the Zionists and it was decided to separate the Grammar School from the Technical College, thus removing the principle bone of contention. In the Grammar School Hebrew was to be used immediately as the unchallengeable language of tuition, while in the College it was to be introduced in the course of four years.[76]

The Zionist organ *Die Welt* (January 1914) maintained that by its excessive zeal the *Hilfsverein* had achieved the opposite effect to that which it desired. By antagonising the liberal sector of Jewry in Palestine it had "artificially created an antipathy for the German language which had not existed before" and as a result the demand to replace German by French became more audible; the *Hilfsverein* had rendered a disservice to German interests.

The Palestinian Zionists too were not idle, Vera Pinczower, headmistress of the Girls' School, endeavoured to impress upon Consul-General Schmidt that the teachers' strike had been misinterpreted as an anti-German move; even in the newly established Hebrew schools, she insisted, German was strongly encouraged, though as a foreign language. Schmidt replied that had he been properly acquainted with the facts, he would not have visited the School in the presence of the police; he was impressed by the "restrained and calm behaviour" of the teachers and the students. This statement, published in the *Neue Jüdische Korrespondenz* (5th January 1914), coupled with the editorial comment that it robbed the *Hilfsverein* of "the last shred of sympathy", enraged James Simon. "The Consul has stabbed us in the back," he wrote to Zimmermann, adding that a "life and death" struggle must now be waged against the Zionists, and

---

[76] *Jüdische Rundschau*, 28th August 1914, *Im Kampf* . . . , pp. 70–72; Weizmann, *op. cit.*, p. 144; Alsberg, *loc. cit.*, p. 169; Rabiwinocz, *op. cit.*, p. 88.

requested Zimmermann's support. Zimmermann received Simon on the same day, but was unable to offer any practical assistance because it had become evident that Schmidt had composed his differences with the Zionists. He had been reassured early in January by two of their leaders (whose names were not given) that "the *Sprachenkampf* was not directed against Germany". Aware of their standing and keen to improve relations, he replied that the pro-Hebrew movement "did not affect German interests *directly*, but was an internal affair". He disapproved of the methods used during the conflict but dismissed the contention that they had violated German interests *"intentionally"*.[77]

The German Embassy also modified its attitude. During the *Sprachenkampf* its former coolness became tinged with positive displeasure but a strongly worded memorandum signed by twenty-seven German Zionists resident in Palestine, made an impression. Von Wangenheim admitted that "if in the signatories' opinion Hebrew enjoys a 'natural superiority' over German and that, if this position 'meets the requirements of Palestine Jewry', then further discussion of the controversial question is futile". The primacy of Hebrew was thus fully recognised. In March 1915 Counsellor Richard von Kühlmann told Richard Lichtheim, the Zionist representative in Constantinople, officially that "Germany would be sufficiently compensated if, besides Hebrew, German would also be cultivated".[78] Kühlmann's opinion was echoed in Brode's memorandum of 26th August 1915 and coincided with views aired in the *Reichstag* and the German press.

The *Sprachenkampf* acquired a place of honour in the annals of the modern *Yishuv*. Professor Ben-Zion Dinaburg (Dinur), a distinguished Israeli historian, referred to it as "the first miracle" on the road towards the rise of Israel.[79] Zvi Scharfstein, another historian, wrote that it signalled "a victory of our cultural independence",[80] while Yoseph Azaryahu, a leading protagonist, described the contest as "one of the finest pages in the history of the Teachers' Union and of the *Yishuv* as a whole".[81] Similar statements appear in memoirs and letters of former participants and witnesses. However, this appraisal was by no means unanimous, Nahum Sokolow, during his visit to Jerusalem in the spring of 1914, expressed misgivings as to the way the struggle was conducted. So did a number of European Zionist leaders like Max Nordau (in the *Jewish Chronicle* of 10th April 1914), Alexander Marmorek, Franz Oppenheimer, Jacobus Kann and others. In Palestine, Yoseph Chaim Brenner, a leading Labour thinker, wrote: "zeal is welcome whenever justifiable . . . but in this case it caused merely demoralisation". Highly critical were also distinguished writers like Mendele Mocher Sforim, Yehuda Burla and Moshe Smilansky, while Chaim Nachman

---

[77] *Türkei* 195, K 176629–31, Simon to Zimmermann, 7th January 1914; K 176626–7, Schmidt to A.A., 13th January 1914.
[78] Lichtheim, *Rückkehr*, pp. 240–242; *Türkei* 195, K 176673–9, memorandum by Ruppin and others, 5th March 1914; K 176672, Wangenheim to A.A., 5th March 1914, tel. no. 809.
[79] Ben Zion Dinaburg, '"Hanes" shel Tkumat Israel . . .' [The Miracle of the rise of Israel . . .] in *Shivat Zion*, vol. I, Jerusalem 1950, p. 44.
[80] Zvi Scharfstein, *Toldoth Hachinuch Ha'ivri B'Eretz Israel* [History of the Hebrew Education in . . .], Tel-Aviv 1965, p. 81.
[81] Yoseph Azaryahu, *Kitvey* . . . [The Writings of . . .], vol. III, Tel-Aviv 1954, p. 67.

Bialik referred to the *Sprachenkampf* as "a misunderstanding" – a characteristic understatement.[82] Cohn-Reiss tells us in his Memoirs that during his seventieth birthday celebration a number of teachers and writers expressed regret for the former acrimonious quarrel. "Perhaps it was we who were mistaken," declared Dr. Itzhak Epstein.[83]

The evidence from official German sources adduced above supports the critics and calls for a thorough-going revision of the established view in Zionist historiography. It shows that Hebrew was in no real danger and that its protagonists, however idealistically motivated, were struggling under an erroneous assumption. Politically, the *Sprachenkampf* could have caused more harm than good, as far as relations with Germany were concerned.[84] How important these relations were, became evident after the outbreak of the First World War when Germany emerged as the Zionists' foremost protector in Palestine.[85]

On the other hand, it is also true that Cohn-Reiss and Finkelstein gave the Hebrew lovers sufficient grounds to divine what their ultimate objectives were. Nathan, though well-meaning, failed to grasp the spirit animating the new *Yishuv*. He accepted Cohn-Reiss's brief uncritically and adopted a moralising and an authoritarian stance which proved self-defeating. Had he followed Loytved-Hardegg's advice given in April 1912,[86] the conflict with the Zionists could well have been avoided. On the whole, the episode is one of the least glorious in the history of the modern *Yishuv*.

The German Government kept wisely away from this internal Jewish controversy. Notwithstanding its former proclivity, it easily came to terms with the Zionists as soon as it was reassured that their struggle was not directed against German *per se*. In contrast, the *Hilfsverein* leaders could hardly stomach the Zionist victory. In April 1914 mutual relations improved noticeably but on 17th July, at the meeting of the *Technikum*'s Board, the *Hilfsverein* representatives managed to carry a resolution declaring the *Technikum* bankrupt. It had run into debt; none the less Nathan advised Jacob Schiff that the *Hilfsverein* would take care of it.[87] But financial difficulties, complicated further by the outbreak of the War, were not the only reason that prompted the *Hilfsverein* to adopt their decision. "If the *Technikum* falls into the hands of the Zionists", Simon told Zimmermann on 27th January, "Hebrew will become the [exclusive] language of instruction." Simon recalled how, during the winter of 1913/14 at the height of the *Sprachenkampf*, the Zionist press endeavoured to discredit the *Hilfsverein* leadership, alleging that

> "it was not concerned with Jewish interests but working in the service of the *Auswärtiges Amt*. I myself was accused of giving our Kaiser a promise to make the *Technikum* a German institution."[88]

[82]Quoted in Cohn-Reiss, *op. cit.*, II, pp. 221–232, 239, 249–250, 320.
[83]*Ibid.*, pp. 291–293.
[84]For the reaction in Britain and France see Friedman, *Germany . . . and Zionism*, pp. 185–186.
[85]*Ibid.*, Chaps. 11, 16 and *passim*.
[86]See above, pp. 299.
[87]*Türkei* 195, K 176920–5, Simon to A.A., 14th March 1915; Cohn-Reiss, *op. cit.*, II, pp. 234–235; Cyrus Adler, *Jacob Schiff. His Life and Letters*, London 1929, vol. II, Nathan to Schiff, 27th July 1914.
[88]*Türkei* 195, K 176774–6, Simon to Zimmermann, 27th January 1915.

Zimmermann, it seems, was not pleased with the *Hilfsverein*'s decision and told Simon that his fears with regard to the *Technikum*'s insolvency were "unjustified", but Simon had made up his mind already. The *Hilfsverein*, he argued, was "the main creditor of the Technical College in Haifa and the most interested party in its future development . . . a further postponement of the date of the auction is undesirable".[89]

Meanwhile the news spread in the United States and Count Johann-Heinrich Bernstorff, the German Ambassador in Washington, cabled Berlin that the American Jews very strongly disapproved of the *Hilfsverein*'s action. The Institute had been founded by joint contributions of American, Russian and German Jews, and the "fictitious bankruptcy" was merely a stratagem to enable the *Hilfsverein* to gain sole possession of the *Technikum*. The German Government was requested to postpone the procedure until after the war. A week later Bernstorff cabled again stating that the affair "was causing a sensation in the entire *English* Press [in the U.S.A.] and was being used against the *Reich* Government . . . The *Hilfsverein*'s conduct is regarded as unfair and not being motivated by objective considerations." Bernstorff forwarded also a copy of a public statement made by Louis D. (later Justice) Brandeis.[90] Brandeis accused the *Hilfsverein* of "taking advantage of conditions arising out of the War. The Russian contributors cannot participate in the proposed auction [while] . . . the Zionists of the United States are perplexed . . ."

In Germany, Major Karl Endres, formerly General Staff officer on von der Goltz's mission to Turkey and later military correspondent of the *Münchener Neueste Nachrichten* and the *Frankfurter Zeitung*, warned that "the sale of the *Technikum* will not serve the German interests in the Orient but the contrary". First it was unprecedented for a public non-profit-making institution to become bankrupt. Second, the whole of Jewry had a moral claim to it and it was intolerable that only one party should take possession of it. Already during the *Sprachenkampf* the *Hilfsverein* had done a disservice to Germany by provoking anti-German sentiments among Palestinian and East European Jews and it would be prudent for the *Reich* Government to prevail upon the *Hilfsverein* to postpone the sale.[91]

The Foreign Ministry forwarded to Simon copies of Bernstorff's correspondence but this infuriated him even more. Simon maintained that the auction of the Technical College was public and that the Zionists were at liberty to make a bid; the judgment of the Embassy was "one-sided and based on Zionist sources". Dr. Isaak Straus, Bernstorff's adviser on Jewish Affairs, was "a notorious Zionist who had misused his position . . . for Zionist purposes". Simon did not confine himself to the specific issue under discussion and attacked his opponents on wider matters of policy. He maintained that the Zionists were unreliable; while those in Berlin were endeavouring to solicit the support of the

---

[89]*Ibid.*, K 176789–90, Zimmermann to Simon, 27th January 1915; K 176853–4, Simon to Zimmermann, 9th February 1915.
[90]*Ibid.*, K 176889–90, K 176855, Bernstorff to A.A., 12th, 19th February 1915.
[91]Franz Karl Endres, 'Das deutsche Interesse am jüdischen Technikum in Haifa', in *Die Jüdische Presse, Konservative Wochenschrift*, Nr. XI, 12th March 1915.

German Government, their colleagues in London and Paris were counting on the possibility of Palestine being taken over by the Entente. The latter had inspired the British to launch a hostile propaganda campaign against Turkey and this had provoked the Porte into undertaking countermeasures which endangered the safety of other Jews. Beha-ed-Din's proclamation of 25th January 1915 showed that resentment was directed "exclusively" against the Zionists and that the Turkish Government "by no means wished to suppress Ottoman Jewry as a whole".[92]

Zimmermann forwarded Simon's letters to Washington but Bernstorff, unable to judge on an internal Jewish controversy, passed them on to Straus.[93] The latter dismissed Simon's allegations as "utterly unfounded"; they were meant to discredit him personally and "to kill the interest of the German Government in the Zionist movement". Simon, Straus went on, was ignorant of the nature of the Zionists' press campaign in the United States and of the principles of their policy "which stemmed from the conviction that loyalty to Turkey should be the first commandment of the [Palestinian] Jews". It was the conduct of the *Hilfsverein* that had alienated American Jewry and thereby harmed Germany's reputation. Straus quoted letters which he had received from leading Jewish personalities like Louis Marshall, Chairman of the American Jewish Committee, Julius Rosenwald of Chicago, Judge Mack and others, who regarded the *Hilfsverein*'s behaviour over the *Technikum* as "dishonest . . . it shook the confidence of the American Jews in their German co-religionists and in German methods".[94]

Count Bernstorff refrained from expressing any opinion but reiterated his confidence in Straus and praised his "useful activities in influencing the Press in general and Jewish circles in particular on [Germany's] behalf."[95]

The *Hilfsverein* persisted in their attacks and on 8th May 1915, in his second memorandum, Straus quoted Djemal Pasha's speeches in Tel-Aviv and in some of the Jewish colonies in which the latter expressed regret for his repressive policy;[96] apparently "the *Hilfsverein* leaders consider themselves to be more efficient guardians of the Turkish interests than the Sublime Porte itself". Straus went on to explain that there were at least a million Jews all over the world who were conscious adherents of the Zionist idea and many millions more who sympathised with it. It was therefore incomprehensible why the *Hilfsverein* leaders should discredit it in the eyes of the German Government as "a movement of political adventurers, bunglers and chauvinists", who operated to the detriment of the Jewish population in Palestine. The *Hilfsverein* was a welfare

---

[92] *Türkei* 195, K 176904, A.A. to Simon, 11th March 1915; K 176857–8, K 176321–35, Simon to Zimmermann, 23rd February, 14th, 17th March 1915. On Straus see Friedman, *Germany . . . and Zionism*, pp. 204–205; on Beha-ed-Din's proclamation, *ibid.*, pp. 219–220, and on Zionist policy during the war, *ibid.*, pp. 228–230, 236–240, 289–292, 322–326, 339–340, 344–345, 418–419.

[93] *Türkei* 195, K 177023–4, Zimmermann to Bernstorff, 12th April; K 177066 Bernstorff to Bethmann Hollweg, 26th April 1915; Lichtheim, *Rückkehr*, pp. 309–310.

[94] *Ibid.*, K 177068–71, Straus to Bernstorff, 23rd April 1915, encl. in Bernstorff to Bethmann Hollwegg, 26th April.

[95] *Ibid.*, Bernstorff to same, 26th April 1915.

[96] Friedman, *Germany . . . and Zionism*, pp. 221–223.

organisation and, though it deserved credit for a number of useful activities, on the whole it was divorced from the Jewish way of life, both religious and secular, and lacked any political influence.[97]

Simon's frustration is understandable. Before the war the *Hilfsverein* had enjoyed almost exclusive access to official circles in all matters regarding the Jews in the Orient but, with the German-Zionist *rapprochement* becoming a reality, they feared that the *Hilfsverein*'s monopoly would be broken. In the circumstances its leadership seemed to welcome Djemal Pasha's régime since it provided them with a unique opportunity to deliver a death blow to their opponents. Their guiding spirit was Ephraim Cohn-Reiss. "Seriously defamed by the Zionists during the *Sprachenkampf*, he found it convenient to take revenge against his opponents by denouncing them early in the war to Beha-ed-Din and Djemal Pasha". He endeavoured also to convince the German Consulate that the Zionists were "the worst enemies of *Deutschtum*". Similarly, he attempted to influence the officers of the German Military Mission. Halberstadter, his subordinate, was even less discreet. When meeting Brode he "ventured to insinuate tactlessly that one should drive the Zionists out of the country by 'pinpricks'". Brode had reason to think that it was Cohn-Reiss who had "clearly and systematically encouraged the suspicions of the Turkish authorities against Zionism".[98] Cohn-Reiss's cousin, who acted as Beha-ed-Din's secretary, busied himself collecting material "to prove the Zionists' disloyalty to Turkey".[99]

In his Memoirs Cohn-Reiss claimed that he tried to avoid Djemal Pasha[100] but Mordechai Ben-Hillel Hacohen, a contemporary writer, attested to the contrary; that he was a *persona grata* with the Ottoman Commander. Djemal demonstrated his regard by dining at Cohn-Reiss's home; in return the latter frequently praised the Commander for "all the favours he had done for the Jews".[101] With the Ottoman archives still unexplored it would be difficult to establish the extent of Cohn-Reiss's collusion with the Turkish authorities but there is no doubt about his intentions. In his letter to Nathan, dated 18th February 1915, Cohn-Reiss wrote:

> "The Turkish Government ought to be enlightened by authoritative quarters that only approximately five per cent of the whole population in Palestine, and in Jerusalem hardly two per cent, adhere to political Zionism, and that the Jewish population would feel relieved to be freed from the terrorism of the Russian-Jewish chauvinists. Should the Government quietly expel the Ottoman and the newly-Ottoman Zionist agents provocateurs . . . it would be a step which nobody will regret. It is Turkey's legitimate right to remove peace-disturbing elements to places where they could be rendered harmless."

Cohn-Reiss suggested that the Zionist Press should be muzzled and that all

---

[97] *Türkei* 195, K 177083–8, Straus to Bernstorff, 8th May 1915, encl. in Bernstorff to Bethmann Hollweg, 13th May 1915, dis. no. A 158.

[98] *Ibid.*, K 177300–41, 'Memorandum über den Zionismus und Weltkrieg', Brode to Bethmann Hollweg, 26th August 1915, encl. to dis. no. 76/1278; Mordechai Ben-Hillel Hacohen, *Milchemet Ha-Amim* [War Among the Nations], Tel-Aviv 1929–1930, vol. I, p. 69.

[99] Menachem Shenkin, *Kitvei . . .* [Writings of . . .], ed. A. Hermoni, Jerusalem 1936, vol. I, p. 57; Abraham Elmaliyach, *Eretz-Israel V'Suria Bimey Milchemet Haolam* [Palestine and Syria during the First World War], Jerusalem 1928–1929, vol. II, p. 105.

[100] Cohn-Reiss, *op. cit.*, II, p. 275.

[101] Ben-Hillel Hacohen, *op. cit.*, IV, p. 39.

branches of the Zionist Bank, the Anglo-Palestine Co., be closed, since "it keeps the business community in a deplorable dependence". Closed also should be "the party schools", and dabbling in politics by the Zionist agents in Constantinople should be terminated. In conclusion,

> "if the Turkish Government declared itself against Zionism and takes the proper measures against it . . . it will become clear how little sympathy Palestinian Jews have for the Zionist chauvinist aspirations."[102]

Richard Lichtheim, the Zionist representative in Constantinople, received reliable reports that "Cohn [had] gone so far as to appear before the Magistrate in Jerusalem with accusations against Zionism and provided the Turkish authorities with arguments against it".[103] It would not be too difficult to detect a similarity between the views expressed by Cohn-Reiss and the wording of Beha-ed-Din's proclamation of 25th January 1915.[104] It was also no coincidence that on 9th February 1915 Ben-Gurion and Itzhak Ben-Zvi, leaders of *Poale Zion*, were detained on charges of being members of a "secret organisation, detrimental to the interests of the State". In vain did they protest that *Poale Zion* was an open organisation, in no way inimical to Turkey. Both were former law students at the University of Constantinople and, following the outbreak of war, tried unsuccessfully to volunteer for the Turkish army. When the Capitulations were abrogated, they were among the first to adopt Ottoman nationality and actively encouraged their fellow Jews in Palestine to follow their example. On 15th March Djemal summoned them and issued a writ of deportation. Deported also were Ben-Zion Mossinsohn, Menahem Shenkin, Yoseph Aaronowitz, Dr. Chaim Bugrashov, Dr. Joseph Lurie and others. It was ironical that these men, who had been espousing the cause of the Central Powers should have been thus condemned. No less astonishing was the deportation of Dr. Bugrashov, the headmaster of the Herzliya High School, who had welcomed Djemal during the official reception given to him there on 2nd March. Closed also were the organs of the Socialist–Zionist parties, the *Ahdut* and *Hapoel Hatzair*, although they had consistently taken a pro-Turkish line in their respective editorials.[105] It would however be worthwhile to point out that most of the deportees were actively involved in the *Sprachenkampf* and that the papers mentioned were formerly bitter opponents of the *Hilfsverein*'s.

Disturbed by the newly found German-Zionist *rapprochement*, Cohn-Reiss vented his wrath again on 16th May 1915:

> "These gentlemen [he told Nathan] are international and want to maintain communica-

---

[102] *Türkei* 195, K 176954–60, Cohn-Reiss to Nathan, 18th February 1915.

[103] *Türkei* 195, K 177107–15, Lichtheim to Wangenheim, 5th June 1915, encl. in K 177106, Wangenheim to Bethmann Höllweg, 6th June 1915. On Lichtheim see Friedman, *Germany . . . and Zionism*, pp. 240–241 and *passim*.

[104] On which see Friedman, *Germany . . . and Zionism*, pp. 219–220. On Beha-ed-Din see *ibid.*, pp. 197–199.

[105] *Ibid.*, pp. 224–225. On Djemal's visit to the Herzliya High School *ibid.*, p. 221. In a letter to Jacob Schiff, Ephraim Cohn-Reiss denied that he had sent the Ottoman authorities a memorandum against the Zionists (CZA, L 2/181/11, Cohn-Reiss to Schiff, 25th November 1915). He denied the same to Consul Brode but the latter doubted the veracity of Cohn-Reiss's statement. (Brode's memo., on which see above, notes 36 and 98.)

tions with both sides, [but] we know very well how antagonistic the Palestinian Zionists are to German interests . . . The Zionist leaders in Palestine are *modern* Russian Jews, who though they may be enemies of the Russian Government, are none the less Russian in sentiment and anti-German in feeling . . . It requires an extraordinary arrogance to claim that Palestinian Zionism furthers German *Kultur*. The Zionist Bank is English, the Jewish National Fund is English, and the first foreign language in Zionist schools in Jaffa and elsewhere is French."

To Cohn-Reiss's consternation the Turks had some difficulty in distinguishing the non-Zionists from the Zionists. He listened in trepidation when Djemal Pasha told him that the *Hilfsverein* institutions "nourished Zionist tendencies also, though in a somewhat milder form." Hence, in order to draw a clear demarcation line, the German Government should advise its ally that it could no longer approve of Zionist work in Palestine. "It cannot be sufficiently emphasised," he concluded his letter, "that the great mass of Jewish population wants to be liberated from Russian-Zionist terrorism."[106]

Cohn-Reiss's correspondence was forwarded through the diplomatic courier service and was perused by the German Consulate in Jerusalem, the Embassy in Constantinople and the Ministry in Berlin. His arguments left a mark on the German diplomats.[107] Particularly influenced was Schmidt. His friendship with Cohn-Reiss was of long-standing. In February 1912 he recommended that Cohn-Reiss be decorated with the *Kgl. Kronen-Orden 4.Klasse* in honour of the forthcoming twenty-fifth anniversary of his educational activity, commenting that, in addition, Cohn-Reiss was "always ready to volunteer information on local Jewish affairs".[108] Schmidt listened readily to Cohn-Reiss and, ignorant of Hebrew, accepted his advice uncritically.[109] Schmidt's dispatches to Constantinople re-echoed Cohn-Reiss's ideas.[110]

The Zionists were outraged when they learned about the *Hilfsverein*'s moves and launched a counter-offensive. Arthur Ruppin, the Head of the Palestine Office, replied to Schmidt,[111] while Lichtheim rebutted most of the points made in the Simon–Cohn-Reiss correspondence. The latters' contention that the old *Yishuv* (the ultra-religious section of the Jewish population in Palestine) supported the *Hilfsverein*'s anti-Zionist campaign was unfounded. The protest lodged by the Chief Rabbi, Moses Franco, against Beha-ed-Din's attempt to drive a wedge between one Jew and another[112] was evidence to the contrary. Telling also was the offer made by the leaders of the Orthodox Jewish community in Frankfurt a. Main to come to Constantinople in order to convince the Turkish Government of the Zionists' loyalty.[113]

[106] *Türkei* 195, K 177248–51, Cohn-Reiss to Nathan, 16th May 1915.
[107] It influenced Richard Kühlmann, the Ambassador to Constantinople, as late as July 1917 (see Friedman, *Germany . . . and Zionism*, p. 311).
[108] Eliav, *Dokumente . . . op. cit.*, Schmidt to Wangenheim, 11th February 1912.
[109] C.Z.A., Z 3/52, Lichtheim to P.E.C. (Provisional Zionist Executive, New York), 30th April 1915.
[110] Friedman, *Germany . . . and Zionism*, pp. 247–248.
[111] *Türkei* 195, K 177260–76, Ruppin to Schmidt, 21st July 1915, encl. in E.A.C. (Zionist Executive) to A.A., 2nd September 1915. On Ruppin see Friedman, *Germany . . . and Zionism*, pp. 132–134 and passim.
[112] *Ibid.*, p. 220.
[113] *Türkei* 195, K 177107–15, Lichtheim to Wangenheim, 5th June 1915, encl. in Wangenheim to

The Straus–Ruppin–Lichtheim response blunted the edge of the *Hilfsverein*'s charges but it was primarily Consul Brode's memorandum of 26th August 1915 that finally enabled the Wilhelmstrasse to formulate its policy. Owing to illness Schmidt's influence was waning, but Brode's ascending. Brode thought that from the German point of view the campaign against the Zionists was "highly undesirable". Cohn-Reiss's intrigues were particularly "disagreeable" since he pretended to be a "victim of his German patriotism . . . and to have suffered personal injury because he had devoted himself fully, heart and soul, to the German propaganda on the *Auswärtiges Amt*'s behalf". Brode denied knowledge of "any agreement" between the Foreign Ministry and the *Hilfsverein* although schools in which German was taught and which were financed by funds from Germany would, as heretofore enjoy Consular support. However, Brode warned Cohn-Reiss that Germany evinced interest also in "other circles which . . . might be important" to her. Pondering about the future he thought that a *modus vivendi* between the two parties would have to be found. In the first place, it was most unlikely that the *Hilfsverein*, accused by the Zionists of resorting to unfair means and deprived of their cooperation, would be able to retain exclusive control of the *Technikum*, unless the students were enrolled solely from the indigenous population. But in this case, Brode concluded, "it would lose its Jewish character as had been originally planned". At all events, he thought it more prudent to leave the question to the Jews themselves. The *Reich* Government should not incur the displeasure of either party and try to use them both to Germany's advantage.[114]

This the German Government did although by now the most favoured party was the Zionist. The new policy was reflected in the instructions to the German Consulate issued by the Embassy in Constantinople on 22nd November 1915. The relevant key passage of this highly important document reads:

> "It seems politically advisable to show a friendly attitude towards Zionism and its aims. Efforts should be made to respect as far as possible, the sensitivity, if any, of the German Jews, particularly those connected with the *Hilfsverein* who, without justification, behave as if interest in the Zionist Movement implies a direct prejudice to their own position."

The Consul was requested to exert his "calming influence" upon the *Hilfsverein* representative, whenever the need might arise.[115]

The position of the German Government was now fixed and on 10th January 1916, when Simon approached Zimmermann again, he was told bluntly that Cohn-Reiss's suggestion to use the *Hilfsverein* as a means to fight Zionism was to his mind a very doubtful step to take.[116] Both parties were urged by the German

---

Bethmann Hollweg, 5th June 1915. See also Lichtheim, *Rückkehr, op. cit.*, pp. 313–315. Lichtheim received copies of Simon's and Cohn-Reiss's letters from Straus. Rabbi Rosenheim of Frankfurt a. Main, the celebrated leader of Orthodox Jewry in Germany, did eventually approach the Foreign Ministry on the Zionists' behalf (Lichtheim, *Rückkehr*, p. 314).

[114] As above, note 98. Brode's statements are further proof that the Zionist suspicions of a "secret agreement" between the *Hilfsverein* and the German Government and of the latter's intention to "germanise" the *Technikum* were misplaced.

[115] *Türkei* 195, K 177404–7, Metternich to Bethmann Hollweg, 22nd November 1915, dis. no. 693 and encls. For the full text see Friedman, *Germany . . . and Zionism*, p. 265.

[116] *Ibid.*, K 177515–6, Zimmermann to Simon, 10th January 1916.

diplomats to compose their differences and by the end of 1916 the truce was concluded. Nathan strongly condemned Cohn-Reiss's "vain insinuations and intrigues which misled James Simon".[117]

It was, however, not until the end of January 1918 that cooperation between the *Hilfsverein* and the Zionists began in earnest. That Jewish factions, formerly at loggerheads with one another, composed their differences, was largely due to the electrifying effect of the Balfour Declaration. As in the Entente and neutral countries, so also in Germany it greatly strengthened the Zionist position and made it respectable. Zionism suddenly became a factor in world politics and a topical subject for debate. It engendered a radical change in Jewish opinion. German Jewry – and this was typical to an even greater degree of the anti-Zionists – watched uneasily as the Entente reaped the rewards of the Balfour Declaration and considered it their patriotic duty to see that the imbalance was righted. The plight of Jews in Eastern Europe, now within the German sphere of interest, was a complementary factor calling for greater unity.

The idea of founding a unified body to represent the interests of German Jews and their co-religionists at the peace negotiations originated with James Simon. On 30th November 1917, he invited a number of notable German Jews but excluded the Zionists, under the pretext that they were an international, not a German organisation. The notables, however, refused to proceed without the Zionists and the latter made it known that unless their programme was accepted, they would not join. It consisted of three points: civic equality (e.g., in Romania); national-cultural autonomy in those countries where the Jews were settled in great numbers; the right to free immigration to Palestine and to cultural autonomy there.

With a common programme thrashed out, the foundation of the *Vereinigung jüdischer Organisationen Deutschlands zur Wahrung der Rechte der Juden des Ostens* (V.J.O.D.) was possible. It was an umbrella organisation for all sections of German Jewry. James Simon was elected President, Oskar Cassel and Franz Oppenheimer, Vice-Presidents, Arthur Hantke and Paul Nathan, Honorary Secretaries.[118]

With the German Government's blessings the V.J.O.D. delegation arrived in Constantinople on 14th July 1918 to negotiate the creation of "a national and religious Jewish centre in Palestine". But Talaat Pasha, the Grand Vizier, although willing to satisfy the Jews, insisted on deleting the word "national". Here the negotiations stumbled and subsequently most of the V.J.O.D. delegates returned home. On 23rd September 1918 Haifa was captured by the British forces and on 31st October an armistice with Turkey was concluded. The Imperial Ottoman era in Asia had come to a close.

The results of the war did not affect Jewish unity. So deep was the shock following Germany's defeat and so high the prestige of the Zionists in the wake of the declaration made by all the belligerent Powers, that former controversies were rendered irrelevant. Cooperation within the V.J.O.D. enhanced mutual trust and in the immediate years after the war German Jewry was united as

---

[117]Lichtheim, *Rückkehr*, pp. 314–315. In midsummer 1917 Cohn-Reiss returned to Germany.
[118]Friedman, *Germany . . . and Zionism*, pp. 392–394.

never before. This was clearly demonstrated early in March 1919, during a meeting with Count Bernstorff, now in charge of Jewish affairs at the Foreign Ministry, when representatives of the *Hilfsverein*, the *Centralverein* and of other German-Jewish organisations expressed their unanimous support of the Zionist Copenhagen Manifesto. Bernstorff thereafter invited Lichtheim to serve as his adviser. Other leaders who joined the advisory committee for the German delegation to the Peace Conference were: Dr. Eugen Fuchs, Head of the *Centralverein*, representing the non-Zionists, and Rabbi Pinchas Cohn of Ansbach representing the Orthodox. Later the programme was expanded and the item on Palestine was changed. It demanded:

> ". . . creation of such political, administrative, and economic conditions in Palestine so that its development into an autonomous Commonwealth (*Gemeinwesen*), supported by the whole of Jewry, be secured."[119]

This wording was a modified version of that submitted by the World Zionist Organization to the Peace Conference in Paris.[120] Such an ideological turnabout by the non-Zionist German Jews would not have been possible before 1918. In 1920, as a gesture of goodwill, the *Hilfsverein* sold the *Technikum* to the Zionist Organization for a small price. They showed their generosity again two years later when they sold the premises of the Lämel School as well as the Girls' School to the Keren Hayesod. Thereafter the *Hilfsverein* discontinued their activities in Palestine.[121]

[119]*Ibid.*, pp. 407, 411–416.
[120]Friedman, *The Question of Palestine, 1914–1918*, p. 318.
[121]Rinot, *op. cit.*, p. 233.

Weimar Germany and the Palestine Question

BY FRANCIS R. J. NICOSIA

In March 1925 *Legationsrat* Moritz Sobernheim, head of the Jewish Affairs section (*Jüdisch-Politische Angelegenheiten*)* in the German Foreign Office, went to Palestine to participate in the opening of the new Hebrew University in Jerusalem.[1] He spent nearly two months touring the country and meeting with Zionist and British officials about matters relating to the Mandate government in Palestine and Zionist work throughout the country. Upon his return to Berlin, Sobernheim filed a lengthy report on his trip which outlines German interests in Palestine after the First World War, attitudes towards the issues involved in the Palestine debate and the policies to be pursued based on those interests and attitudes.[2] Sobernheim's evaluation of the situation in Palestine, his description of Germany's varied interests in the Levant and the policies he recommended to best preserve and promote those interests were the foundation upon which German Palestine policy was formulated before 1933.

Sobernheim dismissed the Arabs at the very beginning. He credited the tremendous growth and development of Palestine since the war to the strength and dynamism of Jewish capital and labour. He described the Arabs as unable and unwilling to do anything to develop the country and as completely unjustified in their claims of being the oppressed component in the Palestine

ABBREVIATIONS IN FOOTNOTES
AA: Auswärtiges Amt (Foreign Office)
ADAP: Akten zur Deutschen Auswärtigen Politik, 1918–1945
BA: Bundesarchiv, Koblenz
DB: Deutsche Botschaft (German Embassy)
DBFP: Documents on British Foreign Policy, 1919–1939
DG: Deutsche Gesandtschaft (German Embassy)
DGK: Deutsches General-Konsulat
DK: Deutsches Konsulat
ISA: Israel State Archives, Jerusalem
PA: Politisches Archiv des Auswärtigen Amts, Bonn
St.S: Staatssekretär (State Secretary)

[1]Until 1936 *Politische Abteilung III-2* (*Orient*) in the German Foreign Office was responsible for the Middle East and South Asia. Two offices within this department dealt directly with Palestine, one responsible for Egypt, the Sudan, Arabia, Palestine, Syria, Iraq and Abyssinia, and the other for Jewish Affairs under Sobernheim. The Jewish Affairs section was set up in early 1918 as part of the last minute effort by the German government to counter the effects of the Balfour Declaration on Jewish opinion in Europe, and to help secure continued Jewish sympathy for Germany. It was eliminated in 1933. Professor Sobernheim, a renowned Orientalist, did not belong officially to the Zionist movement, but he did sympathise with its aims. See: Richard Lichtheim, *Rückkehr. Lebenserinnerungen aus der Frühzeit des deutschen Zionismus*, Stuttgart 1970, Veröffentlichung des Leo Baeck Instituts, p. 377; Arnold Paucker, *Der Jüdische Abwehrkampf gegen Antisemitismus und Nationalsozialismus in den letzten Jahren der Weimarer Republik*, Hamburg 1968/1969, p. 282.

[2]PA: Botschaft Ankara. Pol. 3-Palästina, 1924–1938. 'Bericht über meine Reise nach Palästina im März und April, 1925', III O 1269.

triangle. In Sobernheim's judgment, here was the basis for satisfying one of Germany's major interests in Palestine and elsewhere, namely the quest for markets for German goods. He observed that in the overall picture of world trade Palestine was relatively insignificant; however, it was a country which was opening up and developing as a result of Jewish efforts and which would have substantial economic needs in the coming years that could only be satisfied from the outside. The implications are clear, for Palestine would provide a growing market for the kinds of goods Germany exported most. The natural trade ties between Jewish businesses in Germany and in Palestine would ensure that Germany cornered a considerable part of this market. The Jews of Palestine, industrious, dynamic, progressive, driven by an ideal and financed by a prosperous Jewish community in the West, and not the backward, indolent Arabs, would be the buyers of ever-increasing amounts of German goods.

Sobernheim also stressed the necessity of rebuilding and expanding German cultural interests and prestige in Palestine and the Middle East as the best means of achieving the desired economic goals. Before the war, Germany had exercised considerable cultural influence in Syria and Palestine. German schools, institutes, hospitals, orphanages etc. were numerous and among the best in the Middle East. Furthermore, the presence of some 2,000 German colonists, most of whom were members of the Protestant Temple Society, enjoying friendly relations with their Arab and Jewish neighbours as well as with the Turkish authorities, helped to generate considerable prestige and good will for Germany from all segments of society, Moslem, Christian and Jewish.[3] Indeed, in spite of her war-time alliance with the hated Turks, there does not seem to have been any perceptible decline in German popularity and prestige.

Sobernheim realised the cultural advantages that Germany might reap from the continued success of Zionist efforts and the eventual emergence of a predominantly Jewish Palestine. Only a minority of German Jews opted for Zionism, but those few who actually settled in Palestine tended to occupy the highest professional, business and academic positions within the Jewish community there. This small nucleus of German Jews, combined with the masses of Eastern European Jewish immigrants who were largely German-orientated in culture, language and affection, were seen by Sobernheim as potential agents of German culture in the Middle East. He realised the long-term political and economic advantages that would fall to Germany as a result of this combination.[4]

Finally, Sobernheim emphasised that England was the most important element in the Palestine situation as far as Germany was concerned. Germany had to secure the friendship and cooperation of England if her limited interests and

---

[3] For the best, most comprehensive account of the beginnings and development of the Temple colonies in Palestine in the nineteenth century, see: Alex Carmel, *Die Siedlungen der Württembergischen Templer in Palästina 1868–1918*, Stuttgart 1973. A rather dated work, but useful, is: Hans Seibt, *Moderne Kolonisation in Palästina*, Teil I, Diss., Leipzig 1933. See also: Paul Sauer, *Beilharz-Chronik. Die Geschichte eines Schwarzwälder Bauern- und Handwerkergeschlechts vom 15. Jahrhundert bis Heute in Deutschland, Palästina und Australien*, Ulm 1975.

[4] Klaus Herrmann, 'Political Response to the Balfour Declaration in Imperial Germany. German Judaism', *The Middle East Journal*, 19 (1965), p. 307. See also: Jacob Marcus, *The Rise and Destiny of the German Jew*, Cincinnati 1934, p. 205.

objectives in Palestine as well as her more crucial goals in Europe were to be achieved. Sobernheim addressed himself to Britain's position as Mandatory power in Palestine by urging continued German support for and cooperation with British authorities in their efforts to carry out the provisions of the Mandate. In his view, this was the only way in which to protect and promote German interests in Palestine and in the rest of the Middle East.

It is not known what immediate reaction if any the German government might have had to Sobernheim's report. The report simply outlined policies which were for the most part already being pursued, and would continue to be pursued until 1933. This essay will examine and evaluate in greater detail the fundamentals presented in the Sobernheim report in the light of events as they unfolded in Palestine. German interests in that part of the world, and in the more crucial arena of Europe, were best served by supporting the post-First World War status-quo in Palestine and in the rest of the Middle East. The two political facts of life in post-war Palestine, namely the Balfour Declaration and the growing Jewish presence on the one hand, and British control through the Mandate on the other, were deemed by Berlin to be in the German interest.

With her defeat, Germany lost every advantage she had had in Palestine prior to the war, with the possible exception of the continued good will of the inhabitants.[5] Perhaps the most immediate loss had been the confiscation of all German property and institutions by British authorities in 1918, and the internment of most of the approximately 2,000 *Palästinadeutsche* in camps in Egypt.[6] However, by the beginning of September 1920 the Palestinian Germans had begun returning to their homes and settlements in Palestine.[7]

The problem of the returning *Palästinadeutsche*, the manner of their return and the restoration of their property and rights became the first issue in Anglo-German diplomacy regarding Palestine after the First World War. There was a great deal of suspicion on the part of British officials towards these German natives of Palestine in the early post-war period. To the new English administration in Palestine they represented a rather direct and uncomfortable presence of a recently defeated Germany in a country already demonstrating its potential for conflict and violence. Until the conclusion of the Treaty of Lausanne with Turkey in July 1923 the Palestine Germans were considered by British authorities as dependants of an enemy state. Upon their return to Palestine in 1921 and 1922 the *Palästinadeutsche* were faced with a political situation vastly different from the one which they had left just a few years before. They had to reconstruct their lives in a society already torn by hostilities and conflicts between Arabs and Jews and under the control of a suspicious British administration. From the beginning the Germans of Palestine undertook the almost impossible

---

[5]Carmel, *op. cit.*, pp. 258, 292–294.
[6]For a complete list of all German colonies, schools, hospitals and other institutions in Palestine during the inter-war years, see: Francis R. J. Nicosia, *Germany and the Palestine Question, 1933–1939*, Diss., McGill University 1977, appendices 3, 4 and 5.
[7]PA: Pol. Abt. III, Innere Verwaltung 14-Palästina, Aufzeichnung (author unknown), 23rd September 1920.

task of maintaining strict neutrality between the Arabs and the Jews and demonstrated unconditional loyalty to and support for the British administration.[8] The Arab and Jewish communities were capable of making life difficult for the Germans in Palestine when they suspected that the German settlers were partial to or supporting one side or the other; moreover, these suspicions were fed by a persistent refusal on the part of the German government and the German settlers in Palestine to support either side. England alone was the most important guarantee for the continued existence of the German settlements and institutions in Palestine and she alone possessed the power to protect or eliminate the German presence.

The British government agreed to cover the costs of returning the Palestine Germans from Egypt to Palestine, thanks largely to the efforts of Sir Herbert Samuel, the first British High Commissioner in Palestine. Confiscated property was returned and compensation made for damages or losses incurred during the period of internment in Egypt.[9] A controversy occurred in November 1920 when Britain attempted to send a group of Palestine Germans from Egypt to Germany instead of to their homes in Palestine. The problem was resolved according to Germany's wishes after strong intervention by the German Foreign Office on behalf of the German settlers.[10] By 1925 the German Consul-General Kapp in Jerusalem was able to report to Berlin that the *Palästinadeutsche* were securely re-established in Palestine.[11] They were enjoying friendly relations with Herbert Samuel and the British administration despite the lingering hostility of a few British officials. Kapp reiterated that German neutrality in the Arab–Jewish conflict was the best proof of German loyalty to and cooperation with the administration.[12]

It took about five years for the German Foreign Office to pick up the threads of a policy which had emerged in Berlin immediately after the publication of the Balfour Declaration.[13] The *Palästinadeutsche* were by no means the only

---

[8] PA: Pol. Abt. III, Politik 16-Palästina, Jahresbericht über die Verhältnisse der deutsch-evangelischen Gemeinde zu Jerusalem 1922/1923, III 0 3167/23, 10th October 1923.

[9] PA: Pol. Abt. III, Innere Verwaltung 14-Palästina, Aufzeichnung der Pol. III (author unknown), 10th September 1920; and Pol. Abt. III, Politik 6-Palästina, DK/Triest an AA/Berlin, Nr. 2452, 26th July 1921.

[10] PA: Pol. Abt. III, Innere Verwaltung 14-Palästina, Aufzeichnung der Pol. III (author unknown), 10th November 1920.

[11] During his five-year tenure as High Commissioner Herbert Samuel was especially sympathetic and helpful towards the German settlers in Palestine. PA: Pol. Abt. III, Politik 10-Palästina, Bd. 1., Aufzeichnung Sobernheims, III 0 493, 11th September 1924. British authorities distinguished between German welfare institutions such as hospitals, orphanages, etc. and the Templar settlements. The former were Lutheran and Catholic institutions which were tied to and run by the Churches in Germany for the most part and were regarded by British authorities as German propaganda centres. The documents show that these did not always receive a sympathetic hearing. The Templar settlements, on the other hand, were independent of influence and control from Germany before 1933 and were generally favoured by the British. PA: Gesandtschaft Bern, Palästina 1922–1937, Aufzeichnung des AA über die Lage in Palästina (author unknown), Nr. IIb 245, 8th May 1922.

[12] PA: Pol. Abt. III, Pol. 3-Länder (England), Bd. 1. DGK/Jerusalem an AA/Berlin, 1297/25, 27th June 1925.

[13] See: Alex Carmel, 'Die deutsche Palästinapolitik 1871–1914', *Jahrbuch des Instituts für Deutsche*

agents of German influence in Palestine, nor were they a significant economic factor. The approximately 2,000 German Templars, Lutherans and Catholics living in Palestine represented a rather small vehicle for the promotion of German political, economic and cultural interests; on the other hand, the growing number of Central and Eastern European Jewish immigrants were still culturally and spiritually dependent on the German-speaking world. As early as September 1920 there had been talk in the German Foreign Office of actively renewing support for the German and international Zionist movements as a means of rebuilding German influence in Palestine. Karl von Schubert, State Secretary in the Foreign Office from 1924 until 1930 and an active supporter of the Zionist movement, submitted a memorandum in September 1920 in which he stressed the positive effect that German-Jewish financial help for Palestine would have on Germany's attempts to regain her influence there.[14] He also observed that efforts in Palestine would be of considerable benefit to German foreign policy throughout the Middle East.

On 8th May 1922 the German Foreign Office issued its first comprehensive statement on Palestine to all German diplomatic missions abroad.[15] The statement emphasised the advantages won by Britain in Palestine and throughout the Middle East as a result of the war, namely the Mandate over strategically important Palestine and the sympathy of the world's 14 million Jews. The statement also analysed the difficulties Britain was experiencing as a result of her new position in Palestine; these difficulties were caused by the Arabs and to some extent the French, less from an opposition to Zionist activities at that point than from a more immediate distrust of English intentions. The 8th May statement did not directly criticise or oppose British authority in Palestine; however, it did portray the British position as contradictory and therefore unstable due to a degree of Jewish and French distrust and outright Arab opposition.

The memorandum presented a positive analysis of Germany's position and potential advantages in the economic affairs of Palestine. It referred to the favourable trade position being established, with German imports into Palestine fourth in total volume behind imports from England, Egypt and the United States. German imports into the country were increasing rapidly. Most of the English, Egyptian and American imports into Palestine were consumer goods which Germany was not in a position to export in 1922. Nevertheless, Germany was able to export machinery, heavy industrial products and building materials which would be greatly needed in Palestine as more and more Jewish capital and immigration stimulated the development of the country.[16] It was also

---

Geschichte, IV, Tel-Aviv 1975; Herrmann, *loc. cit.*, pp. 313–318; Lichtheim, *Rückkehr*, pp. 242–252, 376; Leonard Stein, *The Balfour Declaration*, New York 1961, pp. 539, 602; Saadia Weltmann, 'Germany, Turkey and the Zionist Movement, 1914–1918', *Review of Politics*, 1961, pp. 262–269; and Egmont Zechlin, *Die deutsche Politik und die Juden im Ersten Weltkrieg*, Göttingen 1969, pp. 419–426, 434–435.

[14] PA: Pol. Abt. III, Politik 2-Palästina, Aufzeichnung von Schuberts, 2nd September 1920.
[15] PA: Gesandtschaft Bern, Palästina 1922–1937, Aufzeichnung des AA über die Lage in Palästina, Nr. IIb 245, 8th May 1922.
[16] For trade statistics between Germany and Palestine during the Weimar years and for a list of the major exports to Palestine during those years, see: Nicosia, *op. cit.*, appendices 6 and 7

observed that German-Jewish economic and financial cooperation in Palestine would be of considerable value to the German-Christian communities. The spiritual and cultural ties between Germany and the growing numbers of Central and Eastern European Jewish immigrants in Palestine would afford German business the ideal means for promoting German exports to Palestine and the Middle East. The 8th May memorandum announced the renewal of an active policy in Palestine with the intention of securing primarily economic goals for Germany. It was clear that the Foreign Office considered the Zionist movement the best vehicle for securing German aims in the Levant. The memorandum spelled out in detail the major thrust of German Palestine policy during the Weimar years, and concluded:

> "Friendly relations with the Jewish movement, as will doubtless be pursued by their leaders, could be of significance for Germany's economic and even political position."

So strongly did the German government identify its interests in Palestine with the Zionist movement that the Foreign Office in Berlin sought to intercede on behalf of the Zionist cause in its rift with the Vatican after the First World War. In a *Pro-Memoria* delivered to the League of Nations on 4th June 1922 the Vatican expressed its approval of the British Mandate over Palestine but its opposition to the Balfour Declaration which was to be incorporated into the Mandate for Palestine.[17] The Vatican resented any gains made in the Holy Land by Judaism and expressed fears that the Declaration gave Jews a privileged position in Palestine at the expense of other nationalities and religions.

Five months before the Vatican initiative, the German Foreign Office had instructed its Embassy at the Vatican to explore opportunities which might lead to a change in the Vatican's hostile attitude towards the Zionist movement. Berlin suggested talks between Zionist officials and leading personalities of the Roman Curia.[18] The Embassy was told that an understanding between the Vatican and the Zionist movement would be desirable in the light of the close ties between World Jewry and German culture. This effort by the German Foreign Office was not successful. The Vatican did not change its basic opposition, and remained aloof and officially neutral in the Arab–Jewish conflicts of 1929 and later.[19] The German government apparently feared that the Vatican might exercise an anti-Zionist influence at least on Germany's Catholics, which might have jeopardised the efforts of the Foreign Office to forge an alliance between Germany and the Zionist movement.

Before Germany entered the League of Nations in October 1926 there existed no formal treaty relationship, based on a German recognition of the British Mandate, between Germany and Palestine. The Spanish Consulate in Jeru-

---

[17]PA: Botschaft beim Heiligen Stuhl, 51: Palästina-Zionismus, 1919–1943, DB/Heiliger Stuhl an AA/Berlin, Nr. 92, 3rd July 1922.
[18]PA: Botschaft beim Heiligen Stuhl, 51: AA/Berlin an DB/Heiliger Stuhl, Nr. IIa Va46, 20th January 1922.
[19]PA: Pol. Abt. III, Politik 3-Palästina, Bd. 1. DB/Heiliger Stuhl an AA/Berlin, Nr. 204, 4th September 1929.

salem had taken care of German interests in Palestine since the end of the war, until the German Consulate-General was able to reopen in 1924. Palestine was not an independent state, however, and the existence of a German consular mission there did not constitute recognition of the Mandate system.

League membership and acceptance of the principles of the Covenant formally committed Germany to the post-war settlement in Palestine. Germany became bound to the Mandate system as outlined in Article 22 of the League Covenant and to the British Mandate over Palestine as adopted by the League on the 24th July 1922. As a League member, she was treaty-bound to support and promote the provisions embodied in the Balfour Declaration which had been incorporated into the Preamble of the Palestine Mandate and into Articles 2, 4, 6, 11, 22 and 23.[20]

The memorandum of 8th May 1922 had already demonstrated Berlin's intention to promote Zionist interests in Palestine. At that time, however, there was no indication of a specific German commitment to the British presence and the Mandate system. The memorandum had only mentioned the contradictions and conflicts in British war-time and post-war policy; it refrained from taking a position in the debate at that time over the selection of the Mandatory power for Palestine. Although the memorandum had been issued some three months before formal League presentation of the Palestine Mandate to Great Britain, there was little doubt at that time that Britain would receive it.

Events in Europe between 1922 and 1925, their effect on German Foreign policy and more specifically on Germany's relations with Britain and France had an impact on the German approach to Palestine and the Middle East as well. Germany's diplomatic isolation and the importance to her of the tenuous relationship with the Soviet Union were still harsh realities in 1922. This situation gave way to the era of Locarno which embodied cooperation and friendly relations with the West, especially with England, as the best means of promoting German interests in Europe and elsewhere. The Locarno system became the basis of German foreign policy under Stresemann. To grasp the effects of this process on the German approach to Palestine one need only compare the memorandum of 8th May 1922 with the Sobernheim report of April 1925. Sobernheim reiterated the advantages to Germany of supporting the Zionist movement; he also emphasised that the success of the German-Zionist connection as well as the welfare of the German-Christian settlements and institutions were best served by the successful implementation of the British Mandate and Germany's full cooperation with the Mandate authorities.

Germany was accorded Great Power status with a permanent seat on the League Council, and she became a member of the Permanent Mandates Commission.[21] Germany's main interest in securing membership on the Man-

---

[20]For the complete text of the Palestine Mandate and of Article 22 of the League of Nations Covenant, see: J. C. Hurewitz, *Diplomacy in the Near and Middle East. A Documentary Record, 1914–1956*, II, New York 1956, pp. 61–62, 106–111.

[21]At its meeting of 9th September 1927 the League Council increased membership on the Permanent Mandates Commission from nine to ten with the appointment of Dr. Ludwig Kastl from Germany. Dr. Kastl was a former high official from the German Colonial Office. In May 1930 Kastl was replaced by Dr. Julius Ruppel, also a former colonial officer.

dates Commission was her desire to continue working in the colonial field, and the hope of recovering some of her lost colonies which had become Mandates of the victorious Allies. Stresemann pushed especially hard for the seat in the face of much initial opposition from Britain, France, Belgium and Japan, or those powers which stood to lose by colonial revisions.[22] Indeed, Stresemann believed that the colonial question and the return of at least some of Germany's former African colonies, like the other revisions of the Versailles settlement which Germany was pursuing, would be best resolved through patient cooperation and negotiation with the Western powers and membership in the League of Nations.[23]

With her seat on the Mandates Commission, Germany became directly involved in the issues and administration of the Palestine Mandate. Britain administered Palestine in the name of the League of Nations and was responsible in theory for her policies to the Commission of which Germany was a member. The Palestine issue was certainly not as vital to Germany as was the administration and desired return of her former colonies; however, participation in the Commission's deliberations provided her with an instrument through which she could better protect and promote her interests in Palestine and elsewhere.

The task of promoting a pro-Zionist, pro-Mandate policy at home was complicated by the Zionist–anti-Zionist cleavage within the Jewish community in Germany. The ideological conflict and propaganda war between the various liberal/"assimilationist" Jewish organisations and the German Zionists had already reached a high level of intensity during the years immediately before the First World War.[24] By the outbreak of war in 1914 all the principal Jewish organisations in Germany had either actively joined or openly sympathised with the anti-Zionist campaign.[25] When war broke out, however, Zionists and anti-Zionists alike became caught up in the patriotic fervour and national

---

[22]PA: Büro des St. S. X-Kolonialfragen (Mandatsgebiete), Bd. 2, AA/Berlin (Stresemann) an DB/London, DB/Paris u. DG/Brussel, IIIa 1.3305/27, 26th April 1927; and BA: R/43 1–162. Reichstagrede Gustav Stresemanns, 23rd June 1927.

[23]PA: Büro des St. S. X-Kolonialfragen (Mandatsgebiete), Bd. 1, Rundfunkrede Gustav Stresemanns vom 4. November 1925, Nr. 100, 13th April 1926. See also: ADAP: B, I/1, Nr. 230.

[24]Jehuda Reinharz, *Fatherland or Promised Land. The Dilemma of the German Jew, 1893–1914*, Ann Arbor 1975, chapter V; Ismar Schorsch, *Jewish Reactions to German Anti-Semitism, 1870–1914*, New York–London–Philadelphia 1972, pp. 179 ff., 195 ff.; Arnold Paucker, 'Zur Problematik einer jüdischen Abwehrstrategie in der deutschen Gesellschaft', in *Juden im Wilhelminischen Deutschland 1890–1914*. Ein Sammelband herausgegeben von Werner E. Mosse unter Mitwirkung von Arnold Paucker, Tübingen 1976 (Schriftenreihe wissenschaftlicher Abhandlungen des Leo Baeck Instituts 33), pp. 591 ff. See also: Zechlin, *op. cit.*, p. 307.

[25]These included: the *Centralverein deutscher Staatsbürger jüdischen Glaubens*, the *Hilfsverein der deutschen Juden*, the *Vereinigung für das liberale Judentum*, the *Reformgemeinde zu Berlin*, the *Agudat Israel*, the *Deutsch-Israelitischer Gemeindebund*, the *Verband der Deutschen Juden*, the *B'nai B'rith* and the *Verband der jüdischen Jugendvereine Deutschlands*. The campaign was led by an umbrella organisation established in October 1912, known as the *Reichsverband zur Bekämpfung des Zionismus*. The *Reichsverband* was organised mainly by leaders of the *Vereinigung für das liberale Judentum* and had the support of the *Centralverein*. Its name was changed to the *Antizionistisches Komitee* in December 1912. See: Reinharz, *op. cit.*, pp. 218–219.

Foundation Meeting of the Pro-Palästina Komitee on 15th December 1926 in the Hotel Kaiserhof, Berlin

Seated second on left, Leo Baeck; in the centre, Albert Einstein; second row, ninth from left, Eduard Bernstein; at back, standing on left, Robert Weltsch

hysteria of their fellow-citizens; during the war years the bitterness and strife between the two groups for the most part came to a temporary halt.[26]

The struggle between Zionists and anti-Zionists was renewed after the war with an even greater intensity as a result of the political realities of Weimar Germany. Emancipation, and all that the term implies, reached its most advanced stage as a result of the conditions of war and of the subsequent democratic Weimar Republic. At the same time antisemitism as a political weapon and as a socio-political force achieved a hitherto unprecedented level of intensity, openness and public tolerance during the Weimar years. The intensification of both currents in German society further deepened the cleavages among German Jews over the question of Zionism; it also tended to undermine the ability of the German-Jewish community to understand and to accurately assess what was happening around them.[27]

The increasing virulence of the antisemitic movement, coupled with the growing animosity between Zionists and anti-Zionists, tended to politicise the Jewish community as never before. The antisemitism of the day made most Jews either more militant in their Zionism or more militant in their opposition to it. Liberal or "assimilationist" Jews on the one hand and the Zionists on the other believed that their respective positions were the best protection for the entire Jewish community against the antisemitic threat. The older, pre-war representatives of liberal Jewry, the *Centralverein deutscher Staatsbürger jüdischen Glaubens* and the *Vereinigung für das liberale Judentum*, were joined by the ultra-assimilationist, *Verband nationaldeutscher Juden*, and to some extent the *Reichsbund jüdischer Frontsoldaten* in the struggle against Zionism. The liberal/assimilationist forces, which represented the vast majority of German Jewry, attempted to counter Nazi propaganda that the Jews were an alien body in Germany, a charge that had been traditionally accepted by the Zionist movement as part of its ideological argument. The Zionist premise that the Jews were a separate people, that there was a definite link between *Stamm* and nationality and that German Jews were members not only of a separate *Religionsgemeinschaft* but of a distinct *Volksgemeinschaft* as well, with its own language, traditions, culture, heritage and country (Eretz Israel), was viewed with alarm by the liberal majority. The majority maintained that German Jewry was as natural and as integral a part of the German *Volksgemeinschaft* as their Christian fellow-citizens and viewed Zionist ideology as a dangerous ally of antisemitism. This was the futile attempt by the mainstream of German Jewry to counter both antisemitic and Zionist propaganda with the theories and ideals of a pluralistic society which had the façade but not the substance of reality in Weimar Germany.[28]

The German government had to make its *Palästinapolitik* palatable to its Jewish and non-Jewish citizens, particularly to the former, because opposition to Zionism was representative of German-Jewish opinion in general. The government sought to enlist greater popular sympathy for its support of the

---

[26]*Ibid.*, pp. 222 ff.; Schorsch, *op. cit.*, p. 202; Paucker, 'Abwehrstrategie', *loc. cit.*, p. 525.
[27]Kurt Blumenfeld, *Erlebte Judenfrage. Ein Vierteljahrhundert deutscher Zionismus*, Stuttgart 1962, Veröffentlichung des Leo Baeck Instituts, pp. 180–181.
[28]See Paucker, *Der jüdische Abwehrkampf*, *op. cit.*, *passim.*, Reinharz, *op. cit.*, chapter V.

Zionist cause in Germany and in Palestine. The instrument chosen for the domestic promotion of the Zionist cause was the *Pro-Palästina Komitee* (PPK.), which was re-established in December 1926.[29] German Zionists had been urging such a move for some time; with the blessing of the German Foreign Office and with the example of other governments in Europe and overseas, they were able to reconstruct a *Pro-Palästina Komitee* similar to its short-lived war-time predecessor. The PPK. was again composed of prominent Jews and Gentiles[30] and adopted as its goals those that had been pursued by the first PPK.; these included the promotion of Zionist goals in Palestine and the mobilisation of support for those goals within Germany. Its official programme stressed the humanitarian nature of Zionist efforts in Palestine, as well as the necessity of educating German public opinion about those efforts and of strengthening the ties between Germany and Palestine.[31] The official programme also emphasised:

> ". . . daß das jüdische Aufbauwerk in Palästina ein hervorragendes Mittel für die wirtschaftliche und kulturelle Entwicklung des Orients, für die Ausbreitung deutscher Wirtschaftsbeziehungen und für die Versöhnung der Völker ist".

The first chairman of the *Pro-Palästina Komitee* was Count Johann von Bernstorff, the war-time German Ambassador to the United States and to the Ottoman Empire. Bernstorff had spent much of his time in the United States selling the cause of the Central Powers to American Jewry in an effort to keep America neutral. In Constantinople in 1917 and 1918 Bernstorff had been instrumental in the efforts of German Zionist leaders and the German government to persuade the Ottoman government to come out in favour of a Jewish commonwealth in Palestine.[32]

In his Memoirs Bernstorff asserts that the *Pro-Palästina Komitee* had the warm support of the German government and that the Foreign Office in Berlin had urged him to become its chairman.[33] Both he and his Jewish colleagues from the *Zionistische Vereinigung für Deutschland* on the *Pro-Palästina Komitee* misleadingly stressed the belated war-time support for the Zionist cause shown by the German

---

[29] In May 1918 the German government cooperated in the establishment of the *Deutsches Komitee zur Förderung der jüdischen Palästinasiedlung* in Berlin. This was part of the government's attempt to offset the propaganda advantages reaped by Great Britain with the Balfour Declaration in November 1917. The original *Pro-Palästina Komitee* attracted prominent Jewish and non-Jewish Germans of all political and ideological shades, brought together by the common conviction that Germany's political, economic and strategic interests were best served by promoting the Zionist cause in Palestine. The majority of the members of the first *Komitee* were not Jewish. See: Joseph Walk, 'Das Deutsche Komitee Pro-Palästina, 1926–1933', in *Bulletin des Leo Baeck Instituts*, XV (1976), Nr. 52, pp. 162–193; Weltmann, *loc. cit.*, p. 266; Zechlin, *op. cit.*, pp. 434 ff.

[30] Twelve members from the original *Pro-Palästina Komitee* became members of the new organisation. They were Otto Auhagen, Georg Bernhard, Robert Breuer, Otto Eberhard, Adolf Grabowsky, Otto Hoetzsch, Ernst Jaeckh, Carl Meinhof, Lothar Meyer, Werner Sombart, Ludwig Stein and Oskar von Truppel. See: Walk, *loc. cit.*, p. 165, n. 12.

[31] PA: Pol. Abt. III, Nachlaß Sobernheim: Jüdische Angelegenheiten, Deutsches Komitee Pro-Palästina.

[32] Zechlin, *op. cit.*, pp. 493 ff. According to Joseph Walk, Bernstorff originally had been less than sympathetic towards Zionism but had changed his views as a result of the influence of Dr. Isaak Straus and Arthur Ruppin. See: Walk, *loc. cit.*, p. 169, n. 24.

[33] J.-H. Graf von Bernstorff, *Memoirs of Count Bernstorff*, New York 1936, pp. 331–333.

government. Bernstorff attempts to convince his readers that Germany, not England, deserved most of the credit for the success of Zionist efforts in Palestine up to that point and that the German government had actively promoted the Zionist cause before the Balfour Declaration.[34] Besides the usual arguments concerning economic, political and cultural advantages for Germany through support of the Zionist movement, the Foreign Office and the *Pro-Palästina Komitee* both underlined the moral obligation which Germany had undertaken, as a member of the League of Nations, to uphold the provisions of the League Covenant and the Palestine Mandate. This meant among other things the fulfilment of the promises embodied in the Balfour Declaration. In a letter to Georg Mecklenburg of the *Centralverein* Bernstorff emphasised Germany's new international responsibilities as a result of her membership in the League, specifically her responsibility for upholding the provisions of the Palestine Mandate.[35] He also noted:

> "Die Förderung der jüdischen Palästinasiedlung ist ein vom Standpunkt der deutschen Aussenpolitik zu begrüssendes Unternehmen."

In a note to the German Consulate-General in Jerusalem in February 1927 the Foreign Office in Berlin made the same points regarding the re-establishment of the *Pro-Palästina Komitee*.[36]

Non-Jewish support for and membership in the *Pro-Palästina Komitee* came for the most part from the liberal, democratic parties at the centre of the German political spectrum, namely from the Social Democrats (SPD), the *Deutsche Demokratische Partei* (DDP) and the Catholic *Zentrum*.[37] Since Jewish members came almost exclusively from the ranks of the SPD and the DDP, these two parties had by far the strongest representation in the PPK. The long list of prominent personalities from the SPD, the DDP and the *Zentrum*, as well as from the Foreign Office and other government agencies, who became members of the *Pro-Palästina Komitee* reflects the broad and continuing support within the German government for the Zionist cause before 1933. The list includes such figures as the State Secretary in the *Reichskanzlei*, Hermann Pünder, Mayor Konrad Adenauer of Cologne and former Chancellor Josef Karl Wirth of the *Zentrum* Party, Count von Bernstorff, *Regierungspräsident* Hermann Hausmann and Prussian *Kultusminister* Carl Heinrich Becker of the DDP, and Rudolf Breitscheid, Prussian *Ministerpräsident* Otto Braun, *Reichstagspräsident* Paul Löbe and Chancellor Hermann Müller of the SPD. The crucial support of the German Foreign Office was reinforced by the membership of *Ministerialdirigent* Hartmann Freiherr von Richthofen of the *Orient-Abteilung* and State Secretary

---

[34]*Ibid.* See also: PA: Pol. Abt. III, Politik 2a-Palästina, Bd. 1, Denkschrift betr. Gründung eines Deutschen Komitees Pro-Palästina, von der Zionistischen Vereinigung für Deutschland (no date).
[35]PA: Pol. Abt. III, Politik 2a-Palästina, Bd. 1, Bernstorff an Mecklenburg, 3rd October 1927.
[36]PA: Pol. Abt. III, Politik 2a-Palästina, Bd. 1, AA/Berlin an DGK/Jerusalem, III 0 807, 22nd February 1927.
[37]Several members of the conservative parties, including the *Deutsche Volkspartei* (DVP), the *Wirtschaftspartei* and the *Deutschnationale Volkspartei* (DNVP), also joined the *Pro-Palästina Komitee*. For a detailed analysis of the leading members of the *Pro-Palästina Komitee* and their political and occupational affiliations, see: Walk, *loc. cit.*, pp. 168–178.

Karl von Schubert. Other key figures who became members of the PPK included Germany's representatives at the League of Nations and on the Permanent Mandates Commission, Dr. Ludwig Kastl and Dr. Julius Ruppel, as well as the German Consul-General in Jerusalem, Erich Nord, and Dr. Curt Prüfer of the *Orient-Abteilung* in the German Foreign office.

The membership rolls of the *Pro-Palästina Komitee* continued to grow after 1926, and by April 1932 the PPK had secured the participation of 217 of the most prominent Germans, Jewish and non-Jewish, in public life.[38] The extent of non-Jewish participation in the *Pro-Palästina Komitee* was bound to have a positive influence on both Christian and Jewish public opinion; moreover, the active membership of prominent non-Zionist Jews such as Leo Baeck, Albert Einstein, Bernhard Kahn, Eugen Landau, Leo Simon, Moritz Sobernheim and Isak Unna, could only have a positive impact on Zionist fortunes within the still predominantly liberal/assimilationist German-Jewish community.[39]

The only serious opposition to the pro-Zionist policy of the government and to the creation of the *Pro-Palästina Komitee* came from within the German-Jewish community itself. Most German Jews, spiritually, culturally and nationally German to the core, feared that their identity was being torn from them, from within and from without, by the Zionists and by the antisemites. Max Naumann of the *Verband nationaldeutscher Juden* felt that the German government was being drawn into this process by the Zionist side. Immediately following the *Gründungsversammlung* of the *Pro-Palästina Komitee* in December 1926 Naumann expressed the fear that:

> "... selbst hohe Beamte des Reiches und der Staaten unter dem Einfluß zionistischer Ratgeber sich in Gefahr begaben, für die Zwecke der Jüdisch-Nationalen ausgenützt zu werden".[40]

Jewish opposition to the *Pro-Palästina Komitee* centred its efforts on the non-Jewish members of the PPK. The *Vereinigung für das liberale Judentum* sent a sharp protest note to State Secretary Hermann Pünder on 24th December 1926, while the approximately seventy non-Jewish members of the PPK were sent questionnaires early in 1927 asking them to justify their membership in the PPK.[41]

Early in 1927 representatives of various anti-Zionist Jewish organisations and their non-Jewish sympathisers met to organise their campaign against the *Pro-Palästina Komitee* and the Zionist movement as a whole. An official of the *Orient-Abteilung (Abteilung III)* in the German Foreign Office, *Gesandter* R. Diel, attended the meeting and reported that the assembled representatives had completely rejected the concept of a separate Jewish people with a separate identity.[42] Diel further noted that Zionist efforts to revive the Hebrew language as the basis of a separate Jewish culture were also rejected with the argument that to do so would remove Western European Jewry from its only true "Kulturmutterboden". The most critical resolutions at the meeting accused the Zionists of

[38]*Ibid.*, p. 184.
[39]*Ibid.*, pp. 176–178.
[40]*Ibid.*, p. 178.
[41]*Ibid.*, pp. 178–179.
[42]PA: Pol. Abt. III, Politik 2a-Palästina, Bd. 1, Aufzeichnung Diels, 9th February 1927.

playing into the hands of both the antisemites in Germany and the English in Palestine; it was argued that:

> ". . . Zionismus und Antisemitismus sind korrespondierende Erscheinungen, die zu den vielfachen Spaltungen innerhalb des deutschen Volkes noch neue hinzufügten".

Finally, the delegates concluded that Palestine did not belong to the Jewish people and that the Jews of Germany would have to choose between Germany and Palestine.

From the beginning the German government refrained from becoming actively involved in the ideological battle raging within the Jewish community. This was of little consequence in view of the active policy pursued by the government based on its interpretation of the national interest. All of the actions of the German government since 1922 had been predicated on a fundamental support for Zionist efforts in Palestine. Its views were echoed by leading officials of the *Pro-Palästina Komitee* in their response to the pressures of the anti-Zionist Jewish groups against the PPK. At the *Gründungsversammlung* of 15th December 1926 Count von Bernstorff addressed himself to the Jewish opponents of the PPK in the following way:

> "Um so weniger, sollte ich denken, brauchten deutsche Juden, in deren Blut die Erinnerung an diese Urheimat lebendig ist, zu fürchten, in ihrem Deutschtum bezweifelt zu werden."[43]

Other prominent members of the PPK, who were also government officials, spoke out against the anti-Zionist contention that loyalty to the Zionist cause was incompatible with loyalty to the German Fatherland. In a letter to the *Vereinigung für das liberale Judentum* in January 1927 the Prussian *Kultusministere* Carl Heinrich Becker, recognised the dilemma of many Jews over the problem of conflicting loyalties.[44] Becker praised the patriotism and loyalty of groups like the *Centralverein* and others, but observed:

> ". . . daß ich aber auf der anderen Seite auch das Bekenntnis zum Zionismus für durchaus vereinbar halte mit national-deutscher Staatsgesinnung".

State Secretary Pünder had already informed the *Vereinigung für das liberal, Judentum* that it was not out of a desire to rid Germany of her Jewish citizens that the government supported the Zionist cause.[45] In his letter of 30th December 1926 to the *Vereinigung* Pünder observed that German Jews could enjoy full equality in Germany and simultaneously support Jewish colonisation in Palestine, and concluded:

> "Ich sehe auch nicht, inwiefern die Schaffung von Heimstätten für das jüdische Volk in Palästina eine gegen das Deutschtum gerichtete Angelegenheit sein soll."

In his capacity as representative of the German Foreign Office, member of

---

[43]Walk, *loc. cit.*, p. 180.
[44]PA: Pol. Abt. III, Politik 2a-Palästina, Bd. 1, Preußischer Kultusminister Becker an die Vereinigung für das liberale Judentum e.V., III 0 676, 5th January 1927.
[45]PA: Pol. Abt. III, Nachlaß Sobernheim: Jüd. Angelegenheiten, Deutsches Komitee Pro-Palästina, Bd. 1, Der St. S. in der Reichskanzlei an die Vereinigung für das liberale Judentum e.V., 30th December 1926. For more on Pünder's sympathies for Zionism, see: Hermann Pünder, *Von Preußen nach Europa. Lebenserinnerungen*, Stuttgart 1968, pp. 125–126, 138.

the *Pro-Palästina Komitee* and member of the Jewish community, Professor Sobernheim undertook the task of persuading the various non-Zionist and anti-Zionist groups that the PPK had been created first and foremost in the German political interest. He argued that the PPK was not a tool of the international Zionist movement and that, while the first concern of German Jews was and should be Germany, their loyalty would not be compromised or questioned as a result of their support for Zionist efforts in Palestine for purely economic and philanthropic ends.[46] He succeeded in winning over some members of the *Centralverein*, but made no progress whatever with the other organisations.

Both the non-Jewish and the non-Zionist Jewish members of the *Pro-Palästina Komitee* remained faithful allies of the Zionist cause in Germany after 1926, in spite of the pressure put on them by anti-Zionist Jewish groups. With the exception of seven members who died between 1926 and 1932, the PPK lost only one member, as a result of resignation, during those years.[47] Committees similar to the German *Pro-Palästina Komitee* were established in Belgium, France, England, Austria, Italy, Romania, Bulgaria, Hungary, South Africa, Chile and the United States, with all but the Hungarian organisation enrolling prominent non-Jewish members in their ranks. The non-Jewish members of these and the German PPK, who were often important government and political figures, played key roles in the efforts of the Zionist movement in their respective countries.[48] In Germany the PPK was instrumental in spreading information about the Zionist movement and its efforts in Palestine and at the same time in promoting the pro-Zionist policies of the government. In assessing the importance of the non-Jewish members of the PPK and their efforts on behalf of the Zionist cause, Kurt Blumenfeld concluded that the non-Jewish members of the PPK were among the few non-Jewish Germans willing to accept Jewish emancipation without the necessity of depriving the Jewish people of their Judaism at the same time.[49]

The relationship between the German-Christian communities and the incoming Jewish settlers during the 1920s in Palestine is a subject that warrants further research. It is sufficient here to point out that the German Foreign Office considered friendly relations between German-Christian and German-Jewish settlers desirable and necessary. One of the first assignments for the reopened German Consulate-General in Jerusalem in 1924 was to exercise guidance and moral leadership among Jewish and non-Jewish Germans in Palestine and to work to promote better relations and a more cooperative spirit between the two groups.[50] However, both the Temple Society in Palestine and the *Pro-Palästina Komitee* in Germany rejected active cooperation in the form of joint projects and activities. The relationship between German-Christian and German-Jewish settlers in Palestine remained outwardly friendly but reserved; this was largely

---

[46]PA: Pol. Abt. III, Politik 2a-Palästina, Bd. 1, AA/Berlin an DGK/Jerusalem, III O 287, 27th January 1927.
[47]Walk, *loc. cit.*, p. 184.
[48]*Ibid.*, pp. 186 ff.
[49]*Ibid.*, p. 192.
[50]PA: Pol. Abt. III, Politik 10-Palästina, Bd. 1, Aufzeichnung Sobernheims, III O 493, 11th September 1924.

a result of the tense and delicate position of the German Christians caught in the middle of Arab–Jewish hostilities.[51]

In all of the German government's policy statements covered thus far, economic motives, or the desire to corner a large share of the growing Palestine market for German exports, seem to have been primary in promoting an alliance with the Zionist movement. The government sought to cultivate friendly relations with the leading personalities of the world Zionist movement in its pursuit of this policy. Dr. Chaim Weizmann, President of the World Zionist Organization, visited Berlin several times during the 1920s for talks with government and Jewish leaders, primarily on economic matters. Weizmann was received by heads of government and state wherever he went, and Germany was no exception. In a memorandum on his impending visit to Berlin in January 1925, Foreign Minister Stresemann and State Secretary von Schubert recommended that Dr. Weizmann be received by the President and the Chancellor of the *Reich*, both emphasising the need for close contacts with leading circles in the Zionist movement outside Germany.[52] Sobernheim again stressed the necessity for close ties to the World Zionist movement shortly after his report of April 1925.[53]

Jewish immigration into Palestine had reached a peak annual figure of 33,801 in 1925, and thereafter declined rapidly until, in 1927, there was a small net emigration of Jews from the country.[54] The decline in Jewish immigration, due to causes inside and outside Palestine, had a negative impact on the economy of the country. It resulted in a decline in the flow of Jewish capital into the country, thereby reducing the pace of building and economic expansion. It also meant that the demand for German imports was significantly

---

[51]PA: Pol. Abt. III, Politik 2a-Palästina, Bd. 1, Gebietsleitung der Tempelgesellschaft in Deutschland an den Vorsitzenden des Deutschen Komitee Pro-Palästina, Nr. 928/181, 17th February 1928; AA/Berlin an Herrn Botschafter a.D. Graf Bernstorff, III 0 2/53, 18th April 1928; Deut. Komm. Pro-Palästina an die Gebietsleitung der Tempelgesellschaft, 7th April 1928; DGK/Jerusalem an AA/Berlin, N. Pro. 2/28, 8th May 1928. See also: *Jüdische Rundschau*, Nr. 9 (31st January 1933).

[52]PA: Pol. Abt. III, Jüd. Angelegenheiten: Jüd. Pol. 1-Allg., Bd. 6, Aufzeichnung des AA, IIIe39 29th December 1924.

[53]PA: Pol. Abt. III, Jüd. Angelegenheiten: Jüd. Pol. 1-Allg., Bd. 6, Aufzeichnung Sobernheims, `III 0 1191, 3rd June 1925. During an earlier visit to Berlin in 1921 Weizmann had stressed the strong community of interests, especially in the economic sphere, between Germany and the Zionist movement. He placed orders for over RM 1 million worth of German goods and promised to use his influence in London to help remedy the economic chaos in Germany. PA: Pol. Abt. III, Politik 1-Palästina, Bd. 1, Aufzeichnung des AA, IIIe65, 10th January 1922.

[54]For statistics on Jewish immigration into Palestine during the inter-war years, see the following: BA: R/57-26, Deutsches Auslandsinstitut/Stuttgart; Esco Foundation for Palestine Inc., *Palestine, A Study of Jewish Arab and British Policies*, 2 vols., New Haven 1947, I, pp. 406–407, II, p. 674; and Great Britain, *Reports by His Majesty's Government in the United Kingdom of Great Britain and Northern Ireland to the Council of the League of Nations on the Administration of Palestine and Transjordan (1933–1939)*, colonial numbers 94, 104, 112, 129, 146, 166, London 1934–1939. Very few German Jews went to Palestine before 1933. Only about 2,000 emigrated to Palestine during the Weimar years. See: Lucy Dawidowicz, *The War Against the Jews, 1933–1945*, New York 1975, pp. 176–177; and Richard Lichtheim, *Die Geschichte des deutschen Zionismus*, Jerusalem 1954, pp. 234–235.

lowered.⁵⁵ German trade with Palestine had been most successful when Jewish immigration was highest because the plans, capital and activity brought into the country by the immigrants led to purchases of considerable amounts of German goods.

By 1927 the German Consulate-General in Jerusalem was sounding the alarm over the consequences that reduced Jewish immigration were having on the volume of German imports into Palestine.⁵⁶ In a comprehensive economic report to the Foreign Office in Berlin Consul-General Nord noted the decline in Jewish immigration and with it the decline in economic activity. He went on to stress the dependence of Jewish immigrants on German imports, due not only to the high quality of German goods but to the strong spiritual and financial ties they had with Germany as well. Later that year Nord again filed a report in which he lamented the negative impact that declining Jewish immigration and the resulting disillusionment had on German imports into the country.⁵⁷

Another major problem limiting German economic policy in Palestine was the difficulty of competing with British goods. According to Nord, these goods had the unfair advantage of being promoted by the British administration in Palestine at the expense of German products, even when German goods were substantially cheaper.⁵⁸ Article 18 of the Mandate guaranteed economic equality in Palestine and stipulated clearly that there would be no economic discrimination by the mandatory power against other members of the League.⁵⁹ Nord was especially concerned about the obstacles that the British administration was creating for German industry and business which were involved or sought to be involved in such projects as electrification, harbour building in Haifa, railway construction, oil pipeline construction, road building and others. In a memorandum to Berlin in November 1927 Nord complained that the British administration in Palestine created merely the façade of trading equality and in the end usually intervened to promote British economic interests.⁶⁰ The German Foreign Office attempted to ameliorate the situation through its representatives on the Mandates Commission, Dr. Kastl and Dr. Ruppel, but was unable to break the British monopoly over many of the important development projects in Palestine.⁶¹

German *Kulturpolitik* in Palestine during the Weimar years was limited by several factors, the most important of which was limited financial resources. German economic difficulties and an ever-precarious balance of payments problem throughout the inter-war period severely restricted the scope of ac-

---

⁵⁵See: Nicosia, *op. cit.*, appendix 6.
⁵⁶PA: Pol. Abt. III-Wirtschaft, Palästina-Handel 11, Bd. 1, DGK/Jerusalem an AA/Berlin (no date).
⁵⁷ADAP: B, VII, Nr. 129.
⁵⁸PA: Pol. Abt. III-Wirtschaft, Palästina-Handel 11, Bd. 1, Bericht des Deutschen General-Konsuls Nord in Jerusalem (no date).
⁵⁹Hurewitz, *op. cit.*, II, 109.
⁶⁰PA: Pol. Abt. III-Wirtschaft, Palästina-Wirtschaft 7, Bd. 1, DGK/Jerusalem an AA/Berlin, JN 2386/27, 14th November 1927.
⁶¹PA: Pol. Abt. III-Wirtschaft, Palästina-Wirtschaft 7, Bd. 1, AA/Berlin an Ministerialdirektor Ruppel, III 0 1142, 14th March 1931.

tivities designed to promote German cultural influence in Palestine and elsewhere. Large sums of money to subsidise German schools, language instruction and other projects among the Jewish, Christian and Moslem inhabitants were apparently not available.

The teaching of German language and literature was naturally deemed the most important means of promoting German culture in Palestine and it was the only aspect of *Kulturpolitik* actively pursued in the country. German schools in Palestine, in which a German curriculum was followed, were subsidised jointly by the German government, the Temple Society settlements and the Protestant and Catholic parent institutions in Germany.[62]

In 1932 Consul-General Nord filed a lengthy report on the progress of German *Kulturpolitik* during the 1920s in Palestine. He stressed the shortcomings of German policy as a result of limited financial resources.[63] Apart from financial difficulties, however, the fact that English, Hebrew and Arabic were the official languages of the country left little room for a fourth language.[64]

Efforts were made to secure a place for German language instruction in some Jewish educational institutions in Palestine, most notably with the attempt to establish a Chair for German language and literature at the Hebrew University in Jerusalem. Plans were afoot to finance the undertaking through contributions from the Jewish community of Berlin and the *Hilfsverein der deutschen Juden*.[65] Nord was very enthusiastic about the plan, as well as about new prospects for promoting German language and culture in other schools throughout Palestine. By 1930 he had become more optimistic about the chances of securing German language instruction in at least some Jewish schools. After the violence of 1929 many Jewish parents began to send their children back to Germany for their education and this created a need for German instruction in some Jewish elementary schools.[66] The above-cited 1932 report on *Kulturpolitik* contained Nord's optimistic analysis of the changes of the previous four years, which had strengthened Germany's position in Palestine. Nord asserted that the Arab–Jewish violence of 1929 and the debates which followed had only intensified the anti-colonial sentiments of the people of the Middle East; this sentiment portrayed England, France and Italy as the natural enemies of the people of the Levant and tended to favour Germany as the only European power without imperial designs in that part of the world.[67] It is true that Britain, already the object

---

[62] By 1929 German schools in Palestine had a combined enrolment of 1,399 pupils, which made the German school system the third largest non-Arab system in Palestine after the English and French systems, ISA: 67/1359, DGK/Jerusalem an AA/Berlin, Rduc. 1/29, 29th June 1929. For a complete list of the German schools in Palestine during the inter-war years, see: Nicosia, *op. cit.*, appendix 4.
[63] PA: Pol. Abt. III Nachlaß Sobernheim: Jüd. Angelegenheiten – Prof. Sobernheim III Verschiedenes, Bd. 1, DGK/Jerusalem an AA/Berlin, Kult. 10/32, 10th March 1932.
[64] ISA: 67/1359, DGK/Jerusalem an die Akademie zur wissenschaftlichen Erforschung und zur Pflege des Deutschtums/München Spr. 1/28, 30th October 1928.
[65] PA: Pol. Abt. III Politik 16-Palästina, Bd. 1, AA/Berlin an DGK/Jerusalem, III 0 1280, 13th March 1930.
[66] PA: Pol. Abt. III, Politik 17-Palästina, Bd. 1, DGK/Jerusalem an AA/Berlin, Nr. Kult. 1/30, 8th January 1930.
[67] PA: Pol. Abt. III, Nachlaß Sobernheim: Jüd. Angelegenheiten – Prof. Sobernheim III

of Arab hostility before 1929, had incurred the distrust of the Zionists as well. Nord hoped that growing disenchantment in Palestine with British policies, which were more and more viewed as partial to the Arab side, would gradually lead to greater opportunities for German cultural prestige and influence. However, these hopes were dashed the following year by the advent of the Nazis to power.

The almost hopeless state of the German economy during the early 1930s precluded any major effort on the part of the German government to act on Nord's hopes. He was aware of this when he recommended a limited programme in 1932 in which a total of RM 40,000 was requested for cultural purposes; this included RM 1,600 for German language instruction at a few Jewish schools, RM 750 for German lessons at the Priests' Seminar of the Armenian Patriarch and RM 37,650 for the usual subsidy for German schools.[68] This budget indicated that Germany would pursue *Kulturpolitik* in 1932 mainly through Jews and Christian Germans in Palestine and ignore the possibility of gaining support among the dissatisfied Arab majority.

When Winston Churchill visited Palestine in March 1921 the debate over the future of Palestine and the recriminations over the broken promises of the past were at fever pitch. By that time it had become clear that British control over Palestine would continue through the League Mandate and that the provisions of the Balfour Declaration would be implemented. British and Zionist interests were to be carried out through the Mandate, while the Arab cause, after being heard, would be ignored. Arthur Balfour, author of the Declaration, noted in a memorandum in Paris on 11th August 1919:[69]

> "For in Palestine we do not propose even to go through the form of consulting the wishes of the present inhabitants of the country . . . The four Great Powers are committed to Zionism. And Zionism, be it right or wrong, good or bad, is rooted in age-long traditions, in present needs, in future hopes, of far profounder import than the desires and prejudices of the 700,000 Arabs who now inhabit that land."

In 1921 the Arabs could not have known that Balfour had in fact admitted what is contained in the above statement; they were convinced, nevertheless, that Britain had betrayed them, and they were prepared to act on that conviction.

In Haifa Churchill listened to a delegation of Moslem and Christian Arabs who presented their views on the Palestine problem. Their warning to Churchill at that meeting turned out to be a prophecy of profound significance in the troubled history of the Middle East to the present time:[70]

> "Today the Arabs' belief in England is not what it was . . . If England does not take up the cause of the Arabs, other powers will. From India, Mesopotamia, the Hedjaz and Palestine the cry goes up to England now. If she does not listen, then perhaps Russia will take up their call some day, or perhaps even Germany."

Verschiedenes, Bd. 1, DGK/Jerusalem an AA/Berlin, Kult. 10/32, 10th March 1932. The violence of 1929 grew out of tensions and misunderstandings over the Wailing Wall in Jerusalem.
[68] PA: Pol. Abt. III, Nachlaß Sobernheim: Jüd. Angelegenheiten – Prof. Sobernheim III Verschiedenes, Bd. 1, DGK/Jerusalem an AA/Berlin, Kult. 10/32, 10th March 1932.
[69] DBFP: 1, IV, No. 242.
[70] Doreen Ingrams, *Palestine Papers, 1917–1922. Seeds of Conflict*, London 1972, p. 118.

Arab nationalists in Palestine and the Middle East turned increasingly to Germany during the inter-war years for diplomatic and material support in their efforts against the Mandate and its English and Zionist sponsors. This effort was greatly accelerated after Hitler's assumption of power in 1933, as many Arabs mistakenly saw the antisemitism and the potentially anti-English nationalism of the Nazis as allies in their struggle. With help from Germany not forthcoming, and Germany's defeat in 1945, the Arabs turned to the Soviet Union in the 1950s and 1960s.

There is no indication that Germany had lost the basic friendship and good will of the Arabs that had existed prior to the war, in spite of the war-time German alliance with the hated Turks. As mentioned earlier, the first post-war issue involving German diplomatic activity in Palestine was the return of the *Palästinadeutsche* to their homes in Palestine after internment in Egypt. In their efforts to this end, the Foreign Office in Berlin and the German Embassy in London enjoyed the support of Palestinian Arab leaders. Apart from a genuine feeling of sympathy for the *Palästinadeutsche*, the Arabs were interested in soliciting support from an outside source which also had grievances against the post-war settlement. In the autumn of 1921 an Arab delegation from Palestine was in London for negotiations regarding the future Mandate over Palestine. During their stay in London several members of the Arab delegation declared their support for German efforts, then in progress, to secure the return to Palestine and the just compensation of the *Palästinadeutsche*. The German Ambassador in London, Dr. Friedrich Stahmer, reported that the Arabs praised the past relationship between themselves and the German colonists, and the economic benefits which the latter had bestowed on the country:[71]

> "They have never had hostile feelings toward Germany, but rather have trusted Germany more than the other Great Powers because they have always had the impression that Germany never proceeded in a purely egocentric fashion, preferring instead to respect the interests of the native population."

This was the beginning of a long and futile effort by the Arabs of Palestine to enlist the sympathy and support of a revisionist Germany.

Early attempts were made by Syrian Arabs to involve Germany in Syria as a counter force to French domination. Representatives of the Syrian Orthodox Church, hostile to France because of French partiality to the majority Maronite Catholics, visited Germany in 1921 and urged the German government to become involved in Syria again "um verlorengegangenen Boden wieder zu gewinnen".[72] These overtures were immediately rejected in Berlin with the argument that to even appear to oppose French authority in Syria would be disastrous for German economic and cultural interests there.[73] Germany's vulnerable post-war position did not permit "Prestige-Politik" in opposition to other major powers in Syria or elsewhere. Another attempt to involve Germany in Syrian affairs

---

[71]PA: Pol. Abt. III, Politik 6-Palästina, Bd. 1, DB/London an AA/Berlin, K. Nr. 69, 1st September 1921.
[72]PA: Pol. Abt. III, Politik 2-Syrien, Bd. 1, Freistaat Bayern, Ministerium des Äussern, an AA/Berlin, Nr. 44928, 23rd November 1921. ". . . in order to regain lost ground".
[73]PA: Pol. Abt. III, Politik 2-Syrien, Bd. 1, Aufzeichnung des AA, zu III. T. 1478 (no date).

was made in 1927, when Syrian nationalists approached Consul-General Nord in Jerusalem with a request for German weapons. Nord explained the impossibility of that kind of assistance by pointing out that the Treaty of Versailles prohibited Germany from manufacturing most weapons and from exporting any weapons at all. Moreover, there was the strict supervision of the Allied Control Commission of military and related industries.[74] Even if the weapons had been available, their delivery to Syrian Arabs would have been contrary to Germany's obligations as a member of the League of Nations.

Late in 1924 a memorandum was circulated in the Foreign Office by Sobernheim and Baron von Richthofen, Director of the Orient section of *Abteilung III*, which outlined in detail Germany's rejection of all of the basic Arab arguments in the Palestine conflict.[75] It was first observed that the Arabs had done nothing for centuries to develop the land. It was further argued that they had forfeited their rights to the land to the Jews who, with their energy, skill and resources, had already demonstrated a unique capacity for developing the land and making it flower as it had flowered in antiquity. The memorandum criticised the Palestinian Arabs for boycotting the British-proposed Legislative Assembly and asserted that they were not ready for self-government. Arab demands for proportional representation on the proposed Council, based on current population figures, were viewed by the German government as unrealistic in view of widespread illiteracy and lack of education among the Arabs of Palestine. This approach to the issues dividing Jews and Arabs in Palestine indicates the primacy of economic interests in German Palestine policy. The Jews, not the Arabs, were capable of creating conditions in Palestine most favourable to those interests.

The Arab–Jewish unrest of 1929 disrupted the state of relative peace which had prevailed in Palestine since the pre-Mandate violence of 1921.[76] Until the violence of August 1929 the German government had been free to pursue its aims in Palestine without being subjected to the kind of pressure which erupts in a crisis situation and which calls for public policy positions. So long as relative calm prevailed the German Foreign Office simply ignored the Arab population of Palestine, supported the Zionist cause and cultivated friendly relations with Great Britain. By virtue of the Mandate system a crisis in Palestine became an international one, involving the member states of the League of Nations and, more specifically, those states on the Permanent Mandates Commission. They became involved in the issues surrounding the Arab–Jewish conflict, as well as the examination and questioning of the policies of the Mandatory power. In the debate which followed in late 1929 and throughout most of 1930 Germany was forced not only to publicly define in a more precise manner her own position on the Arab–Jewish conflict but to confront the fundamental contradictions in-

[74] PA: Geheim-Akten, 1920–1936, Politik 2-Syrien, DGK/Jerusalem an AA/Berlin, JN 145/27, 24th January 1927.
[75] PA: Pol. Abt. III, Politik 5-Palästina, Bd. 1, Aufzeichnung Sobernheims, III O 844, 8th December 1924.
[76] See: John Marlowe, *The Seat of Pilate. An Account of the Palestine Mandate*, London 1959, chapter 8; and Christopher Sykes, *Crossroads to Israel*, London 1965, chapter 6.

herent in British war-time and post-war policy in Palestine. British policy, with all of its contradictions, had served German interests as long as peace had been maintained.

The disturbances of 1929 were detrimental to German interests in several ways. The unrest and violence would eventually impede economic activity and expansion in Palestine. It would frighten off prospective Jewish immigrants and induce some Jewish settlers already in Palestine to leave. This was bound to have a negative impact on the volume of business between Germany and Palestine which, by 1928, had slowly begun to recover from the unsuccessful years of 1926 and 1927. Both Ziemke and Sobernheim of *Abteilung III* reached the following conclusion late in 1929:

> "Deutschland hat hauptsächlich das Interesse, daß bald in Palästina Ordnung geschaffen und die wirtschaftliche Entwicklung gefördert wird."[77]

The unrest of 1929 seriously threatened the security of the *Palästinadeutsche* as well. In a report from Jerusalem on 21st June 1930 Consul-General Nord outlined the precarious position of the German-Christian communities in the conflict. He reported that the strict neutrality professed and practised by the German communities in Palestine was not always accepted by Arabs and Jews, who often interpreted an unwillingness to become involved as a sign of sympathy for the other side.[78] During the height of the violence in August 1929 the German Consulate-General in Jerusalem was attacked by a Jewish group which, according to Nord, had mistaken German neutrality in the conflict for antisemitic, pro-Arab inclinations.[79]

In the international debate over Palestine in late 1929 and 1930 the German government, as a member of the Permanent Mandates Commission, was forced to take a position more critical of British Mandate policy. Events in Germany and Europe were beginning to influence the general thrust of German foreign policy. Stresemann died in October 1929 and with him went the era of close cooperation with Britain and France. His successors were able to take a more independent approach as a result of Stresemann's foreign policy accomplishments; with the Young Plan reparations were to be regulated in a way more favourable to Germany, Allied military control had been ended and the Rhineland was to be evacuated in 1930. Moreover, the dramatic electoral successes of the Right no doubt put pressure on the government to pursue a tougher, more independent foreign policy aimed at completing the revision of the Versailles settlement. Finally, there were changes in *Abteilung III* in the German Foreign Office which to some extent altered the tone of Germany's *Palästinapolitik*. Professor Sobernheim, the man most responsible for German Palestine policy during the 1920s, lost much influence and retired in 1932; Arabists such as Fritz Grobba began to exert more influence on German Middle East policy as a

---

[77]PA: Pol. Abt. III, Politik 5-Palästina, Bd. 3, Aufzeichnung Ziemkes, A.O. 6577, 23rd December 1929.
[78]PA: Pol. Abt. III, Politik 5-Palästina, Bd. 3, DGK/Jerusalem an AA/Berlin, Nr. Polit. 34/40, 21st June 1930.
[79]PA: Pol. Abt. III, Politik 10-Palästina, Bd. 2, Telegramm, DGK/Jerusalem an AA/Berlin, Nr. 12, 31st August 1929.

whole, which tended to be somewhat more critical of British policy than had previously been the case.

Basic German support for the Jewish National Home and for the British Mandate was not altered by these changes. The German government did become openly critical of past and current British policies in Palestine during the deliberations of *Abteilung III* and during the League debates on Palestine. British policy was held to be essentially responsible for the outbreak of violence in Palestine in 1929. Moreover, Germany demonstrated a greater flexibility by urging the Zionist side to understand the frustrated nationalism of the Arabs and to seek accommodation with them for their mutual benefit. At the 16th Session of the Permanent Mandates Commission from 6th to 26th November 1929 Germany outlined her view of the events in Palestine in a way which was critical – yet supportive – of England, and conciliatory – yet non-committal – towards the Arab cause.[80] The German delegation criticised the conflicting promises made to both the Jews and the Arabs by Britain during the war. It asserted that, while Germany wholeheartedly supported the idea of a Jewish National Home in Palestine and the concept of Arab national self-determination, it was clear that both concepts had been simply instruments for the conduct of war against Germany and her allies and not ideals sincerely promoted for their moral worth. Germany further noted that England alone was responsible for the consequences of these policies. The German government rejected outside intervention in the settlement of the conflict, observing that Britain alone was responsible for and capable of working out a solution.

It would not be appropriate here to discuss in detail the diplomatic aftermath of the 1929 unrest in Palestine, involving as it did the various commissions of enquiry and reports on the causes and the possible solutions.[81] It is sufficient to note that Germany was prepared to acknowledge Britain's responsibility for the Palestine conflict and perhaps enjoy some consolation in the knowledge that those war-time policies which England had so successfully employed against Germany were now backfiring. At the same time she unrealistically encouraged Britain to somehow show support for Jews and Arabs in a way which would leave standing as the basis of policy those contradictory war-time promises which were under attack by Berlin. It is clear that Germany was concentrating her criticism on the anti-German motives behind Britain's war-time promises to the Jews and the Arabs; after that point was made, she felt that reconciliation could be achieved without eliminating the contradictions. The task of making peace between Jews and Arabs, proceeding as if the provisions of the Balfour Declaration and the concept of Arab national self-determination could be made compatible, would be left to Britain. This approach is evident in a memorandum prepared by *Legationsrat* Ziemke of *Abteilung III*; it formulated the German acceptance of the findings and recommendations of the Shaw Commission regarding the 1929 violence.[82]

---

[80]PA: Pol. Abt. III, Politik 3-Länder (England), Bd. 2, Aufzeichnung des AA (author unknown), III 0 6430, 30th December 1929.

[81]See: Marlowe, *op. cit.*, pp. 115–126; and Sykes, *op. cit.*, pp. 112–120.

[82]PA: Pol. Abt. III, Politik 5-Palästina, Bd. 3, Aufzeichnung Ziemkes zu III 0 2110/30, 9th

The events of 1929 in Palestine had a similar impact on German and English Palestine policy. The Arabs demonstrated among other things their capacity to disrupt life considerably in Palestine, which in turn could have a damaging effect on the interests and policies of the individual European powers. To avoid such disruptions and yet avoid altering fundamentally the post-war status quo, both England and to a lesser extent Germany had to pay greater heed to Arab frustrations and demands.

Weimar Germany consistently if somewhat critically supported Britain's position in Palestine. Germany was obviously not in a position, politically, economically or militarily, to change the post-war facts of life in that or any other part of the world; this fact was recognised by Stresemann in a speech at Hannover in the spring of 1924.[83] In that speech Stresemann admitted that these facts were not likely to change in the near future. It is generally accepted that from 1924 on Stresemann acted on the premise that rapprochement with England and France would make it possible to gradually gain concessions that would do away with many of the most objectionable provisions of the Versailles settlement.[84]

The consent of both Britain and France was necessary in any revision of the settlement in Europe. Germany's policy towards the post-war positions of Britain and France in the Middle East was, therefore, to uphold the status quo and to support the legitimacy of both the British and French Mandates. This would avoid incurring the wrath of either power and still preserve the post-war rivalry and distrust which existed between them in the Middle East. Sources of friction in the Levant between Britain and France were certainly not harmful to German efforts to break down Versailles solidarity.[85]

Post-war Anglo-French rivalry in the Middle East had the potential of involving Germany. In March 1927 the German Consulate in Beirut reported to Berlin that French authorities in Syria suspected an English attempt to eliminate the French Mandate over Syria and to create the British war-time dream of a Greater Arab Empire under British protection.[86] The report described the intense anti-British attitude of the French civilian and military authorities in Syria and their paranoid fears that all of the intrigues and unrest among the various national and religious groups within Syria were instigated by England. It also contained a French request for German support at the League of Nations in upholding the integrity of the French position in Syria. Consul Schwörbel's recommendation that Germany provide France with the active

---

May 1930. A Royal Commission on Palestine under Sir Walter Shaw began its work in September 1929. Its task was to enquire into the causes of the Wailing Wall riots and the subsequent unrest. See: Sykes, *op. cit.*, pp. 141 ff.

[83]Eric Sutton (ed. and transl.), *Gustav Stresemann. His Diaries, Letters and Papers*, I, London 1935, p. 317.

[84]See: Henry Ashby Turner, *Stresemann and the Politics of the Weimar Republic*, Princeton 1963, pp. 175–176.

[85]See: Gordon Craig, *From Bismarck to Adenauer. Aspects of German Statecraft*, Baltimore 1958, p. 54–55.

[86]ADAP: B, IV, Nr. 252.

support she was seeking was based on hints from French authorities in Syria that they would favour expansion of German schools and institutions to counter the growing influence and prestige of English and American educational institutions in Syria.

Berlin's reaction to Schwörbel's suggestion was completely negative. In a memorandum to the Consulate in Beirut, copies of which were forwarded to German consular missions in Paris, London, Rome, Constantinople, Cairo, Jerusalem and Baghdad, the German Foreign Office rejected as premature and unfounded allegations that England planned to oust France from Syria and cautioned that German interests were best served by strict neutrality in Anglo-French disputes and by the maintenance of the post-war status quo in the Middle East.[87]

Palestine and the Middle East were not crucial in the foreign policy objectives of the various governments of Weimar Germany, but stood on the periphery of Germany's immediate sphere of national interest. Yet Germany had specific political, economic and cultural interests in Palestine and the rest of the Middle East, and pursued specific policies designed to preserve and promote those interests. German policy was double-edged; economic and cultural interests were best served by supporting the Zionist movement and the implementation of the Balfour Declaration, while overall political interests in Europe and the Middle East were served by supporting the British Mandate in Palestine. Since Germany's major interests in Palestine and the Middle East were of an economic and cultural nature, support for Zionist aims in Germany and Palestine became the most important element in German Palestine policy.

German sympathy for Zionist efforts remained consistent from Rathenau through Stresemann and Schubert, to Neurath and Bülow.[88] This was effectively summed up by State Secretary von Bülow in 1931 in a letter to the *Pro-Palästina Komitee* in the following way:[89]

> "The German government and the Foreign Office have repeatedly expressed their sympathy for the goals and efforts of your committee. My predecessor had indicated on several occasions, both verbally and in writing, that with you we view the work in Palestine as an excellent means for the economic and cultural development of the Orient, for the expansion of Germany's economic relations and for the reconciliation of the people."

The close ties between the German Zionist leadership and German government circles enabled the Zionist minority within the Jewish community to compensate somewhat for its traditional popular disadvantage in relation to the non-Zionist and anti-Zionist majority. Considerable support from the German government,

---

[87]PA: Pol. Abt. III, Politik 2-Syrien, Bd. 1, AA/Berlin an die Deutschen Botschaften bezw. Konsulate in Paris, London, Rom, Konstantinopel, Kairo, Jerusalem und Bagdad, zu III O 1455, 20th April 1927.

[88]Ernst Marcus, 'The German Foreign Office and the Palestine Question in the Period 1933–1939', *Yad Vashem Studies*, 2 (1958), p. 181.

[89]PA: Pol. Abt. III, Politik 2a-Palästina, Bd. 2, AA/Berlin an das Pro-Palästina Komitee, III O 161, 16th January 1931.

and the central role in German Middle East policy assigned to the Zionist movement, enabled German Zionists to neutralise the fears of many Jews that Zionism merely reinforced antisemitic charges that Jewry was an alien body in Germany. As a result, Zionism had already become firmly rooted in the Jewish community in Germany when the tumult and tragedy of the 1930s brought a rapidly growing stream of adherents to the Zionist option.

Jewish Nationalism

Siegfried Bernfeld's Jewish Order of Youth, 1914–1922

BY PHILIP L. UTLEY

I. INTRODUCTION

Siegfried Bernfeld was a Viennese left-wing intellectual whose life (1892–1953) was devoted to writing and action on behalf of youth, psychoanalysis and libertarian socialism. From 1914 to 1922, his leftist intellectual activity had more direct influence on others than before or after. There were two reasons: during the period he was primarily concerned with what youth and Jewish nationalism[1] could do for each other; and he was a realist.

Conditions during and just after the First World War meant that the focus of Bernfeld's organising activity and political thought was the young Jewish people living in Vienna. He had developed tactical and theoretical skills in the radical pre-war *Anfang* youth movement; and later put these skills at the disposal of the Zionist Organisation and other institutions concerned with Jewish youth. In so doing, he influenced people upon whom chance was to bestow the task of shaping some of the earliest and most important Jewish institutions in Palestine, especially the *Kibbutzim*.

Bernfeld was often accused of being a "dreamer"[2] with far-fetched ideas like those of other left-wing intellectuals who shared his aversion to the party functionary role.[3] Some of his ideas were far-fetched, but basically he had a realistic attitude whose major traits were flexibility and originality.

To an unusual extent, he had the tactical and ideological flexibility characteristic of many Viennese, especially the Austro-Marxist Social Democrats. His flexibility enabled him to work with, and use ideas from, very different kinds of people under changing circumstances. Thus he could deal with young people as well as adults, and with socialists as well as capitalists. His flexibility made him especially willing to revise theory on the basis of practice. Thus he could actualise and reshape his ideas experimentally in the institutions he created with the help of youthful followers and sponsoring adult organisations.

His originality lay in his ability to devise new intellectual and institutional

---

[1]He preferred the term to Zionism. Siegfried Bernfeld, *Kinderheim Baumgarten. Bericht über einen ernsthaften Versuch mit neuer Erziehung*, Vienna 1921, pp. 14–19.
[2]Willi Hoffer, 'Siegfried Bernfeld and "Jerubbaal". An episode in the Jewish Youth Movement', in *LBI Year Book X* (1965), pp. 156, 161–162, 166. Hoffer was Bernfeld's *aide-de-camp* at Baumgarten; his writings generally confirm Bernfeld's factual statements but tend to attribute difficulties to personal traits like pupil indiscipline and lack of diplomacy; his denial that Bernfeld was a dreamer is to some extent counteracted by the impression he gives that Bernfeld was too permissive *vis-à-vis* pupils. The difference between the two reflects the still-extant divergence of psychoanalytic viewpoints on treatment of unmotivated patients and character disorders.
[3]See Istvan Deak, *Weimar Germany's Left-wing Intellectuals*, Berkeley, California 1968, pp. 1–134; and George L. Mosse, *Germans and Jews. The Right, the Left and the Search for a "Third Force" in Pre-Nazi Germany*, New York 1970, pp. 184–186.

syntheses. This ability had unusual practical value in his Jewish nationalist period; changing times required new syntheses to replace the monarchical–aristocratic–clerical order, not just in the wider sphere of the Austrian Empire but in every part of Central European society. He had the perceptiveness to address himself to the pressing issues of the post-traditional order: how to bring into the political process the newly vocal young people, women, creative artists and proletarians; how to reconcile the claims of direct and parliamentary democracy as replacements for monarchy; and how, without monarchy and its clerical or aristocratic agents, to cope with the problems of crime, economic need, nationalism and religion.

Bernfeld was able to tackle these issues concretely among young people because he was a youth leader who thought that youthful activity was not just a matter for education and welfare specialists but a political and social microcosm. He disagreed with the vast majority of educators in his view that most education was a hypocritically idealistic "superstructure" whose function was to teach obedience to the authority of teachers and state officials – and thereby inculcate lifetime obedience to governmental and economic authority in the adult social order.[4] His own efforts were devoted to making youthful institutions an autonomous microcosm foreshadowing what adult society should be.[5]

Bernfeld's Jewish nationalist period had a war-time and a post-war phase. During the war, he hopefully awaited the fall of monarchical traditionalism, interacted with the Jewish youth movement and put forward his ideas in the books *The New Youth and Women* (1914) and *The Jewish Volk and its Youth* (written before November 1918).[6] Many of these ideas were realistic, but some were unworkable and, because of war-time conditions, untested in practice. His realism deepened when his ideas were tested in the sobering post-war atmosphere of 1918–1922; at that point his activity revolved about the brief actualisation of his political thought: the experimental Jewish orphans' school *Kinderheim Baumgarten*, described in his book of the same name (1921).[7]

II. WAR-TIME HOPE

During the war, Bernfeld was optimistic because he hoped the war would lead to a leftist revolution with youth in the vanguard. Because of the Russian pogroms in Galicia, 1914–1917, refugees swarmed to Vienna, but there was no ensuing mood of desperation. Instead, there was a surge of optimism among Bernfeld and likeminded figures, who made plans for revolution based on Jewish national unity and youthful settlement in Palestine. By 1916–1917, Allied and German talk of self-determination, especially Britain's Balfour

[4] Bernfeld, *Baumgarten*, p. 47.
[5] Bernfeld, *Das jüdische Volk und seine Jugend*, Leipzig 1919, p. 148.
[6] *Ibid.*; for dating see Bernfeld, 'Selbstanzeige', *Jerubbaal. Eine Zeitschrift der jüdischen Jugend*, I (November/December 1918), Heft 8/9, pp. 346–348; Bernfeld, *Die neue Jugend und die Frauen*, Vienna 1914.
[7] Bernfeld, *Baumgarten*.

Declaration, helped reinforce the hopeful mood.[8] So did the nationalities' self-organisation for autonomy in the Austria–Hungary of the new, more tolerant Emperor Charles, who acceded to the throne in 1916.

Bernfeld had the opportunity to be politically active. After receiving his doctorate in psychology (1915), he acquired a Viennese military clerical post suited to his pacifist convictions because it kept him out of combat.[9] His spare-time efforts on behalf of Jewish nationalism gradually became more and more enthusiastic, time-consuming and public. As the Vienna Zionist Organisation's youth representative, he became the major Viennese leader of middle-class Zionist youth of university and especially secondary-school age. These belonged to many organisations; the most important were the *Bünde* ("leagues") *Blau-Weiss* and the more socialist, less romantic and more lasting and influential *Hashomer Hatzair*, largely composed of East European refugees.[10]

Bernfeld's war-time political thought included a concern for political structure, the mechanism of political change and nationalism. These concerns will be discussed; then the ideas which influenced Bernfeld's synthesis will be analysed; finally, the workability of his programme will be examined.

The transitional "Order of Youth" was Bernfeld's term for a political structure he described in *The New Youth and Women* before he had much interest in Jewish nationalism. He assumed the structure would develop along parallel lines among all nationalities, but its major practical impact was among Jews. He encouraged participation in the order's various communities by most young people he knew, but they were seldom aware that the order existed in his mind as an organisational schema.[11]

The order's highest and commanding layer was the secret "struggle community" of older youth. The struggle community was "dangerous" – that is, somewhat authoritarian, since it was designed to centralise and lead a revolution. Early on in the war, Bernfeld formed the *Zielgemeinde*, a struggle community designed to coordinate a Viennese revolution with the twin goals of socialism and youthful autonomy. The *Zielgemeinde* debated a good deal but never developed a significant following among middle-class or proletarian youth groups which it hoped would join the revolutionary vanguard.[12] His efforts among Jews were more successful. Towards the end of the war, he formed the "Order *Jerubbaal*", a struggle community for Jewish youth. The order employed masonic-style ranks, oaths, and secret insignia; it led less committed age-peers in the *Kreis Jerubbaal*; and it published the journal *Jerubbaal*.[13]

---

[8]Elkana Margalith, 'Die sozialen und intellektuellen Ursprünge der jüdischen Jugendbewegung "Haschomer Hazair", 1913–1920', *Archiv für Sozialgeschichte*, X (1970), pp. 261–289; Hoffer, *loc. cit.*, pp. 157–158.
[9]Hoffer, *loc. cit.*, p. 155.
[10]Margalith, *loc. cit.*; Bernfeld, 'Jugendbewegung', *Der Jude*, V (1920–1921), Heft 5/6, pp. 351–353.
[11]Bernfeld, *Neue Jugend*, pp. 55–71.
[12]*Ibid.*; YIVO Institute Bernfeld Archive File 3916 (cited hereafter as YIVO with file number). I am grateful to Marek Web for access to the Archive.
[13]Named after a youthful generational revolt led by Gideon and described in *Judges*. Hoffer, *loc. cit.*, pp. 151–167; YIVO 3905; Rudolf Glanz, Interview with Philip Utley, 9th April 1976.

He called the Order of Youth's next layer "youth communities" or "groups" – small selective communities about the size of boy scout patrols, organised in *Bünde* such as *Hashomer Hatzair* and *Blau-Weiss*. Bernfeld particularly valued the groups' communitarian spirit and their selection of *Führer* as first among equals – and symbols of a consensus which was broader than majority feeling and hence defined each group. The groups were coordinated by a pyramidal structure of representative assemblies of *Führer*. Bernfeld hoped these groups would submit fully and virtually spontaneously to the struggle community's leadership, but they never did.[14]

Nor did the next layer of organised youth, the "idea community". The idea community's hallmark was free intellectual discussion – in this case, at a Viennese "youth home" where Jewish youth met to read, exchange ideas and take courses organised by Bernfeld under the auspices of the Zionist Organisation. That which was considered as the lowest layer of youth – not really part of the order but unorganised and apathetic – was eventually to be converted to enthusiastic participation.[15]

Bernfeld also designed institutions for university students and young adults sympathetic to the Jewish Order of Youth. One was the *Kreis Jerubbaal*. Another was the *Pädagogium*, a Bernfeld-led teacher-training institute founded in 1917; it received financial support from the Zionist Organisation and was designed to supplement standard teacher-training courses with material on Judaism and youthful autonomy.[16]

The transitional Order of Youth was to struggle for a future Order of Youth, that is, a "Pedagogic Province" in Palestine (or perhaps in Europe in preparation for Jewish autonomy). Bernfeld described this autonomous youthful province as a "utopia" in *The Jewish Volk* because he knew the future could not be depicted with full accuracy. In the future utopia, the struggle community's authority was unneeded because youthful activity was virtually all voluntary. The province was a federation in which all youth, now converted, lived apart from adults in youth communities – selective "groups" belonging to the various *Bünde* and organised by locality. Government was coordinated by the groups' *Führer*; law-making based on free speech and interparty debate took place in representative assemblies of *Führer* and large direct democratic assemblies.[17]

In Bernfeld's Palestinian utopia, the idea community was organised around the homes of teaching "Doctors", adults sympathetic to youthful autonomy – selected and trained by a pedagogic university faculty of like sympathies, then voluntarily chosen as teachers, administrators, and higher-ranking "Masters" by the youth of the locality to be served. The Doctors, and especially Masters, had great political influence, but on an informal basis: youth as well as the

---

[14]Bernfeld, *Neue Jugend*, pp. 58–71; Bernfeld, 'Die Jugendgemeinde', *Die freie Schulgemeinde*, V (October 1914/January 1915), Heft 1/2, pp. 52–58.

[15]Bernfeld, *Neue Jugend*, pp. 58–71; Bernfeld, 'Sprechsaal', *Jüdische Jugendblätter*, I (1919), Heft 1, pp. 17–20; YIVO 3891.

[16]Hoffer, *loc. cit.*, pp. 151–159; YIVO 3910.

[17]Bernfeld, *Volk*, pp. 71–123; Bernfeld, 'Zum Problem der jüdischen Erziehung', *Der Jude*, I (1916/1917), Heft 3, pp. 169–182.

adults outside the Pedagogic Province came voluntarily to ask advice on political and other matters.[18]

The primary mechanism of political change, for Bernfeld, was morality. He believed that morality derived from the Hegelian *Geist* ("spirit" or "intellect"), a religious category he learned about from the progressive educator Gustav Wyneken and applied in his own secular terms.

People who were *geistig* valued individual freedom, anti-materialism, communitarian obligation, universalism and social justice; inspired by creative greatness, they were dialectically opposed to the status quo. Bernfeld used psychoanalytic categories to define true youthfulness: a tendency to sublimate puberty's increased instinctual energy. Hence the truly youthful had a "natural inclination to morality" – a *geistig* "sense of reverence, of the sublime, of truth, of justice". Young people became truly youthful and belonged to the Order of Youth if they could avoid their peers' all-too-frequent surrender to instinctual impulse, moral degeneracy and apathy.[19] Bernfeld also believed the Jewish *Volk* was potentially the most *geistig* of nations because it was the only one with a *geistig* myth of origin and prophetic tradition. Moreover, great creative men – the Jewish prophets and the "Doctors" of the future Order of Youth – expressed *geistig* values in their teaching and works of art.[20]

For Bernfeld, *geistig* self-selection was the crux of the process of revolutionary political change. The transitional Order of Youth was unconsciously modelled on the spontaneously self-selected circles of individuals – youth, Zionists and creative intellectuals, frequently emigrés with characteristic idealist revolutionary fervour – who came together in cosmopolitan Vienna.[21] He said that only youth were really revolutionary; and that in the face of adult opposition, *geistig* Jewish youth would convert all other Jewish youth and make the revolutionary transition to a future Order of Youth through school strikes and emigration to the Palestinian (or, temporarily, European) countryside. There they would establish the Pedagogic Province, whose only resident adults would be creative intellectual "Doctors".[22] Revolutionary violence would have to be prepared for but would only be used in self-defence.[23]

Morality would prevail in the Pedagogic Province. The Doctors' moral probity would keep them from becoming an entrenched bureaucracy and employing the curricular rigidity and verbal and physical violence of the European secondary school. There would be an end of crime; youthful wrong-doers and "non-achievers" would reform because tribunals composed of *Führer* would substitute for punishment a combination of psychoanalysis and new educational techniques. The economic order would be feminist and socialist: women could work while children were supervised by professionals; youth would be guaran-

---

[18]Bernfeld, *Volk*, pp. 123–149.
[19]*Ibid.*, pp. 45, 109.
[20]*Ibid.*, pp. 1–70.
[21]See Michael Walzer, *The Revolution of the Saints. A Study in the Origins of Radical Politics*, Cambridge, Mass. 1965, pp. 66–147.
[22]Bernfeld, 'Zum Problem der jüdischen Erziehung', *loc. cit.*, pp. 169–182; Bernfeld, *Volk*, pp. 71–149.
[23]Bernfeld, *Neue Jugend*, pp. 55–71.

teed autonomy, the necessities of life and freedom from productive work until the age of twenty-one.[24]

At that age, most young people would become adults – far less *geistig* than they had been as youth or than the few adult Doctors who remained in the Pedagogic Province. For adults, immersed in *ungeistig* economic pursuits and the Philistinism of everyday life, crime (and hence courts) remained a possibility; particularly the crime of trying to lure youth out of the Pedagogic Province into economic activity – though perhaps adults might become fully *geistig* in the remote future.[25] In short, youth and Doctors would be an unproductive, moral, *geistig* aristocracy in what might be called a reverse slave society reminiscent of Plato's *Republic*.

Bernfeld's most important efforts on behalf of Jewish nationalism were attempts to bridge old divisions between religious and secular Jews. He tried to make secular, heretofore "assimilationist" Jews like himself comfortable with Jewish traditions. When speaking and writing, he communicated emotionally with both religious and non-religious Jews by using Biblical metaphors in a secular sense.[26] He said that the specifically Jewish aspect of the school curriculum, that is, religious instruction should henceforth be in the hands of teachers who were acceptable to youth and had secular pedagogical rather than just religious training; the content – Hebrew language, literature and history, based primarily on the Bible – should be taught without ritual or rote.[27] As director of the *Pädagogium* and Youth Courses, he sought to develop an educational system according to this plan and to establish cooperation between the secular and religious individuals concerned.[28] It is clear that he was attempting to make such instruction part of the secular curriculum – the ubiquitous cultivator of national sentiment.

He believed festivals – once purely religious, now also symbols of secular nationalism – to be an effective and exciting means of forging emotional bonds among participants. With this thought in mind, he organised the culminating event of his war-time activity, the "Austrian Jewish Youth Conference (*Jugendtag*)" in Vienna, 18th–20th May 1918, where participants heard *geistig* talks by Martin Buber and Bernfeld, debated freely and at length, hiked in small groups through the Vienna Woods, and were moved to a sense of unity formalised by their *Führer*. The *Führer* met to establish the "Federation of Austrian Jewish Youth Groups"[29] – clearly an institutionalisation of the transitional Order of Youth. Bernfeld led this federation, edited its journal and so gave formal unity to Jewish national youth, secular and religious, in the various *Bünde*, until May 1919, when post-war disappointments dampened the unifying enthusiasm.[30]

---

[24]Bernfeld, *Volk*, pp. 71–149.
[25]*Ibid*.
[26]Bernfeld, *Volk*, p. 70.
[27]Bernfeld, 'Vom Religionsunterricht an den Mittelschulen', *Jüdische Zeitung*, XI (5th and 12th January 1917), Nos. 1, 2.
[28]YIVO 3910.
[29]Bernfeld, 'Der österreichisch-jüdische Jugendtag in Wien', *Jerubbaal*, I (June 1918), Heft 3, pp. 119–121.
[30]'Sprechsaal', *Jüdische Jugendblätter*, I (1918/1919), pp. 142–143. This was the Federation's journal.

A striking characteristic of Bernfeld's war-time political thought is the tendency to draw on widely varying anti-traditionalist political ideas as the basis for his synthesis. The parliamentary state; leftist programmes; his pre-war *Anfang* youth movement; German *völkisch* ideology; enlightened humanism; and the Jewish heritage – all provided ideas that he used.

Bernfeld was familiar with the Western Allies' parliamentary states. Yet he mistrusted the formal apparatus of the parliamentary state: it was often a façade for monarchist traditionalism in Austria and Germany; nor had it ever guaranteed full satisfaction of the needs of the non-established sectors of the population with which he identified – youth, Jews and proletarians. Thus, to achieve fairness and the eradication of crime, the future Order of Youth relied primarily on morality, voluntary cooperation and the exclusion of adults. Bernfeld desultorily conceded the usefulness of some parliamentary assemblies for youth and courts for adults; but the future Order of Youth was not a state because it did not retain a centralised executive able to coerce like the revolutionary struggle community. He was a virtually uncompromising advocate of the right to free self-expression most widely practised in the West, but, in his experience, the parliamentary state was not especially concerned with guaranteeing this right.

He had more faith in the guarantees of leftist groups and programmes. Voluntary federalism through a structure of direct democratic small communities; free party debate; freely accessible idea communities with unlimited intellectualised political discussion – all were vigorously demanded by anarchists and other left-wing libertarians, especially in Central Europe and especially from 1917 to 1922, when such institutions sprang up frequently and spontaneously, with the Soviets of Russia as inspiration. When making plans for the Order of Youth, Bernfeld was influenced by such leftist ideas, which were advocated by his friends Martin Buber and Gustav Landauer as well as by Austro-Marxism.[31] There was always tension between this leftist voluntarism and the party discipline required to channel the spontaneously released energy into concerted political action. Bernfeld's struggle community was his own version of the centralised party executives by which twentieth-century Socialists and Communists achieved various degrees of coordinated direction; in using ranks, oaths and insignia, the Order *Jerubbaal* resembled the Jacobin and other secret societies which had an analogous function in the French Revolutionary and early industrial era.

The concept of youthful revolution had been a major tenet of the pre-war Bernfeld-led movement whose journal was *Der Anfang*; the movement had publicised its ideas enough to suffer police bans and had to operate in secret by the beginning of the war.[32] The *Anfang* movement's ideas owed something to feminism, to Social Democracy, to Freud and to Expressionist art.[33] During the

---

[31]See Hans Kohn, *Martin Buber. Sein Werk und seine Zeit*, Köln 1961, Veröffentlichung des Leo Baeck Instituts, pp. 13–210; Charles A. Gulick, *Austria. From Hapsburg to Hitler*, Berkeley 1948, II, pp. 1363–1400; Lily Bernfeld Stross, Interview with Philip Utley, 23rd November 1975.

[32]Bernfeld, *Die Schulgemeinde und ihre Funktion im Klassenkampf*, Berlin 1928, pp. 18–23.

[33]Bernfeld, *Neue Jugend*, pp. 55–71.

war, Bernfeld maintained the focus by insisting that revolution produce a feminist, socialist Order of Youth which employed psychoanalysis. Many Expressionists thought that *avant-garde* artists' visions should determine politics; he echoed that Expressionist cry when he said that creative intellectuals differed enough from other adults to be entrusted with leadership in the Order of Youth.

The idea of youth's *geistig* moral superiority and right to autonomy had been the *Anfang* movement's most important tenet. The rationale had been supplied by Gustav Wyneken, who merely formalised a feeling characteristic of some middle-class youth movements. The members of such movements tend to define themselves as morally purer than the older generation because they differ primarily in age, i.e., they lack responsibility for worldly decisions, which involve political compromise and economic self-interest; they fantasise about an autonomous moral order without compromise or materialism. Yet youth is dependent on adult authorities, usually their own parents and teachers, to satisfy their need for economic and psychological support; and there is a constant turnover of personnel within the youthful age-group; hence youth are usually submissive to adults. Occasionally, moved and united by moral outrage, youth can massively advocate, and create public consciousness of, new ideas; they can threaten and sporadically apply tactics likely to influence adults who need, and often love, them: school strikes, demonstrations, leaving home to join rural youth communities are such tactics. Thus the *Anfang* movement created awareness of the need for school reform. But such sporadic enthusiasms are no substitute for the political and economic purposefulness of adult parties and interest-groups, which can pursue goals over long periods; youth can hope to put new ideas into practice only by becoming an appendage of an adult movement.[34] During the war, Bernfeld tacitly acknowledged this fact by placing the struggle for youthful autonomy in an adult Zionist framework.

At first glance it seems that Bernfeld's Jewish nationalism is a carbon copy of German *völkisch* nationalism. This impression is in line with much valuable recent scholarship which concludes that the German *völkisch* tradition was the dominant influence on Zionist practice, particularly in the Jewish youth movement, during the war and the twenties.[35] But Bernfeld consciously resisted the temptation to let German influence suffocate enlightened and traditional Jewish values; rather, he synthesised the various influences.

Bernfeld had more concrete experience with German *völkisch* nationalism than did most of his Jewish contemporaries. In October 1913, he attended the "Free German Youth Day" on the Meissner mountains, where Wyneken was the major unifying speaker. Spurred by the seeming acceptance of Wyneken's *geistig* humanism, he attempted to gain support for the *Anfang* movement in the *Freideutsche Jugend* federation founded there. The federation dissociated itself

---

[34]See Bernfeld, 'Über Schülervereine', *Zeitschrift für angewandte Psychologie*, XI (1916), pp. 167–213.

[35]Mosse, *Germans and Jews*, pp. 89–102; Hermann Meier-Cronemeyer, 'Jüdische Jugendbewegung', *Germania Judaica*, Neue Folge, VIII (1969), pp. 1–122, the most recent and extensive work; Walter Laqueur, 'The German Youth Movement and the "Jewish Question". A Preliminary Survey', in *LBI Year Book VI* (1961), p. 205.

from Wyneken and the largely Jewish *Anfang* movement in an antisemitic, anti-revolutionary purge during March 1914; to a great extent, the purge resulted from a German *völkisch* tide[36] which engulfed Central Europe increasingly thenceforth.[37] German *völkisch* thought contrasted the German *völkisch* self-image with a Jewish antitype, which was frequently cast in racist terms; Jews were depicted as an ugly dark-haired desert people and hence sterile: urban, materialistic, intellectualised, politically schismatic, given to ritualistic religion, and therefore mentally and physically weak.[38]

Bernfeld reacted to the traumatic *Freideutsche* experience by preoccupying himself with Jewish nationalism. His Austrian Jewish Youth Day and Federation of April 1918 clearly owe much to the German model. So do his assertions, in April–May 1918, that Jews possess hereditary beauty and racial superiority[39] (though it is probable that East European refugee racial consciousness also affected him at this point). Yet before and after that peak of excitement, he eschewed racism, which was inconsistent with his basically universalist worldview. Buber, who, like Bernfeld, shared responsibility for the German influence on Jewish nationalism, sent a letter with the editorial suggestion that Bernfeld acknowledge the influence in *The Jewish Volk* (written just before November 1918). Bernfeld declined on technical grounds, but the main reason was his negative experience with German *völkisch* nationalism. Instead, he dedicated the book to the German Wyneken, the Berlin Jew Berthold Otto, the Italian Maria Montessori and the American Granville Stanley Hall, creative progressive educators none of whom were associated with nationalist excess. Rather, in their juxtaposition, they symbolised universalism.[40]

Analysis of the 1918 Federation and the Order of Youth, as described by Bernfeld, confirms the fact that his ideal was a synthesis of ideas. The new Jewish youth did not fit the antisemitic antitype. They approximated the German *völkisch* self-image – yet they nevertheless retained attributes of traditional Jews and enlightened humanists. They went hiking and yearned to live on the land yet their war-time locus was urban and their future Order of Youth urbanised.[41] They had anti-materialist *geistig* values – yet their institutions received material aid from *ungeistig* adult Jews.[42] They centred their lives on emotionally satisfying, selective youth communities inspired by creative personalities – yet the free intellectual discussion of the idea community and even

---

[36]Bernfeld, *Schulgemeinde*, pp. 20–23.
[37]Walter Laqueur, *Young Germany. A History of the German Youth Movement*, New York 1962, pp. 74–83; George L. Mosse, *The Crisis of German Ideology. Intellectual Origins of the Third Reich*, New York 1964, pp. 145, 171–189.
[38]Mosse, *Crisis*, pp. 126–145.
[39]Bernfeld, 'Eine Zeitschrift der jüdischen Jugend', *Jerubbaal*, I (April 1918), Heft 1, p. 3; Bernfeld, 'Grundsätze für die Organisation eines Bundes der jüdischen Jugend', *Jerubbaal*, I (April 1918), Heft 1, p. 33.
[40]Bernfeld to Buber, n.d., Martin Buber Archive, Jewish National Library, attributed to late in the First World War on basis of content and postage stamp. I am grateful to the Jewish National Library for access to this material.
[41]Bernfeld, *Volk*, pp. 71–140.
[42]*Ibid.*; Bernfeld, 'Zum Problem der jüdischen Erziehung', *loc. cit.*, pp. 169–182; YIVO 3892, 3893.

the freedom not to join a youth community characterised the Federation and the Order of Youth.[43] For the sake of unity they accepted the *Führer* principle (which originated among *völkisch* German youth to whom, more and more, the principle meant unconditional obedience between 1900 and 1945) – yet for the new Jewish youth the *Führer* was a freely chosen first among equals.[44] The new Jewish youth employed the fertile religious tradition of the *Volk*'s earliest ancestors as a source of national revival – yet they did not exchange Judaeo-Christian-Enlightenment values for the Nordic-style paganism admired in *völkisch* thought.[45] They were strong, self-confident, struggle-orientated nationalists, not "formless, characterless assimilationists"[46] – yet according to Bernfeld the Jewish *Volk*, especially its youth, had the "vanguard" task, not of denigrating, fighting or dominating, but of setting an example for other nations: the universal human mission of the chosen people.[47]

Bernfeld's war-time ideas were influential partly because of the individuals with whom he communicated. His influence also stemmed from the realistic workability of his intellectual synthesis.

It was largely members of *Hashomer Hatzair* who transmitted Bernfeld's ideas to Palestine. Their war-time Viennese exile experience resembled that which Michael Walzer has found characteristic of sixteenth-century Puritans and pre-revolutionary Russian Leninists: uprooted from their homes and traditions, they were particularly susceptible to sustained enthusiasm for ideology – new ideas as well as their own established beliefs.[48] Members of the *Hashomer Hatzair* saw their war-time hopes shattered after the war by the chauvinistic régimes of East Europe; certain members emigrated to realise their ideas in Palestinian *Kibbutzim*. Some of these ideas are directly attributable to Bernfeld, as Elkana Margalith's recent studies testify.[49] But Bernfeld's own direct influence was increasingly forgotten between the early twenties and the seventies. Probably the main reason was that his own writings and speeches took such pains to proclaim the creative greatness of his intellectual mentors, notably Freud and Wyneken. Another reason was that public opinion, in Israel and world-wide, came increasingly to recognise the importance of leftist, psychoanalytic, German *völkisch*, and even Wyneken's ideas – and to acknowledge their influence in the Palestine of the twenties. Bernfeld was seen more as a conduit for such influences[50] than what he really seems to have been – a synthesiser of influential new programmes in his own right.

[43]Bernfeld, *Neue Jugend*, pp. 58–62; Bernfeld, *Volk*, pp. 71–149.
[44]Laqueur, *Young Germany*, pp. 1–74; Bernfeld, *Volk*, pp. 47, 64–70, 99–113.
[45]Bernfeld, 'Vom Religionsunterricht an den Mittelschulen', *loc. cit.*
[46]Bernfeld, *Volk*, pp. 7–15.
[47]Bernfeld, 'Eine Zeitschrift der jüdischen Jugend', *loc. cit.*, pp. 1–4; Bernfeld, *Volk*, pp. 7–15; Bernfeld, 'Die jüdische Jugendbewegung und ihre Bedeutung für die Internationale der Jugend', *Die Junge Schweiz*, I (1919), pp. 352–356.
[48]Walzer, *op. cit.*
[49]Margalith, *loc. cit.*
[50]See Hoffer, *loc. cit.*, p. 166; Laqueur, 'The German Youth Movement and the "Jewish Question" ', *loc. cit.*, p. 205; Meier-Cronemeyer, *loc. cit.*, pp. 21–25, 28–32, 37, 40, 44–47, 95–96; Mosse, *Crisis*, p. 124.

Bernfeld's Order of Youth

The Order of Youth theory contained many ideas that were workable after the First World War; often these ideas turned out to be necessary for the functioning of the post-monarchical order.

The most striking war-time Bernfeld concept is that of a federation of rural communities based on the principles of youthful independence, feminism, socialist cooperation, progressive education and psychoanalysis. Paradoxically, he arrived at the idea in 1914 before he was much concerned with its application among Jews; it was largely chance that put him in touch with *Hashomer Hatzair*. This *Bund*, already influenced by similar concepts, was able to adapt Bernfeld's idea for realisation in Palestine. The idea was to prove unworkable in the near future in Europe's centralising states, for which it was originally conceived; but it proved an ideal framework for settlement under the frontier conditions of Palestine.

Other Bernfeld ideas were more widely applicable. The *Führer* concept often masked non-traditional authoritarianism in *völkisch* (especially Nazi) thought. The struggle community (party discipline) idea sometimes masked leftist authoritarianism. But Bernfeld used the concepts as accurate assessments of how non-traditional institutions really function – through leaders whose authority derives from group consensus, not hereditary right.

As Bernfeld suggested, in politics generally, non-traditional society has used intellectuals' skills and taken some account of the interests of youth, women and organised working people. Whether or not the "order" *per se* is revered (as in the fascist corporate state), these new function-, sex- and age-based "orders" have gained a socio-political role similar to that of the hereditary estates or orders of monarchical-aristocratic society. Bernfeld also sensed post-traditional society's tendency to grant special rights to youth and creative intellectuals and, in its educational and cultural institutions, to intertwine the fate of the two groups. Traditional class- and patronage-based relationships have waned; youth has gained some freedom from labour; and artists and intellectuals have achieved a certain professional autonomy while increasingly being institutionalised as teachers (if not in the exact manner envisaged). Moreover, the importance of creative intellectuals in nation-building is universally apparent. Bernfeld thought there were not enough such figures among Jews and showed how they could have a role in the Jewish nation.[51] His belief that they could have some such role was accurate, for as Jewish national consciousness has grown in the twentieth century, the output of creative Jewish intellectuals has grown in quantity and significance, though to a great extent parallel to rather than within institutions for secondary school youth and the Zionist movement.

Shared ethical codes are the cement of political structures. Bernfeld accurately perceived that the post-traditional order, including the new Jewish nation, needed such a code. Creative intellectuals and youth have a tendency to experiment with such codes ("life-styles") and hence are likely to pioneer any new code which later achieves general acceptance (though the tendency hardly makes them morally pure).

He sensed the growing twentieth-century tendency towards secular–religious

---

[51]Bernfeld, 'Der jüdische Künstler und die Jugend', *Der Jude*, I (1916/1917), Heft 8, pp. 563–564.

compromise to establish constitutional ground-rules for post-traditional nations. Just as Social Democrats were about to form their first alliances with Catholic parties in Germany and Austria, he was attempting to form the same kind of alliance in the Jewish nation.

He was especially perceptive in his awareness of the dangers of German nationalism at a time when others were still primarily concerned with East European pogroms. He sensed that a Jewish nationalism synthesising German, Jewish and universal-human elements resembled the relatively tolerant, long-lived national traditions which unified Switzerland, France and America. When he and Buber, each in his own way, advocated such nationalism, they provided Palestinian settlers with workable ideas. These ideas were more likely to survive than the self-centred German *völkisch* enthusiasm and its East European counterparts – which, even then, were tearing Austria–Hungary asunder in a prelude to relatively brief total domination in successor nations between the twenties and 1945.

Though realistic in these ways, Bernfeld's war-time beliefs also had an air of unreality because they were the residue of hopeful conversations among the sort of powerless, frequently emigré youth and intellectuals who gather and organise during wars, and, in their isolation, attribute uncanny power to their own thought. Thus he did not perceive that the parliamentary state's judiciary and centralising executive might be politically valuable in the near future; he believed in the myth of youth's moral purity; and he thought Jewish nationalist unity would persist after the war.

III. POST-WAR VICISSITUDES

In Bernfeld's post-war Jewish nationalist period, November 1918 to 1922, his optimism faded and his realism deepened. He had to take account of sobering conditions affecting Jews and youth, and he was affected by his personal experiences.

By then, it was becoming clear that settlement in Palestine would be a lengthy process unlikely to alleviate the problems of Jews in successor nations. Post-monarchical Austria could not fully control verbal and physical acts of anti-semitism. Polish pogroms were encountered by returning Galician refugees whom Bernfeld had known. American relief, which replaced the Allied blockade of Austria in January 1919, could not fully assuage the misery of post-war inflation and concurrent depression. One result of the hard times was a schism in the Zionist movement between capitalist and socialist elements.

Another consequence was that the youthful revolution which Bernfeld had hoped the Federation would lead[52] never materialised; most of the middle-class youth in question – their *geistig* disdain for materialism having been made possible through adult subsidy – could not sustain long-term defiance of adult authority, especially at a time of economic distress. Instead, war-weariness, economic misery, the end of traditional authority and the Russian example con-

---

[52]Bernfeld, 'Jugendbewegung', *loc cit*.

tributed to spontaneous mass self-organisation for revolution by adults in leftwing trade unions and direct democratic Soviets (*Räte*). This new movement was counteracted by a sobering antithetical phenomenon – protofascist paramilitary veterans' groups. Instead of letting the opposing sides fight it out, the Social Democrats in Austria gained a majority in the Soviets and incorporated the Soviets' innovative spirit sufficiently to prevent the development of a significant German- or Hungarian-style Communist party. In that spirit, the Social Democratic Renner Ministry (March 1919–June 1920) permitted small-scale direct democratic experiments, among them boarding schools like Bernfeld's *Kinderheim Baumgarten*.[53] The sad fact was that only adult politics made it possible to satisfy the needs of youth along lines Bernfeld proposed.

His personal achievements were marred by illness and material setbacks. War-time and post-war economic crises irretrievably reversed Bernfeld's material circumstances. He briefly led a defence against antisemitic agitation during November 1918. In December, he began devoting himself to gaining sponsorship and funding for the orphans' home; now, for the first time, his political activism dovetailed with an effort to secure paid employment. After numerous rebuffs, in mid-October 1919, under the auspices of the American Joint Distribution Committee (Vienna Branch), *Baumgarten* was established, with Bernfeld as educational director and Erna Patak as administrator, in a former military barracks on the outskirts of Vienna. His programme was the basis for the home's functioning from then until 17th April 1920; at that point, because of administrative objection to his programme, a new teaching staff and programme replaced his. He went on leave to a tuberculosis sanatorium on 1st March 1920. After August 1920, he found employment and continued recuperating as Buber's secretary and assistant editor of *Der Jude* in Heppenheim/Bergstrasse. In May 1921, with Freud's strong support, he returned to Vienna and became a lay psychoanalyst.[54] Throughout the period, he became increasingly less optimistic and more materialist in both a personal and a philosophical sense.

His post-war Jewish nationalist period was marked by new attempts to actualise the Order of Youth idea; because he was flexible in the face of new circumstances, the idea now contained adaptations. In some articles and in the book *Kinderheim Baumgarten*, he described his modified attitude to political structure, the mechanism of change, and nationalism. After a discussion of his post-war activities in terms of these categories, the influence and workability of his new synthesis will be analysed.

His post-war conception of youthful political structure showed greater regard than before for state and organisational centralisation based on adult leadership. The changed attitude emerged while he commanded Vienna's "Jewish National Guard" and underlay the structure he established for the *Baumgarten* microcosm.

He organised the Guard at the request of the Zionist Organisation immediately

---

[53]Gulick, *op. cit.*, I, pp. 69–83, 544–582.
[54]Stross, *loc. cit.*; YIVO 3892; Hoffer, *loc. cit.*, pp. 151–157; Bernfeld, *Baumgarten*, pp. 9–22, 113–126; Sigmund Freud to Bernfeld, 28th March 1921, Martin Buber Archive, Jewish National Library.

after the November 1918 armistice, when disorder on a massive scale threatened Jewish life and property. His leadership of a tightly structured military organisation surprised many because they did not know that his secret "struggle community" activities – planning revolutionary emigration – entailed preparation to defend the revolution. The Guard had four companies, one each for students, members of the *Blau-Weiss*, of the *Hashomer Hatzair* and returned Galician Jewish veterans, all quartered at the Youth Home. It is clear that he had in mind youthful revolution as well as Jewish self-defence. But military experience was imperative for the task at hand, so within a month, all but the soldiers were "sent home", and the independent guard was reduced to a branch of the Viennese auxiliary police.[55] He later blamed the influx of returning veterans – more "adult" than "youthful" in outlook – for the failure of Austrian-Jewish youth to achieve revolutionary change.[56] Thus an enterprise which began as a compromise between left-wing Soviet-style revolutionary spirit and statist centralisation became useless for Bernfeld's larger purposes by acquiring some of the character of a paramilitary veterans' group and then becoming a segment of the established government.

Baumgarten contained 300 proletarianised Jewish orphans aged six to sixteen, but mostly under fourteen; he felt that, because they were younger and less bourgeois than the youth he had led during the war, he had to provide them with more organisation. Still, the home's political structure, which developed from mid-October 1919 to 17th April 1920,[57] was basically a modification of the Order of Youth concept.

Baumgarten's "school community" was an institution originated by Wyneken and at the same time a descendant of the war-time "idea community". Established two weeks after the founding of the home itself, the school community functioned as a direct democratic legislature. Laws regulated conduct on the basis of compromise between the will of the teachers and the will of the pupils, all of whom participated in the institution's free debates and votes. The school community's substructure consisted of seven selective, mutually competitive *Kvutzot*, descendants of the "youth community" or Youth Movement "group"; the *Kvutzot* were led by adult *Führer* (*Manhigim*) and provided camaraderie as well as activities ranging from sport to voluntary labour.[58]

The "pupil committee", an executive elected by the school community, was a descendant of the war-time "struggle community". The committee coordinated such officials as the elected police (*Ordner*) and also acted as the law court when the school community began passing laws. The teachers belonged to Bernfeld's *Kreis* or Order *Jerubbaal*, the war-time struggle community, and their centralised co-ordination made them an effective force *vis-à-vis* the pupils and the outside world. Unlike the mild, freely chosen Doctors of the future Order of Youth, but like a political party, they stayed organised and stated their

---

[55]Bernfeld, *Neue Jugend*, pp. 55–71; Bernfeld, 'Die Selbstwehr', *Blätter aus der jüdischen Jugendbewegung*, I (November/December 1918), Nr. 11/12, pp. 11–12; Peter Paret, 'Preface', Bernfeld, *Sisyphus or the Limits of Education*, tr. Frederic Lilge, Berkeley 1973, pp. xvi–xvii.

[56]Bernfeld, 'Jugendbewegung', *loc. cit.*

[57]Bernfeld, *Baumgarten*, pp. 9–32.

[58]*Ibid.*, pp. 33–82.

collective moral viewpoint within the school community, to which they taught the technique of organisation and delegated their disciplinary function.[59] It is fair to say that they encouraged the school community to develop as a centralised state out of the "creative chaos" of unruly orphans.

The mechanism of change was morality at *Baumgarten* as in the Order of Youth, but in a different sense. No longer were *geistig* youth and creative Doctors considered inherently superior to ordinary adults and expected to form an ideal society; instead, the main event in the pupils' life was the process of learning to act morally – on the basis of enlightened, universally self-evident principles. Bernfeld ceased to use the word *geistig* extensively when he described the home; he still called the home's community-building a creative process, but he was proud that the process was carried out by ordinary adults and pupils without special creative ability.[60]

The moral condition of the pupils upon moving to *Baumgarten* from other orphanages was hardly *geistig*. Full of lice and inured to filthy living quarters, they had an indifference to dirt equalled only by their impulsive aggressiveness, most forcefully expressed when they noisily ingested food, stole and fought. Today most would be diagnosed as having various character disorders ranging from the neurotic to the more severe.[61]

The *Baumgarten* teachers refused to impose a moral code through rules or punishments. Instead they asserted verbally and demonstrated by example the values they considered important. Chaos resulted, though a *Kvutzah* of older boys, the *Histadrut Haavodah*, briefly imposed some violent vigilante justice. Two weeks after *Baumgarten* opened, the school community began meeting regularly. The first laws echoed the teachers' views, but later laws showed that the pupils had learned the necessity of law and the technique of proposing statutes reflecting their own will. They legislated on such things as cleanliness, undisturbed classrooms and orderly mealtimes, at the same time adopting rules for orderly sports and channelling uninhibited aggressiveness into sublimated competition among the *Kvutzot*.[62]

Through its fairness, the court also contributed to the development of a moral community. The court eliminated most theft, fighting and other serious crimes among individuals, then, aided by an administrative decision to provide more food, proceeded against the theft of this and other kinds of communal property. After some pupil resistance the first week, the relatively minimal punishments – return and replacement of property, brief exclusion from sports, classes and the school community, and in two extreme cases, expulsion – were accepted and feared less than the actual verdict of guilty. Like all real courts an institution of drama as well as the state, the court, at pupil insistence, tried cases with great formality on a theatrical stage before the enraptured school community, which, according to Bernfeld, was "cleansed and cheered":

---

[59]*Ibid.*; YIVO 3905.
[60]Bernfeld, *Baumgarten*, pp. 46, 124.
[61]*Ibid.*, pp. 23–45. On character disorders, Otto Kernberg, *Borderline Conditions and Pathological Narcissism*, New York 1975.
[62]Bernfeld, *Baumgarten*, pp. 33–72; Hoffer, *loc. cit.*, p. 164.

through catharsis (which he understood in both classical and psychoanalytic terms), the conviction and punishment of one individual convicted and punished in everybody the generally unconscious wish to commit crimes.[63]

Between the school community's formation and February 1920, the pupils gradually accepted the self-evident moral principles minimally necessary for community living; in February, the pupils had so deeply internalised the principles that they could no longer be called "institution children".[64] According to Bernfeld, they then became genuinely enthusiastic about the school community and imposed a higher level of common morality, a kind of experimental socialist "Terror" like that of the Jacobins, whereby "community feeling" purged the individual selfishness acceptable in bourgeois society. Adults were brought to court regularly for violating laws, there was an interest in obligatory manual labour for the sake of the community, and the school community legislated the distribution of extra food to pupils who received nothing from relatives.[65]

A major catalyst for the creation of a moral community was the teachers' attitude. The teachers partook of the post-war vogue for progressive education but were in one respect unique: Bernfeld instilled in them a psychoanalytic awareness of the dynamics at work in the pupil–teacher relationship. Teachers assumed the role of enlightened parents; care was taken to ensure that each pupil developed an affectionate relationship with at least one teacher (generally, the *Kvutzah Führer*) and that the teachers' own ethical positions were clearly stated. Teachers also employed psychoanalytically orientated therapeutic techniques. Pupils were allowed freedom to express thoughts and feelings without inhibition; the result was emotional catharsis of orally and anally fixated instinctual energy (which had produced character traits like excessive concern for food and disregard of dirt). Moreover, teachers facilitated what is now called group therapy: in *Kvutzot* and the school community, pupils gained insight into themselves and abandoned destructive traits because of peer pressure. Catharsis and insight put energy at the disposal of the ego and strengthened the individual conscience. The energy could thus be channelled into sublimated activities and relationships with friends, teachers and the moral "collective ego", that is, the community.[66]

As Bernfeld's conception of morality became more sophisticated in relation to youth and creative intellectuals, he no longer attributed the origin of evil to adults as such. *Baumgarten*'s community-creation process ended in April 1920, when a long-festering dispute culminated between the educational staff and an independent, inefficient administration led by a social worker, Erna Patak, who wanted no part of Bernfeld's methods. On 17th April, the teachers resigned because neither she nor the Joint Distribution Committee would agree to make the director, Bernfeld, the final authority subject to the Committee in administrative as well as educational matters.[67] He did not attribute the blame to adults

[63]Bernfeld, *Baumgarten*, pp. 33–72; YIVO 3947 (the court's records).
[64]Hoffer, *loc. cit.*, p. 165.
[65]Bernfeld, *Baumgarten*, pp. 64–67.
[66]*Ibid.*, pp. 33–36.
[67]*Ibid.*, pp. 112–126.

generally; he recognised that blame was shared by many, including the administrator and anti-socialist Zionists on the Committee, who were suspicious of his methods. Yet his Kafkaesque account of the dispute betrays the feeling that, in the last analysis, he was dealing with an irrational, insuperable phenomenon, a bureaucratic resistance that could neither be controlled nor explained, but finally only described:

> "The administration was simply bad, unbelievably bad ... the antithesis of all rational organisation, [lacking] a usable inventory of stock ... a list of regular requirements ... and an organised purchasing procedure ... [For example], 80 plates and 300 toothbrushes were needed and the administrator provided two dozen toothbrushes; now only 276 toothbrushes and 80 plates were needed; finally she provided 30 plates and two dozen more toothbrushes, and that took care of these requirements for a while ... In the end I bought a mass of plates and toothbrushes [with money collected from charitable fund-raising]."[68]

Bernfeld's attitude on Jewish nationalism became much more sober after the war. He said that the Jewish *Volk* had won the struggle for recognition from "imperialist Europe and the Second International"; he assumed a Jewish state would be established in due course. Since the overriding goal was no longer national recognition, he felt that party conflict within the *Volk* could emerge. From his left-wing viewpoint, the Zionist Organisation was now merely a party which had lost its youthful revolutionary vigour and which represented bourgeois class interest within the *Volk*.[69]

He had become aware, from settling his own financial problems, fund-raising among Jewish capitalists and coping with administrators, that power depended on money. From dealing with proletarianised orphans, he learned that a minimum level of material comfort was a prerequisite for eliminating crime and creating a moral community. As a result, he gradually adopted a more and more materialist position, which asserted that moral communities developed not in an *élite* of *geistig* youth and "Doctors" relieved of manual labour, but among those recognising the dignity and duty of labour. Less willing to compromise principle than most Social Democrats and tolerant of the Leninist model but not its authoritarianism, especially for young people,[70] he put his libertarian socialism in a materialist framework.

Between the end of the war and July 1919, therefore, Bernfeld's plan for an orphan settlement envisaged a socialist community where the older pupils and *Chalutzim*, aged fourteen to twenty-one, would combine liberal and vocational education and learn the value of labour through participating in agriculture, cooking, making clothes and all the administrative and manual work necessary for socialist economic self-sufficiency. According to Bernfeld, almost all leading Viennese Zionists opposed the plan as inimical to Jewish capitalism; consequently, the Joint Distribution Committee agreed in July to fund the *Baumgarten* proposal only with conditions: there would be neither community self-sufficiency nor work-study for participants over the age of fourteen. Instead, to encourage respect for labour, Bernfeld had to make do with craft workshops

[68]*Ibid.*, pp. 120–121.
[69]*Ibid.*, pp. 9–22.
[70]*Ibid.*, p. 46.

for the *Baumgarten* pupils, all but a few under fourteen. To the same end, he furthered the development of communitarian morality, which he considered antithetical to capitalist egotism and which grew in tandem with the pupils' awareness that they wanted to do constructive labour for the group.[71]

Bernfeld's dispute with official Zionism extended into the sphere of Jewish national activity at the home. Official Zionism, in the person of the administrator, forced on the pupils the forms and symbols of what Bernfeld considered superficial patriotism; pupils were expected to enjoy blue-and-white bunting, admire pictures of Herzl and be extraordinarily orderly, well-behaved and quiet in the presence of Zionist officials. Bernfeld said that he and most of the teachers tried to penetrate deeper: the affection they bestowed, the freedom they allowed and the statements they made were designed to make the orphans feel inwardly comfortable with the emotions of early childhood in Jewish families and overcome unease about the personal and collective Jewish past – an unease acquired in non-Jewish orphanages before *Baumgarten*. In the *Kvutzot*, labour, contemporary politics and Palestine were discussed in terms of personal experience; the school community celebrated the Sabbath and Jewish holiday festivals with great fervour when outside officials were absent; in history and literature classes and general ethical discussion, teachers' narration of biblical episodes – allowing but not imposing a religious interpretation – proved the most effective way of relating the Jewish past to pupil fantasy. Appreciation of national forms and symbols followed rather than preceded this internalisation of national consciousness.[72]

Bernfeld's nationalism continued to evolve after he left *Baumgarten*. At the end of 1920, he still thought that pupils – spurred to inward national consciousness, communitarian morality and respect for labour by teachers such as *Baumgarten*'s – might carry out a youthful socialist revolution within the Jewish nation.[73] By 1922, he completed his journey away from official Zionism and from the Order of Youth concept: he decided that youthful revolutionaries should not aim for autonomy *per se* but instead should further the socialist strivings of the adult proletariat – the only force strong enough to be able to guarantee the eventual satisfaction of youth's needs in school communities. He became a supporter of *Hapoel Hatzair*, the party then grouping together the most significant socialist currents in Jewish nationalism.[74]

Bernfeld's post-war ideas were influential in a more diffuse manner than those of the war period because of the individuals he dealt with. But the new ideas were just as effective in reality – in fact, more so, because they were tested in practice.

He did not have the opportunity to communicate with young people as organised or susceptible to ideological commitment as those of the war-time *Hashomer Hatzair*. He was known and his ideas had a diffuse impact through

[71] *Ibid.*, pp. 9–22.
[72] *Ibid.*, pp. 103–111.
[73] *Ibid.*, pp. 19–22.
[74] Bernfeld, 'Über den Begriff der sozialistischen Erziehung', *Die Arbeit. Organ der zionistischen volkssozialistischen Partei Hapoel Hazair*, III (1921), pp. 86–91.

Baumgarten pupils and teachers who, as individuals, emigrated to Palestine or settled throughout Europe and America.[75]

Bernfeld's post-war ideas were a synthesis workable in macrocosmic and microcosmic post-monarchical politics. He rapidly came to acknowledge the need for armed Jewish national self-defence and the intractability of some crime; to cope with these problems he recognised the value of the centralised state; to cope with the state's potential arbitrariness, he employed the parliamentary state's popularly based executive, legislature and fair judiciary. Yet he did not disavow spontaneous libertarianism, a workable but often scorned aspect of his leftism; *Baumgarten* was based on direct democracy. He ruled out the authoritarian socialism adopted by less developed countries as inapplicable in his milieu, but he showed a characteristic post-war responsiveness to proletarian needs; *Baumgarten* was a miniature welfare state which combated personal unhappiness and crime by satisfying material needs and also by providing compassion, free self-expression and even the beginnings of a right to work.

His belief in community morality became practicable after the war because he had the flexibility and originality to synthesise ideas from various sources. He discarded Wyneken's simple adult–youth contrasts, which were applicable only in a middle-class milieu, and not very applicable even there. He institutionalised free leftist self-expression. In so doing, he produced a mutual generational respect more likely to prevail in the enlightened Jewish families he knew than in other families or state institutions of his milieu. Psychoanalytic knowledge gave him confidence that the results would not be destructive; *Baumgarten* was the first institution which employed extensive psychoanalytic insight as justification for modes of child-rearing typical of advanced segments of post-traditional twentieth-century society.[76] Thus pupils' morality involved less submissive obedience and more self-assertion than they would otherwise have acquired; consequently, they could cope with the doubts and vicissitudes of a libertarian milieu.

Bernfeld's Kafkaesque description of *Baumgarten*'s administration suggests a growing awareness that what had traditionally been considered evil must be coped with as an existential fact. In 1925, he formulated this perception in terms of Freud's death-instinct theory and (before Camus) the myth of Sisyphus; he said the task of coping with the child's destructive instincts and with social injustice was Sisyphean.[77]

He had a number of accurate insights about Jewish nationalism. He recognised that adherence would not develop overnight but was a psychologically complex attitude which resulted from things like mutual suffering, childhood experience and emotional attachment to small communitarian groups; Zionist loyalty developed as he foresaw, at first in East Europe and Palestine and subsequently world-wide. He was aware that there would necessarily be party conflict within Zionism after the First World War, since he conceived of the Jewish

---

[75] YIVO 3905.
[76] See Lloyd de Mause, ed., 'The Evolution of Childhood', in *The History of Childhood*, New York 1974, pp. 51–54.
[77] Bernfeld, *Sisyphus*, pp. 85–87.

nation on the model of the Western rather than Central and East European nationalisms of the time. Finally, he saw that the proletariat and the satisfaction of its material needs would be particularly important factors in the Jewish nation's development; the self-assertiveness of such institutions as the Palestinian *Histadrut* bore out his contention.

IV. CONCLUSION

Bernfeld was influential during 1914–1922 because he interacted with Jewish youth and teachers who settled throughout the world – and especially members of the *Hashomer Hatzair* who settled in Palestine. His influence also stemmed from his flexible, original attitude, which led to syntheses of political ideas workable in the post-monarchical order. During the war he believed youth were morally superior to adults; he proposed that a transitional Jewish "Order of Youth" employ self-selection, strikes and emigration to consummate a revolution ensuring autonomy in a future Palestinian "Order of Youth". His theory showed awareness that the post-monarchical order would grant certain rights to youth, women, the proletariat and the intelligentsia; that consensus-based leaders would replace traditional ones; that nations would have to develop new moral-legal codes; that politics would include more of the free self-expression advocated by the libertarian Left; that Jewish nationalism would rest on secular-religious compromise and incorporate German elements but not neglect the Jewish and Enlightenment heritage; and that federations of rural socialist youth communities would settle Palestine. After the war he revised the theory because of sobering post-war antisemitism, economic conditions and the experience of testing his ideas at the orphans' home *Baumgarten*. He emphasised the need for state centralisation to handle self-defence and crime; he gave up the idea of youth's moral superiority; and he showed how psychoanalytically informed teachers and libertarian institutions could lead chaotic pupils to become a moral community. He articulated the need for party conflict, psychological depth and concern for proletarian and material needs within Jewish nationalism.

Profile of a Local Zionist Association 1903–1904
On the Social History of German Zionism

BY JOSEPH WALK

In his thorough and informative introduction to the Letters of Kurt Blumenfeld,[1] who was the spokesman of the Zionist Organisation of Germany, Jochanan Ginat cites Blumenfeld's reference to the "comparatively small" circle of Zionist students which he had joined at the age of twenty-one: "They were young people, students, without money or political influence and without any aspirations to either, but rich in unfulfilled longing."[2] Like Blumenfeld himself, most of them were what he calls "post-assimilation Jews". Ginat thus subscribes to the prevalent view that it was mainly the sons of assimilated German-Jewish parents who were attracted to Zionism, although he prefaces this generalisation with the remark:

> "Certainly not all German Zionists are to be regarded as post-assimilation Jews; a not inconsiderable section came from families in which Jewish tradition was still alive, albeit in different forms; and these people reached Zionism without the need to discover their Jewishness anew. However, a fairly large section – no one today can determine its actual extent – belonged to assimilated German-Jewish families, and it was they who gave German Zionism its characteristic stamp."[3]

In the light of this view I shall attempt here to retrace the profile of one local Zionist Association in the first years of the movement. Among the papers of my late father, Max Walk, who joined the Zionist Association in 1903 at the age of twenty, there is a list of members and contributors of the Breslau Zionist Association for 1903–1904. The list contains 211 names with addresses and, in most cases, occupations.[4] In order to get as accurate a picture as possible of the sociological make-up of this group, I sent the list to the few surviving Breslau Zionists of the period, or to their descendants, with a request for the following information: country of birth (Germany or abroad); religiously observant or liberal; occupation (in so far as this was not already indicated in the list). In this way I succeeded in obtaining information about the geographical background and religious identification of nearly 45 per cent of the Breslau Zionists on the list and in drawing up a table of the occupations of 65 per cent. These figures should permit a fairly reliable analysis.

The Breslau association, founded in 1898, was one of the oldest and most

---

[1]Kurt Blumenfeld, *Im Kampf um den Zionismus. Briefe aus fünf Jahrzehnten*, ed. by Miriam Sambursky and Jochanan Ginat, Stuttgart 1976, Veröffentlichung des Leo Baeck Instituts.
[2]*Ibid.*, p. 9.
[3]*Ibid.*, p. 10.
[4]Report of the Breslau Zionist Association, Breslau, June 1904–Tammuz 5664. Apart from the list of members and contributors the report contains an address by Hugo Schachtel, first president of the association, and a list of nine publications under the heading "recommended reading".

active in Germany. Its founders included Dr. Ernst Kalmus (later of Hamburg), Dr. Aron Sandler (later of Berlin), both physicians, and above all Dr. Hugo Schachtel, by profession a dentist but also a well-known journalist and editor of the first Zionist paper in Germany.[5] Hugo Translateur, ninety-six years old at the time of writing (whose detailed answers to my questionnaire bear witness to an excellent memory) states in his recollections of his Zionist activity in Breslau,[6] which were written in 1963, that at the turn of the century the Breslau Zionist Association had over one hundred members, including several Rabbinical students of the Breslau Seminary. The list of members for 1903–1904 contains only one rabbinical student. This apparent discrepancy can be explained, in my view, by a phenomenon well known from the history of other non-conformist groups, viz. the assumption that some adherents of Zionism shrank from openly expressing their sympathy for a movement decried as "revolutionary". Thus the name of Solomon Gottschalk, who worked as an editor on the liberal *Breslauer Zeitung* and was a "quiet collaborator" of the Zionist Association, does not appear in the list of members; and like him some future rabbis will, no doubt, have preferred to keep their political views secret. If in our calculations we have counted "contributors" as members – in the list they are not kept apart – this inaccuracy is probably counterbalanced by the fact that there were in 1903–1904 a number of "uncounted" adherents of the movement. But even without these anonymous fellow travellers the annual report was able to speak of a "gratifying increase in membership". The Zionist Organisation of Germany, according to the *Jüdische Rundschau*, numbered 4,500 paid-up members (shekel-payers) in 1903. On the basis of this figure the Breslau group formed 4·7 per cent of the total, which exceeds the proportion of the Breslau community in the Jewish population of Germany (1905: 20,365 out of 607,862=3·3 per cent) by 1·4 per cent. The number of anonymous contributors was probably even higher than the membership; but, since it was naturally above all in the big cities that Zionist associations had been formed, we may regard the Breslau group as a more or less typical example.

It may be objected that the Jewish community of Breslau, a city situated in East Germany, was likely to contain a disproportionately large number of East European Jews, who would be more easily drawn to Zionism than their West European co-religionists. (My father, who was born in Lithuania, often told me how he became a Zionist in 1903 after reading the Proceedings of the Sixth Zionist Congress: "Every word seemed to express my innermost thoughts and feelings.") Unfortunately I do not have exhaustive figures concerning

[5]See my article ' "Der Zionist". *Zur Geschichte der ältesten zionistischen Zeitung Deutschlands*', MB, *Wochenzeitung des Irgun Olej Merkas Europa*, Tel Aviv, 14th April 1976. The first of Blumenfeld's published letters, dated 28th April 1911, is addressed to Schachtel (Blumenfeld, *op. cit.*, p. 39).

[6]*Erinnerungen aus meiner ersten zionistischen Tätigkeit in Breslau von 1898–1904*. The manuscript belongs to the Leo Baeck Institute of New York. After I had completed this article, Yaakov Tsur (of Eyn Hanatziv) drew my attention to the memoirs of Hugo Hillel Schachtel, *Die ersten zwanzig Jahre* (Central Zionist Archives, Jerusalem, K 13/30, MS.). His detailed account confirms some of my surmises, e.g., my observations about the students of the Rabbinical seminary (Schachtel, pp. 1–4). Schachtel also remarks that there was sometimes an identity of interest between the Zionist Association and the Conservatives in community politics.

East European Jews in Breslau. In 1910 only 351 out of 20,212 Jews in the city (i.e., 1·7 per cent) did *not* speak German as their mother tongue,[7] but this figure signifies little, since many Jews born outside Germany – like, for example, my father's family – had spoken German in their country of origin. In 1925 there were only 2,006 aliens out of a Jewish population of 23,240 (i.e., 8·6 per cent),[8] but even this figure represents only foreign citizens rather than foreign-born Jews, most of whom had been naturalised by then. At the same time, the proportion of foreign Jews in the total Jewish population of Germany came to 19·1 per cent,[9] so that, surprisingly enough, Breslau was below average in this respect. It may be assumed that foreign-born East European Jews did not unduly dominate the general picture of the community in 1903–1904 either; accordingly our calculations below will be based on an estimate of a maximum of 6–7 per cent East European Jews for that year. (For Germany as a whole the figures were 7 per cent in 1900, 12·8 per cent in 1910.)

In contrast to Frankfurt a. Main, Berlin and Cologne, the Breslau Jewish community was organised as a "united congregation" (*Einheitsgemeinde*), i.e., one that included conservative and liberal Jews. Since there were few definitely "orthodox" Jews in Breslau, but many people who can be regarded as "positively Jewish" (a term that owed its popularity in Breslau to the influence of Frankel's Rabbinical Seminary), we shall use the term "observant" and include in this concept those whom Max Wiener described as identifying themselves emotionally as Jews; unlike liberal Jews, who had gone far on the road towards assimilation, these still had a sense of Jewish national identity; and they still comprised in the nineteenth century an important part of German Jewry. In the words of Wiener, "In the last generation the social groups with which we are here concerned formed the recruiting ground of Zionism in Western Europe."[10] In what follows we shall investigate how far this statement applies to Breslau Jewry, estimating the percentage of observant Jews at 20 per cent.[11]

For the occupational grouping of Breslau Jewry we have accurate figures for 1907,[12] which can serve as a basis for comparison with the figures provided by our list. The occupations indicated in the original list or subsequently supplied

---

[7]Bruno Blau, 'Zur Statistik der Juden in Breslau', *Zeitschrift für Demographie und Statistik der Juden*, 11. Jahrgang, Heft 2/3, (Februar/März 1915), p. 35.
[8]Heinrich Silbergleit, *Die Bevölkerungs- und Berufsverhältnisse der Juden im Deutschen Reich*, vol. I, Freistaat Preussen, Berlin 1930, p. 24.
[9]S. Adler-Rudel, *Ostjuden in Deutschland 1880–1940. Zugleich eine Geschichte der Organisationen, die sie betreuten*, Tübingen 1959 (Schriftenreihe wissenschaftlicher Abhandlungen des Leo Baeck Instituts 1), p. 164. (Cf. also p. 26).
[10]Max Wiener, *Jüdische Religion im Zeitalter der Emanzipation*, Berlin 1933, p. 238.
[11]In 1926 the Committee of Representatives (*Repräsentantenversammlung*) of the Breslau Jewish Congregation consisted of 13 Liberals, 4 Zionists (including 1 Mizrachi), 3 Conservatives and 1 Orthodox member. (*Jüdische Rundschau*, 22nd January 1926). The "observant" therefore accounted for 23·8 per cent, a figure that corresponds to the estimates of Jewish statisticians. Cf. Felix Theilhaber, *Der Untergang der deutschen Juden*, Munich 1911, p. 43. Theilhaber uses the term "*gesetzestreu*" ("observant") for those who observe the Sabbath and the dietary laws; this definition applies to conservative members of the Breslau community.
[12]*Statistik des Deutschen Reichs*, Bd. 203, *Berufs- und Betriebszählung vom 12. Juni 1907*, Berlin, 1910, pp. 594–598. I am grateful to Professor Schmelz for making this document available to me.

in the questionnaire have been classified in accordance with the grouping underlying the official census. This classification is fraught with a number of difficulties, however, some of which could not be overcome. Thus, in the government statistics, doctors, lawyers and teachers – professions which are particularly important for our enquiry – are subsumed under the heading "public service, liberal professions", while students are included in the group "no profession".

Let us now turn to the results of our questionnaire, bearing in mind the reservations mentioned above:[13]

1. *Country of birth:* We received exact data about 95 (=45 per cent) members of the Breslau Association. Of these 80 (=84·2 per cent) were born in Germany, 15 (=15·8 per cent) abroad. Against my estimate of 6·7 per cent foreign Jews it turns out, therefore, that the proportion of foreign-born Jews in the Zionist Organisation was more than twice as high as their proportion in the Breslau Jewish community. Even if we correct this result by taking into account the fact that, as stated previously, many foreign-born Jews were by this time German citizens, we may still safely surmise that these figures justify the view that East European Jews were especially attracted to Zionism.

2. *Religious identification:* We have detailed data for only 94 (=44 per cent) of the 211 names. 41 (=43·6 per cent) are described as "observant", 53 (56·4 per cent) as "liberal". (In doubtful cases the questionnaire was followed by oral questions in order to attain greater accuracy.) Hence the proportion of traditional Jews in the group was nearly twice as high as their proportion in the Jewish population as a whole; moreover, this result is not decisively influenced by foreign-born Jews (see above), nearly all of whom belonged to the conservative trend. For at least twenty-eight of the eighty-one native-born Jews (i.e. 34·6 per cent) are identified as "observant". These results cast doubt on Ginat's claim that "assimilated, German-Jewish families . . . gave German Zionism its characteristic stamp",[14] at any rate as far as Breslau is concerned; rather, they appear to confirm Wiener's view. It is true that the leadership of the movement in Breslau – and in Germany as a whole – was in the hands of men coming from "assimilated German-Jewish families". The rank-and-file membership of the organisation, however, contained a higher percentage of "positively Jewish" individuals than is generally assumed. This leaves open the question which section of a movement – the leaders or the led – give it its character.

3. *Occupations:* The 137 members whose occupations are given in the original list or in our questionnaire belong to the following categories (our use and definition of these categories being dictated by the government statistics for 1907, which serve as the basis of comparison):

---

[13]Often the answers referred to the same people, so that we were usually able to base ourselves on two or three sources of information. In doubtful cases we decided according to the majority of answers received.
[14]See note 3.

Occupational group	Zionist Association		Jewish population		
	Number	%	Number	%	+/−
Self-employed business men and industrialists	77	56·2	2,931	31·1	+25·1
Employees	9	6·6	1,710	18·2	−11·6
Manual workers and artisans	5	3·7	1,553	16·4	−12·7
Liberal professions and public service	21	15·3	833	8·8	+6·5
No profession	25	18·2	2,406	25·5	−7·3
Total=	137	100	9,443	100	

From this comparison we may, I think, draw the following conclusions:

a) Those groups that were either dependent on employers or independent but comparatively weak economically (employees, manual workers and artisans) represented only 10 per cent in the Zionist Association, whereas their proportion in the community as a whole came to 25 per cent. It may be surmised that their under-representation was due in part to a, not unjustified, fear of social or even economic sanctions.

b) On the other hand self-employed, more or less independent business men and industrialists – a group that comprised a quarter of Breslau Jews – formed the majority of the Association, without, however, exercising a corresponding influence on the leadership, as shown by the composition of the executive.

c) The leadership was in the hands of the academically educated (listed under "liberal professions" in the table), who were likewise represented more strongly in the Zionist Association than in the Jewish population as a whole, but were less numerous than the self-employed.

d) Since nearly all those listed under "no profession" were students (the twenty-five members of this group included two people of independent means, the rest being students) we may disregard the difference of 7·3 per cent. On the other hand most of the 2,406 Breslau Jews who are listed under "no profession" were probably people living on capital or investment income. The proportion of students and rabbinical candidates would hardly have been more than 4·5 per cent, so that their share in the Zionist Association was probably,[15] like that of the liberal professions, higher than the average.

---

[15] In 1925 70·3 per cent of the category "no profession" were people "living on capital, investment income or pensions" (and this was after the great inflation!). Only 11·8 per cent of this category were students (including rabbinical students and high-school pupils) not living at home, and it may be assumed that only (or mainly) such students could dare to join the Zionist movement. (Silbergleit, *op. cit.* (see note 8), p. 201.)

In sum, it emerges that members of the liberal professions and students were the spokesmen of the group, while the majority of members were middle-class business men. Without the financial and moral support of these mainly conservative "baale batim",[16] the intellectual leaders of German Zionism would have been reduced to the status of generals without an army. If the social history of German Zionism is ever written, it should take into account these conclusions regarding one of the most active local associations.

[16] 54·5 per cent of the category "business men and industrialists" were observant.

Post-War Publications on German Jewry

A Selected Bibliography of Books and Articles 1978

Compiled by
BERTA COHN

Leo Baeck Institute
4 Devonshire Street
London W.1.

CONTENTS

		Page
I.	HISTORY	
	A. General	377
	Linguistics	379
	B. Communal and Regional History	380
	1. Germany	380
	1a. Alsace	383
	2. Austria	383
	3. Czechoslovakia	384
	4. Hungary	385
	5. Romania	385
	6. Switzerland	385
	C. German Jews in Various Countries	386
II.	RESEARCH AND BIBLIOGRAPHY	
	A. Libraries and Institutes	387
	B. Bibliographies and Catalogues	388
III.	THE NAZI PERIOD	
	A. General	389
	B. Jewish Resistance	395
IV.	POST WAR	
	A. General	396
	B. Restitution	397
	C. Antisemitism, Judaism, Nazism in Education and Teaching	397
V.	JUDAISM	
	A. Jewish Learning and Scholars	398
	B. The Jewish Problem	404
	C. Jewish Life and Organisations	404
	D. Jewish Art and Music	406
VI.	ZIONISM AND ISRAEL	406
VII.	PARTICIPATION IN CULTURAL AND PUBLIC LIFE	
	A. General	408
	B. Individual	410
VIII.	AUTOBIOGRAPHY, MEMOIRS, LETTERS, GENEALOGY	430
IX.	GERMAN-JEWISH RELATIONS	
	A. General	432
	B. German-Israeli Relations	433
	C. Church and Synagogue	433
	D. Antisemitism	435
	E. Noted Germans and Jews	437
	INDEX	439

BIBLIOGRAPHY 1978

I. HISTORY

A. General

14992. ALTER, ROBERT: *Modernism, the Germans and the Jews.* [In]: 'Commentary', Vol. 65, No. 3, March. New York: The American Jewish Committee, 1978. Pp. 61–67.

14993. ANGRESS, WERNER T.: *The German Army's 'Judenzählung' of 1916.* Genesis–Consequences–Significance. [In]: LBI Year Book XXIII. London, 1978. Pp. 117–137, illus., facsim., tabs. [See No. 15111 and see also No. 13383/YB. XXII.]

14994. BELKE, INGRID: *Liberal Voices on Antisemitism in the 1880s.* Letters to Moritz Lazarus, 1880–1883. [In]: LBI Year Book XXIII. London, 1978. Pp. 61–87. [See No. 15111].

14995. BIEBERSTEIN, JOHANNES ROGALLA VON: *Aufklärung, Freimaurerei, Menschenrechte und Judenemanzipation in der Sicht des Nationalsozialismus.* [In]: Jahrbuch des Instituts f. Deutsche Geschichte. Bd. VII. Tel Aviv, 1978. Pp. 339–354. [See No. 15109].

14996. GAY, PETER: *Freud, Jews and other Germans.* Masters and Victims in Modernist Culture. New York: Oxford University Press, 1978. xx, 289 pp., ports., illus., facsims. [Incl. I. Sigmund Freud: A German and his Discontents. II. Encounter with Modernism: German Jews in Wilhelminian Culture. III. The Berlin-Jewish Spirit: A Dogma in Search of some Doubts. IV. Hermann Levi. V. Aimez-vous Brahms? On Polarities in Modernism. VI. For Beckmesser: Eduard Hanslick, Victim and Prophet.] [All essays are revised reprints. 'Encounter with Modernism (Begegnung mit der Moderne)' appeared in 'Juden im Wilhelminischen Deutschland 1890–1914', see No. 13387/YB. XXII. 'The Berlin-Jewish Spirit' was published in 1972 as the Leo Baeck Memorial Lecture, 15, see No. 10185/YB. XVIII.] [Cf. also: Danke, Herr Doktor (Philip Toynbee) in: 'The Sunday Observer', April 16, London, 1978. Deutsch/Jüdisch. Neue Betrachtungen in Amerika (Sigrid Bauschinger) in: 'FAZ', 6. Mai, Frankfurt/M. 1978. 'The Economist', July 8, London, 1978 and the Review Article by Robert Alter, see No. 14992].

14997. GILAM, ABRAHAM: *A Reconsideration of the Politics of Assimilation.* [In]: 'Journal of Modern History'. Vol. 50, No. 1, March. Chicago: University of Chicago Press, 1978. Pp. 103–111. [With reference to the article: European Jewry and the Politics of Assimilation. Assessment and Reassessment by Michael R. Marrus [see No. 14185/YB. XXIII.]

14998. GILBERT, FELIX: *Bismarckian Society's Image of the Jew.* New York: Leo Baeck Institute, 1978. 31 pp., notes pp. 30–31. (The Leo Baeck Memorial Lecture, 22).

14999. JERSCH-WENZEL, STEFI: *Juden und 'Franzosen' in der Wirtschaft des Raumes Berlin-Brandenburg zur Zeit des Merkantilismus.* Berlin: Colloquium, 1978. 308 pp. (Einzelveröffentlichungen der Historischen Kommission zu Berlin).

15000. KAPLAN, MARION A.: *The Campaign for Women's Suffrage in the Jewish Community in Germany.* New York: YIVO Institute for Jewish Research, Max Weinreich Centre for Advanced Jewish Studies, 1976. 24 pp. (Working Papers in Yiddish and East European Jewish Studies, 18). [Mimeog.]

15001. KATZ, JACOB: *Out of the Ghetto.* The Social Background of Jewish Emancipation, 1770–1870. New York: Schocken, 1978. [New Paperback ed. For a 1973 ed. see No. 11054/YB. XIX.]

15002. KISCH, GUIDO: *Forschungen zur Rechts- und Sozialgeschichte der Juden in Deutschland während des Mittelalters.* Nebst Bibliographien. Zweite, erw. Auflage. Sigmaringen: Jan Thorbecke, 1978. 336 pp., Bibliographie zur Rechts-und Sozialgeschichte der Juden in Deutschland während des Mittelalters, pp. 269–299. (Guido Kisch. Ausgewählte Schriften, Bd. 1). [Eine rev. und völlig erweiterte Zusammenfassung mehrerer 1948 und 1954 veröffentlichten Schriften].

The Editors of the Year Book wish to express their thanks to The Ridgefield Foundation which as in previous years has given generous financial support to this Bibliography.

15003. LAMBERTI, MARJORIE: *Jewish Activism in Imperial Germany*. The Struggle for Civil Equality. New Haven and London: Yale Univ. Press, 1978. xii, 235 pp., notes pp. 193–220, bibl. (pp. 221–235). (Yale Historical Publications, Miscellany, 119). [Cont. 1) The Leadership Establishment of the Jewish Communities. 2) The Breakthrough to Political Activism. 3) Alignment with the Progressives. 4) The Dilemma of the Jewish Left Liberals: the Years of the Bülow Bloc. 5) The Conflict between Party Affiliation and the Imperatives of Jewish Honor and Loyalty. 6) A New Generation and the Reorientation of the Defense Movement. 7) Jewish Lobbying and Government School Policies. 8) Conclusion].

15004. LAMBERTI, MARJORIE: *The Jewish Struggle for the Legal Equality of Religions in Imperial Germany*. [In]: LBI Year Book XXIII. London, 1978. Pp. 101–116. [See No. 15111].

—— LEUSCHEN-SEPPEL, ROSEMARIE: *Sozialdemokratie und Antisemitismus im Kaiserreich*. Die Auseinandersetzungen der Partei mit den konservativen und völkischen Strömungen des Antisemitismus 1871–1914. [See No. 15780].

15005. LEVINE, YITZHAK: *Die 'Agudat Haorthodoxim' in Poilen*. Kapiteln zu der Forgeschichte fun Agudat Yisroel. Fun Haraw Dr. Yitzhak Levine. [In]: 'Dos Yiddische Vort'. Leading National Orthodox Jewish Magazine. New York, Tishri 5739. Pp. 23–27, ports. [of Rabbi Dr. Pinhas Cohn and Rabbi Dr. Emanuel Carlebach (in military uniform), illus. [The article deals with the activities of the two rabbis in occupied Poland during World War I. (Emanuel Carlebach, 1874 Lübeck – 1927 Köln).]

15006. LIEBESCHÜTZ, HANS: *Past, Present and Future of German-Jewish Historiography*. [In]: LBI Year Book XXIII. London, 1978. Pp. 3–21. [See No. 15111.] [Prof. Hans Liebeschütz, Historian, Mediaevalist, Member of the Executive of the London Board of the Leo Baeck Institute, born 1893 in Hamburg, died Oct. 28, 1978 in Liverpool. Obs. in: 'The Times', Nov. 13, London, 1978. 'AJR Information' (Arnold Paucker), Dec., London, 1978. 'LBI News', Winter, New York 1978/79. 'Allgemeine', 24. Nov., Düsseldorf, 'Isr. Wochenblatt' (IW), Nov. 10, Zürich 1978. and Hans Liebeschütz zum Gedenken (Hans Tramer) in: 'MB', 1. Dez., Tel Aviv, 1978. See also No. 15113.]

15007. MEYER, MICHAEL A.: *The Origins of the Modern Jew*. Jewish Identity and European Culture in Germany, 1749–1824. Detroit: Wayne State University Press, 1975. 249 pp., bibl. (pp. 220–243). (Wayne Books, No. 32). [First publ. 1967. See No. 6416/YB. XIII.]

15008. MOSSE, GEORGE L.: *Rassismus*. Ein Krankheitssymptom in der europäischen Geschichte des 19. und 20. Jahrhundert. Aus dem Englischen von Elfriede Bureau. Deutsche Erstausgabe. Königstein/Ts.: Athenäum, 1978. 228 pp. [Engl. original]: *Towards the Final Solution*. A History of European Racism. London: Dent, 1976, New York: Howard Fertig, 1978. 277 pp., illus., bibl. notes pp. 239–265. [Cf. Rassismus. Ein rechtes Gruselkabinett. Die Geschichte antisemitischer Wahnideen (Hermann Glaser) in: 'Die Zeit', 9. März, Hamburg, 1979, illus. [and]: From Gobineau to Hitler (Lucy S. Dawidowicz) in: 'Commentary', Vol. 66, No. 6, Dec., New York, 1978. Pp. 86–88.]

15009. SCHOLEM, GERSHOM: *Zur sozialen Psychologie der Juden in Deutschland 1900–1930*. [In]: Die Krise des Liberalismus zwischen den Weltkriegen. [See No. 15015.]

15010. SIEVERS, LEO: *Juden in Deutschland*. Die Geschichte einer 2,000 jährigen Tragödie. Ein Stern-Buch. Hamburg: Gruner & Jahr, 1977. 230 pp., 120 ports., illus. [Cf. The Jewish Past through German Eyes (F. Hellendall) in: 'AJR Information', August, London, 1978. In response to the review some letters by Hans Joachim Schoeps, H. D. Feldheim, G. Schmerling, Henry Morland in: 'AJR', October 1978.]

15011. STERN, F[RITZ]: *The Burden of Success*. Reflections on German Jewry. Pp. 124–144 in: Art, Politics and Will. Essays in Honor of Liolel Trilling. Ed. by Quentin Anderson a.o New York: Basic Books, 1977. viii, 295 pp., illus.

15012. STERN, FRITZ: *Gold und Eisen*. Bismarck und sein Bankier Bleichröder. Aus dem Engl. von Otto Weith. Berlin: Ullstein, 1978. 754 pp., 16 pp. ports., illus. [Engl. original see Nos. 13400/YB. XXII and 14192/YB. XXIII. Further reviews of the work: Golo Mann in: 'NZZ', Nr. 203, 2.-3. Sept., Zürich, 1978. Pp. 61–62, ports. Theodor Eschenburg in: 'Die Zeit', 9. Juni, Hamburg, 1978, ports. Banker who could not buy acceptance (Elon Salmon) in: 'Jewish Observer and Middle East Review', May 5, London, 1977. Banker to the Chancellor (Jonathan Steinberg) in: 'TLS', Aug. 12, London, 1977. Bismarck und Bleichröder. Ein Beitrag zur Tragik des deutsch-jüdischen Verhältnisses (Hans Tramer) in: 'MB', Nr. 36/37, 29. Sept., Tel Aviv, 1978. Pp. 7–8.

15013. TAL, URIEL: *'Political Faith' of Nazism Prior to the Holocaust*. Annual Lecture of the Jacob M. and Shoshana Schreiber Chair of Contemporary Jewish History. Tel Aviv University, Faculty of Humanities, Tel Aviv: Israel Press, 1978. 50 pp., 5 facsims.
15014. TAL, URIEL: *Tradition and Modernisation: Aspects of Social Ethics in Contemporary Jewish History and Thought*. Inaugural lecture at the dedication ceremony of the Jacob M. and Shoshana Schreiber Chair of Contemporary Jewish History at Tel Aviv University, on June 7, 1978. Issued by the Information and Public Relations Department Tel Aviv University, 1978. Pp. 15–24. [Prof. Tal is the incumbent of the chair].
15015. THADDEN, RUDOLF VON, ed.: *Die Krise des Liberalismus zwischen den Weltkriegen*. Göttingen: Vandenhoeck & Ruprecht, 1978. 300 pp. [Incl. contributions by S. N. Eisenstadt, Martin Seliger, Yehoshua Arieli, Werner Jochmann, Rudolf Vierhaus, Hans-Paul Bahrdt, Zwi Werblowsky, Nathan Rotenstreich (see No. 15315), Ernst Simon: Die Krise des Liberalismus im 'Untertan', im 'Zauberberg' und im 'Mann ohne Eigenschaften', Gershom Scholem (see no. 15009).]
15016. VIERHAUS, RUDOLF, ed.: *Am Hof der Hohenzollern*. Aus dem Tagebuch der Baronin Spitzemberg 1895–1914. Notizen aus der Ära Wilhelms II. München: Deutscher Taschenbuch Verlag, 1978. (dtv Dokumente, Bd. 2911). [Contains many references to Jews. [First publ. 1961. For a 1976 ed. see No. 13401/YB. XXII.]
15017. WASSERMANN, HENRY: *Jews and Judaism in the Gartenlaube*. [In]: LBI Year Book XXIII. London, 1978, Pp. 47–60, facsim. [See No. 15111].
15018. WENNINGER, MARKUS J[OHANNES]: *Die Vertreibung der Juden aus den deutschen Reichsstädten im 15. Jahrhundert*. Geisteswiss. Diss., Universität Salzburg, 15. Dez. 1977. 235 pp., map. [Typescript].
——— ZIMMERMANN, MOSHE: *Two Generations in the History of German Antisemitism*. The Letters of Theodor Fritsch to Wilhelm Marr. [See No. 15799.]

Linguistics

15019. DINSE, HELMUT/SOL LIPTZIN: *Einführung in die jiddische Literatur*. Stuttgart: Metzler 1978. x, 180 pp., bibl. (Sammlung Metzler, 165, Abt. D. Literaturgeschichte).
15020. DREESSEN, WULF-OTTO/HERMANN-JOSEF MÜLLER, eds.: *Doniel. Das atljiddische Danielbuch nach dem Basler Druck von 1557*. Band I: Transkription. Band II: Faksimile. Göppingen: Alfred Kümmerle, 1978. Bd. 59/I: vi, 122 pp., Bd. 59/II: v, 104 pp. [2 vols.] (Litterae. Göppinger Beiträge zur Textgeschichte hrsg. von Ulrich Müller, Franz Hundsnurscher und Cornelius Sommer). [See No. 14200/YB. XXIII.]
15021. HEIDE, MANFRED GERNOT: *Graphematisch-Phonematische Untersuchungen zum Altjiddischen, der Vokalismus*. Bern: H. Lang, 1974. v, 442 pp., bibl. (pp. 435–442). [Europäische Hochschulschriften, Reihe 1, Deutsche Literatur und Germanistik, Bd. 106. Zugl. Philolog. Diss., Hamburg). [Reviewed by Manfred Caliebe in: 'Germanistik', 17. Jg., H.1, Tübingen: Niemeyer, 1976. Pp. 92–93.]
15022. KAPLAN, ANATOLI L'VOVIČ: *Variationen zu jiddischen Volksliedern*. Hrsg. von Beate Jahn-Zechendorff. 1. Aufl. Leipzig: Insel, 1976. 47 pp., 32 coloured illus. (Insel Bücherei, 1012).
15023. RÖLL, WALTER: *Die Pluralbildung im Jiddischen und im Deutschen*. [In]: Akten des V. Internationalen Germanisten-Kongresses Cambridge 1975. Bern, Frankfurt M.: Herbert Lang, [1978?]. Pp. 211–220.

B. Communal and Regional History

1. Germany

15024. GENERAL REGIONAL HISTORY. LOWENTHAL, E. G.: *In the Shadow of Doom.* Post-War Publications on Jewish Communal History in Germany (III). [In]: LBI Year Book XXIII. London, 1978. Pp. 283–308. [See No. 15111.] [For part I see No. 5600/YB. XII, for part II No. 8449/YB. XVI.]

15025. BERLIN. MAAYAN, SHMUEL: *The Elections in the Jewish Community of Berlin in the Years 1901–1920.* (Habechirot Bakehillah Berlin Beschanim 1901–1920). Givat-Havira: The Zvi Lurie Institute for the Study of Zionism and Diaspora, 1977. 246 pp. [In Hebrew].

15026. MUNK, MICHAEL L. (Brooklyn, N.Y.): *Austrittsbewegung und Berliner Adass Jisroel-Gemeinde 1869–1939.* [In]: 'Udim', Bd. VII/VIII. Frankfurt/M., 1977–1978. Pp. 77–94. [See No. 15323.]

15027. TERGIT, GABRIELE: *Die Effingers.* Roman. Eine Schicksalschronik aus dem Berliner Bürgertum von 1870 bis 1942. Frankfurt/M.: Krüger, 1978. 736 pp. [First publ. 1951]. [Cf. Eine Familie in Berlin wieder zu entdecken (Christa Rotzoll) in: 'FAZ', 21. Dez., Frankfurt/M., 1978.]

15028. TERGIT, GABRIELE: *Käsebier erobert den Kurfürstendamm.* Ein Berlin Roman. Frankfurt./M.: Fischer Taschenbuch Verlag, 1978. 286 pp., port. (Fischer Taschenbuch Nr. 2158). [First publ. 1931]. [Cf. Aktualität nach fünfzig Jahren (M.Nk.) in: 'NZZ', 29. Juli, Zürich, 1977.] [Gabriele Tergit, i.e. Elise Reifenberg, born 1894 in Berlin, lives in London].

15029. BRESLAU. BRILLING, BERNHARD: *Die ersten Beamten der Breslauer jüdischen Gemeinde zur Preussischen Zeit (1744–1751).* [In]: 'Mitteilungen des Verbandes ehemaliger Breslauer und Schlesier in Israel'. Nr. 43, Tel Aviv, 1978. Pp. 31–32. [See No. 15060.]

15030. DIAMANT, ADOLF: *Einige Thorarollen kamen nach Israel.* Zur Geschichte der Synagogen in Breslau. [In]: 'Allgemeine', 3. März, Düsseldorf, 1978. [And in]: 'Mitteilungen des Verbandes ehemaliger Breslauer und Schlesier in Israel'. Nr. 43, 1978. [See No. 15060.]

15031. SCHEYER, ERNST: *Breslau, so wie es war.* Ein Bildband. Vorwort von Günther Grundmann. 4. Aufl. Düsseldorf: Droste, 1977. 101 pp., 174 illus. [For 1969 ed. see No. 7636/YB. XV.]

15032. ERLANGEN. SPONSEL, ILSE: *Drei Lebensbilder – Jüdische Schicksale in unserer Stadt.* Zur Woche der Brüderlichkeit 1978 veröffentlicht in: 'Das Neue Erlangen'. Zeitschrift für Wissenschaft, Wirtschaft und kulturelles Leben. H, 45, März. Erlangen: Merkel, 1978. (Die drei Lebensbilder: Chirurg Jakob Herz (1816–1871). Physiologe Isidor Rosenthal (1836–1915). Mathematikerin Emmy Noether (1882–1935). [The vol. incl. further: Einleitung: Überblick über das Werden und Vergehen der Gemeinde (Shlomo Lewin), Über christlich-jüd. Zusammenarbeit in Erlangen (Georg Künzel), Möglichkeiten und Grenzen jüdisch-christlicher Verständigung (Hans Joachim Schoeps), Gesetz und Gerechtigkeit nach dem Alten Testament (Georg Fohrer), Die Geschichte des Erlanger Israelitischen Friedhofes und eine Zeittafel 1831–1971 zusammengestellt von Ilse Sponsel.]

15033. ESSEN. VEREIN FÜR DIE ERHALTUNG DES ESSENER MÜNSTERS, ed.: *Biographien der vier an der Essener Synagoge an der Steeler Strasse tätig gewesenen Rabbiner*: Salomon Samuel (1867–1942) (H. J. Samuel). Paul Lazarus, sein Leben und Wirken in Deutschland, 1888–1951 (L. Baerwald). Paul Lazarus in Israel (M. Elk). Emil Cohn, Kämpfer und Poet, 1881–1948 (B. Cohn). Hugo Hahn, 1893–1967 (F. S. Brodnitz). [In]: 'Das Münster am Hellweg', 21. Jg., H. 6, Juni. Essen: Münster Bauverein, 1978. Pp. 81–115, ports.

15034. FLOSS. *Historisch-topographische Beschreibung des Judenberges bey Floss.* Israelitische Kirchengeschichte. Conferenzaufgabe bearb. von dem hebr. Sprach- und Jüdischen Religionslehrer Joseph Goldmann allda, Floss, den 15. März 1845. Pp. 335–345, illus. [of the synagogue and cemetery] [And]: Die Flosser Juden in der neueren Zeit (Fred Lehner), pp. 343–345 [In]: 1000 Jahre Floss (Adolf Wolfgang Schuster). Floss, 1976.

15035. FRANKEN. ENDRES, RUDOLF: *Juden in Franken.* Vortrag ... auf der Herbsttagung der Gesellschaften für christlich-jüdische Zusammenarbeit in Bayern. Würzburg: 'Die Schwestern-Revue', 1977. 8 pp.

15036. ENDRES, RUDOLF: *Jüdische Gemeinden in Franken 1100 bis 1975.* [In]: Frankenland, Zeitschrift für fränkische Landeskunde und Kulturpflege. Sondernummer. [And]: *Jüdische Landgemeinden im 18./19. Jahrhundert.* (Hartmut Heller). Würzburg (Hofstr. 3), 1978. Pp. 5–13 [See also No. 15055.]

15037. JENKS, STUART: *Judenverschuldung und Verfolgung von Juden im 14. Jahrhundert: Franken bis 1349.* [In]: Vierteljahrschrift für Sozial- und Wirtschaftsgeschichte. Bd. 65, H.3. Wiesbaden: Steiner, 1978. Pp. 309–356.

15038. FRANKFURT/MAIN. *Bibliographie zur Geschichte der Frankfurter Juden 1781–1945.* Hrsg. von der Kommission zur Erforschung der Geschichte der Frankfurter Juden. Bearb. von Hans-Otto Schembs mit Verwendung der Vorarbeiten von Ernst Loewy und Rosel Andernacht. Frankfurt a.M.: Kramer, 1978. 680 pp.

15039. HYAMS-PETER, HELGE-ULRIKE: *Vor den Trümmern einer Jugend.* Die Welt der Frankfurter Juden und ihr berühmtes 'Philanthropin'. [In]: 'Frankfurter Rundschau', 11. Nov., Frankfurt/M., 1978, illus. [A talk with Betty Rand-Schleifer, who now lives in Jerusalem, on a visit to her birthplace where she was a pupil and later, for sixteen years, a teacher at the Philanthropin.]

15040. GLÜCKSTADT (Schleswig Holstein). KÖHN, GERHARD: *Die portugiesischen Juden in Glückstadt bis 1652.* Pp. 127–152 [in]: Die Bevölkerung der Residenz, Festung und Exulantenstadt Glückstadt von der Gründung 1616 bis zum Endausbau 1652. Neumünster: Wachholtz, 1974. 206 pp., plans. (Quellen und Forschungen zur Geschichte Schleswig-Holsteins, Bd. 65. Zugl. Diss., Univ. Hamburg.

15041. GÖTTINGEN, ROSDORF, GEISMAR. WILHELM, PETER: *Die Synagogengemeinde Göttingen, Rosdorf und Geismar 1850–1942.* Göttingen: Vandenhoeck & Ruprecht, 1978. 124 pp., illus. (Schriften zur Geschichte der Stadt Göttingen, herg. von der Stadt Göttingen, Bd. 11.)

15042. HAMBURG. *Die Synagogen in Hamburg.* Erforscht und zusammengestellt von Ruben Maleachi, (Engel), Jerusalem. [In]: 'Mitteilungen des Verbandes ehemaliger Breslauer und Schlesier in Israel'. Nr. 44, 1978, pp. 26–28, and 40. [To be cont.] [See No. 15060.]

15043. HILDESHEIM. JAN, HELMUT VON: *Zur Geschichte der Hildesheimer Juden von 1800 bis 1815.* [In]: Alt-Hildesheim. Nr. 48. Hildesheim: Lax, 1977. Pp. 44–59, 4 illus., plan, facsims, footnotes.

15044. KIRCHEN (Efringen-Kirchen, Kreis Lörrach im Markgräflerland). HUETNER, AXEL: *Die jüdische Gemveinde von Kirchen (Efringen-Kirchen, Kreis Lörrach) 1736–1940.* Beitrage zur geschichtlichen-, politschen-, wirtschaftlichen und religiösen Situation der Juden im Markgräflerland. 2., verb. Aufl. Grenzach/Heidelberg: Im Selbstverlag, 1978. 371 pp. + 45 ports., illus., facsims, tabs., bibl. (pp.332–350). [Cf. Denkmal für eine Gemeinde in Markgräflerland (Bruno Stern, New York) in: 'Das Neue Israel', H.5, Novj., Zürich, 1978.]

15045. KÖNIGSBERG. (East Prussia). MATULL, WILHELM: *Damals in Königsberg 1919–1939.* Ein Buch der Erinnerung an Ostpreussens Hauptstadt. München: Gräfe und Unzer, 1978. 140 pp. [Incl. chap. Unsere jüdischen Mitbürger. Also other references to Jews.]

15046. LIPPE. BÖDEKER, HEINRICH: *Schmerzliches Gedenken.* [In]: Heimatland Lippe. Zeitschrift des Lippe'schen Heimatbundes. 71. Jg., Nr. 6, Nov./Dez. Detmold, 1978. Pp. 269–280, illus., facsims. [Jewish cemeteries, tomb stones and memorial tablets were mostly destroyed by the Nazis but as far as possible restored. The first victim in Lippe was the editor of the 'Volksblatt', Felix Fechenbach, who was shot dead on March 5, 1933. For the history of Jews in Lippe see Nos. 11099–11101/YB. XIX.]

15047. LOWER SAXONY. Bückeburg. BRILLING, BERNHARD: *Jüdische Goldschmiede in Bückeburg im 19. Jahrhundert.* Ein Beitrag zur Geschichte der Juden in Bückeburg. [In]: Schaumburg-Lippische Mitteilungen. H. 24, hrsg. vom Schaumburg-Lippischen Heimatverein, Bückeburg und Stadthagen, 1978. Pp. 105–127.

15048. HEUTGER, NICOLAUS: *Niedersächsische Juden.* Eine Einführung zum 40. Jahrestag des 9. November 1938. Mit einem Votum von Landesbischof Prof. D. Eduard Lohse, Abt zu Loccum. Hildesheim: August Lax, 1978. xii, 103 pp. + [36 pp.] ports., illus., facsims., bibl. (pp. ix-xii.)

15049. LEUENBERGER, WALTER: *Eine hebräische Pergamenthandschrift in Burgdorf* (Niedersachsen). Sonderdruck aus dem Burgdorfer Jahrbuch, 1978. Pp. 100–130, illus.

15050. LUCKENWALDE (Regierungsbezirk Potsdam). DIAMANT, ADOLF: *Die Synagoge von Luckenwalde.* Zur Einweihung vor 80 Jahren. [In]: 'Allgemeine', Nr. XXXII/40, 7.

Okt. Düsseldorf, 1977., illus. [The last Jews were deported in 1940 and the damaged synagogue rebuilt into three flats.]

15051. MAINZ. *Juden in Mainz.* Katalog zur Ausstellung der Stadt Mainz im Rathaus-Foyer, November 1978. Bearb. von Friedrich Schütz, gestaltet von Valy Schmidt-Heinicke. Unter Leitung von Anton M. Keim. Schirmherr der Ausstellung S.E. Yohanan Meroz, Botschafter des Staates Israel in der BRD. Mainz: Bernd Hesse, 1978, 215 pp., ports. illus., facsims., bibls., maps. [Incl. Geschichte der Juden in Mainz (Ludwig Falck). Neugründung der Gemeinde. Die Zeit des Absolutismus um 1583 bis 1763 (Otto Böcher). Aufklärung und Befreiung durch die Franzosen. Die Mainzer Judenschaft von 1763 bis 1814 (Friedrich Schütz). Emanzipation und Gleichberechtigung (1814–1933) (Anton M. Keim). Der Weg in die Vernichtung (1933–1945) (Ursula von Dietze). Nach dem Nationalsozialismus 1945 bis heute (Alfred Epstein). Spuren jüdischer Kultur in Mainz (Otto Böcher). Ein Anfang in der neuen Heimat Israel. Mainzer Juden in Israel (Ernst Gerth). Vorläufige Liste von Archivalien Mainzer Provenienz im Central Archives for the History of the Jewish People, Jerusalem (Daniel J. Cohen). Verzeichnis von Schriften zur Geschichte der Mainzer Juden in der Stadtbibliothek Mainz (Michael Real and Hans-Werner Ginkel).]

15052. MAINZ. MAIMON, ARYE: *Der Judenvertreibungsversuch Albrechts II. von Mainz und sein Misserfolg (1515/1516).* [In]: Jahrbuch für westdeutsche Landesgeschichte, 4. Koblenz: Selbstverlag der Landesarchivverwaltung Rheinland-Pfalz, 1978. Pp. 191–220, bibl.

15053. RAPP, EUGEN: LUDWIG: *Chronik der Mainzer Juden.* Die Mainzer Grabdenkmalstätte. Hrsg. von der Jüd. Gemeinde Mainz mit Unterstützung d. Kultusministeriums Rheinland-Pfalz und der Stadt Mainz. Grünstadt: Emil Sommer, 1977. 79 pp., illus., Namen der Mainzer Inschriften pp. 66–76, bibl. (pp. 77–79).

15054. MARK BRANDENBURG. HEISE, WERNER: *Die Juden in der Mark Brandenburg bis zum Jahre 1571.* Nachdr. d. Ausg. Berlin, Ebering, 1932. Vaduz: Kraus, 1965. xix, 367 pp., bibl. (pp. iii-xii). (Historische Studien, H. 220). Lizenz d. Matthiesen-Verl. Lübeck.

15055. NÜRNBERG-FÜRTH. ENDRES, RUDOLF: *Geschichte der jüdischen Gemeinden Nürnberg-Fürth im 19. und 20. Jahrhundert.* Pp. 23–31 [in]: 'Frankenland'. Sondernummer. [See No. 15036.]

15056. OFFENBACH AM MAIN. ROTH, ERNST und MAX WILLNER: *Die Juden im 1000jährigen Offenbach am Main. Teil I* [In]: 'Udim', Bd. VII-VIII. Frankfurt/M. 1977/78. Pp. 159–174. [See No. 15323.]

—— OLDENBURG. SCHICKEL, HARALD: *Gesuche um Änderungen jüdischer Familiennamen zur Verhinderung antisemitischer Geschäftsschädigungen.* Beispiele aus dem Lande Oldenburg, 1870–1931. [See No. 15793.]

15057. PADERBORN (Westphalia). BRILLING, BERNHARD: *Zur Geschichte des Rabbinats in Paderborn 1809–1869.* [In]: 'Udim', Bd. VII-VIII. Frankfurt/M. 1977/78. Pp. 25–45. [For part I: (1809–1826) see No. 13432/YB. XXII.] [See No. 15323.]

15058. RODALBEN (Landkreis Pirmasens). WEBER, ALOIS: *Die israelitische Schule zu Rodalben.* [In]: Heimatkalender 1978. Hrsg. vom Landkreis Pirmasens. Weissenthurm (Rheim): Dokter Verlag, 1978. Pp. 189–192.

15059. SCHWETZINGEN. LOHRBÄCHER, ALBRECHT/MICHAEL RITTMANN: *'Sie gehörten zu uns.'* Geschichte und Schicksal der Schwetzinger Juden. Schwetzingen: Bürgermeisteramt, 1978. 125 pp. + [21 pp.] list of names, ports., illus., facsims., bibl. (pp. 123–125). [Mimeog.] [Incl. Simon Eichstetter – eine jüd. Persönlichkeit als Beispiel für eine gelungene Integration jüdischer Mitbürger. Fritz Hirsch – ein Jude aus Schwetz. Ehrenbürger. Heinrich Bloch, der letzte Kantor und Lehrer in der Schw. isr. Gemeinde.]

15060. SILESIA. *'Mitteilungen des Verbandes ehemaliger Breslauer und Schlesier in Israel'.* Hrsg. Erich Lewin. Nr. 43–44, Apr.-Oct. Tel Aviv, 1978. [2 issues]. [Nr. 43 incl.: Erinnerungen an Martin Buber (Walter B. Goldstein). Ein Pessach an der Westfront (Leopold Heinemann). Julius Sachs 85 Jahre. Geschichte der Familie Nothmann (Forts.) Beiträge zur Geschichte der Juden in Oberschlesien (Louis Lewin). Breslauer Jüdisches Gemeindeblatt, 10. Jahrg. Juli 1933, Nr. 7 (Albert Rosenthal). Innerjüd. Verhältnisse in Oberschlesien (Hans Chanoch Meyer). Ein altbürgerliches Handelshaus in Tarnowitz. Aus dem Leben und der Geschichte der Familie Panofsky.) Pioniere der Industrie in Naharia (Erich M. Lehmann). Rudolf Küstermeier: er schlug eine Brücke nach

Israel (Erich Lüth). Dr. Max Elk, Rabbiner und Erzieher (Heinzwerner Goldstein). Dr. Ludwig Nelken 80 Jahre (Zvi Schaal). Erinnerungen (Hans Margolius, Forts. in Nr. 44). Erinnerung aus meiner Jugend. Ergänzung zum Bericht von den Johanneern (Luis Meyer). Die Juden von Breslau (Georg Less). Breslau-Wroclaw, die jüdische Geschichte einer Stadt (Jehuda Ben Awner [Markt]). Oberkantor Magnus Davidsohn. Zur 100. Wiederkehr seines Geburtstages (E. G. Lowenthal). Prof. Abraham (Adolf) Fränkel (1891–1965) liebte Breslau nicht... (Mordechai Noy). Nr. 44 incl.: Uber die Wissenschaft des Judentums in Deutschland (Zum 40. Jahrestag nach der Kristallnacht 1938) (E. M. Hauschner). Geschichte der Familie Nothmann (Schluss). Die deutschen Juden in Israel. Bodensee Hefte Juni 1978 (Else Levi-Mühsam). Die Emanzipation der Juden in Deutschland im 19. Jahrhundert (Jehuda Ben Awner [Markt]). Ein Leben für den Frieden: Max Tau, 1897–1976 (Caroline Cossina). Hermann Vogelstein – Gemeinderabbiner in Breslau – 35 Jahre später. Im Gedenken an Herbert Bileski (1909–1942) und Adalbert Saretzki (1911–1942) (Rabb. I. Löwenstein). Breslau im September 1977 (Kurt Jacques Gadiel). Das Johaneum – und die Judenfrage (Jisrael (Rudi) Jutkowski).]

15061. SILESIA – PRAUSNITZ – TRACHENBERG. BRILLING, BERNHARD: *Die Judenakten des Schlossarchivs von Trachenberg.* Ein Beitrag zur Geschichte der Juden in Prausnitz. (Darin eine Liste der Prausnitzer Juden vom August 1805). [In]: Jahrbuch der Schlesischen Friedrich-Wilhelms-Universität zu Breslau. Bd. XIX. Würzburg: Holzner, 1978. Pp. 21–44.

15062. SPEYER. SCHECKENBACH, ACHIM with GÜNTER STEIN: *Speyer und die Juden.* [In] Vierteljahresheft des Verkehrsvereins. Frühjahr. Speyer, 1977. Pp. 2–12, illus.

15063. WARTENBURG (East Prussia now Poland). DIAMANT, ADOLF: *Die Synagoge wurde Gefängnis.* Von den Juden aus Wartenburg. [In]: 'Aufbau', Oct. 7, New York, 1977.

15064. WESTPHALIA. BRILLING, BERNHARD: *Das Judentum in der Provinz Westfalen 1815–1945.* [In]: Kirchen und Religionsgemeinschaften in der Provinz Westfalen (B. Brilling, E. Hegel, R. Stupperich). Beiträge zur Geschichte der Preussischen Provinz Westfalen, Bd. 2. Münster: Aschendorf, 1978. Pp. 105–143, bibl. footnotes. (Veröffentlichungen der Historischen Kommission für Westfalen, Bd. 38). [Cont. Überblick über die Entwicklung der jüdischen Gemeinden von 1815 bis zur zwangsweisen Auflösung (1942) and: Der Kampf der westfälischen Juden um die Gleichberechtigung.]

15065. WRONKE (formerly Provinz Posen) DIAMANT, ADOLF: *Erinnerung an die Juden von Wronke.* [In]: 'Allgemeine', 3. Nov. Düsseldorf, 1978.

15066. ZIEGENHAIN, KREIS. HÖCK, ALFRED: *Steuerliste der Synagogengemeinden des Kreises Ziegenhain aus dem Jahre 1840.* [In]: 'Schwälmer Jahrbuch 1978'. Schwalmstadt-Ziegenhain: Schwälmer Heimatbund (Postfach 2244), 1978.

1a. Alsace

15067. *Jalons pour une histoire des Juifs en Alsace* [by] F. Raphaël, R. Weyl, M. Warschawski, S. Schlesinger, S. Picard. [In]: Revue des Sciences Sociales de la France de l'Est. Revue Publiée avec le Concours du Centre National de la Recherche Scientifique. No. 4, Strasbourg, 1975.

2. Austria

15068. *Austro-Marxismus.* Texts transl. and ed. by Tom Bottomore and Patrick Goode. With an introduction by Tom Bottomore. London: Oxford University Press, 1978. [This book provides an introduction to the work of important Marxist thinkers, among them Max Adler, Otto Bauer, Rudolf Hilferding.]

15069. *Judentum im Mittelalter.* Ausstellung im Schloss Halbturn, 4. Mai – 26. Okt. 1978, veranstaltet von d. Kulturabteilung des Amtes der Burgenländischen Landesregierung.

Katalog. Hrsg.: Kurt Schubert u.a. Eisenstadt: Kulturabteilung . . ., 1978. 268 pp., 28 pp. illus., bibls.
—— POPPER-LYNKEUS, JOSEF. BELKE, INGRID: *Die sozialreformerischen Ideen von Josef Popper-Lynkeus (1838–1921).* [See No. 15656].
—— HELLIN, FREDERICK P. und ROBERT PLANK: *Der Plan des Josef Popper-Lynkeus.* [See No. 15657.]

15070. SONNENFELS, JOSEPH, FREIHERR VON. KARNIEL, JOSEF: *Joseph von Sonnenfels. Das Welt- und Gesellschaftsbild eines Kämpfers um ein 'glückliches Österreich'.* [In]: Jahrbuch des Instituts für Deutsche Geschichte. Bd. VII. Tel Aviv, 1978. Pp. 111–158. [See No. 15109.] [J. v. S., statesman and writer, 1733 Nikolsburg (Moravia) – 1817 Vienna. The younger son of Lipmann Berlin (Perlin) who, after conversion in 1735 changed his name to Alois Wienner. Ennobled in 1746 he became 'Von Sonnenfels'.]

15071. VIENNA. LOHRMANN, KLAUS: *Die Juden Wiens im Mittelalter.* 65. Kleinausstellung des Wiener Stadt- und Landesarchivs, Rathaus, Okt.-Dez., 1977. 7 pp., bibl. [Mimeog.]

15072. *Das Wiener Kaffeehaus.* Einleitender Essay von Hans Weigel. Text und Bildausw. von Christian Brandstätter u. Werner J. Schweiger. Wien: Molden, 1978. 152 pp., 121 illus. [The views of writers like Kraus, Schnitzler, Polgar, Hofmannsthal, Torberg and others on the 'institution'.]

3. Czechoslovakia

15073. '*Judaica Bohemiae*'. Publication du Musée Juif d'État, Prague. Rédacteur en chef: Miroslav Jaroš. Sécrétaire de la rédaction: Jiřina Sedinová. Vol. XIV, Nos. 1–2. Praha: Státni Zidorské Muzeum v Praze, 1978. 67 pp. + 4 pp. illus.; pp. 71–123 + 4 pp. illus. [No 1 incl.: Das Kinderheim I in L 417 im Konzentrationslager Terezin (Jarmila Škochová). Débuts du mouvement assimilateur tchéco-juif (Vlastimila Hamácková). From the Mss Collection of the State Jewish Museum. Miscellanea II (Vladimir Sadek, Jiřina Sedinová). Auswahlkatalog Hebräischer Drucke Prager Provenienz aus d. 18. Jahrhundert in d. Sammlungen des Staatl. Jüd. Museums in Prag. 3. Teil: 1700–1799 (Bedrich Nosek-Schluss der Studie). Exhibition of Karel Fleischmann's Creations from Terezin, 1942–1944. Exhibition 'The Old Jewish Cemetery and its Restoration and Protection'. Restoration of the Tombstone of David Oppenheimer (1664–1736) in the Old Jewish Cemetery. No. 2 incl.: Grabsteine mit Figuralmotiven auf dem alten Jüd. Friedhof (Vladimir Sadek). Old Czech Legends in the work of David Gans (1592) (Jiřina Sedinová). Die Kunst im Konzentrationslager Theresienstadt als Form des antifaschistischen Widerstandkampfes (Anita Franková).]

15074. PRAGUE. BOCK, EVE: *The German-Jewish Writers of Prague.* Interpreters of Czech Literature. [In]: LBI Year Book XXIII. London, 1978. Pp. 239–246. [See No. 15111.]

15075. *Das jüdische Prag.* Eine Sammelschrift mit Texten von Max Brod, Martin Buber, Albert Ehrenstein, Theodor Herzl, Franz Kafka, Paul Kornfeld, Else Lasker-Schüler, Isidor Pollak, Robert Weltsch, Franz Werfel, Oskar Wiener u.a. Mit einer Einführung von Robert Weltsch. Kronberg/Ts.: Jüdischer Verlag im Athenäum Verlag, 1978. ix, 56 pp., ports., illus., facsims. (Neuausgabe des 1917 im Verlag der Jüdischen Selbstwehr, Prag, erschienenen Buches. Mit einer Einführung von Robert Weltsch (Mai 1978), pp. v-ix].

15076. PAZI, MARGARITA: *Fünf Autoren des Prager Kreises.* Frankfurt/M.-Bern: Lang, 1978. 316 pp., bibl. (pp. 303–306). (Würzburger Hochschulschriften zur neueren deutschen Literaturgeschichte. Hrsg. von Anneliese Kuchinske-Bach. Bd. 3). [Cont. das Prag des 'Prager Kreises'. Ernst Weiβ, Oskar Baum, Ernst Sommer, Paul Kornfeld, Ludwig Winter].

15077. SLOVAKIA. JELINEK, YESHAYAHU: *The Jews in Slovakia, 1945–1949.* [In]: 'Soviet Jewish Affairs'. Vol. 8, No. 2, London: The Institute of Jewish Affairs, 1978. Pp. 45–56, bibl. (pp. 54–57).

4. Hungary

15078. EPPLER, ELIZABETH E.: *The Hungarian Contribution to Jewish Life and Letters.* The Meir Gertner Memorial Lecture, delivered on the opening of Jewish Book Week 1977. London: Jewish Book Council, 1978. 12 pp. [Mimeog.]

15079. IGNOTUS, PAUL: *Hungary.* London: Ernest Benn, 1972. 333 pp., ports., illus., bibl. (pp. 311–318). [The book bears witness to the important role Jews played in the economic and social life in Hungary. Paul Ignotus, whose grandfather was the chief editor of the German language 'Pester Lloyd', was born in 1901. A writer and political journalist he lived from 1956 on as a refugee in England. He died on the 1st of April, 1978 in London.]

15080. KATZBURG, NATHANIEL: *The Hungarian Jewish Situation during the late 1930's.* Bar Ilan. Reprint from the Annual of Bar-Ilan University in Judaica and the Humanities. Vol. 14–15, pp. 73–79.

15081. PAÁL, J.: *Die Hochschule jüdischer Wissenschaft in Osteuropa.* Zur Hundertjahrfeier des Rabbinerseminars zu Budapest. [In]: 'Emuna-Israel Forum'. H. 1, 1978. Pp. 17–24, illus. [See No. 15759.]

15082. ROTH, ERNST: *Zum 100jährigen Bestehen der Landesrabbinerschule in Ungarn.* [In]: 'Udim', Bd. VII-VIII, Frankfurt/M., 1977/78. Pp. 109–144. [See No. 15323.] [Also]: *100 Jahre segensreichen Wirkens,* [In]: 'Allgemeine', 7. Okt. Düsseldorf, 1977. [Die Landesrabbinerhochschule in Budapest was opened on Oct. 4, 1877 and was, until 1945, called Franz Josef Landesrabbinerschule after the emperor Franz Josef I.]

15083. *Studien zum ungarischen Judentum.* Studia Judaica Austriaca, Bd. III. Hrsg.: Verein 'Österr. Jüdisches Museum in Eisenstadt.' Ed. Kurt Schubert. Institut für Judaistik der Universität Wien. Eisenstadt: Edition Roetzer, 1976. 79 pp., cover ports., bibl. [Cont. Judengesetze im Burgenland von Stefan dem Heiligen bis Maria Theresia (1001–1780) (Ivan Hacker), pp. 7–15, bibl. Das Judentum Ungarns 1780–1914 (Wolfdieter Bihl, pp. 17–31). Assimilation und Emanzipation des ungarischen Judentums um die Mitte des 19. Jahrhunderts (Wolfgang Häusler, pp. 33–79, bibl. footnotes).] [Fxpanded entry 13456/YB. XXII.]

5. Romania

15084. IANCU, CAROL: *Les Juifs en Roumanie (1866–1919).* De L'Exclusion à L'Émancipation. Aix-en-Provence (France): Éditions de L'Université de Provence (29, avenue Robert Schuman, 13621 Aix-en-Provence 1978. ports., illus., facsims., maps, chron., bibl. (Études historiques 4).

15085. ROSEN, MOSES. FISCHER, ALFRED: *Moses Rosen – dreissig Jahre rumänischer Oberlandesrabbiner.* Beispielgebende Position einer jüdischen Gemeinde in der sozialistischen Welt. [In]: 'Das Neue Israel'. 30. Jg., H. 12, Juni. Zürich, 1978. Pp. 745–749, port. [on p. 725].

6. Switzerland

15086. BONJOUR, EDGAR: *Geschichte der Schweizerischen Neutralität.* Bd. 8: Dokumente 1939–1945. Bd. 9: Dokumente 1939–1946. Basel: Helbing & Lichtenhahn, 1975/76. 374, 428 pp. [Vols. 8–9. For vol. 7 see No. 12043/YB. XX.]

15087. KÜLLING, FRIEDRICH: *Antisemitismus -? bei uns wie überall?* Judenfeindschaft in der Schweiz zwischen 1866 und 1900. Zürich: Juris Druck und Verlag, 1977. xxv, 412 pp., illus., maps, diagrs., bibl. (pp. 399–404). [Expanded entry No. 14245/YB. XXIII.]

15088. WOHLMANN-MEYER, CLÄRE/ALEX IZBICKI (Fotos): *Wiedersehen nach 33 Jahren.* Die Flüchtlingskinder von Heiden trafen sich jetzt in Israel. [In]: 'IW', Nr. 21, 26. Mai, Zürich, 1978. Pp. 10–11, ports. [Shortly following the November pogrom 40 children left Frankfurt/M. and were received into the Jewish children's home in Heiden. 21 came from all parts of the world for a reunion meeting in Israel.]

C. German Jews in Various Countries

15089. ARONSFELD, C. C.: *B'nai B'rith Leo Baeck (London) Lodge 1593. The First Thirty Years*. Ed.: Arnold Horwell. London, 1976. 32 pp., illus. [Founded in 1943 by Jews from Germany.]

15090. ARONSFELD, C. C.: *In the Land of the Incas*. Early German Jews in Peru. [In]: 'AJR Information'. Vol. XXXIII, No. 1, January. London, 1978. [Between 1830 and 1870 a small number of Jews from Posen settled in Peru].

15091. BAUM, CHARLOTTE, PAULA HYMAN and SONYA MICHEL: *The German Jewish Woman in America*. Pp. 17–53 in: The Jewish Woman in America. New York: New American Library, 1977. xiii, 219 pp., ports., illus., bibl. (pp. 263–281).

15092. DOBKOWSKI, MICHAEL N.: *'The Fourth Reich' – German-Jewish Religious Life in America Today*. [In]: 'Judaism'. Issue No. 105, Vol. 27, No. 1, Winter. New York: The American Jewish Congress and World Jewish Congress, 1978. Pp. 80–95.

15093. EISENBERG, AZRIEL, HANNAH GRAD GOODMAN, eds.: *The German Immigration 1800–1875*. Part II of 'Eyewitnesses to American Jewish History, a History of American Jewry [vol. 2]. New York: Union of American Hebrew Congregations, 1977. viii, 148 pp., ports., illus., facsims.

15094. FABIAN, RUTH/CORINNA COULMAS: *Die deutsche Emigration in Frankreich nach 1933*. München: Saur, 1978. 136 pp. [Cf. Where Exodus Failed. German Jews in Occupied France (W. Rosenstock) [In]: 'AJR Information'. Vol. XXXIX, No. 4 (April), London, 1979. Pp. 1–2.

15095. FEINGOLD, HENRY/Michael Dobkowsky: *A Century of German Jewish Immigration to America, 1840–1940*. [In]: 'keeping posted', vol. XXIII, No. 2, Oct. New York, 1977. 24 pp., ports., illus.

15096. FIGES, EVA: *Little Eden*. A Child at War. London: Faber, 1978. 140 pp. [A memoir of her experience as a war time evacuee from London. Eva Figes née Unger, born in 1932 in Berlin, is a well known novelist.]

15097. GEORGE, MANFRED. STEINER, FRANK CHARLES: *Manfred George. His Life and Works*. Dissertation [pres. to] the State University of New York, 1977. Ann Arbor, Mich.: University Microfilms, 1978. v, 240 pp., bibl. M. G. pp. 224–240. [Manfred George, originally Manfred Cohn, born 1893 in Berlin, was from 1939 until his death, Dec. 1965, chief editor of the 'Aufbau'.]

15098. *(The)* GUGGENHEIMS. DAVIS, JOHN H.: *The Guggenheims*. An American Epic. New York: Morrow, 1978. 608 pp., 32 pp. ports., illus. [Cf. Ein Lengnauer in Amerikas Big Business. Die Geschichte von Simon Meyer Guggenheim. Mit einer verhinderten Hochzeit fing es an, mit Blei-, Silber- und Kupferminen in Amerika endete es (E. B.) in: 'Isr. Wochenblatt', Nr. 23, 9. Juni, Zürich, 1978, pp. 17–19, illus.]

15099. *Jewish Immigrants of the Nazi Period in the U.S.A.* Sponsored by the Research Foundation for Jewish Immigration. Vol. I: Archival Resources. Vol. II: Oral History. London-München: K. G. Saur, 1978. 2 vols. [Vols. III-VI to appear in 1979.]

15100. HUBERT, ARTHUR. KALISCH, SIMON: *A Builder of Judaism*. The Story of Arthur Hubert and his Family. Prefaces by Chief Rabbi Immanuel Jakobovits and Sir Israel Brodie, and by Lord Fisher of Camden, President of the Board of Deputies. Manchester: Boaz House, 1978. 144 pp. [Cf. A. Philanthropist's Story (Margot Pottlitzer) in: 'AJR Information', Nov., London, 1978.]

15101. KISSINGER, HENRY. MAZLISH, BRUCE: *Kissinger: The European Mind in American Policy*. London: Harper and Row, 1977. 330 pp., ports. [An attempt to explain Mr. Kissinger's public policies against his personal background.] [Heinz Kissinger, born May 27, 1923 in Fürth/Bavaria.]

15102. KARP, ABRAHAM J.: *Golden Door to America*. The Jewish Immigrant Experience. Harmondsworth (Middsex). England: Penguin Books, 1978. 272 pp. [A short introduction to the history of Jewish immigration to America starting with the flow of German Jews (1830–1880).]

15103. LOEBL, HERBERT, OBE, B.Sc.: *Government-Financed Factories and the Establishment of Industries by Refugees in the Special Areas of the North of England 1937–1961*. Thesis submitted to the University of Durham, 1978. 345 pp., annex of documents. [Typescript]. [Incl. Nazi persecution, emigration, refugee history, internment, special legislation in

Britain concerning immigrants, a collection of case histories of firms. Cf. Refugee Industries in the North of England. A Proud Record (Margot Pottlitzer) [In]: 'AJR Information', May, London, 1978. Pp. 1–2 and some additional remarks in the AJR June issue.]

15104. MOSER, SIR CLAUS. COLEMAN, TERRY *Interviews Sir Claus Moser* who is retiring as director of the Central Statistical Office, about his extraordinary career to date, about his future as vice chairman of Rothschild, and about his abiding interest as chairman of the Royal Opera House, Covent Garden. Pictures of Sir Claus Moser by E. Hamilton-West [in]: 'The Guardian', July 26, London 1978, ports.

15105. HENNESSY, PETER: *Man in the News: Sir Claus Moser*. Whitehall Statistician, Polymath looking to a third career. [In]: 'The Times', 7 June, London, 1978, port. [Sir Claus Moser was born 1921 in Berlin into a banker's family that emigrated to England.]

15106. NEY, FRITZ. NEY, FRITZ: *Quarenta E Três Anos No Brasil*. (Documentos E Fotos). Sao Paulo: Empresa Gráfica Da Revista Dos Tribunais, 1978. 82 pp., ports., illus., facsims., curriculum vitae. [Dr. Fritz Ney, born 1897 in Halberstadt, son of Gustav and Martha Ney née Löwenthal, lawyer in Berlin 1925–1927, Syndic of Circus Sarrasani 1928–1935. Since May 1934 with Sarrasani in Brazil where he eventually became a teacher of English.]

15107. STRAUSS, LEVI. MASSON, IRMA LOTTE/URSULA VON WIESE: *Die Levi Strauss Saga*. Die märchenhafte Geschichte des Mannes, der die Jeans erfand. München: Kindler, 1978. 248 pp., ports., illus. [Levi Strauss (1830 Windsheim (Bavaria) – 1902 San Francisco), arrived 1850 in USA, some bales of canvas his only possession. The blue jeans which he manufactured, are known as 'Levis' throughout the world.]

15107a. THORWALD, JÜRGEN: *Das Gewürz. Die Saga der Juden in Amerika*. München: Droemer-Knaur, 1978. 640 pp., ports. [Incl. many portraits and biographies of prominent immigrants from Germany of the last century followed by the mass immigration from Eastern Europe. [Cf. Stärkstes Gewürz im Völkerkochtopf. Legende und Wirklichkeit. Die wechselvolle Geschichte der Juden in Amerika (Margrit Gerste) in: 'Die Zeit', 19. Jan., Hamburg, 1979, ports.]

II. RESEARCH AND BIBLIOGRAPHY

A. Libraries and Institutes

15108. CONFERENCE ON JEWISH MATERIAL CLAIMS AGAINST GERMANY, ed.: *Report for the period Jan. 1, 1973–Sept. 30, 1975*. New York, 1976. 32 pp., tabs. [Corrected entry No. 14254/YB. XXIII.]

15109. *Jahrbuch des Instituts für Deutsche Geschichte*. Bd. 7. Hrsg. u. eingel. von Walter Grab. Ed. Sekr. M. Techniczek. Institut f. Deutsche Geschichte, Universität Tel Aviv, Ramat Aviv, 1978. 555 pp. xiii pp. Hebrew Resumés. [Incl. Zeitgeist und deutsche Althistoriker in der ersten Hälfte des 19. Jahrhunderts (Zvi Yavetz, pp. 255–276). Wirtschaftliche Grundanschauungen und Ziele der N.S.D.A.P. (Ein unveröffentlichtes Dokument aus dem Jahre 1931). (Avraham Barkai, pp. 355–385). Heinrich Bürgers über die 'Familie' Marx, Engels und Hess im Jahre 1846. Ein Beitrag zur Kritik der neuen MEGA (Marx Engels Gedächtnisausgabe) (Shlomo Na'aman, pp. 447–456).] [Some selected contributions are listed according to subject.]

15110. LEO BAECK INSTITUTE. *Bulletin des Leo Baeck Instituts*. Hrsg. Hans Tramer. 16./17. Jg., Neue Folge, Nr. 53/54. Tel Aviv: Bitaon, 1977/78. 188 pp., ports., illus., facsim., list of names. [Individual contributions are listed according to subject.] Dr. Hans Tramer, Executive Vice President of the Leo Baeck Institute, born 1908 in Bunzlau (Niederschlesien) died on January 6, 1979 in Tel Aviv. Obituary Notes in: AJR Information, February, London, 1979. Allgemeine, Jan. 19, Düsseldorf, 1979. Aufbau, Jan. 19, New York, 1979. Isr. Wochenblatt, 19. Jan., Zürich, 1979. Neue Jüd. Nachrichten, 19. Jan., München, 1979. Dr. Hans Tramer s.A. in Memoriam. Zu den Schloschim. Statt eines Nachrufs Auszüge aus einigen seiner Schriften. [In]: 'MB', 9. Febr., Tel Aviv, 1979. Pp. 4–6.

15111. *Year Book XXIII*. Antisemitism and Philosemitism. An annual Collection of Essays on the history and activity of Jews in Germany during the past century. Founder Editor: Robert Weltsch. Co-Editor: Arnold Paucker. Introduction by Robert Weltsch. London: Secker & Warburg, 1978. xii, 402 pp., frontispiece (William II visiting Jewish-owned stationer's), port. [of Hanns G. Reissner (1902–1977), ports., illus., facsims., bibl. (pp. 309–388). [Individual contributions are listed according to subject.]

15112. LBI NEW YORK. *Library and Archives News.* Ed.: Gabrielle Bamberger. No. 7 (January), No. 8 (May). New York: Leo Baeck Institute, 1978. [8 pp., 8 pp.] [2 vols.]

15113. *LBI News.* Ed.: Gabrielle Bamberger. Vol. XIX, Summer 1978, Winter 1978/79. 12 pp., ports., illus., facsims.; 16 pp., ports., illus., facsims. [2 vols.] [The summer issue is dedicated to the memory of Martin Buber, one of the founders of the LBI. The material from the LBI collections was selected to present an impression of the many facets of Buber's life and work. The issue further incl.: Hermann Struck at the LBI. In the Winter issue are 14 Nobel Prize winners – Men of Science – pictured in connection with the 100th birthday of Albert Einstein (1879–1955). Axel Springer recipient of the first award of the Leo Baeck Medal. Obituaries Hans Liebeschütz (1893–1978) [see also No. 15006.] and Max Kreutzberger (1900–1978). Dr. Kreutzberger was Executive Director of the Institute and, after moving, in 1967, to Switzerland, its General Consultant. Further obituaries by Robert Weltsch [in]: 'MB', Nr. 47, 29. Dez. Tel Aviv, 1978 and by Eva G. Reichmann [in]: 'AJR Information', January, London, 1979. By Ernst G. Lowenthal: Sozialarbeiter – Historiker [in]: 'Die Gemeinde', 7. Febr., Wien, 1979.]

B. Bibliographies and Catalogues

15114. *A Dictionary of Jewish Names and their History.* Comp. by Benzion C. Kaganoff. New York: Schocken Books, 1977. London: Routledge and Kegan Paul, 1978. xiii, 250 pp., bibl. (pp. 212–213).

15115. *Bibliographie zur deutschen Revolution 1918/19.* [Comp. by] Georg P. Meyer. Göttingen: Vandenhoeck und Ruprecht, 1977. 188 pp. (Arbeitsbücher zur modernen Geschichte, Bd. 5). [Appr. 2,500 works are listed.]

15116. *Der deutsche Widerstand im Spiegel von Fachliteratur und Publizistik seit 1945.* Bericht und Bibliographie von Regine Büchel. München: Bernard & Graefe, 1976. vii, 215 pp. (Schriften der Bibliothek für Zeitgeschichte, Stuttgart. Neue Folge der Bibliographien der Weltkriegsbücherei, H. 15).

15117. *German Jewry: Part II.* Additions and Amendments to Catalogue No. 3, 1959–1972. Ed. Helen Kehr. London: The Institute of Contemporary History, 1978. 363 pp. (The Wiener Library Catalogue Series No. 6).

15118. *Guide to Unpublished Materials of the Holocaust Period.* Ed. Yehuda Bauer. Co-Eds.: Shmuel Krakowski, Aharon Weiss. Comp. by Ora Alcalay, Esther Blumenzweig, Chaja Lifsshitz. Vol. IV. Jerusalem: The Hebrew University, The Institute of Contemporary Jewry, Division of Holocaust Studies, Yad Vashem Martyrs' and Heroes' Remembrance Authority, 1977. 389 pp. [For Vols. I and II, ed. by J. Robinson and Y. Bauer see Nos. 8559/YB. XVI and 10261/YB. XVIII. For vol. III (1975), ed. by Y. Bauer, see No. 13492/YB. XXII.]

15119. *The Holocaust.* An Annotated Bibliography. Comp. by Harry James Cargas. Haverford, Pa.: Catholic Library Assoc., 1977. 86 pp., illus.

15120. *KC Adress-Buch.* (Kartell-Convent der Verbindungen deutscher Studenten jüdischen Glaubens (1896- Zwangsverbot 1936). Comp. by Richard J. Auerbach. Hrsg. von American-Jewish KC Fraternity und Max Mainzer Memorial Foundation. Flushing, N.Y., 1978. 62 pp.

15121. *Neue Deutsche Biographie.* Hrsg. von der Historischen Kommission bei der Bayerischen Akademie der Wissenschaften. Bd. 11: Kafka-Kleinferchen. Berlin: Duncker & Humblot, 1977. 784 pp.

15122. *Österreichisches Biographisches Lexikon 1815–1950.* Hrsg. von d. Österr. Akademie d. Wissenschaften. Redigiert von Eva Obermayer-Marnach. Bd. VI: [Maier] Stefan – Musger, August. Wien: Verlag d. Österr. Akademie d. Wissenschaften, 1975. xxx, 448 pp. [For vol. V see No. 10274/YB. XVIII.]

15123. *Persecution and Resistance under the Nazis.* Part I: Reprint of Catalogue No. 1 (Second Ed.) Ed. by Ilse R. Wolff. Part II: New Material and Amendments. Comp. and ed. by Helen Kehr. London: The Institute of Contemporary History, 1978. 500 pp. (The Wiener Library Series No. 7).
15124. *Post-War Publications on German Jewry.* A Selected Bibliography of Books and Articles 1977. Compiled by Bertha Cohn. [In]: LBI Year Book XXIII. London, 1978. Pp. 309–388.
15125. *The Weimar Era and Hitler, 1918–1933.* A Critical Bibliography. Comp. by Peter D. Stachura. Oxford: Clio Press, 1977. xvii, 275 pp.
15126. *Who's Who in World Jewry.* A Biographical Dictionary of Outstanding Jews. Chief ed.: I. J. Carmin Karpman. 4th edition. Tel Aviv: Olive Books of Israel, 1978. xxx, 974 pp. [For previous eds. see No. 9365/YB, xvii.]

III. THE NAZI PERIOD

A. General

15127. ADAM, UWE DIETRICH: *Persecution of the Jews, Bureaucracy and Authority in the Totalitarian State.* [In]: LBI Year Book XXIII. London, 1978. Pp. 139–148, facsims. [See No. 15111.]
15128. ARONSFELD, C. C.: *The Extermination of the Jews was no 'War Crime'.* [In]: 'Jewish Frontier'. Vol. XLIV, No. 7 (477). Aug./Sept. New York, 1977. Pp. 18–20.
15129. ARONSFELD, C. C.: *The Path of Hate.* [In] Jewish Affairs. Vol. 32. No. 9 (Sept.). Johannesburg, 1977. Pp. 73–77.
15130. AUSCHWITZ. HÖSS, RUDOLF: *Kommandant in Auschwitz.* Autobiographische Aufzeichnungen. Hrsg. von Martin Broszat. 4. Aufl. München: Dt. Taschenbuch Verlag, 1978. (dtv-dokumente, Bd. 2908).
15131. SMOLEN, KAZIMIERZ: *Auschwitz 1940–1945.* Guide-Book through the Muzeum. Transl. from the Polish, text by Krystyna Michalik, 6th ed. Auschwitz: Państwowe Muzeum w Oświęcimin, 1976. 118 pp., illus., plans.
15132. AUSTRIA. ROSENKRANZ, HERBERT: *Verfolgung und Selbstbehauptung der Juden in Österreich von 1938–1945.* Wien: Herold, 1978. 424 pp.
15133. WEIS, GEORG: *Arisierungen in Wien.* [In]: Forschungen und Beiträge zur Wiener Stadtgeschichte. 2, 1978. [Glückwunsch für Dr. Georg Weis zum 80. Geburtstag am 28. Mai 1978 (Hans Tramer) in: 'MB', 26. Mai, Tel Aviv, 1978. The Czech born jurist was from 1948–1956 co-director of IRSO].
15134. BAUER, YEHUDA: *The Holocaust in Historical Perspective.* Seattle: University of Washington Press, 1978. 174 pp. [Four essays which are an important contribution to Holocaust historiography].
15135. BAVARIA. BROSZAT, MARTIN, et al eds.: *Bayern in der NS-Zeit.* Soziale Lage und politisches Verhalten der Bevölkerung im Spiegel vertraulicher Berichte. Veröff. im Rahmen d. Projekts 'Widerstand und Verfolgung in Bayern 1933–1945'. Im Auftrag d. Bayerischen Staatsministeriums f. Unterricht und Kultus bearb. vom Institut für Zeitgeschichte in Verbindung mit den Staatlichen Archiven Bayerns. München: Oldenbourg, 1977. 712 pp., maps, tabs., bibl. [Part V deals with the persecution of the Jews].
15136. JAEGER, HARALD and RUMSCHÖTTEL, HERMANN: *Das Forschungsprojekt 'Widerstand und Verfolgung in Bayern 1933–1945'.* Ein Modell für die Zusammenarbeit von Archivaren und Historikern. [In]: 'Archivalische Zeitschrift', Bd. 73, Köln: Böhlau, 1977. Pp. 209–220.
15137. BERNETT, HAJO: *Der jüdische Sport im nationalsozialistischen Deutschland 1933–1938.* 7060 Schorndorf: Karl Hofmann, 1978. 182 pp., bibls. pp. 9–11. 173–175, facsims., list of names pp. 176–182. (Schriftenreihe des Bundesinstituts für Sportwissenschaft, Bd. 18). (Dem Andenken der in München 1972 ermordeten israelischen Olympia Kämpfern). [Incl. Joe Jacobs, the Jewish manager of Max Schmeling, Alfred Flatow, gymnastic Olympic victor of 1896 (died in Theresiendtadt), Helene Mayer, fencing Olympic victor of 1928, Daniel Prenn, the tennis star who emigrated to England. Cf. Die jüd.

Sportbewegung im 'Dritten Reich'. 'Max Schmeling schlägt Hitler k.o.' Des Führers 'boxender Diplomat': kein Verzicht auf den jüd. Manager (Manfred Lehnen) in: 'Die Zeit', 9. März, Hamburg, 1979, illus.]

15138. BUCHENWALD. HANNSMANN, MARGARETE: *Aufzeichnungen über Buchenwald*. Mit Holzschnitten von HAP Grieshaber und Zeichnungen von Herbert Sandberg. Frankfurt/M.: Röderberg-Verlag, 1978. 93 pp., ports., illus. [H. Sandberg is a former prisoner of Buchenwald].

—— CARGAS, HARRY JAMES, comp.: *The Holocaust*. An Annotated Bibliography. [See No. 15119.]

15139. DACHAU. SELZER, MICHAEL: *Deliverance Day*. The Last Hours at Dachau. New York: Lippincott, 1978. [An hour-by-hour account of Dachau's liberation].

15140. DAWIDOWICZ, LUCY S.: *The War against the Jews, 1933–1945*. Harmondsworth (Middx.): Penguin, 1977. 552 pp., tabs., maps, notes, bibl. [Paperback edition. For previous eds. see No. 13512/YB. XXII.]

15141. DEKEL, EPHRAIM: *B'riha*. Flight to the Homeland. Transl. from the Hebrew by Dina Ettinger. Ed. by Gertrude Hirschler. New York: Herzl Press, 1978. 352 pp., illus., B'riha chronology. [The exodus of the holocaust survivors from German and Austrian DP camps and other European countries.]

15142. DEUTSCHKRON, INGE: *'Ich trug den gelben Stern'*. Köln: Verlag Wissenschaft und Politik, 1978. 216 pp., illus. [Cf. Als Jüdin in Berlin. Den unbesungenen Helden. Inge Deutschkrons ungewöhnliches Überleben in schrecklicher Zeit (Rolf W. Schloss) in: 'Die Zeit', 9. März, Hamburg, 1977, illus. Rolf W. Schloss, journalist, ARD-correspondent in Tel Aviv, born 1918 in Frankfurt/M., died February 1979 in Israel.]

15143. ECKARDT, ALICE and ROY: *Studying the Holocaust's Impact Today*. Some Dilemmas of Language and Method. [In]: 'Judaism', Issue No. 106, Vol. 27, No. 2, Spring. New York: The American Jewish Congress and World Jewish Congress, 1978. Pp. 222–232, bibl. footnotes.

15144. EZRAHI, SIDRA DEKOVEN: *The Holocaust in Literature*. A comparative study of modes of literary response to the holocaust. Waltham, Mass., 1976. v, 478 pp. Diss., Brandeis University, Microfilm copy of typescript Ann Arbor, Mich. University Microfilms, 1976.

15145. FEST, JOACHIM: *The Face of the Third Reich*. Portraits of the Nazi leadership. Transl. from the German by Michael Bullock. New York: Pantheon Books, 1970. xiii, 402 pp., bibl. (pp. 386–391). New German edition: Das Gesicht des Dritten Reiches, 1977. See No. 14287/YB. XXIII.]

15146. DORTMUND. KNIPPING, ULRICH: *Die Geschichte der Juden in Dortmund während der Zeit des Dritten Reiches*. Dortmund: Verlag des Historischen Vereins, 1977. 255 pp., illus., facsims. tabs. (Monographien zur Geschichte Dortmunds und der Grafschaft Mark, Bd. 6). [Incl. Verzeichnis der Mitglieder d. Jüd. Kultusvereinigung Dortmund nach dem Stand vom 1. Juni 1941 (1200 names). Theresienstadt-Liste 1942–1944 (mit 331 names). Eye witness accounts by Jeanette Wolff and others.]

15147. FLEISCHNER, EVA, comp.: *Select Annotated Bibliography on the Holocaust*. [In]: 'Horizons', 4, spring. New York: American Heritage Publ. Co., 1977. Pp. 61–83.

15148. GILBERT, MARTIN: *The Holocaust*. A Record in Maps and Photographs of the Destruction of Jewish Life in Europe during the dark years of Nazi Rule. London: Board of Deputies of British Jews, 1978. v, 60 pp., illus., maps, bibl. [Incl. also details of the persecution of gipsies and other non-Jewish minorities by the Nazis.]

15149. GOEBBELS, JOSEPH. *The Diaries of Joseph Goebbels*. The Final Entries 1945. Ed. and with an Introduction by Hugh Trevor-Roper. Transl. by Richard Barry. New York: Putnam, London: Secker and Warburg, 1978. 368 pp. [For German original see No. 14294/YB. XXIII.]

15150. GUTMAN, YISRAEL and LIVIA ROTHKIRCHEN, eds.: *The Catastrophe of European Jewry. Antecedents – History – Reflections*. Selected Papers. Jerusalem: Yad Vashem, 1976. x, 757 pp., chronol. table of events 1933–1945 (Shmuel Krakowski, pp. 705–738), index of names and places, bibl. (pp. 756–757). [Incl. European Jewry before and after Hitler (Salo W. Baron). The Holocaust (Jacob Robinson). The 'Final Solution' in its last stages (Livia Rothkirchen). The Dignity of the Destroyed. Towards a Definition of the Period of the Holocaust (Shaul Esh). The Attitude of the Judenrats to the Problems of Armed Resistance against the Nazis (Isaiah Trunk). The 'Righteous Among the

Nations' and their Part in the Rescue of Jews (Moshe Bejski). The Holocaust and the Struggle of the Yishuv as Factors in the Establishment of the State of Israel (Yehuda Bauer). The Holocaust in Jewish Historiography (Leni Yahil). The Mission of the Survivors (Abba Kovner). For other contributions see No. 15775.]

15151. GUTMAN, YISRAEL and EFRAIM ZUROFF, eds.: *Rescue Attempts during the Holocaust.* Proceedings of the Second Yad Vashem International Historical Conference, Jerusalem, April 9–11, 1974. Jerusalem: Yad Vashem, 1977. 679 pp., facsims., indexes of names, places, major organizations involved in rescue attempts, pp. 659–679. [Incl. The Negotiations between Saly Mayer and the Representatives of the S. S. in 1944–1945 (Yehuda Bauer, pp. 5–45). The Rescue Work of the World Jewish Congress during the Nazi Period (Elizabeth E. Eppler, pp. 47–69). The British Government and the Fate of Hungarian Jewry in 1944 (Bela Vago, pp. 205–223). The Problem of the Rescue of German Jewry during the years 1933–1939: the reasons for the Delay in their Emigration from the Third Reich (Abraham Margaliot, pp. 247–265). The Emigration of Jews from Worms (Nov. 1938–Oct. 1941); Hopes and Plans. A Statistical Analysis of the Impact of Immigration Policies on the Fate of German Jewry (Henry R. Huttenbach, pp. 267–288, tabs.) The Role of the Czech and Slovak Jewish Leadership in the Field of Rescue Work (Livia Rothkirchen, pp. 423–434). The Uniqueness of the Rescue of Danish Jewry (Leni Yahil, pp. 617–625). The 'Righteous among the Nations' and their Part in the Rescue of Jews (Moshe Bejski, pp. 627–647).]

15152. HAHN, FRED, ed.: *Lieber Stürmer.* Leserbriefe an das NS-Kampfblatt 1924 bis 1945. Bearbeitung der deutschen Ausgabe von Günther Wagenlehner. Stuttgart: Seewald, 1978. 263 pp., ports., illus., facsims., notes pp. 261–263. (Zeitpolitische Schriftenreihe, Bd. 19). [The letters are taken from the Bernhard Kolb collection in the LBI in New York.]

15153. HESSE. MORITZ, KLAUS und ERNST NOAM: *NS-Verbrechen vor Gericht 1945–1955.* Dokumente aus hessischen Justizakten mit e. Nachwort von Richard Schmid. Wiesbaden: Kommission für die Geschichte der Juden in Hessen, 1978. 374 pp., tabs., graphs., map, bibl. (pp. 344–348), notes pp. 349–361. (Schriften der Kommission f.d. Geschichte der Juden in Hessen II, Justiz und Verfolgung, Bd. 2). [For vol. 1: Juden vor Gericht 1933–1945 see No. 14337/YB. XXIII.] [Ernst Noam, orig. Nussbaum, 1908 Hanau–1977 Vassin (Switzerland).]

15154. HOLOCAUST – FILM. FRANKEL, WILLIAM: *Holocaust: can the truth ever be told?* Television documentary on the examination of Europe's Jews: but how much is fact and how much fiction? [In]: The Times, Aug. 31, London, 1978 [And]: *Six Million Reasons.* William Frankel, former editor of the 'Jewish Chronicle', on why they had to make a television drama out of Holocaust. [In]: 'Evening Standard', Sept. 7, London, 1978.

15155. GREEN, GERALD: *Holocaust.* The Book of the TV Series. London: Corgi Books, A Division of Transworld Publs., 1978. 408 pp. (Deutsche Buchausgabe): *Holocaust – Endlösung.* Roman. Bayreuth: Hestia, 1978. 424 pp., ports., illus. (Der Roman zur vieldiskutierten Fernsehserie).

15156. *Holocaust.* The Facts behind the TV Fiction. Taken from Byron L. Shervin's contribution to the background material prepared in America and distributed prior to the showing of the film. [In]: 'Jewish Chronicle', Sept. 1, London, 1978. Pp. 19–21, illus.

15157. *The Holocaust in History 1933–1945.* [In]: 'The Record'. Publ. by The Anti-Defamation League of B'nai B'rith and the National Council for the Social Studies. New York and Washington, 1978. 16 pp., illus., maps, chronology, bibl.

15158. *'Holocaust' on small screen.* On the discussion that arose after the showing of the film. [In]: 'AJR Information', No. 10, Oct. London, 1978.

15159. *Holocaust: A Book of the Dead in the Style of Best-Seller Yuk.* (Dennis Potter) on the BBC's American serial about the massacre of the Jews. [In]: 'Sunday Times', 10th Sept., London, 1978.

15160. *Judenvernichtung als Fernsehspiel.* [In]: 'MB', 21. Juli, Tel Aviv, 1978. Pp. 5–6.

15161. LETTAU, REINHARD: *Und dann . . . Und dann . . . Judenvernichtung als Fernsehspiel –* jetzt in den USA, demnächst bei uns. [In]: 'Die Zeit', 16. Juni, Hamburg, 1978, illus.

15162. LIETZMANN, SABINA: *Diskussion über Holocaust. Die Judenvernichtung als Seifenoper.* [In]: 'FAZ', 20. April, Frankfurt/M., 1978 [and] Kritische Fragen, in: 'FAZ', 28.

Sept. 1978. [And]: *Holocaust, eine Prüfung* (Karl Heinz Bohner) in: 'FAZ', 3. Sept. 1978.

15163. RÜHLE, GÜNTHER: *Wenn Holocaust kommt*. Vor der Fernsehsendung über die Massenvernichtung der Juden – Ein Ereignis, das die Meinungen spalten wird. [In]: 'FAZ', 17. Jan., Frankfurt/M., 1979, illus.

15164. WIESEL, ELIE: *Wie erzählt man eine Story, die nicht erzählt werden kann?* Trivialisierter Holocaust. [In]: 'Isr. Wochenblatt', Nr. 21, 26. Mai, Zürich, 1978. Pp. 7–10, ports.

15165. HORBACH, MICHAEL: *So überlebten sie den Holocaust*. Zeugnisse der Menschlichkeit 1933–1945. München: Goldmann, 1978. [Jews who survived thanks to the assistance of Germans who often risked their own lives in such rescue attempts.]

15166. *Justiz und NS-Verbrechen*. Sammlung deutscher Strafurteile wegen nationalsozialistischer Tötungsverbrechen 1945–1966. Bearb. von Irene Sagel-Grande, H. H. Fuchs, C. F. Rüter. Bd. XVIII: Die vom 21. 11. 1961 bis zum 10.01. 1963 ergangenen Strafurteile. Lfd. Nr. 523–547. Bd. XIX: Die vom 10.01. 1963 bis zum 12.04. 1964 ergangenen Strafurteile, Lfd. Nr. 547–569. Amsterdam: University Press, 1978. v, 864 pp.; v, 847 pp., tabs. [2 vols. For previous vols. see No. 14325/YB. XXIII.]

15167. KLARSFELD, SERGE (Rechtsanwalt), ed.: *Die Endlösung der Judenfrage in Frankreich*. Deutsche Dokumente 1941–1944. Verlegt und veröffentlicht von Beate und Serge Klarsfeld, Paris 16 (Rue de Versailles 196), 1977. 244 pp., cover ports., biogr. notes (pp. 231–241). (Dokumentationszentrum für Jüdische Zeitgeschichte (DJC Paris).

15168. KOEHN, ILSE: *'Mischling, Second Degree'*. My childhood in Nazi Germany. New York: Greenwillow Books, London: Hamish Hamilton, 1977. 240 pp.

15169. KRÖGER, ULLRICH: *Die Ahndung von NS-Verbrechen vor westdeutschen Gerichten und ihre Rezeption in der deutschen Öffentlichkeit 1958–1965*, unter besonderer Berücksichtigung von 'Spiegel', 'Stern', 'Zeit', 'SZ', 'FAZ', 'Welt', 'Bild', 'Hamburger Abendblatt', 'NZ' und 'Neue Deutschland'. Hamburg, 1973. xiv, 457 pp., bibl. (pp. 440–457). (Diss. Hamburg, 1973).

15170. LEUNER, H[EINZ] D[AVID]: *When Compassion was a Crime*. Germany's Silent Heroes, 1933–45. Foreword by Terence Prittie. London: Oswald Wolff, 1978. 168 pp., chronology, bibl. index. [First publ. 1966. See No. 5702/YB. XII. Transl. into German by Hans Lamm: 'Als Mitleid ein Verbrechen war' (1967), see No. 6332/YB. XIII. In his Foreword to the new edition Terence Prittie pays tribute to the author, who died in 1977, and his work for the cause of Christian-Jewish relations. [See also Nos. 15765–15766.]

15171. MÜNDEN. PETZOLD, JOHANN DIETRICH VON: *Judenverfolgung in Münden 1933–1945*. Eine Dokumentation aus dem Archiv der Stadt Münden, 1978.

15172. NATZWEILER. VORLÄNDER, HERWART, ed.: *Nationalsozialistische Konzentrationslager im Dienst der totalen Kriegführung*. Sieben württembergische Aussenkommandos des Konzentrationslagers Natzweiler/Elsass. Stuttgart: Kohlhammer, 1978. xix, 270 pp., documents [56 pp.], bibl. (pp. xi-xvii). (Veröffentlichungen der Kommission f. geschichtliche Landeskunde in Baden-Württemberg, Reihe B, Forschungen, Bd. 91).

15173. NEU-ISENBURG. REBENTISCH, DIETER/ANGELIKA RAAB, eds.: *Neu-Isenburg zwischen Anpassung und Widerstand*. Dokumente über Lebensbedingungen und politisches Verhalten 1933–1945. Neu-Isenburg: Magistrat der Stadt, 1978. 343 pp., ports., illus., tabs., facsims. [Kap. VI: *Die Verfolgung der Juden*, pp. 229–288, ports. [of Bertha Pappenheim], bibl. (pp. 243–244). Die Tätigkeit des Jüd. Kinderheimes, Liste de jüd. Bürger Neu-Isenburgs.]

15174. NEUENGAMME. BRINGMANN, FRITZ: *Kindermord am Bullenhuserdamm*. (Aussenkommando des Kz Neuengamme). SS-Verbrechen in Hamburg 1945: Menschenversuche an Kindern. Hrsg. von der Arbeitsgemeinschaft Neuengamme für die BRD, Hamburg. Frankfurt/M.: Röderberg, 1978. 64 pp., illus., ports., facsims., bibl. (pp. 63–64).

15175. NOVEMBER POGROM. DIAMANT, ADOLF: *Zerstörte Synagogen vom November 1938*. Eine Bestandsaufnahme. Frankfurt/M.: Im Selbstverlag, 1978. xvi, 227 pp., 100 illus. (pp. 127–226), facsims., bibl. (pp. 118–122).

15176. ESSEN. SCHRÖTER, HERMANN: *Die 'Reichskristallnacht' in Essen*. [In]: Das Münster am Hellweg. 32. Jg., H.1/4, Jan. Essen, 1979. Pp. 48–54.

15177. DÖSCHER, HANS JÜRGEN: *Die Reichskristallnacht 1938*. Materialien zur Geschichte der Judenverfolgung. Ausstellung 9. Nov.–1. Dez. 1978 in Schwedenspeicher-Museum, Stade.

15178. *Erinnerung* (Arnulf H. Baumann) [and] *Umkehr und Erneuerung.* Zum Gedenken an den 9. November 1938 (Eduard Lohse) [In]: Friede über Israel. Zeitschrift für Kirche und Judentum. 61. Jg., H.4, Dez. Hannover, 1978. Pp. 145–153.
15179. FREIMARK, PETER/WOLFGANG KOPITZSCH: *Der 9./10. November 1938 in Deutschland.* Dokumentation zur 'Kristallnacht'. Hamburg: Landeszentrale für politische Bildung, 1978. 104 pp., illus., facsims., bibls.: Unterrichtsmaterialien; Publikationen, Autovisuelle Medien. (Veröffentlichung der Landeszentrale f. politische Bildung, Hamburg, in Zusammenarbeit mit dem Institut für die Geschichte der deutschen Juden, Hamburg. Redaktion: Hartmut Hohlbein). [Incl. chaps.: Nationalsozialismus als Unterrichtsthema. Die 'Kristallnacht' – Möglichkeiten der Unterrichtsgestaltung. Anregungen für die Unterrichtsplanung].
15180. GALINSKI, HEINZ: *9. November 1938. Fakten und Folgerungen.* [In]: 'Isr. Wochenblatt', 3. Nov., Zürich, 1978. Pp. 11–16, illus.
15181. GALINSKI, HEINZ: *9. November 1938 – ein noch immer aktuelles Datum.* [And]: *Gedanken zum 9. November 1938* (Joachim March) [In]: 'Die Mahnung'. Hrsg. Bund der Verfolgten des Naziregimes. 25. Jg., Nr. 11, Nov. Berlin, 1978. Pp. 1–3, illus.
15182. HANOVER. *'Reichskristallnacht' in Hannover.* Eine Ausstellung zur 40. Wiederkehr des 9. Nov. 1938 (7. Nov. 1978–21. Jan. 1979). Beiträge zur Ausstellung hrsg. vom Historischen Museum, Redaktion Waldemar R. Röhrbein. Hannover, 1978. 136 pp., cover illus., ports., illus., facsims., Zeittafel 'Kristallnacht' pp. 79–81, bibl. (pp. 132–135). [Cont. Die jüd. Gemeinde in Hannover seit der Emanzipation (Helmut Zimmermann). Emanzipation und Antisemitismus in Hannover zwischen 1842 und 1918 (Waldemar R. Röhrbein). Antisemitismus 1918–1945 (Friedrich Wilhelm Rogge). Die 'Reichskristallnacht', Zeittafel 'Reichskristallnacht' (Klaus Mlynek). Ghettoisierung, Deportation und Ermordung der hannoverschen Juden (Marlis Buchholz/Herbert Obenaus). Deutsche und Juden nach 1945 (Klaus Mlynek, Herbert Obenaus, Helmut Zimmermann).]
15183. HESSE. *Materialien zum 40. Jahrestag der Synagogenzerstörungen in Hessen.* Hrsg. von der Jüdischen Gemeinde Frankfurt am Main und dem Landesverband der Jüdischen Gemeinden in Hessen, 1978. 36 pp., illus.
15184. HUTTER, CLEMENS M.: *Die 'Kristallnacht' – Auftakt zur Endlösung.* '... bis der letzte Jude Münchens ausgetilgt ist' (Hitler im Jahr 1922). [In]: 'Jüd. Rundschau Maccabi'. Nr. 42, 19. Okt. Basel, 1978. Pp. 2 & 8, illus.
15185. KAMPEN, WILHELM VON, comp.: *Holocaust Dokumentenmaterial.* Bundeszentrale für politische Bildung in Bonn, 1978. 60 pp., illus.
15186. KREMERS, HEINZ: *Mauer des Misstrauens durchbrochen.* Interview zu zwei Symposien über den Holocaust. [In]: 'Allgemeine', 10. Nov. Düsseldorf, 1978. Pp. 5 & 6.
15187. LOWENTHAL, E. G.: *Zum 9. November 1978.* Was war die 'Kristallnacht'? [In]: 'Das Neue Israel'. 31. Jg., H. 4, Okt. Zürich, 1978. Pp. 201–202.
15188. *Mahnung und Verpflichtung des 9. November 1938.* Gedenken an die Judenverfolgung in Deutschland. Erklärung des Bundespräsidenten Walter Scheel. Ansprache des Bundeskanzlers Helmut Schmidt in der Kölner Synagoge. Gedenken des Deutschen Bundestages: Erklärung des Präsidenten Prof. Karl Carstens zur Eröffnung der Sitzung am 9. November 1978 [In]: Bulletin. Nr. 130, 10. November. Presse- und Informationsamt der Bundesregierung, Bonn, 1978. Pp. 1213–1218. Ein Bericht von Hermann Lewy über die zentrale Veranstaltung in der Synagoge von Köln *'Bekenntnis zum Miteinander'* auch in: 'Allgemeine', 17. Nov., Düsseldorf, 1978. Pp. 1, 3, 4, ports., illus. [Incl. Die Ansprache von Nahum Goldmann.]
15189. MAYER, HANS: *Die verbrannte Synagoge.* Gedanken zur Kristallnacht 1938. [In]: 'Die Zeit', 10. Nov., Hamburg, 1978. Pp. 49–50, illus. (Skulptur von Rolf Szymanski).
15190. METZGER, HARTMUT: *Kristallnacht.* Dokumente von gestern zum Gedenken heute. Stuttgart: Calwer, 1978. 64 pp., illus., maps. (Calwer Paperback). [Augenzeugenberichte, Zeitungsartikel, eine Busstagspredigt, Reaktionen der Kirche, Briefe jüdischer Kinder, die 'Kleine Dachauer Passion'. Ein Interview mit Joseph Walk (Breslau jetzt Israel) setzt die Ereignisse von damals in Beziehung zu den Aufgaben, die wir heute vor uns haben].
15191. *Die Nacht im November – Judenpogrom 1938: Als ein ganzes Volk schuldig wurde* (Karl-Heinz Janßen). Befehl der SA-Gruppe 'Nordsee': Sofort zerstören!' (Aus dem Archiv des Instituts für Zeitgeschichte in München). 'Ihr seid hier in einem Krematorium',

Augenzeugenbericht aus dem Konzentrationslager Sachsenhausen, Aus: Judenverfolgung im Dritten Reich (Wolfgang Scheffler, Berlin 1960).) O Land, höre des Herrn Wort! Busstagspredigt 1938 des Pfarrers Julius von Jan, Oberlenningen (Auszug). Der 9. November 1938 in Zahlen: Opfer, Kosten, Folgen der Kristallnacht [In]: 'Die Zeit', 3. Nov. Hamburg, 1978. Pp. 17–21, illus., facsim.

15192. *November Pogroms Remembered.* Wide Coverage in Germany. [In]: 'AJR Information', December, London, 1978.
15193. OESTREICHER, PAUL: *Terror on Berlin's Night of Broken Glass.* A boy's memory of Germany, 1938, when Nazis smashed Jewish shops and the 'Final Solution' began ... [In]: 'The Times', Nov. 9, London, 1978, illus.
—— *Die Reichskristallnacht. 9. Nov. 1938–9. Nov. 1978.* Eine Arbeitshilfe für Unterricht und Gemeindearbeit. Hrsg. Evangelischer Arbeitskreis Kirche und Israel in Hessen und Nassau. [See No. 15238].
15194. ROSENSTOCK, WERNER: *Prelude to Holocaust.* The November 1938 Pogroms. [And]: *Pogroms Planned Well in Advance* (Janet Langmaid) [In]: 'AJR Information'. Vol. XXXIII, No. 11 (Nov.), London, 1978. Pp. 1–2.
15195. SCHEFFLER, WOLFGANG: *Ausgewählte Dokumente zur Geschichte des Novemberpogroms 1938.* I. Zur Situation der nationalsozialistischen Judenpolitik im Jahre 1938. II. Dokumente: A. Zur Befehlsgebung. B. Zur Durchführung des Pogroms. C. Zur wirtschaftlichen Entrechtung. [In]: Aus Politik und Zeitgeschichte. Beilage zur Wochenzeitung 'Das Parlament'. B 44/78, 4. Nov. Hrsg. von der Bundeszentrale für politische Bildung, Bonn, 1978. Pp. 3–30.
15196. STEINITZ, HANS: *40. Jahrestag der 'Kristallnacht' – eine Nachlese.* [In]: 'Aufbau', 15. Dez. New York, 1978.
15197. STELZER, WERNER: *Kapitulation am 9. November 1938.* Deutsches Versagen vor dem Bösen. (pp. 3–10). Vierzig Jahre danach ... Theologische Erwägungen zur 'Reichskristallnacht' (Rudolf Pfisterer, pp. 11–20). Dokumentation zur 'Reichskristallnacht', pp. 22–60, facsim.' tabs. [In]: 'Tribüne', H. 68, 1978. [See No 15751]
15198. *Vierzig Jahre danach. Zum 9. November 1938* (Alexander Ginsburg). *Anlass zur Gewissenserforschung.* Ein Schreiben von Joseph Kardinal Höffner, Vors. d. deutschen Bischofskonferenz. '*Nur Gott kann unsere Schuld vergeben*', Erklärung vom Rat d. Evangelischen Kirche in Deutschland. *Ehre und Recht ausser Kraft gesetzt.* Der Pogrom vom 9. Nov. 1938 (Hermann Lewy). *Das Zeichen unter den Völkern.* Aus einer unveröffentlichten Rede aus dem Jahre 1958 von Rabbiner Dr. R. R. Geis s.A. *Brennende Seele.* Zum 40. Jahrestag der Synagogenverbrennung (Rabb. H. I. Grünewald). '*Ich möchte jetzt kein Jude sein*' (Wolfgang Nitsche) [In]: 'Allgemeine', 3. Nov., Düsseldorf, 1978. Pp. 1–2, 7–10, illus. pp. 8–9.
15199. *Vor vierzig Jahren ....* (Ernst Vogt) [and]: Material aus Zeitungsberichten über die Vorgänge in Deutschland gesammelt unter d. Titel 'Der Pogrom' mit einem Vorwort von Heinrich Mann vom Verlag für Soziale Literatur, Zürich-Paris 1939 veröffentlicht [In: 'Emuna-Israel Forum', H.4, 1978. Pp. 37–41 [to be cont.] [See No. 15759.]
15200. *Vor vierzig Jahren: das Reichskristallnacht-Pogrom.* Ausarbeitung der EKD-Kirchenkanzlei und andere Texte. [In]: Dokumentation. Evangelischer Pressedienst (epd), Nr. 44/78, 16. Okt. Hrsg. vom Gemeinschaftswerk der Evangelischen Publizistik, ed. Hans-Wolfgang Hessler. Frankfurt/M., 1978. 136 pp., tabs., facsims., bibl. [Mimeog.] [Incl. Zur Verfolgung des Judentums durch den Nationalsozialismus. (Aus Anlass des 40. Jahresgedenktages der November-Pogrome 1938) (Holger Maiwald, pp. 1–22), bibl. pp. 19–22). Die Vernichtung des Europäischen Judentums im Spiegel Jüdisch-Theologischen Denkens der Gegenwart (Stefan Schreiner, pp. 23–32). Die Zahl der Opfer der 'Endlösung' und der Korherr-Bericht (Georges Wellers, pp. 57–74). Gerhard Kittel und die Judenfrage, pp. 79–93).]
15201. POLIAKOV, LÉON/JOSEF WULF, eds.: *Das Dritte Reich und die Juden.* Dokumente und Aufsätze. 2., durchges. Aufl., berecht. Nachdr. München, New York, London, Paris: Saur, Berlin: Arani, 1978. xii, 457 pp. [First ed. 1955. See No. 126/YB. I.]
15202. ROBINSOHN, HANS: *Justiz als politische Verfolgung.* Die Rechtsprechung in 'Rasseschandefällen' beim Landgericht Hamburg 1936–1943. Schriftenreihe der Vierteljahrshefte für Zeitgeschichte, Stuttgart: Deutsche Verlagsanstalt, 1978. 168 pp. [Cf. 'Rasseschandefälle', Liebe als Verbrechen (Werner Steltzer) [In]: 'Tribüne', H. 68, 1978. Pp. 155–158. See No. 15751.]

15203. SCHOENBERNER, GERHARD: *Der Gelbe Stern*. Die Judenverfolgung in Europa 1933–1945. Neu überarbeitete Bilddokumentation. München: Bertelsmann, 1978. 224 pp., 200 photo documents, facsims., map. [First ed. 1960. See No. 2035/YB. VI.]
15204. SOBIBOR. NOVITCH, MIRIAM: *Sobibor*. Martyre et révolte. Documents et témoignages. Université Paris: Centre de Publication Asie Orientale, 1978. 170 pp., ports., illus,. bibl. (pp. 169–170).
15205. THERESIENSTADT–TEREZIN. EISENKRAFT, CLARA: *Damals in Theresienstadt*. Erlebnisse einer Judenchristin. Wuppertal: Aussaat Verlag, 1977. 103 pp. (ABC-Team, 3005).
15206. GREEN, GERALD: *The Artists of Terezin*. Illustrations by the inmates of Terezin. New York: Hawthorn Books/Schocken, 1978. ix, 193 pp., illus.
15207. TRUNK, ISAIAH: *Judenrat*. The Jewish Councils in Eastern Europe under Nazi Occupation. New York: Stein and Day, 1978. 664 pp. [Cf. Doch nicht mitschuldig? Die Judenräte im historischen Urteil der Nachwelt (Julius H. Schoeps) [In] : 'Die Zeit', 24. Nov., Hamburg, 1978, illus.
15208. *Das verspottete Tausendjährige Reich*. Witze gesammelt von Alexander Drozdzynski. Düsseldorf: Droste, 1978. 220 pp., illus. [Incl. Konzentrationslager oder das 'Lachen' hinter Stacheldraht. Die Juden im Dritten Reich oder der Witz als Kunst des Überlebens. Exil oder wie man sich gegen Heimweh tröstet.] [The author, born 1925 in Poland, deported 1944 to Auschwitz, studied philosophy in Cracow and Breslau and has lived since 1968 in West Germany.]
15209. WELLERS, GEORGES: *Die Zahl der Opfer der 'Endlösung' und der Korherr-Bericht*. [In]: Aus Politik und Zeitgeschichte. Beilage zur Wochenzeitung 'Das Parlament'. B 30/78, 29. Juli. Bonn: Bundeszentrale für Politische Bildung, 1978. Pp. 22–39, bibl. notes. [The 'Inspekteur für Statistik' der SS Richard Korherr was ordered by Himmler in January 1943 to write a report on the 'final solution' of the European Jewish question.]
15210. WIESEL, ELIE: *The Holocaust as Literary Inspiration*. [In]: Dimensions of the Holocaust. Lectures at North-Western University. Evanston, Ill.: North-Western University. Distributed by the Center for Studies on the Holocaust, Anti-Defamation League of B'nai B'rith, New York, 1977. 63 pp. [Other lectures incl.: The Holocaust as historical record (L. S. Dawidowicz). The H. as living memory (D. Rabinowitz). The H. as a problem in moral choice by dimensions of the Holocaust (R. McFee Brown.]
15211. YAD VASHEM, comp.: *Liste von Publikationen, in denen die Ermordung von Sechs Millionen Juden im Zweiten Weltkrieg abgestritten wird*. [Also]: Literature Denying the Holocaust and Reactions to this Literature. Jerusalem: Yad Vashem Bibliothek, Jan. 1977, 3 pp.; Sept. 1978, 3 pp. [Type-script].

B. Jewish Resistance

15212. AUSTRIA. MAASS, WALTER B.: *The Years of Darkness*. The Austrian Resistance Movement, 1938–1945. Transl. by John Wilde. Vienna: Federal Press Service, 1975. 68 pp., ports., illus. [Incl. The terror, pp. 10–18. The 'Final Solution' in Austria, pp. 19–25.]
15213. BUCHENWALD. DROBISCH, KLAUS: *Widerstand in Buchenwald*. Frankfurt/M.: Röderberg, 1978. 175 pp., ports., illus. Lizenz d. Dietz-Verl., Berlin East.
15214. KOWALSKI, ISAAC: *A Secret Press in Nazi Europe*. The story of a Jewish United Partisan Organisation. Third ed., rev. for paperback. New York: Shengold, 1978. 352 pp., front. map, ports., illus., facsims., bibl. (pp. 346–347). First publ. 1969. See No. 7756/YB. XV.]
15215. KRAKOWSKI, SHMUEL: *Jewish Resistance to the Nazis*. [In]: Soviet Jewish Affairs. Vol. 5, No. 2. London: The Institute of Jewish Affairs in association with the World Jewish Congress, 1975. Pp. 94–102. [A review article.]
15216. LEVIN, DOV: *Die Beteiligung der litauischen Juden im Zweiten Weltkrieg*. [In]: Acta Baltica, XVI. Königstein/Ts.: Institutum Balticum, 1976. Pp. 172–184.
15217. LEVIN, DOV: *They Fought Back*. Lithuanian Jewry's Armed Resistance to the Nazis, 1941–1945. Ed. by Yad Vashem Martyrs' and Heroes' Remembrance Authority,

The Institute of Contemporary Jewry, The Hebrew University. Jerusalem, 1974. vii, 267 pp. [See also No. 14353/YB. XXIII.]
15218. RÜCKERL, ADALBERT: *Begriff des Widerstandes und der Verfolgung aus der Gegenwartsperspektive.* Vortrag von A. R., Leiter der Zentralen Stelle zur Aufklärung von NS-Verbrechen, geh. auf d. Delegiertentag des BVN, Berlin am 7. Mai 1978. [In]: 'Die Mahnung'. Hrsg. Bund der Verfolgten des Naziregimes. 25. Jg. Nr. 6, 7, 8. Berlin, 1978.
15219. SYRKIN, MARIE: *Blessed is the Match.* The Story of Jewish Resistance. Philadelphia: Jewish Publication Society of America, 1977. xviii, 366 pp. [A new paperback ed. Original first publ. 1948.]

IV. POST WAR

A. General

15220. CZECHOSLOVAKIA. *'Informationsbulletin'.* Hrsg.: Rat d. Jüd. Gemeinden in d. Tschechischen Sozialistischen Republik zu Prag und vom Zentralverband d. Jüd. Religionsgemeinden in d. Slowakischen Republik zu Bratislava. Ed.: Rudolf Iltis. Nr. 2. Prag: Kirchenzentralverlag, 1977. 42 pp. [Incl. Zum Thema Theresienstadt. Vom Staatl. Jüd. Museum zu Prag.] [The editor Rudolf Iltis died aged 77, 1977 in Prague.]
15221. DIAMANT, ADOLF: *Filme über die Geschichte der Juden.* Rückblick auf deutsche Produktionen nach 1945. [In]: 'Allgemeine', 21. Okt., Düsseldorf, 1977.
15222. FEDERAL GERMAN REPUBLIC. BRODER, HENRYK M.: *Deutschland erwacht.* Die neuen Nazis – Aktionen und Provokationen. Nachwort von Jean Améry. Querheft 5. 5303 Bornheim Merten: Lamuv Verlag (Martinstr. 7), 1978. 120 pp., ports., illus., facsims.
15223. *Die Juden in Deutschland.* Sonderdruck. 'Rheinischer Merkur', aus den Ausgaben 48–50 vom. 1.–15.12. 1978. Koblenz, [16 pp.], ports., illus.
15224. *Die jüdische Minderheit in der Bundesrepublik Deutschland.* Eine Analyse. Philos. Diss., Universität Köln, [submitted by] Doris Kuschner. Köln, 1977. viii, 321 pp., tabs., bibl. (pp. 266–300).
15225. KAHE, JOACHIM, ed.: *Etty, Peter und Silvia Gingold.* Porträt einer Familie. Ein Bilderbuch über deutsche Zustände. Köln: Pahl-Rugenstein, 1978. 104 pp., illus. [In 1933 the Gingolds, Jewish Communists, fled to Paris. They worked in the French Resistance and were decorated for their services.
15226. STROTHMANN, DIETRICH: *Hitlers Harlekine von heute.* Der Bundesrepublik droht keine Gefahr von rechts. [In]: 'Die Zeit', 28. April, Hamburg, 1978. Pp. 33–37, illus., facsims. [Eine Antwort auf die Frage: Wie gefährlich sind die neuen Nazis?].
15227. GERMAN DEMOCRATIC REPUBLIC. *'Nachrichtenblatt'* d. Jüd. Gemeinde von Gross-Berlin und d. Verb. d. Jüd. Gemeinden in der Deutschen Demokratischen Republik. Eds. Helmut Aris, Peter Kirchner, Herbert Ringer. Berlin–Dresden, März, Juni, Sept., Dez. 1978. 39 pp., illus.; 25 pp., ports., illus.; 40 pp., ports., illus.; 40 pp., ports., illus. [4 issues.] [No. 1 incl.: Martin Buber zum 100. Geburtstag (Peter Heidrich). Die jüd. Position in der Welt (Peter Kirchner). 100 Jahre Rabbiner-Seminar in Budapest (Helmut Aris). Eröffnung einer jüd. Bibliothek in Berlin (Renate Kirchner). Die Geschichte der Juden in Magdeburg: Der Sklavenmarkt in Magdeburg (Hans Bekker, 2. Forts. see No. 14362/YB. XXIII). Die Synagoge der Roland-Stadt (Nordhausen) (Herbert Gerhardt). Im Herzen von Berlin (Julius Rodenberg, orig. Levy, 1831–1914) aus 'Bilder aus dem Berliner Leben (1891). Jüdische Gemeinde zu Halle/Saale. Erste Barmizwoh seit 1945. No. 2 incl.: Die Geschichte der Juden in Magdeburg: Das Heilige Römische Reich Deutscher Nation (Hans Bekker, 3. Forts.) Aus der Geschichte der Juden in Erfurt (Karl Heilbrunn s.A., written 1951). Forts. u. Schluss in Nr. 3 u. 4. Ein Beschneidungsbuch des 19. Jahrhunderts aus der Mark Brandenburg. Quellentext zur jüd. Geschichte (Heinrich Simon, 1.u.2. Forts, in Nr. 3 u.4.) No. 3 incl.: Judentum im Mittelalter (Peter Kirchner). Tagung gegen Faschismus und Neonazismus (Peter Kirchner). Die Reichskristallnacht, ein Wort zum 40. Jahrestag

des 9. Nov. 1938 (Erich Cohn). Helmut Aris 70 Jahre. No. 4 incl.: Besinnen wir uns. Gedenkpredigt zum Jahrestag der Kristallnacht (Martin Riesenburger s.A.) Chronik eines Pogroms (Klaus Drobisch). Arnold Zweig, 10. Nov. 1887–26. Nov. 1968 (Renate Kirchner).]

15228. STEELE, JONATHAN: *Inside East Germany.* The State that came in from the Cold. New York: Urizen Books, 1978. 256 pp. [Incl. East Germany's attitude to the Jews.]

B. Restitution

15229. LEWIN, ISAAC: *On the Use of Heirless Jewish Property in Germany.* Essay. [In]: Unto the Mountains. [See No. 15309.]

C. Antisemitism, Judaism, Nazism in Education and Teaching.

— FREIMARK, PETER/WOLFGANG KOPITZSCH: *Der 9./10. Nov. 1938 in Deutschland.* Dokumentation zur Kristallnacht. [Incl. chaps.: Nationalsozialismus als Unterrichtsthema. Die 'Kristallnacht'-Möglichkeiten der Unterrichtsgestaltung. Anregungen für die Unterrichtsplanung. Bibls.: Unterrichtsmaterialien, Publikationen, Autovisuelle Medien, pp. 95–101. [See No. 15179.]

15230. GÖSSMANN, WILHELM, ed.: *Heine im Deutschunterricht.* Ein literaturdidakt. Konzept. Düsseldorf: Pädagogischer Verlag Schwann, 1978. 164 pp., illus., bibl. (pp. 158–164).

15231. GÖSSMANN, WILHELM/WINFRIED WOESLER, eds.: *Politische Dichtung im Unterricht.* 'Deutschland. Ein Wintermärchen' von Heinrich Heine. Text-Kommentare, Unterrichtshinweise, Materialien. Düsseldorf: Pädagogischer Verlag Schwann, 1974.

15232. HASUBEK, PETER: *Ausbürgerung – Einbürgerung?* Heinrich Heine als Schullektüre. Ein Beitrag zur Rezeptionsgeschichte. Pp. 305–332 [In]: Heinrich Heine. Artistik und Engagement (Wolfgang Kuttenkeuler). [See No. 15525.]

15233. HOFFMANN, GERD: *Sein Name ist ein Ärgernis . . .* Heinrich Heine im Deutschunterricht der BRD. [In]: Wissenschaftl. Zeitschrift der Martin-Luther-Universität Halle-Wittenberg, 1975. Pp. 75–84. (Gesellschafts- und sprachwissen. Reihe, Halle 24).

15234. *Judenverfolgung/'Reichskristallnacht'.* Unterrichtsmaterialien. H.3. 2000 Hamburg 13: GEW (Rothenbaumchaussee 15), 1978. 65 pp. [Didaktische Hinweise, Film- und Literaturlisten, eine Aufstellung von Kinder- u. Jugendbüchern zum Thema Faschismus].

15235. KEMPNER, ROBERT M. W.: *Holocaust-Unterricht in der Schule:* USA und Deutschland. [In]: 'Aufbau', July 14, New York, 1978.

15236. KREMERS, HEINZ: *Internationale Zusammenarbeit bei der Erforschung der Darstellung des Judentums im Schulunterricht.* [In]: 'Emuna-Israel Forum'. H.1, 1978. P. iv. [See No. 15759.]

15237. *Nationalsozialismus und Schule.* [Replies to relevant questions from several Ministers of Education], pp. 21–32. *Zur Darstellung der Schoah im deutschen Schulbuch der Gegenwart* (E. Horst Schallenberger, pp. 33–58, bibl. (pp. 56–57), tab.) [In]: 'Tribüne', H. 67, 1978. [See No. 15751.]

15238. *Die Reichskristallnacht – 9. Nov. 1938/9. Nov. 1978.* Eine Arbeitshilfe für Unterricht und Gemeindearbeit. Ed. Pfarrer René Leudesdorff für Evang. Arbeitskreis Kirche und Israel in Hessen und Nassau. Vors. Pfarrer Ulrich Schwemer. Mainz: Hans Krach, 1978. 81 pp., illus., facsims., illus., tabs., map, bibl. (pp. 79–81). [Incl. Die Reichskristallnacht (Hermann Graml). Vom Antisemitismus zur 'Endlösung' der Judenfrage (Rita Thalmann). Die Judenverfolgung im Dritten Reich (Hans-Georg Vorndran). Protokoll der Wannseekonferenz am 20.1.1942 (Auszug). Besuch von Bundeskanzler Schmidt in Auschwitz 1977 (Pressebericht). Gesetze, Verordnungen und Massnahmen gegen jüd. Bürger 1933–1945 (chronol. Aufstellung). Fragen, Suche nach Spuren. Zur Erschliessung des in diesem Heft vorgelegten Materials (Martin Stöhr). Stimmen aus der Geschichte (1) . . . für die Juden, (2) . . . gegen die Juden. Das Gedächtnis nicht verlieren (Martin Stöhr). Gottesdienst zum Gedächtnis des 9.11.1938 (Dieter Trautwein).]

15239. RIEMENSCHNEIDER, RAINER: *Die Judenverfolgung im Dritten Reich*. Eine Dokumentation aus westdeutschen Geschichtsbüchern unseres Jahrzehnts. Braunschweig: Georg-Eckert-Institut für Internationale Schulbuchforschung, 1977.
15240. SCHALLENBERGER, E. HORST/GERD STEIN: *Juden, Judentum und Staat Israel in deutschen Schulbüchern*. [In]: 'Lebendiges Zeugnis'. Themenheft: Judentum und Christentum. 32. Jg., H. 1/2, Febr. Paderborn, 1977. Pp. 44–51.
15241. *Teaching about the Holocaust*. [In]: Social Education, Official Journal of the National Council for the Social Studies. Vol. 42, No. 4, April. Washington D.C., 1978. Pp. 253–325, illus., bibl. [Incl. Why teach about the Holocaust? (Theodor Freedman). The Holocaust 1933–1945. A Chronology. Then and Now: The Experiences of a Teacher (Elie Wiesel). Confronting the Moral Implications of the Holocaust (Raul Hilberg). Sources and Resources for Teaching about the Holocaust. Prepared by the Anti-Defamation League of B'nai B'rith. The Holocaust: A Study in Inhumanity.]
15242. *The Teaching of Holocaust History*. I. Inadequacies in Textbooks (Glen S. Pate). II. The Wider Setting (Robert R. Spillane and Dorothy Levenson). III. Why the Subject is Shunned (Lawrence Fuchs). IV. The Message through Imaginative Literature (Alfred Hoelzel). V. A Project Unit (Margot Stern Strom and William S. Parsons [In]: 'Patterns of Prejudice'. Vol. 12, No. 5. London, 1978. Pp. 1–16. [Some of the views expressed at a National Conference on Teaching in Secondary Schools about Genocide and the Nazi Holocaust]. [See No. 15787.]
15243. *Teaching the Holocaust to Children*. A Guide for Teachers in: The Second Jewish Catalogue. Philadelphia: The Jewish Publication Society of America, 1978. [Incl. European Jewry before the Holocaust. How Hitler Came to Power. Final Solution Carried out. What is Resistance? Who Helped? How? Why? When?]
15244. UHDE, BERNHARD/FELIX BÖHL, eds.: *Judentum im Religionsunterricht Sekundarstufe II*. Einführung, Texte, Unterrichtsmodelle, Arbeitsmaterial. München: Don Bosco Verlag, 1978. 212 pp., bibl.

V. JUDAISM

A. Jewish Learning and Scholars

15245. ARONSFELD, C. C.: *The Return of the Jews to Spain*. German Rabbi's Pioneering Work. [In]: 'AJR Information', August, London, 1978. [Dr. Ludwig Philippson (1811 Dessau-1889 Bonn) one time rabbi of Magdeburg and editor of the 'Allgemeine Zeitung des Judenthums' which he founded in 1837, exerted himself to bring about a Jewish–Spanish 'reconciliation'.]
15246. BAECK, LEO. BAKER, LEONARD: *Days of Sorrow and Pain... Leo Baeck and the Berlin Jews*. New York/London: Macmillan/Collier MacMillan Publ., 1978. xiii, 396 pp., ports., illus., facsims., notes pp. 351–378, bibl. (pp. 339–350).
15247. BAMBERGER, RAW SELIGMANN BAER ('Würzburger Raw'). STERN, WILLIAM: *Der Würzburger Raw s.A.*: Zum 100. Jahrzeitstag. Pp. 183–194 [and]: *Einige Noten über die vielverzweigte Tätigkeit des Würzburger Raws* (S. B. Bamberger) [In]: 'Udim', Bd. VII-VIII, 1977/78. [See No. 15323.] [The 'Würzburger Raw' (1807–1878) founded, in 1864, the Isr. Lehrerbildungsanstalt and was its director until his death.]
15248. BLOCH, ELIESER F. GRÜNEWALD, RABBINER H. I.: *Letzter Vertreter einer rabbinischen Schule in Deutschland*. Landesrabbiner Dr. Elieser F. Bloch zu seinem 75. Geburtstag. [In]: 'Allgemeine', 17. März, Düsseldorf, 1978. Pp. 5–6.
15249. BREUER, MORDECHAI: *Emancipation and the Rabbis*. [In]: Niv Hamidrashia. Publ. by Friends of the Midrashia in Israel. Vol. 13–14. Tel Aviv, 5738/9–1978/9.
—— BUBER, MARTIN Febr. 8, 1878 Vienna – June 13, 1965 Jerusalem. A Selection only from the many Buber Centenary Publications are listed here.
15250. BUBER, MARTIN: *Des Baal-Schem-Tow Unterweisung im Umgang mit Gott*. 4., durchges. Aufl. Heidelberg: Lambert Schneider, 1977. 117 pp.
15251. BUBER, MARTIN: *Begegnung*. Autobiographische Fragmente. Mit e. Nachwort von Albrecht Goes. Neuausgabe. 3., verb. Aufl. Heidelberg: Schneider, 1978. 114 pp.

15252. BUBER, MARTIN: *Between Man and Man*. With an Afterword by the author 'The History of the Dialogical Principle'. Introd. by Maurice Friedman. Transl. by Ronald Gregor Smith. Afterword transl. by Maurice Friedman. New York: Macmillan, 1975. xxx, 229 pp. [First publ. 1965.]

15253. BUBER, MARTIN: *The Legend of the Baal-Shem*. Transl. from the German by Maurice Friedman. New York: Schocken, 1977. 223 pp. [Previously publ. 1969. See No. 8620/YB. XVI. First publ. in German 1908.]

15254. BUBER, MARTIN: *Reden über Erziehung*. 10. verb. Aufl. Heidelberg: Lambert Schneider, 1978. 76 pp. [Cont. Über das Erzieherische. Bildung und Weltanschauung. Über Charaktererziehung. 1964 ed. No. 4489/YB. X.]

15255. *Die Schrift*. Verdeutscht von Martin Buber gemeinsam mit Franz Rosenzweig. Heidelberg: Lambert Schneider, [1978]. 4 vols. Bd.1: *Die fünf Bücher der Weisung* [See No. 14385/YB. XXIII]. Bd. 2: *Bücher der Geschichte*. 7., abermals durchges. u. verb. Aufl. d. Ausg. von 1955. 1978. 519 pp. Bd. 3: *Bücher der Kündung*. 7., abermals durchges. u. verb. Aufl. d. Ausg. von 1957. 1978. 780 pp. Bd. 4: *Die Schriftwerke. Das Buch der Preisungen*. [See No. 14386/YB. XXIII.]

15256. BUBER, MARTIN: *Urdistanz und Beziehung*. 4., verb. Aufl. Erw. um einen editorischen Anhang mit ergänzenden Texten von Lothar Stiehm. Heidelberg: Schneider, 1978. 57 pp. (Beiträge zu einer philosophischen Anthropologie, 1).

15257. BUBER, MARTIN: *Zwiesprache*. Traktat vom dialogischen Leben. Mit e. Anhang: Zur Editionsgeschichte von 'Zwiesprache' von Lothar Stiehm. Neuausgabe (3. Aufl.) Heidelberg: Schneider, 1978. 86 pp., Anhang pp. 79–86.

15258. BUBER, MARTIN: *Zwischen Zeit und Ewigkeit. Gog und Magog*. Eine Chronik. 3., durchges. Aufl. Mit e. editor. Anhang. Heidelberg: Schneider, 1978. 423 pp. Nachw. pp. 401–408, ed. Anhang (Lothar Stiehm, pp. 413–419), notes pp. 420–424. [First German ed. 1949, Hebrew ed. 1941]. [Cf. Gog und Magog. Buber's only novel (Schalom Ben-Chorin) in: 'MB', 20. Okt., Tel Aviv, 1978.]

15259. BEN-CHORIN, SCHALOM: *Martin Buber heute*. Zum 100. Geburtstag am 8. Februar 1978. [In]: 'Isr. Wochenblatt', 3, Febr. Zürich, 1978. Pp. 61–63, port.

15260. BENDKOWER, SIGMUND: *Der verdrängte Buber*. [In]: 'Das Neue Israel', 30. Jg., H.9 (März), Zürich, 1978. Pp. 490–493. [On Buber's political teachings and activities.]

15261. BERRY, DONALD L.: *Buber's View of Jesus as Brother*. [In]: 'Journal of Ecumenical Studies', Philadelphia Pa., 14, 1977. Pp. 203–218.

15262. BLOCH, JOCHANAN: *Die Aporie des Du*. Probleme der Dialogik Martin Bubers. Heidelberg: Schneider, 1977. 347 pp., list of names, Begriffsregister comp. by Gerhard Mahr, pp. 320–347. (Phronesis. Eine Schriftenreihe, Bd. 2). (Gedruckt mit Unterstützung der Dt. Forschungsgemeinschaft Bonn-Bad Godesberg und des LBI Jerusalem). [Jochanan Bloch, Prof. at the Ben-Gurion-University in Beersheba, born March 17, 1919 in Berlin, was fatally injured in a motor car accident, on Febr. 26, 1979. Ob. (Ralph Schweiger) in: 'Allgemeine', März 16, Düsseldorf, 1979.]

15263. BLUMENTHAL-WEISS, ILSE: *Begegnung mit Martin Buber*. [In]: 'Allgemeine', 3. März, Düsseldorf, 1978. Pp. 20–21.

15264. BORRIES, ACHIM VON: *Martin Buber – 'Defaitist' für den Frieden*. Der unvollständige Ruhm. [In]: 'Merkur', 32. Jg., H. 8(363), Aug. Stuttgart: Klett-Cotta, 1978. Pp. 807–819.

15265. COHEN, B. H.: *Le Centenaire de la Naissance de Martin Buber (1878–1978)*. [And]: *Martin Buber, der Künder des Chassidismus zu seinem 100. Geburtstag* (Meir Faerber). [In]: 'Das Neue Israel', 30. Jg., H.8 (Febr.), Zürich, 1978. Pp. 445–449, port.

15266. *Coming to Terms with Buber*. An assessment by Rabbi Dow Marmur on the centenary of the philosopher's birth. [In]: 'Jewish Chronicle', Febr. 10, London, 1978, port.

15267. ECKERT, WILLEHAD PAUL: *Martin Buber – Gesprächspartner für Christen?* [In]: 'Emuna-Israel Forum'. H.4, 1978. Pp. 18–28, bibl. notes. [See No. 15759.]

15268. FAERBER, MEIR: *Martin Buber*. Zu seinem 100. Geburtstag. [And]: Ein Brief Martin Bubers an Fritz Naschitz in Tel Aviv. Dank für den Glückwunsch zu seinem 85. Geburtstag. [In]: 'Aufbau', Jan. 27, New York, 1978. Pp. 15 & 17.

15269. *Festakt* zum 100. Geburtstag von Martin Buber. Veranstaltet von der hessischen Landesregierung und der Karl-Hermann-Flach-Stiftung in der Frankfurter Paulskirche. Ansprachen von Walter Wallmann, Hölger Börner, Laudatio von Minister Karry für Walter Hesselbach, Martin-Buber-Preis Empfänger der Karl-Hermann-

Flach-Stiftung, Shmaryahu Talmon und die Danksworte des Vorsitzenden der Bank für Gemeinwirtschaft, Walter Hesselbach. Ein Bericht in: 'deutschland-berichte', 14. Jg., Nr.3, März. Bonn, 1978. Pp. 22–29. [See No. 15752.]

15270. GOES, ALBRECHT: *Erinnerungen an Martin Buber*. [In]: Tagwerk. 2. Aufl., Frankfurt/M.: Fischer, 1978.

15271. GORDON, HAIM: *An Approach to Martin Buber's Educational Writings*. [In]: 'Journal of Jewish Studies'. Ed. Geza Vermes. Vol. XXIX, No. 1, Spring. Oxford: Centre for Postgraduate Hebrew Studies, 1978. Pp. 85–97.

15272. GRUENEWALD, MAX: *Jewish-Christian 'Dialogue' of 1933*. Reminiscences in the Buber Centenary Year. [In]: 'AJR Information', Vol. XXXIII, No. 10, Oct. London, 1978. Pp. 1–2.

15273. HORWITZ, RIVKA: *Buber's Way to 'I and Thou'*. An Historical Analysis and the First Publication of Martin Buber's Lectures 'Religion als Gegenwart'. Heidelberg: Schneider, 1978. 301 pp., facsims., bibl. (pp. 271–274). (Phronesis, Bd. 7). [Buber's Lehrhaus-Lectures of 1922.]

15274. KEMPSKI, JÜRGEN V.: *Die zwei Seiten des Zionismus*. Zu dem Briefwechsel von Martin Buber. [In]: 'Merkur', H.8 (363), Aug. Stuttgart: Klett-Cotta, 1978. Pp. 819–823. [Martin Buber, Briefwechsel aus sieben Jahrzehnten, see No. 12826/YB. XXI.]

15275. LAMM, HANS: *Bubers Standort im Geistesleben des 20. Jahrhunderts*. Zu seinem 100. Geburtstag am 8. Febr. 1978. [In]: 'Allgemeine', 3. Febr. Düsseldorf, 1978. [And]: *Der Zionist Martin Buber* (Stefan Schwarz), pp. 5–6, port., illus.

15276. LAMM, HANS: *Buber (teilweise) ernst genommen*. Zur internationalen Konferenz von Beerscheba. [And]: Vorschau auf die Woche der Brüderlichkeit, das Jahresthema 1978: Martin Buber – Zwiesprache heute (Wolfgang Zink) [In]: 'Allgemeine', 20. Jan., Düsseldorf, 1978.

15277. LINK-SALINGER (HYMAN), RUTH: *Friends in Utopia: Martin Buber and Gustav Landauer*. [In]: 'Midstream', XXIV, No. 1, Jan., New York: The Theodor Herzl Foundation, 1978. Pp. 67–72, bibl. footnotes.

15278. *Martin Buber, 1878–1978. Leben, Werk und Wirkung*. Eine Ausstellung. Veranstalter: Deutscher Koordinierungsrat der Gesellschaft für Christlich-Jüdische Zusammenarbeit. Katalog von Elisabeth Oggel und Mitarbeit von Hans Lamm und Pnina Navé Levinson. Worms, 1978. 139 pp., ports., illus., facsims., Literatur über M.B. pp. 129–133. [Cf. Judentum und deutsche Kultur. Buber Ausstellung in Worms (Arianna Giachi) in: 'FAZ', 27. Juli, Frankfurt/M., 1978. Eine beglückende Begegnung in Worms nahe des 'Heissen Sandes', dem ältesten europäischen Juden-Friedhof (Gerhard E. Habermann) in: 'Neue Jüdische Nachrichten', 28. Juli, München, 1978, ports.

15279. *Martin Buber, 1878–1978*. Exhibition, arranged by Margot Cohn and Moshe Catanne with the cooperation of the staff of the Dept. of Manuscripts and Archives of the Jewish National and University Library. Introductions: Akiva Ernst Simon. English version: Toni Shimoni and Mira Reich. Catalogue. Jewish National and University Library, Berman Hall, April, Jerusalem, 1978. 75 pp. + 61 pp. in Hebrew, cover port and facsim., ports., illus., facsims., bibl. (pp. 69–75). [Cf. Die Martin Buber-Ausstellung in Jerusalem (Erich Gottgetreu) in: 'MB', 26. Mai, Tel Aviv, 1978, pp. 4 & 7.]

15280. *Martin Buber on his Centennial. A Tribute and an Evaluation*. [In]: Judaism. Vol. 27, Issue No. 106, No. 2 (Spring). New York: The American Jewish Congress and World Jewish Congress, 1978. Pp. 131–132, 135–213. [Cont. Encounter: The Thought of Martin Buber (Eva Jospe, pp. 135–147). The Builder of Bridges (Ernst Simon, transl. by David Wolf Silverman, pp. 148–160). On Mordecai M. Kaplan's Critique of Buber (Meir Ben-Horin, pp. 161–174). The Mysticism of M.B.: An Essay on Methodology (William E. Kaufman, pp. 175–183). M.B. as an Interpreter of the Bible (Michael Fishbane, pp. 184–195). M.B. and the Drama of Otherness: The Dynamics of Love, Art and Faith (Edward K. Kaplan, pp. 196–206). Buber, the Man of Letters (Ruth Link-Salinger, pp. 207–213 (see also No. 15277).]

15281. MENDES-FLOHR, PAUL R.: *Buber und das nachtraditionelle Judentum*. Überlegungen aus Anlass seines 100. Geburtstages. Pp. 118–121). *Buber und die amerikanisch-jüdische Gegenkultur* (Yizhak, Ahren, pp. 122–130). *Buber ist tot – es lebe Buber*. Ausmass und Deutung seiner Renaissance (Hans Lamm, pp. 131–136) [In]: 'Tribüne', H.66, 1978. Pp. 118–136. [See No. 15751.]

15282. MENDES-FLOHR, PAUL R.: *Von der Mystik zum Dialog*. Martin Bubers geistige Entwick-

lung bis hin zu 'Ich und Du'. Mit einem Vorwort von Ernst Simon. Königstein i.Ts.: Jüdischer Verlag im Athenäum Verlag, 1978.
15283. MOSER, ROGER, OFMCAP.: *Gotteserfahrung bei Martin Buber*. Eine theologische Untersuchung. Heidelberg: Schneider, 1978. (Schriftenreihe Phronesis, Bd. 5).
15284. OSTEN-SACKEN, PETER VON DER, ed.: *Leben als Begegnung*. Ein Jahrhundert Martin Buber (1878–1978). Vorträge und Aufsätze. Vorwort des Herausgebers. Berlin: Selbstverlag Institut Kirche und Judentum, 1978. 160 pp., bibl. M.B. comp. by Christian Bartsch, pp. 155–160. (Veröffentlichungen aus dem Institut ... bei der Kirchlichen Hochschule Berlin, Bd.7). [Incl. M.B. (1878–1965). Ein Lebensabriss (Ursula Bohn). M. B., Helfer in sprachloser Zeit, Aspekte seines Werkes (Marianne Awerbuch). Angst und Vertrauen bei M.B. (Ernst Simon). M.B. als Bibel-Interpret (Shemaryahu Talmon). M.B. über Moses Hess. Anmerkungen zu einem Denkanstoss (Christian Bartsch). M.B.'s Bedeutung für die protestantische Theologie (Helmut Gollwitzer). M.B.'s Fragen zum ökumenischen Gespräch (Franz v. Hammerstein). M.B. als sozialistischer Zionist (Friedrich Wilhelm Marquardt). M.B.'s Mitarbeit am Freien Jüd. Lehrhaus in Frankfurt (Annemarie u. Reinhold Mayer). Begegnung im Widerspruch. Text und Deutung des Zwiegesprächs zwischen Karl Ludwig Schmidt und M.B. im Jüd. Lehrhaus in Stuttgart am 14. Januar 1933. (Text): Kirche, Staat, Volk, Judentum (Peter von der Osten-Sacken, pp. 116–144). M.B.'s Bibelübersetzung (Rolf Rendtorff).]
15285. RÜBNER, TUVIA, ed.: *Martin Buber und Ludwig Strauss*. Ein Lebenszeugnis in Briefen. Hrsg. u. eingel. von ... Heidelberg: Lambert Schneider, 1978. 240 pp., ports., facsims. [Ludwig Strauss (1892 Aachen – 1953 Jerusalem) 'returned' to Palestine in 1934 and then wrote his lyric and other works in Hebrew.]
15286. SCHATZKER, CHAIM: *Martin Buber's Influence on the Jewish Youth Movement in Germany*. [In]: LBI Year Book XXIII. London, 1978. Pp. 151–171. [See No. 15111.]
15287. SHESTOV, LEV: *Martin Buber*. [In]: 'Midstream'. Vol. XXIV, No. 9, Nov. New York: The Theodor Herzl Foundation, 1978. Pp. 41–48. [And]: *Meetings with Buber* (Avraham Shapira, pp. 48–54. [The essay by Shestov originally appeared in the Russian journal 'Put' (The Path), Paris, June 1933.]
15288. SIMON, ERNST: *Martin Bubers lebendiges Erbe*. Heidelberg: Lambert Schneider, 1978. 150 pp., port. [Cont. M.B. und das deutsche Judentum. Scholem und Buber. Martin Buber, der Erzieher. Martin Buberslebendiges Erbe.]
15289. THEUNISSEN, MICHAEL: *Der Weg der Sprache in das Sprechen*. Bemerkungen zur Philosophie Martin Bubers aus Anlass seines 100. Geburtstages. [In]: 'FAZ', 8. Febr., Frankfurt/M., 1978, port.
15290. TRAMER, HANS: *Zum 100. Geburtstag von Martin Buber*. Bubers Werk in dieser Zeit. *Erbe der Propheten und der Pharisäer* (Pinchas Rosenblüth). *Das Prinzip der Bibelübersetzung von Buber-Rosenzweig* (Rahel Freund). [And]: Das Buber-Jahr in der BRD. Vom Martin Buber-Symposium in Beer-Schewa [In]: 'MB', 3. Febr. Tel Aviv, 1978. Pp. 5–9, port.
15291. ZINK, WOLGANG, ed.: *Martin Buber 1878–1978*. Bonn: Hohwacht in Zusammenarbeit mit Inter Nationes, 1978. 127 pp., front. port., ports., illus., chron. comp. by Wolfgang Henrich pp. 104–121, bibl. M.B. u. bibl. pp. 122–123. [Also in an English ed., translations by Patricia Crampton.] [Incl. Mehr als ein Menschenleben – ein Vorwort (Wolfgang Zink). Deutsche, Juden, Christen – ein Gespräch mit M.B. (Rudolf Küstermeier). Gruss an M.B. (Theodor Heuss). M.B.'s Bedeutung für das jüdische Bewusstsein im 20. Jahrhundert (Robert Weltsch (1958). Lebendige Legende (Albrecht Goes). M.B. als Erzieher (Ernst Simon). Ich und Du – Die Welt M.B.'s (Paul Schallück). M.B.'s hebräischer Humanismus (Grete Schaeder). (1966). M.B. – ein jüdischer Denker und Humanist (N. Peter Levinson (1966). Zionismus – Ideal und Verwirklichung bei M.B. (Pinchas Erich Rosenblüth (1968). M.B. als Bibel-Interpret (Shemaryahu Talmon (1975). M.B. in Jerusalem (Schalom-Ben-Chorin (1978.)]
15292. COHEN, CARL: *The Impact of the Protestant Reformation on the Jews*. Introduction by George Huntston Williams. Heidelberg: Schneider, 1978. 350 pp. (Bibliotheca Judaica, Bd. 5).
15293. COHEN, HERMANN. HOLZHEY, HELMUT: *Das Hermann-Cohen-Archiv in Zürich*. [In]: Zeitschrift für philosophische Forschung. Bd.31, H.3. Meisenheim am Glan: Hain, 1977. Pp. 443–452. [Author is director of the H.-C.-Archiv.]

15294. OLLIG, HANS-LUDWIG: *Aporetische Freiheitsphilosophie.* Zu Hermann Cohens philosophischem Ansatz. [In]: Philosophisches Jahrbuch. Im Auftrag der Görres-Gesellschaft hrsg. von Hermann Krings u.a. 85. Jg., 2. Halbband. Freiburg/München: Hans Alber, 1978. Pp. 359–371, bibl. notes. [Hermann Cohen, 1842 Coswig (Anhalt–1918 Berlin.]
15295. EMDEN, JACOB, RABBI. GREENBERG, BEN: *Rabbi Jacob Emden: The Views of an Enlightened Traditionalist on Christianity.* [In]: 'Judaism', Vol. 27, Issue No. 107, No. 3, Summer. New York: The American Jewish Congress and World Jewish Congress, 1978. Pp. 351–362. [J. E., 1697–1776.]
15296. GEIS, ROBERT RAPHAEL: *Vom unbekannten Judentum.* 2. Aufl. Freiburg i.Br.: Herder, 1977. 235 pp. [The anthology was first publ. in 1961, reprinted in 1975. See No. 12850/YB. XXI. – R. R. Geis, 1906–1972.]
15297. GUTMANN, JOSEPH. *Joseph Gutmann, Von Westfalen nach Berlin.* Lebensweg und Werk eines jüdischen Pädagogen. Redigiert und bearbeitet von Hans Chanoch Meyer. Haifa: Im Selbstverlag, 1976. 127 pp., front. port., illus., bibl. (Documenta Judaica, Bd. 5).
15298. HIRSCH, SAMSON RAPHAEL. GRÜNEWALD, PINCHAS PAUL: *Eine jüdische Offenbarungslehre.* Samson Raphael Hirsch. Bern, Frankfurt/M.: Lang, 1978. 261 pp., notes, bibl. (Reihe 'Judaica et Christiana, ed. by Simon Lauer and Clemens Thoma, Bd. 2).
15299. *Judaism Eternal.* Selected Essays from the Writings of Rabbi Samson Raphael Hirsch. Transl. from the German original and annotated, with an introduction and a short biography by I[sidor] Grunfeld. 4th ed., vol. 1–2. London: Soncino Press, 176. lxi, 270 pp.; xii, 315 pp., bibl. S.R.H. pp. xlix–lxi. [2 vols.] [Samson Raphael Hirsch, rabbi, 1808 Hamburg – 1888 Frankfurt/M.]
15300. JOËL, DAVID HEIMANN: *Die Religionsphilosophie des Sohar und ihr Verhältnis zur allgemeinen jüdischen Theologie.* Nachdr. d. Ausg. Leipzig 1849. Hildesheim: Olms Reprints, 1977. xvi, 394 pp., port. [David Hei[y]mann Joël (1815–1882, Provinz Posen), rabbi and scholar.]
15301. JOËL MANUEL: *Beiträge zur Geschichte der Philosophie.* Reprograph. Druck d. Ausg. Breslau 1876. Hildesheim: Gerstenberg, 1978. 638 pp. [2 vols. in 1]. [M.J., 1826 Birnbaum-1890 Breslau, rabbi, scholar.]
15302. KAUFMAN, WILLIAM E., ed.: *Contemporary Jewish Philosophies.* New York: Reconstructionist Press, 1976. xii, 276 pp., bibl. (p. 272). [Incl.: Toward an Existential Jewish Theology (Franz Rosenzweig). Can God be encountered? (Martin Buber). The Encounter with Nothingness (L. Rubenstein). From Covenant Theology to Commanding Voice (Eugene B. Borowitz and Emil L. Fackenheim). The Far yet Near God (Leo Baeck). The Meaning Beyond Mystery (A. J. Heschel).]
15303. KRESSEL, G.: *The Heritage of German Jewry.* [In]: Gesher, Quarterly Review of Jewish Affairs. Publ. by the Israel Executive of the World Jewish Congress. No. 3/4, Oct. Tel Aviv/Jerusalem, 1977. Pp. 191–195. [In Hebrew]. Reprinted in 'Hadoar', publ. by the Hebrew Organisation of America, vol. 57, No. 1. [A tribute to the work and achievements of the Leo Baeck Institute in the first twenty years of its existence.]
15304. MENDELSSOHN, MOSES. BOUREL, DOMINIQUE: *Les Exigences du Libéralisme de Mendelssohn.* [In]: 'Recherches de Science Religieuse'. No. 4, Paris, 1978. Pp. 517–532.
15305. BOUREL, DOMINIQUE: *Moses Mendelssohn et l'Aufklärung.* [In]: 'Dix-Huitième Siècle'. No. X, Paris, 1978. Pp. 13–26.
15306. BOUREL, DOMINIQUE: *La Purification du Spinozisme chez Mendelssohn.* [In]: 'Archivio di Filosofia'. Roma, 1978. Pp. 133–145.
15307. BOUREL, DOMINIQUE: *Les Réserves du Mendelssohn, Rousseau, Voltaire et le Juif de Berlin.* [In]: 'Revue Internationale de Philosophie'. No. 2–3. Bruxelles, 1978. Pp. 309–326.
15308. POPKIN, RICHARD H.: *Moses Mendelssohn and Francisco De Miranda.* [In]: 'Jewish Social Studies'. Vol. XL, No. 1, Winter. New York: Conference on Jewish Social Studies, 1978. Pp. 41–48, notes pp. 47–48. [Colonel De Miranda, a Venezuelan, was the leading revolutionary thinker in Latin America. In 1785 he called on Mendelssohn, an event of historical interest at that time.]
15309. ROSENHEIM, JACOB. LEWIN, ISAAC: *Jacob Rosenheim. Man of Spirit and Action.* [In]: Unto the Mountains. Essays. New York: Hebrew Publ. Co., 1975. 127 pp., ports., illus. [J. R., orthodox rabbi, 1870 Frankfurt/M. – 1965 Jerusalem. From 1905 until 1935 he was editor of the 'Israelit'.] [See also No. 15229.]

15310. ROSENZWEIG, ADELE. HORWITZ, RIVKA: *Adele Rosenzweigs Jugenderinnerungen.* [In]: LBI Bulletin. No. 53/54. Tel Aviv, 1977/78. Pp. 133–146. [See No. 15110.] [A. R. née Alsberg, 1867–1933, mother of Franz Rosenzweig.]
15311. ROSENZWEIG, FRANZ. ROSENZWEIG, FRANZ: *Briefe und Tagebücher.* Hrsg. von Rachel Rosenzweig und Edith Scheinmann unter Mitwirkung von Bernhard Casper. Den Haag: Martinus Nijhoff, 1978. 2 Bände und 1 Registerband. (Franz Rosenzweig. Der Mensch und sein Werk. Ges. Schriften I. [Ges. Schriften II see No. 14429/YB. XXIII.]
15312. KOCHAN, LIONEL: *Franz Rosenzweig.* [In]: 'Jewish Chronicle Literary Supplement', June 9, London, 1978. [The progressive re-publication of Rosenzweig's works gives rise to a reconsideration of the outlook of one of the greatest of the 20th century Jewish thinkers.]
15313. OPPENHEIM, MICHAEL D.: *Death and Man's Fear of Death in Franz Rosenzweig's 'The Star of Redemption'.* [In]: 'Judaism', Vol. 27, Issue No. 108, No. 4 (Fall). Publ. by the American Jewish Congress and World Jewish Congress. New York, 1978. Pp. 458–467.
15314. VEIT, REINHARD: *Der didaktische Ansatz von Franz Rosenzweig.* Heidelberg: Lothar Stiehm, 1978. 160 pp. (Phronesis, Bd. 3).
15315. ROTENSTREICH, NATHAN: *Die Verschiedenheit der Religionen.* Judentum und Christentum in den Systemen Kants, Cohens und Rosenzweigs. [In]: Die Krise des Liberalismus zwischen den Weltkriegen (Rudolf von Thadden, ed.). [See No. 15015.]
15316. SCHOLEM, GERSHOM. *Bibliography of the Writings of Gershom G. Scholem,* comp. by Moshe Catane. Presented on the occasion of his 80th birthday by the Israel Academy of Sciences and Humanities and the Hebrew University of Jerusalem. Jerusalem: The Hebrew University, The Magnes Press, 1977. 86 pp., port. [Contains all his printed writings from his first work in 1915 up to his 80th birthday, in German, Hebrew, English and other languages. A rev. ed. of the bibliography which was incl. in 'Studies in Mysticism and Religion'. See No. 7087/YB. XIV.]
15317. SCHOLEM, GERSHOM: *Fidélité et Utopie.* Essais sue le Judaisme Contemporain. Transl. by Marguerite Delmotte and Bernard Dupuy. Préface, notes and bibl. by Bernard Dupuy. Paris: Calman-Lévy, 1978. 288 pp. (Collection 'Diaspora').
15318. SCHOLEM, GERSHOM: *Verschollene jüdische Mystiker: Ephraim Joseph Hirschfeld – Abenteurer und Theosoph.* Von Pinchas Rosenblüth aus dem Hebräischen übersetzter Extrakt der 2. Siegfried Moses Memorial Lecture, geh. am 15. Febr. in Jerusalem. [In]: 'MB', 24. Febr. Tel Aviv, 1978.
15319. PACHTER, HENRY: *Masters of Cultural History.* Gershom Scholem – The Myth of the Mythmaker. [In]: 'Salmagundi'. A Quarterly of the Humanities and Social Sciences. Publ. by Skidmore College. No. 40, Winter. Saratoga Springs, N.Y.: Skidmore College, 1978. Pp. 9–39.
15320. *Studies in Maimonides and St. Thomas Aquinas.* Selected with an Introduction and Bibliography by Jacob I. Dienstag. New York: Ktav, 1975. lix, 350 pp., bibl. (pp. 334–345). (Bibliotheca Maimonidica, vol. I). [Texts in English, German or French]. [Incl.: Judaism and Jewry in the Social Doctrine of Thomas Aquinas (Hans Liebeschütz). Etwas über den Einfluss der jüdischen Philosophie auf die christliche Scholastik (Manuel Joel). Thomas von Aquin (Jacob Guttmann). Eine Polemik des Thomas von Aquin gegen Maimonides (Hans Liebeschütz). [Thomas Aquinas, Saint, 1225?–1274. Moses ben Maimon, Maimonides, 1135–1204. Hans Liebeschütz 1893–1978. Manuel Joel, 1826–1890. Jacob Guttmann 1845–1919.]
15321. T[RAMER], H[ANS]: *Eduard Strauss und seine Freundschaft mit Franz Rosenzweig und Martin Buber.* [In]: LBI Bulletin. Nr. 53/54. Tel Aviv, 1977/78. Pp. 147–158. [Eduard Strauss (ß), biochemist and Scholar, 1876 Frankfurt/M. – 1952 New York.]
15322. TREPP, LEO: *Das Judentum, Geschichte und lebendige Gegenwart.* Aus d. Amerik. übers. von Karl-Heinz Laier. 2., vom Autor durchges. u. erg. Aufl. Reinbek: Rowohlt, 1976. 254 pp., bibl. (pp. 243–246). (Rowohlts Deutsche Enzyklopädie, 325). [See No. 7838/YB. XV for 1969 edition. Author was prior to his emigration to USA, the last Rabbi of the Oldenburg district.]
15323. '*Udim*', Zeitschrift der Rabbinerkonferenz in der Bundesrepublik Deutschland. Bd. VII–VIII. Frankfurt/M., 1977/78. [Incl. Distrikts-Rabbiner S. B. Bamberger (Naftalie Bar-Giora Bamberger). Juden im Odenwald 1469 der 'Hostienschändung' verdächtigt (Ernst Roth). Von den Bräuchen der Aschkenasischen Juden (Miminhagei jehudei

aschkenas) (Viktor Awigdor Unna), Chanan Lehrmann, wie wir ihn kannten (Graziella Sara Lehrmann).] [Ch. Lehrmann, from 1960–1971 Rabbi in West Berlin, died Sept. 1977 in Luxemburg.] [See also Nos. 15056, 15082, 15247, 15341.]

15324. WISE, ISAAC MAYER. RUBINSTEIN, ARYEH: *Isaac Mayer Wise*, A new appraisal. [In]: Jewish Social Studies. Vol. XXXIX, Nos. 1–2, Winter-Spring. New York: Conference on Jewish Social Studies, 1977. Pp. 53–74. [The prominent reform Rabbi (1819 Steingrub/Böhmen – 1900 Cincinnati) arrived in the USA from Bohemia in 1846.]

15325. ZINBERG, ISRAEL: *A History of Jewish Literature*. Vol. 10: The Science of Judaism and Galician Haskalah. Transl. from the Yiddish and ed. by Bernard Martin. Cincinnati: Hebrew Union College Press, New York: Ktav, 1977. xxi, 249 pp., illus. [For vols. 1–9 see No. 14448/YB. XXIII.]

B. The Jewish Problem

15326. FLEISCHHAUER, INGE/HILLEL KLEIN: *Über die jüdische Identität*. Eine psycho-historische Studie. Königstein/Ts.: Jüdischer Verlag, 1978. 167 pp.

15327. MENDES-FLOHR, PAUL R.: *The Throes of Assimilation: Self-Hatred and the Jewish Revolutionary*. [In]: 'European Judaism'. Vol. 12, No. 1, Spring. London: European Judaism, 1978. Pp. 34–39, bibl. footnotes.

15328. SCHULTZ, HANS JÜRGEN, ed.: *Mein Judentum*. Stuttgart: Kreuz Verlag, 1978. 286 pp., 20 ports. (Das Buch liegt einer Sendereihe d. Südd. Rundfunks zugrunde). [The twenty contributors who state what it has meant to them to be Jews are: Jureck Becker, Yehuda Amichai, Jeanne Hersch, Alfred Grosser, Günther Anders (i.e. Stern), Jean Améry, Ernst Simon, Hilde Domin, Samuel Bak, Michael Landmann, Lily Pincus, Alfons Rosenberg, Manès Sperber, Schalom Ben-Chorin, Max Fürst, Isca Salzberger-Wittenberg, György Ligeti, Hans Mayer, Wolfgang Hildesheimer, Robert Jungk.] [Reviewed by Eva Michaelis-Stern in: 'Das Neue Israel', H.8. Febr. Zürich, 1979. Pp. 437–439. Reiner Bernstein in: Tribüne, H.69, Frankfurt/M., 1979. Horst Krüger: Was es heisst, ein Jude zu sein. Selbstprüfungen mit unterschiedlichem Ergebnis [In]: 'Die Zeit', 9. Febr., Hamburg, 1979, illus.]

C. Jewish Life and Organisations

15329. BAR KOCHBA BERLIN UND MAKKABI. *80 Jahre Bar Kochba Berlin und Makkabi 1898–1978*. [In]: Bar Kochba-Hakoah Nachrichten. Verantwortlich für den Inhalt: Fritz A. Lewinson. Dez. Tel Aviv, 1978. 17 pp. [in German], 5 pp. [in Hebrew], ports., illus. [Incl. contributions by Hans Friedenthal: Idee und Verwirklichung. Fritz A. Lewinson: Bar Kochba in der Bewährung (1933–1938). Ernst Jokl: Zum 80 jährigen Jubiläum des Bar Kochba. Erinnerungen. Robert Atlasz: Vom Turnverein zur Kampfmannschaft. Erinnerungen an die Frühzeit des B. K. (Ernst Nehab, port.) Deutsche Makkabim in Israel (Fritz Lewinson).]

15330. JOKL, ERNST: *Zum 80jährigen Jubiläum des Bar Kochba – Erinnerungen*. [In]: 'Mitteilungen des Verb. ehemaliger Breslauer und Schlesier in Israel. Nr. 44, 1978. port. [of Prof. Ernst Jokl]. [See No. 15060].

15331. BRAUDE, JACOB. CARLEBACH, ALEXANDER: *Dr. Jacob Braude*. [In]: Niv Hamidrashia, a journal devoted to halachah, Jewish thought, education and literature. Publ. by Friends of the Midrashia in Israel. Ed. Israel Sadan, Engl. ed.: Alexander Carlebach. Vol. 13/14, Tel Aviv, 1978/79. Pp. 12–25. [Dr. Jacob Braude, born 1902 in Fürth, obtained his doctorate in law at Leipzig University. He came to England in 1938 and built up a highly successful export business. Amongst many important Jewish offices he held, he was chairman of the world presidium of the Friends of Midrashia. He died Jan. 1978 in Hendon. Ob. in AJR Information, February, London, 1978.]

15332. GLÜCKEL OF HAMELN. *The Memoirs of Glückel of Hameln*. Transl. by Marvin

Lowenthal. With a new introduction by Robert S. Rosen. New York: Schocken, 1977. 205 pp. [Paperbound ed.] [The Memoirs were written 1690 in Yiddish. First transl. into German by Bertha Pappenheim in 1910. First English transl. by Marvin Lowenthal in 1932. Glückel of Hameln 1645 Hamburg-1724 Metz.]

15333. HILFSVEREIN DER DEUTSCHEN JUDEN. PRINZ, ARTHUR: *Was der 'Hilfsverein' geleistet hat.* November 1938 – Wendepunkt der jüdischen Auswanderung aus Mitteleuropa. [In]: 'MB', Nr. 41, 17. Nov. Tel Aviv, 1978. Pp. 3–4. (Zur Wiederkehr des 40. Jahrestages der November Pogrome in Deutschland).

15334. HINRICHSEN, KLAUS ERNST: *Die Anfänge der Ebräer-Schule in Riga seit 1835.* [In]: LBI Bulletin. Nr. 53/54. Tel Aviv, 1977/78. Pp. 159–181. [See No. 15110] [Dr. Ludwig Philippson (1811 Dessau – 1889 Bonn), Rabbi in Magdeburg, supported the aspirations and interests of the Riga Jews in the 'Allgemeine Zeitung des Judenthums' which he had founded in 1837.]

—— JEWISH SPORT. BERNETT, HAJO: *Der jüdische Sport im nationalsozialistischen Deutschland 1933–1938.* [See No. 15137]

—— JEWISH YOUTH MOVEMENT. SCHATZKER, CHAIM: *Martin Buber's Influence on the Jewish Youth Movement in Germany.* [See No. 15286.]

15335. JÜDISCH–LITERARISCHE GESELLSCHAFT. *Jahrbuch der Jüdisch-Literarischen Gesellschaft* (Sitz Frankfurt a.M.) Unv. Nachdr. d. Original-Ausg. Bd. 10–22. Frankfurt/M. J. Kauffmann. Amsterdam: John Benjamins, 1975. Bd. 10:1912, 1913; Bd. 11: 1916 [incl. Inhaltsverzeichnis d. Bde. 1–10]. Bd. 12: 1918; Bd. 13: 1920; Bd. 14: 1921. Bd. 15: 1923; Bd. 16: 1924; Bd. 17: 1926; Bd. 18: 1927: Bd. 19: 1928; Bd. 20: 1929 [enth. Inhalts- und Autoren-Verzeichnis zu den Bden 1–20]; Bd. 21: 1930; Bd. 22: 1931/32.]

—— KAGANOFF, BENZION C., comp.: *A Dictionary of Jewish Names and their History.* [See No. 15114.]

15336. LEVIN, NORA: *Jewish Socialist Movements (1871–1917).* While Messiah Tarried. New York: Schocken Books, London: Routledge & Kegan Paul, 1978. xi, 554 pp., ports., illus., maps, bibl. notes. (The Littman Library of Jewish Civilization). [IV. Socialist Zionism. Ruppin and the first Kvutzot].

—— MEIDNER, LUDWIG. TRAMER, HANS: *Das Judenproblem im Leben und Werk Ludwig Meidners.* [See No. 15621.]

—— OLDENBURG. SCHIECKEL, HARALD: *Gesuche um Änderungen jüdischer Familiennamen zur Verhinderung antisemitischer Geschäftsschädigung. Beispiele aus dem Lande Oldenburg.* [See No. 15793.]

—— OPPENHEIM, MORITZ DANIEL. COHEN, ELISHEVA: *Moritz Daniel Oppenheim.* [See No. 15645.]

15337. *Families and Feasts.* Paintings by Moritz Daniel Oppenheim and Isidor Kaufmann. Exhibition. Apr. 24–June 19, 1977. (Catalogue). Text by Alfred Werner. New York: Yeshiva University Museum, 1977. 15 pp., illus. [See also No. 15645 and No. 14461/YB. XXIII.]

15338. (*Der*) REICHSBUND JÜDISCHER FRONTSOLDATEN. DUNKER, ULRICH: *Der Reichsbund jüdischer Frontsoldaten, 1919–1938.* Geschichte eines jüd. Abwehrvereins. Düsseldorf: Droste, 1977. 354 pp., illus., facsims., notes pp. 219–339, bibl. (pp. 340–354). Zugl. Geschichtswiss. Diss., F. U. Berlin, 1976 u.d.T. Nationalismus contra Antisemitismus. [Cf. Weighed and Found Wanting. A Study of the 'Frontbund' (Eva G. Reichmann) [In]: 'AJR Information', Nov. London, 1978. Evaluation of the 'Frontbund' (Paul Yogi Mayer) [In]: 'AJR Information', Jan., London, 1979. [Also]: Versagen vor der Geschichte. Das war der 'Reichsbund jüdischer Frontsoldaten' (R. J. F.) (Eva G. Reichmann) [In]: 'Isr. Wochenblatt', 23. Juni, Zürich, 1978. Pp. 13–16, illus., [and in]: 'MB', 21. April, Tel Aviv, 1978. [Also]: Jews for the Fatherland (Arnold Paucker) [In]: 'TLS', July 28, London, 1978.]

15339. ROSENSTOCK, WERNER. *Werner Rosenstock 70 on 10th of April 1978.* Birthday tributes in: 'AJR Information', Vol. XXXIII, No. 4 (April), London, 1978. Pp. 8–12:

15340. (*The*) SCHWARZES FÄHNLEIN. RHEINS, CARL J.: *The Schwarzes Fähnlein, Jungenschaft 1932–1934.* [In]: LBI Year Book XXIII. London, 1978. Pp. 173–197, illus. [See No. 15111.]

15341. STERN, WILLIAM: *Jüdische Familiennamen.* Weitere Untersuchungen. [In]: 'Udim',

Zeitschrift der Rabbinerkonferenz in der Bundesrepublik Deutschland. Bd. VI. Frankfurt/M. 5736/37–1975/76. Pp. 107–124. [English version see No. 14465/YB. XXIII.]

D. Jewish Art and Music

15342. GRADENWITZ, PETER: *Die Musikgeschichte Israels*. Von den biblischen Anfängen bis zum modernen Staat. Kassel: Bärenreiter, 1978. 240 pp., ports., illus.
15343. *Judaica*. Kult und Kultur des europäischen Judentums. Die Sammlung [Max] Berger. Katalog. Text: Wolfgang Häusler. Bilder: Erich Lessing. Wien: Jugend und Volk, 1978. 299 pp., 200 illus., bibl. (pp. 297–299). English, French, Spanish and Hebrew summaries, [Cf. Max Berger – Judaicasammler aus Leidenschaft (Fritz L. Brassloff) [In]: 'Das Neue Israel', 31. Jg., H.7 (Januar), Zürich, 1979. Pp. 369–370.] [Born in Galicia, Max Berger lives in Vienna].
—— MEIDNER, LUDWIG. TRAMER, HANS: *Das Judenproblem im Leben und Werk Ludwig Meidners*. [See No. 15621.]
—— OPPENHEIM, MORITZ DANIEL. COHEN, ELISHEVA: *Moritz Daniel Oppenheim*. [See No. 15645.]
15344. *Tora-Wimpel*. Zeugnisse jüdischer Volkskunst aus dem Braunschweigischen Landesmuseum. Sonderausstellung vom 10.9.–26.11.1978. Braunschweig, 1978. (Katalog), 66 pp., illus. (Veröffentlichungen des Braunschweigischen Landesmuseums, 17).

VI. ZIONISM AND ISRAEL

15345. AGNON, SHMUEL YOSEPH: *To S.Z. Schocken after the 1929 Riots*. (A Letter). [In]: The Jerusalem Quarterly. Publ. by the Middle East Institute. No. 9, Fall. Jerusalem, 1978. [Schocken became Agnon's publisher].
15346. BEN-CHORIN, SCHALOM: *Fremdheit und Verfremdung*, [In]: 'Isr. Wochenblatt', 31. März, Zürich, 1978. Pp. 9–11. [Arnold Zweig, Else Lasker-Schüler, Joseph Kastein a.o.]
15347. BLUMENFELD, KURT. TRAMER, HANS: *Kurt Blumenfeld s.A., 1884–1963*. [In]: 'MB', 9. Juni, Tel Aviv, 1978. Pp. 4 & 6. [Some recently discovered letters addressed by K. B. to Dr. Ludwig Pinner.]
15348. BODENHEIMER, HENRIETTE HANNAH, ed.: *Der Durchbruch des politischen Zionismus in Köln 1890–1900*. Eine Dokumentation. Briefe, Protokolle, Flugblätter, Reden. Köln: Bund-Verlag, 1978. 312 pp., front. port., facsims., list of names pp. 291–302.
15349. FISCH, HAROLD: *The Zionist Revolution*. A new perspective. London: Weidenfeld and Nicolson, 1978. vii, 197 pp., notes and bibl. (pp. 171–189). [A study of the spiritual roots of Zionism. Moses Hess, A. D. Gordon, Martin Buber.]
15350. GILBERT, MARTIN: *Exile and Return*. The Emergence of Jewish Statehood. London: Weidenfeld and Nicolson, 1978. xii, 364 pp., ports., illus., maps, bibl. (pp. 325–331). [Israel dispersed. An historical survey. Chap.: Holocaust, Resistance and Flight. Arthur Ruppin, Pioneer of the Kibbutz Movement. The Fate of Bertha Pappenheim under the Nazis. Gerson Bleichröder, Buber, Herzl, Baron Hirsch.]
15351. GOLDMANN, NAHUM. GOLDMANN, NAHUM: *Das jüdische Paradox*. Zionismus und Judentum nach Hitler. Aus d. Französ. übers. von Michel R. Lang. Köln: Europäische Verlagsanstalt, 1978. 288 pp. [Original: Le paradoxe Juif. See No. 13675/YB. XXII.]
15352. ALPERIN, AHARON: *Dr. Nachum Goldmann*. Tel Aviv: World Jewish Congress, 1978. 64 pp., front. port., ports. [In Hebrew]. Also: Transl. from Yiddish by Marcelo Sneh.. Buenos Aires: Congreso Judío Latinamericano, 1976. 48 pp., ports., illus. (Grandes Figuras del Judaismo, 100).
15353. GUGGENHEIM, WILLY: *30 mal Israel*. München: Piper, 1977. 419 pp., cover maps, chronology. [Stresses the achievements of the West European, especially the German-Jewish immigration. First publ. 1973. See No. 11344/YB. XIX.]

15354. HABE, HANS: *Wie einst David: Entscheidung in Israel.* Ein Erlebnisbericht. Genehmigte, ungek. Taschenbuchausg. München: Heyne, 1978. 287 pp. (Heyne Taschenbuch, 5453). [First publ. 1971. See No. 9555/YB. XVII.] [Hans Habe, orig. J. Bekessy, (1911 Budapest-1977 Locarno) visited Israel for the first time in 1970.]
15355. HERZL, THEODOR: '*Wenn ihr wollt, ist es kein Märchen*'. Altneuland/Der Judenstaat. Nach den Erstausgaben von 1902 und 1896 hrsg. und eingel. von Julius Schoeps. Kronberg/Ts.: Jüdischer Verlag, 1978. vi, 252 pp., illus.
15356. HESS, MOSES. FREI, BRUNO (orig. Benedikt Freistadt): *Die sieben Kehrtwendungen des Moses Hess.* Sonderdruck aus 'Israel-Nachrichten', Tel Aviv vom 17., 24. Febr., 3., 10. März 1978. Wien: [priv. pr.], 32 pp.
15357. KOLLEK, TEDDY: *For Jerusalem.* A Life by Teddy Kollek, with his son, Amos Kollek. London: Weidenfeld and Nicolson, 1978, x, 269 pp., front. maps, ports., illus. [German ed.]: *Ein Leben für Jerusalem.* Hamburg: Hoffmann und Campe, 1978.
15358. KRÄMER-PREIN, GABRIELE: *Der Buchhandel in Israel* (aus deutscher Sicht). Beispiel: Buchhandlung Mayer in Jerusalem. [In]. 'Börsenblatt für d. Dt. Buchhandel', 34: Jg., Nr. 69, 29. Aug., Frankfurt/M., 1978. illus. [Ludwig Mayer, born Febr. 1879 in Prenzlau, emigrated to Palestine in 1908. He died June 1978 in Jerusalem.]
15359. PETZOLD, GÜNTHER und LESLIE: *Shavei Zion.* Blüte in Israel aus schwäbischer Wurzel. Ein Bericht in Wort und Bild. Gerlingen: Bleicher, 1978. 96 pp., ports., illus.
15360. POPPEL, STEPHEN M[URRAY]: *Zionism in the Diaspora – The Case of Germany.* [In]: Proceedings of the Sixth World Congress of Jewish Studies. Vol. II. Jerusalem, 1975. [For 'Zionism in Germany 1897–1933' by same author see No. 14489/YB. XXIII.]
15361. RABIN, ESTHER: *Schattenbilder.* Jerusalem-Tel Aviv: Massada, 1975. 140 pp. [Corrected index entry No. 13311/YB. XXI]. [E. R., whose husband was Rabbi and lecturer at the 'Jüdisch-Theologisches Seminar in Breslau, died 1978 in Israel. Cf. Abschied von Esther Rabin (Anni Loewenstein) in: Mitteilungen des Verb. ehemaliger Breslauer und Schlesier in Israel, Nr. 44, 1978. See No. 15060.]
15362. REINHARZ, JEHUDA: *Three Generations of German Zionism.* (In memory of Dr. Karl Rothschild). [In]: 'The Jerusalem Quarterly', No. 9, Fall. Publ. by The Middle East Institute, Jerusalem, 1978. Pp. 95–110, front. illus.
15363. ROER, EMANUEL. ROTHSCHILD, ELI: *Ein Pionier ging von uns.* In memoriam Emanuel Roer (1891–1977). [In]: 'MB', 10. Febr., Tel Aviv, 1978. Pp. 4 & 7. [Emanuel Roer belonged to the group of 42 German Zionists who visited Palestine in 1913 in order to work for the establishment of the Jewish National Homeland after their return to Germany. Only 2 members of this group are still alive today: Nahum Goldmann and John Levy.]
15364. ROSEN, PINCHAS. ISTOR, H.: *Zum Tode von Dr. Pinchas Rosen* (1. Mai 1887 Berlin – 3. Mai 1978 Jerusalem). [In]: 'Allgemeine', 26. Mai, Düsseldorf, 1978. *Pinchas Rosen s.A.* (Hans Tramer) in: 'MB', 12. Mai, Tel Aviv, 1978. Ex-Justizminister Pinchas Rosen gestorben (Cläre Wohlmann-Meyer) in: 'IW', 9. Juni, Zürich, 1978. In memoriam. Zu den Schloschim (Kurt Kanowitz) in: 'MB', 2. Juni, Tel Aviv, 1978. [Orig. Felix Rosenblüth].
15365. ROSENBLÜTH, CESSI: *Von Berlin nach Ginegar.* Ein Lebensbericht. Hrsg. Kibbutz Hameuchad. Tel Aviv, 1978. 173 pp., cover port. [In Hebrew]. [Born 1898 in Berlin, C. R. emigrated 1924 to Palestine. Cf. Das Bild einer Epoche in den Augen eines menschlichen Menschen. Die Memoiren von C. R. (Ernst Simon) in: 'MB', Nr. 36/37, 29. Sept. Tel Aviv, 1978. Pp. 5–6.]
15366. ROTHSCHILDS. SCHAMA, SIMON: *Two Rothschilds and the Land of Israel.* New York: Knopf, London: Collins, 1978. 399 pp., ports. [The work, efforts and wealth devoted by Edmond de R. (1845–1934) and his son James (1878–1957) to the creation of Jewish settlements in Palestine and their relationship with Zionist leaders like Herzl and Weizmann.]
15367. SHARON, ARIEH: *Kibbuz + Bauhaus.* An Architect's Way in a New Land. Stuttgart: Krämer, 1978. 260 pp., ports., illus., maps, diagrs., index of buildings and projects., biogr. data. [Biographical descriptions of his work at the Bauhaus in Dessau, in international planning, in Zionism and in the Kibbuz-Movement.]
15368. SHATIL, JOSEF: *Die Geschichte von Hasorea während der ersten zehn Jahre.* Ein wichtiger Beitrag zur Geschichte der Einordnung der deutschen Juden in Israel. Publ. in Israel, 1978. [In Hebrew]. [Josef Shatil, formerly Ernst Stillmann, died a few days after his

68th birthday. Cf. Abschied von Josef Shatil (Werner Rosenstock) in: 'MB', 3. Febr., Tel Aviv and in: 'AJR Information', February, London, 1978.]
15369. VOGT, ERNST: *Zionismus und Sozialismus*. Zur Rolle der jüdischen Arbeiterbewegung bis zur Gründung des Staates Israel. Bonn: Bundeszentrale für politische Bildung, 1977. 31 pp., bibl. footnotes. [Incl. Wegbereiter des Arbeiterzionismus: Moses Hess, Nahman Syrkin, Ber Borochow.]
15370. WEIZMANN, CHAIM. *The Letters and Papers of Chaim Weizmann*. Gen. Ed.: Barnet Litvinoff, Series A. Vol. XII, Aug. 1923–March 1926. Ed. Joshua Freundlich, 1977. 493 pp., front. port., ports., illus. biogr. index. [Incl. Meyer W. Weisgal: A Tribute (Barnet Litvinoff). The late gen. editor died 1977.] Vol. XIII, March 1926–July 1929. Ed.: Pinhas Ofer, 1978. xxx, 591 pp., front. port., ports., illus. Vol. XIV, July 1929–Oct. 1930. Ed.: Camillo Dresner, 1978. xli, 408 pp., front. illus., ports., facsim. Jerusalem: Transaction Books, Rutgers University, Israel Universities Press, 1977/78. Vols. XII–XIV. [For vols. I–XI see No. 14493/YB. XXIII.]

VII. PARTICIPATION IN CULTURAL AND PUBLIC LIFE

A. General

15371. BLUMENBERG, WERNER: *Kämpfer für die Freiheit*. 3. Aufl. Berlin: Dietz, 1977. 179 pp., facsims. (Internationale Bibliothek, Bd. 72). (Nachdr. d. 1959 erschienenen 1. Aufl.) [Incl. chaps. on: Johann Jacoby, Karl Marx, Ferdinand Lassalle, Eduard Bernstein.]
15372. BRAUNTHAL, JULIUS: *Geschichte der Internationale*. Bd. 1–2, 3. Aufl. unveränd. Nachdr. d. 1974 erschienenen 2. Aufl.; Bd. 3, 2. Aufl., unv. Nachdr. d. 1971 erschienenen 1. Aufl. Berlin-Bonn: Dietz, 1978. 401, 613, 723 pp. [3 vols.] [For German and English eds. see No. 9593/YB. XVII. Julius Braunthal died May 1972, aged 81.]
15373. BUBER-NEUMANN, MARGARETE: *Die erloschene Flamme*. Schicksale meiner Zeit. Frankfurt/M.: Fischer Taschenbuch Verlag, 1978. (FTB, Bd. 2073). [Also]: München: Langen Müller, 1976. 207 pp. [Incl. Milena [Jesenska] aus Prag, Kafka's friend, died 1944 in Ravensbrück] and: Die Geschichte der Bella Rosenkranz, born 1921, deported from the Jewish orphanage in Fürth, 1938.]
15374. EXILE LITERATURE. BERENDSOHN, WALTER A.: *Die humanistische Front*. Einführung in die deutsche Emigranten-Literatur. Erster Teil: Von 1933 bis zum Kriegsausbruch 1939. Worms: Heintz, 1978. 204 pp. [Reprint, first publ. Zürich, Europa Verlag, 1946.] Zweiter Teil: Vom Kriegsausbruch 1939 bis Ende 1946. See No. 13700/YB. XXII.]
15375. DAHLKE, HANS: *Geschichtsroman und Literaturkritik im Exil*. Berlin [East]: Aufbau-Verlag, 1976. 451 pp., notes pp. 393–419, bibl. zum Geschichtsroman des Exils (pp. 420–444), list of names pp. 445–450. [Incl. chaps.: Zur Bedeutung des Geschichtsromans im Exil, Einige theoretische Positionen bei der Rechtfertigung des historischen Stoffes: Lion Feuchtwanger, Alfred Döblin, Stefan Zweig. Literaturkritische Arbeiten zu Thomas Manns 'Joseph und seine Brüder' und 'Lotte in Weimar'.]
15376. KANTOROWICZ, ALFRED: *Politik und Literatur im Exil*. Deutschsprachige Schriftsteller im Kampf gegen den Nationalsozialismus. Hamburg: Christians, 1978. 346 pp. (Hamburger Beiträge zur Sozial-und Zeitgeschichte, Bd. 14). [Cf. Wir sind die Letzten. A.K. über Exil-Literatur (Ulrich Weinzierl) in: 'FAZ', 7. Okt., Frankfurt/M., 1978.] [*Emigrant der ersten und der letzten Stunde*. Heimatlos in Deutschland: Alfred Kantorowicz, geb. am 12. August 1899 gestorben am 27. März 1979 in Hamburg (Fritz J. Raddatz) in: 'Die Zeit', 6. April, Hamburg, 1979, port. [And]: *Der schreibende Zeitgenosse*. Zum Tode von A.K. (Marcel Reich-Ranicki) in: 'FAZ', 29. März, Frankfurt/M., 1979.]
15377. MAAS, LISELOTTE: *Die Exilpresse in Lateinamerika*. Frankfurt/M.: Buchhändler-Vereinigung, 1978. 88 pp. (Kleine Schriften der Deutschen Bibliothek, Bd. 3).
15378. *Österreicher im Exil, 1934 bis 1945*. Protokoll des Intern. Symposiums zur Erforschung des Österr. Exils von 1934 bis 1945, abgehalten vom 3. bis 6. Juni 1975 in Wien. Hrsg.: Dokumentationsarchiv des Österr. Widerstandes u. Dokumentationsstelle f. Neuere

Österr. Literatur. Red.: Helene Maimann, Heinz Lunzer. Vorw. von Bruno Kreisky. Wien: Österr. Bundesverlag, 1977. xxxvii, 618 pp., bibl.

15379. WALTER, HANS-ALBERT: *Exilpresse*. Deutsche Exilliteratur 1933–1950. Bd.4. Stuttgart: Metzler, 1978. xii, 842 pp., bibl. and notes pp. 731–821, names index pp. 822–842. [Incl. Politisch-kulturelle Zeitschriften der jüdischen Massenemigration: 'Aufbau', pp. 543–678; 'Orient' (Haifa), pp. 679–733.] [For vols. 1, 2, 7, 8 see No. 12177/YB. XX.] [Cf. Zum Stand der Exilforschung in der BRD. Neue Bücher von Alfred Kantorowicz [see No. 15376.] and Hans-Albert Walter (Konrad Feilchenfeldt) in: 'NZZ', 16. März, Zürich, 1979.]

15380. WINKLER, MICHAEL, ed.: *Deutsche Literatur im Exil 1933–1945*. Texte und Dokumente. Stuttgart: Reclam, 1977. 512 pp., authors, titles and bibl. (pp. 449–512). (Universal–Bibliothek Nr. 9865 [6]. [Der Weg ins Exil. Stationen der Flucht. Politik und Propaganda. Schreiben im Exil. Permanenz des Exils.]

15381. (*The*) FRANKFURT SCHOOL. ARATO, ANDREW/Eike GEBHARDT, eds.: *The Essential Frankfurt School Reader*. Introduction by Paul Piccone. New York: Urizen; Oxford: Basil Blackwell, 1978. xxiii, 558 pp. [An introduction to the Frankfurt School for the English-speaking reader. Incl. essays by Adorno, Benjamin, Fromm, Horkheimer and Marcuse.]

15382. BUCK-MORSS, SUSAN: *The Origin of Negative Dialectics*: Theodor W. Adorno, Walter Benjamin and the Frankfurt Institute. New York: Free Press, 1977. xv, 335 pp., bibl. (pp. 307–322).

15383. *Kritik und Interpretation der kritischen Theorie*. Aufsätze über Adorno, Horkheimer, Marcuse, Benjamin, Habermas. l.Aufl. (Repr.) Giessen: Achenbach, 1975. 383 pp. (theorie + kritik, 4).

15384. SCHMIDT, ALFRED: *Die kritische Theorie als Geschichtsphilosophie*. München: Hanser, 1976. 111 pp., bibl. (pp. 108–[112]). (Reihe Hanser, 207).

15385. TIBI, BASSAM: *Der Terrorismus und die Frankfurter Schule*. [In]: Die Neue Gesellschaft. Jg. 25, H.5, Mai. Bonn: Neue Gesellschaft, 1978. pp. 382–386. [Ist kritisches Denken terroristisch?]

15386. WIGGERSHAUS, ROLF: *Die Geschichte der Frankfurter Schule*. [In]: 'Neue Rundschau'. 89. Jg., H.4. Berlin: S. Fischer, 1978. P.p 571–587. At all times, from the official opening of the Institute in 1924, during the time of it's emigration in New York and with the return to Frankfurt in 1948, Jews were closely connected with it: Felix Weil, Friedrich Pollock, Max Horkheimer, Leo Löwenthal, Theodor W. Adorno, Karl Mannheim, Erich Fromm, Herbert Marcuse.

15387. GOLDSCHMIDT, HERMANN LEVIN: *Hiob einst und immer*. Das kollektive jüdische Zeugnis. Von Margarete Susman bis Karl Wolfskehl. Aussagen von Nelly Sachs und Martin Buber, von Heine bis Goll [Yvan], Bloch und Jung. [In]: 'Allgemeine', 3. Nov., Düsseldorf, 1978. Pp. 6 and 11.

15388. HERMANN, ARMIN: *Die Jahrhundertwissenschaft*. Werner Heisenberg und die Physik seiner Zeit. Stuttgart: Deutsche Verlagsanstalt, 1978. 275 pp. [Incl. Einstein, Bohr, Born, Pauli.]

15389. INGOLD, FELIX PHILIPP: *Literatur und Aviatik*. Europäische Flugdichtung 1909–1927. Mit e. Exkurs über die Flugidee in der modernen Malerei und Architektur. Basel: Birkhäuser, 1978. 505 pp., ports., illus., bibl. [Incl. Kafka, Karl Kraus, Hofmannsthal. See also No. 15544.]

15390. KREILER, KURT, ed.: *Traditionen deutscher Justiz*. Politische Prozesse 1914 bis 1932. Ein Lesebuch zur Geschichte der Weimarer Republik. Berlin: Klaus Wagenbach, 1978. 312 pp., ports. [Incl. Die Verteidigungsrede, das 'letzte Wort' vor Gericht von Rosa. Luxemburg (Februar 1914). Äusserungen und Vernehmungen Ernst Tollers. Das Schlusswort Levinés mit dem bekannten Ausspruch 'Wir Kommunisten sind alle Tote auf Urlaub'. Die Ermordung Eisners. Attentat auf Rathenau. Der Prozess wegen des Attentats auf Maximilian Harden (Juli 1922). Der Prozessbericht von Kurt Tucholsky. Das Plädoyer Paul Levis u.a. Cf. Dokumente zur Justizgeschichte der Weimarer Republik (Richard Schmid) in: 'Merkur', 32. Jg., H.11 (366), Nov. Stuttgart: Klett-Cotta, 1978. Pp. 1152–1155.]

15391. KREILER, KURT: *Die Schriftstellerrepublik*. Zum Verhältnis von Literatur und Politik in der Münchner Räterepublik. Ein systemat. Kapitel politischer Literaturgeschichte. Berlin: Guhl, 1978. 228 pp., ports., bibl. (pp. 217–228). [Incl. Die 'Proklamation' der bayerischen Räterepublik am 7. April 1919: literarische Profile: Mühsam, Toller, Landauer, Eisner. Modelle literarpolitischen Handelns. Die Verteidigungsreden von Erich Mühsam und Ernst Toller].

15392. SCHULZE, HAGEN: *Otto Braun oder Preussens demokratische Sendung*. Eine Biographie. Frankfurt/M.–Berlin: Ullstein, 1977. 1094 pp., front. port. [by Max Liebermann], notes pp. 864–1027, bibl. (pp. 1030–1056), list of names pp. 1057–1094. (Eine Veröffentlichung der Stiftung Preussischer Kulturbesitz). [Pp. 19–22: In Erinnerung an Otto Braun (Herbert Weichmann). Many Jewish socialist politicians figure in this biography and in the essay listed below.]

15393. SCHULZE, HAGEN: *Stabilität in der politischen Ordnung von Weimar*. Die sozialdemokratischen Parlamentsfraktionen im Reich und in Preussen. [In]: Vierteljahrshefte für Zeitgeschichte. Hrsg. von Karl Dietrich Bracher und Hans-Peter Schwarz. H.3. Stuttgart: Dt. Verlags-Anstalt, 1978. Pp. 419–432, tab.

15394. STRESEMANN, WOLFGANG: *Philharmonie und Philharmoniker*. Berlin: Stapp Verlag. 1977. 116 pp. ports., illus. [Many Jewish personalities played a prominent part in the orchestra's history. Cf. History of Berlin's 'Philharmonie' (H. W. Freyhan) in: 'AJR Information', Dec. London, 1978.]

15395. '*Die Weltbühne*'. Wochenschrift für Politik-Kunst-Wirtschaft. Begründet und bis 1926 geleitet von Siegfried Jacobsohn. Von 1927 unter Mitarbeit von Kurt Tucholsky geleitet von Carl v. Ossietzky. Verlag der Weltbühne, Charlottenburg, Kantstrasse 152. Vollständiger Nachdruck der Ausgaben 1918 bis 1933. Mit e. Begleitband von Axel Eggebrecht und Dietrich Pinkerneil. Königstein/Ts.: Athenäum, 1978. 25000 pp. [in 16 vols.] Paperback or library edition. [Der Begleitband (100 pp.) enthält eine kurze Einführung in die Geschichte der Zeitschrift, Berichte über die wichtigsten Mitarbeiter, insbesondere eine Würdigung des Gründers und Herausgebers Siegfried Jacobsohn (1881 Berlin – 1926 Berlin), und ein Gesamtregister. Axel Eggebrecht war ein Mitarbeiter der Zeitschrift.]

15396. WIEGAND, WILFRIED, ed.: *Uber Chaplin*. Zürich: Diogenes, 1978. 338 pp., 22 ports., illus., chronol., list of 81 Chaplin films. (Reihe detebe Bd. 159). [27 contributions, the earliest text from the year 1916. Authors incl. Siegfried Kracauer, Kurt Tucholsky, Egon Erwin Kisch, Hannah Arendt, Adorno and the clown Grock (orig. Adrian Wettach).]

15397. *Zeit und Ewigkeit*. Tausend Jahre österreichische Lyrik. Hrsg. u. eingel. von Joachim Schondorff. Mit e. Nachw. von Heinz Politzer. Düsseldorf: Claassen, 1978. 600 pp., [Authors incl. are: Rose Ausländer, Broch, Brod, Celan, Ehrenstein, Fried, Kafka Kraus, Mahler, Musil, Salten, Schnitzler, Stefan Zweig.]

B. Individual

15398. ADLER, ALFRED: *Lebenskenntnis*. Mit e. Einführung von Wolfgang Metzger. Aus d. Amerik. von Willi Köhler. Frankfurt/M.: Fischer-Taschenbuch-Verlag, 1978. 158 pp. (F. Taschenbücher, Bd. 6392, Bücher des Wissens). [The Science of Living.]

15399. ADLER, ALFRED: *Menschenkenntnis*. Frankfurt/M.: Fischer, 1978. 254 pp. (Fischer–Taschenbücher, Bd. 6080, Bücher des Wissens).

15400. ADLER, ALFRED: *Der Sinn des Lebens*. Mit e. Einführung von Wolfgang Metzger. Ungek. Ausg. Frankfurt/M.: Fischer-Taschenbuch-Verlag, 1978. 191 pp. (Fischer Taschenbücher, Bd. 6179, Bücher des Wissens). [See No. 14517/YB.XXIII.] [A.A. 1870 Vienna–1937 Aberdeen, Scotland.]

15401. ADLER. FELIX. BÖCHER, OTTO: *Felix Adler (1851–1933)*. [In]: 700 Jahre Stadt Alzey. Festschrift, hrsg. im Auftrage der Stadt Alzey von Friedrich Karl Becker. Alzey, 1977 Pp. 313–314. [Born in Alzey the philosopher and teacher died in New York where, in 1876, he had founded the Society for Ethnic Culture (Gesellschaft für ethische Kultur.]

15402. ADLER, H. G.: *Gedichte vom Tod in schlimmen Zeiten*. [In]: 'Europäische Ideen'. Hrsg. Andreas W. Mytze. H.43, Berlin, 1978. Pp. 32–34. [Poems written between 1942 and 1945 in Theresienstadt and Langenstein.]

15403. ADLER, H. G.: *Spuren und Pfeiler*. Gedichte. Mit Zeichnungen von Friedrich Daniels. London: Alphabox Press, 1978. [H. G. Adler, born July 2, 1910 in Prague.]

15404. ADLER, MAX. MERCHAV, PERETZ: *Otto Bauer und Max Adler*. [In]: 'Die Neue Gesellschaft'. 24. Jg., Nr. 12 (Dez.). Bonn: Verlag Neue Gesellschaft, 1977. Pp. 1034–1041. [M.A. 1873–1937. O.B. 1882–1938.]
15405. ADORNO, THEODOR W.: *Musikalische Schriften, I–III*. Hrsg. von Rolf Tiedemann. 1. Aufl. Frankfurt/M.: Suhrkamp, 1978. 683 pp. (Ges. Schriften, Bd. 16). [Cont. 1. Klangfiguren. 2. Quasi una fantasia. 3. Musikalische Schriften.]
15406. ADORNO, THEODOR W.: *Philosophie der neuen Musik*. Hrsg. von Rolf Tiedemann. Frankfurt/M.: Suhrkamp, 1978. 200 pp. (Suhrk. Taschenbücher Wissenschaft, Bd. 239).
15407. HERMANN, BERNDT: *Theodor W. Adorno: Seine Gesellschaftstheorie als ungeschriebene Erziehungslehre*. Ansätze zu einer dialektischen Begründung der Pädagogik als Wissenschaft. Bonn: Bouvier, 1978. vi, 121 pp., bibl. (pp. 117–121). (Abhandlungen zur Philosophie, Psychologie und Pädagogik, Bd. 126).
15408. JAY, MARTIN: *Adorno and Kracauer: Notes on a Troubled Friendship*. [In]: 'Salmagundi', A Quarterly of the Humanities and Social Sciences. No. 40, Winter. Saratoga Springs, N.Y.: Skidmore College, 1978. Pp. 42–66.
15409. MARCUSE, HERBERT: *Zum 75. Geburtstag von Theodor W. Adorno*. Nach seinem Tode ist die Welt ärmer. [In]: 'Die Zeit', 8. Sept., Hamburg, 1978, port., facsim. [Theodor W. Adorno, orig. Wiesengrund, born 11. Sept. 1903 in Frankfurt/M., died August 1969 in Frankfurt/M. Philosopher, sociologist, musicologist.]
15410. SCHMUCKER, JOSEPH F.: *Adorno – Logik des Zerfalls*. Stuttgart/Bad Cannstadt: Frommann–Holzboog, 1977. 154 pp., bibl. Th. W. A. und bibl. pp. 149–154.
15411. AGNON, SHMUEL YOSEPH. MIRON, DAN: *German Jews in Agnon's Work*. [In]: LBI Year Book XXIII. London, 1978. Pp. 265–280. [See No. 15111.] [Sh.Y. Agnon, (orig. Czaczkes) 1888 Galicia – 1970 Israel.]
15412. AMÉRY, JEAN: *Charles Bovary, Landarzt*. Porträt eines einfachen Mannes. Stuttgart: Klett-Cotta, 1978. 162 pp. [Cf. Roman und Diskurs. Jean Amérys 'Charles Bovary' (François Bondy) [in]: 'Merkur', Jg. 33, H.1(368) Januar. Stuttgart: Klett-Cotta, 1979. Pp. 87–89. [Also]: Biographie eines möglichen Helden. Amüsantes Denkspiel (Fritz J. Raddatz) [in]: 'Die Zeit', 20. Okt., Hamburg, 1978. [And]: Der Unglückliche ist unter den Glücklichen allein. Jean Améry und sein letztes Buch. Statt einer Rezension (Hans J. Fröhlich) in: 'FAZ', 25. Nov., Frankfurt/M., 1978.
15413. AMÉRY, JEAN: *Jenseits von Schuld und Sühne*. Bewältigungsversuche eines Überwältigten. Mit einem Vorwort des Autors zur Neuausgabe. Stuttgart: Klett-Cotta, 1977. 156 pp. [First ed. 1966. See No. 6118/YB. XII.]
15414. AMÉRY, JEAN: *Lessingscher Geist und die Welt von heute*. [In]: 'Merkur', 32. Jg., H.12(367), Dez. Stuttgart: Klett-Cotta, 1978. Pp. 1194–1206. (Dies ist die letzte Rede, die J.A., Träger des Lessingpreises der Freien und Hansestadt Hamburg, am 15. April 1978 zur Eröffnung des Wolfenbütteler Lessinghauses gehalten hat).
15415. HEISSENBÜTTEL, HELMUT/BERND JENTZSCH, eds.: *Hermannstrasse 14*. Sonderheft Jean Améry. Stuttgart: Klett-Cotta, 1978. 60 pp., ports., illus.
15416. *Jean Améry* (orig. Hans Mayer), born 1812 in Vienna committed suicide on October 17, 1978 in Salzburg. Obituaries:– Heute hätte ich ihn treffen sollen ... (Wolfgang Kraus) in: Jüd. Rundschau Maccabi, 19. Okt., Basel, 1978, ports. Allein in der Sprache zu Hause. Ein Nachwort auf Jean Améry (Horst Krüger) in: 'Merkur', 32. Jg., H.12(367), Dez. Stuttgart: Klett-Cotta, 1978. Pp. 1283–1287. Stille Klage um Jean Améry (Hans Lamm) in: 'Allgemeine', 27.Okt., Düsseldorf, 1978, port. Interruption – von und für Jean Améry (Hans Paeschke) in: 'Merkur', 32.Jg., H.11(366), Nov. Stuttgart: Klett-Cotta, 1978. Pp. 1103–1105. Er leistete 'Trauerarbeit' für andere – Jean Amérys gedenkend (Hety Schmitt-Maass) in: Die Neue Gesellschaft'. 25. Jg., H.12 (Dez.), Bonn, 1978, Pp. 1000–1002. Jenseits der Grenze (Uwe Schultz) in: 'FAZ', 20. Okt., Frankfurt/M., 1978. Stolz und auch sehr melancholisch. Nachruf auf einen Freund (Horst Krüger) [In]: 'Die Zeit', 27.Okt., Hamburg, 1978, port., bibl.
15417. ANDERS, GÜNTHER: *Kosmologische Humoreske (1954) und andere Erzählungen*. Frankfurt/M.: Suhrkamp, 1978. 335 pp. (st Bd. 432). [Cont. the philosophical stories Learsi (1933), Der Hungermarsch (1935), Rigonia (1966), Zirkus Xaret (1973) and Politische Humoreske (1973).] [Günther Anders, orig. Stern, born 1902 in Breslau.]
15418. ARENDT, ERICH: *Zeitsaum*. Gedichte. 1.Aufl. Leipzig: Insel, 1978. 122 pp., port.
15419. LASCHEN, GREGOR/MANFRED SCHLÖSSER, eds.: *Der zerstückte Traum*. Für Erich Arendt zum 75. Geburtstag am 15. April 1978. Berlin: Agora, 1978. 270 pp., graphics. [Incl.

contributions by Thomas Brasch, Volker Braun, Sarah Kirsch, Reinhard Lettau, Heinz Piontek a.o.]

15420. RADDATZ, FRITZ J.: *An alle Scheiben blutig klopfen*. 'Getrieben und verschlagen'. Ein Dichter der DDR, dessen Ruhm wächst – nur noch nicht bei uns – Erich Arendt, Person und Werk. [In]: 'Die Zeit', 7. April, Hamburg, 1978, port., bibl. [E.A. emigrated 1933 via Switzerland to Spain, fought from 1936–1939 in the Spanish Civil War, was from 1941 until 1950 in Columbia when he returned to East Berlin.]

15421. ARENDT, HANNAH: *The Jew as Pariah*. Jewish Identity and Politics in the Modern Age. Ed. and with an Introduction by Ron H. Feldman. New York: Grove Press, 1978. 288 pp. [Cf. H.A. and the Jews (Werner J. Dannhauser) [In]: 'Commentary', Vol. 67, No. 1 (Jan.), New York: American Jewish Committee, 1979. Pp. 70–72.]

15422. ARENDT, HANNAH: *The Life of the Mind*. Vol. I: Thinking. Vol. II: Willing. Ed. and a postface by Mary McCarthy. London: Secker & Warburg, 1978. 272, 288 pp. [2 vols.] [Posthumously published Gifford lecture.] H.A. died before the third vol. 'Judging' was completed. [Cf. The Passionate Thinker (George Steiner) [In]: 'The Sunday Times', July 30, London, 1978, ports.]

15423. McCARTHY, MARY: *Hannah Arendt, meine schöne Freundin*. Ein postumes Porträt. Aus d. Amerik. übers. von Mark W. Rien. [In]: 'Die Zeit', 13. Jan., Hamburg, 1978, ports. [H.A. 1906 Hanover–1975 New York.]

15424. ARNSTEIN, FANNY VON. SPIEL, HILDE: *Fanny von Arnstein oder Die Emanzipation*. Ein Frauenleben an der Zeitwende 1758–1818. Frankfurt/M.: Fischer Taschenbuch Verlag, 1978. 537 pp., front. port., ports., illus., fascims., tab., bibl. (Fischer Taschenbuch, Bd. 2131). [First publ. 1962. See No. 3236/YB. VIII.] [Fanny v. Arnstein, daughter of Daniel Itzig, 1758 Berlin–1818 Wien.]

15425. ARONS, MARTIN LEO. BEUTLER, KURT/UWE HENNING: *Friedrich Paulsen und der 'Fall' Leo Arons*. Dokumente zur Diskussion um die 'Freiheit von Forschung und Lehre' nach der Aufhebung des Sozialistengesetzes (1890). [In]: Die Deutsche Schule, Darmstadt, Jg. 69, H.5., 1977. Pp. 270–279, bibl. footnotes.

15426. BEUTLER, KURT/UWE HENNING: *Der Professoren Geist und das 'Ministerium des Geistes'*. Zur Rolle von Wissenschaft und Staat in Preussen-Deutschland unter dem 'System Althoff' (1882–1907). [In]: 'Neue Sammlung', Göttinger Zeitschrift für Erziehung und Gesellschaft. 17. Jg., H.1. Göttingen: Vandenhoeck und Ruprecht, 1977. Pp. 1–26, bibl. footnotes. [1. Der Fall Arons und das Prinzip der Wissenschaft.]

15427. BEUTLER, KURT/UWE HENNING: *Zum Problem der 'Freiheit von Forschung und Lehre' im Kaiserreich und innerhalb der Sozialdemokratischen Partei nach 1890*. [In]: 'Literatur/Manuskript', 4, H.12-13. Köln, 1976. Pp. 68–77, bibl. notes pp. 75–77. [Prof. Leo Arons, physicist, (1860 Berlin–1919 Berlin) was, because of his socialist views and activities, suspended in 1899 from his lectureship at Berlin University on the basis of the Prussian 'Lex Arons' especially introduced for this purpose.]

15428. BECKER, JUREK: *Schlaflose Tage*. Roman. Frankfurt/M.: Suhrkamp, 1978. 158 pp. [The writer was born in 1937, spent his childhood in the Ghetto Lodz and concentration camps, came 1945 to Berlin where he now lives.]

15429. BENJAMIN, WALTER: *Reflections: Essays, Aphorisms, Autobiographical Writings*. Selected by Hannah Arendt. Transl. by Edmund Jephcott. Introduced and ed. by Peter Demetz. New York/London: Harcourt Brace Jovanovich, 1978. xliii, 348 pp.

15430. FULD, WERNER: *Agesilaus Santander oder Benedix Schönflies*. Die geheimen Namen Walter Benjamins. [In]: 'Neue Rundschau', 89. Jg., H. 2. Berlin: S. Fischer, 1978. Pp. 253–263, facsims. relating to the deprivation of his citizenship in 1939. [And]: Besuch in Port Bou. Auf der Suche nach dem Grabe Benjamins (Helmut Niemeyer), pp. 264–267.

15431. *Die geheimen Namen Walter Benjamins*. Eine Zuschrift Gershom Scholems. Die Antwort Werner Fulds. [In]: 'Neue Rundschau', 89. Jg. H.4. Berlin: S. Fischer, 1978. Pp. 663–667.

15432. HASELBERG, PETER V.: *Der Deutsche Walter Benjamin*. [In]: 'Merkur', 32. Jg., H.6(361), Juni. Stuttgart: Klett-Cotta, 1978. Pp. 592-600.

15433. UNGER, PETER: *Walter Benjamin als Rezensent*: Die Reflexion eines Intellektuellen auf d. zeitgeschichtliche Situation. Frankfurt/M., Bern: Lang, 1978. 281 pp. (Europ. Hochschulschriften, Reihe 1: Dt. Literatur und Germanistik, Bd. 241). Zugl. philolog. Diss., Univ. Frankfurt/M., 1976.

15434. BERENDSOHN, WALTER A. GARAGULY, BRITA VON, comp.: *Walter A. Berendsohn*.

Verzeichnis seiner 1908–1978 erschienenen Veröffentlichungen anlässlich seines 94. Geburtstages am 10. September 1978. Mit einem Vorwort von Gustav Korlén. Stockholm: Nyblo., 1978. 103 pp., front. port. [Acta Bibliothecae Regiae Stockholmiensis XXXI.)

15435. BERNFELD, SIEGFRIED: *Trieb und Tradition im Jugendalter.* Kulturpsychologische Studien an Tagebüchern. Nachdr. d. Ausg. Barth, Leipzig 1931. Frankfurt/M.: Päd.-Extra-Buchverlag, 1978. 181 pp., bibl. (pp. 171–179). (Reprint, 2). (Ursprünglich hrsg. als Beihefte zur Zeitschrift für angewandte Psychologie, Beiheft 54).

15436. UTLEY, PHILIP LEE: *Siegfried Bernfeld, Left-Wing Youth Leader, Psychoanalyst and Zionist 1910–April 1918.* Madison, Wis., 1975. vi, 433 pp. Diss., The University of Wisconsin, Microfilm copy of type-script. Ann Arbor, Mich., University Microfilms, 1975. [Siegfried Bernfeld, 1892 Vienna–1953 San Francisco].

15437. BERNSTEIN, EDUARD: *Sozialdemokratische Lehrjahre.* Nachdr. d. 1928 bei Der Bücherkreis, Berlin, erschienenen 1. Aufl. Berlin–Bonn: Dietz, 1978. xx, 196 pp. (Internationale Bibliothek, Bd. 118). [E.B. 1850 Berlin–1932 Berlin.]

15438. BETTELHEIM, BRUNO: *Der Weg aus dem Labyrinth:* Leben lernen als Therapie. Ungek. Ausg. Frankfurt/M.: Ullstein, 1978. 464 pp. (Ullstein Buch Nr. 3506). [An account of his life's work, the Orthogenic School in Chicago. Born 1903 in Vienna, child psychologist, after a year in Dachau, went in 1939 to USA.]

15439. BLOCH, ERNST: *Texte aus der DDR.* Berlin: Verlag Europäische Ideen, 1977. 50 pp. (Europ. Ideen, H. 26).

15440. BLOCH, ERNST: *Tendenz – Latenz – Utopie.* Ergänzungsband zur Gesamtausgabe. Frankfurt/M.: Suhrkamp, 1978. 424 pp. [Incl. works written between 1902 and 1977 not contained in the 'Gesamtausgabe', see No. 14553/YB.XXIII.]

15441. BLUM, ROBERT. HIRSCH, HELMUT: *Robert Blum.* Märtyrer der Freiheit. Köln: Nachrichtenamt der Stadt Köln, 1977. 56 pp., port. (Kölner Biographien, 8). [R.B. 1807 Cologne, sentenced to death and shot 1848 in Vienna.]

15442. BÖRNE, LUDWIG: *Briefe aus Paris.* Auswahl, Anmerkungen und Nachw. von Manfred Schneider. Stuttgart: Reclam, 1977. 264 pp. (Universal Bibliothek Nr. 9850[3]. [The 'Briefe aus Paris' (to Jeanette Wohl) were publ. 1832/34 in 2 vols.]

15443. BÖRNE, LUDWIG: *Sämtliche Schriften.* Neu bearb. u. hrsg. von Inge u. Peter Rippmann. Bd. 1: xxx, 1221 pp.; Bd. 2: ix, 1239 pp.; Bd. 3: viii, 1053 pp.; Bd. 4: Briefe I: cxx, 1366 pp.; Bd. 5: Briefe II, Nachträge: xxviii, 1164 pp. Dreieich: Abi Melzer, 1977. [5 vols.]

15444. MARCUSE, LUDWIG: *Ludwig Börne.* Aus der Frühzeit der deutschen Demokratie. Zürich: Diogenes, 1977. 262 pp., port., list of names. (detebe Bd. 21/VIII). [The book was first publ. 1929 under the title: Revolutionär und Patriot]. [L.B., orig. Löb Baruch, 1786 Frankfurt–1837 Paris.]

15445. BORCHARDT, RUDOLF. *Rudolf Borchardt, Alfred Walter Heymel, Rudolf Alexander Schröder:* Eine Ausstellung d. Deutschen Literaturarchivs im Schiller-Nationalmuseum, Marbach am Neckar, 8. Apr.–31. Okt. 1978. Ausstellung und Katalog: Reinhard Tgahrt. München: Kösel, 1978. 631 pp., ports., illus., music, bibls. (Sonderausstellungen des Schiller-Nationalmuseums, Katalog Nr. 29, hrsg. von Bernhard Zeller.) [Cf. Alles war möglich, auch das Unmögliche. Eine esoterisch Trias: Borchardt – Heymel – Schröder (Clara Menck). Zu der Ausstellung im Marbacher Literaturarchiv. [In]: 'FAZ', April 27, Frankfurt/M., 1978, port. [of R. Borchardt.]

15446. VORDTRIEDE, WERNER: *Rudolf Borchardt und die europäische Tradition.* [And]: *'Deutschland ist Kain'. Der Dichter Rudolf Borchardt* (Helmut Heissenbüttel) [In]: Jahrbuch der Deutschen Schillergesellschaft. Hrsg. von Fritz Martini. Walter Müller-Seidel u. Bernhard Zeller. 22. Jg., Stuttgart: Kröner, 1978. [xii, 784 pp., ports.] [R.B. 1877 Königsberg–1945 Sterzing.]

15447. BRAHM, OTTO. SEIDLIN, OSKAR: *Der Theaterkritiker Otto Brahm.* 2. Aufl. Bonn: Bouvier, 1978. 226 pp. (Studien zur Literatur der Moderne, Bd. 6). [Otto Brahm, orig. Abrahamsohn, critic, theatre director, 1856 Hamburg–1912 Berlin.]

15448. BROCH, HERMANN: *Menschenrecht und Demokratie.* Politische Schriften. Hrsg. u. eingel. von Paul Michael Lützeler. Frankfurt/M.: Suhrkamp, 1978. 285 pp., bibl. (pp. 281–284). (Bibliothek Suhrkamp, Bd. 588). [See also Nos. 8821 & 8828/YB. XVI.]

15449. BROCH, HERMANN: *Politische Schriften.* Frankfurt/M.: Suhrkamp, 1978. 516 pp. (Kommentierte Werkausgabe, hrsg. von Paul Michael Lützeler, Bd.11).

15450. BROCH, HERMANN: *Die Schlafwandler*. Eine Romantrilogie. Frankfurt/M.: Suhrkamp, 1978. 768 pp. bibl. (Kommentierte Werkausgabe in 16 Bänden. Hrsg. von Paul Michael Lützeler, Bd. 1). [For other vols. in this ed. see No. 14567/YB. XXIII. The trilogy was first publ. 1931/32. Also in a Suhrkamp Taschenbuch ed., 1978, Bd. 472.]

15451. BROCH, HERMANN: *Der Tod des Vergil*. Roman. Mit e. Nachwort von Dietrich Simon. Berlin [East]: Volk und Welt, 1978. 602 pp. Lizenzausg. d. Suhrkamp Verl., Frankfurt/M. [For English and another German ed. see No. 14566/YB. XXIII.]

15452. BROD, MAX: *Der Meister*. Roman. 1. Aufl. Berlin: Evangelische Verlagsanstaltz 1977, 402 pp.

15453. BROD, MAX: *Tycho Brahes Weg zu Gott*. Mit e. Vorw. von Stefan Zweig. Frankfurt/M.: Suhrkamp, 1978. 275 pp. (st Nr. 490). [The novel was first publ. in 1915].

15454. *Erinnerungen an Max Brod zum 10. Todestag (20. 12. 1978)*. (Ben-Chorin) in: 'MB', Nr. 45, 15. Dez., Tel Aviv, 1978. Pp. 5–6 [and]: Nur Liebe, von nichts anderem weiss ich (Ben-Chorin) in: 'IW', 22. Dez. Zürich, 1978. Pp. 19–21. Max Brod, Herold und Beispiel der Nächstenliebe (Meir Faerber) in: 'Das Neue Israel', H. 7, Jan. Zürich, 1979. Max Brods 'streitbares' Leben (Stefan Schwarz) [and] Zum Gedenken (Meir Reubeni) in: 'Neue Jüd. Nachrichten', Nr. 1–2, 12. Jan., München, 1979.

—— PAZI, MARGARITA: *Arnold Zweig and Max Brod*. – 1929, 1939, 1949. [In]: LBI Year Book XXIII. [See No. 15717.]

15455. CANETTI, ELIAS: *Die Blendung*. Roman. Mit e. Essay des Autors und e. Nachwort von Annemarie Auer. 3. Aufl. Berlin [East]: Volk und Welt, 1978. 597 pp. Lizenzausg. d. Hanser-Verl. München. [First publ. München, Hanser 1963 and cf. No. 11458/YB. XIX. See also No. 10585/YB. XVIII and 9704/YB. XVII.]

15456. CASSIRER, ERNST: *Descartes, Lehre, Persönlichkeit und Wirkung*. Nachdr. d. Ausgabe Stockholm, 1939. Hildesheim: Gerstenberg, 1978. 44 pp.

15457. CASSIRER, ERNST: *Der Mythus des Staates*. Philosophische Grundlagen politischen Verhaltens. Mit e. Vorwort von Walter Rüegg. Zürich: Artemis, 1978. 412 pp. (Erasmus–Bibliothek).

15458. LIPTON, DAVID R.: *Ernst Cassirer*. The Dilemma of a Liberal Intellectual in Germany, 1914–1933. Toronto: University of Toronto Press, 1978. xi, 212 pp., notes pp. 177–195, bibl. (pp. 197–207). [E.C., philosopher, 1874 Breslau – 1945 New York.]

15459. CELAN, PAUL. CHALFEN, ISRAEL: *Paul Celan*. Eine Biographie seiner Jugend. Frankfurt/M.: Insel, 1978. 240 pp., ports., illus.

15460. PETUCHOWSKI, ELIZABETH: *A new Approach to Paul Celan's 'Argumentum e silentio'*. [In]: Deutsche Vierteljahrsschrift für Literaturwissenschaft und Geistesgeschichte. Vol. 52, No. 1. Stuttgart, 1978. Pp. 111–136, bibl. notes.

15461. SCHULZ, GEORG-MICHAEL: *Negativität in der Dichtung Paul Celans*. Tübingen: Niemeyer, 1977. vi, 283 pp. (Studien zur deutschen Literatur, Bd. 54). Zugl. Neuphilolog. Diss., Univ. Tübingen, 1975. [P.C., orig. Paul Antschel also Antzel, 1920 Czernowitz–1970 Paris (suicide).]

15462. DÖBLIN, ALFRED: *Flucht und Sammlung des Judenvolks*. Aufsätze und Erzählungen. Neudruck d. Ausgabe Amsterdam 1935. Hildesheim: Gerstenberg, 1977. 232 pp. (Exilliteratur, Bd. 1, ed. by Werner Berthold und Hans-Albert Walter). Lizenz d. Walter-Verl., Olten.

15463. DÖBLIN, ALFRED: *Der neue Urwald*. Roman. Neudr. d. Ausgabe Baden-Baden 1948. Hildesheim: Gerstenberg, 1977. 193 pp. (Das Land ohne Tod. Südamerikatrilogie, 3) (Exilliteratur, Bd. 2, ed. by Werner Berthold und Hans-Albert Walter).

15464. DÖBLIN, ALFRED: *November 1918*. Eine deutsche Revolution. Mit e. Nachw. von Heinz D. Osterle. Erzählwerk in 4 Bänden. 1. Bürger und Soldaten, 360 pp.; 2. Verratenes Volk, 416 pp.; 3. Heimkehr der Fronttruppen, 486 pp.; 4. Karl und Rosa, 700 pp. München: Dt. Taschenbuch Verlag, 1978. [4 vols.] (dtv 1389 [4].] Lizenzausg. d. Walter-Verl., Olten. [Vol. 1 was publ. 1939 by Berman-Fischer, Stockholm and Querido, Amsterdam. Vols. 2–4 between 1948 and 1950, but the work remained unnoticed and is also not contained in the Jubilee Edition, published 1977 for Döblin's 100th birthday, see No. 14575/YB. XXIII. 'Die wiederentdeckte Roman-Chronik eines Augenzeugen, Döblins Panorama der Deutschheit' (Gerhard Schulz) in: 'FAZ', 21. Okt. Frankfurt/M. 1978.]

15465. DÖBLIN, ALFRED: *Der Oberst und der Dichter oder Das menschliche Herz. Die Pilgerin Ätheria*. Zwei Erzählungen. Olten: Walter, 1978. 356 pp. (Ausgewählte Werke in Einzelausgaben). [Not cont. in the Jubilee Ed.]

15466. DÖBLIN, ALFRED: *Pardon wird nicht gegeben.* Roman. Reinbek b. Hamburg: Rowohlt, 1978. 282 pp. (rororo Bd. 4243). [Recounts his youth and the hard times in Berlin].
15467. *Alfred Döblin: 1878–1978.* Eine Ausstellung d. Dt. Literaturarchivs im Schiller Nationalmuseum, Marbach am Neckar vom 10. Juni–31. Dezember. Ausstellung und Katalog: Jochen Meyer in Zusammenarbeit mit Ute Doster. Marbach: Deutsche Schillergesellschaft; München: Kösel (in Kom.), 1978. 540 pp., ports., illus., bibl. (Sonderausstellungen des Schiller-Nationalmuseums, Katalog Nr. 30). [Cf. *Späte Wiedergutmachung* (Otto Keller) in: 'NZZ', FA Nr. 174, 30./31. Juli, Zürich, 1978. *Eine zweite Heimkehr für Alfred Döblin?* (Günther Rühle) in: 'FAZ', 2. Aug., Frankfurt/M., 1978.]
15468. *Alfred Döblin zum 100. Geburtstag:* Der schnoddrige Visionär (Marcel Reich-Ranicki). Laufe, mein Ich oder: Der lange Tag nimmt kein Ende (Wolfgang Koeppen). Weltbewegter Atemstrom (Peter Rühmkorf). Tusch auf dem elektrischen Klavier (Wolfdietrich Schnurre) in: 'FAZ', 5. Aug., Frankfurt/M., 1978, port., biogr. data. *Doeblin Centenary* (Fritz Friedlander) in: 'AJR Information', Aug., London, 1978. [And]: *Auch er trug die Fackel* (Erich Gottgetreu) in: 'MB', Nr. 31, 11. Aug., Tel Aviv, 1978. Pp. 5 & 7. [Also]: *Ich bin am Ziel. An welchem Ziel? Der Widerspruch, das bin ich* (Richard Hey) in: 'Die Zeit', 11. Aug., Hamburg, 1978. Pp. 34–35, port. [A.D., 10. Aug. 1878 Stettin–16. Juni 1957 Emmendingen nr. Freiburg/Br.]
15469. PROSKAUER, PAUL F.: *Alfred Döblin, ein Schicksal unseres Jahrhunderts.* Zur Jubiläumsausgabe der Werke von A. D. [In]: 'Aufbau', July 21, New York, 1978. port. drawing.
15470. RASCH, WOLFDIETRICH: *'Man lernt von mir und wird noch mehr lernen'.* Zur Wirkung Alfred Döblins auf die Literatur nach 1945. [In]: 'FAZ', 12. Aug., Frankfurt/M., 1978.
15471. REICH-RANICKI, MARCEL: *'Heldenvater Doblin'.* [In]: 'FAZ', 20. Aug., Frankfurt/M., 1978, illus. [Döblin's son 'Vincent Doblin', i.e. alias Wolfgang Döblin, born 1915 in Berlin, volunteered for the French army. In order not to be taken prisoner by the Germans he committed suicide in 1940 and is buried in Housseras/Alsace by the graves of his parents.]
15472. REICH-RANICKI, MARCEL: *Die wunderlichen Bewandtnisse mit Döblins Grab und Grabschrift* [In]: 'FAZ', 20. August 1978.
15473. SCHRÖTER, KLAUS: *Alfred Doblin in Selbstzeugnissen und Bilddokumenten.* Dargestellt von... Den Anhang besorgte der Autor unter Mitarbeit von Helmet Riegel. Reinbek: Rowohlt, 1978. 156 pp., ports., illus., bibl. A.D. pp. 145–152. (Rowohlts Monographien, 266).
15474. SERKE, JÜRGEN: *Drei Frauen und nur ein Leben.* Der unbekannte Döblin. [In]: 'Zeit-Magazin'. Nr. 22, 26. Mai. Hamburg, 1978. Pp. 1, 18–28, ports., illus., bibl.
15475. ELIAS, NORBERT: *The Civilizing Process. The History of Manners.* Vol. I. Transl. from the German by Edmund Jephcott. Oxford: Basil Blackwell, 1978. 328 pp. [German orig.: Über den Prozess der Zivilisation. See No. 13026/YB. XXI. Cf. *Western Man and his Manners* (Robert M. Adams) in: 'TLS', Sept. 15, London, 1978.]
15476. *Materialien zu Norbert Elias' Zivilisationstheorie.* Hrsg. von Peter Gleichmann, Johan Goudsblom und Herman Korte. Frankfurt/M.: Suhrkamp Taschenbuch Verlag, 1978. (st wissenschaft, Bd. 233). [N.E. sociologist, born 1897 in Breslau, is the first recipient of the 'Theodor W. Adorno-Preis' of Frankfurt/M.]
15477. ELKAN, BENNO. MENZEL-SEVERING, HANS: *Benno Elkan, 2. 12. 1877 (Dortmund)–10. 1. 1960 (London).* Eine monographische Skizze zum 100. Geburtstag des Dortmunder Künstlers. Dortmund: Stadtbücherei, 1977. 27 pp., ports., fascisms., bibl. B. E. and bibl. pp. 20–22. (Dortmunder Autoren und Künstler. Eine Verzeichnisreihe, Folge 3. Hrsg. von Hedwig Bieber).
15478. EMIN PASCHA. KRAFT, RUDOLF: *Emin Pascha. Ein deutscher Arzt als Gouverneur von Äquatoria.* Darmstadt: Turris Verlag, 1978. 447 pp., port., illus. (Deutsche unter anderen Völkern). [Adventurer, explorer, born 1840 in Oppeln/Upper Silesia as Eduard Schnitzer. He studied medicine and natural science, converted to Islam and was murdered 1892 in the Belgian Congo.]
15479. EINSTEIN, ALBERT. HERNECK, FRIEDRICH: *Einstein privat.* Herta W. erinnert sich an die Jahre 1927 bis 1933. Berlin: Der Morgen, 1978. 169 pp., ports., facsims., plan.
15480. SEELIG, CARL, ed.: *Albert Einstein: Ideas and Opinions.* Based on 'Mein Weltbild' and other sources. New translations and revisions by Sonja Bargmann. New York: Dell, 1978. 366 pp. (Dell, 34150, Laurel Edition). [Cont.: Ideas and Opinions. On Politics. Government and Pacifism. On the Jewish People. On Germany. Contributions to Science.

Material from 'The World as I see it'. 'Out of my later years'. Some texts have not been publ. in book form before.] [A. E. 1879 Ulm–1955 Princeton (USA).]

15481. EINSTEIN, ALFRED: *Mozart. Sein Charakter. Sein Werk.* Frankfurt/M.: Fischer Taschenbuch Verlag, 1978. 475 pp., 99 music samples, Werkverzeichnis W. A. Mozart pp. 447–460. (Fischer Tb. Bd. 2039). [A. E., musicologist, 1880 Munich–1952 El Cerrito (Calif.).]

15482. EISLER, HANNS. *Hanns Eisler – A Rebel in Music.* Selected Writings. Ed. and with Introduction by Manfred Grabs. Transl. by Majorie Meyer. Berlin: Seven Seas Publ., 1978. 223 pp., bibl. (Seven Seas Book).

15483. ROTHSCHILD, THOMAS: *Der Pomp hielt sich in Grenzen.* 'Mit fortschrittlichem Bewusstsein ist dem Komponisten noch nicht geholfen'. Ost-Berlin feiert den 80. Geburtstag von Hanns Eisler, dem Komponisten der DDR-Nationalhymne. [In]: 'Die Zeit', 7. Juli, Hamburg, 1978, port. [Born 1898 in Leipzig, H.E. died 1962 in East Berlin. For the monography 'H.E.' by Albrecht Betz see No. 13797/YB. XXII.]

15484. SCHEBERA, JÜRGEN: *Hanns Eisler im USA-Exil 1938–1948.* Zu den politischen, ästhetischen und kompositorischen Positionen des Komponisten 1938 bis 1948. Meisenheim: Anton Hain, Berlin [East]: Akademie Verlag, 1978. 234 pp., bibl. H. E. u. bibl. pp. 224–229. (Literatur und Gesellschaft).

15485. FEUCHTWANGER, LION: *Jew Süss.* A Historical Romance. Transl. from German by Willa and Edwin Muir. London: Henry Pordes, 1977. 424 pp. [First publ. in German 1925, see No. 13803/YB. XXII.]

15486. BRÜCKNER, EGON/KLAUS MODICK: *Lion Feuchtwangers Roman 'Erfolg'.* Leistung und Problematik schriftstellerischer Aufklärung in der Endphase der Weimarer Republik. Kronberg/Ts.: Scriptor, 1978. 202 pp., bibl. (pp. 196–202). (Monographien: Literaturwiss. Bd. 42). ['Erfolg' was first published in 1930. See No. 13027/YB XXI.]

15487. PETUCHOWSKI, ELIZABETH M.: *Some Aspects of the Judaic Element in the Work of Lion Feuchtwanger.* [In]: LBI Year Book XXIII. London, 1978. Pp. 213–226, port. [See No. 15111.]

15488. RADDATZ, FRITZ J.: *Weihnachten gingen wir zu Brecht.* Am 21. Dez. 1958 starb der Schriftsteller Lion Feuchtwanger im katholischen Exil. [And]: *An den Bewohner meines Hauses in Berlin* (Lion Feuchtwanger) [In]: 'Die Zeit', Nr. 52, 22. Dez., Hamburg, 1978. Pp. 37–38, ports., illus., facsim. [After having had to flee from his houses in Berlin-Grunewald (1933 confiscated by the Nazis), and the South of France (1940), L. F. built a third one near Los Angeles, Calif. (in 1941), where he kept his private library of appr. 40,000 books, and which, donated, and financed by his widow Martha, will be an American Research Centre for German Exile Literature.]

15489. FRANKL, VIKTOR E.: *Das Leiden am sinnlosen Leben.* Psychotherapie für heute. In Memoriam Leo Baeck. Freiburg i. Br.: Herder, 1977. (Bd. 615). [Prof. Frankl is the founder of the '3. Wiener Schule für Psychotherapie' and recipient of the Karl-Innitzer-Preis for his outstanding scientific life work.]

15490. FREUD, SIGMUND: *Werkausgabe in zwei Bänden.* Hrsg. u. mit Kommentaren versehen von Anna Freud und Ilse Grubrich-Simitis. Bd. 1: Elemente der Psychoanalyse. Bd. 2: Anwendungen der Psychoanalyse. Frankfurt/M.: Fischer, 1978. 590, 616 pp., 3 ports., bibls. [2 vols.]

15491. DECKER, HANNAH S.: *Freud in Germany.* Revolution and Reaction in Science, 1893–1907. New York: International Universities Press, 1977. xi, 360 pp., 19 ports., bibl. (pp. 331–346). (Psychological issues, monograph 41).

15492. GÖRLICH, BERNARD, ed.: *Der Stachel Freud.* Eine Kontroverse zwischen Otto Fenichel, Erich Fromm und Herbert Marcuse. Mit Nachträgen von Alfred Lorenzer und Alfred Schmit. Frankfurt/M.: Suhrkamp, 1978.

15493. ROAZEN, PAUL: *La Pensée Politique et Sociale de Freud.* Paris: Presses Universitaires de France, 1976. 231 pp. (Collection 'Textes'). [For the English ed.: Political and Social Thought see No. 6562/YB. XIII and for the German transl. No. 9750/YB. XVII.]

15494. SIMON, ERNST: *Sigmund Freud el Judío.* Transl. from Hebrew by Jehoschua Faigon. Buenos Aires: Congresso Judío Mundial, 1977. 48 pp., ports. (Grandes Figuras del Judaísmo). [The Hebrew original was publ. by the Hebrew University, Jerusalem, in a vol. 'Azereth Freud', 1956. Pp. 70–111. Transl. into English by Aubrey Hodos 'Sigmund Freud, the Jew' in: LBI Year Book II, 1957. Pp. 270–305.]

15495. *A Visit to Dr. Freud.* A collection of photographs and a personal memoir by Edmund

Engelman. [In]: 'Observer Magazine', Oct. 8, London, 1978. Pp. 34–39 & 72, ports., illus. [Photographs of Freud's home secretly taken in 1938 before he was forced to flee. 'Berggasse 19' is publ. in New York: Basic Books, 1978 (distributed in the U.K. by Harper & Row). German ed. see No. 14600/YB. XXIII.]
15496. ZWEIG, STEFAN: *Freud*. Paris: Stock et Plus, 1978. [La brève étude date de 1931.]
15497. FREUNDLICH, OTTO. BAUERMEISTER, VOLKER: *Ausstellung in Bonn: Otto Freundlich*. Abstraktion als Befreiung [In]: 'Die Zeit', 19. Jan., Hamburg, 1979, illus. [And]: In der Malerei wird die Materie zum Geist. Otto Freundlich aus Anlass seiner Wanderausstellung (Edith Hoffmann) in: 'NZZ', 15/16. Okt. Zürich, 1978. Eine Ausstellung im Israel-Museum in Jerusalem. [In]: 'MB', 20. Okt., Tel Aviv, 1978. [O.F., painter and sculptor, born 1878 in Stolp/Pommern, deported March 1943.]
15498. FRIEDELL, EGON. DENCKER, KLAUS PETER: *Der junge Friedell*. Dokumente der Ausbildung zum genialen Dilettanten. München: Beck, 1978. 69 pp., ports., illus. (Egon Friedell zum 100. Geburtstag.)
15499. OBERMAIER, WALTER: *Egon Friedell zum 100. Geburtstag*. Ausstellung Rathaus. Jan.–März 1978. Katalog, Gestaltung und Text: Walter Obermaier. Wien: Stadt- und Landesbibliothek, 1978. 16 pp. [And]: *Egon Friedell, der gläubige Freigeist*. Zur hundertsten Wiederkehr seines Geburtstags (Hilde Spiel) [In]: 'FAZ', 21. Jan., Frankfurt/M., 1978. [E. F. 21. Jan. 1878 Wien–16. März 1938 Wien (suicide).]
15500. FROMM, ERICH: *Psychoanalyse und Ethik*. Ungek. Ausg. Berlin: Ullstein, 1978. 272 pp. (Ullstein-Buch Nr. 3507).
15501. FROMM, ERICH: *Psychoanalyse und Religion*. München: Goldmann, 1978. (Goldmann Sachbuch Bd. 11211).
15502. PIEL, EDGAR: *Im Teufelskreis von Haben und Sein*. [In]: 'Merkur'. 32. Jg., H. 6 (261), Juni. Stuttgart: Klett-Cotta, 1978. Pp. 619–622. [E.F.: Haben oder Sein/To Have or to Be see No. 13829/YB. XXII.]
15503. REIF, ADELBERT, ed.: *Erich Fromm: Materialien zu seinem Werk*. Wien: Europaverlag, 1978. 336 pp. (Paperback). [17 contributions considering the works: The Anatomy of Human Destructiveness (1973, No. 11515/YB. XIX) and 'To Have or to Be' (1976, 13829/YB. XXII.] [E. F., born 1900 in Frankfurt/M.]
15504. FROMM-REICHMANN, FRIEDA: *Psychoanalyse und Psychotherapie*. Eine Auswahl aus ihren Schriften. Hrsg. von Dexter M. Bullard. Vorw. von Edith V. Weigert. 1. Aufl. Stuttgart: Klett-Cotta, 1978. 432 pp. (Konzepte der Humanwissenschaften).
15505. FÜRNBERG, LOUIS. POSCHMANN, HENRI: *Louis Fürnberg: Leben und Werk*. 2., bearb. Aufl. Berlin [East]: Volk und Wissen, 1977. 183 pp., port., illus., bibl. L. F. p. 183. (Schriftsteller der Gegenwart, 21). [L. F., 1909–1957].
15506. GOLL, CLÄRE: *Gedichte. 1924–1950*. München: Dt. Taschenbuch Verlag, 1977. (Sonderreihe dtv Bd. 5437).
15507. GOLL, CLÄRE: *Memoiren eines Spatzes des Jahrhunderts*. Erzählungen und Lyrik. München: Langen Müller, 1978. 364 pp. [C.G. 1901 Nuremberg–1977 Paris].
15508. GOLL, YVAN. BERG, PHYLLIS: *Jüdische Themen und das Hiob Schicksal im Werke Yvan Golls*. Diss. . . . University of Cincinnati, Ohio, 1976. 331 pp. Microfilm copy of typescript, Ann Arbor, Mich., University Microfilms, 1977.
15509. GOMBRICH, ERNST H.: *Kunst und Fortschritt–Wirkung und Wandlung einer Idee*. Köln: DuMont, 1978. 136 pp., 62 illus., bibl. E.H.G. (DuMont Taschenbücher, Bd. 70).
15510. GOMBRICH, ERNST H.: *Kunst und Illusion – Zur Psychologie der bildlichen Darstellung*. Aus dem Engl. von Lisbeth Gombrich. Stuttgart: Belser, 1978. 504 pp., 319 illus. (Eine Studie über die Psychologie von Abbild und Wirklichkeit in der Kunst). [Engl. title: Art and Illusion]. [Sir Ernst H[ans] Gombrich, art historian, born 1909 in Vienna.]
15511. HACHENBURG, MAX: *Lebenserinnerungen eines Rechtsanwalts und Briefe aus der Emigration*. Hrsg. und bearb. von Jörg Schadt. Stuttgart: Kohlhammer, 1978. 260 pp., ports., illus., facsims., gen. table, list of names. (Veröffentlichungen des Stadtarchivs Mannheim, Bd. 5). [Briefe aus der Emigration 1946–1951. Max Hachenburgs Beitrag zum deutschen Rechtsleben.] [M.H., 1860 Mannheim–1951 Berkeley, USA.]
15512. HASENCLEVER, WALTER: *Irrtum und Leidenschaft – Erziehung durch Frauen*. Ein Bekenntnisroman. Mit einem Nachwort als Einführung hrsg. von Kurt Pinthus. Erstmals mit dokumentarischem Bildteil. München: Herbig, 1977. 338 pp., ports., illus. (Lizenz d. Universitas-Verl. Berlin). [First publ. 1969, written between 1934 and

1940 in exile. W.H., 1890 Aachen–1940 committed suicide in Aix-en-Provence concentration camp.]
15513. HEARTFIELD, JOHN. SIEPMANN, ECKHARD, ed.: *Montage John Heartfield*. Vom Club Dadda zur Arbeiter-Illustrierten Zeitung. Dokumente, Analysen, Berichte. Im Zusammenhang mit der Wanderausstellung und dem Film 'John Heartfield, Fotomonteur' hrsg. von der Elefanten-Press-Galerie. Montiert von Jürgen Holtfreter. 3., verb. Aufl. Berlin-West: Elefanten-Press-Galerie, Frankfurt/M.: Zweitausendeins (Vertrieb), 1977. 299 pp., ports., illus., facsims., bibl. J.H. and bibl. pp. 291–297. [J.H., orig. Helmut Herzfelde, 1891–1968 Berlin East, pioneer of photo-montage, publicist, writer and initiator of the Malik Verlag in Berlin.]
15514. HEIMANN, EDUARD. HEYDER, ULRICH: *Der sozialwissenschaftliche Systemversuch Eduard Heimanns*. Darstellung und Kritik der Möglichkeit einer einheitlichen Theorie der modernen Wirtschafts- und Sozialsysteme. Frankfurt/M., Bern: Lang, 1977. 297 pp. (Beiträge zur Politikwissenschaft, Bd. 7). Zugl. Wirtschaftswiss. Diss., Univ. Hamburg, 1975. [E. H., economist, 1889–1967].
15515. HEINE, HEINRICH: *Buch der Lieder*. Nach dem Text der Ausgaben letzter Hand. Mit einer Einführung von Werner Vordtriede in das Gesamtwerk Heines. Zürich: Artemis & Winkler, 1978. 492 pp.
15516. HEINE, HEINRICH: *Der Rabbi von Bacherach*. Ein Fragment. Mit 11 Faksimiles nach Farblithographien von El Lissitzky zum 'Chad Gadya' (Lied vom Zicklein). Hrsg. von Hans Marquardt. Berlin [East]: Der Morgen, 1978. 69 pp., illus.
15517. HEINE, HEINRICH: *Shakespeares Mädchen und Frauen*. Mit Illustrationen der Ausgabe von 1838. Hrsg. von Volkmar Hansen. Frankfurt/M.: Insel, 1978. 242 pp., illus. (insel taschenbuch Bd. 331).
15518. HEINE, HEINRICH: *Werke in einem Band*. Ausgew. u. eingel. von Walther Vontin. 9. Aufl. Hamburg: Hoffmann und Campe, 1978. 787 pp. (Campe-Klassiker).
15519. HEINE, HEINRICH: *Werke in zwei Bänden*. Hrsg. u. kommentiert von Stuart Atkins und (bei Band II) von Oliver Boeck. Bd. I: 1973, vi, 973 pp. Bd. II: 1978, viii, 1296 pp. München: Beck, 1973/1978. [2 vols.] (Beck's kommentierte Klassiker).
15520. BARKAI, JEHOSCHUA: *Heinrich Heine und das Judentum*. Vortrag am 27. Dez. 1976 vor der David-Yellin-Loge in Jerusalem. Jerusalem: Schriftenreihe der David-Yellin-Loge, 1977.
15521. BEIN, ALEX: *Heinrich Heine, der 'Schamlose'*. [In]: Heine-Jahrbuch 1978. Pp. 152–174, bibl. notes. [See No. 15522.] (Die überarbeitete Fassung eines Exkurses aus dem Buch des Verfassers 'Die Judenfrage. Biographie eines Weltproblems', das 1979 bei der Dt. Verlags-Anstalt, Stuttgart, erscheinen wird.]
15522. *Heine-Jahrbuch 1978*. 17. Jg. Hrsg. von Joseph A. Kruse, Heinrich-Heine-Institut der Landeshauptstadt Düsseldorf. Hamburg: Hoffmann und Campe, 1978. 330 pp., ports., illus., facsims., Heine-Literatur mit Nachträgen 1976/77 comp. by Heinfried Heitmann, pp. 298–313. (Heine-Jahrbuch, begründet von Eberhard Galley. Hrsg. in Verbindung mit der H.-H.-Gesellschaft). [Incl. Die Bedeutung von Goethes Pantheismus und seiner satirischen Brechung für Heines Demokratiebegriff (Sara Ann Malsch). Views on Heine in Russia in the Beginning of the 20th Century (Clara Hollosi). Nachruf auf Fritz H. Eisner (Eberhard Galley). See also No. 15521.]
15523. HEINEGG, PETER: *Heine's Conversion and the Critics*. [In]: 'German Life and Letters'. New Series. Vol. 30, No. 1. Oxford, 1976. Pp. 45–51.
15524. JACOBI, RUTH L[ISBAND]: *Heinrich Heines jüdisches Erbe*. Bonn: Bouvier, 1978. viii, 184 pp., bibl. (pp. 178–184). (Abhandlungen zur Kunst-, Musik- und Literaturwissenschaft, Bd. 243).
15525. KUTTENKEULER WOLFGANG, ed.: *Heinrich Heine. Artistik und Engagement* Stuttgart: Metzler, 1977. X. 332 pp. [See No. 15232.
15526. PETERS, ECKEHARD/EBERHARD KIRSCH: *Religionskritik bei Heinrich Heine*. Leipzig: Sankt-Benno-Verlag, 1976. 140 pp., bibl. (pp. 135–139). (Erfurter theologische Schriften, 13). [Cont.: Religionskritik bei H. H. (E. Peters). Die Religionskritik in den philosophischen Schriften H. Heines (E. Kirsch).]
15527. ROSE, MARGARET A.: *Die Parodie*. Eine Funktion der biblischen Sprache in Heines Lyrik. Meisenheim am Glan: Hain, 1976. 138 pp. (Deutsche Studien, 27). [English orig. title: The Functions of Biblical Language in the Poetry of H.H.]
15528. ROSENTHAL, LUDWIG (Guatemala): *Heinrich Heines Grossoheim Simon von Geldern*. Ein historischer Bericht mit bisher meist unveröffentlichtem Quellenmaterial. Kastellaun:

Aloys Henn, 1978. 210 pp. (Veröffentlichungen des H.-H.-Instituts Düsseldorf, hrsg. von Joseph A. Kruse).

15529. HEINE, THOMAS THEODOR: *Die Märchen.* Fotomechan. Nachdr. d. Ausg. Amsterdam, Querido, 1935. Berlin [East]: Aufbau, 1978. 64 pp., illus.

15530. ALLEN TAYLOR, ANN: *Sex and Satire in Wilhelmine Germany: 'Simplicissimus' looks at Family Life.* [In]: 'Journal of European Studies'. Vol. 7, Part 1, No. 25, March. Chalfont St. Giles, Bucks.: Alpha Academic, 1977. Pp. 19–40 + cartoons by Th.Th. Heine, bibl. (pp. 37–40). (Science History Publications). [Th.Th. Heine (1867 Leipzig–1948 Stockholm) was, in 1896, a co-founder of the 'Simplicissimus' and until 1933 its chief cartoonist and satirical caricaturist.]

15531. HERMLIN, STEPHAN. ERTL, WOLFGANG: *Stephan Hermlin und die Tradition.* Bern, Frankfurt: Lang, 1977. 151 pp. (Europ. Hochschulschriften, Reihe 1, Dt. Literatur u. Germanistik, Bd. 206). [Stephan Hermlin, orig. Rudolf Leder, born 1915 in Chemnitz, lives in the GDR.]

15532. HERZ, HENRIETTE. FÜRST, J[ULIUS], ed.: *Henriette Herz, ihr Leben und ihre Erinnerungen.* Fotomechan. Neudruck d. Orig.-Ausg. 1850. Leipzig: Zentralantiquariat d. Dt. Demokratischen Republik, 1977. 248 pp., port. [Berlin Hostess, 1764 Berlin–1847 Berlin.]

15533. HEYM, STEFAN: *Erich Huckniessel und das fortgesetzte Rotkäppchen.* Märchen für kluge Kinder. Mit Linoschnitten von Erich Schönig und Wolfgang Jörg. Berlin: Berliner Handpresse, 1977. 34 pp., illus. (Berliner Handpresse, Druck 48). [Born 1913 in Chemnitz, St. H. returned 1953 from American exile to the GDR.]

15534. HILLER, KURT. WURGRAFT, LEWIS D.: *The Activists.* Kurt Hiller and the Politics of Action on the German Left 1914–1933. Philadelphia: American Philosophical Society, 1977. 114 pp. (Transactions of the American Philosophical Society, No. 67, part 8). [K.H., publicist, 1885 Berlin–1972 Hamburg.]

15535. HIRSCH, BARON ROBERT VON. HODGART, SUZANNE: *The Sale of the Century.* A Profile of Baron Robert von Hirsch and the Auction in London at Sotheby's of his Art Collection. [In]: 'The Sunday Times Magazine', June 18, London, 1978. Pp. 19–25, port., illus. [Robert v. Hirsch, born 1883 in Frankfurt/M., was, in 1913, awarded by the Grand Duke of Hesse the title of baron for his achievements in the Offenbach leather industry. When only 20 he started his art collection which he took with him to Basle in Jan. 1933, where he died in 1977. The auction, expected to fetch 7 million, in fact raised over 18 Million Pounds.]

15536. HIRSCHBERG, JULIUS: *Geschichte der Augenheilkunde.* Nachdr. mit e. Nachw. von Heinrich Schipperges. Hildesheim–New York: Olms, 1977. 7 vols. [J.H., 1843 Potsdam–1925 Berlin, publ. his main work between 1877 and 1919.]

15537. HORKHEIMER, MAX. LIENERT, FRANZ: *Theorie und Tradition.* Zum Menschenbild im Werke Max Horkheimers. Bern, Frankfurt/M.: Lang, 1977. 141 pp., bibl. (pp. 135–141). (Basler u. Berner Studien zur historischen und systematischen Theologie, Bd. 27).

15538. ISOLANI, GERTRUD: *Ich lege keinen Wert auf posthume Ehrungen.* Interview Ronald Goldberger mit der Schriftstellerin Gertrud Isolani. [In]: 'Jüdische Rundschau Maccabi'. Nr. 32, 11. Aug., Basel, 1977, port.

15539. ISOLANI, GERTRUD: *Schwiegermütter! Schwiegermütter!* Eine psychologische, kulturhistorische, soziologische und humoristische Studie. Liebevoll boshaft illustriert von Jüsp (pseud). Basel: Gissler, 1975. 92 pp., illus. [Pp. 60–75: Naemi, die klassische Schwiegermutter der Bibel].

15540. JESSNER, LEOPOLD. PERRY, ALFRED: *Die glücklosen Jahre eines grossen Regisseurs.* Der doppelte Sturz und der Traum vom neuen Anfang. Erinnerung an Leopold Jessner zum 100. Geburtstag. [In]: 'FAZ', 6. April. Frankfurt/M., 1978, port. [Author was a close friend of L.J.]

15541. SEELMANN-EGGEBERT, ULRICH: *Leopold Jessners unbekannte Jahre.* Die frühe Zeit in Konigsberg und die späte Zeit in Tel Aviv. [In]: 'NZZ', FA Nr. 249, 27. Okt. Zürich, 1978. Pp. 39–40, port. [Born 1878 in Königsberg, L.J. emigrated to London in 1933, to Palestine in 1936, where he worked with Habima, to USA in October 1937. He died on Dec. 13, 1945 in Los Angeles.]

15542. KAFKA, FRANZ: *Ein Bericht für eine Akademie.* Mit 7 Holzschnitten von Hans Fronius. Wien, Zürich: Molden, 1977. 31 pp., illus.

15543. CAPUTO-MAYS, MARIA LUISE, ed.: *Franz Kafka.* Eine Aufsatzsammlung nach einem

Symposium in Philadelphia. Hrsg. u. eingel. von . . . Editorielle Assistenz: William W. Langebartel. Darmstadt: Agora, 1978. xvi, 245 pp. (Schriftenreihe Agora, Bd. 29). [17 contributions.]

15544. EGGER, CHRISTOPH: *Herr K. und die Liebe zur Aeronautik*. Kleists und Kafkas Interesse am Fliegen. [In]: 'NZZ', FA Nr. 142, 23. Juni, Zürich, 1978. illus. [See No. 15389, also No. 14667/YB. XXIII.]

15545. FLORES, ANGEL, comp.: *A Kafka Bibliography, 1908–1976*. New York: Gordian Press, 1976. 193 pp. [See also No. 14670/YB. XXIII: The Kafka Debate by same author.]

15546. KELLER, KARIN: *Gesellschaft in mythischem Bann*. Studien zum Roman 'Das Schloss' und anderen Werken Franz Kafkas. Wiesbaden: Athenaion, 1977. 273 pp., bibl. (pp. 271–273). (Athenaion-Literaturwiss., Bd. 7). Zugl. Germanist. Diss., F.U. Berlin, 1976.

15547. MENSE, JOSEF HERMANN: *Die Bedeutung des Todes im Werk Franz Kafkas*. Frankfurt/M., Bern: Lang, 1978. 278 pp. (Kasseler Arbeiten zur Sprache und Literatur, Bd. 4).

15548. MILFULL, HELEN: *Franz Kafka – The Jewish Context*. [In]: LBI Year Book XXIII London, 1978. Pp. 227–238. [See No. 15111.]

15549. NAGEL, BERT: *Kafka und Goethe*. Stufen der Wandlung von der Klassik zur Moderne. Berlin: Erich Schmidt, 1978. 306 pp.

15550. NICOLAI, RALF R.: *Ende oder Anfang*. Zur Einheit der Gegensätze in Kafkas 'Schloss'. München: Fink, 1977. 205 pp.

15551. POLITZER, HEINZ: *Franz Kafka, der Künstler*. Neuausgabe. Frankfurt/M.: Suhrkamp, 1978. 583 pp. (sk tb., Bd. 433).

15552. POLITZER, HEINZ: *In einen geschlossenen Mund kommt keine Fliege*. Franz Kafka und die Wissenschaft. Zu fünf Neuerscheinungen. [Review article in]: 'FAZ', 8. Juli, Frankfurt/M., 1978. [See Nos. 15543, 15549, 15550, 15554, 15555.]

15553. RIES, WIEBRECHT: *Transzendenz als Terror*. Eine religionsphilosophische Studie über Franz Kafka. Heidelberg: Schneider, 1977. 159 pp., bibl. (pp. 149–152). (Phronesis, Bd. 4).

15554. SIEFKEN, HINRICH: *Kafka: Ungeduld und Lässigkeit*. Zu den Romanen 'Der Prozess' und 'Das Schloss'. München: Fink, 1977. 118 pp., bibl. (pp. 112–114). [See No. 15552.]

15555. STEINMETZ, HORST: *Suspensive Interpretation*. Am Beispiel Franz Kafka. Göttingen: Vandenhoeck & Ruprecht, 1977. 153 pp. [See No. 15552.]

15556. URZIDIL, GERTRUDE: *Notes on Kafka*. Pp. 11–16, ports. [In]: Franz Kafka. His Place in World Literature. [See No. 9812/YB. XVII.] [G. Urzidil née Thieberger, died June 1977 in New York.]

15557. KALÉKO, MASCHA: *In meinen Träumen läutet es Sturm*. Gedichte und Epigramme aus dem Nachlass. Hrsg. u. eingel. von Gisela Zoch-Westphal. München: Dt. Taschenbuch Verlag, 1977. 159 pp. (dtv Bd. 1294).

15558. KALÉKO, MASCHA: *Verse für Zeitgenossen*. Hrsg. u. mit einem Nachw. vers. von Gisela Zoch-Westphal. Düsseldorf: Eremiten-Presse, 1978. 76 pp. (Broschur, 81). (Neudr. d. amerik. Erstausgabe von 1945). [Reviewed by Alfred Frankenstein [in]: 'Das Neue Israel', H. 2, Aug. Zürich, 1978 and in: 'Allgemeine', 3. Nov., Düsseldorf, 1978.] Born 1912 M.K. died 1975 in Zurich.]

15559. KAYSER, RUDOLF: *The Saints of Qumrân*. Stories and Essays on Jewish Themes. Ed. Harry Zohn. Transl. by Tali Perlman, Heni Wenkart, Harry Zohn. Cranbury, N.J./London: Associated University Press, 1977. 198 pp., ports. [Die Heiligen von Qumrân was written in 1963. – R.K., essayist, biographer, philosopher (1889 Parchim/Mecklenburg – 1964 New York) was from 1923–1933 editor of 'Die Neue Rundschau'. Corrected entry No. 14677/YB. XXIII.]

15560. KERR, ALFRED: *Sätze meines Lebens*. Über Reisen, Kunst und Politik. Hrsg. von Helga Bemmann. Berlin [East]: Buchverlag Der Morgen, 1978. 639 pp., ports., illus., facsims., bibl. (pp. 638–639). [Incl.: Alfred Kerr, Dichter und Demokrat (H. Bemmann), pp. 612–631.]

15561. KESTEN, HERMANN. WINKLER, ANDREAS: *Hermann Kesten im Exil (1933–1940)*. Sein politisches und künstlerisches Selbstverständnis und seine Tätigkeit als Lektor in der deutschen Abteilung des A. de Lange Verlages. Mit e. Anhang unveröffentl. Verlagskorrespondenz von und an H. Kesten. Hamburg: Lüdke, 1978. iii, 304 pp. Zugl. Diss., Univ. Hamburg, 1977.

15562. KISCH, EGON ERWIN: *Reportagen*. Auswahl u. Nachw. von Erhard Schütz. Stutt-

gart: Reclam, 1978. 326 pp. (Univ.-Bibliothek Nr. 9893[4]. Lizenz d. Aufbau Verl., Berlin East.
15563. *Erinnerungen an Egon Erwin Kisch.* Das war der 'Rasende Reporter' (Leo Brod) in: 'Aufbau', Sept. 30, New York, 1978. Nach seinem Tode siegte die Partei. Zum 30. Todestag von E. E. Kisch (Meir Faerber) in: 'Isr. Wochenblatt', Nr. 8, 24. Febr., Zürich, 1978, port. [And in]: 'Allgemeine', 31. März, Düsseldorf, 1978. Der 'rasende Reporter' und die Macht der Experten (Ulrich Greiner) in: 'FAZ', 7. Nov., Frankfurt/ M., 1977. [E.E.K. 1885 Prag–1948 Prag.]
15564. KISCH, GUIDO: *Immanuel Kant im Medaillenbild.* Sigmaringen: Thorbecke, 1977. 28 pp. mit 28 illus., bibl. (G.K. 1889 Prag.]
15565. KOESTLER, ARTHUR: *Janus.* A Summing Up. New York: Random House, London: Hutchinson, 1978. 354 pp. [Cf. Irrational Man (Jeffrey Marsh) in: 'Commentary', Vol. 66, No. 5, Nov., New York: American Jewish Committee, 1978. Pp. 78–80].
15566. KOESTLER, ARTHUR: *Sonnenfinsternis.* Roman. Einzig autoris. Übertr. aus dem Engl. Wien: Europaverlag, 1978. 313 pp. [Engl. original: Darkness at Noon.]
15567. KOESTLER, ARTHUR: *La Treizième Tribu.* L'empire khazar et son héritage. Tr. de l'anglais par Georges Fradier. Paris: Calmann-Lévy, 1976. 300 pp., front. map, bibl. (pp. 284–289). [For Engl. original and German transl. see No. 14682/YB. XXIII.]
15568. KOLMAR, GERTRUD: *Eine jüdische Mutter.* Nachbemerkung von Friedhelm Kemp. 2. Aufl. München: Kösel, 1978. 247 pp. [1. Aufl. 1965 u.d. T. Eine Mutter. Prosawerk aus dem Nachlass veröffentlicht. See No. 5359/YB. XI.
15569. KOLMAR, GERTRUD: *Das Wort der Stummen.* Ein Gedichtzyklus. Berlin [East]: Buchverlag Der Morgen, 1978. 53 pp.
15570. LANGER, LAWRENCE L.: *Survival Through Art.* The Career of Gertrud Kolmar. [In]: LBI Year Book XXIII. London, 1978. Pp. 247–258. [Gertrud Kolmar, i.e. Gertrud Chodziesner, 1894 Berlin–1943 Auschwitz.] [See No. 15111.]
15571. KRAFT, WERNER: *Das sterbende Gedicht, 1972–1975.* Frankfurt/M.: Corvus, 1976. 40 pp. (Colloquium poeticum, Bd. 4). [Poems with Jewish motifs.]
15572. *'Ich bin an meinen Punkt gebannt'.* Werner Kraft im Gespräch mit Jörg Drews. München: edition text + kritik, 1978. 32 pp., bibl. W.K. [Writer, essayist, born 1896 in Brunswick, has lived in Jerusalem since 1934.]
15573. KRAUS, KARL: *Half-Truths and One-and-a-half Truths.* Selected Aphorisms by Karl Kraus. Ed. and Transl. by Harry Zohn. Montreal: Engendra Press, 1976. [Corrected entry No. 14692/YB. XXIII.]
15574. *Kraus-Hefte.* Hrsg. von Sigurd Paul Scheichl und Christian Wagenknecht. H. 1: 1933–1936. Januar. H. 2, April. München: edition text + kritik, 1977. 16 pp., 16 pp. [H. 1 cont.: 'Man frage nicht' (K. Kraus). Ein Brief aus Prag (K. Kraus). Nachträgliches zur 'Fackel' (Ch. Wagenknecht). Karl Kraus und der Prager 'Sozialdemokrat' (J. W. Bruegel). 'Ad Spectatores'. Zu 'Wichtiges von Wichten' (S. P. Scheichl). Kommentierte Auswahlbibliographie K.K. (S. P. Scheichl). H. 2 incl.: Information on 'Kultur und Presse', a book by K.K. that was never publ. Contributions by Friedrich Torberg, J. J. Braakenburg, J. W. Bruegel, Hans Eberhard Goldschmidt, Sophie Schick.]
15575. KREISKY, BRUNO: *Die Zeit, in der wir leben.* Betrachtungen zur internationalen Politik. Hrsg. von Manuel Luchert. Wien: Molden, 1978. 207 pp. [Cf. Kreisky's persönliches Credo zu seiner umstrittenen Stellungnahme zum Judentum (R. Astor) in: 'Das Neue Israel', 31. Jg., H. 6, Dez. Zürich, 1978.]
15576. AMERONGEN, MARTIN VAN: *Kreisky und seine unbewältigte Gegenwart.* Aus dem Hollandischen übers. von Gerhard Hartmann. Graz/Wien: Styria, 1977. 128 pp., notes pp. 123–127.
15577. KUCZINSKI, JÜRGEN: *Studien zu einer Geschichte der Gesellschaftswissenschaften.* Bd. 8: Zur Geschichte der Wirtschaftsgeschichtsschreibung. Bd. 9: Theodor Mommsen, Porträt eines Gesellschaftswissenschaftlers. Mit e. Kap. über Mommsen, d. Juristen von Hermann Klenner. Berlin [East]: Akademie Verlag, 1978. 230, 277 pp. [For vols. 1–7 see No. 14694/YB. XXIII.]
15578. LANDAUER, GUSTAV: *Rechenschaft.* Aufsätze aus der Zeitschrift 'Der Sozialist'. (Sammlung). Bremen: Verlag Impuls, 1977. 205 pp. [Landauer was the editor of 'Der Sozialist'.]
15579. LANDAUER, GUSTAV: *Der Todesprediger.* Roman. Münster: Verlag Büchse der Pandora, 1978. 126 pp. [G.L. 1870 Karlsruhe – 1919 murdered in Munich.]

15580. LANDMANN, MICHAEL: *Entfremdete Vernunft.* [And]: *Anklage gegen die Vernunft.* Stuttgart: Klett, 1976. 235 pp., 1977, 230pp. [2 vols.] (Edition Alpha).
15581. LANDMANN, MICHAEL: *Neugestaltung der hebräischen Schrift.* Mit e. Vorwort von James W. Marchand. Bonn: Bouvier, 1977. iv, 222 pp. [Prof. Landmann, born 1913 in Basle.]
15582. LASSALLE, FERDINAND. BECKER, BERNHARD: *Geschichte der Arbeiter–Agitation Ferdinand Lassalles.* Nach authentischen Aktenstücken. Nachdr. d. Ausg. Braunschweig, Bracke, 1874. Neudruck mit einer Einl. von Toni Offermann. Berlin, Bonn: Dietz, 1978. vii, 312 pp. (Reprints zur Sozialgeschichte). [B. Becker (1826–1882), Nachf. Lassalles als Präsident des von L. begründeten Allgemeinen Deutschen Arbeitervereins. F.L., 1825 Breslau–1864 Genf.]
15583. LESSMAN, DANIEL. KAHN, LOTHAR: *Daniel Lessman.* [In]: LBI Year Book XXIII. London, 1978. Pp. 201–212. [See No. 15111.] [D.L., orig. Daniel Lewin Philipp, poet and non-practising physician, born 1798 in Soldin nr. Frankfurt/Oder, committed suicide in 1831. See also No. 10752/YB. XVIII.]
15584. LEVISON, WILHELM. HÜBINGER, PAUL EGON: *Wilhelm Levison (1876–1947).* [In]: Rheinische Lebensbilder, Bd. 7. Köln: Rheinland Verlag, 1977. Pp. 227–251, bibl. [W.L. medievalist, historian. See also No. 14711/YB. XXIII.]
15585. LEWIN, LUDWIG. *Ludwig Lewin und die Lessing-Hochschule.* Festschrift zum zehnjährigen Bestehen nach der Neugründung im Jahre 1965. Berlin: Lessing Hochschule, 1975. 47 pp., port., illus. [The Hochschule, founded in 1899, closed down in 1945. Dr. phil. Ludwig Lewin (1887–1967 Berlin) was its director until his emigration in 1933. After his return from America in 1964 he became its director again. For his 'Zur Geschichte der L.-H., Berlin 1914–1933' see No. 4126/YB. IX.]
15586. LIEBERMANN, MAX. ACHENBACH, SIGRID: *Die Druckgraphik Max Liebermanns.* Diss., Univ. Heidelberg, 1974. 318 pp., bibl. (pp. 167–176). [Cont. L. als Graphiker. Die stilistische Entwicklung der Graphik L's. Das Spätwerk seit 1914. Die Illustrationen.] [M.L. Berlin 1847–1935.]
15587. LIEPMANN, MORITZ: *Die Todesstrafe.* Ein Gutachten. Nachdr. Berlin–New York: De Gruyter, 1978. 220 pp. [M.L., 1869–1928 Hamburg, expert on penal law and noted opponent of the death penalty, publ. this work in 1912.]
15588. LÖWENTHAL, RICHARD. HORN, HANNELORE, ed.: *Sozialismus in Theorie und Praxis.* Festschrift für Richard Löwenthal zum 70. Geburtstag am 15. April 1978. Berlin, New York: De Gruyter, 1978. vii, 687 pp., port., bibl. R.L. pp. 667–683. [Contributions in German, English, French.]
15589. LUKÁCS, GEORG: *Politische Aufsätze.* Hrsg. von Jörg Kammler und Frank Benseler. Aus d. Ungar. übers. von Janos Györkös [et al]. Bd. III: 1921–1924: Organisation und Illusion. Bd. V: 1925–1929: Demokratische Diktatur. Neuwied: Luchterhand, 1977. 2 vols. (SL Bd. 209, 221). [For vols. I and II see No. 13919/YB. XXII.]
15590. SCHMITT, HANS-JÜRGEN, ed.: *Der Streit mit Georg Lukács.* Frankfurt/M.: Suhrkamp, 1978. 235 pp. (ES, Bd. 579). [7 contributions showing differences and concurrences in the thirties between Lukács, A. Seghers, Brecht, Eisler, Bloch a.o.] [G.L. orig. Löwinger, literary historian, 1885–1971 Budapest.]
15591. LUXEMBURG, ROSA. MUTIUS, BERNHARD VON: *Die Rosa-Luxemburg-Legende.* Bd. 1. Frankfurt/M.: Verlag Marxistische Blätter, 1978. 280 pp. (Marxistische Taschenbücher: Reihe Marxismus aktuell, 123).
15592. SILBERNER, EDMUND: *Rosa Luxemburg, ihre Partei und die Judenfrage.* [In]: Jahrbuch des Instituts für Deutsche Geschichte. Bd. VII. Tel Aviv, 1978. Pp. 299–337. [See No. 15109.]
15593. MAHLER, GUSTAV. BLAUKOPF, KURT: *Gustav Mahler.* Sinfonie und Wirklichkeit. Graz: Universal Edition, 1977. 216 pp., music. (Studien zur Wertungsforschung, Bd. 9).
15594. GARTENBERG, EGON: Mahler: *The Man and his Music.* New York: Schirmer Books, 1978. x, 406 pp., ports., illus., facsim., bibl. (pp. 379–386).
15595. *Gustav Mahler-Dokumentation.* Sammlung Eleonore Vondenhoff (Wien). Materialien zu Leben und Werk. Hrsg. von Bruno und Eleonore Vondenhoff. Geleitwort von Franz Grasberger. Tutzing: Hans Schneider, 1978. xxii, 676 pp., ports., illus.
15596. KARBUSICKY, VLADIMIR: *Gustav Mahler und seine Umwelt.* Darmstadt: Wissenschaftl. Buchgesellschaft, 1978. viii, 158 pp. (Impulse der Forschung, Bd. 28).
15597. KRAVITT, EDWARD F.: *Mahler's Dirges for his Death: Feb. 24, 1901.* [In]: The Musical

Bibliography

Quarterly. Vol. 64, No. 3. New York: Schirmer, 1978. Pp. 329–353, facsim., music, bibl. footnotes.

15598. REILLY, EDWARD R.: *Gustav Mahler und Guido Adler*. Wien: Universal-Edition, 1978. 70 pp. (Schriftenreihe der Gustav-Mahler-Gesellschaft, hrsg. von Herta Singer-Blaukopf). [The material for the study on the friendship between the composer and the musicologist was found in the Adler-estate kept in the University of Georgia in Athens, USA.] [G.M., 1860 Kalischt, Bohemia–1911 Vienna.]

15599. MARCUS, ERNST: *Logik*. Der kategorische Imperativ Die. Zeit – und Raumlehre Kants. Bonn: Bouvier, 1978. 500 pp. (Bd. 2 der Ausgewählten Schriften in 4 Bden., hrsg. von Gottfried Martin und Gerd Hergen Lübben.) [For vol. I see No. 8145/YB. XV.] [E.M., 1856 Kamen, Westf.–1928 Essen.]

15600. MARCUSE, HERBERT: *Frühe Aufsätze*. Frankfurt/M.: Suhrkamp, 1978. 594 pp. (Schriften, Bd. 1). [Incl. Der deutsche Künstlerroman, the hitherto upubl. diss., Univ. Freiburg/Br. 1922.]

15601. AMÉRY, JEAN: *Herbert Marcuse, der grosse Neinsager*. Zu seinem 80. Geburtstag am 19. Juli. [In]: 'Aufbau', July 14, New York, 1978. *Philosoph der Revolte wird 80* (Fritz J. Raddatz) in: 'Die Zeit' 21. Juli, Hamburg, 1978. *Lange Umwege* (mey) in: 'NZZ', 14. Juli, Zürich, 1978. *Der erste Heidegger-Marxist* (Alfred Schmidt) in: 'FAZ', 19. Juli, Frankfurt/M., 1978, port.

15602. HABERMAS, JÜRGEN/SILVIA BOVENSCHEN u.a.: *Gespräche mit Herbert Marcuse*. Frankfurt/ M.: Suhrkamp, 1978. 152 pp., front. port., ports. (es Bd. 938, Zeitfragen).

15603. MARCUSE, LUDWIG, ed.: *Ein Panorama europäischen Geiste s*. Teste aus drei Jahrtausenden. Ausgewählt und vorgestellt von ... Mit e. Vorw. von Gerhard Szczesny. Bd. 1: Von Diogenes bis Plotin. Bd. 2: Von Augustinus bis Hegel. Bd. 3: Von Karl Marx bis Thomas Mann. Zürich: Diogenes, 1977. 400, 436, 450 pp. (3 Sonderbände).

15604. MARCUSE, LUDWIG: *Die Welt der Tragödie*. Nachdr. d. Ausg. 1923. München: F. Schneider, 1977. 180 pp., illus. [L.M. 1894 Berlin–1971 München.]

15605. MARX, KARL. BERLIN, ISAIAH: *Karl Marx: His Life and Environment*. New fourth edition. London: Oxford University Press, 1978. xii, 228 pp., bibl. (Opus series). [First publ. in 1939. For German translation see No. 1783/YB. V.]

15606. CARLEBACH, JULIUS: *Karl Marx and the Radical Critique of Judaism*. London: Routledge & Kegan Paul, 1978. xi, 466 pp., notes pp. 370–437, annotated bibl. pp. 438–449, bibl. (pp. 451–459). (The Littman Library of Jewish Civilization. Eds.: Louis Jacobs, David Goldstein, Lionel Kochan). [Cont. Part I: Citizen Jews in a Christian State. II: The Radical Critique of Judaism. III: On the Jewish Question and on the Question of Jews. IV.: Marx and the Problem of Antisemitism.]

15607. FRÄNTZKI, EKKEHARD: *Der missverstandene Marx*. Seine metaphysisch-ontologische Grundstellung. Pfullingen: Neske, 1978. 294 pp. [Der verstandene Marx. Eine Interpretation der Marxschen Metaphysik (Will Klunker) in: 'NZZ', 26. Okt., Zürich, 1978.]

15608. HORNUNG, KLAUS: *Der faszinierende Irrtum*. Karl Marx und die Folgen. Freiburg/Br.: Herder, 1978. 159 pp., bibl. (pp. 156–[160]. (Herderbücherei, Bd. 645).

15609. MOREAU, PIERRE-FRANÇOIS: *Marx und Spinoza*. Versuch e. materialist. Lektüre. Hamburg: VSA, 1978. 144 pp. (Reihe Positionen, Bd. 4).

15610. PADOVER, SAUL K.: *The Baptism of Karl Marx's Family*. [In]: 'Midstream'. Vol. XXIV, No. 6 (June–July). New York: The Theodor Herzl Foundation, 1978. Pp. 36–44.

15611. PADOVER, SAUL K.: *Karl Marx*. An Intimate Biography. New York: McGraw-Hill, 1978. xix, 667 pp., ports., illus., facsims., bibl. (pp. 644–651).

15612. RADDATZ, FRITZ J.: *Karl Marx*. A Political Biography. London: Weidenfeld and Nicolson, 1978. 256 pp. [German orig. No. 13166/YB. XXI.]

15613. SEIGEL, JERROLD: *Marx's Fate*. The Shape of a Life. London: Princeton University Press, 1978.

15614. THAIDIGSMANN, EDGAR: *Falsche Versöhnung*. Religion und Ideologiekritik beim jungen Marx. Vorarbeit zu e. ideologiekrit. Hermeneutik d. Evangeliums. München: Kaiser, 1978. 273 pp. (Beiträge zur evangelischen Theorie, Bd. 81).

15615. ZANDER, JÜRGEN: *Das Problem der Beziehung Max Webers zu Karl Marx*. Frankfurt/M.: Haag und Herchen, 1978. 186 pp.

15616. MAYER, HANS, ed.: *Deutsche Literaturkritik*. Bd. 1: Von Lessing bis Hegel (1730–1830). 967 pp. Bd. 2: Von Heine bis Mehring (1830–1900). 1040 pp., bibl. (pp. 1022–1024).

Bd. 3: Vom Kaiser-reich bis zum Ende der Weimarer Republik (1889–1933), 858 pp. Bd. 4: Vom Dritten Reich bis zur Gegenwart (1933–1968), 1049 pp. Frankfurt/M.: Fischer-Taschenbuch-Verlag, 1978. [4 vols.] (Frischer-Taschenbücher Nr. 2008–2011).

15617. MAYER, HANS: *Nach Jahr und Tag*. Reden 1945–1977. Frankfurt/M.: Suhrkamp, 1978. 300 pp., notes pp. 287–288, bibl. (pp. 289–293). [Incl.: Das Wort der Verfolgten (Zürich 1945). Nach dem Urteil im Nürnberger Prozess (Frankfurt 1947). Die deutsche Literatur und der Scheiterhaufen. Bücherverbrennung nach 15 Jahren (Berlin 1948). Ernst Bloch und die Heimat (Ludwigshafen 1977).]

15618. *Hans Mayer zu Ehren*. Festschrift. Mit Beiträgen von Max Bill, Michael Hamburger u.a. Frankfurt/M.: Suhrkamp, 1978. 109 pp., port. [21 contributions].

15619. *Hans Mayer zum 19. März 1977*. Beiträge von Raymond Aron, Peter Beckmann, Pierre Boulez, Ernst H. Gombrich, Joachim Kaiser, Anna Mahler, Fritz J. Raddatz, Günther Uecker. Stuttgart–Zürich: Belser, 1977. 131 pp. [H.M., literary historian, born 1907 in Cologne.]

15620. UEDING, GERT, ed.: *Materialien zu Hans Mayer 'Aussenseiter'*. Frankfurt/M.: Suhrkamp, 1978. 216 pp. (Suhrkamp Tb. Bd. 448). [See No. 14442/YB. XXIII.]

15621. MEIDNER, LUDWIG. TRAMER, HANS: *Das Judenproblem im Leben und Werk Ludwig Meidners*. [In]: LBI Bulletin. No. 53/54. Tel Aviv, 1977/78. Pp. 75–132, illus. [See No. 15110.] [L.M., painter, poet, 1884 Bernstadt/Silesia–1966 Darmstadt.]

15622. MENDELS[S]OHN, ERIC[H]. BERCKENHAGEN, EKHART: E. *Mendelsohns Architekturzeichnungen in Berlin*. [In]: Jahrbuch Preuss. Kulturbesitz 1976. Bd. XIII. Hr sg. im Auftrag des Stiftungsrats vom Präsidenten der Stiftung Preuss. Kulturbesitz Hans-Georg Womit. Berlin: Gebr. Mann, 1977. Pp. 253–258 + 2 pp. illus. [E.M., architect, 1887 Allenstein – 1953 San Francisco.]

15623. MENDELSSOHN, PETER DE. FREUND, J. HELLMUT, ed.: *Unterwegs*. Peter de Mendelssohn zum 70. Geburtstag. Frankfurt/M.: S. Fischer, 1978. Bibliographie 1929–1977 [comp. by] Klaus W. Jonas. [20 contributions].

15624. *Peter de Mendelssohn zum Siebzigsten* (Richard Friedenthal). Der Geist in der Diaspora (Joachim Kaiser). Von der Bewahrung des Lebens für die Geschichte (Jürgen Busche) [in]: Jahrbuch 1978. Deutsche Akademie für Sprache und Dichtung, Darmstadt. Heidelberg: Lambert Schneider, 1978. Pp. 98–102, 103–104, 105–107. [P. de M., born 1908 in Munich.]

15625. MENDELSSOHN-BARTHOLDY, FELIX. JENKINS, DAVID/MARK VISOCCHI: *Mendelssohn in Scotland*. London: Chappell, Elm Tree Books, 1978. 160 pp., port., illus. [The composer's 1829 tour of Scotland.] [1809 Hamburg–1847 Leipzig.]

15626. MISES, LUDWIG VON: *Erinnerungen*. Stuttgart. New York: Fischer, 1978. xvi, 118 pp. [Economist, sociologist, 1881 Lemberg–1973 New York.]

15627. MISES, LUDWIG VON: *Im Namen des Staates oder die Gefahren des Kollektivismus*. Vorw.: Alfred Müller-Armack. Stuttgart: Verlag Bonn Aktuell, 1978. 262 pp.

15628. MOLNAR, FRANZ: *Die Jungen der Paulstrasse*. Roman. Aus dem Ungarischen von Edmund Alkalay. Nachw. von Hans Weigel. Köln: Styria, 1978. 218 pp. [Written in 1907.] [Cf. Viel Edelmut und Heldentum. Wie wirkt Franz Molnars Roman heute? (Egon Schwarz) in: 'FAZ', 26 Sept., Frankfurt/M., 1978.] [F.M., orig. Neumann, dramatist, 1878 Budapest–1952 New York.]

15629. MÜHSAM, ERICH: *Ausgewählte Werke*. Band 1: Gedichte, Prosa Stücke. Band 2: Publizistik, Unpolitische Erinnerungen. Hrsg. von Christlieb Hirte unter Mitarb. von Roland Links und Dieter Schiller. Mit e. Nachw. von Dieter Schiller. Berlin [East]: Volk und Welt, 1978. 1368 pp., 16 ports., illus. [In 2 vols.] (Auslieferung Berlin: Helios).

15630. MÜHSAM, ERICH: *Brennende Erde*. Verse eines Kämpfers. Nachdr. d. Ausg. München, Wolff, 1920. Berlin: Guhl, 1978. 92 pp.

15631. MÜHSAM, ERICH: *Scheinwerfer; oder, Färbt ein weisses Blütenblatt sich schwarz*. Politische Essays, Gedichte, Briefe, Flugblätter. Geleitwort von Gerd W. Jungblut. Hrsg. von Hugo Fidus. Berlin: Klaus Guhl, 1978. 174 pp., ports., illus., facsims., bibl. notes.

15632. EMIG, GÜNTHER, ed.: *Erich Mühsam*. Gesamtausgabe zum 100. Geburtstag am 6. April 1978. Berlin: Verlag Europäische Ideen, 1977/78. [5 vols.] Bd. 1: Gedichte. Bd. 2: Dramen, 1977. 459 pp., Bd. 3: Prosaschriften I, 469 pp., Bd. 4: Prosaschriften II, 481 pp. [Incl. Ascona (1905), Die Jagd auf Harden (1908), Das Standrecht in Bayern

(1923). Die Aufsätze aus 'Alarm' (1925) und aus 'Sammlung' 1898–1928). Von Eisner bis Leviné (1929). Unpolitische Erinnerungen (1931). Die Befreiung der Gesellschaft vom Staat (1933). Bd. 5: Verstreute Aufsätze.] [E.M., 1878 Berlin, murdered 1934 in Oranienburg concentration camp.]
15633. OSCHILEWSKI, WALTHER G.: *Zwischen Utopie und Wirklichkeit*. Erich Mühsam und der Anarchismus. [In]: 'Die Neue Gesellschaft', 25. Jg., H. 4, April. Bonn: Verlag Neue Gesellschaft, 1978. Pp. 308–314.
15634. *Was können wir heute von Erich Mühsam Lernen?* [Replies by]: Augustin Souchy, Alfred Kantorowicz. Gerald K. Zschorsch, Gerhard Zwerenz, Bruno Frei, Jean Améry, Heinrich Böll, Arno Reinfrank. [In]: 'Erich Mühsam Blätter', 3. Folge, Berlin: Europäische Ideen, 1978. 10 pp., illus., facsim.
15635. MÜHSAM, PAUL: *Glaubensbekenntnis*. Hrsg. von Else Levi-Mühsam. Konstanz: Priv. Printed [Gottfried v. Herder Weg 2], 1978. 71 pp. [Written 1946. P.M., 1876 Brandenburg/Havel, lawyer in Görlitz until 1933, died 1960 in Jerusalem.]
15636. MYNONA [i.e. Salomo Friedlaender]: *Katechismus der Magie*. Mit Kommentar: Das magische Prinzip der Natur von Martin Schönberger. Unv. Wiedergabe. Freiburg/Br.: Aurum, 1978. xxiii, 123 pp. (Edition imago solis). [Philosopher, satirist, 1871 Posen–1946 Paris.]
15637. NELSON, LEONARD. *Leonard Nelson-Gedenkfeier*. Reden, gehalten bei d. Zusammensein d. politischen Anhänger Leonard Nelsons aus Anlass seines 50. Todestages am 29. Okt. 1977 in Göttingen. Kassel: Philos.-Polit.-Akademie, 1978. 47 pp. [L.N., 1882 Berlin–1927 Göttingen.]
15638. NEUMANN, FRANZ LEOPOLD: *Wirtschaft, Staat, Demokratie*. Aufsätze 1930–1954. Hrsg. von Alfons Söllner. [Essays orig. written in English are transl. by Sabine Gwinner and Alfons Söllner]. Frankfurt/M.: Suhrkamp, 1978. 467 pp., bibl. F.L.N. pp. 460–467 comp. by Wolfgang Luthardt. (es, Bd. 892). [Incl. F.L. Neumann, Skizzen zu einer intellektuellen und politischen Biographie (Alfons Söllner); pp. 7–56, notes pp. 49–56.]
15639. NEUMANN, SIEGFRIED: *Nacht über Deutschland*. Vom Leben und Sterben einer Republik. Ein Tatsachenbericht. München: List, 1978. 131 pp. [Cf. Die Hoffnung im Nazi-Deutschland verloren (Adolf Diamant) [in]: 'Aufbau', July 14, New York, 1978.]
15640. NEUMANN, SIEGFRIED: *Vom Kaiserhoch zur Austreibung*. Aufzeichnungen aus dem Leben eines jüdischen Rechtsanwalts in Deutschland. Bonn: Bundeszentrale für politische Bildung, 1978. 131 pp. (Schriftenreihe d. Bundeszentrale ... Bd. 129). [S.N., born 1899.]
15641. NICK, DAGMAR: *Fluchtlinien*. Gedichte seit 1945. Zeichnungen von Klaus Bertelsmann. München: Delp, 1978. 170 pp., illus. [D.N., born 1926 in Breslau, lives in Israel.]
15642. NISSEN, RUDOLF: *Fünfzig Jahre erlebter Chirurgie*. Ausgew. Vorträge und Schriften. Stuttgart, New York: Schattauer, 1978. 357 pp. [The noted surgeon, born 1896 in Neisse (Silesia) retired in 1967 as the director of the 'Chirurgische Universitätsklinik in Basle'.]
15643. NORDAU, MAX. INGOLD, FELIX PHILIPP: *Leo Tolstoi und Max Nordau*. [In]: 'NZZ', FA Nr. 207, 8. Sept., Zürich, 1978. [In 1892/93 Nordau publ. 'Entartung' [in 2 vols.] which was translated into Russian. Tolstoi disapproved of the theses of 'the little Jew'.] [M.N., orig. Südfeld, 1849 Budapest–1923 Paris, physician, author, Zionist.]
15644. OPHÜLS, MAX. RIVETTE, JACQUES FRANÇOIS TRUFFAUT: *Max Ophüls im Gespräch*. [And]: Der letzte Drehtag (Max Ophüls) in: 'Filmkritik'. Jg. 21, H. 11. München: Filmkritiker-Kooperative, 1977. Pp. 525–586, illus. [M.O., orig. Oppenheimer, film director, author, 1902 Saarbrücken–1957 Hamburg.]
15645. OPPENHEIM, MORITZ DANIEL. COHEN, ELISHEVA: *Moritz Daniel Oppenheim*. [In]: LBI Bulletin. No. 53/54. Tel Aviv, 1977/78. Pp. 42–74, illus., facsim. [See No. 15110, also No. 15337]. [M.D.O., 1800 Hanau–1882 Frankfurt/M.]
15646. PAEPCKE, LOTTE: *Ein kleiner Händler, der mein Vater war*. Gütersloh: Mohn, 1978. 112 pp. (Gütersloher Tb. Siebenstern, Bd. 276). [First publ. 1972. See No. 10819/YB. XVIII. The story of a German Jew, soldier in the First World War, then an emigrant, who returned to Germany as an old man.]
15647. PAPPENHEIM, BERTHA. KAPLAN, MARION: *Bertha Pappenheim: Founder of German-Jewish Feminism*. Pp. 149–163, bibl. [in]: The Jewish Woman. New Perspectives. Ed. by

Elizabeth Koltun. New York: Schocken, 1976. 294 pp., bibl. (pp. 283–289). [B.P. 1859 Vienna–1936 Neu Isenburg.]

15648. PICARD, MAX: *Fragmente.* Aus dem Nachlass 1920 bis 1965. Hrsg. u. eingel. von Michael Picard. Konstanz: Rentsch, 1978. 208 pp. [M.P., physician and author, 1888 Schopfheim (Baden)–1965 Neggio (Switzerland). He converted to Catholicism in 1939, but later returned to the Jewish faith.]

15649. PINCUS, LILY: ... *bis dass der Tod euch scheidet.* Zur Psychologie des Trauerns. Aus d. Engl. übers. von Gudrun Hansen. Stuttgart: Dt. Verlags-Anstalt, 1977. 310 pp. [L.P., born 1898 in Karlsbad, social therapist at the London Tavistock Clinic.]

15650. POPPER, SIR KARL R[AIMUND]: *Die beiden Grundprobleme der Erkenntnistheorie.* Auf Grund von Manuskripten aus den Jahren 1930 bis 1932 hrsg. von Troels Eggers Hansen. Tübingen: J. C. B. Mohr (Paul Siebeck), 1978. 520 pp. (Die Einheit der Gesellschaftswissenschaften, 18). [The first part of the work was publ. in 1934 under the title 'The Logic of Scientific Discovery' (Logik der Forschung), see No. 11707/YB. XIX.]

15651. POPPER, KARL R./JOHN C. ECCLES: *The Self and its Brain.* Berlin, Heidelberg, London: Springer International, 1977. xvi, 597 pp., 66 graphics, bibl.

15652. BAYERTZ, KURT/JOSEF SCHLEIFSTEIN: *Mythologie der 'kritischen Vernunft'.* Zur Kritik der Erkenntnis- und Geschichtstheorie Karl Poppers. Köln: Pahl-Rugenstein, 1977. 270 pp. (Kleine Bibliothek, 86).

15653. GRÜNBAUM, ADOLF: *Is Psychoanalysis a Pseudo-Science?* Karl Popper versus Sigmund Freud. [In]: 'Zeitschrift für philosophische Forschung'. Nr. 31 und 32. Meisenheim am Glan: Hain, 1977, pp. 333–353; 1978, pp. 49–69.

15654. HOCHKEPPEL, WILLY: *Karl Popper und die Politik.* [In]: 'Merkur', 32. Jg., H. 12 (367), Dez. Stuttgart: Klett-Cotta, 1978. Pp. 1257–1264.

15655. SPINNER, HELMUT F.: *Popper und die Politik.* Rekonstruktion und Kritik d. Sozial-Polit- und Geschichtsphilosophie d. kritischen Rationalismus. 1. Geschlossenheitsprobleme. Berlin, Bonn: Dietz, 1978. xv, 624 pp., bibl. (Internationale Bibliothek, Bd. 106).

15656. POPPER-LYNKEUS, JOSEF. BELKE, INGRID: *Die sozialreformerischen Ideen von Josef Popper-Lynkeus (1838–1921) im Zusammenhang mit allgemeinen Reformbestrebungen des Wiener Bürgertums um die Jahrhundertwende.* Tübingen: J. C. B. Mohr (Paul Siebeck), 1978. vii, 296 pp., front. port., ports., illus., bibl. (pp. 265–290). Zugl. Philos.-Histor. Diss., Univ. Basel 1975.

15657. HELLIN, FREDERICK P./ROBERT PLANK: *Der Plan des Josef Popper-Lynkeus.* Vorw. von Richard Coudenhove-Kalergi. Bern, Frankfurt/M.: Lang, 1978. 76 pp. (Europäische Hochschulschriften 29, Sozialökonomie, Bd. 7).

15658. RATHENAU, WALTHER. WILLIAMSON, D. G.: *Walther Rathenau and the K.R.A. August 1914–March 1915.* [In]: 'Zeitschrift für Unternehmensgeschichte'. Hrsg. im Auftrag der Gesellschaft für Unternehmensgeschichte von Wilhelm Treue und Hans Pohl. 23. Jg., H. 2, Wiesbaden: Steiner, 1978. Pp. 118–136, tabs., bibl. footnotes. [KRA – Kriegs Rohstoff Abteilung].

15659. REICH, WILHELM: *Christusmord.* Die emotionale Pest des Menschen. Aus d. Amerik. von Bernd Laska. Olten-Freiburg: Walter, 1978. 398 pp. [Cf. Christusmord oder die Unmöglichkeit der Befreiung des Menschen durch sich selbst. Gedanken zu einem ungewöhnlichen Buch (Heinz Müller-Pozzi) in: 'NZZ', 8. Dez., Zürich, 1978.] [W.R., born 1897 in Galicia, died 1957 in an American jail.]

15660. REIK, THEODOR: *Der unbekannte Mörder.* Psychoanalytische Studien. Hamburg: Hoffmann und Campe, 1978. 320 pp. [Th.R., psychologist and close co-worker of Freud, 1888 Vienna–1969 USA.]

15661. ROTH, JOSEPH: *Perlefter.* Die Geschichte eines Bürgers. Romanfragment aus dem Berliner Nachlass. Hrsg. und mit e. Nachwort von Friedemann Berger. Köln: Kiepenheuer & Witsch, 1978. 166 pp. [Cf. Joseph Roth und die Stützen der Gesellschaft. 'Perlefter', ein bisher unbekannter Roman (Ulrich Greiner) [in]: 'FAZ', 10. Juni, Frankfurt/M., 1978.]

15662. ROTH, JOSEPH: *Zipper und sein Vater.* Roman. Ungek. Ausg. München: Dt. Taschenbuch-Verlag, 1978. 132 pp. (dtv, 1376). Lizenz d. Verl. Kiepenheuer u. Witsch, Köln.

15663. RADDATZ, FRITZ J.: *In Hässlichkeit sterbende Welt.* Kein bedeutender Romancier, aber ein bohrender Menschenbeobachter und grosser Polemiker. Joseph Roth – Romane, Briefe und Fragmente aus dem Nachlass. Porträt-Essay [in]: 'Die Zeit', 28. Juli,

Hamburg, 1978. Pp. 31–32, port. drawing. [J.R., 1894 Schwabendorf (Galicia)–1939 Paris (suicide).]
15664. SALOMON, ERICH: *Berühmte Zeitgenossen in unbewachten Augenblicken*. München: Schirmer-Mosel, 1978. 144 pp., 104 photos. [Dr. E. Salomon, one of the first photo journalists (1886 Berlin–1944 Auschwitz), published this album, the document of an epoch, in 1931 in Berlin. Cf. Erich Salomon unvergessen (E. G. Lowenthal) in: 'Aufbau', Sept. 8, New York, 1978.]
15665. SAPHIR, MORITZ GOTTLIEB: *Mieder und Leier*. Gedankenblitze aus dem Biedermeier. Zur Erde geleitet, gebündelt und in gute Nachrede gebracht von Manfred Barthel. Olten, Freiburg/Br.: Walter, 1978. 180 pp. [Satirical writer, 1795 nr. Budapest–1858 Baden nr. Vienna. Editor of the journal 'Der Humorist']
15666. SCHÄFFER, HANS. DANZL, ERNA: *Erinnerungen Hans Schäffers an Ernst Trendelenburg*. [In]: 'Vierteljahrshefte für Zeitgeschichte'. 25. Jg., H. 4, Okt. Stuttgart: Dt. Verlags Anstalt, 1977. Pp. 865–888. [H.Sch. 1886 Breslau–1967 Jönköping (Sweden).]
15667. SCHNITZLER, ARTHUR: *The little Comedy and other Stories*. Transl. from the original German. Foreword by Frederick Ungar. New York: Ungar Publ. Co., 1977, xii, 234 pp. [Cont. The little comedy. Riches. The Son. The judge's wife. Dying.]
15668. BERLIN, JEFFREY, B., comp.: *An Annotated Arthur Schnitzler Bibliography, 1965–1977*. With an Essay on 'The Meaning of the Schnitzler Renaissance'. Introduction by Sol Liptzin. München: Fink, 1978. 80 pp. [This bibliography forms a direct continuation of Richard H. Allen's 'Annotated Schnitzler Bibliography, 1879–1965'. See No. 6039/YB. XII.]
15669. DAVIAN, DONALD, ed.: *Modern Austrian Literature: Special Arthur Schnitzler Issue*. Vol. 10, No. 314. Publ. by Department of Literature and Languages, University of California, Riverside, Ca., 1977. 339 pp.
15670. GUTT, BARBARA: *Emanzipation bei Arthur Schnitzler*. Berlin: Spiess, 1978. 198 pp., bibl. (pp. 185–195). Zugl. Germanistik Diss., F.U. Berlin, 1975 u.d.T.: Die Emanzipation der Frau bei A.Sch.
15671. SCHEIBLE, HARTMUT: *Arthur Schnitzler und die Aufklärung*. München: Fink, 1977. 124 pp. [Cf. Der späte Bürger A.Sch., Hartmut Scheibles Untersuchung (Christa Melchinger) in: 'FAZ', 11. Okt., Frankfurt/M., 1977.]
15672. SCHOEPS, HANS-JOACHIM: *Deutsche Geistesgeschichte der Neuzeit*. Ein Abriss in 5 Bänden. Bd. 1: Das Zeitalter der Reformation. Bd. 2: Das Zeitalter des Barock. Zwischen Reformation und Aufklärung. Mainz: v. Hase und Koehler, 1977, 379 pp.; 1978, 343 pp. [2 vols.]
15673. SCHWERIN, KURT: *Bibliographie rechtswissenschaftlicher Schriftenreihen*. A Bibliography of German Language Legal Monograph Series. München–New York: Verlag Dokumentation, 1978. xvi, 383 pp.
15674. SEGHERS, ANNA. NEUGEBAUER, HEINZ: *Anna Seghers. Leben und Werk*. Wissenschaftl. Mitarbeiter: Irmgard Neugebauer. 6., stark veränd. Aufl. Berlin [East]: Volk und Wissen, 1978. 239 pp., port., illus., bibl. A.S. pp. 222–224. (Schriftsteller der Gegenwart, 4).
15675. ROSS, PETER/FRIDERIKE J. HASSAUER-ROSS, eds.: *Anna Seghers Materialienbuch*. Darmstadt: Luchterhand, 1977. 187 pp. (Sammlung Luchterhand, Bd. 242).
15676. SAUER, KLAUS: *Anna Seghers*. München: Beck, Edition text und kritik, 1978. 183 pp. (Autorenbücher, 9).
15677. SILBERGLEIT, ARTHUR: *Der ewige Tag*. Gedichte. Mit einem Nachw. hrsg. von Horst Bienek. Faksimiledruck nach der Erstausgabe der Künstlerhilfe der Jüdischen Gemeinde zu Berlin (1935). Berlin: Verlag Europäische Ideen, 1978. 40 pp. [Cf. Ein vergessener Schriftsteller: Arthur Silbergleit (Horst Bienek) in: 'NJN', Nr. 19. 19. Mai, München, 1978.] [A.S., poet, 1881 Gleiwitz–1943 Auschwitz.]
15678. SIMMEL, GEORG: *Philosophie des Geldes*. 7. Aufl., unv. Nachdr. d. 1958 ersch. 6. Aufl. Berlin: Duncker und Humblot, 1977. xv, 585 pp. (Ges. Werke, Bd. 1). [Publ. in Berlin in 1900. For the first transl. into English see No. 14819/YB. XXIII.] [G.S., philosopher, sociologist, 1858 Berlin–1918 Strassburg.]
15679. SOMMER, ERNST: *Revolte der Heiligen*. Roman. Gewidmet den Helden des Warschauer Gettos. Reprint. Berlin: LitPol mit Verlag Europäische Ideen, 1978. 240 pp. [First publ. 1944 in Mexico, Verlag El Libro Libre.] [E.S., poet and writer, 1889 Iglau (CSR)–1955 London.]

15680. SPERBER, MANÈS: *Dieses mein Judentum*. Die Ereignisse in Nazi-Deutschland haben meinen Nacken versteinert. Versuch eines Selbstporträts. [In]: 'Die Zeit', Nr. 39, 22. Sept., Hamburg, 1978. [A reprint from his contribution to 'Mein Judentum', see No. 15328.] [Author and psychologist, born 1905 in East Galicia.]
15681. SPERBER, MANÈS: *Individuum und Gemeinschaft* – Versuch einer sozialen Charakterologie. Stuttgart: Klett-Cotta, 1978. 326 pp. (Konzept der Humanwissenschaften). [A collection of lectures given between 1927 and 1932 at the 'Individualpsychologische Institut' in Berlin.]
15682. SPIRO, EUGEN. *Eugen Spiro (1874 Breslau–1972 New York)*. Retrospektive. Gemälde, Aquarelle, Zeichnungen, Druckgraphik. Ausstellung der Galerie Von Abercron, Jan. 1978 in Köln. (Catalogue). 62 pp., mostly illus.
15683. SCHEYER, ERNST: *Eugen Spiro, Clara Sachs*. Beiträge zur neueren schlesischen Kunstgeschichte. Ein Text-Bildband. München: Delp, 1977. 100 pp., ports., illus., bibl. E.S., chronologies. [Cf. Zwei jüdische Künstler aus Schlesien [in]: 'Emuna-Israel Forum', H. 2, 1978. Pp. 67–69, illus. See No. 15759]. [E.S., 1874 Breslau–1972 New York. C.S., 1862 Breslau–1921.]
15684. STEINER, GEORGE: *Heidegger*. London: Fontana, 1978. 150 pp., port.
15685. TELLER, EDWARD. BLUMBERG, STANLEY A./GWINN OWENS: *Energy and Conflict*. The Life and Times of Edward Teller. New York: Putnam's Sons, 1976. xvii, 492 pp., ports. [Physicist, born 1908 in Budapest.]
15686. TOLLER, ERNST: *Gesammelte Werke*. Hrsg. von Wolfgang Frühwald und John M. Spalek. Bd. 1: Kritische Schriften, Reden und Reportagen. Bd. 2: Dramen und Gedichte aus dem Gefängnis, 1918–1924. Bd. 3: Politisches Theater und Dramen im Exil, 1927–1939. Bd. 4: Eine Jugend in Deutschland. Bd. 5: Briefe aus dem Gefängnis. München: Carl Hanser, 1978. 1444 pp. [5 vols.] (Reihe Hanser, Bd. 250–255). [Ein Kommentarband erscheint in 1979.] [Cf. Endlich eine Toller-Werkausgabe (Norbert Schachtsieck-Freitag) in: 'Tribüne' H. 67, 1978. See No. 15751.] [E.T., 1893 Samotschin nr. Bromberg – 1939 committed suicide in New York.]
15687. TORBERG, FRIEDRICH: *Die Erben der Tante Jolesch*. München–Wien: Langen–Müller, 1978. 317 pp. + facsims. (Ges. Werke in Einzelausgaben, Bd. IX). [For vol. VIII: Die Tante Jolesch oder der Untergang des Abendlandes in Anekdoten see No. 13260/YB. XXI.]
15688. TORBERG, FRIEDRICH: *... und glaubten, es wäre die Liebe*. Roman Wien–München: Langen–Müller, 1978. 504 pp.
15689. STRELKA, JOSEF, ed.: *Der Weg war schon das Ziel*. Festschrift für Friedrich Torberg zum 70. Geburtstag. 277 pp., front. port., biogr. notes on the 22 contributors. [Friedrich Torberg, orig. Kantor Berg, born 1908 in Vienna.]
15690. TUCHOLSKY, KURT: *Zwischen Gestern und Morgen*. Eine Auswahl aus seinen Schriften und Gedichten. Hrsg. von Mary Gerold-Tucholsky. Ungek. Ausg. Reinbek: Rowohlt, 1978. 202 pp. (rororo, 50).
15691. BECKER, HANS J.: *Mit geballter Faust: Kurt Tucholskys 'Deutschland, Deutschland über alles'*. Bonn: Bouvier, 1978. ii, 126 pp., ports., illus., bibl. (pp. 123–126). (Abhandlungen zur Kunst-, Musik- und Literaturwissenschaft, Bd. 240).
15692. GODER-STARK, PETRA, ed.: *Das Kurt Tucholsky Archiv*. Ein Bericht. Marbach a. Neckar: Deutsche Schillergesellschaft, 1978. 163 pp., ports., illus. (Deutsches Literaturarchiv, Verzeichnisse, Berichte, Informationen, 5).
15693. PHILIPPOFF, EVA: *Kurt Tucholskys Frankreichbild*. München: Minerva-Publikation, 1978. xvi, 155 pp., port., bibl. K.T. and bibl. pp. 143–151. (Minerva-Fachserie Geisteswissenschaften). [K.T., 1890 Berlin–1935, committed suicide in Hindas (Sweden).]
15694. UNGAR, HERMANN: *Die Klasse*. Roman. Mainz: v. Hase & Koehler, 1978. 212 pp. (Die Mainzer Reihe. Hrsg. Akademie der Wissenschaften und der Literatur, Mainz, Nr. 36). [H.U., writer, 1893 Boskowitz (Moravia)–1929 Prague.]
15695. URZIDIL, JOHANNES. PISTORIUS, HEDWIG: *Johannes Urzidil und das Exil*. Geisteswiss. Diss., Univ. Wien, 1977. x, 209 pp. [Typescript]. [J.U., 1896 Prague–2nd Nov. 1970 Rome (on a lecture tour).]
15696. VARNHAGEN, RAHEL. SCURLA, HERBERT: *Rahel Varnhagen, die grosse Frauengestalt der deutschen Romantik*. Düsseldorf: Claassen, 1978. 524 pp., 17 pp. ports., illus. Lizenzausg. d. Verlag der Nation, Berlin [East], publ. under the title: Begegnungen mit Rahel. Der Salon der Rahel Levin. [R.V. 1771 Berlin—1833 Berlin.]

15697. VIERTEL, BERTHOLD. *Berthold Viertel im amerikanischen Exil*. Eine Ausstellung im Deutschen Literaturarchiv zu Marbach am Neckar. [In]: 'Marbacher Magazin', comp. by Friedrich Pfäfflin. Nr. 9. Schiller Nationalmuseum und Deutsches Literaturarchiv, 1978. 36 pp., 42 ports., illus., facsims. [B.V., 1885 Vienna–1953 Vienna.]

15698. WALDEN, HERWARTH. OSCHILEWSKI, WALTHER G.: *Marc Chagall, Waldens 'Sturm' und Berlin*. Zum 100. Geburtstag von Herwarth Walden am 16. 9. 1978. [In]: 'Europäische Ideen', Hrsg. Andreas W. Mytze. H. 40. Berlin, 1978. Pp. 63–71, bibl. notes pp. 70–71. [Chagall's relationship with Walden, ed. of 'Der Sturm' in Berlin 1910–1932, and promoter of several Chagall exhibitions. H.W., 1878 Berlin, perished in Russia 1941.]

15699. WALLICH, HERMANN AND PAUL. *Zwei Generationen im deutschen Bankwesen, 1833–1914*. Hermann Wallich: Aus meinem Leben. Paul Wallich: Lehr- und Wanderjahre eines Bankiers. Mit einer Einführung von Henry C. Wallich. Frankfurt/M.: Knapp, 1978. 432 pp., ports., register. bibl. P.W. p. 28. (Schriftenreihe des Instituts für Bankhistorische Forschung, Bd. 2). [Hermann W., 1833–1928. Paul W., 1882–1938 (suicide). Henry C, the son of Paul, born 1914 in Berlin, since 1935 in USA. Paul W. was co-author of Berliner Grosskaufleute und Kapitalisten, see No. 6906/YB. XIV.]

15700. WARBURG, ABBY M.: *Ausgewählte Schriften und Würdigungen*. In Verbindung mit Carl Georg Heise und mit einer Einführung hrsg. von Dieter Wuttke. Baden-Baden: Valentin Koerner, 1978.

15701. WUTTKE, DIETER: *Aby M. Warburgs Methode als Anregung und Aufgabe*. Öffentlicher Abendvortrag aus Anlass des XIV. Deutschen Kunsthistorikertages geh. am 7. Okt. 1974... Univ. Hamburg. 2. Aufl. Göttingen: Selbstverlag der Arbeitsstelle für Renaissanceforschung am Seminar f. Deutsche Philologie der Universität Göttingen, 1978. (1. Aufl. 1977). 69 pp., cover port., illus., facsims., bibl. (pp. 57–67). (Gratia, Schriften d. Arbeitsstelle... H. 2).

15702. (M. M.) WARBURG & CO., BANKHAUS. ROSENBAUM, E[DUARD] and A. J. SHERMAN: *Das Bankhaus M. M. Warburg & Co. 1978–1938*. 2. Aufl. Hamburg: Christians, 1978. 235 pp., ports., illus., facsims., bibl. (pp. 215–222). [First ed. 1976, see No. 14026/YB. XXII.]

15703. WARBURG, OTTO. KREBS, HANS: *Otto Warburg*. Zellphysiologe, Biochemiker, Mediziner, 1883–1970. Stuttgart: Wissenschaftl. Verlags G.m.b.H., 1978. 170 pp., 31 ports., illus. (Grosse Naturforscher, Bd. 41). [Sir Hans Krebs was an assistant of Warburg.]

15704. WASSERMANN, CHARLES: *Insulin – Der Kampf um eine Entdeckung*. München: Langen-Müller, 1978. 272 pp. [Charles Wassermann, born 1924 in Vienna, son of Jakob W., died shortly before the publication of this book in Canada.]

15705. WASSERMANN, JAKOB: *Caspar Hauser oder Die Trägheit des Herzens*. Roman. München: Langen-Müller, 1978. 381 pp. [Written 1908. Cf. Ein langlebiger Findling. J.Ws. Roman 'Caspar Hauser' wieder erschienen (Rolf Schneider) in: 'FAZ', 4. Sept., Frankfurt/M. 1978.] [J.W., 1873 Fürth–1934 Alt-Aussee.]

15706. WEIGEL, HANS: *Das Land der Deutschen mit der Seele suchend*. Bericht über eine ambivalente Beziehung. München, Zürich: Artemis & Winkler, 1978. 255 pp., port. [Publicist, author, born 1908 in Vienna, emigrated 1938 to Switzerland.]

15707. WEININGER, OTTO: *Sexe et Caractère*. Tr. de l'allemand par Daniel Renaud. Avant-propos de Roland Jaccard. Lausanne: L'Age d'Homme, 1975. 291 pp. (Collection 'Sphinx'. [German orig. was publ. 1903. O.W., philosopher, 1880 Vienna–1903 Vienna (suicide).]

15708. WEISS, PETER: *Die Ästhetik des Widerstands*. Roman. Zweiter Band. Frankfurt/M.: Suhrkamp, 1978. 326 pp. [Vol. I of the planned trilogy appeared 1975. See No. 13271/YB. XXI.] [Cf. Blasen aus der Wort-Flut (Fritz J. Raddatz) in: 'Die Zeit', 17. Nov., Hamburg, 1978. Pp. 1–2, port. [Also] Der verschollene Peter Weiss (Gert Ueding) in: 'FAZ', 9. Dez., Frankfurt/M., 1978.]

15709. WEIß, ERNST: *Der andere Augenzeuge und eine Auswahl aus seinen Werken*. Eingel. und hrsg. von Klaus-Peter Hinze. Wiesbaden: Steiner, 1978. 147 pp. (Reihe: Verschollene und Vergessene).

15710. WEIß, ERNST: *The Eyewitness*. Transl. by Ella R. W. McKee with a foreword by Rudolph Binion and a postscript by Klaus-Peter Hinze. Boston: Houghton Mifflin, London: Proteus, 1978. viii, 206 pp. [For German orig.: Der Augenzeuge, mit e. Vorw. von

Hermann Kesten see No. 4187/YB. IX (1963) and No. 14861/YB. XXIII for a 1977 ed.]
[E.W., physician and author, born 1884 Brünn (Brno), committed suicide 1940 in Paris.] [Cf. also: Ernst Weiß – der "Augenzeuge", Ein früher Hitler-Roman und sein Autor (Margarita Pazi) in: 'Aufbau,' Apr. 20, New York 1979].

15711. WOLFF, THEODOR. KÖHLER, WOLFRAM: *Der Chef-Redakteur Theodor Wolff*. Ein Leben in Europa 1868–1943. Düsseldorf: Droste, 1978. 320 pp., port., bibl. (pp. 309–313).

15712. WAGNER, ERICH: *T. W.: Vermächtnis und Lorbeer*. [In]: Börsenblatt f.d. Dt. Buchhandel. Nr. 71, 5. Sept. Frankfurt/M., 1978. Pp. 1826–1828, port. (Vor der Verleihung des 1961 von der Axel-Springer-Stiftung begründeten Theodor-Wolff-Preises als posthume Ehrung des grössten deutschen Journalisten.)

15713. ZUCKMAYER, CARL: *Auf einem Weg im Frühling*. Erzählung. Wiedersehen mit einer Stadt (Salzburg). Aus dem Stegreif erzählt. Mit 11 Zeichnungen von Anton Steinhart. München: Dt. Taschenbuch-Verlag, 1978. (dtv 2518).

15714. BALINKIN, AUSMA: *The Central Women Figures in Carl Zuckmayer's Dramas*. Bern, Frankfurt/M.: Lang, 1978. 120 pp. (Europ. Hochschulschriften, Reihe 1, Dt. Literatur u. Germanistik, Bd. 235).

15715. *Carl Zuckmayer '78*. Ein Jahrbuch. Hrsg. von Barbara Glauert. Frankfurt/M.: Fischer, 1978. 160 pp. [Incl. Worte des Gedenkens by Karl Holzamer, Harry Buckwitz u.a. The textcritical version of the drama 'Pankraz erwacht', written 1923, first performed 1925. A critical report on the 'Zuckmayerforschung 1961–1977', reviews of Z.'s publications 1976–1977, a bibl. for the years 1971–1977.]

15716. MEWS, SIEGFRIED: *Carl Zuckmayer, Der Hauptmann von Köpenick*. Grundlagen und Gedanken zum Verständnis des Dramas. München: Diesterweg, 1978. 87 pp., bibl. C.Z. u. bibl. pp. 84–87.

15717. ZWEIG, ARNOLD-BROD, MAX. PAZI, MARGARITA: *Arnold Zweig and Max Brod – 1929, 1939, 1949*. [In]: LBI Year Book XXIII. London, 1978. Pp. 259–264. [See No. 15111.]

15718. WENZEL, GEORG, ed.: *Arnold Zweig 1887–1968*. Werk und Leben in Dokumenten und Bildern. Mit unveröffentlichten Manuskripten und Briefen aus dem Nachlass. Berlin [East]: Aufbau, 1978. vii, 673 pp., ports., illus., facsims., bibl. (pp. 643–649). (Veröffentlichung der Akademie der Künste der Deutschen Demokratischen Republik).

15719. ZWEIG, STEFAN: *Leporella*. Novellen. Mit e.Nachw. von Manfred Wolter. Berlin [East]: Aufbau, 1977. 355 pp. (Taschenbibliothek der Weltliteratur).

15720. ZWEIG, STEFAN: *Magellan, der Mann und seine Tat*. Eine Biographie. Ungek. Ausg. Frankfurt/M.: Fischer-Taschenbuch-Verlag, 1977. 211 pp., ports., illus. (Fischer Tb. Bd. 1830).

VIII. AUTOBIOGRAPHY, MEMOIRS, LETTERS, GENEALOGY

15721. BENJAMIN, URI: *Die Welt als Vaterland*. Teil III. [In]: Aus dem Antiquariat. Börsenblatt für den Deutschen Buchhandel. Nr. 24, 25. März. Frankfurt/M., 1977. Pp. A 95–A 104, port. (Antiquare im Exil). [For parts I–II see No. 14883/YB. XXIII.] [Uri Benjamin, i.e. Walter Zadek, born 26th March, 1900 in Berlin, lives in Israel.]

15722. BENJAMIN, WALTER: *Briefe*. Hrsg. und m. Anmerkungen vers. von Gershom Scholem und Theodor W. Adorno. 1. Aufl. Frankfurt/M.: Suhrkamp, 1978. 484 pp., pp. 485–884, port. [2 vols.] (Edition Suhrkamp, 930). [Letter written between July 1910 and August 1940.]

15723. BERGNER, ELISABETH: *Bewundert viel und viel gescholten* . . . Elisabeth Bergner's unordentliche Erinnerungen. München: C. Bertelsmann, 1978. 344 pp., with 40 pp. ports., illus.

15724. BORN, MAX: *My Life*. Recollections of a Nobel Laureate by Max Born. London: Taylor and Francis, 1978. [For the German translation see No. 13281/YB. XXI.] [The atom physicist (1882 Breslau–1970 Göttingen) received the Nobel prize in 1954. During the Nazi period he lived in England. His literary estate is now in the Staatsbibliothek Preuss. Kulturbesitz in Berlin.]

15725. FISCHER, BRIGITTE B.: *Sie schrieben mir oder Was aus meinem Poesie-Album wurde.* Zürich, Stuttgart: Classen, 1978. 360 pp., ports., illus. [The memories of the daughter of Samuel Fischer (1859–1934) and wife of the publisher Gottfried Bermann Fischer.]
15726. FÜRST, MAX: *Talisman Scheherezade. Die schwierigen zwanziger Jahre.* München: Dt. Taschenbuch-Verlag, 1978. (dtv 1407). [First publ. München, Hanser, 1976. For this and the first part of his autobiography 'Gefilte Fisch'. Eine Jugend in Königsberg, see Nos. 14056–14058/YB. XXII. Born 1905 in Königsberg, M.F. died June 21, 1978 in Stuttgart. Cf. Ein Wanderer kommt zur Ruhe (Erwin Lichtenstein) in: 'MB', 21. Juli, Tel Aviv, 1978. His last writing was his contribution to 'Mein Judentum', see No. 15328.]
15727. FÜRSTENBERG, CARL. *Carl-Fürstenberg-Anekdoten:* Ein Unterschied muss sein. Gesammelt und erzählt von Hans Fürstenberg. Düsseldorf: Econ, 1978. 112 pp. [C.F., banker, 1850 Danzig–1933 Berlin. Die Lebensgeschichte eines deutschen Bankiers, told by his son Hans, was first publ. 1931, reprinted 1961. See No. 2756/YB. VII.]
15728. GOLDZIHER, IGNAZ: *Tagebuch.* Hrsg. von Alexander Scheiber. Leiden: Brill, 1978. 341 pp. [Cf. The Prisoner of Budapest (W. Montgomery Watt) in: 'TLS', Sept. 8, London, 1978.] [I.G., Islamist, 1850 Stuhlweissenburg–1921 Budapest. The diary is an important historical document for the state of Hungarian Jewry and of Hungarian academic life.]
15729. GOLL, CLAIRE and YVAN: *Meiner Seele Töne.* Das literarische Dokument eines Lebens zwischen Kunst und Liebe, aufgezeichnet in den Briefen von Yvan und Claire Goll. München: Scherz, 1978. 304 pp., ports., illus., facsims.
15730. GUNDOLF, FRIEDRICH/ERICH VON KAHLER. *Aus dem Briefwechsel Erich von Kahler/Friedrich Gundolf.* Mitgeteilt von Klaus-Gerhard Pott. [In]: Jahrbuch 1978. Deutsche Akademie für Sprache und Dichtung Darmstadt. Heidelberg: Lambert Schneider, 1978. Pp. 84–97.
15731. HERTZ, HEINRICH: *Memoirs, Letters, Diaries.* Arranged by Johanna Hertz. Engl. translation by Lisa Brinner. With a biogr. introduction by Max von Laue. 2., enlarged ed. Prepared by Mathilde Hertz and Charles Susskind. San Francisco, Calif.: San Francisco Press/Weinheim: Physik Verlag, 1977. xxxvii, 361 pp., ports., illus., bibl. (pp. 354–359). Paralleltitel: Erinnerungen, Briefe, Tagebücher. Text deutsch u. englisch.
15732. KESTEN, HERMANN: *Briefe an J.R. Becher.* (München, Berlin 1957). Aus aktuellem Anlass [in]: 'Europäische Ideen', Hrsg. Andreas W. Mytze. H.40, Berlin, 1978. Pp. 48–54. [Letters concerning German authors in GDR prisons.]
15733. LIEBESCHÜTZ, RAHEL: *Im Wandel der Zeit.* Briefe von zwei Generationen aus der Biedermeier-Epoche. [In]: LBI Bulletin. No. 53/54. Tel Aviv, 1977/78. Pp. 1–41. [See No. 15110.]
15734. LUXEMBURG, ROSA: *Briefe aus dem Gefängnis.* 9., erw. Aufl. Berlin [East]: Dietz, 1977. 103 pp., port. [For collections of R.L. letters see Nos. 14068/YB. XXII, 13301/13302/YB. XXI, 11809/YB. XIX, 10044/YB. XVII.]
15735. MAHLER, GUSTAV: *Briefe 1879–1911.* Hrsg. von Alma Maria Mahler. Nachdr. d. Ausg. Wien/Berlin 1925. Hildesheim: Olms Reprints. 1978. xiv, 494 pp., port.
15736. MISES, LUDWIG VON: *Erinnerungen.* Mit e. Vorwort von Margit v. Mises und e. Einleitung von Friedrich August von Hayek. Stuttgart/New York: Fischer, 1978. xvi, 112 pp., port., bibl. (pp. 92–109). [National economist, sociologist, 1881 Lemberg–1973 New York.]
15737. MÜHSAM, PAUL: *Mein Weg zu mir.* Aus Tagebüchern. Hrsg. und kommentiert von Else Levi-Mühsam. Geleitwort von Werner Volke. Konstanz: Rosgarten Verlag, 1978. xiv, 250 pp., ports., illus. [The development of a Prussian citizen and Jew, by profession a lawyer, by his inner calling a poet.]
15738. SPERBER, MANÈS: *Den Tod überleben.* Erinnerungen an Freunde. [In]: 'Merkur', 31. Jg., H. 8 (351), August. Stuttgart: Klett, 1977. Pp. 735–748. [Friends remembered incl. Arthur Koestler, Anna Seghers, André Malraux.]
15739. HIEBER, JOCHEN: *Selbstzeugnis und Zeitgeschichte.* Manès Sperbers Memoirenwerk. [In]: 'Neue Rundschau', 89. Jg., 3. H. Frankfurt/M.: Fischer, 1978. Pp. 465–469. [See No. 14915/YB. XXIII.]
15740. Ross, WERNER: *Innere Wahrhaftigkeit.* Zu Manès Sperbers Autobiographie. [In]: 'Merkur', 32. Jg., H. 5, Mai. Stuttgart: Klett, 1978. Pp. 528–531. [See No. 14915/YB. XXIII.]

15741. STERNBERGER, HARRY: *Tolle Jahre.* Begegnungen in 88 Jahren. Teil V. Tel Aviv: Priv. Printed (21, Keren Kayemeth Blvd.), 1978. 54 pp. [For parts I–IV see No. 13317/YB. XXI.]
15742. STERNHEIM, CARL: *Briefe Carl Sternheims an Thea.* Mitgeteilt und eingel. von Wolfgang Wendler. [In]: 'NZZ', 1./2. April, Zürich, 1978. Pp. 63–64, port. [Thea Löwenstein née Bauer became, in 1907, Sternheim's second wife. Appr. 600 letters he had written to her between 1904 and 1942 have been since 1965 in the 'Deutsches Literaturarchiv in Marbach', but can only be published now after St.'s 100th birthday. C.St., 1878 Leipzig–1942 Brüssel. Erste Auszüge aus den Briefen an Thea und Dorotha (his daughter 'Mopsa') also in: 'FAZ', 1. April, Frankfurt/M., 1978, port. drawing [by B. F. Dolbin.]
15743. TUCHOLSKY, KURT: *Die Q-Tagebücher, 1934–1935.* Hrsg. von Mary Gerold-Tucholsky und Gustav Huonker. Reinbek b. Hamburg: Rowohlt, 1978. 448 pp., illus. [Das Q steht für Quatsch. Addressed to a Swiss lady doctor friend the diary entries begin Sept. 1934 and end on the 18th/19th Dec. 1935, two days before his suicide. Cf. Der Hass, der aus der Liebe kommt. Gut Nacht, Deutschland (Erich Fried) in: 'Die Zeit', March 31, Hamburg, 1978.]
15744. ZWEIG, ARNOLD-LOUIS FÜRNBERG: *Briefwechsel zwischen Louis Fürnberg und Arnold Zweig.* Dokumente einer Freundschaft. Hrsg. im Auftrag der Akademie der Künste der DDR von Rosemarie Poschmann und Gerhard Wolf. Berlin [East]: Aufbau, 1978. 397 pp., ports. [Cf. Dokumente des Exils. Genossen nur in der Not? (Hans-Albert Walter) in: 'Die Zeit', 6. April, Hamburg, 1979. – Zweig and Fürnberg were in Palestine during the same period. The German Zionist, the Czech Communist – both disappointed in Palestine returned to East Berlin.]
15745. ZWEIG, STEFAN: *Briefe an Freunde.* Hrsg. von Richard Friedenthal. Frankfurt/M.: Fischer, 1978. viii, 420 pp., facsim., notes pp. 355–401, list of letter recipients. [Cf. Stefan Zweigs Lebenstragödie in Selbstzeugnissen (Paul F. Proskauer) in: 'Aufbau', Jan. 19, New York, 1979, port.]
15746. *Richard Strauss/Stefan Zweig: A Confidential Matter.* An exchange of letters during 1931–1935. Transl. from the German by Max Knight. Foreword by Edward E. Lowinsky. Berkeley, Calif.: University of California Press, 1977. xxxi, 122 pp., ports., facsims. [Expanded entry No. 14924/YB. XXIII.]

IX. GERMAN-JEWISH RELATIONS

A. General

15747. BERGLAR, PETER, ed.: *Die Juden in Deutschland.* Schatten-Schuld. Ein neuer Anfang. Sonderdruck aus' Rheinischer Merkur aus den Ausgaben 48 bis 50 vom 1. bis 15. 12. 1978. 54 Koblenz (Görgenstr. 11), n.p., ports., illus. [Incl. I.: Nach dem Abgrund des 'Dritten Reiches' kann es, opportun oder inopportun, im Verhältnis zwischen Juden und Deutschen keine Neutralität geben. II. Das moderne Israel gibt selbstbewusste Antworten auf Jahrhunderte von Verfolgung und Assimilation. Die Staatsnation integriert die Einwanderer. III. Endstation Sehnsucht. IV. Wechselvoll ist die Geschichte der Juden in Deutschland. Erst die Emanzipation zu Anfang des 19. Jahrhunderts brachte eine Wende zu relativer Sicherheit für die Juden. V. Weg von der Legende. Der europäische Judenhass nahm die verschiedensten Formen an. VI. Die Besonderheiten des deutschen Antisemitismus konzentrierten sich immer mehr auf 'gleichartiges Blut'. In Blut endete zunächst alles. Letzte Antworten auf die tiefsten Fragen bleiben versagt.]
15748. BLASIUS, DIRK: *'Judenfrage' und Gesellschaftsgeschichte.* [In]: Neue Politische Literatur. Berichte über das internationale Schrifttum. XXIII. Jg., H. 1 (Jan.–März). Wiesbaden: Steiner, 1978. Pp. 17–33. [Review article of works concerning the history of German-Jewish relationship].
15749. LEA, CHARLENE A.: *Emancipation, Assimilation and Stereotype.* The Image of the Jew in German and Austrian Drama (1800–1850). Bonn: Bouvier, 1978. viii, 171 pp., notes pp. 118–155, bibl. (pp. 156–169), names index pp. 167–169. (Modern German Studies, vol. 2).

15750. RENGSTORF, KARL HEINRICH: *Christen und Juden in Nordwestdeutschland.* Gemeindevortrag, geh. am 29. Mai 1978 bei der Jahrestagung der Ges. f. niedersächsische Kirchengeschichte . . . [In]: Jahrbuch d. Ges. f. Niedersächsische Kirchengeschichte, Bd. 76, Nienburg, 1978. Pp. 31–40, bibl.
15751. 'TRIBÜNE', Zeitschrift zum Verständnis des Judentums. Hrsg. von Elisabeth Reisch. Chief Ed. Axel Silenius. 17. Jg., H. 65–68. Frankfurt/M.: Tribüne Verlag, 1978. [4 issues.] [H. 65 incl.: Vergangenheitsbewältigung – Hilfe für die Zukunft? (Rudolf Schroers). H. 67: Majdanek – Ein Prozess macht Geschichte. Ursprung-Stand-und keine Folgen (Heiner Lichtenstein). Dokumentation: Antisemitismus und Majdanek-Prozess. Knessetdebatte über neonazistische und antisemitische Tendenzen (in deutscher Übersetzung, pp. 88–114). H. 68: 'Holocaust' – Fiktion des Erlebten. Einige Fakten und Gedanken zur Fernsehsendereihe 'Holocaust' des WDR (Tilman Ernst, pp. 76–88). Widerstandspresse und Nationalsozialismus (Gerd Renken, pp. 89–108). Unbekannter Widerstand gegen Hitler (Günter Markscheffel, pp. 109–122). In Erinnerung an Jean Améry (Hermann Glaser).] [Some selected contributions are listed according to subject. See Nos. 15197, 15202, 15237, 15281, 15686, 15754.]

B. German–Israeli Relations

15752. '*deutschland-berichte*'. Hrsg. Rolf Vogel. 14. Jg., Nr. 1–12. Bonn, 1978. [Twelve issues.]
15753. DOERDELMANN, BERNHARD: *30 Jahre Staat Israel.* Gedanken zum deutsch-israelischen Verhältnis. [In]: 'Emuna-Israel Forum'. H. 1, 1978. Pp. 58–62.
15754. *30 Jahre Israel. Die deutsch-israelischen Beziehungen.* Grussworte und Stellungnahme zum deutsch-israelischen Verhältnis von Helmut Schmidt, Helmut Kohl, Willy Brandt, Hans-Dietrich Genscher, Annemarie Renger, Rolf Rodenstock, Heinz Oskar Vetter, Matthias Wissmann. Pp. 3–30. Verpflichtung und Politik. Zum Verhältnis zwischen der Bundesrepublik Deutschland und Israel (Reiner Bernstein, pp. 32–46). Die deutsche Mark in Israel (Christoph von Imhoff, pp. 48–62). Die theologische Bedeutung des Staates Israel (Rudolf Pfisterer, pp. 74–90). Religion und Politik in Israel (Rolf Rendtorff, pp. 91–101). Die Förderung der deutsch-israelischen Beziehungen (M. G. Hess, pp. 114–116) [In]: 'Tribüne', H. 66, 1978. Pp. 3–116. [See No. 15751.]
15755. SCHOENBERNER, GERHARD: *Die Situation der Bibliothek des Deutschen Kulturzentrums.* [In]: 'Börsenblatt für den Dt. Buchhandel'. 34. Jg., Nr. 69, 29. Aug. Frankfurt/M., 1978. Pp. 1775–1776. [The origin was the 'Deutsche Bibliothek Prof. Walter Hirsch' in Tel Aviv, a private collection of appr. 2000 volumes.]
15756. STEIN, GUSTAV, ed.: *Menschenrechte in Israel und Deutschland.* Ein Symposon der Gesellschaft zur Förderung der wissenschaftlichen Zusammenarbeit mit der Universität Tel Aviv. Köln: Verlag Wissenschaft und Politik, 1978. 175 pp. [Lectures and discussions at the 2nd German Israeli symposion, held in Nov. 1976 in Munich. Ten contributions German or English.]

C. Church and Synagogue

15757. '*Christian Attitudes on Jews and Judaism*'. A Bi-Monthly Documentary Survey. Ed. C. C. Aronsfeld. No. 58–63. London: Institute of Jewish Affairs in Association with the World Jewish Congress, 1978. [6 issues.] [No. 58 incl.: Theological Impact of the Holocaust (Peter F. Gilbert). No. 59: All Life is Meeting. On the Centenary of Martin Buber's Birth (C. Witton-Davies). Oberammergau – Prelude to 1980. No. 60: Jerusalem Conference Paper on the Church and the Jewish People. The Antisemitism of Martin Luther. No. 61: Theology of the Holocaust (Clemens Thoma). After Auschwitz (Charlotte L. Klein). No. 62: Views of The 'Holocaust' TV Film (Philip Schofield). German Christian Reaction to the Burning of the Synagogues in 1938. No. 63: Young Germans' Work for Christian-Jewish Understanding (Elke Floris). German Christians' Heart-Searching. Antisemitism in the New Testament (W. E. B. Jones). Chagall Window in a German Church [St. Stephan's Church in Mainz], the artist's first work for a church in Germany.]

15758. EHRLICH, ERNST LUDWIG: *Die christlichen Kirchen und das Judentum*. Der Spannung standhalten (Lukas Vischer). Die christliche Komponente im modernen Antisemitismus (Jacob Katz). Gegenwart der Propheten? (Max Schoch). Das orthodoxe Christentum und das Judentum. Der Stand ihrer Beziehungen (Damaskinos Papandreon). Die Identität der Dialogiker (Clemens Thoma). [In]: 'NZZ', FA Nr. 243, 20. Okt., Zürich, 1978. Pp. 33–36.

15759. '*Emuna-Israel Forum*'. Vereinigte Zeitschriften über Israel und Judentum. Hrsg. Deutscher Koordinierungsrat d. Gesellschaften f. Christl.-Jüd. Zusammenarbeit. Deutsch Israelische Gesellschaft (DIG). Eds.: Willehad Paul Eckert, Erika Doerdelmann-Kolbe, Erich Rotter. H. 1–4. Rothenburg ob der Tauber: Verlag Israel-Forum, 1978. [4 issues.] [H. 1 incl.: Begegnungen mit Martin Buber (Pnina Navé). Martin Buber in Königsfeld. Eine persönliche Erinnerung (Leopold Marx). Else Lasker-Schüler zum 30jährigen Todestag (J. Tolkes). Egon Erwin Kisch – 30. Todestag (Meir Reubeni). Martin Buber, dem Künder des Chassidismus, zu seinem 100. Geburtstag (Meir Reubeni). H. 2: Martin Bubers Lehre über Geschichte und Gesellschaft (Wolf-Dieter Gudopp, pp. 1–12, bibl.) Buber in Gesprächen (Arye Ben-David). Kafka im Kloster (Willehad Paul Eckert). Nes Ammim – Eine christliche Siedlung in Israel (Heinz Kremers). Die Musik im jüdischen Gottesdienst (Kantor Julius Stolberg). Martin-Buber-Jahr 1978. Eindrücke vom Martin Buber-Symposion in Beer Sheva (Ernst Vogt, illus.) Gerschom Scholem–80 Jahre (Meir Reubeni). H. 3: Ein Jude kämpfte für die Rettung von einer Million armenischer Christen. Die Taten des Henry Morgenthau sen. (Robert M. W. Kempner). Die Massenvernichtung der Juden wird geleugnet! (Erich Kulka, pp. 37–47). H. 4: Die Zukunft des jüdischen Volkes aus christlicher Sicht (Willehad Paul Eckert, pp. 29–36. To be continued). Heinrich Heine und die Bolkerstrasse in Düsseldorf (Emilie Schüssler). Zu Alfred Döblins 100. Geburtstag (Meir Reubeni). Bitteres Gedenken und farbige Lebenslust im Werke des Malers Heinrich Sussmann (Meir Faerber.) [The painter, born 1904 in Tarnopol, is a survivor of Auschwitz.] [Some selected contributions are listed according to subject. See Nos. 15081, 15199, 15236, 15267, 15683, 15753.]

15760. '*Freiburger Rundbrief*'. Beiträge zur christlich-jüdischen Begegnung. Hrsg. (mit Unterstützung der Deutschen Bischofskonferenz und des Deutschen Caritasverbandes) von Willehad P. Eckert, Rupert Giessler, Georg Hüssler, Ludwig Kaufmann, Gertrud Luckner, Clemens Thoma, Anton Vögtle. XXIX. Folge, Nr. 109–112. Freiburg i. Br.: Freiburger Rundbrief, 1977. 208 pp., Literaturhinweise pp. 113–159. (1 vol.) [Incl. 30 Jahre Freiburger Rundbrief 1948–1978. Versuch einer Zwischenbilanz der Reformbemühungen des Redens von den Juden im christlichen Religionsunterricht (Ingrid Maisch). Der Architekt der Versöhnung. Erinnerungen an Franz Böhm (Moshe Tavor, Vorbemerkung von Gertrud Luckner). Judentum im heutigen Religionsunterricht (Hildegard Gollinger). Juden und Christen auf dem XVII. Deutschen Evangelischen Kirchentag, Berlin West, Juni 1977. Zum 100. Geburtstag von Jules Isaac (18.11.1877–5.9.1963). Einzige und letzte Nachricht aus dem KZ Drancy, Sept. 1943, von Laura Isaac an ihren Gatten vor ihrer Ermordung in Auschwitz. Ansprache von Bundeskanzler Helmut Schmidt in Auschwitz-Birkenau am 23. Nov. 1977. Antisemitismus kritisch betrachtet. Kritik und Gegenkritik an Christentum und Jüdentum (Rita Egger). Statt Reformpassion ein Versöhnungsspiel. Oberammergauer Passionsspiele nun doch mit revidiertem Text. See also Nos. 15763, 15766, 15802.]

15761. GOLLWITZER, HELMUT/ROLF RENDTORFF: *Thema Juden, Christen, Israel*. Ein Gespräch. Mit e. Entgegnung von Nathan Peter Levinson. Didaktische Skizze mit e. Projektidee zum Thema Judentum von Helga Sorge. Stuttgart: Radius Verlag, 1978. 128 pp.

15762. GRUENEWALD, MAX: *Jewish-Christian 'Dialogue' of 1933*. Reminiscences in the Buber Centenary Year. [In]: 'AJR Information'. Vol. XXXIII, No. 10, Oct. London, 1978. Pp. 1–2.

15763. '*Immanuel*'. Dokumente des heutigen religiösen Denkens und Forschens in Israel. Hrsg.: Ökumenisch-Theologische Forschungsgemeinschaft in Israel und Freiburger Rundbrief. VI, 1977. Jerusalem-Freiburg i. Br., 1977. Pp. 169–208 im 'Freiburger Rundbrief' [see No. 15760]. (Hebräische Veröffentlichungen aus Israel in deutscher Übersetzung). [Incl.: Gershom Scholem und die 'Wissenschaft des Judentums'. Prof. Scholem zum 80. Geburtstag am 5.12.1977 (Zeev Levi, aus dem Hebr. übers. von A. D. von Kries, Jerusalem, pp. 170–172). Buber im heutigen Israel (Rivka Horwitz, aus d. Hebr.

übers. von A. D. von Kries, Jerusalem, pp. 172–176). Die verschiedenen Strömungen innerhalb des deutschen Judentums konfrontiert mit der allgemeinen Kultur (Moshe Schwarcz s.A., aus dem Hebr. übers. von Angela von Kries, Jerusalem, pp. 176–183). [This is the first chapter from the author's book 'Jüdisches Denken und allgemeine Kultur', Tel Aviv, 1966]. [Moshe Schwarcz, prof. of philosophy at Bar Ilan University, Tel Aviv, died Nov. 1977 in Lucerne.]

15764. KÜNG, HANS/PINCHAS LAPIDE: *Brother or Lord?* A Jew and a Christian talk together about Jesus. Transl. from the German by E. Quinn. London: Collins, 1977. 44 pp. [For German original: 'Jesus im Widerstreit' see No. 14102/YB. XXII.]

15765. LEUNER, HEINZ DAVID: *Zwischen Israel und den Völkern.* Vortrag eines Judenchristen. Berlin: Institut Kirche und Judentum, 1978. 148 pp. (Veröffentlichungen aus dem Institut K. u. J. bei der Kirchlichen Hochschule, Berlin, 6).

15766. *Heinz David Leuner.* Special Memorial Issue of 'Der Zeuge'. Hrsg.: International Hebrew Christian Alliance. Jg. XXIX, No. 57, April. Ramsgate, Kent: Internationale Judenchristliche Allianz, 1978. 24 pp., port. (Der Beitrag: Rev. Heinz David Leuner zum Gedenken (15.9.1906 Breslau–23.9.1977 London). Eine theologische Würdigung von Peter von der Osten-Sacken, pp. 6–8, ist ein Nachdruck aus 'Veröffentlichungen des Instituts Kirche und Judentum, H. 6, Berlin, und ist auch abgedruckt in 'Freiburger Rundbrief'. See No. 15760). [See also No. 15170.]

15767. *Treue zur Thora.* Beiträge zur Mitte des christl.-jüd. Gesprächs. Festschrift für Günther Harder zum 75. Geburtstag. Hrsg. von Peter von der Osten-Sacken. Berlin: Institut Kirche und Judentum, 1977. 223 pp., port., bibl. G.H. pp. 207–220. (Veröffentlichungen aus dem Institut Kirche und Judentum bei der Kirchlichen Hochschule Berlin, Nr. 3).

D. Antisemitism

— ANGRESS, WERNER T.: *The German Army's 'Judenzählung' of 1916.* Genesis-Consequences-Significance. [See No. 14993.]

15768. ANONYMOUS: *The Myth of the Six Million.* The Truth about the Greatest Lie in History. 3rd. ed. Torrance, Ca.: Noontide Press, 1978. 119 pp. [See Der Auschwitz-Betrug, No. 12580/YB. XX and No. 11859/YB. XIX.]

15769. ANTI-ROEDER-ARBEITSKREIS, ed.: *'NSDAP' – Propagandisten unter der Lupe.* Dokumentation antisemit., antidemokrat. und offener NS-Provokationen der Schönborn-Roeder-Christophersen-Bande und ihre Deckung seitens staatl. Organe. Hamburg: Reents, 1978. 203 pp., ports., illus. (Anti-faschistische Russell-Reihe, 3).

— BELKE, INGRID: *Liberal Voices on Antisemitism in the 1880s.* Letters to Moritz Lazarus, 1880–1883. [See No. 14994.]

15770. BENTLEY, JAMES: *The Most Irresistible Temptation.* [British Theologians and the Third Reich/The Tübingen Theologian Gerhard Kittel and National Socialism]. A radio broadcast printed in: 'The Listener', 16 Nov., London, 1978. Pp. 635–636. [What made Kittel's support for Hitler all the more dangerous was his international reputation].

15771. BERNSTEIN, GEORGE: *Anti-semitism in Imperial Germany, 1871–1914.* Selected Documents. New York, 1973. iv, 433 pp. Diss., Columbia University, Microfilm copy of typescript. Ann Arbor, Mich., University Microfilms, 1974.

15772. BIEBERSTEIN, JOHANNES ROGALIA VON: *Die These von der Verschwörung 1776–1945.* Philosophen, Freimaurer, Juden, Liberale und Sozialisten als Verschwörer gegen die Sozialordnung. 2., verb. u. verm. Aufl. Frankfurt/M., Bern: Lang, 1978. 294 pp., bibl. (pp. 236–284). (Europ. Hochschulschriften, Reihe 3, Geschichte und ihre Hilfswiss., Bd. 63). [See also No. 14945/YB. XXIII.]

15773. BURG, J. G. [i.e. Josef Ginsburg]: *Der jüdische Eichmann.* 1977, 8 pp. Offener Brief an den bayerischen Landesrabbiner H. I. Grünewald, 1977, 12 pp. Das Tagebuch (der Anne Frank), 1978, 20 pp., illus. Terror und Terror: Gift oder Honig, Wahrheit oder Lüge? 1977, 22 pp. Troika: Das Dreigespann Goldmann, Bengurion (sic), Adenauer, 1978, 19 pp., illus. München: Ederer, 1977/78. [5 vols.]

15774. FREI, BRUNO [originally Benedikt Freistadt]: *Sozialismus und Antisemitismus.* Wien, München: Europaverlag, 1978. 50 pp.

15775. GUTMAN, YISRAEL and LIVIA ROTHKIRCHEN, eds.: *The Catastrophe of European Jewry*. Antecedents-History-Reflections. Selected Papers. Jerusalem: Yad Vashem, 1976. x, 757 pp., chron. table of events 1933–1945 comp. by Shmuel Krakowski, pp. 705–738, index of names, bibl. (pp. 756–757). [Incl. The Origins of Modern Anti-Semitism (Shmuel Effinger). The Jewish Question in Modern Anti-Semitic Literature: Prelude to the 'Final Solution' (Alex Bein). Anti-Christian anti-Semitism (Uriel Tal). Mission and Testimony: The Universal Significance of Modern Anti-Semitism (Jacob L. Talmon). European Jewry before and after Hitler (Salo W. Baron). The Holocaust (Jacob Robinson). The 'Final Solution' in its Last Stages (Livia Rothkirchen). The Dignity of the Destroyed. Towards a Definition of the Period of the Holocaust (Shaul Esh). The Attitude of the Judenrats to the Problems of Armed Resistance against the Nazis (Isaiah Trunk). The 'Righteous among the Nations' and their part in the Rescue of Jews (Moshe Bejski). The Holocaust and the Struggle of the Yishuv as Factors in the Establishment of the State of Israel (Yehuda Bauer). The Holocaust in Jewish Historiography (Leni Yahil). The Mission of the Survivors (Abba Kovner.] [For a Hebrew edition (1973) see No. 11191/YB. XIX.]

15776. HARWOOD, RICHARD [pseud.]: *Nuremberg and Other War Crimes Trials.* A new look. Chapel Ascote, Ladbroke Southam, Warks. England: Historical Review Press, 1978. 69 pp., illus., bibl. (Historical Fact No. 2).

15777. HUNGARY. BRAHAM, RANDOLPH L.: *The Hungarian Labor Service System 1939–1945*. Boulder, Colo.: East European Quarterly, 1977. 159 pp. [Study reflecting anti-semitic aspects of this phase of Hungarian policies.]

15778. KUBINZKY, JUDIT: *Political antiszemitizmus Magyarorszagon 1875–1890*. Budapest: Kossruth, 1976. 273 pp.

15779. LEISTNER, REINHOID: *Antijudaismus im Johannisevangelium?* Bern, Frankfurt/M.: Lang, 1974. 227 pp.

15780. LEUSCHEN-SEPPEL, ROSEMARIE: *Sozialdemokratie und Antisemitismus im Kaiserreich*. Die Auseinandersetzungen der Partei mit den konservativen und völkischen Strömungen des Antisemitismus 1871–1914. Bonn: Verlag Neue Gesellschaft, 1978. 340 pp., ports., illus. (Reihe Politik und Gesellschaftsgeschichte).

15781. LEVENBERG, S.: *Antisemitismus – Illusion und Wirklichkeit*. [In]: 'Jüdischer Presse Dienst'. Informationen des Zentralrats der Juden in Deutschland. Nr. 7/8, Dez., Düsseldorf, 1978. Pp. 17–19.

15782. LILL, RUDOLF: *Zu den Anfängen des Antisemitismus im Bismarck-Reich*. [In]: 'Saeculum'. Bd. 26, H. 2. Freiburg/Br.: Alber, 1975. Pp. 214–231, bibl. footnotes.

15783. LÖWE, HEINZ-DIETRICH: *Antisemitismus und reaktionäre Utopie*. Hamburg: Hoffmann und Campe, 1978. 300 pp.

15784. MICHAELIS, MIRJAM: *Rassenantisemitismus vor neunzig Jahren*. [In]: 'Das Neue Israel' 31. Jg., H. 1, Juli. Zürich, 1978. Pp. 22–23. [Racial antisemitism propagated by Friedrich Lange, chief editor of the 'Tägliche Rundschau' and founder, in 1894, of the 'Deutschbund'.]

—— MOSSE, GEORGE L.: *Rassismus*. Ein Krankheitssymptom in der europäischen Geschichte des 19. und 20. Jahrhunderts. [See No. 15008.]

15785. MÜLLER, JOSEF: *Die Entwicklung des Rassenantisemitismus in den letzten Jahrzehnten des 19. Jahrhunderts*. Dargestellt hauptsächlich auf Grundlage der 'Antisemitischen Korrespondenz'. Nachdr. d. Ausg. Berlin, Ebering, 1940. Vaduz: Kraus, 1965. 95 pp., bibl. (Historische Studien, H. 372).

15786. OPPENHEIMER, MAX/HORST STUCKMANN/RUDI SCHNEIDER: *Als die Synagogen brannten*. Zur Funktion des Antisemitismus gestern und heute. Mit e. Vorw. von Willy Bleicher. Frankfurt/M.: Röderberg Verlag, 1978. 156 pp., ports., illus., facsims.

15787. *'Patterns of Prejudice'*. Ed. C. C. Aronsfeld. Publ. Bi-Monthly. Vol. 12, No. 1–6. London: Institute of Jewish Affairs, 1978. [6 vols.] [No. 1 incl.: Obsession and Realpolitik in the 'Final Solution' (Erich Goldhagen, pp. 1–16, footnotes pp. 12–16). Germans, Poles and Auschwitz. Reconciliation in Europe. No. 3: The West and the Holocaust (Michael Mashberg, pp. 19–32, footnotes pp. 30–32). Vol. 4: 'Holocaust' Film's Impact on Americans (Sander A. Diamond, pp. 1–9 & 19, footnotes). No. 5: 'Perish Judah'. Nazi Extermination Propaganda 1920–1945 (C. C. Aronsfeld, pp. 17–26, footnotes pp. 25–26). No. 6: Nazi Shadows are Lengthening over Germany (Eva Kolinsky, pp. 25–32, footnotes pp. 31–32). See also No. 15242.]

Bibliography

15788. POLIAKOV, LÉON: *Geschichte des Antisemitismus.* I. Von der Antike bis zu den Kreuzzügen. II. Das Zeitalter der Verteufelung und des Ghettos. Mit e. Anhang: Zur Anthropologie der Juden. Aus dem Franzos. von Rudolf Pfisterer. Worms: Heintz, 1976–1978. 93, 239 pp. [2 vols.] [See also No. 14956/YB. XXIII.]
15789. POLIAKOV, LÉON: *Histoire de l'antisémitisme.* Vol. 4: L'Europe Suicidaire 1870–1933. Paris: Calmann-Lévy, 1977. 364 pp.
15790. RAGINS, SANFORD: *Jewish Responses to Antisemitism in Germany, 1870–1914.* Philos. Diss., pres. to . . . Brandeis University, 1972. Ann Arbor, Mich.: University Microfilms, 1978. 280 pp. + 17 pp. notes + 18 pp. bibl. [Photocopy of typescript.]
15791. ROTHE, WOLF DIETER: *Die Endlösung der Judenfrage.* Bd. 2: Dokumente. Frankfurt/M.: Bierbaum, 1978. 208 pp. [Documentary proof that the gas chambers, f. i. in Mauthausen, never existed. For vol. I: Zeugen, see No. 12592/YB. XX.]
15792. RUETHER, ROSEMARY: *Faith and Fraticide: The Theological Roots of Anti-Semitism.* Introduction by Gregory Baum. New York: The Seabury Press, 1974. ix, 293 pp., notes pp. 262–285. Transl. into German by Ulrike Berger: *Nächstenliebe und Brudermord – Die theologischen Wurzeln des Antisemitismus.* Hrsg. von Helmut Gollwitzer. München: Kaiser, 1978. 269 pp., notes pp. 252–269. (Abhandlungen zum christlich-jüdischen Dialog, Bd. 7).
15793. SCHIECKEL, HARALD: *Gesuche um Änderungen jüdischer Familiennamen zur Verhinderung antisemitischer Geschäftsschädigungen.* Beispiele aus dem Lande Oldenburg 1870–1931. [In]: 'Genealogie', Deutsche Zeitschrift für Familienkunde. 27. Jg., Bd. 14, H. 11, Nov. Neustadt (Aisch): Degener, 1978. Pp. 337–348.
15794. SPIRA, LEOPOLD: *Antisemitismus in Österreich.* Erscheinungen, Wurzeln, Träger. [In]: Weg und Ziel. Sept. Hrsg.: Kommunistische Partei Österreichs. Wien: Stern Verlag, 1965. 47 pp.
15795. SUZMAN, ARTHUR/DENIS DIAMOND: *Der Mord an sechs Millionen Juden.* Die Wahrheit ist unteilbar. Aus dem Engl. übers. von Ingemarie Grabendorff. [In]: Aus Politik und Zeitgeschichte. Beilage zur Wochenzeitung 'Das Parlament'. B 30/78, 29. Juli. Bonn: Bundeszentrale für Politische Bildung, 1978. Pp. 4–21. [Translated excerpts from the English original 'Six Million Did Die. The Truth shall prevail' Foreword by Nahum Goldmann. See No. 14346/YB. XXIII.] [A refutation of the antisemitic brochure: Did six million really die? by Richard Harwood (pseud.).]
15796. VOGT, JUDITH: *Historien Om Et Image.* Antisemitisme og antizionisme i karikaturer. Oslo: J. W. Cappelens Forlag/Kobenhavn: Samlerens Forlag, 1978. 276 pp., facsims., notes pp. 257–272, bibl. (pp. 273–276). [Antisemitism and anti-Zionism in caricature. The author has reproduced about 500 cartoons from medieval times up to the present day, and supplied a commentary and analysis.]
15797. VOLKOV, SHULAMIT: *Antisemitism as a Cultural Code.* Reflections on the History and Historiography of Antisemitism in Imperial Germany. [In]: LBI Year Book XXIII. London, 1978. Pp. 25–46. [See No. 15111.]
— WASSERMANN, HENRY: *Jews and Judaism in the Gartenlaube.* [In]: LBI Year Book XXIII. London, 1978. Pp. 47–60, facsim. [See No. 15017.]
15798. WAWRZINEK, KURT: *Die Entstehung der deutschen Antisemitenparteien (1873–1890).* Nachdr. d. Ausg. Berlin, Ebering 1927. Vaduz: Kraus, 1965. 97 pp., bibl. (pp. 84–97). (Historische Studien, H. 168).
15799. ZIMMERMANN, MOSHE: *Two Generations in the History of German Antisemitism.* The Letters of Theodor Fritsch to Wilhelm Marr. [In]: LBI Year Book XXIII. London, 1978. Pp. 89–99. [See No. 15111.]

E. Noted Germans and Jews

15800. FORSTER, GEORG. GORDON, JOSEPH S.: *Georg Forster und die Juden.* [In]: Jahrbuch des Instituts für Deutsche Geschichte. Bd. VII. Tel Aviv, 1978. Pp. 215–253. [See No. 15109.] [G.F. (1754–1794), the most prominent German Jacobin.]
15801. GRILLPARZER, FRANZ. BAUER, ROGER: *Grillparzers 'Jüdin von Toledo' oder der verbotene Garten Eden.* [In]: 'NZZ', FA Nr. 142, 23. Juni, Zürich, 1978.
15802. KÜSTERMEIER, RUDOLF. LUCKNER, GERTRUD: *Rudolf Küstermeier (1903 Bielefeld–1977 Tel Avi:).* [In]: 'Freiburger Rundbrief', 1977. [See No. 15760.]

15803. LÜTH, ERICH: *Er schlug eine Brücke nach Israel.* [In]: 'Mitteilungen des Verbandes ehemaliger Breslauer und Schlesier in Israel'. Nr. 43, Tel Aviv, April 1978. [See No. 15060.]
15804. LUTHER, MARTIN. SUCHER, C. BERND: *Luthers Stellung zu den Juden.* Eine Interpretation aus germanistischer Sicht. Nieuwkoop: De Graaf, 1977. xii, 316 pp., bibl. (pp. 294–316). (Bibliotheca Humanistica & Reformatorica, Vol. XXIII).
15805. MANN, THOMAS: *Die Briefe Thomas Manns: Regesten und Register.* Bearb. und hrsg. unter Mitwirkung des Thomas-Mann-Archivs d. Eidgen. Techn. Hochschule Zürich von Hans Bürgin und Hans-Otto Mayer. Bd. 1: Die Briefe von 1889 bis 1933 hrsg. unter Mitarbeit von Yvonne Schmidlin. Mit e. Vorw. von Hans Wysling. Bd. 2: Die Briefe 1934–1943. Frankfurt/M.: Fischer, 1977. xxxix, 761 pp., bibl.; 1978, 800 pp., bibl. [2 vols.] [Vol. 3, 4 and Addenda to follow.]
15806. MANN, THOMAS: *Tagebücher.* Hrsg. von Peter de Mendelssohn. Bd. 1: 1933–1934. 1977, xxi, 817 pp.; Bd. 2: 1935–1936. 1978, 732 pp. Frankfurt/M.: Fischer, 2 vols. [Bd. 3: 1918–1921, Bd. 4: 1937–1955 to follow.]
15807. HARTUNG, RUDOLF: *Mensch und Werk.* Zu den Tagebüchern 1933–1934 von Thomas Mann. [In]: 'Die Neue Rundschau'. 89. Jg., H. 2, 1978. Pp. 285–291.
15808. TRAMER, HANS: '*Als Papale einen Juden nachmachte*'. Bemerkungen zu Thomas Manns Tagebüchern. [In]: 'MB'. 21. April. Tel Aviv, 1978. Pp. 12–14.
15809. THOMAS MANN – ERICH VON KAHLER: *Briefwechsel.* Hrsg. und kommentiert von Gerhard Mahr. Heidelberg: Stiehm, 1978. 220 pp. [The correspondence was translated into English by Richard and Clara Winston and published in 1975 under the title: An Exceptional Friendship. See No. 13363/YB. XXI.]
15810. WAGNER, RICHARD. WAGNER, COSIMA: *The Diaries.* Vol. I: 1869–1877. Ed. and annotated by Martin Gregor-Dellin and Dietrich Mack. Transl. by Geoffrey Skelton. London: Collins, 1978. 1199 pp., ports., illus. [For German orig. vol. I and II see No. 14975/YB. XXIII.] [Cf. Days in the Life of a Genius (George Steiner) in: 'The Sunday Times', Oct. 8, London, 1978, port. 'The record of Wagner's conversation and of Cosima's feelings are literally charged with hatred of Jews. It is the Jews who are ruining Europe. They must be eliminated if art and society are to be restored'.]
15811. WAGNER, RICHARD: *Schriften.* Ein Schlüssel zu Leben, Werk und Zeit. Ausgewählt, kommentiert und eingel. von Egon Voss. Ungek. Ausg. Frankfurt/M.: Fischer, 1978. 217 pp. (Fischer Taschenbücher, 2075).
15812. MAYER, HANS: *Richard Wagner. Mitwelt und Nachwelt.* Stuttgart: Belser, 1978. 448 pp. (Einleitung von Hans Mayer: Wir Wagnerianer.) [All the author's studies on Wagner written between 1955 and 1978.]
15813. *Wie antisemitisch darf ein Künstler sein?* Schriften über Richard Wagner. Musik-Konzepte Band 5. Hrsg. von Heinz-Klaus Metzger und Rainer Riehn. München: Edition text und kritik, 1978. 112 pp. [Incl. contributions (reprints) by Peter Viereck, Thomas Mann, Klaus-Uwe Fischer, Michel-François Demet. Further a 'Diskussion über Recht, Unrecht und Alternativen' with Hans Mayer. [And]: Die Verdrängung Heinrich Heines aus Werk und Bewusstsein Richard Wagners (Karl Richter).]
15814. WEGNER, ARMIN T. LAMM, HANS: *In memoriam Armin T. Wegner (1886 Elberfeld–17. Mai 1978 Rom).* [In]: Isr. Wochenblatt', Nr. 26, 30. Juni, Zürich, 1978. *Einer der Gerechten der Völker.* Hermann Lewy) in: 'Allgemeine', 26. Mai, Düsseldorf, 1978. *Ein Mann, der sich nicht beugen wollte* (Ernst Johann) in: 'FAZ', 19. Mai, Frankfurt/M., 1978, port. Armin T. Wegners '*Offener Brief an Hitler*', Ostern 1933 und Nachruf in 'Die Zeit', 26. Mai, Hamburg, 1978.

Index to Bibliography

Achenbach, Sigrid, 15586
Acta Baltica, 15216
Adam, Uwe Dietrich, 15127
Adams, Robert M., 15475
Adler, Alfred, 15398–15400
Adler, Felix, 15401
Adler, Guido, 15598
Adler H[ans] G[ünther], 15402–15403
Adler, Max, 15068, 15404
Adorno, Theodor W. (orig. Wiesengrund), 15381, 15382, 15383, 15386, 15396, 15405–15410, 15722
Adventurers, Jewish, 15478
Agnon, Shmuel Yoseph, 15345, 15411
Ahndung von NS-Verbrechen, 15169
Ahren, Yizhak, 15281
Aix-en-Provence (France) University, 15084
'AJR Information', London, 15006, 15010, 15090, 15094, 15100, 15103, 15110, 15113, 15158, 15192, 15194, 15245, 15272, 15331, 15338, 15339, 15394, 15468, 15762
Akademie der Künste, Berlin [East], 15718, 15744
Akten des V. Intern. Germanisten-Kongress Cambridge 1975, 15023
Alkalay, Edmund, 15628
Alkalay, Ora, 15118
Allen, Richard H., 15668
Allen Taylor, Ann, 15530
'Allgemeine' Wochenzeitung d. Juden in Deutschland, 15006, 15030, 15050, 15065, 15082, 15110, 15186, 15188, 15198, 15221, 15248, 15263, 15275, 15276, 15364, 15387, 15416, 15558, 15563, 15814
'Allgemeine Zeitung des Judenthums', 15334
Alperin, A[h]aron, 15352
Alsace, 15067
Alter, Robert, 14992, 14996
Alzey, 15401
American Jewish Committee, 14992, 15421, 15565
American Jewish Congress, 15092, 15143, 15280, 15295, 15313
American Jewish KC Fraternity, 15120
Amerongen, Martin van, 15576
Améry, Jean (i.e. Hans Mayer), 15222, 15328, 15412–15416, 15601, 15634, 15751
Amichai, Yehuda, 15328
Andernacht, Rosel, 15038
Anders, Günther (i.e. Günther Stern), 15328, 15417
Anderson, Quentin, 15011
Angress, Werner T., 14993
Anonymous, 15768

Anti-Defamation League of B'nai B'rith, 15157, 15210, 15241
Anti-faschistische Russell-Reihe, 15769
Anti-Roeder-Arbeitskreis, 15769
Antisemitism, 14993, 14994, 15087, 15182 (Hanover), 15238, 15606, 15747, 15751, 15757 (Martin Luther), 15758, 15760, 15768–15799
— Austrian, 15794
— Christian, 15779, 15792
— Hungarian, 15777–15778
— Imperial Germany, in, 15771, 15782, 15790, 15797
— Nazi, 15768, 15769, 15773, 15791
— Parties, in, 15780, 15798
— Racial, 15784, 15785
— Swiss, 15087
'Antisemitische Korrespondenz', 15785
Antisemitism, Judaism, Nazism in Education and Teaching, 15179, 15230–15244
Aquinas, St. Thomas, 15320
Arato, Andrew, 15381
Architects, Jewish, 15367, 15622
'Archivalische Zeitschrift', Köln, 15136
'Archivio di Filosofia', Roma, 15306
Arendt, Erich, 15418–15420
Arendt, Hannah, 15396, 15421–15423, 15429
Arieli, Yehoshua, 15015
Armenian Christians, 15759
Aris, Helmut, 15227
'Arisierung', 15133 (in Vienna)
Arnstein, Fanny von, 15424
Aron, Raymond, 15619
Arons, Martin Leo, 15425–15427
— 'Lex Arons', 15427
Aronsfeld, C. C. A., 15089, 15090, 15128, 15129, 15245, 15757, 15787
'Art behind barbed wire', 15073, 15206
Art Historians (Jewish), 15509, 15700
Arts and Crafts, Jews in, 15477, 15497
As[c]hkenasim, 15323
Assimilation, 14997, 15327, 15747, 15749
— 15073 (Czech-Jewish), 15083 (Hungarian)
Astor, R., 15575
Atkins, Stuart, 15519
Atlasz, Robert, 15329
Auser, Annemarie, 15455
Auerbach, Richard J., 15120
'Aufbau', 15063, 15110, 15196, 15236, 15268, 15379, 15469, 15563, 15601, 15639, 15664, 15745
Aufklärung see Enlightenment
'aus politik und zeitgeschichte', Bonn, 15195, 15209, 15795

Auschwitz, 15130–15131, 15238, 15757, 15787
— Museum, Staatliches, 15131
Ausländer, Rose (Scherzer-Ausländer), 15397
Austria, 15068–15072, 15132–15134, 15212 (resistance), 15378, 15397, 15794 (Kommun. Partei)
— Antisemitism, in, 15794
— Emigration, 14497
Austrian Lyric, 15397
Austromarxismus, 15068, 15404
Aviatik, Aeronautik, 15389, 15544
Awerbuch, Marianne, 15284
Awner, Jehuda Ben (Markt), 15060

Baden Markgrafschaft, 15044
Baden-Württemberg, 15172
— Komission f. Geschichtliche Landeskunde, in, Veröffentlichungen der, 15172
Baeck, Leo, 15246, 15302, 15489
Baerwald, Leo, Rabb., 15033
Bahrdt, Hans-Paul, 15015
Bak, Samuel, 15328
Baker, Leonard, 15246
Balinkin, Ausma, 15714
Baltic Jews, 15216, 15217
Bamberger, Gabrielle, 15112, 15113
Bamberger, Raw Seligmann Baer, 15247
Bamberger, S. B., 15247, 15323
Bankers, Jewish, 15012, 15699, 15702, 15727
Bar-Giora Bamberger, Naftalie, 15323
Bar Ilan University, Annual, 15080
Bar Kochba Makkabi-Berlin, 15329, 15330
Bargmann, Sonja, 15480
Barkai, A[vraham], 15109
Barkai, Jehoschua, 15520
Baron, Salo W[ittmayer], 15150, 15775
Barthel, Manfred, 15665
Bartsch, Christian, 15284
Basle University, 15656
Bauer, Otto, 15068, 15404
Bauer, Roger, 15801
Bauer, Yehuda, 15118, 15134, 15150, 15151, 15775
Bauermeister, Volker, 15497
Baum, Charlotte, 15091
Baum, Gregory, 15792
Baum, Oskar, 15076
Baumann, Arnulf H., 15178
Bauschinger, Sigrid, 14996
Bavaria (Bayern), 15035–15037, 15135–15136
— Räterepublik, 15391
— Staatliche Archive, 15135
— Staatsministerium f. Unterricht u. Kultus, 15135
Bayerische Akademie d. Wissenschaften, Histor. Kommission bei der, 15121
Bayertz, Kurt, 15652
Becher, J. R., 15732
Becker, Bernhard, 15582

Becker, Friedrich Karl, 15401
Becker, Hans J., 15691
Becker, Jurek, 15328, 15428
Beckmann, Peter, 15619
Bein Alex[ander], 15521, 15775
Bejski, Moshe, 15150, 15151, 15775
Bekker, Hans, 15227
Belke, Ingrid, 14994, 15656
Bemmann, Helga, 15560
Ben Chorin, Schalom, 15258, 15259, 15291, 15328, 15346, 15454
Ben-David, Arye, 15759
Ben-Horin, Meir, 15280
Bendkower, S., 15260
Benjamin, Walter, 15381, 15382, 15383, 15429–15433, 15722
— Die geheimen Namen, 15430, 15431
Benjamin, Uri [i.e. Walter Zadek), 15721
Benseler, Frank, 15589
Bentley, James, 15770
Berendsohn, Walter A., 15374, 15434
Berg, Phyllis, 15508
Berger, Friedemann, 15661
Berger, Max, 15343
Berger, Ulrike, 15792
Berglar, Peter, 15747
Bergner, Elisabeth, 15723
Berkenhagen, Ekhart, 15622
Berlin, 15025–15028, 15193, 15227, 15246, 15329
— Freie Universität, 15338, 15546, 15670
— Staatsbibliothek Preuss. Kulturbesitz, 15724
Berlin East, 15227
Berlin, Isaiah, 15605
Berlin, Jeffrey B., 15668
Bernett, Hajo, 15137
Bernfeld, Siegfried, 15435–15436
Bernstein, Eduard, 15371, 15437
Bernstein, George, 15771
Bernstein, Reiner, 15328, 15754
Berry, Donald L., 15261
Bertelsmann, Klaus, 15641
Berthold Werner, 15462, 15463
Bettelheim, Bruno, 15438
Betz, Albrecht, 15483
Beutler, Kurt, 15425, 15426, 15427
Bibliothek d. Dt. Kulturzentrums, Tel Aviv, 15755
Bibliothek f. Zeitgeschichte, Stuttgart, Schriften d., 15116
Bibliotheca Judaica, Heidelberg, 15292
Bibliotheca Maimonidica, 15320
Bieber, Hedwig, 15477
Bieberstein, Johannes Rogalla von, 14995, 15772
Bienek, Horst, 15677
Bihl, Wolfdieter, 15083
Bileski, Herbert, 15060

Index to Bibliography 441

Bill, Max, 15618
Binion, Rudolph, 15710
Bismarck, Otto von, 15012, 15782
Blasius, Dirk, 15748
Blaukopf, Kurt, 15593
Bleicher, Willy, 15786
Bleichröder, Gerson von, 15012, 15350
Bloch, Elieser F[ritz], 15248
Bloch, Ernst, 15387, 15439–15440, 15590, 15617
Bloch, Heinrich, 15059
Bloch, Jochanan, 15262
Blum, Robert, 15441
Blumberg, Stanley A., 15685
Blumenberg, Werner, 15371
Blumenfeld, Kurt, 15347
Blumenthal-Weiss, Ilse, 15263
Blumenzweig, Esther, 15118
B'nai B'rith Leo Baeck (London) Lodge, 15089
Board of Deputies of British Jews, 15148
Bock, Eve, 15074
Bodenheimer, Henriette Hannah, 15348
Böcher, Otto, 15051, 15401
Boeck, Oliver, 15519
Bödeker, Heinrich, 15046
Böhl, Felix, 15244
Böhm, Franz, 15760
Böll, Heinrich, 15634
Börne, Ludwig, 15442–15444
Börner, Hölger, 15269
Börsenblatt f.d. Dt. Buchhandel, 15358, 15712, 15721, 15755
Bohn, Ursula, 15284
Bohner, Karl Heinz, 15162
Bohr, Niels, 15388
Bondy, François, 15412
Bonjour, Edgar, 15086
Book Trade, Jews in, 15358, 15721
Borchardt, Rudolf, 15445–15446
Born, Max, 15388, 15724
Borochov, Ber, 15369
Borowitz, Eugene B., 15302
Borries, Achim von, 15264
Bottomore, Tom, 15068
Boulez, Pierre, 15619
Bourel, Dominique, 15304–15307
Bovenschen, Silvia, 15602
Braakenburg, Johannes J., 15574
Bracher, Karl Dietrich, 15393
Braham, Randolph L., 15777
Brahm, Otto, 15447
Brandeis Univ. (Waltham, Mass.), 15144, 15790
Brandenburg (Mark), 15054
Brandstätter, Christian, 15072
Brandt, Willy, 15754
Brasch, Thomas, 15419
Brassloff, Fritz Lothar, 15343
Bratislava, Zentralverb. d. Jüd. Religionsgemeinden zu, 15220
Braude, Jacob, 15331

Braun, Otto, 15392
Braun, Volker, 15419
Braunschweigisches Landesmuseum, Veröffentlichungen d., 15344
Braunthal, Julius, 15372
Brecht, Bertolt, 15590
Breslau, 15029–15031, 15060, 15361
— Schles. Friedrich-Wilhelms Univ., Jahrbuch Bd. XIX, 15061
— Verband ehemaliger Breslauer und Schlesier in Israel, 15029, 15030, 15042, 15060, 15330, 15361, 15803
Breuer, Mordechai, 15249
Brilling, Bernhard, 15029, 15047, 15057, 15061, 15064
Bringmann, Fritz, 15174
Brinner, Lisa, 15731
Broch, Hermann, 15397, 15448–15451
Brod, Leo, 15563
Brod, Max, 15075, 15397, 15452–15454, 15717
Broder, Henryk M., 15222
Brodie, Sir Israel, 15100
Brodnitz, Friedrich S., 15033
Broszat, Martin, 15130, 15135
Brückner, Egon, 15486
Brügel, Johann Wolfgang, 15574
Buber, Martin, 15060, 15075, 15113, 15227, 15250–15291, 15302, 15321, 15349, 15350, 15387, 15757, 15759, 15762, 15763
— Symposium in Beer-Sheba, 15276, 15290, 15759
Buber-Neumann, Margarete, 15373
Buchenwald, 15138, 15213
Buchholz, Marlis, 15182
Buck-Morss, Susan, 15382
Buckwitz, Harry, 15715
Budapest, Rabbinerseminar, 15081, 15082, 15227
Büchel, Regine, 15116
Bückeburg, 15047
Bürgers, Heinrich, 15109
Bürgin, Hans, 15805
Bullard, Dexter M., 15504
Bullock, Michael, 15145
Bund d. Verfolgten d. Naziregimes (B.V.N.), Berlin, 15181, 15218
Bundesinstitut f. Sportwissenschaft, Schriftenreihe d., 15137
Bundesrepublik Deutschland see Federal German Republic
Bundeszentrale f. Politische Bildung, Bonn, 15185, 15195, 15209, 15369, 15640, 15795
Bureau, Elfriede, 15008
Burg, J. G. (i.e. Josef Ginsburg), 15773
Burgdorf, Niedersachsen, 15049
Burgenland, 15069, 15083
Burning of the Synagogues, German Christian Reaction to, 15757, 15786
Busche, Jürgen, 15624

Caliebe, Manfred, 15021
Canetti, Elias, 15455
Caputo-Mays, Maria Luise, 15543
Cargas, Harvy James, 15119
Carlebach, Alexander, 15331
Carlebach, Emanuel, 15005
Carlebach, Julius, 15606
Carstens, Karl, 15188
Cartoonists, Caricaturists, Jewish, 15530
Casper, Bernhard, 15311
Cassirer, Ernst, 15456–15458
Catane, Moshe, 15279, 15316
Celan, Paul (orig. Antschel also Antzel), 15397, 15459–15461
Cemeteries (Jewish), 15032 (Erlangen), 15034 (Floss), 15046 (Lippe), 15053 (Mainz). 15073 (Prag)
Center for Studies on the Holocaust, New York, 15210
Central Archives for the History of the Jewish People, Jerusalem, 15051
Centre National de la Recherche Scientifique in Paris, 15067
Chagall, Marc, 15698, 15757
Chalfen, Israel, 15459
Chaplin, Charlie (Charles), 15396
Children, 15174, 15243
'Christian Attitudes on Jews and Judaism', 15757
Christian–Jewish Cooperation, 15032 (Erlangen), 15035 (Bavaria)
Christian–Jewish Relations, 15170
Church and Synagogue, 15757–15767
Cincinnati (Ohio), University, 15508
Clowns, Jewish, 15396
Cohen, B. H., 15265
Cohen, Carl, 15291
Cohen, Daniel J., 15051
Cohen, Elishewa, 15645
Cohen, Hermann, 15293–15294, 15315
— Archives at Zurich University, 15293
Cohn, B[ernhard], 15033
Cohn, Bertha, 15124
Cohn, Emil, 15033
Cohn, Erich, 15227
Cohn, Margot, 15279
Cohn, Pinhas, 15005
Coleman, Terry, 15104
Cologne (see also Köln), 15348
'Commentary', 14992, 15008, 15421, 15565
Conference on Jewish Material Claims against Germany, 15108
Conference on Jewish Social Studies, New York, 15308, 15324
Congreso Judío Latinoamericano, Buenos Aires, 15352, 15494
Cossina, Caroline, 15060
Coudenhove-Kalergi, Graf Richard N., 15657
Coulmas, Corinna, 15094

Crampton, Patricia, 15291
Critics, Jewish (Art, Literary), 15447, 15560, 15616
Czechoslovakia, 15073–15077, 15220
— Czech and Slovak Jewish Leadership, 15151

Dachau, 15139
Dahlke, Hans, 15375
Daniels, Friedrich, 15403
Dannhauser, Werner J., 15421
Danzl, Erna, 15666
Davian, Donald, 15669
David Yellin-Loge, Jerusalem, Schriftenreihe d., 15520
Dawidowicz, Lucy S., 15008, 15140, 15210
Davidsohn, Magnus, 15060
Davis, John H., 15098
Decker, Hannah S., 15491
Dekel, Ephraim, 15141
Delmotte, Marguerite, 15317
Demet, Michel-François, 15813
Demetz, Peter, 15429
Dencker, Klaus Peter, 15498
Denmark, Danish Jewry, 15151
Deutsch-Israelische Gesellschaft, 15759
Deutsche Akademie f. Sprache u. Dichtung, Darmstadt, Jahrbuch d., 15624, 15730
Deutsche Bibliothek Prof. Walter Hirsch, Tel Aviv, 15755
Deutsche Bischofskonferenz, 15198, 15760
Deutsche Forschungsgemeinschaft, 15262
Deutsche Schillergesellschaft, Marbach, 15467, 15692 Jahrbuch d., 15446
'(Die) Deutsche Schule', Darmstadt, 15425
'Deutsche Vierteljahrsschrift f. Literaturwissenschaft und Geistesgeschichte, Stuttgart, 15460
Deutscher Caritas-Verband, 15760
Deutscher Evangelischer Kirchentag (XVII.), 15760
Dt. Koordinierungsrat d. Gesellschaften f. christl.-jüd. Zusammenarbeit, 15278, 15759
Deutsches Literaturarchiv, Marbach, 15445, 15467, 15692, 15697, 15742
Deutschkron, Inge, 15142
'deutschland-berichte', 15269, 15752
Diamant, Adolf, 15030, 15050, 15063, 15065, 15175, 15221, 15639
Diamond, Denis, 15795
Diamond, Sander A., 15787
Dienstag, Jacob I., 15320
Dietze, Ursula von, 15051
Dinse, Helmut, 15019
'Dix Huitième Siècle', Paris, 15305
Dobkowski, Michael N., 15092, 15095
Documenta Judaica, Haifa, 15297
Döblin, Alfred, 15375, 15462–15474, 15759
Doerdelmann, Bernhard, 15753

Doerdelmann-Kolbe, Erika, 15759
Döscher, Hans Jürgen, 15177
'Dokumentation', Evangelischer Pressedienst, 15200
Dokumentationsarchiv d. österr. Widerstandes, 15378
Dokumentationsstelle f. Neuere Österr. Literatur, 15378
Dokumentationszentrum f. Jüd. Zeitgeschichte (DJC), Paris, 15167
Dolbin, B[enedikt] F[red], 15742
Domin, Hilde, 15328
Dortmund, 15146
— Stadtbücherei, 15477
Doster, Ute, 15467
Dramatists, Jewish, 15628 (Molnar), 15632 (Erich Mühsam)
Drancy c.c., 15760
Dreeßen, Wulf-Otto, 15020
Dresner, Camillo, 15370
Drews, Jörg, 15572
Drobisch, Klaus, 15213, 15227
Drozdzynski, Alexander, 15208
Düsseldorf, 15759
Dunker, Ulrich, 15338
Dupuy, Bernard, 15317
Durham University, 15103

'East European Quarterly', New York, 15777
East Prussia (Province), 15045, 15063
Ebräer-Schule in Riga, 15334
Eccles, John C., 15651
Eckardt, Alice, 15143
Eckardt, Roy, 15143
Eckert, Willehad P[aul], 15267, 15759, 15760
Economists, Jewish, 15514, 15736
Educationalists, Pedagogues, 15297, 15435
Effinger, Shmuel, 15775
Eggebrecht, Axel, 15395
Egger, Christoph, 15544
Egger, Rita, 15760
Ehrenstein, Albert, 15075, 15397
Ehrlich, Ernst Ludwig, 15758
Eichstetter, Simon, 15059
Einstein, Albert, 15113, 15388, 15479–15480
Einstein, Alfred, 15481
Eisenberg, Azriel, 15093
Eisenkraft, Clara, 15205
Eisenstadt (Burgenland), 15069, 15083
Eisenstadt, Samuel N., 15015
Eisler, Hanns, 15482–15484, 15590
Eisner, Fritz H., 15522
Eisner, Kurt, 15390, 15391, 15632
Elefanten-Press-Galerie, Frankfurt/M., 15513
Elias, Norbert, 15475–15476
Elk, M., 15033, 15060
Elkan, Benno, 15477
Emancipation (Jewish), 15001, 15051, 15060, 15083, 15084, 15182, 15249, 15670, 15747, 15749
Emden, Jacob, 15295
Emig, Günther, 15632
Emin Pascha (orig. Isaak Eduard Schnitzer), 15478
'Emuna—Israel Forum', 15081, 15199, 15236, 15267, 15683, 15753, 15759
Endres, Rudolf, 15035, 15036, 15055
Engelman, Edmund, 15495
Engels, Friedrich, 15109
Enlightenment, 15305, 15671, 15672
Eppler, Elizabeth E., 15078, 15151
Epstein, Alfred, 15051
Erfurt, 15227
Erfurter Theologische Schriften, 15526
Erlangen, 15032
Ernst, Tilman, 15751
Ertl, Wolfgang, 15531
Eschenburg, Theodor, 15012
Esh, Shaul, 15150, 15775
Essayists, Jewish, 15072, 15559, 15572
Essen, 15033, 15176
Ettinger, Dina, 15141
'Europäische Ideen', Berlin, 15402, 15439, 15632, 15634, 15677, 15679, 15698, 15732
'European Judaism', 15327
Evangel. Kirche in Deutschland, Rat d., 15198
Evangel. Kirchenkanzlei, 15200
Evanston, Ill., University, 15210
Exile Literature, 15374–15380
Explorer, Jewish, 15478
Ezrahi, Sidra Dekoven, 15144

Fabian, Ruth, 15094
'(Die) Fackel', 15574
Fackenheim, Emil L., 15302
Faerber, Meir, 15265, 15268, 15454, 15563, 15759
Faigon, Jehoschua, 15494
Falck, Ludwig, 15051
Fechenbach, Felix, 15046
Federal German Republic, 15222–15224, 15226, 15233, 15290, 15754
Feilchenfeldt, K[onrad], 15379
Feingold, Henry L., 15095
Feldheim, H. D., 15010
Feldman, Ron H., 15421
Fenichel, Otto, 15492
Fest, Joachim C., 15145
Feuchtwanger, Lion, 15375, 15485–15488
Feuchtwanger, Martha, 15488
Fidus, Hugo, 15631
Figes, Eva, 15096
'Filmkritik', München, 15644
'Final Solution', 15150, 15167, 15209, 15212, 15238, 15775, 15787, 15791
Fisch, Harold, 15349

Fischer, Alfred, 15085
Fischer, Brigitte B[ermann], 15725
Fischer, Klaus-Uwe, 15813
Fishbane, Michael A., 15280
Fisher of Camden, Baron Samuel, 15100
Flach, Karl Hermann, Stiftung, 15269
Flatow, Alfred, 15137
Fleischhauer, Inge, 15326
Fleischmann, Karel, 15073
Fleischner, Eva, 15147
Flores, Angel, 15545
Floris, Elke, 15757
Floss (Upper Palatinate), 15034
Fohrer, Georg, 15033
Forster, Georg, 15800
Fradier, Georges, 15567
Fraenkel, Abraham Adolf, 15060
Fräntzki, Ekkehard, 15607
France, 15094, 15167
Franconia, 15035, 15036, 15037, 15055
Frank, Anne, 15773
Frankel, William, 15154
Franken, see Franconia
Frankenstein, Alfred, 15558
Frankfurt/M., 15038, 15039
— Jüd. Gemeinde, 15183
— Kommission zur Erforschung d. Geschichte d. Frankfurter Juden, 15038
— Lehrhaus, 15284
— Paulskirche, 15269
— Philanthropin, 15039
— University, 15433
'(Die) Frankfurter Schule', 15381–15386
Frankl, Viktor E., 15489
Franková, Anita 15073
Freedman, Theodor, 15241
Frei, Bruno (orig. Freistadt), 15356, 15634, 15774
Freiburg/Br., University, 15600
'Freiburger Rundbrief', 15760, 15763, 15766, 15802
Freimark, Peter, 15179
Freud, Anna, 15490
Freud, Sigmund, 14996, 15490–15496, 15653
Freund, Joachim Hellmut, 15623
Freund, Rahel, 15290
Freundlich, Joshua, 15370
Freundlich, Otto, 15497
Freyhan, H. W., 15394
Fried, Erich, 15397, 15743
'Friede über Israel', Zeitschrift f. Kirche u. Judentum, 15178
Friedell, Egon (orig. Friedmann), 15498–15499
Friedenthal, Hans, 15329
Friedenthal, Richard, 15624, 15745
Friedländer, Salomo (Mynona), 15636
Friedlander, Fritz, 15468
Friedman, Maurice, 15252, 15253

Fritsch, Theodor, 15799
Fröhlich, Hans-Jürgen, 15412
Fromm, Erich, 15381, 15386, 15492, 15500–15503
Fromm-Reichmann, Frieda, 15504
Fronius, Hans, 15542
Frühwald, Wolfgang, 15686
Fuchs, H. H., 15166
Fuchs, Lawrence, 15242
Fürnberg, Louis, 15505, 15744
Fürst, Julius, 15532
Fürst, Max, 15328, 15726
Fürstenberg, Carl, 15727
Fürstenberg, Hans, 15727
Fürth (Bavaria), 15055, 15373
Fuld, Werner, 15430, 15431

Gadiel, Kurt Jacques, 15060
Galinski, Heinz, 15180, 15181
Galley, Eberhard, 15522
Gans, David, 15073
Garaguly, Brita von, 15434
Gartenberg, Egon, 15594
'Gartenlaube', 15017
Gay, Peter, 14996
Gebhardt, Eike, 15381
Geis, Robert Raphael, 15198, 15296
Geismar, 15041
Geldern, Simon von, 15528
'(Die) Gemeinde', 15113
'Genealogie', Neustadt (Aisch), 15793
Genscher, Hans-Dietrich, 15754
Georg-Eckert-Institut f. Intern. Schulbuchforschung, Braunschweig, 15239
George, Manfred (orig. Manfred Cohn), 15097
Gerhardt, Herbert, 15227
German Democratic Republic (GDR), 15227, 15228
German–Israeli Relations, 15752–15756
German-Jewish Relations, 15747–15751
German Jews in Israel, 15051, 15060, 15329, 15346, 15359, 15362, 15365, 15368
German Jews in Various Countries, 15089–15107a
'German Life and Letters', Oxford, 15523
Gerold-Tucholsky, Mary, 15690, 15743
Gerste, Margrit, 15107a
Gerth, Ernst, 15051
Gertner, Meir, Memorial Lecture, 15078
Gesellsch. f. Christl.-Jüd. Zusammenarbeit, see Christian–Jewish Cooperation, Society for
Ges. f. niedersächs. Kirchengeschichte, Nienburg, Jahrbuch d., 15750
Ges. zur Förderung d. wissenschaftl. Zusammenarbeit mit der Universität Tel Aviv, 15756
'Gesher' Review, Jerusalem, 15303
Giachi, Arianna, 15278
Giessler, Rupert, 15760

Gilam, Abraham, 14997
Gilbert, Felix, 14998
Gilbert, Martin, 15148, 15350
Gilbert, Peter F., 15757
(The) Gingold Family, 15225
Ginkel, Hans-Werner, 15051
Ginsburg, Alexander, 15198
Gipsies, 15148
Glaser, Hermann, 15008, 15751
Glauert, Barbara, 15715
Gleichmann, Peter, 15476
Glückel of Hameln, 15332
Glückstadt, 15040
Goder-Stark, Petra, 15692
Goebbels, Josef, 15149
Görlich, Bernard, 15492
Görres Gesellschaft, 15294
Goes, Albrecht, 15251, 15270, 15291
Gössmann, Wilhelm, 15230, 15231
Göttingen, 15041
— Universität, Seminar f. Deutsche Philologie, d., 15701
Goldberger, Ronald, 15538
Goldhagen, Erich, 15787
Goldmann, Joseph, 15034
Goldmann, Nahum, 15188, 15351–15352, 15363, 15795
Goldschmidt, Hans Eberhard, 15574
Goldschmidt, Hermann Levin, 15387
Goldstein, David, 15606
Goldstein, Heinzwerner, 15060
Goldstein, Walter B[enjamin], 15060
Goldziher, Ignaz, 15728
Goll, Claire, 15506–15507, 15729
Goll, Yvan (orig. Lang), 15387, 15508, 15729
Gollinger, Hildegard, 15760
Gollwitzer, Helmut, 15284, 15761, 15792
Gombrich, Sir E[rnst] H[ans], 15509–15510, 15619
Gombrich, Lisbeth, 15510
Goode, Patrick, 15068
Gordon, A. D., 15349
Gordon, Haim, 15271
Gordon, Joseph S., 15800
Gottgetreu, Erich, 15279, 15468
Goudsblom, Johan, 15476
Grab, Walter, 15109
Grabendorff, Ingemarie, 15795
Grabs, Manfred, 15482
Grad Goodman, Hannah, 15093
Gradenwitz, Peter, 15342
Graml, Hermann, 15238
Grandes Figuras del Judaísmo, 15352, 15494
Grasberger, Franz, 15595
Green, Gerald, 15155, 15206
Greenberg, Ben, 15295
Gregor-Dellin, Martin, 15810
Greiner, Ulrich, 15563, 15661
Grieshaber, HAP, 15138

Grillparzer, Franz, 18501
'Grock' (orig. Adrian Wettach), 15396
Grosser, Alfred, 15328
Grubrich-Simitis, Ilse, 15490
Grünbaum, Adolf, 15653
Grünewald, H. I., 15198, 15248, 15773
Gruenewald, Max, 15272, 15762
Grünewald, Pinchas Paul, 15298
Grundmann, Günther, 15031
Grunfeld, Isidor, 15299
Gudopp, Wolf-Dieter, 15759
Guggenheim, Simon Meyer, 15098
(The) Guggenheims, 15098
Guggenheim, Willy, 15353
Gundolf, Friedrich, 15730
Gutman, Yisrael, 15150, 15151, 15775
Gutmann, Joseph, 15297
Gutt, Barbara, 15670
Guttmann, Jakob, 15320
Gwinner, Sabine, 15638
Györkös, Janos, 15589

Habe, Hans, 15354
Habermann, Gerhard E., 15278
Habermas, Jürgen, 15383, 15602
Hachenburg, Max, 15511
Hacker, Ivan, 15083
Häusler, Wolfgang, 15083, 15343
Hahn, Fred, 15152
Hahn, Hugo, 15033
Halle, 15227
— Universität, Wissenschaftl. Zeitschrift d., 15233
Hamácková, Vlastimila, 15073
Hamburg, 15042
— Institut f.d. Geschichte d. Deutschen Juden, 15179
— Landeszentrale f. Polit. Bildung, Veröffentlichung d., 15179
— Universität, 15021, 15040, 15169, 15514, 15561
Hamburger, Michael, 15618
Hamilton-West, E., 15104
Hammerstein, Franz von, 15284
Handicraft, Jews in, 15047
Hannsmann, Margarete, 15138
Hanover, Jüd. Gemeinde, 15182
Hansen, Gudrun, 15649
Hansen, Troels Eggers, 15650
Hansen, Volkmar, 15517
Hanslick, Eduard, 14996
Harden, Maximilian, 15390, 15632
Harder, D. Günter, 15767
Hartmann, Gerhard, 15576
Hartung, Rudolf, 15807
Harwood, Richard (pseud.), 15776, 15795
Haselberg, Peter V., 15432
Hasenclever, Walter, 15512
Hasidism, 15759

Hasorea, 15368
Hassauer-Ross, Friderike J., 15675
Hasubek, Peter, 15232
Hauschner, E. M., 15060
Hayek, Friedrich August v., 15736
Heartfield, John (orig. Helmut Herzfelde), 15513
(The) Hebrew University, Jerusalem, 15118, 15217, 15316
Hegel, E., 15064
Hegel, Georg Wilh. Friedrich, 15616
Heide, Manfred Gernot, 15021
Heidegger, M., 15684
Heidelberg, Universität, 15586
Heidrich, Peter, 15227
Heilbrunn, Karl, 15227
Heimann, Eduard, 15514
Heine, Heinrich, 15230, 15231, 15232, 15233, 15387, 15515–15528, 15616, 15759, 15813
— Heinrich-Heine-Gesellschaft, 15522
— Heinrich-Heine-Institut, Düsseldorf, 15522, 15528
— Heine-Jahrbuch 1978, 15521, 15522
Heine, Thomas Theodor, 15529–15530
Heinegg, Peter, 15523
Heinemann, Leopold, 15060
Heise, Carl Georg, 15700
Heise, Werner, 15054
Heisenberg, Werner, 15388
Heissenbüttel, Helmut, 15415, 15446
Heitmann, Heinfried, 15522
Hellendall, F., 15010
Heller, Hartmut, 15036
Hellin, Frederick P., 15657
Hennessy, Peter, 15105
Henning, Uwe, 15425–15427
Henrich, Wolfgang, 15291
Hermann, Armin, 15388
Hermlin, Stephan, 15531
Herneck, Friedrich, 15479
Herrmann, Berndt, 15407
Hersch, Jeanne, 15328
Hertz, Heinrich, 15731
Hertz, Johanna, 15731
Hertz, Mathilde, 15731
Herz, Henriette, 15532
Herz, Jakob, 15032
Herzfelde, Helmut see Heartfield, John
Herzl, Theodor, 15075, 15350, 15355, 15366
Heschel, Abraham J[oshua], 15302
Hess, Moses, 15109, 15284, 15349, 15356, 15369
Hess, M. G., 15754
Hesse, 15153, 15183
— Kommission f.d. Geschichte d. Juden in, 15153
— Landesregierung, 15269
— Landesverband d. Jüd. Gemeinden in, 15183

Hesse-Nassau, Evang. Arbeitskreis Kirche und Israel, 15238
Hesselbach, Walter, 15269
Hessler, Hans-Wolfgang, 15200
Heuss, Theodor, 15291
Heutger, Nicolaus, 15048
Hey, Richard, 15468
Heyder, Ulrich, 15514
Heym, Stefan (i.e. Hellmuth Fliegel), 15533
Heymel, Alfred Walter, 15445
Hieber, Jochen, 15739
Hilberg, Raul, 15241
Hildesheim, 15043
Hildesheimer, Wolfgang, 15328
Hilferding, Rudolf, 15068
Hilfsverein der Deutschen Juden, 15333
Hiller, Kurt, 15534
Himmler, Heinrich, 15209
Hinrichsen, Klaus Ernst, 15334
Hinze, Klaus-Peter, 15709, 15710
Hirsch, Fritz, 15059
Hirsch, Helmut, 15441
Hirsch, Moritz (Maurice), Baron de, 15350
Hirsch, Baron Robert von, 15535
Hirsch, Samson Raphael, 15298–15299
Hirsch, Walter, 15755
Hirschberg, Julius, 15536
Hirschfeld, Ephraim Joseph, 15318
Hirschler, Gertrude, 15141
Hirte, Christlieb, 15629
Historians (Jewish), 15006, 15584
Historische Kommission zu Berlin, 14999
Historiography (Jewish), 15006, 15150, 15775
Hitler, Adolf, 15125
Hochkeppel, Willy, 15654
Hodgart, Suzanne, 15535
Hodos, Aubrey, 15494
Höck, Alfred, 15066
Höffner, Joseph, Kardinal, 15198
Hoelzel, Alfred, 15242
Hoess, Rudolf, 15130
Hoffmann, Edith, 15497
Hoffmann, Gerd, 15233
Hofmannsthal, Hugo von, 15072, 15389
Hohlbein, Hartmut, 15179
Hollosi, Clara, 15522
Holocaust, 15118, 15119, 15134, 15141, 15143, 15144, 15147, 15148, 15150, 15151, 15165, 15210, 15211, 15235, 15241–15243, 15350, 15757, 15775, 15787
— Denial of, 15128, 15211, 15759, 15768, 15773, 15776, 15791, 15795
— Film, 15154–15164, 15751, 15757, 15787
— Theological Impact of, 15757
Holtfreter, Jürgen, 15513
Holzamer, Karl, 15715
Holzhey, Helmut, 15293
Horbach, Michael, 15165
Horkheimer, Max, 15381, 15386, 15537

Horn, Hannelore, 15588
Hornung, Klaus, 15608
Horwell, Arnold, 15089
Horwitz, Rivka G., 15273, 15310, 15763
Hubert, Arthur, 15100
Hübinger, Paul Egon, 15584
Hüssler, Georg, 15760
Huettner, Axel, 15044
'Humour Behind Barbed Wire', 15208
Hundsnurscher, Franz, 15020
Hungary, 15078–15083, 15151, 15728, 15777–15778 (Antisemitism)
Huonker, Gustav, 15743
Huttenbach, Henry R., 15151
Hutter, Clemens M., 15184
Hyams-Peter, Helge-Ulrike, 15039
Hyman, Paula, 15091

Ianku, Carol, 15084
Ignotus, Paul, 15079
Iltis, Rudolf, 15220
Imhoff, Christoph von, 15754
'Immanuel', Dokumente d. heutigen religiösen Denkens und Forschens in Israel, 15763
Imperial Germany, 14996, 15003, 15530, 15616
— Antisemitism in, 15771, 15780, 15782, 15790, 15797
'Informationsbulletin', Prag, 15220
Ingold, Felix Philipp, 15389, 15643
Institut f. Bankhistorische Forschung, Frankfurt/M., 15699
Institut f. Dt. Geschichte, Jahrbuch VII d., 14995, 15070, 15109, 15592, 15800
Institut f.d. Geschichte d. deutschen Juden, Hamburg, 15179
Institut f. Zeitgeschichte, München, 15135, 15191
Institut 'Kirche und Judentum',
— Veröffentlichungen aus dem, 15284, 15765, 15766, 15767
Institute of Contemporary History—The Wiener Library, London, 15117, 15123
Institute of Contemporary Jewry, Jerusalem, 15118, 15217
Institute of Jewish Affairs, London, 15077, 15215, 15757, 15787
Inter Nationes, Bonn, 15291
International Hebrew Christian Alliance, 15766
Isaac, Jules and Laura, 15760
Isenburg, Jüd. Kinderheim, 15173
Isolani, Gertrud, 15538–15539
Israel, State of, 15150, 15240, 15342, 15353, 15354, 15366, 15369, 15747, 15753, 15754, 15775
Israel Academy of Sciences and Humanities, 15316
Israel, German Jews in, 15051, 15060, 15346, 15359, 15362, 15365, 15368

'Isr. Wochenblatt' (IW), Schweiz, 15006, 15088, 15098, 15110, 15164, 15180, 15259, 15338, 15346, 15364, 15454, 15563, 15814
Istor, H., 15364
Izbicki, Alex, 15088

Jaccard, Roland, 15707
Jacob M. and Shoshana Schreiber Chair, 15013, 15014
Jacobi, Ruth L[isband], 15524
Jacobin, German, 15800
Jacobs, Joe, 15137
Jacobs, Louis, Rabbi, 15606
Jacobsohn, Siegfried, 15395
Jacoby, Johann, 15371
Jaeger, Harald, 15136
Jahn-Zechendorff, Beate, 15022
Jahrbuch d. Instituts f. Deutsche Geschichte, Tel Aviv, see Institut f. Deutsche Geschichte
Jahrbuch f. Westd. Landesgeschichte, Koblenz, 15052
Jakobovits, Immanuel, Chief Rabbi, 15100
Jan, Helmut von, 15043
Jan, Julius von, Pfarrer, 15191
Janßen, Karl-Heinz, 15191
Jaros, Miroslav, 15073
Jay, Martin, 15408
Jelinek, Y[eshayahu], 15077
Jenkins, David, 15625
Jenks, Stuart, 15037
Jentzsch, Bernd, 15415
Jephcott, Edmund, 15429, 15475
Jersch-Wenzel, Stefi, 14999
Jerusalem, 15279, 15357
— Central Archives for the History of the Jewish People, 15051
— University, 15118, 15217, 15316
'(The) Jerusalem Quarterly', 15345, 15362
Jesenska, Milena, 15373
Jessner, Leopold, 15540–15541
'Jewish Affairs', Johannesburg, 15129
Jewish Art and Music, 15342–15344, 15759
Jewish Book Council, London, 15078
Jewish Book Week 1977, 15078
Jewish–Christian Dialogue, 15032, 15272, 15762, 15767, 15792
'Jewish Chronicle', London, 15156, 15266, 15312
Jewish General Regional History in Germany, 15024
Jewish Councils see Judenräte
'Jewish Frontier', New York, 15128
(The) Jewish National and University Library, Jerusalem, 15279
'Jewish Observer and Middle East Review', London, 15012
(The) Jewish Problem, 15326–15328, 15606, 15621

(The) Jewish Publication Society of America, Philadelphia, 15219, 15243
Jewish Question, 15060, 15606
Jewish Restitution Successor Organisation (JRSO), 15133
Jewish Self-Hatred, 15327
'Jewish Social Studies', New York, 15308, 15324
Jochmann, Werner, 15015
Joël, David Hei[Y]mann, 15300
Joel, Manuel, 15301, 15320
Jörg, Wolfgang, 15533
Johaneum (Johannes Gymnasium), Breslau, 15060
Johann, Ernst, 15814
Jokl, Ernst, 15329, 15330
Jonas, Klaus W., 15623
Jones, W. E. B., 15757
Jospe, Eva, 15280
'Journal of Ecumenical Studies', Philadelphia, 15261
'Journal of European Studies', 15530
'(The) Journal of Jewish Studies', Oxford, 15271
'Journal of Modern History', 14997
Journalists, Jewish, 15079, 15097, 15354, 15562
'Judaica Bohemiae', 15073
'Judaica et Christiana', 15298
'Judaism', New York, 15092, 15143, 15280, 15295, 15313
Judaism, Critique of, 15606
'Judenfrage', 15200, 15238, 15592, 15606, 15748, 15791
'Judenräte', 15150, 15207, 15775
Jüdisch-Literarische Gesellschaft, Jahrbuch d., 15335
Jüdische Arbeiterbewegung, 15369
'Jüdische Rundschau Maccabi', Basel, 15184, 15416, 15538
'Jüdischer Pressedienst', Düsseldorf, 15781
'Jüsp' (Pseud.), 15539
Jung, Carl Gustav, 15387
Jungblut, Gerd W., 15631
Jungk, Robert, 15328
Justiz und NS-Verbrechen, 15166
Jutkowski, Jisrael (Rudi), 15060

Kafka, Franz, 15075, 15389, 15397, 15542–15556, 15759
Kaganoff, Benzion C., 15114
Kahe, Joachim, 15225
Kahler, Erich, 15730, 15809
Kahn, Lothar, 15583
Kaiser, Joachim, 15619, 15624
Kaléko, Mascha, 15557–15558
Kalisch, Simon, 15100
Kammler, Jörg, 15589
Kampen, Wilhelm von, 15185

Kanowitz, Kurt, 15364
Kant, Immanuel, 15315, 15564, 15599
Kantorowicz, Alfred, 15376, 15379, 15634
Kaplan, Anatoli L'vovič, 15022
Kaplan, Edward K., 15280
Kaplan, Marion A., 15000, 15647
Kaplan, Mordecai Menahem, 15280
Karbusicky, Vladimir, 15596
Karl-Hermann-Flach-Stiftung, 15269
Karniel, Josef, 15070
Karp, Abraham J., 15102
Karpman, I. J. Carmin, 15126
Karry, —, Minister, 15269
(K.C.) Kartell Convent Deutscher Studenten Jüd. Glaubens, 15120
Kastein, Josef (orig. Julius Katzenstein), 15346
Katz, Jacob, 15001, 15758
Katzburg, Nathaniel, 15080
Kaufman, William E., 15280, 15302
Kaufmann, Isidor, 15337
Kaufmann, Ludwig, 15760
Kayser, Rudolf, 15559
'Keeping Posted', New York, 15095
Kehr, Helen, 15117, 15123
Keim, Anton M., 15051
Keller, Karin, 15546
Keller, Otto, 15467
Kemp, Friedhelm, 15568
Kempner, Robert M. W[assili], 15235, 15759
Kempski, Jürgen von, 15274
Kerr, Alfred (orig. Alfred Kempner), 15560
Kesten, Hermann, 15561, 15710, 15732
'Kibbuz', 15350 (Movement), 15367
Kibbuz Hameuchad, 15365
Kirchen (Place), 15044
Kirchner, Peter, 15227
Kirchner, Renate, 14537
Kirsch, Eberhard, 15526
Kirsch, Sarah, 15419 '
Kisch, Egon Erwin, 15396, 15562–15563, 15759
Kisch, Guido, 15002, 15564
Kissinger, Henry A., 15101
Kittel, Gerhard, 15200, 15770
Klarsfeld, Beate and Serge, 15167
Klein, Charlotte L. (i.e. Louis Gabriel M.), 15757
Klein, Hillel, 15326
Klenner, Hermann, 15577
Klunker, Will, 15607
Knight, Max, 15746
Kochan, Lionel, 15312, 15606
Köhler, Willi, 15398
Köhler, Wolfram, 15711
Köhn, Gerhard, 15040
Koehn, Ilse, 15168
Köln (Cologne), Nachrichtenamt d. Stadt, 15441

— Universität, Forschungsinst. f. Soziologie d., 15224
Königsberg (East Prussia), 15045
Köppen, Wolfgang, 15468
Köstler, Arthur, 15565–15567, 15738
Kohl, Helmut, 15754
Kolb, Bernhard (Collection), 15152
Kolinsky, Eva, 15787
Kollek, Amos, 15357
Kollek, (Teddy) Theodor, 15357
Kolmar, Gertrud (i.e. Chodziesner), 15568–15570
Koltun, Elizabeth, 15647
Kopitzsch, Wolfgang, 15179
Korherr [Richard]-Bericht, 15200, 15209
Kornfeld, Paul, 15075, 15076
Korte, Herman, 15476
Kovner, Abba, 15150, 15775
Kowalski, Isaac, 15214
Kracauer, Siegfried, 15396, 15408
Krämer-Prein, Gabriele, 15358
Kraft, Rudolf, 15478
Kraft, Werner, 15571–15572
Krakowski, Shmuel, 15118, 15150, 15215, 15775
Kraus, Karl, 15072, 15389, 15397, 15573–15574
Kraus, Wolfgang, 15416
Kravitt, Edward F., 15597
Krebs, Sir Hans Adolf, 15703
Kreiler, Kurt, 15390, 15391
Kreisky, Bruno, 15378, 15575–15576
Kremers, Heinz, 15186, 15236, 15759
Kressel, G., 15303
Kreutzberger, Max, 15113
Kries, Angela von, 15763
Krings, Hermann, 15294
'Kritische Theorie', 15382, 15383, 15384, 15385
Kröger, Ullrich, 15169
Krüger, Horst, 15328, 15416
Kruse, Joseph A., 15522, 15528
Kubinzky, Judit, 15778
Kuchinske-Bach, Anneliese, 15076
Kuczynski, Jürgen, 15577
Külling, Friedrich, 15087
Küng, Hans, 15764
Künzel, Georg, 15032
Küstermeier, Rudolf, 15060, 15291, 15802–15803
Kulka, Erich, 15759
Kuschner, Doris, 15224
Kuttenkeuler, Wolfgang, 15232, 15525

Laier, Karl-Heinz, 15322
Lamberti, Marjorie, 15003, 15004
Lamm, Hans, 15170, 15275, 15276, 15278, 15281, 15416, 15814
Landauer, Gustav, 15277, 15391, 15578–15579

Landmann, Michael, 15328, 15580–15581
Lang, Michel R., 15351
Langebartel, William W., 15543
Langer, Lawrence L., 15570
Langmaid, Janet, 15194
Lapide, Pinchas E., 15764
Laschen, Gregor, 15419
Laska, Bernd, 15659
Lasker-Schüler, Else, 15075, 15346, 15759
Lassalle, Ferdinand, 15371, 15582
Laue, Max von, 15731
Lauer, Simon, 15298
Lazarus, Moritz, 14994
Lazarus, Paul, Rabbi, 15033
Lea, Charlene A., 15749
Leder, Rudolf see Hermlin, Stephan
Legal Profession, Jews in, 15511, 15587, 15638, 15640, 15673
Lehmann, Erich M., 15060
Lehnen, Manfred, 15137
Lehner, Fred, 15034
Lehrmann, Chanan L., 15323
Lehrmann, Graziella Sara, 15323
Leistner, Reinhold, 15779
Leo Beck Institute, 15110–15113, 15303
— Bulletin, 15110, 15310, 15321, 15334, 15621, 15645, 15733
— Jerusalem, 15262
— Year Book XXIII, 14993, 14994, 15004, 15006, 15017, 15024, 15074, 15111, 15124, 15127, 15286, 15340, 15411, 15487, 15548 15570, 15583, 15717, 15797, 15799
— New York, 14998, 15112–15113, 15152
— Leo Baeck Memorial Lecture (22), 14998
— Library and Archives News, 15112
— News, 15113
Less, Georg, 15060
Lessing, Erich, 15343
Lessing, Gotthold Ephraim, 15616
Lessing-Hochschule, Berlin, 15585
Lessmann, Daniel, 15583
Lettau, Reinhard, 15161, 15419
Leudesdorff, René, 15238
Leuenberger, Walter, 15049
Leuner, Heinz David, 15170, 15765, 15766
Leuschen-Seppel, Rosemarie, 15780
Levenberg, S., 15781
Levenson, Dorothy, 15242
Levi, Hermann, 14996
Levi, Paul, 15390
Levi, Zeev, 15763
Levi-Mühsam, Else, 15060, 15635, 15737
Levin, Dov, 15216, 15217
Levin, Nora, 15336
Levine, Yitzhak, 15005
Leviné-Nissen, Eugen [orig. Nissen Berg], 15390, 15632
Levinson, N[athan] P[eter], 15291, 15761
Levison, Wilhelm, 15584

Levy, John, 15363
Lewin, Erich, 15060
Lewin, Isaac, 15229, 15309
Lewin, Louis, 15060
Lewin, Ludwig, 15585
Lewin, Shlomo, 15032
Lewinson, Fritz A., 15329
Lewy, Hermann, 15188, 15198, 15814
Lichtenstein, Erwin, 15726
Lichtenstein, Heiner, 15751
Liebermann, Max, 15392, 15586
Liebeschütz, Hans, 15006, 15113, 15320
Liebeschütz, Rahel, 15733
Lienert, Franz, 15537
Liepmann, Moritz, 15587
Lietzmann, Sabina, 15162
Lifsshitz, Chaja, 15118
Ligeti, György, 15328
Lill, Rudolf, 15782
Link-Salinger (Hyman), Ruth, 15277, 15280
Links, Roland, 15629
Lippe, 15046
Lipton, David R., 15458
Liptzin, Sol[omon], 15019, 15668
Lissitzky, El[iezer], 15516
'(The) Listener', 15770
Literary Historians, Jewish, 15589, 15619, 15623
'Literatur/Manuskript', Köln, 15427
'Litterae', Göppinger Beiträge zur Textgeschichte, 15020
(The Joseph Aaron) Littman Library of Jewish Civilization, 15336, 15606
Litvinoff, Barnet, 15370
Loebl, Herbert, OBE, B.Sc., 15103
Lörrach (Kreis), 15044
Löwe, Heinz-Dietrich, 15783
Löwenstein (Evenari), Anni, 15361
Löwenstein, I[saak], Rabbi, 15060
Löwenstein, Thea née Bauer, 15742
Lo[e]wenthal, Leo, 15386
Löwenthal, Richard, 15588
Loewy, Ernst, 15038
Lohrbächer, Albrecht, 15059
Lohrmann, Klaus, 15071
Lohse, D. Eduard, Landesbischof, 15048, 15178
Lorenzer, Alfred, 15492
Lowenthal, E[rnst] G[ottfried], 15024, 15060, 15113, 15187, 15664
Lowenthal, Marvin, 15332
Lower Saxony, 15047–15049
Lowinsky, Edward E., 15746
Luchert, Manuel, 15575
Luckenwalde (Reg. Bezirk Potsdam), 15050
Luckner, Gertrud, 15760, 15802
Ludwig, Max (pseud.) see Oppenheimer, Max
Lübben, Gerd Hergen, 15599

Lüth, Erich, 15060, 15803
Lützeler, Paul Michael, 15448, 15449, 15450
Lukács, Georg (orig. Löwinger), 15589–15590
Lunzer, Heinz, 15378
Luthardt, Wolfgang, 15638
Luther, Martin, 15757, 15804
Luxemburg, Rosa, 15390, 15591–15592, 15734
Lyric Writers (Jewish), 15632, 15677

Maas, Lieselotte, 15377
Maass, Walter B., 15212
Maayan, Shmuel, 15025
McCarthy, Mary, 15422, 15423
McFee Brown, R., 15210
Mack, Dietrich, 15810
McKee, Ella R. W., 15710
Magdeburg, 15227
Mahler, Alma Maria, 15735
Mahler, Anna, 15619
Mahler, Gustav, 15397, 15593–15598, 15735
— Gustav-Mahler-Gesellschaft, Schriftenreihe, d., 15598
'(Die) Mahnung', 15181, 15218
Mahr, Gerhard, 15262, 15809
Maimann, Helene, 15378
Maimon, Arye (orig. Herbert Fischer), 15052
Maimonides, Moses ben Maimon, 15320
Mainz, 15051–15053, 15757
— Akademie d. Wissenschaften und d. Literatur, 15694
— Stadtbibliothek, 15051
Maisch, Ingrid, 15760
Maiwald, Holger, 15200
Majdanek, 15751
Maleachi, Ruben, 15042
'Malik' Verlag, 15513
Malraux, André, 15738
Malsch. Sara Ann, 15522
Mann, Golo, 15012
Mann, Heinrich, 15199
Mann, Thomas, 15375, 15603, 15805–15809, 15813
— Archives, Zürich, 15805
Mannheim, Stadtarchiv, Veröffentlichungen d., 15511
Mannheim, Karl, 15386
Manufacturers, Jewish, 15106
'Marbacher Magazin, 15697
March, Joachim, 15181
Marchand, James W., 15581
Marcus, Ernst, 15599
Marcuse, Herbert, 15381, 15383, 15386, 15409, 15492, 15600–15602
Marcuse, Ludwig, 15444, 15603–15604
Margaliot, Abraham, 15151
Margolius, Hans, 15060
Mark Brandenburg, 15054
Markgrafenland, Markgraeflerland, 15044
Markscheffel, Günter, 15751

Marmur, Dow, Rabbi, 15266
Marquardt, Friedrich Wilhelm, 15284
Marquardt, Hans, 15516
Marr, Wilhelm, 15799
Marrus, Michael R., 14997
Marsh, Jeffrey, 15565
Martin, Bernard, 15325
Martin, Gottfried, 15599
Martini, Fritz, 15446
Marx, Karl, 15109, 15371, 15603, 15605–15615
— Family, 15610
Marx, Leopold, 15759
Mashberg, Michael, 15787
Masson, Irma Lotte, 15107
Mathematics, Jews in, 15032, 15060
Matull, Wilhelm, 15045
Max Mainzer Memorial Foundation, 15120
Mayer, Annemarie and Reinhold, 15284
Mayer, Hans see Améry, Jean
Mayer, Hans, 15189, 15328, 15616–15620, 15812, 15813
Mayer, Hans-Otto, 15805
Mayer, Helene, 15137
Mayer, Ludwig, 15358
Mayer, Sali, 15151
Mazlish, Bruce, 15101
'MB'-Wochenzeitung d. Irgun Olej Merkas Europa, Tel Aviv, 15006, 15012, 15110, 15113, 15133, 15160, 15258, 15279, 15290, 15318, 15333, 15338, 15347, 15363, 15364, 15365, 15368, 15454, 15468, 15497, 15726, 15808
Medicine, Jews in, 15032, 15536, 15583, 15642, 15648, 15709
'MEGA' (Marx Engels Gedächtnisausgabe), 15109
Mehring, Walter, 15616
Meidner, Ludwig, 15621
Melchinger, Christa, 15671
Menck, Clara, 15445
Mendels[s]ohn, Eric[h], 15622
Mendelssohn, Moses, 15304–15308
Mendelssohn, Peter de, 15623–15624, 15806
Mendelssohn-Bartholdy, Felix, 15625
Mendes-Flohr, Paul, R., 15281, 15282, 15327
Mense, Josef Hermann, 15547
Menzel-Severing, Hans, 15477
Merchav, Peretz, 15404
'Merkur', Stuttgart, 15264, 15274, 15390, 15412, 15414, 15416, 15432, 15502, 15654, 15738, 15740
Meroz, Yohanan, 15051
Metzger, Hartmut, 15190
Metzger, Heinz-Klaus, 15813
Metzger, Wolfgang, 15398, 15400
Mews, Siegfried, 15716
Meyer, Georg P., 15115
Meyer, Hans Chanoch, 15060, 15297

Meyer, Jochen, 15467
Meyer, Luis, 15060
Meyer, Majorie, 15482
Meyer, Michael A., 15007
Michaelis, Mirjam, 15784
Michaelis-Stern, Eva, 15328
Michalik, Krystyna, 15131
Michel, Sonja, 15091
Middle East Institute, Jerusalem, 15345, 15362
'Midstream', New York, 15277, 15287, 15610
Milful, Helen, 15548
Minerva-Fachserie Geisteswissenschaften, 15693
Miranda, Francisco de, Colonel, 15308
'Mischling', 15168
Mises, Ludwig von, 15626–15627, 15736
Mises, Margit von, 15736
'Mitteilungen d. Verb. ehemaliger Breslauer u. Schlesier in Israel', 15029, 15030, 15042, 15060, 15330, 15361, 15803
Mlynek, Klaus, 15182
M. Nk., 15028
Modick, Klaus, 15486
Molnár, Franz (orig. Neumann), 15628
Mommsen, Theodor, 15577
Moreau, Pierre-François, 15609
Morgenthau sen., Henri, 15759
Moritz, Klaus, 15153
Morland, Henry, 15010
Moser, Sir Claus, 15104–15105
Moser, Roger, OFMCap., 15283
Moses, Siegfried, l. Gedenkvorlesung, 15318
Moses ben Maimon, Maimonides, 15320
Mosse, George L., 15008
Mühsam, Erich, 15391, 15629–15634
— 'Erich Mühsam Blätter', Berlin, 15634
Mühsam, Paul, 15635, 15737
Müller, Hermann-Josef, 15020
Müller, Josef, 15787
Müller, Ulrich, 15020
Müller-Armack, Alfred, 15627
Müller-Pozzi, Heinz, 15659
Müller-Seidel, Walter, 15446
Münden, 15171
Münster am Hellweg, Jahrbuch, 15033, 15176
Muir, Willa and Edwin, 15485
Munich, Räterepublik, 15391
Munk, Michael L., 15026
Music, Jews in, 15394, 15482, 15593, 15625
'(The) Musical Quarterly', New York, 15597
Musicologists, Jewish, 15394, 15405, 15481, 15598
Musil, Robert, 15397
Mutius, Bernhard von, 15591
Mynona see Friedländer, Salomo
Mytze, Andreas W., 15402, 15698, 15732

Na'aman, Shlomo, 15109
'Nachrichtenblatt', d. Jüd. Gemeinde von

Gross-Berlin u. d. Verbandes d. Jüd. Gemeinden in der DDR., 15227
Nagel, Bert, 15549
Nahariya, 15060
Names, Jewish, 15114, 15341, 15793
Naschitz, Fritz, 15268
National Council for Social Studies, New York, 15157
NSDAP, 15109, 15769
Natzweiler, 15172
Navé Levinson, Pnina, 15278, 15759
Nazi Period, 15123, 15127–15211, 15617
Nehab, Ernst, 15329
Nelken, Ludwig, 15060
Nelson, Leonard, 15637
Neo-Nazismus, 15751
Nes Ammin, 15759
Neu Isenburg, 15173
Neue Deutsche Biographie (NDB), 15121
'(Die) Neue Gesellschaft', Bonn, 15385, 15404, 15416, 15633
'(Das) Neue Israel', Zürich, 15044, 15085, 15187, 15260, 15265, 15328, 154343, 15454, 15558, 15575, 15784
'Neue Jüdische Nachrichten' (N.J.), München, 15110, 15278, 15454, 15677
'Neue Politische Literatur', Wiesbaden, 15748
'Neue Rundschau', 15386, 15430, 15431, 15559, 15739, 15807
'Neue Sammlung', Göttingen, 15426
Neuengamme Kz, 15174
Neugebauer, Heinz, 15674
Neugebauer, Irmgard, 15674
Neumann, Franz L., 15638
Neumann, Siegfried, 15639, 15640
New York, Columbia University, 15771
— State University, 15097
Ney, Fritz, 15106
Nick, Dagmar, 15641
Nicolay, Ralf R., 15550
Niedersachsen see Lower Saxony
Niemeyer, Helmut, 15430
Nissen, Rudolf, 15642
Nitsche, Wolfgang, 15198
'Niv Hamidrashia', 15249, 15331
Noam, Ernst (orig. Nussbaum), 15153
Nobel Prize, 15113, 15724
Noether, Emmy, 15032
Nordau, Max, (orig. Südfeld), 15643
Nordhausen (now Roland Stadt), 15227
Nosek, B[ederich], 15073
(The) Nothmann Family, 15060
November Pogrom, 15175–15200, 15227, 15234, 15238, 15757, 15786
Novitch, Miriam, 15204
Noy, Mordechai, 15060
Nürnberg-Fürth, 15055
Nuremberg Trial, 15617, 15776

Obenaus, Herbert, 15182
Oberammergau, 15757, 15760
Obermaier, Walter, 15499
Obermayer-Marnach, Eva, 15122
Oberschlesien see Upper Silesia
'Observer Magazine', London, 15495
Ökumenisch-Theologische Forschungsgemeinschaft in Israel, 15763
Österreicher im Exil, 15378
Oesterreicher, Paul, 15193
Österr. Akademie d. Wissenschaften, 15122
Österr. Biographisches Lexikon, 15122
Österr. Jüdisches Museum in Eisenstadt, Verein, 15083
Ofer, Pinhas, 15370
Offenbach a. M., 15056
Offermann, Toni, 15582
Oggel, Elisabeth, 15278
Oldenburg (District), 15322, 15793
Ollig, Hans-Ludwig, 15294
Ophüls, Max (orig. Oppenheimer), 15644
Oppenheim, Michael D., 15313
Oppenheim, Moritz Daniel, 15337, 15645
Oppenheimer, David (also Oppenheim), 15073
Oppenheimer, Max (pseud. Max Ludwig), 15786
'Orient', Haifa, 15379
Orientalists (Jewish), 15728
Oschilewski, Walther G[eorg], 15633, 15698
Ossiestzky, Carl von, 15395
Osten-Sacken, Peter von der, 15284, 15766, 15767
Osterle, Heinz D., 15464
Owens, Gwinn, 15685
Oxford Centre for Postgraduate Hebrew Studies, 15271

Paál, J[anos], 15081
Pachter, Henry M., 15319
Paderborn, 15057
Padover, Saul K., 15610, 15611
Paepke, Lotte, 15646
Paeschke, Hans, 15416
Painters (Jewish), 15328, 15337, 15497, 15586, 15621, 15645, 15683, 15759
(The) Panofsky Family, 15060
Papandreon, Damaskinos, 15758
Pappenheim, Bertha, 15173, 15332, 15350, 15647
Paris Université, Centre de Publication Asie Orientale, 15204
'(Das) Parlament', Bonn, 15195, 15209, 15795
Parsons, William S., 15242
'Patterns of Prejudice', 15242, 15787
Paucker, Arnold, 15006, 15111, 15338
Pauli, Wolfgang, 15388
Paulsen, Friedrich, 15425

Pazi, Margarita, 15076, 15710, 15717
Perlman, Tali, 15559
Perry, Alfred, 15540
Peru, Jews in, 15090
Peters, Eckehard, 15526
Petuchowski, Elizabeth M., 15460, 15487
Petzold, Günther and Leslie, 15359
Petzold, Johann Dietrich von, 15171
Pfäfflin, Friedrich, 15697
Pfisterer, Rudolf, 15197, 15754, 15788
Philanthropists, Jewish, 15100
Philippoff, Eva, 15693
Philippson, Ludwig, 15245, 15334
Philosophisches Jahrbuch, Freiburg/Br., 15294
Philosophy and Learning, Jews in, 15250, 15293, 15328, 15401, 15407, 15456, 15599, 15601, 15636, 15637, 15650, 15707
Photographers, Photo Reporters, 15513, 15664
Phronesis, Eine Schriftenreihe, 15262, 15273, 15283, 15314, 15553
Picard, Max, 15648
Picard, Michael, 15648
Picard, Salomon, 15067
Piccone, Paul, 15381
Piel, Edgar, 15502
Pincus, Lily, 15328, 15649
Pinkerneil, Dietrich, 15395
Pinner, Ludwig, 15347
Pinthus, Kurt, 15512
Piontek, Heinz, 15419
Pirmasens (Landkreis), 15058
Pistorius, Hedwig, 15695
Plank, Robert, 15657
Plate, Glen S., 15242
Pohl, Hans, 15658
Polgar, Alfred, 15072
Poliakov, Léon, 15201, 15788, 15789
Politics, Jews in, 15101, 15575, 15578, 15592, 15632, 15658, 15666
Politzer, Heinz, 15397, 15551, 15552
Pollak, Isidor, 15075
Pollock, Friedrich, 15386
Popkin, Richard H., 15308
Poppel, Stephen M[urray], 15360
Popper, Sir Karl R[aimund], 15650–15655
Popper-Lynkeus, Josef, 15656–15657
Portuguese Jews, 15040
Poschmann, Henri, 15505
Poschmann, Rosemarie, 15744
Pott, Klaus-Gerhard, 15730
Potter, Dennis, 15159
Pottlitzer, Margot, 15100, 15103
'Prager Kreis', 15076
'Prager Selbstwehr', 15075
Prague, 15073, 15074–15076
— Rat d. Jüd. Gemeinden in der CSR, 15220
— Staatliches Jüd. Museum, 15073
Prausnitz, 15061

Prenn, Daniel, 15137
Press- und Informationsamt d. Bundesregierung, Bonn
— Bulletin d., 15188
Preuss. Kulturbesitz, Stiftung, 15392, 15622 (Jahrbuch)
Prinz, Arthur, 15333
Prittie, Terence, 15170
Proceedings of the 6th World Congress of Jewish Studies, 15360
Proskauer, Paul F., 15469, 15745
Psychoanalysts, Psychologists, Jewish, 15436, 15438, 15490, 15500, 15504, 15660, 15681
Psychotherapists, Jewish, 15328, 15489, 15649
Public Service, Jews in, 15666
Publicists, Journalists, Jewish, 15534, 15698, 15706, 15711

Quinn, Edward, 15764

Raab, Angelika, 15173
Rabbis, 15033, 15060, 15085, 15198, 15245, 15247, 15248, 15249, 15266, 15295, 15298, 15300, 15301, 15309, 15322, 15323, 15324
Rabin, Esther, 15361
Rabinowitz, Dorothy, 15210
Racism, 15008, 15202
Raddatz, Fritz Joachim, 15376, 15412, 15420, 15488, 15601, 15612, 15619, 15663, 15708
Ragins, Sanford, 15790
Rand-Schleifer, Betty, 15039
Raphael, F[reddy], 15067
Rapp, Eugen Ludwig, 15053
Rasch, Wolfdietrich, 15470
'Rassenschande', 15008, 15202
Rathenau, Walther, 15390, 15658
Real, Michael, 15051
Rebentisch, Dieter, 15173
'Recherches de Science Religieuse', Paris, 15304
'(The) Record', 15157
Reich, Mira, 15279
Reich, Wilhelm, 15659
Reich-Ranicki, Marcel, 15376, 15468, 15471, 15472
Reichmann, Eva G., 15113, 15338
Reichsbund Jüdischer Frontsoldaten (R.J.F.), 15338
Reif, Adelbert, 15503
Reik, Theodor, 15660
Reilly, Edward R., 15598
Reinfrank, Arno, 15634
Reinharz, Jehuda, 15362
Reisch, Elisabeth, 15751
Reissner, Hanns G[ünther], 15111
Religious Currents and General Culture, 15763
Renaud, Daniel, 15707
Rendtorff, Rolf, 15284, 15754, 15761
Renger, Annemarie, 15754

Rengstorf, Karl Heinrich, 15750
Renken, Gerd, 15751
Research Foundation for Jewish Immigration, New York, 15099
Resistance, Jewish, 15073, 15123, 15150, 15212 (Austrian), 15213–15219, 15751, 15775
—, Spiritual, 15073, 15206, 15208
Restitution, 15229
Reubeni, Meir, 15454, 15759
Revolutionaries, Jewish, 15327, 15427, 15441, 15632
'Revue Internationale de Philosophie', Bruxelles, 15307
'Rheinischer Merkur', Koblenz, 15223, 15747
Rheins, Carl J., 15340
Richter, Karl, 15813
Riegel, Helmut, 15473
Riehn, Rainer, 15813
Riemenschneider, Rainer, 15239
Rien, Mark W., 15423
Ries, W[iebrecht], 15553
Riesenburger, Martin, 15227
'Righteous Among the Nations', 15142, 15150, 15151, 15165, 15170, 15775
Ringer, Herbert, 15227
Rippmann, Inge, 15443
Rippmann, Peter, 15443
Rittmann, Michael, 15059
Riverside, University of California, 15669
Rivette, Jacques, 15644
Roazen, Paul, 15493
Robinsohn, Hans, 15202
Robinson, Jacob, 15118, 15150, 15775
Rodalben (Pirmasens), 15058
Rodenberg, Julius, 15227
Rodenstock, Rolf, 15754
Röhrbein, Waldemar R., 15182
Röll, W[alter], 15023
Roer, Emanuel, 15363
Rogge, Friedrich Wilhelm, 15182
Roland-Stadt (Nordhausen), 15227
Romania, 15084–15085
Rosdorf, 15041
Rose, Margaret A., 15527
Rosen, Moses, 15085
Rosen, Pinchas, 15364
Rosen, Robert S., 15332
Rosenbaum, Eduard, 15702
Rosenberg, Alfons, 15328
Rosenblüth, Cessi, 15365
Rosenblüth, Felix see Rosen, Pinchas
Rosenblüth, Pinchas (Erich), 15290, 15291, 15318
Rosenheim, Jacob, 15309
Rosenkranz, Bella, 15373
Rosenkranz, Herbert, 15132
Rosenstock, Werner, 15094, 15194, 15339, 15368

Rosenthal, Albert, 15060
Rosenthal, Isidor, 15032
Rosenthal, Ludwig, 15528
Rosenzweig, Adele, 15310
Rosenzweig, Franz, 15255, 15290, 15302, 15310, 15311–15315, 15321
Rosenzweig, Rachel, 15311
Ross, Peter, 15675
Ross, Werner, 15740
Rotenstreich, Nathan, 15015, 15315
Roth, Ernst, 15056, 15082, 15323
Roth, Joseph, 15661–15663
Rothe, Wolf Dieter, 15791
Rothkirchen, Livia, 15150, 15151, 15775
Rothschild, Edmond, 15366
Rothschild, Eli, 15363
Rothschild, James de, 15366
Rothschild, Karl, 15362
Rothschild, Thomas, 15483
(The) Rothschilds, 15366
Rotter, Erich, 15759
Rotzoll, Christa, 15027
Rousseau, Jean Jacques, 15307
Rubenstein, L., 15302
Rubinstein, Aryeh, 15324
Rübner, Tuvia, 15285
Rückerl, Adalbert, 15218
Rüegg, Walter, 15457
Rühle, Günther, 15163, 15467
Rühmkorf, Peter, 15468
Rüter, C. F., 15166
Ruether, Rosemary, 15792
Rumschött, Hermann, 15136
Ruppin, Arthur, 15336, 15350

Sachs, Clara, 15683
Sachs, Julius, 15060
Sachs, Nelly, 15387
Sachsenhausen, 15191
Sadan, Israel, 15331
Sadek, Vladimir, 15073
'Saeculum' (Freiburg), 15782
Sagel-Grande, Irene, 15166
'Salmagunde', 15319, 15408
Salmon, Elon, 15012
Salomon, Erich, 15664
Salten, Felix (orig. Siegmund Salzmann), 15397
Salzberger-Wittenberg, Isca, 15328
Salzburg, University, 15018
Samuel, H. J., 15033
Samuel, Salomon, Rabbi, 15033
Sandberg, Herbert, 15138
Saphir, Moritz (Moishe) Gottlieb, 15665
Saretzki, Adalbert, 15060
Satirical Writers, Jewish, 15636, 15665
Sauer, Klaus, 15676
Schaal, Zvi, 15060
Schachtsieck-Freitag, Norbert, 15686

Schadt, Jörg, 15511
Schaeder, Grete, 15291
Schäffer, Hans, 15666
Schallenberger, E. Horst, 15237, 15240
Schallück, Paul, 15291
Schama, Simon, 15366
Schatzker, Chaim, 15286
Schaumburg-Lippe, 15047
Schebera, Jürgen, 15484
Scheckenbach, Achim, 15062
Scheel, Walter (Bundespräs.), 15188
Scheffler, Wolfgang, 15191, 15195
Scheiber, Alexander [Sandor], 15728
Scheible, Hartmut, 15671
Scheichl, Sigurd Paul, 15574
Scheinmann-Rosenzweig, Edith, 15311
Schembs, Hans-Otto, 15038
Scheyer, Ernst, 15031, 15683
Schick, Sophie, 15574
Schieckel, Harald, 15793
Schiller, Dieter, 15629
Schiller-Nationalmuseum, Marbach/N., 15445, 15467, 15697
Schipperges, Heinrich, 15536
Schleifstein, Josef, 15652
Schlesinger, S., 15067
Schlösser, Manfred, 15419
Schloss, Rolf W[alter], 15142
Schmerling, G., 15010
Schmid, Richard, 15153, 15390
Schmidlin, Yvonne, 15805
Schmidt, Alfred, 15384, 15601
Schmidt, Helmut (Bundeskanzler), 15188, 15238, 15754, 15760
Schmidt, Karl Ludwig, 15284
Schmidt-Heinicke, Valy, 15051
Schmit, Alfred, 15492
Schmitt, Hans-Jürgen, 15590
Schmitt-Maass, Hety, 15416
Schmuckler, Joseph F., 15410
Schneider, Manfred, 15442
Schneider, Rolf, 15705
Schneider, Rudi, 15786
Schnitzler, Arthur, 15072, 15397, 15667–15671
Schnurre, Wolfdietrich, 15468
Schock, Max, 15758
Schocken, Salman, 15345
Schönberger, Martin, 15636
Schoenberner, Gerhard, 15203, 15755
Schönig, Erich, 15533
Schoeps, Hans Joachim, 15010, 15032, 15672
Schoeps, Julius Hans, 15207, 15355
Schofield, Philip, 15757
Scholars, Jewish, 15006, 15320, 15321, 15763
Scholem, Gershom [also Gerhard], 15009, 15015, 15288, 15316–15319, 15431, 15722, 15759, 15763
Schondorff, Joachim, 15397

Schreiner, Stefan, 15200
Schröder, Rudolf Alexander, 15445
Schroers, Rudolf, 15751
Schröter, Hermann, 15176
Schröter, Klaus, 15473
Schubert, Kurt, 15069, 15083
Schüssler, Emilie, 15759
Schütz, Erhard, 15562
Schütz, Friedrich, 15051
Schultz, Hans Jürgen, 15328
Schultz, Uwe, 15416
Schulz, Georg-Michael, 15461
Schultz, Gerhard, 15464
Schulze, Hagen, 15392, 15393
Schuster, Adolf Wolfgang, 15034
Schwarcz, Moshe, 15763
Schwarz, Hans-Peter, 15393
Schwarz, Stefan, 15275, 15454
'(The) Schwarzes Fähnlein', 15340
Schweiger, Werner J., 15072
Schwemer, Ulrich, Pfarrer, 15238
Schwerin, Kurt, 15673
Schwetzingen, 15059
Science, Jews in, 15032, 15113, 15388, 15427, 15685, 15703, 15704, 15724, 15731
Scurla, Herbert, 15696
'(The) Second Jewish Catalogue', Philadelphia, 15243
Sedinová, Jiřina, 15073
Seelig, Carl, 15480
Seelmann-Eggebert, Ulrich, 15541
Seghers, Anna, 15590, 15674–15676, 15738
Seidlin, Oskar, 15447
Seigel, Jerrold, 15613
Seliger, Martin, 15015
Selzer, Michael, 15139
Serke, Jürgen, 15474
Shapira, Avraham, 15287
Sharon, Arieh, 15367
Shatil, Josef [f'ly Ernst Stillmann], 15368
Shavei Zion, 15359
Shermann, A. J., 15702
Shervin, Byron L., 15156
S[c]hestov, Lev [orig. Schwarzmann], 15287
Shimoni, Toni, 15279
Siefken, Hinrich, 15554
Siepmann, Eckhard, 15513
Sievers, Leo, 15010
Silbergleit, Arthur, 15677
Silberner, Edmund, 15592
Silenius, Axel, 15751
Silesia, 15060, 15061
Silverman, David W[olf], 15280
Simmel, Georg, 15678
Simon, Dietrich, 15451
Simon, Ernst Akiba, 15015, 15279, 15280, 15282, 15284, 15288, 15291, 15328, 15365, 15494
Simon, Heinrich, 15227

'Simplizissimus', 15530
Singer-Blaukopf, Herta, 15598
Sixth World Congress of Jewish Studies, 15360
Skelton, Geoffrey, 15810
Škochová, Jarmila, 15073
Slesvig-Holstein, 15040
Slovakia, 15077, 15151, 15220
Smith, Ronald Gregor, 15252
Smolen, Kazimierz, 15131
Sneh, Marcello, 15352
Sobibor, Camp, 15204
Social Reformers, Jewish, 15656
Socialism, 15369, 15774
Socialist Zionism, 15336, 15369
Socialists, Jewish, 15392, 15427, 15534, 15578, 15582, 15591
Sociologists, Jewish, 15476, 15577, 15626, 15678
Society for Ethnic Culture, New York, 15401
Söllner, Alfons, 15638
Sommer, Cornelius, 15020
Sommer, Ernst, 15076, 15679
Sonnenfels, Joseph von, 15070
Sorge, Helga, 15761
Souchy, Augustin, 15634
'Soviet Jewish Affairs', 15077, 15215
Spain, 15245
Spalek, John M., 15686
Sperber, Manès, 15328, 15680–15681, 15738–15740
Speyer, 15062
Spiel, Hilde, 15424, 15499
Spillane, Robert R., 15242
Spinner, Helmut F., 15655
Spinoza, Baruch, Spinozisme, 15306, 15609
Spira, Leopold, 15794
Spiro, Eugen, 15682–15683
Spitzemberg, Baronin, 15016
Sponsel, Ilse, 15032
Sports, Jews in, 15137, 15329, 15330
Springer, Axel, 15113, 15712 (Stiftung)
Stachura, Peter D., 15125
Státní Židovské Muzeum v Praze, 15073, 15220
Steele, Jonathan, 15228
Stein, Gerd, 15240
Stein, Günther, 15062
Stein, Gustav, 15756
Steinberg, Jonathan, 15012
Steiner, Frank Charles, 15097
Steiner, George, 15422, 15684, 15810
Steinhart, Anton, 15713
Steinitz, Hans, 15196
Steinmetz, Horst, 15555
Stelzer, Werner, 15197, 15202
Stern, Bruno, 15044
Stern, Fritz, 15011, 15012
Stern, Günther see Anders, Günther
Stern Strom, Margot, 15242
Stern, William, 15247, 15341

Sternberger, Harry, 15741
Sternheim, Carl, 15742
Stiehm, Lothar, 15256, 15257, 15258
Stöhr, Martin, 15238
Stolberg, Julius, 15759
Strauss, Eduard, 15321
Strauss, Levi, 15107
Strauss, Ludwig, 15285
Strauss, Richard, 15746
Strelka, Joseph [f], 15689
Stresemann, Wolfgang, 15394
Strothmann, Dietrich, 15226
Struck, Hermann, 15113
Stuckmann, Horst, 15786
Studia Judaica Austriaca, 15083
'(Der) Stürmer', 15152
Stupperich, R., 15064
'(Der) Sturm', 15698
Stuttgart, Jüd. Lehrhaus, 15284
Sucher, C. Bernd, 15804
Susman, Margarete, 15387
Susskind, Charles, 15731
Sussmann, Heinrich, 15759
Suzman, Arthur, 15795
Switzerland, 15806–15088
Synagogues, 15030 (Breslau), 15033 (Essen), 15034 (Floss), 15042 (Hamburg), 15050 (Luckenwalde), 15227 (Nordhausen)
Syrkin, Marie, 15219
Syrkin, Nachman, 15369
'System Althoff', 15426
Szczesny, Gernard, 15603
Szymanski, Rolf, 15189

Tal, Uriel, 15013, 15014, 15775
Talmon, Jacob L., 15775
Talmon, Shemaryahu, 15269, 15284, 15291
Tau, Max, 14255, 14835
Tavor, Moshe, 15760
Techniczek, M., 15109
Tel Aviv University, 15013, 15014, 15756
Teller, Edward, 15685
Terezin, 15073, 15146, 15205, 15206
Tergit, Gabriele (i.e. Reifenberg, Elise), 15027–15028
Tgahrt, Reinhard, 15445
Thadden, Rudolf von, 15015, 15315
Thaidigsmann, Edgar, 15614
Thalmann, Rita, 15238
Theatre, Cinema, Cabaret, Radio, Jews in, 15072, 15447, 15540, 15560, 15644, 15697, 15723
Theodor Herzl Foundation, 15277, 15287, 15610
Theresienstadt, 15073, 15146, 15205, 15206, 15220, 15402
Theunissen, Michael, 15289
Thoma, Clemens, 15298, 15757, 15758, 15760
Thorwald, Jürgen, 15107a

Tibi, Bassam, 15385
Tiedemann, Rolf, 15405
'T.L.S.' (Times Literary Supplement), 15012, 15338, 15475, 15728
Tolkes, Jerucham, 15759
Toller, Ernst, 15390, 15391, 15686
Tolstoi, Leo, 15643
Torberg, Friedrich (orig. Kantor Berg), 15072, 15574, 15687–15689
Toynbee, Philip, 14996
Trachenberg, 15061
Tramer, Hans, 15006, 15012, 15110, 15133, 15290, 15321, 15347, 15364, 15621, 15808
Trautwein, Dieter, 15238
Trendelenburg, Ernst, 15666
Trepp, Leo, 15322
Treue, Wilhelm, 15658
Trevor-Roper, Hugh R., 15149
'Tribüne', 15197, 15202, 15237, 15281, 15328, 15686, 15751, 15754
Trilling, Lionel, 15011
Truffaut, François, 15644
Trunk, Isaiah, 15150, 15207, 15775
Tucholsky, Kurt, 15390, 15395, 15396, 15690–15693, 15743
Tübingen, Universität, 15461

'Udim', Zeitschrift d. Rabbinerkonferenz, 15026, 15056, 15057, 15082, 15247, 15323, 15341
Uecker, Günther, 15619
Ueding, Gert, 15620, 15708
Uhde, Bernhard, 15244
Ungar, Frederick, 15667
Ungar, Hermann, 15694
Unger, Peter, 15433
Union of American Hebrew Congregations, New York, 15093
Unna, Viktor Awigdor, 15323
Upper Silesia, 15060
Urzidil, Gertrude, 15556
Urzidil, Johannes, 15695
Utley, Philip Lee, 15436

Vago, Bela, 15151
Varnhagen, Rahel, 15696
Veit, Reinhard, 15314
Verband ehemaliger Breslauer und Schlesier in Israel, 15029, 15030, 15042, 15060, 15330, 15361, 15803
Vermes, Geza, 15271
Vetter, Heinz Oskar, 15754
Vienna, 15071–15072, 15133, 15656
— University, 15083 (Institut f. Judaistik), 15695
Viereck, Peter, 15813
Vierhaus, Rudolf, 15015, 15016
Viertel, Berthold, 15697
Vierteljahrshefte für Zeitgeschichte, Stuttgart, 15202, 15393, 15666

Vierteljahrsschrift f .Sozial- u. Wirtschaftsgeschichte, Wiesbaden, 15037
Vischer, Lukas, 15758
Visocchi, Mark, 15625
Vögtle, Anton, 15760
Vogel, Rolf, 15752
Vogelstein, Hermann, Rabbi, 15060
Vogt, Ernst, 15199, 15369, 15759
Vogt, Judith, 15796
Volke, Werner, 15737
Volkov, Shulamit, 15797
Voltaire, François-Marie, 15307
Vondenhoff, Bruno and Eleonore, 15595
Vontin, Walther, 15518
Vordtriede, Werner, 15446, 15515
Vorländer, Herwart, 15172
Vorndran, Hans-Georg, 15238
Voss, Egon, 15811

Wagenknecht, Christian Johannes, 15574
Wagenlehner, Günther, 15152
Wagner, Cosima, 15810
Wagner, Erich, 15712
Wagner, Richard, 15810–15813
Walden, Herwarth (i.e. Lewin, Georg), 15698
Walk, Joseph, 15190
Wallich, Henry C., 15699
Wallich, Hermann, 15699
Wallich, Paul, 15699
Wallmann, Walter, 15269
Walter, Hans-Albert, 15379, 15462, 15463, 15744
'Wannsee-Protokoll', 15238
Warburg, Aby Moritz, 15700–15701
Warburg, M. M. & Co., Hamburg, 15702
Warburg, Otto, 15703
Warschawski, M., 15067
Wartenburg (East Prussia), 15063
Wassermann, Charles, 15704
Wassermann, Henry, 15017
Wassermann, Jakob, 15704, 15705
Watt, W. Montgomery, 15728
Wawrzinek, Kurt, 15798
Weber, Alois, 15058
Weber, Max, 15615
'Weg und Ziel', Wien, 15794
Wegner, Armin T., 15814
Weichmann, Herbert, 15392
Weigel, Hans, 15072, 15628, 15706
Weigert, Edith V., 15504
Weil, Felix, 15386
Weimar Republic, 15125, 15390, 15391, 15393, 15486
— Justiz in d., 15390, 15391
Weininger, Otto, 15707
Weinreich, Max, M.W. Center for Advanced Jewish Studies, 15000
Weinzierl, Ulrich, 15376
Weis, Georg, 15133

Weisgal, Meyer W., 15370
Weiss, Aharon, 15118
Weiss, Peter, 15708
Weiß, Ernst, 15076, 15709–15710
Weith, Otto, 15012
Weizmann, Chaim, 15366, 15370
Wellers, Georges, 15200, 15209
'(Die) Weltbühne', 15395
Weltsch, Robert, 15075, 15111, 15113, 15291
Wendler, Wolfgang, 15742
Wenkart, Heni, 15559
Wenninger, Markus J[ohannes], 15018
Wenzel, Georg, 15718
Werblowsky, Zwi, 15015
Werfel, Franz, 15075
Werner, Alfred, 15337
West Germany see Federal German Republic
'Westdeutscher Rundfunk' (WDR), 15751
Westphalia, 15057, 15064
— Historische Kommission Westfalens, Veröffentlichungen d., 15046
Weyl, Robert, 15067
Who's Who in World Jewry, 15126
Wiegand, Wilfried, 15396
Wien see Vienna
(The) Wiener Library Catalogue Series, 15117, 15123
Wiener, Oskar, 15075
Wienner, Alois, 15070
Wiese, Ursula von, 15107
Wiesel, Eli, 15164, 15210, 15241
Wiggershaus, R[olf], 15386
Wilde, John, 15212
Wilhelm, Peter, 15041
Wilhelm II., German Emperor, 15016, 15111
Williams, George Huntston, 15292
Williamson, D[avid] G[raham], 15658
Willner, Max, 15056
Winkler, Andreas, 15561
Winkler, Michael, 15380
Winston, Clara and Richard, 15809
Winter, Ludwig, 15076
Wisconsin, University of, 15436
Wise, Isaac M[ayer], 15324
'Wissenschaft des Judentums', 15763
Wissmann, Matthias, 15754
Witton-Davies, Carlyle, 15757
Woche der Brüderlichkeit 1978 (Erlangen), 15032
Woesler, Winfried, 15231
Wohl, Jeanette, 15442
Wohlmann-Meyer, Cläre, 15088, 15364
Wolf, Gerhard, 15744
Wolff, Ilse R., 15123
Wolff, Jeanette, 15146
Wolff, Theodor, 15711–15712
— Th.-W.-Preis d. Axel Springer Stiftung, 15712
Wolfskehl, Karl, 15387

Wolter, Manfred, 15719
Women, 15000, 15647, 15670
Womit, Hans-Georg, 15622
World Jewish Congress, 15092, 15143, 15151, 15215, 15280, 15295, 15303, 15313
Worms, 15151, 15278
Wroclaw see Breslau
Wronke (f'ly Poznań Province), 15065
'Würzburger Raw', 15247
Wulf, Josef, 15201
Wurgraft, Lewis D., 15534
Wurttemberg, 15172
Wuttke, Dieter, 15700, 15701
Wysling, Hans, 15805

Yad Vashem, Jerusalem, 15118, 15150, 15151, 15211, 15217, 15775
— Second Intern. Historical Conference 1974, Proceedings of, 15151
Yahil, Leni, 15150, 15151, 15775
Yavetz, Zvi, 15109
'Yellow Star', 15203
Yiddish, 15019–15023
Yivo Institute for Jewish Research, 15000
Youth (German), 15757
Youth Movement, Jewish (in Germany), 15286, 15436

Zadek, Walter (see Benjamin, Uri), 15721
Zander, Jürgen, 15615
'Zeit-Magazin', Hamburg, 15474
Zeitschrift f. philosophische Forschung, 15293, 15653
Zeitschrift f. Unternehmensgeschichte, Wiesbaden, 15658
Zeller, Bernhard, 15445, 15446
Zentralrat d. Juden in Deutschland, 15781
Zentrale Stelle Ludwigsburg zur Aufklärung nationalsozialistischer Verbrechen, 15218
Ziegenhain (District), 15066
Zimmermann, Helmut, 15182
Zimmermann, Moshe, 15799
Zinberg, Israel, 15325
Zink, Wolfgang, 15276, 15291
Zionism, 15336, 15348, 15349, 15351, 15360, 15369
— in Germany, 15348, 15362, 15363
— Socialist, 15336, 15369, 15436
Zoch-Westphal, Gisela, 15557, 15558
Zohn, Harry, 15559, 15573
Zschorsch, Gerald K., 15634
Zuckmayer, Carl, 15713–15716
Zurich, University, (E.T.H.), 15805
Zuroff, Efraim, 15151
Zvi Lurie Institute, 15025
Zweig, Arnold, 15227, 15346, 15717–15718, 15744
Zweig, Stefan, 15375, 15397, 15453, 15496, 15719–15720, 15745–15746
Zwerenz, Gerhard, 15634

List of Contributors

CARLEBACH, Julius, M.Lit., D.Phil., b. 1922 in Hamburg. Reader and Chairman – Sociology, University of Sussex. Author of a.o. *The Jews of Nairobi* (1962); *Caring for Children in Trouble* (1970); *Karl Marx and the Radical Critique of Judaism* (1978). Member of the London Board of the LBI. (Contributor to Year Book XVIII.)

ENGEL, Eva Johanna, Ph.D., b. 1919 in Dortmund. Formerly University teacher, Universities of Cambridge, Keele, Boston etc. Now teacher and editor, Research Fellow, Wellesley College, Wellesley, Mass. Co-Editor of *Moses Mendelssohn Jubiläumsausgabe* and Editor of vol. IV (1977). Editor of *German Narrative Prose*, vol. I (1965) and other German literary texts and author of numerous articles on German literature and philosophy.

FRAENKEL, Peter Joachim, B.A., b. 1926 in Breslau. Broadcaster, Head of East European Service of the BBC. Author of *Wayaleshi* (1958). Peter Fraenkel is the great-great-grandson of B. L. Monasch.

FREIMARK, Peter, Dr. phil., b. 1934 in Halberstadt. Director of the Institut für die Geschichte der deutschen Juden in Hamburg. Author (with Wolfgang Kopitzsch) of *Der 9./10. November 1938* (1978) and of books and numerous articles on rabbinical, onomastical and historical subjects. Editor (since 1974) of *Hamburger Beiträge zur Geschichte der deutschen Juden*.

FRIEDMAN, Isaiah, Ph.D., b. 1921 in Lutzk (formerly Poland). 1971–1977, Professor of History, The Dropsie University, Philadelphia. Now Research Professor of History, Ben-Gurion Institute of the University of the Negev, Beersheba. Author of *The Question of Palestine, 1914–1918, British-Jewish-Arab Relations* (1973); *Germany, Turkey and Zionism, 1897–1918* (1977); and of numerous essays on Palestine, Zionism etc.

GERNSHEIM, Helmut Erich Robert, b. 1913 in Munich. Educated at the University of Munich and the State School of Photography, Munich. Diploma summa cum laude. Historian of Photography, Visiting Professor, University of Texas. Author of numerous books (some in collaboration with Alison Gernsheim), a.o. *Beautiful London* (1950–1965, 6 eds.); *Victorian Photography* (1951); *Julia Margaret Cameron* (1948, 1975); *Historic Events 1839–1939* (1960); *Concise History of Photography* (1965, 1971); *Bibliography of Early British Photography* (1979); and of over 200 articles. Producer of the Festival of Britain Exhibition, *Masterpieces of Victorian Photography from the Gernsheim Collection*, in 1951.

KWIET, Konrad, Dr. phil., b. 1941 in Swinemünde. Senior Lecturer, School of German, University of New South Wales, Sydney and Privatdozent at the

Technische Hochschule, Berlin. Author of *Reichskommissariat Niederlande* (1968); *Van Jodenhoed tot Gele Ster* (1973); and of various essays in historical journals. (Contributor to Year Book XXI.)

LOWENSTEIN, Steven Mark, Ph.D., b. 1945 in New York. Archivist, Leo Baeck Institute, New York. Author of a.o. 'Results of Atlas Investigations among Jews of Germany', *Field of Yiddish* (1969); 'The Remnants of Franconian Yiddish', *Yidishe Shprakh* (1973–1975, in Yiddish); 'A Western Yiddish Drama of the early nineteenth century', *YIVO Bleter* (1975, in Yiddish); 'Voluntary and Involuntary fertility limitation among 19th century Bavarian Jews', *Jewish Fertility* (1979). (Contributor to Year Book XXI.)

MEYER, Michael A., Ph.D., b. 1937 in Berlin. Professor of Jewish History, Hebrew Union College-Jewish Institute of Religion, Cincinnati, Ohio. Author of a.o. *The Origins of the Modern Jew: Jewish Identity and European Culture in Germany, 1749–1824* (1967, 1972); *Ideas of Jewish History* (1974); and of numerous articles on Judaism and Jewish History. Fellow of the LBI, New York, and Member of its Board. (Contributor to Year Books XI and XVI.)

MICHAELIS, Dolf, (A.P.), b. 1906 in Magdeburg. Retired banker. Co-editor of and contributor to: *Haavara-Transfer nach Palästina und Einwanderung deutscher Juden 1933–1939* (1972); and author of various essays on banking and other subjects in economic and historical journals. Member, Executive Committee, Board of Governors of the Hebrew University of Jerusalem. Member of the Jerusalem Board of the LBI. (Contributor to Year Book XXI.)

MOSSE, Werner, E., Ph.D., Fellow of the Royal Historical Society, b. 1918 in Berlin. Since 1964 Professor for European History at the University of East Anglia, Norwich. Author of a.o. *The European Powers and the German Question 1848–1871* (1958); *Alexander II and the Modernization of Russia 1855–1881* (1959); *The Rise and Fall of the Crimean System 1855–1871* (1963); *Liberal Europe – The Age of Bourgeois Realism 1848–1875* (1974). Editor (in collaboration with Arnold Paucker) of *Entscheidungsjahr 1932. Zur Judenfrage in der Endphase der Weimarer Republik* (2nd edition 1966); *Deutsches Judentum in Krieg und Revolution 1916–1923* (1971); and of *Juden in Wilhelminischen Deutschland 1890–1914* (1976). Member of the Executive Committee of the LBI, London. (Contributor to Year Books IV and XV.)

NICOSIA, Francis R. J., Ph.D., b. 1944 in Pennsylvania. Assistant Professor of History, St. Michael's College, Vermont. Author of 'Zionism in National Socialist Jewish Policy in Germany 1933–1939', *Journal of Modern History* (1978).

PELLI, Moshe, Ph.D., b. 1936 in Haifa. Taught Modern Hebrew Language and Literature at the University of Texas, Austin, University of the Negev, Beersheba, the Hebrew University in Jerusalem, Cornell University and Yeshiva University, New York. Formerly editor, *NIV*, Hebrew Literary Quarterly; and

Lamishpahah, Hebrew Monthly. Author of *Moses Mendelssohn: Bonds of Tradition* (1972, in Hebrew); *The Age of Haskalah* (1978); and of novels, short stories and numerous papers on the Hebrew Enlightenment and modern Hebrew literature. (Contributor to Year Books XX and XXII.)

REINHARZ, Jehuda, Ph.D., b. 1944 in Haifa. Associate Professor of History, University of Michigan. Author of *Fatherland or Promised Land: The Dilemma of the German Jew 1893–1914* (1975); Editor of Volume IX of *The Letters and Papers of Chaim Weizmann* (1977); Co-Editor of (and contributor to) *Essays in Jewish Intellectual History* (1979); Editor of *Dokumente zur Geschichte des deutschen Zionismus* (in print) to be published by the Leo Baeck Institute; Co-Editor (with Paul R. Mendes-Flohr) of a forthcoming documentary volume in modern Jewish history. Author of reviews and articles in scholarly periodicals. (Contributor to Year Book XXII.)

SCHOFER, Lawrence, Ph.D., b. 1940 in Baltimore. Historian, at present in Health Administration. Author of *The Formation of a Modern Labor Force. Upper Silesia 1865–1914* (1975); and of articles on German social history and the history of European Jews.

UTLEY, Philip Lee, Ph.D., b. 1940 in Columbia, Ohio. Psychoanalytic Therapist, Affiliation: Theodor Reik Consultation Center, New York. Author of 'Radical Youth: Generational Conflict in the *Anfang* Movement, 1912– January 1914', *History of Education Quarterly* (1979); currently writing a book on Siegfried Bernfeld.

WALK, Joseph, Ph.D., b. 1914 in Breslau. Senior Lecturer for Jewish History, Bar Ilan University and Director of the Leo Baeck Institute, Jerusalem. Author of *The Education of the Jewish Child in Germany – The Law and its Execution* (1976, in Hebrew). Editor of *Shaul Esh: Studies in Holocaust and Contemporary Jewry* (1973, in Hebrew); *Als Jude in Breslau – Aus den Tagebüchern von Studienrat a.D. Dr. Willy Israel Cohn* (1975). (Contributor to Year Book VI.)

Correction to Year Book XXIII

Essay on the Schwarzes Fähnlein
The top left corner photograph opposite page 181 shows the Jewish youth leader Günter Holzmann and not Günther Ballin together with Yogi Mayer

---

Abstracts of articles in this Year Book are included in *Historical Abstracts* and *America: History and Life*.

General Index to Year Book XXIV of the Leo Baeck Institute

Aaranowitz, Yoseph, 315
Aaronson, Aaron (agronomist), 277
Académie Royale des Sciences et des Belles Lettres de Berlin, 64, 65, 69, 77
Acosta, Uriel, 62
Adam, Jacob (merchant), 24
Adelung, Johann Christoph (grammarian), 158
Adenauer, Konrad (German statesman), 331
Adler, H. G., 38, 50n
Adler, Nathan Marcus (Chief Rabbi of Great Britain), 246
Adler-Rudel, Shalom (Director of the Leo Baeck Institute), 38
Agudat Israel, 328n
Ahad Ha'am (Zionist leader, philosopher and Hebrew writer), 275n, 297, 303
Ahavass Zijon, Hamburg, 262, 267
'Ahdut' (Hebrew paper), 315
Alexander II (Czar of Russia), 261
Alexander III (Czar of Russia), 261
Allgemeine Elektrizitätsgesellschaft (AEG), 11, 23
'Allgemeine Zeitung des Judentums', 172, 273, 274n
Alliance Israélite Universelle, 263n, 270, 276, 292, 293, 296, 301, 302, 307, 309
Alsatian Jewry, 119–120
Altenstein, Karl von (Prussian Minister of Religion), 145–154
Altmann, Alexander, 71, 119, 131n
American Jewish Committee, 313
American Joint Distribution Committee, 361, 365
Anfang, youth movement, 349, 355–357
Anglo-Jewish Association, 292, 309
Anglo-Palestine Company, 277, 278, 284, 288, 315
Argens, Jean Baptiste de Boyer, Marquis d' (philosopher), 65, 69
Antisemitism, 11, 20, 25, 28, 37–57, 108, 133, 162, 177, 185, 186, 191, 292, 329, 332, 333, 339, 345; Dinter, 162n; Fichte, 133; Freytag, 162n; in German youth movement, 357; Jewish defence against, 38; in Poland, 28. See also boycott, pogroms, racism and antisemitism, German post-war historiography on.
Antisemitism, German, post-war historiography on, general (western-bourgeois, Jewish), 37–57 passim; Marxist (GDR), 37, 40, 53
Arnhold, Eduard (banker), 241
Arnstein family, 227, 228, 236
Arnstein, Fanny von, 226, 227
Assimilation, 12, 40, 57, 122, 160, 163

Auerbach, Isaak Levin (preacher and educationalist), 139, 141, 149
Auhagen, Otto, 330n
Auschwitz, 37
Avé-Lallemant, F. C. B. (criminologist) 162, 163, 169n
Azaryahu, Yoseph, 310

Babel, Isaac, 33
Baden Jewry, 171; Oberrath der Israeliten, 171
Baeck, Leo, 43, 47, 332
Balfour, Arthur (British statesman), 338
Balfour Declaration, 279, 318, 321, 323, 324, 326, 327, 330n, 331, 338, 342, 344, 350–351
Ball-Kaduri, Kurt Jakob (historian), 38, 39
Ballin, Albert (Director of HAPAG), 241
Ballin, Günther (leader of Schwarzes Fähnlein), 461
Bamberger, Ludwig (Liberal politician), 11n
Bamberger, Seligmann Baer (rabbi), 190, 191
Bambus, Willy (Zionist writer and editor), 267, 269, 270, 271, 272, 273, 274, 275, 276, 280, 283
Bankers, Jewish, 4–11 passim, 23, 237–240
Baptism see Conversion
Baron, Salo, 17, 109
Batocki family, 240
Bauer, Bruno (Protestant theologian and historian), 122
Baum, Herbert, 39
Baum Group, 39, 40, 49, 53
Baumgarten, Alexander Gottlieb (writer), 69, 77
Bavarian Jewry, 182n, 183
Beausobre, Louis, 65
Bebel, August (leader of German Socialists), 108, 124n
Becker, Carl Heinrich (Prussian Minister of Cultural Affairs), 331, 333
Beer family, 242
Beer, Jacob Herz see Herz Beer, Jacob
Beha-ed Din (Turkish adminstrator of Palestine), 313, 314, 315, 316
Behrend, Benzion (author and translator), 212, 213–214, 215, 216, 218, 223
Behrend, Julia (Julie) née Monasch, 202, 211, 212, 223
Beit, Ferdinand, 168
Belkind, Israel (writer and Zionist leader), 277
Ben-Gurion, David, 315
Ben-Zvi, Itzhak, 315
Bergier, J. F., 111
Berlin Jewish community, 20n, 29, 30, 139–155, 239

Bernays, Isaak (Chacham) (Chief Rabbi of Hamburg), 149n, 168
Bernfeld, Siefried (educationalist and psychoanalyst), 349–368; and Buber, 354–361 *passim*; Jerubbaal, 351–368 *passim*; Kinderheim Baumgarten, 349n, 350, 361–368; and Wyneken, 353–367 *passim*
Bernfeld, Simon, 144n
Bernhard, Georg (editor of 'Vossische Zeitung'), 330n
Bernhard, Isaac (manufacturer), 69
Bernstein (Rebenstein), Aron (writer), 188, 245
Bernstorff, Andreas Christian (Danish statesman), 227
Bernstorff, Count Christian (Danish diplomat), 227
Bernstorff, Count Johann-Heinrich (German diplomat), 227, 312, 313, 314n, 319, 330–331, 333, 335n
Bethmann Hollweg, Theobald von (German Imperial Chancellor), 291n, 298n, 300n, 304n, 305n, 313n, 314n, 315n, 317n
Bialik, Chaim Nachman (Hebrew poet), 310–311
Bierbaum, Otto Julius (writer), 254, 257
Bilu, 262–263, 277
Birnbaum, Nathan (Jewish politician and writer), 272
Bismarck, Otto von, 23, 241, 291
Blackall, E. A., 160
Blau-Weiss, in Germany, 52, 289; in Austria, 351, 352, 362
Bleichröder family, 8, 11
Bleichröder, Gerson von (banker), 23, 240n
Blumenfeld, Kurt (German Zionist leader), 334, 369, 370n
B'nai B'rith, 11n, 262, 267, 328n
Boccaccio, 119
Bodenheimer, Max Isidor (German Zionist leader), 269, 271, 273, 274, 275, 279n
Bodmer, Johann Jakob (poet), 74
Börne, Ludwig (writer), 130, 166n
Bonin, von (Prussian Minister of Finance), 216
Borochow-youth, 52
Bosch, Robert (industrialist), 47
Bosch circle, 47n
Boycott, in Germany, 1st April 1933, 42–43, 57, 241n–242n
Brahms, Johannes (composer), 251, 252, 253
Brandeis, Louis D. (Justice), 312
Braun, Otto (Prime Minister of Prussia), 331
Breitscheid, Rudolf (Socialist politician), 331
Brenner, Yoseph Chaim (Jewish labour leader), 310
Brentano, Lujo (economist and sociologist), 5
Breslau Jewish community, 369–374; Zionist Association, 369–374
Breslau Rabbinical Seminary, 218, 370, 371
'Breslauer Zeitung', 370
Breuer, Robert, 330n
Briesen Jewish community, 30
Brinckmann, Carl Gustav von (diplomat and writer), 228
Brode, Heinrich (German consul), 299–300, 306, 307n, 308, 310, 314, 315n, 317

Bruch, Max (composer), 253, 254, 255
Brünn (physician), 278
Brun, Friederike Christiane, 228
Brunschwig, Henri, 112, 117
Buber, Martin, 187, 354, 355, 357, 360, 361
Bülow, Bernhard, Fürst von (Imperial German Chancellor), 241, 293
Bülow, Bernhard Wilhelm von (Staatssekretär, German Foreign Office), 344
Bülow, Hans von (pianist and conductor), 253, 295n
Bugrashov, Chaim (headmaster), 315
Burke, Edmund (writer and politician), 77, 78
Burla, Yehuda (Jewish writer), 310

Campe, Joachim Heinrich von (educationalist), 114
Capitalism, Jews and, 3–15, 17–36 *passim*, 115–116
Carpenter, Mary (English writer and philanthropist), 108
Cassel, Oskar (democratic politician), 318
Centralverein deutscher Staatsbürger jüdischen Glaubens (C.V.), 274n, 292, 319, 328n, 329, 333, 334
Cerfberr, Herz (Jewish politician), 119–120
Chassidism *see* Hasidism
Churchill, Winston, 338
Clermont-Tonnerre, Stanislav, Count of (French statesman), 132
Cohn, J., 264n
Cohn, Pinchas (rabbi), 319
Cohn-Reiss, Ephraim (education director of Hilfsverein), 295, 296, 301, 306, 307, 311, 314, 315, 316, 317, 318
'(Der) Colonist', 262
Concentration Camps, 37–57 *passim*
Condorcet, Jean Antoin (mathematician and encyclopaedist), 124–125
Conversion, 11, 141, 150, 153, 225, 226, 235; of Mendelssohn's descendants, 236
Court Jews, 6, 160, 225, 236, 240

David, Ferdinand (musician), 251
Dayan, Haim Bar, 67
Defoe, Daniel (writer), 88n, 89n, 112
Department stores, Jewish, 12, 22–24, 26
Dettensee Jewish community, 117–118, 137–138
Deutsch, Felix (industrialist), 23
Deutsche Bank, 11
Deutsch-Israelitischer Gemeindebund, 328n
Deutsche Demokratische Partei (DDP), 331
Deutsches Komitee zur Förderung der jüdischen Palästinasiedlung, 330n
Diderot, Denis (writer), 108
Diel, R. (diplomat), 332
Dinaburg (Dinur), Ben-Zion, 310
Dinter, Artur (antisemitic writer), 162n
Djemal Pasha, Ahmed (Turkish Governor of Palestine), 279, 313, 314, 315, 316
Döblin, Alfred (novelist), 32
Dohm, Christian Wilhelm von (writer and archivist), 119n, 120–123, 126–127, 129, 133, 234

General Index

Dorn, Moritz (President of Esra), 269, 279, 286, 288
Düwell, Kurt, 39
Dubnow, Simon (historian), 131n
Dufresne (Jacob Ephraim), 243–244

Eberhard, Otto, 330n
Ebers family, 230, 238n, 239, 240–241, 242, 243
Ebers, Martin (Moses Heimann Ephraim), 242
Ebers, Moritz (Egyptologist), 242
Ebers, Viktor (Veitel Heimann (Heine) Ephraim), 239, 242
Eberty family, 235, 242, 243
Education, Jewish, in Germany, 39, 43, 163–172, 203, 245
Education, Jewish, in Palestine, 261–289 *passim*, 291–319
Ehrenpreis, Markus M. (rabbi), 269n, 272
Eichendorff, Joseph, Freiherr von (poet), 130
Eichmann, Adolf (Nazi war criminal), 37
Einstein, Albert, 332
Emancipation, 18, 46, 160, 191, 225, 334; of German Jewry, and women's question, 107–138; Prussian Edict of 1812, 139, 140, 161, 225
Emigration, Jewish from Germany, 30, 42, 45, 55–56
Endres, Karl (military correspondent), 312
Engels, Friedrich, 110, 112, 132
Enlightenment, 62, 83–103, 107–136, 161, 165, 171, 175, 185, 189, 368
Ephraim family (bankers, merchants, and manufacturers), 225–246
Ephraim, Benjamin Veitel, 232, 237
Ephraim, David, 238
Ephraim, Ephraim Marcus, 243
Ephraim, Ephraim Heine, 243–244
Ephraim, Jacob *see* Dufresne
Ephraim, Joachim Heimann Marcus, 243
Ephraim, Marcus Heine, 243
Ephraim, Moses Heimann *see* Ebers, Martin
Ephraim, Nathan Heine, 225
Ephraim, Nathan Veitel Heine, 226, 240, 243
Ephraim, Veitel Heimann (Heine) *see* Ebers, Viktor
Ephraim, Zacharias Veitel, 237
Ephraim Veitel Stiftung, 243
Epstein, Itzhak, 311
Eschwege, Helmut, 40
Esh, Shaul (historian), 38
Eskeles family, 227, 228
Eskeles, Cecilie von, 227, 229
Esra, Sammelbüchse für Palästina *later* Verein zur Unterstützung Ackerbautreibender Juden in Palästina und Syrien, 264–289
Esrat Nidachim, 266
Ettlinger, Jakob (rabbi and Judaist), 168n
Euchel, Isaac (Hebrew writer and editor), 84–103, 183, 184; 'The Letters of Isaac Euchel', 98–103; 'The Letters of Meshulam', 84–103; and Mendelssohn, 86, 102–103; and Montesquieu, 84–103; Yiddish writings, 183, 184

Eulenburg, Philipp, Fürst zu Eulenburg und Hertefeld (diplomat and writer), 291
Euler, Johann Albrecht (mathematician), 64, 70
Euler, Leonhard (mathematician), 64, 66
Eybenberg, Marianne von, née Mayer (Meyer), 226–235, 236, 237; Goethe and, 228–232

Fascism, 37–57
Feuchtwanger, Lion (writer), 9
Fichte, Johann Gottlieb (philosopher), 127, 128n, 131, 132–135
Finkelstein, Alfons, 300, 306, 311
Fliess, Eleonore von, 226, 229
Förster, Christian (cartoonist), 162
Fontane, Theodor (novelist), 244
Fraenkel (banking family), 237–238, 240
Fränkel, David (rabbi), 63, 69
Franco, Moses (rabbi), 316
Frankel, Zacharias (rabbi and religious leader), 218, 371
Franklin, Benjamin (American statesman and writer), 112, 114, 115–116
'Frankfurter Zeitung', 295, 309, 312
Franz Joseph (Emperor of Austria), 254
Fraternities, Jewish, 269
Frederick II (Frederick the Great) (King of Prussia), 63, 64, 69, 120, 121, 228, 238, 240, 242, 243
Frederick III (Emperor of Germany), 238
Frederick William I (King of Prussia), 238
Frederick William II (King of Prussia), 142n, 234
Frederick William III (King of Prussia), 139–150, 196, 225
Freeden, Herbert, 38, 39
Freideutsche Jugend, 356–357
French Revolution, 124–129 *passim*, 225
Freud, Martha, née Bernays, 7n
Freud, Sigmund, 7, 11n, 355, 358, 361, 367
Freuthal, Selig, 262
Freytag, Gustav (novelist), 162n
Friebe family, 238, 239–240
Friedemann, Adolf (jurist and Zionist politician), 273, 281n
Friedländer, David (reformer of Judaism), 131, 140, 144n, 188, 189, 237
Friedländer, Michal, 98, 99, 102
Friedländer, Moses, 237
Friedlander, Yehuda, 85n
Fuchs, Eugen (chairman of C.V.), 319
Fürstenberg, Carl (banker), 8
Fürstenthal, Raphael L. (poet and translator), 195, 210n, 223

Gandhi, Mahatma, 43
Gans, Eduard (jurist and philosopher), 235
Gans, Isaac Jacob, 243
Gans'sche Stiftung, 243
Gans, Salomon Nathan, 243
Gans family, 243
Geiger, Abraham (religious philosopher), 245
Geiger, Ludwig (literary historian), 139, 228, 232n
Gellert, Christian Fürchtegott (poet), 74

Genossenschaft für Reform im Judentum, 244
Gentz, Friedrich von (publicist and statesman), 236
German literature, Jewish figures in, 161–162
Gernsheim family, 247–257
Gernsheim, Alfred, 250
Gernsheim, Eugen, 250
Gernsheim, Friedrich (physician), 247
Gernsheim, Friedrich (composer), 250–255
Gernsheim, Josef 250
Gernsheim, Michael (Judenbischof) (manufacturer), 247–249
Gernsheim, Michael (banker), 249
Gernsheim, Michael (rabbi), 249–250
Gernsheim, Regina, 249
Gernsheim, Salomon, 247, 248
Gernsheim, Wilhelm (composer), 255–257
Gerstenberg, Heinrich Wilhelm von (writer), 78
Gesellschaft der Freunde, Berlin, 86, 140
Gessner, Salomon (poet and painter), 77, 79
Gestapo, 39, 45n, 46, 48, 50, 52, 55, 250
Ginat, Jochanan (Hans Gaertner) (eductionalist and Director of the Leo Baeck Institute), foll. preface, 38, 369, 372
Gleim, Johann Wilhelm Ludwig (poet), 74, 77, 79
Glückel von Hameln, 179n, 243
Goerdeler, Carl (German nationalist politician), 47
Goerdeler Circle, 46
Göring, Hermann, 45n
Goethe, Johann Wolfgang von, 78, 130n, 226, 228–232, 233
Goldschmidt, Hermann (printer and publisher), 196, 218
Goldschmidt, J. (physician), 166
Goldschmidt, Martin, 195
Goldschmidt, Moritz B. (banker), 4–5
Goldschmidt, Rosa, née Monasch, 218, 220, 221, 223
Gottschalk, Solomon (editor), 370
Gottsched, Johann Christoph (writer), 64n, 69, 158, 159
Grabowsky, Adolf (writer), 330n
Graetz, Heinrich (historian), 167, 211n, 213, 216, 217, 218, 221
Graetz, Maria (Marie), née Monasch, 202, 212–213, 216, 217, 223
Grimm, Jacob (grammarian and philologist), 159
Grobba, Fritz (Arabist), 341
Groth, Klaus (poet), 166n
Grotthus, Ferdinand Dietrich Wilhelm, Baron von, 226
Grotthus, Sara von, née Mayer (Meyer), 226–235, 237; Goethe and, 228–232
Grüber, Heinrich, 56
Grunwald, Max (rabbi and historian), 187
Gumpertz, Aaron Emmerich (physician and scholar), 62–63, 65, 68n, 69, 72
Gumpertz, Ruben Samuel (elder of Berlin Jewish community), 140, 148

Habonim, 52
Hacohen, Mordechai Ben-Hillel (writer), 314

Hall, Granville Stanley (educationalist), 357
Haller, Albrecht von (poet), 79
Hamann, Johann Georg (writer), 62, 78, 127, 131
Hamburg Jewish community, 164–172; Israelitische Freischule, 163n, 165n, 167; Talmud-Tora-Schule, 168; Unterrichts-Anstalt für arme israelitische Mädchen, 169
'Hamburgischer Correspondent', 172
'Hame'asef' (Hebrew periodical), 84, 86, 98, 99, 100, 101n, 183n
Hantke, Arthur (German Zionist leader), 280n, 318
Hapoel Hatzair, 366
'Hapoel Hatzair' (Hebrew paper), 301, 315
Hardenberg, Friedrich, Freiherr von (Novalis) (poet), 130
Hardenberg, Karl August von (Prussian statesman), 142, 144n, 225, 239, 240
Hashomer Hatzair in Austria, 351, 352, 358, 362, 366, 368; in Germany, 52
Haskalah (Hebrew Enlightenment), 83–103, 160
Hasidism, 211n
Hauptmann, Gerhart (writer), 177n
Hauptmann, Moritz (musician), 251
Hausmann, Hermann (Regierungspräsident), 331
Hebbel, Friedrich (poet), 171
Hebrew, 13, 64, 83–103, 142–154, 160n, 161, 169, 173, 179n, 181, 190, 195–223 passim, 296–319 passim, 332, 337, 354
Hebrew literature, in Germany, 83–103
Hebrew University, Jerusalem, 321, 337
Hegel, Georg Wilhelm Friedrich (philosopher), 242, 244
Heine, Heinrich, 110n, 136n, 166n
Heinius (educationalist), 65
Heinrich XIV, Prince of Reuss, 227
Helfft, Gottschalk, 145, 146
Hell, François, 119–120
Herder, Johann Gottfried (writer), 77, 78, 227
Hermann, Georg (novelist), 188
Hertzberg, Arthur, 119
Herz, Henriette, 226, 236
Herz, Joseph (Jewish writer), 184
Herz Beer, Jacob (banker), 140, 141n, 142–143, 144, 145, 146, 147, 242
Herzl, Theodor, 235, 263, 270–271, 272, 273, 274, 281, 283, 366
Hess, Michael (educationalist), 245
Hesse Jewry, 185
Heymann, Aron Hirsch (Jewish writer), 187n
Heymann, Hans Gideon, 281
Hibbat Zion movement, 262–263
Hildesheimer, Esriel (rabbi, leader of orthodoxy), 264, 266, 268n
Hildesheimer, Hirsch (leader of orthodoxy), 266, 267n, 268, 270, 271, 273, 276
Hilfsverein der deutschen Juden, 267n, 277, 292–319, 328n, 337; Language Conflict in Palestine, 296–319
Hilfswerk für Palästina, 279
Hillebrand, Karl (writer), 236
Hiller, Ferdinand (pianist and composer), 251, 252

General Index

Hippel, Theodor Gottlieb von (writer), 124, 125–129, 131n, 134n, 135
Hirsch, Otto (Director of Reichsvertretung), 43
Hirsch family, 11
Hirschfeld, Dr. H., 264n, 265, 266
Hirschfeld, Max (editor of 'Esra'), 265n, 266
Historiography, German-Jewish, 3–57
Hitler, Adolf, 12, 38, 49, 109, 339
Hobsbawm, E. J., 116
Höchheimer, S. (Jewish writer), 161
Hoetzsch, Otto (historian and politician), 330n
Hoffer, Willi (psychoanalyst), 349n
Hohenlohe-Schillingsfürst, Chlodwig, Fürst zu (German Imperial Chancellor), 294
Holl, Karl, 254
Holzer, Charlotte, 53n
Holzmann, Günter (Jewish youth leader), 461
Holzmann, Jehuda, 270
Holzschuher, Friedrich, Freiherr von (writer), 185, 186
Homberg, Herz (educationalist), 188
Hovevei Zion, 262, 263, 264, 267, 268, 269, 270, 271, 273, 276, 280, 281
Huch, Ricarda (writer), 254
Hüttenberger, Peter, 41
Huhn, Arthur von (journalist), 293
Humboldt, Alexander von (naturalist), 236, 240, 242
Humboldt, Wilhelm von (Prussian statesman), 62, 159, 236, 237
Humperdinck, Engelbert (composer), 251, 253
Hurwitz, Judah, 83

Industrialisation, Jews and, 10–15 *passim*, 17–36 *passim*
Intermarriage, 11, 225
'(Der) Israelit', 273
Israelitischer Verein zur Kolonisation von Palästina, 262
Itzig family, 235
Itzig, Daniel (banker), 226, 236, 237
Itzig, Max (banker), 268

Jacobson, Israel (religious reformer), 139, 141, 142, 152
Jaeckh, Ernst, 330n
Jaffe, Mordechai Michael (rabbi), 209
'Jahrbuch für jüdische Volkskunde', 187
Jenisch, Daniel (writer), 63–64, 66, 67, 71
'Jerubbaal' (periodical), 351
Jerubbaal, Kreis, Order, 351–368 *passim*
'(The) Jewish Chronicle, 270–271, 310
Jewish Colonial Trust, 274–275, 281n
Jewish Colonisation Association (ICA), 270, 276
Jewish National Fund, 286, 316
Jewry, Eastern, 14, 17–36 *passim*, 49, 173, 174, 176, 261–289 *passim*, 318, 351–368; in Germany, 19, 25, 32, 35, 174, 370–372
Jewry, German, and colonisation of Palestine, 262–289, 291–319 *passim*, 321–345; communal administration, 206–208; defence against antisemitism, 38; demographic dis-

Jewry – *continued*
tribution, 17–36 *passim*, 370–371; deportations, 44–57 *passim*; and Eastern Jewry, 176–177, 187, 261–287 *passim*; education, 39, 43, 122, 163–172, 203, 245; emigration, 30, 42, 45, 55–56; extermination of, 37–57 *passim*; fight for civil rights, 107–138; migration, 17–36 *passim*, 196; occupational structure, 13–15 *passim*, 17–36 *passim*, 122, 196, 203, 371–374; patriotism, 328–329; persecution, 37–57; philanthropy, 34, 261, 264–289, 282–319; resistance to Nazism, 37–57; social mobility, 17–36 *passim*, 115, 116–117, 176; urbanisation, 17–36 *passim*, 116–117; vocational training, 43, 288–289; attitude to Yiddish, 161–177 *passim*; and Zionism, 268–289, 291–319, 322, 325, 328–335, 336–345 *passim*. *See also* Alsatian, Baden, Bavarian, Hesse, Poznań Jewry *and under* individual communities.
Johlson (preacher, grammarian and translator), 210, 211, 223
Jost, Isaak Markus (historian), 131n, 174n, 245
Judaeo-German *see* Yiddish
Judaism, 83, 86, 131, 133, 147, 150, 151, 226, 244
'(Der) Jude', 361
Judendeutsch *see* Yiddish
Jüdisch-deutsch *see* Yiddish
Jüdische Humanitätsgesellschaft, 269
'(Die) Jüdische Presse', 266, 268, 274n
'Jüdische Rundschau', 281, 370
Jüdisches Arbeitsamt, Berlin, 289
'Jüdisches Volksblatt', 267n
'Jüdische Volkszeitung, früher Selbst-Emancipation', 268
Jung Israel, 268, 269
(Das) Junge Deutschland, 166
Jungmann, Max, 269n

Kafka, Franz (writer), 174n
Kahan, Arcadius, 21
Kahn, Bernhard (General-Secretary of Hilfsverein), 295, 307, 332
Kahn, Zadoc (Grand Rabbin), 270n
Kalisch, Clara, née Stern, 246
Kalisch, Marcus (Hebrew scholar), 246
Kalmus, Ernst (physician), 370
Kant, Immanuel (philosopher), 78, 97, 127, 131n, 132, 133–134
Kann, Jacobus (Zionist politician), 310
Kapp (German consul), 324
Karfunkel, Max (journalist), 264n, 265, 266
Karpeles, Gustav (literary historian), 266
Kartell jüdischer Verbindungen, 269
Kastl, Ludwig (German civil servant), 327n, 332, 336
Katz, Albert, 267
Katz, Jacob, 109n, 119n, 128n, 133
Kaufman, E. M., née Monasch, 195
Kaufmann, David (Jewish scholar), 179n
Kaulla family, 250
Kellner, Leon (philologist), 272
Keren Hayessod, 279, 319
Kestner, Charlotte, 250

Kiderlen-Wächter, Alfred von (German Foreign Minister), 295, 297n
Kinderheim Baumgarten, 349n, 350, 361–368
Kirnberger, Johann Philipp (musician), 66–68
Kisch, Abraham, 66, 68, 69
Kleist, Ewald Christian von (poet), 79
Kleist, Heinrich von (poet and dramatist), 130, 227
Kley, Eduard (preacher and headmaster), 144, 167
Klopstock, Friedrich Gottlieb (poet), 77
'Kölnische Zeitung', 293
Kohn, Hans (historian), 160n
Kommunistische Partei Deutschlands (KPD), Communists, 47, 49, 52, 53, 55
Kreisauer Circle, 46
Kreutzberger, Max (publicist, social worker and Director of the Leo Baeck Institute), foll. preface
Kristallnacht *see* Pogroms, Germany, November 1938
Krotoschin Jewish community, 195–223
'Krotoschiner Kreisblatt', 196
Kühlmann, Richard von (German diplomat), 310, 316n
Kuhn, Loeb & Co. (banking house), 249

Lämel School, 296n, 307, 319
Lämel, Simon Edler von (industrialist), 232
Landau, Eugen (financier and philanthropist), 292, 332
Landau, Leopold (physician), 277, 286
Landauer, Gustav (Anti-Marxist Socialist), 355
Landes, David, 10, 11
Langenbach, Alfred, 249
'Laubhütte', 273
Lazarus, Louis, 265
Leibniz, Gottfried Wilhelm (philosopher), 68
Lemaan Zion, 268n
Leo Baeck Institute, VII, 38, 57; Year Book, VII, 37, 40, 246
Lepsius, Richard (Egyptologist), 242
Leskien, August (philologist), 159
Lessing, Gotthold Ephraim, 61–80, 119, 135, 227, 230, 231, 234
Lessing, Karl, 72
Lestschinsky, Jakob (economist and writer), 115n, 117
Leven, Narcisse (politician and philanthropist, 270
Levi, Hermann (conductor), 251, 253
Levin, Shmarya (Zionist politician), 296, 297, 302, 303, 305, 306n, 309
Levontin, Salman David (Zionist leader), 277, 278, 284
Lewin, Louis (rabbi), 195
Lichtheim, Richard (Zionist politician), 310, 315, 316, 317, 319
Liebeschütz, Hans (historian), foll. preface
Ligne, Charles Joseph, Prince de, 228, 232–235
Limburg-Stirum, Frédéric Adrian, Graf von, 240–241
Limburg-Stirum, Friedrich Wilhelm, Graf von (Conservative politician), 241

Liszt, Franz von (pianist and composer), 251
Literature *see* German, Hebrew, Yiddish literature
Locke, John (philosopher), 65, 66, 68
Löbe, Paul (Socialist politician), 331
Loewe, Heinrich (historian and Zionist politician), 268, 269n, 270n, 274n–275n
Loewe, Richard, 269n
Louis Ferdinand, Prince of Prussia, 228
Louise (Queen of Prussia), 130
Loytved-Hardegg (German consul), 298–299, 300, 304, 305, 306, 307n, 308, 311
Lurie, Joseph, 315
Luther, Martin, 10n, 171
Luzzatto, Ephraim (Hebrew poet), 101

Mahler, Gustav (composer), 254, 255
Mahler, Raphael, 17, 18
Maimonides, 64, 65, 68
Mankiewitz, Paul (banker), 11n
Mannheimer, Isaak Noah (rabbi), 149
Maoz, Eliyahu, 53n
Mapu, Abraham, 99
Margaliot, Abraham, 38
Margalith, Elkana, 358
Mark, Bernhard, 39
Marks, Michael (owner of department store), 23
Marks & Spencer (department store), 23
Marmorek, Alexander (bacteriologist), 310
Marpurg (musician and editor), 70
Marranos, 90n, 97, 100n
Marschall von Bieberstein, Adolf, Freiherr (German diplomat), 294, 295, 296, 297, 298
Marshall, Louis (American Jewish politician), 313
Martin, Rudolf, 14
Marx, Karl, 13, 19, 110, 111, 112, 115, 122, 128, 132
Maskilim, 83–103, 140, 160, 188, 189
'Masur Qohelet' (Hebrew periodical), 83
Maupertuis, Pierre Louis Moreau de (philosopher and mathematician), 64, 69
Mayer (Meyer), Aron Moses, 226
Mayer, Hans, 109
Mayer, Paul 'Yogi' (leader of Schwarzes Fähnlein), 461
Mayer Hacker, Helen, 109n
Mecklenburg, Georg, 331
Mehring, Franz (writer and Socialist politician), 124n
Meinhof, Carl, 330n
Mendele Mocher Sforim (Sh. Y. Abramovitsh) (Jewish writer), 310
Mendelssohn family, 11, 235, 236, 237–238, 240, 242, 243
Mendelssohn, Abraham (banker), 237, 238
Mendelssohn, Franz von (banker), 238
Mendelssohn, Fromet, née Gugenheim, 69
Mendelssohn, Joseph (banker), 6n, 71, 147, 237, 240
Mendelssohn, Moses, 6n, 61–82, 83, 86, 103, 108, 119, 120, 122, 131, 136, 183, 188, 226, 230, 231, 234, 236, 237, 265; Bible translation, 179, 180, 188–189, 190, 191; early writings, table of, 81–82; and Gumpertz,

62–63, 65, 69, 72; and Lessing, 61–80; as literary critic, 61–80; and Nicolai, 61–79
Mendelssohn & Co. (banking house), 237–238, 240
Mendelssohn-Bartholdy, Felix (composer), 66, 251, 252, 253, 254
'Menorah', 269
Meydell, Bodo, Freiherr von, 237
Meyer, Eduard, 243
Metastasio, Pietro (Italian poet), 101
Meyer, Lothar, 330n
Meyerbeer family, 242–243
Meyerbeer, Giacomo (composer), 237, 242, 243
Meyerson, Émile (philosopher, Director of ICA), 270n, 276n
Michaelis, E. (headmaster), 167
Michaelis, Johann David, 65, 74
Michaelis-Stern, Eva, 246
Middle Ages, 135
Mieses, Mathias (writer), 173, 175
Mill, John Stuart (philosopher), 127
Miquel, Hans von (German diplomat), 291, 292
Mirabeau, Honoré Gabriel Victor Riquetti, Count of (French statesman and philosopher), 234
Mohiliwer, Samuel (rabbi), 270
Monasch family, 197–223
Monasch, Baer Loew (printer and publisher), 195–223
Monasch, Isidor, 214, 218, 223
Monasch, Julius, 218, 219, 223
Monasch, Louis, 204, 211, 217–218, 219–220, 223,
Monasch, Mathilde, née Wiener, 201–220
Monasch, Moritz, 216, 218
Monash, Sir John (Australian general) (grandson of B. L. Monasch), 204n
'Monatsschrift für die Geschichte und Wissenschaft des Judentums', 195, 212n
Montefiore, Moses (philanthropist), 108
Montesquieu, 9, 10, 14, 84–103, 109, 132; 'Lettres Persanes', 84–103
Montessori, Maria (educationalist), 357
Moritz, Karl Philipp (writer), 78
Moscheles, Ignaz (musician), 251
Moses, Moritz, 262, 267, 272
Moses, Walter, 289
Mosse, George L., 160n
Mossinsohn, Ben-Zion (headmaster), 307, 315
Motzkin, Leo (Zionist politician), 269n, 274
Müller, Hermann (Socialist German Chancellor), 331
Müller, Johannes von, 236
'Münchener Neueste Nachrichten', 312
Mukhtar, Mahmud, 279n
Munich Jewish community, 273
Mylius, Christlob (writer), 62, 65

Nahoum, Haim Effendi (Chief Rabbi of Turkey), 296, 301
Napoleon I, 12, 197n, 233, 239, 240, 247, 248
National-Jüdische Vereinigung für Deutschland, 273
Nathan, Paul (politician and writer), 292, 293, 294, 295, 297, 298n, 299, 302, 303, 304, 305, 307, 309, 311, 314, 315n, 316n, 318
'(Die) Nation', 292
National-Jüdische Vereinigung, Köln, 273
Nauensche Stiftung, 243
Naumann (friend of Lessing), 70
Naumann, Friedrich (Liberal politician), 292
Naumann, Max (leader of Verband nationaldeutscher Juden), 332
Nazism, 25, 32, 35, 37–57, 247, 250, 256, 329, 338, 339, 359
Neiman, Morris, 85n, 91n, 92n, 97n, 99
Netter, Charles (merchant and philanthropist), 263n
Neu-Beginnen, 52
'Neue Jüdische Korrespondenz', 309
Neumark, David (philosopher), 269n
Neurath, Konstantin, Freiherr von (German Foreign Minister), 344
Nicolai, Christoph Friedrich (writer and bookseller), 61–79
Nikolai II (Czar of Russia), 261
Nord, Erich (German consul), 332, 336, 337, 338, 340, 341
Nordau, Max (writer and Zionist leader), 310
Norwitzky, H., 264n, 265
Nossig, Alfred (publicist and sculptor), 277n
Nuremberg Laws, 55, 56, 57

Ophir, Baruch Zvi, 38
Oppenfeld, Moritz von, 240
Oppenheimer, Franz (economist and sociologist, 310, 318
Oppenheimer, Max, 269
'Orient', 169
Oster Circle, 46
Ottensoser, David (Jewish writer), 189, 191
Otto, Berthold (educationalist), 357

Pädagogium, Vienna, 352, 354
Paine, Thomas (English radical writer), 125
Palästina Amt, 281
Palästinadeutsche see Palestine, German settlements in
Palestine, education, 261–289 passim, 291–319 passim; German policies and, Weimar, 321–345, Wilhelminian, 291–319; German settlements in, 321–345 passim; Jewish settlements in 261–289, 291–319 passim
Panizel, E. M. (rabbi), 296
Patak, Erna (social worker), 361, 364
Paucker, Arnold, 38
Perl, Joseph, 99
Pfuël, Ernst von (Prussian statesman), 216n
Philanthropin, Frankfurt a. Main, 245
Picard, Jacob (writer), 188
Pikarski, Margot, 53n
Pinczower Vera (headmistress), 309
Pinsker, Leon (physician and Jewish politician), 262, 267n
Poale Zion, 52, 315
Pogroms, Germany, November 1938, 55, 56, 57, 245; in Poland, after World War I, 360; Russian, 261, 277
Poznań Jewry, 21, 22, 25, 26–30 passim, 195–223

Printing, of Jewish books in Germany, 179–223
Pro-Palästina Komitee (PPK), 330–335, 344
Prüfer, Curt (German Foreign Office official), 332
Pünder, Hermann (Staatssekretär), 331, 332, 333

Racism, 357
Ramler, Karl Wilhelm (poet), 70, 79
Rashi, 195, 210n
Rast-Organisation, 56
Rathenau, Emil (industrialist), 23, 241
Rathenau, Walther, (statesman and philosopher), 23, 344
Rée, Anton (educationalist and politician), 158, 166, 167, 169, 170, 171, 172
Reformgemeinde, Berlin, 245, 328n
Reform Judaism, Reform movement, 139–155, 243, 244
'Reformzeitung, Organ für den Fortschritt im Judentum', 245
Reichsbund jüdischer Frontsoldaten (RjF), 43n, 54, 329
Reichsverband zur Bekämpfung des Zionismus, 328n
Reichsvertretung der deutschen Juden, 39, 43
Renner, Karl (Austrian statesman), 361
Resistance, in Germany, Jews in, 37–57
Reuter, Fritz (writer), 166n, 177n
Revolution of 1848, 129, 186, 212n, 215–216
Richarz, Monika, 8, 12, 24n, 116
Richter, Jean Paul Friedrich (writer), 127
Richthofen, Hartmann, Freiherr von (Ministerialdirigent, German Foreign Office), 331, 340
Richthofen, Oswald, Freiherr von (Staatssekretär, German Foreign Office), 294
Riemer, Friedrich Wilhelm (scholar, friend of Goethe), 229
Riesser, Gabriel (politician), 151, 245
Rietz, Julius (composer), 251
Romanticism, 115, 129–136, 225–226, 236
Roon, Ger van, 41
Rosen, Friedrich (German consul), 294
Rosenbaum, Dr. (editor of 'Israelitisches Familienblatt'), 308
Rosenberg, Hans von (German civil servant), 308
Rosenberg, Hans, 27n
Rosenheim, Jacob (leader of Jewish orthodoxy), 317n
Rosenthal, A. L. (Jewish writer), 184
Rosenwald, Julius (industrialist and philanthropist), 313
Roter Stoß-Trupp, 52
Rothschild, Albert de (banker), 23
Rothschild, Amschel (banker), 4
Rothschild, Baron Edmond de (banker and philanthropist), 263, 270, 275, 276
Rothschilds, 8, 11, 108, 190n, 206n, 240, 246
Rousseau, Jean Jacques (philosopher), 78, 79, 80, 119, 125, 132
Rubinstein, Anton (pianist and composer), 251

Rülf, Isaak (rabbi and Jewish politician), 252
Rürup, Reinhard, 115n
Ruppel, Julius (German civil servant), 327n, 332, 336
Ruppin, Arthur (sociologist and Zionist leader), 116, 279, 280, 281, 287–289, 316, 317, 330n
Russischer Jüdischer Wissenschaftlicher Verein, 268

Saaz, Johann von (medieval German poet), 256
Sabbatai Zvi, 271
Sagarra, Eda, 111
Salvendi, Adolf (rabbi), 266
Salz, Abraham, 272
Salzmann, Christian Gotthilf (educationalist), 125
Samocz, Israel, 65, 66
Samuel, Sir Herbert (British High Commissioner in Palestine), 324
Sandheim, Adolf, 265n, 267n
Sandler, Aron (physician), 370
Schach, Fabius, 275n
Schachtel, Hugo (journalist and editor), 369n, 370
Schapira, Hermann (mathematician and Jewish politician), 262
Scharfstein, Zvi, 310
Schatz, Boris (sculptor), 277
Schenda, R., 159
Schiff, Jacob Henry (financier and philanthropist), 296–297, 311, 315n
Schiller, Friedrich von, 62, 78, 228
Schlegel, August Wilhelm von (writer), 236
Schlegel, Dorothea, 136, 236
Schlegel, Friedrich von (writer), 136, 236, 244
Schleiermacher, Friedrich Ernst Daniel (Protestant theologian and philosopher), 123n, 130, 225–226, 227, 236, 242, 244
Schlesinger, Liebermann (banker), 144n
Schmeller, Joseph Andreas (Germanist), 159
Schmidt, Edmund (German consul), 294, 295n, 300, 301, 307, 308, 309, 310, 316
Scholl, Hans, 46
Scholl, Sophie, 46
Schorsch, Ismar, 117
Schottel (grammarian), 158
Schramm, Gottfried, 14, 15n
Schuckmann, Friedrich, Freiherr von (Prussian Minister of the Interior), 141–155
Schubert, Karl von (diplomat), 325, 332, 335, 344
Schudt, Johann Jacob (orientalist), 157, 174n
Schultheiss-Patzenhofer (brewery concern), 13n
Schulverein für die Juden des Orients (der deutsche) *see* Hilfsverein der deutschen Juden
Schutzjuden, 126
Schwabach, Paul von (banker), 241–242n
Schwarzes Fähnlein, 461
Schwarzer Haufen, 52
Schwersenz, Jizchak, 56
Schwörbel (German consul), 343
Seitz, A. (educationalist), 166, 170, 171

'Selbst-Emancipation', 268
Sermon, Jewish in Germany, 139–155
'Serubabel' (periodical), 267, 268
Sessa, Borromäus Karl (writer), 185
Sha'anan, Avraham, 85, 91n, 92n, 96n, 97n, 99n
Shaftesbury, Anthony Ashley Cooper, Earl of (philosopher), 68, 71, 77, 78, 79, 80
Shapira, Moshe, 43
Shaw, Sir Walter, 342, 343n
Shenkin, Menahem, 315
Simion, J., 245
Simon, Ernst, 39, 109n
Simon, James (merchant and philanthropist), 292, 294, 297, 298n, 299n, 302, 303, 309, 310, 311, 312, 313, 314, 316, 317, 318
Simon, Joachim "Schuschu", 56
Simon, Leo, 332
Singer, Isaac Bashevis, 33
Sklower, David (printer), 209
Smilanksy, Moshe (Jewish writer), 303n, 310
Sobernheim, Moritz (orientalist and German Foreign Office official), 321–323, 327, 332, 334, 335n, 338n, 340, 341
Social Democrats, Austrian, 349, 360
Sokolow, Nahum (writer and Zionist politician), 310
Solmssen, Georg (banker), 11n
Sombart, Werner (economist), 330n; on Jews and capitalism, 3–8, 13, 110–111, 112, 114, 115
Sonntagsverein im Tunnel über der Spree, 244
Soskin, Selig (agronomist), 269n
Sozialdemokratische Partei Deutschlands (SPD), Social Democrats, 47, 52, 53, 331, 360
Sozialistische Arbeiterpartei Deutschlands (SAPD), 52
Spanish Civil War, 52
Spickermann, Dr. (Prosecutor-General), 51n
Spinoza, Baruch, 62, 65, 68
Spyro (rabbi of Tscharnikau), 209
SS, 44, 48
Staël-Holstein, Germaine (French writer), 108
Stahmer, Friedrich (diplomat), 339
Stein, Charlotte von, 232
Stein, Baron Karl von (Prussian statesman), 149n, 225
Stein, Ludwig, 330n
Steinberg, Lucien, 39–40
Steiner, George, 229
Steinhardt, Menahem Mendel, 143n
Steinthal, Heymann (philologist), 169n
Steinthal, Max (banker), 11n
Stemrich (German civil servant), 295n, 296, 301n
Stern, Fritz, 116n
Stern, Ida, née Fürstenberg, 244
Stern, Sigismund (educationalist and leader of Reform Judaism), 244–246
Stern, William (psychologist and philosopher), 246
Stern-Anders, Günther, 246
Stieglitz (banking family), 237
Straus, Isaak, 312, 313, 314n, 317, 330n

Stoever, Johann Hermann (writer), 164, 165
Stresemann, Gustav (German statesman), 327, 328, 335, 341, 343, 344
Struck, Hermann (painter), 187
Sulzer, Johann Georg (philosopher), 65, 67, 68, 70, 74, 75
Synagogue architecture, 9

Talaat Pasha (Turkish Minister of Interior), 318
Talleyrand-Périgord, Charles Maurice de (French statesman), 124, 127
Talmud, 5, 6, 68, 95, 195, 197, 200, 201
Tawney, R. H., 10
Technikum, Haifa, 297, 298, 299, 300, 302–309, 311, 312, 317, 319
Teller, Wilhelm Abraham (Protestant theologian), 131, 225
Tendlau, Abraham Moses (teacher and writer), 187
Thannhäuser, Isaac, 8
Theilhaber, Felix (sociologist), 371n
Thiele, A. F., 162
Thon, Osias (Jewish writer and politician), 269n, 272, 279n
Tietz family, 11
Tietz, Hermann (owner of department store), 23
Tietz, Leonhard (owner of department store 24
Tocqueville, Alexis de (French statesman and historian), 122
Toury, Jacob, 9, 10n, 160n
Tramer, Hans (publicist, editor and Vice-President of the Leo Baeck Institute), foll. preface
Translateur, Hugo, 370
Treitschke, Heinrich von (historian), 108
Treue, Wilhelm, 240
Troeltsch, Ernst (Protestant theologian), 3
Truppel, Oskar von, 330n
Tschlenow, Yehiel (Zionist leader), 297, 305
'Tse'ena Ure'ena', 181, 182, 191
Turoff, Isaak (Jewish writer), 264n, 267, 270, 280, 288

Uhland, Ludwig (poet), 183n
Ullmann, Ber Bernhard (Yiddish writer), 182–183
Unger, Louis, 270n
Unna, Isak (rabbi), 332
Urbach (rabbi of Lenschütz), 209
Ussishkin, Menachem Mendel (Zionist politician), 303n
Uz, Johann Peter (poet), 74

Varnhagen von Ense, Karl August (diplomat and writer), 226, 227, 228
Varnhagen von Ense, Rahel (Rahel Levin), 226, 227, 229
Veit, David (physician), 229, 232
Veit, Moritz (writer and politician), 245
Veit, Simon, 236
Veit, Solomon (elder of Berlin Jewish community), 140, 144, 146n
Verband der Deutschen Juden, 292, 328n

Verband der jüdischen Jugendvereine Deutschlands, 328n
Verband nationaldeutscher Juden (VnJ) 43n, 54, 329, 332
Verein für Geschichte und Literatur, 267n
Verein jüdischer Studenten an der Universität Berlin, 269
Verein für Wahrung jüdischer Interessen, 212n
Vereinigung jüdischer Organisationen Deutschlands zur Wahrung der Rechte der Juden des Ostens (V.J.O.D.), 318
Vereinigung jüdischer Studierender, 269
Vereinigung für das liberale Judentum, 328n, 329, 332, 333
Voltaire, 64, 65, 68, 72, 93n, 108
Voss (bookseller), 70

Wagner, Richard (composer), 251, 253
Walk, Max, 369
Walk, Joseph, 39, 330n
Wallich, Hermann (banker), 11n
Walz, Hans (industrialist), 46
Walzer, Michael, 358
Wangenheim, Hans, Freiherr von (diplomat), 301–302, 307n, 308n, 310, 315n, 316n
Warburg Institute, London, 244
Warburg, Otto (Zionist leader), 279, 281, 286–287, 305
Warschauer brothers (printers), 208
Wassermann, Jakob (novelist), 188
Wassermann, Oskar (banker), 11n
Weber, Marianne (feminist), 132
Weber, Max (sociologist), 3, 7, 8, 13, 110n–111n, 112, 120; on Jews and capitalism, 3, 7, 8, 13
Weinreich, Max (philologist), 172, 173, 184n
Weizmann, Chaim, 305, 335
Weitz, Paul (journalist), 295
'(Die) Welt', 309
Weltsch, Robert, VII
Werkleute, 52
Wertheimer (department store), 24
Westerweel, Joop, 56
Weyl, Meyer Simon (rabbi), 140, 146n, 148, 149, 150
Wieland, Christoph Martin (poet), 77, 79
Wienbarg, Ludolf (writer), 166, 170, 171
Wiener Library, 51
Wiener, Max (rabbi and historian), 371, 372
William I (Emperor of Germany), 241
William II (Emperor of Germany), 241–242, 254, 291–293, 311
Winckelmann, Johann Joachim (art historian), 78
Wirth, Josef Karl (German Chancellor and Minister of the Interior), 331
Wissotsky family, 304
Wissotzky, Kalman (Russian tea magnate), 296–297

Wittkower family, 244
Wittkower, Rudolf (art historian), 244
Wittkower, Werner (architect), 244
Witwe Heimann Zacharias Epraimsche Stiftung, 243
Witzleben, Job Wilhelm Karl Ernst von (Prussian general), 147, 155
Wohlwill, Immanuel (writer and headmaster), 163n
Wolff, Christian (philosopher), 64n, 68, 72
Wolff, Edith, 56
Wolff, Ferdinand, 267
Wolff, Jacob (businessman), 226, 230
Wolffsohn, David (Zionist leader), 273
Wolfssohn, Aron Halle (Jewish writer), 183, 184, 189
Wollstencroft, Mary (writer and feminist), 124, 125, 135
Woog, Meyer (Jewish writer), 186
World Zionist Organization, 263–264, 275–276, 279, 319
Worms Jewish community, 247–250
Wulff, Liebmann Meyer (banker), 239, 242–243
Wyneken, Gustav (educationalist), 353, 356, 357, 358, 362, 367

Yad Vashem, 51, 57
Yiddish language, 13, 86, 102n, 161–177, 179–192, 195–223 passim, 294, 299
Yiddish literature, in Germany, 86, 179–192
Youth movement, German, 356–357
Youth movement, Jewish, in Austria, 349–368 passim. See also under Anfang, Blau-Weiss, Hashomer Hatzair.
Youth movement, Jewish in Germany, 39, 52, 289, 328n., 461. See also under Blau-Weiss, Hashomer Hatzair, Schwarzes Fähnlein, Werkleute, etc.

Zamosc, Israel, 83
Zelter, Karl Friedrich (composer), 228
Zentrumspartei (Germany), 331
Zielenziger, Kurt (economic adviser), 7n
Ziemke (German Foreign Office official), 341, 342
Zimmermann, Arthur (German civil servant), 297n, 298n, 301–302, 303, 304, 309–310, 311, 312, 313, 317
Zimmermann, Johann Georg (writer), 74
Zion (organisation), 262
'Zion' (periodical), 267n, 272, 274, 283
Zionism, 39, 40, 268–289, 291–319, 321–345, 349–374
Zionistische Vereinigung für Deutschland, 273, 274, 275, 278, 279, 280, 281, 330
Zlocisti, Theodor (physician and writer), 269n, 271
Zunz, Leopold (Jewish scholar), 150n